ISBN 978-0-266-14309-3
PIBN 10932449

1 MONTH OF
FREE
READING

at

www.ForgottenBooks.com

By purchasing this book you are eligible for one month membership to ForgottenBooks.com, giving you unlimited access to our entire collection of over 1,000,000 titles via our web site and mobile apps.

To claim your free month visit:

www.forgottenbooks.com/free932449

English
Français
Deutsche
Italiano
Español
Português

www.forgottenbooks.com

Mythology Photography **Fiction**
Fishing Christianity **Art** Cooking
Essays Buddhism Freemasonry
Medicine **Biology** Music **Ancient**
Egypt Evolution Carpentry Physics
Dance Geology **Mathematics** Fitness
Shakespeare **Folklore** Yoga Marketing
Confidence Immortality Biographies
Poetry **Psychology** Witchcraft
Electronics Chemistry History **Law**
Accounting **Philosophy** Anthropology
Alchemy Drama Quantum Mechanics
Atheism Sexual Health **Ancient History**
Entrepreneurship Languages Sport
Paleontology Needlework Islam
Metaphysics Investment Archaeology
Parenting Statistics Criminology
Motivational

REPORTS OF CASES

ARGUED AND DETERMINED

IN THE

/ ω ... ...

SURROGATES' COURTS

OF THE

STATE OF NEW YORK.

BY

THEODORE F. C. DEMAREST.

VOL. III.

NEW YORK:
BANKS & BROTHERS, LAW PUBLISHERS,
No. 144 Nassau Street.
ALBANY, N. Y.:
Nos. 473, 475 Broadway.
1885.

TABLE OF CASES REPORTED
IN THIS VOLUME.

———•———

TABLE OF CASES REPORTED.

Page

NAMES OF DECEDENTS AND WARDS.

REPORTS OF CASES

ARGUED AND DETERMINED

IN THE

SURROGATES' COURTS

OF THE

STATE OF NEW YORK.

ALBANY COUNTY.—HON. FRANCIS H. WOODS, SUR-
ROGATE.—April, 1885.

TRACEY *v.* SLINGERLAND.

In the matter of the estate of PETER W. TEN EYCK, *deceased.*

Under Code Civ. Pro., § 2706, relating to a special proceeding to discover
property of a decedent withheld from his representative, and providing
that "*an* executor or administrator" may present to the Surrogate's
court a petition praying an inquiry, one of two co-representatives may
proceed alone, without alleging a demand upon and refusal of the
other to unite with him, or otherwise explaining the non-joinder.

The substitution, in the section cited, of the words quoted, in place of
"*any* executor or administrator," used in the original act (L. 1870,
ch. 394, § 1), is a mere change in phraseology, which has effected no
alteration in the law.

PETITION of James T. Tracey, an administrator of
the estate of decedent, for the examination of Cor-
nelius H. Slingerland, under Code Civ. Pro., § 2706,

respecting certain personal property belonging to that estate, alleged to be in the possession of the latter. There was also an administratrix of decedent's estate, who had duly qualified and was acting; but the petition did not show a demand upon or refusal by her to join in instituting the special proceeding, nor did it, or the accompanying affidavit, mention or in any manner refer to her. The objections taken are stated in the opinion.

MATTHEW HALE and JAS. FENIMORE COOPER, *for petitioner.*

N. C. MOAK and WM. C. McHARG, *for respondent.*

THE SURROGATE.—This is a proceeding begun by one of the administrators of Peter W. Ten Eyck, deceased, to discover property of the deceased, alleged to be withheld from the petitioner. There are two objections made to the proceeding, one on the ground that the petition does not set forth sufficient facts, and another that the petition is defective, in that, as there are two administrators of this estate, and only one of them petitions, the proceedings cannot go on without joining the other administrator.

As to the first objection, I am of opinion that the allegations of the petition relating to the withholding of the property and describing the property withheld, are sufficient, *and* I so hold.

As to the second question, which has been earnestly urged and ably argued, I am not so clear. I do not find any decision directly in point, nor do I find that such an objection has been raised since the adoption of the Code of Civil Procedure. I am of opinion, however, that one of two may maintain these proceedings under § 2706 of the Code, without bringing in his co-administrator.

In many respects they may act separately. One may sell personal property without the consent of the other; one may receive and hold the funds of the estate, and is not responsible for the waste or misconduct of the other, unless he directly or indirectly makes himself a party thereto, and is chargeable with all the assets which he actually receives. In a word, each has control of the estate, and may release, pay or transfer, without the agency of the other. In view of this relation between them, it may be reasonably said that any one of them may institute a proceeding under § 2706 of the Code, which provides, in brief, that *an* executor or administrator may present to the Surrogate's court a written petition, tending to show that money or other personal property which ought to be included in the inventory is withheld from the administrator, and thereupon the Surrogate may issue his citation accordingly.

This section of the Code was taken from chapter 394 of the laws of 1870, which gave power to any administrator to begin these proceedings. The substitution in the Code of the words " an administrator " for " any administrator," used in the statute of 1870, was merely a change of phraseology, without changing the meaning of the law. And it has been expressly held that when *any* administrator might begin a proceeding, a single administrator, where he has an associate, has the right to call in the aid of the Surrogate (Jackson v. Robinson, 4 *Wend.*, 436).

And it seems to me that this is a proper construction to give to this section of the Code, for the additional reason that one administrator might refuse to proceed, or might be in collusion with the party withholding the property.

On principle then, as well as by construction of § 2706 of the Code, I am of the opinion that the administrator who began these proceedings had the legal right to do so.

Objections overruled.

ALLEGANY COUNTY.—HON. C. A. FARNUM, SURRO GATE.—November, 1884.

TOMPKINS *v.* FANTON.

In the matter of the judicial settlement of the account of DAVID FANTON, *as executor of the will of* ESTHER FANTON, *deceased.*

The testator of testatrix, by his will, gave to the latter "all my (his) real estate of every name and nature, whatsoever, and all my (his) personal estate, goods and chattels of every kind, together with all book accounts and debts due, etc., and also a lawful right to buy and sell and dispose of a part or all of the above mentioned real estate, personal property, goods and chattels, as long as she retains her sound mind, and is capable of doing business and is not insane, during her natural life;" and, after her death, all the rest, residue and remainder of the estate "which is above willed and bequeathed to my (his) wife" to another and his heirs and assigns.—

Held, that this provision expressly created a life estate in testatrix, with a power of disposition during her life; that so much of the personalty as remained undisposed of at the time of her death constituted no part of her estate; and that the executor of her will was not bound to account therefor.

Cases where a will bestows property without specifying the nature of the estate, and gives to the donee a power of disposition—distinguished.

CONSTRUCTION of the will of the testator of decedent, upon the judicial settlement of the account of the executor of the will of the latter. The facts appear in the opinion.

H. L. JONES and B. C. RUDE, *for executor.*

HAMILTON WARD and IRA MYERS, *for Lydia A. Tompkins and others, legatees.*

THE SURROGATE.—The chief controversy in this accounting has been whether the executor should account for all the personal property in the possession of the testatrix at the time of her death, or for that only which came to her otherwise than by the will of her husband, Daniel Fanton. Counsel for the legatees claim that the testatrix became the absolute owner of all the property bequeathed to her by the will of said Daniel, while counsel for the executor contend that she took a life estate only, and that, upon her death, it passed to the executor herein, David Fanton.

Esther Fanton devised all her real property to David Fanton, and bequeathed all her personal property to her sisters, the legatees who are now objecting to the account of the executor as rendered. The will of Daniel Fanton was duly admitted to probate by the Surrogate of Steuben county, June 5th, 1866, and this controversy arises over the following clauses contained therein:

"*First.* I give and bequeath to my wife, Esther Fanton (the testatrix herein), all my real estate, of every name and nature whatsoever, and all my personal estate, goods and chattels of every kind, together with all book accounts and debts due, etc., and also a lawful right to buy and sell and dispose of a part or all of the above mentioned real estate, personal property, goods and chattels, as long as she retains her sound mind, and is capable of doing business and is not insane, during her natural life. And after her death I will and bequeath to my nephew, David Fanton, (the executor herein), and his heirs and assigns, all the rest, residue and remainder of my real estate, goods and chattels, book accounts, debts due, of whatsoever kind or nature, and personal estate, which is above willed and bequeathed to my wife, Esther Fanton. I request and bind said David Fanton to pay all my lawful debts against the estate, and also ten dollars to the ten lawful heirs, that is to say, one dollar to (naming each of ten persons), which is to be paid when coming in possession of the estate, and I hereby appoint my nephew, David Fanton sole executor of this my last will and testament."

Although this will is quite inartistic there is no serious difficulty in ascertaining the intent of the testator. He gave his wife Esther, *in express terms*, his real and personal estate *for life*, with a power of disposition during life, or so long as she was of sound mind, and, upon her death, the property undisposed of by her passed to David. It would not be claimed in this case that Esther Fanton took more than a life estate under the will of Daniel Fanton, if the will had not given her the power to dispose of the property, for it is expressly stated that the property is given to her " during her natural life " with "a lawful right to buy and sell and dispose of a part or all, so long as she retains her sound mind, and is capable of doing business, and is not insane."

Redfield says : " A power of sale attached to an express life estate will not have the effect to enlarge it to a fee" (2 Redf. on Wills [*2nd ed.*], 345). "Where property, whatever be its nature, is expressly limited to the first taker for life, there is not, it is believed, any case in which such expressions have been held to render the ultimate gift void" (1 Jarman on Wills [*R. & T.*], 654).   Cruise, in his Digest of Real Property (*vol.* 6, *p.* 279, *N. Y.* ed., 1834), says: "Although a devise to a person generally, with a power to give and dispose of the estate devised as he pleases, creates an estate in fee simple, yet when an estate is devised to a person *expressly for life,* with a power of disposal, the devisee will only take an estate for life, with a power to dispose of the reversion."

From the numerous authorities cited and examined on this hearing, I think the following rule can be extracted, viz.: That, where property is willed *without specifying the nature of the estate,* and the donee is given a power of disposition, the latter takes the absolute title to the property, but where the donee takes an estate *expressly for life,* with a power of disposal, during life, he takes a life estate only, and whatever is left of that estate at the time of the death of the life tenant, passes to the remainderman.   This principle is elementary and has been acted upon frequently of late years by our courts, although the rule itself has been rarely stated.

In the case at bar, Esther Fanton took her estate in express terms *for life*, with a power of disposition so long as she lived or was of sound mind, but she is not given the right to make a testamentary disposition of the property received by her under the will of Daniel Fanton. "So if an estate be given to a person generally, or indefinitely, with a power of disposition, it carries a fee; unless the testator gives to the first taker an estate for life only, and annexes to it a power of disposition of the reversion. In that case, the *express* limitation *for life* will control the operation of the power, and prevent it from enlarging the estate to a fee (4 Kent, 319, 536).

In Candler v. Candler (2 *Dem.*, 124), Mrs. Candler was given a certain sum "to have and to hold for her separate use during her natural life, and to be disposed of by her at her death among her lawful issue in such proportions as she shall direct and appoint. But if she shall die without making such appropriation, then I direct the same to be divided among such issue, in the same proportion as if it had been her property at the time of her death." Mrs. Candler contended that the bequest to her was absolute, but the court held that she took a life estate only, subject to the power of disposal by will among her issue.

Colt v. Heard (10 *Hun*, 189) contained these provisions: "I give and bequeath and devise, all the rest, residue and remainder of my estate, real and personal and wheresoever situate unto my beloved husband, Thomas Scott; but such part thereof as he may have at the time of his decease I give, devise and bequeath unto my niece Mary Louise Ledyard," etc. It was there held that the intent of the testatrix was that her husband should enjoy the full benefit which he could derive from the estate willed to him, while he lived, and such of it as was left at his decease should go to the relatives of the testatrix, as stated in her will. See, also, Terry v. Wiggins (47 *N. Y.*, 512). Campbell v. Beaumont (91 *N. Y.*, 464) does not infringe upon the proposition above stated, for in that case the property disposed of by will to the widow was not in express terms given to her for life. It was given to her *generally*, without any words of qualification or limitation.

In Stuart v. Walker (72 *Maine*, 145; *S. C.*, 2 *Am. Prob. R.*, 79), the testator's will contained these provisions: "I give, devise and bequeath unto my wife, Mary Berry, all the rest and residue of my estate, real and personal, of what kind soever and wherever situate, with the right to use, occupy, lease, exchange, sell or otherwise dispose of the same, and the increase and income thereof, according to her own will and pleasure during her lifetime, meaning and intending hereby that the said Mary Berry, during her lifetime, shall have the absolute right, power and authority to use and dispose of, by sale or otherwise, all said devised estate, real and personal, for her own support and for any and all other purposes to which she may choose to appropriate it. And so much of said estate, so devised to my said wife, together with the increase, income and proceeds thereof, as may remain unexpended and undisposed of by her at her decease, I give, devise and bequeath unto the said Frances L. Sargeant, her heirs and assigns forever, if she shall be then living; and if not living, then to such children or child of said Frances as may be living at that time." The court unanimously held that the widow took a life estate only, and upon her death the property passed to the residuary legatee and devisee. The authorities bearing upon this question are here very fully discussed and collected, and the court say: "In no case in this State has it been directly or indirectly held that, where there is a devise for life in *express terms*, a power of disposal annexed can enlarge it to a fee."

From all the cases examined, I am satisfied that the testatrix herein had no power to dispose of, by will, the property which came to her through the will of Daniel Fanton.

From the testimony given before me upon this accounting, I am satisfied that Esther Fanton died possessed of personal property which came from means of her own, received from other sources than from her deceased husband, amounting to upwards of $1,200. For this the executor has not accounted. He should be charged with this, and the avails thereof distributed to the sisters of the testatrix, and to the representatives of the two sisters deceased since these proceedings were instituted.

The contestants have failed in part, and succeeded in part, in their claim. No bad faith can be imputed to the executor in the position he assumed. Neither party should be charged with costs as against the other. A decree should be entered accordingly.

ALLEGANY COUNTY.—HON. C. A. FARNUM, SURRO-
GATE.—January, 1885.

MATTER OF WISNER.

In the matter of the guardianship of the property of
BLANCHE WISNER, *and others, infants.*

In order that a petition, sworn to in another state, as permitted by Code
Civ. Pro., § 844, be deemed *duly verified*, the certificate authenticating
the act of the administering officer must show that the latter was
authorized by the laws of that state to take and certify the acknowledgment and proof of deeds to be recorded therein.

APPLICATION, by Adeline J. Wisner for ancillary
letters of guardianship.   The facts appear in the
opinion.

STANLEY C. SWIFT, *for petitioner.*

THE SURROGATE.—This is an application by Adeline
J. Wisner for ancillary letters of guardianship of the
property of Blanche Wisner and three others, infants
for whom she was appointed the guardian by the
circuit court of Huntington county, Indiana.

By § 2838 of the Code of Civil Procedure, the
application must be by a written petition, *duly verified,* setting forth certain facts.   The paper presented
sets forth all the facts required to be stated, and is
accompanied by exemplified copies of the petition,
bond of guardian, letters of guardianship and other
papers, showing her appointment by the Indiana
court, duly certified under the great seal of the state
of Indiana, as required by § 2705 of the Code.

The petition herein purports to have been verified by Mrs. Wisner before a notary public, in and for the county of Huntington, Indiana; and has attached thereto a certificate of the clerk of the circuit court of said Huntington county, stating that the person "whose certificate of acknowledgment is affixed to the instrument in writing to which this is attached, was a notary public in and for said county, and that full faith and credit ought to be given to his official acts; that the signature purporting to be his is genuine; and that said certificate is issued in accordance with the laws of the state of Indiana."

This certificate does not state that the notary public was authorized by the laws of the state of Indiana, to take and certify the acknowledgment and proof of deeds to be recorded in that state, as required by § 844 of the Code of Civil Procedure. The affidavit of the petitioner must be taken before an officer who has such authority, and the certificate of the clerk of the circuit court should show that he had such authority. The petition as presented to this court is the same as if unverified (Harris v. Derkeu, 5 *Browne*, 376).

The petitioner will have to procure a proper certificate, before this court can act upon the petition.

ALLEGANY COUNTY.—HON. C. A. FARNUM, SURRO-
GATE.—January, 1885.

MATTER OF CORTWRIGHT.

In the matter of the probate of the will of PHILENA
A. CORTWRIGHT, *deceased.*

Code Civ. Pro., § 2527, providing, among other things, that a Surrogate,
where he has reasonable grounds to believe that a person to be cited is
mentally incapable to protect his rights, although not judicially declared
to be incompetent, may "make an order requiring that a copy of the
citation be delivered, in behalf of that person, to a person designated
in the order," authorizes an *additional* service; the regular and ordinary service is not dispensed with. Hence, where application was
made for an order for such delivery, in behalf of a resident of another
state, alleged to be of unsound mind,—

Held, upon granting the application, that, in order to acquire jurisdiction,
the citation must *also* be served upon the non-resident, by publication, or by delivering to him personally a copy, without the State,
pursuant to § 2524.

APPLICATION, under Code Civ. Pro., § 2527, for an
order directing delivery of a copy of a citation, in
behalf of one incompetent, to a person designated.
The facts appear in the opinion.

C. S. DWINELLE, *for petitioner.*

THE SURROGATE.—Upon the return of the citation
herein, it appears that Lorenzo Cortwright, who is one
of the heirs at law and next of kin of the testatrix,
resides in Kansas, and has not been served with the
citation.

The petitioner now presents an affidavit tending to
show that the absent party is of unsound mind and

mentally incapable adequately to protect his rights, although he has not been judicially declared to be incompetent to manage his affairs.

He asks the Surrogate, under § 2527 of the Code of Civil Procedure, to make an order requiring that a copy of the citation be delivered, in behalf of Lorenzo, to a person designated in the order.

The Surrogate is willing to grant the order asked for, but the petitioner now insists that, if the citation be served on the person designated in the order, this court will acquire jurisdiction of the absent person, although he be not in fact served with the citation. He wishes to serve the citation upon the person to be designated in the order, and then proceed with this matter.

There is no foundation for such a contention. Until a person is judicially declared to be incompetent to manage his affairs, he must be treated, so far as the service of process is concerned, as if he was competent, although he be in fact incompetent.

It was not the intention of the legislature, in enacting § 2527, to take away any safeguard for the protection of one not competent to protect himself, but to give the incompetent person additional protection. Service of the citation upon him personally if within the State, or by publication if without the State, is not dispensed with. The petitioner will have to take an order, under § 2524 of the Code of Civil Procedure, for service of the citation upon Lorenzo Cortwright, by publication or by delivering to him personally without the State a copy of the citation herein. If he wish an order for the *additional* service of the citation upon a person to be designated in the order, he may take it, and in such case the citation should be served at least eight days before the return day thereof.

CATTARAUGUS COUNTY.—HON. ALFRED SPRING, SUR-
ROGATE.—November, 1884.

REFORM SOCIETY v. CASE.

In the matter of the judicial settlement of the account of THOMAS CASE, *and another, as executors of the will of* JOHN C. REYNOLDS, *deceased.*

Testator, who was an illegitimate child, and died leaving no parent or issue, by his will gave his property to his executors in trust, directing that, after the death of A., who was to have the use of his farm for life, the same "be sold, and the proceeds be let out at interest, and the said interest be annually paid to" a charitable corporation named, but making no provision for the management of the property after the death or resignation of the trustees selected by him. A. having died, the executors converted the real property into money which they invested, and paid the interest annually to the corporation legatee. Upon the judicial settlement of their account, had upon their application for leave to resign their trust,—

Held, that the bequest was not void, as contravening the statute against perpetuities, but that the principal of the fund should be transferred to the corporation, after deduction of commissions and the expenses of the accounting.

CONSTRUCTION of will upon executor's accounting. The facts appear in the opinion.

E. T. BARTLETT *and* W. W. WARING, *for the Reform Society.*

THE SURROGATE.—The deceased, John C. Reynolds, was an illegitimate person and left no issue.   In his

last will and testament, the testator leaves his property in trust to his executors therein named, and,
after giving one Ann Reynolds the use of his farm
during her life, directs his executors to make the following disposition thereof: "From and after the
decease of the said Ann Reynolds I do further direct
that the said farm be sold and the proceeds be let
out at interest and the said interest be annually paid
to the American Female Reform Society."

The executors duly qualified, and, in the execution
of their trust, and in compliance with the provision
quoted, converted the real estate into cash, and, since
the decease of the said Ann Reynolds, which occurred
in November, 1869, have paid the interest annually
to said legatee, the said Reform Society.

The executors have recently resigned, and, in proceedings for the judicial settlement of their account,
have presented and filed their account in this court,
showing a fund in their hands of about $1,300, the
proceeds arising from the sale of the farm. The
Reform Society appear in response to a citation in
this proceeding, and ask that the *corpus*, the principal, of this fund be paid over to the society, instead
of having the same invested and the interest paid
through the medium of an administrator with the will
annexed.

In construing a will, the testator's real intention is
the primary and paramount object to be sought (4
Kent Com., 534). An examination of testator's
surroundings, in connection with the will itself, frequently gives some clue to his probable intention on
the disposition of his property as set forth in his will.

In this case, testator had no children and left no parent, and after the death of the life tenant there was no one in any way dependent upon him, or having claims upon his bounty, so that the equitable claims of this residuary legatee, this charitable institution, are not inferior to those of any one else. He does not limit or qualify this bequest to the Reform Society, and this is a significant circumstance, indicating that he desired the Reform Society to receive all of his property after the expiration of the life tenancy.

He makes no provision for the management of this property after the death or resignation of the trustees selected by him—an omission not liable to be made if it was intended to keep this fund forever invested and controlled by others than the beneficiary.

The testator never intended to die intestate as to the bulk of his property. With no next of kin, a man of his intelligence would not go through the formality of executing a will and still designedly leave the residuum, the major part, of his property undisposed of, to pass to the State. Persons in his unfortunate condition would be particular to a finical degree in making an unequivocal and permanent disposition of their property. Intestacy to them means a dissipation of their estates.

It has been repeatedly held that, where a testator devises the income and rents of certain real estate, without qualification, and without disposing of the body of the land, the devise carries with it the land itself (4 Kent Com., 536 ; Jennings v. Conboy, 73 *N. Y.*, 230 ; Hatch v. Bassett, 52 *N. Y.*, 359 ; Monarque v. Monarque, 80 *N. Y.*, 320 ; Patterson v. Ellis'

Ex'rs, 11 *Wend.*, 200; Parker v. Plummer, *Cro. Eliz.*, 190; Smith v. Post, 2 *Edw. Ch.*, 523; 3 Wash. Real Prop., 450).

The analogous doctrine, that a bequest of the interest of personal property carries with it the principal itself, where there is no limit or qualification to such bequest, is equally well established by authority (Earl v. Grim, 1 *Johns. Ch.*, 494; Hatch v. Bassett, 52 *N. Y.*, 359; Thompson v. Conway, 23 *Hun*, 621; Adamson v. Armitage, 19 *Vesey*, 416).

The fact that the corporation in this case is the legatee does not alter the rule, as that is endued with the power of perpetual existence (Angel & Ames on Corporations, *Sec.* 8).

Eleemosynary corporations are organized for the purpose of perpetually distributing funds entrusted to them, and hence partake of the "immortal" character attributable to all corporations (Angel & Ames [*supra*], *Sec.* 39).

The Revised Statutes of this State provide that "the absolute ownership of property shall not be suspended by any limitation or condition whatever, for more than two lives in being at the death of the testator" (2 R. S. [*6th ed.*], 1167, § 1).

Either this bequest is absolutely and unqualifiedly a gift to the Reform Society, or else it is void *in toto*, as being repugnant to the statute. Inasmuch as a gift can readily be spelled out of the will itself, there is no necessity for the strained construction required to avoid the will.

A decree may be entered adjusting and allowing the account filed, and directing the transfer, to the society, of the body, the principal, of the fund remaining after the expenses of this accounting and the commissions of the executors.

CATTARAUGUS COUNTY.—HON. ALFRED SPRING, SURROGATE.—March, 1885.

TURNER *v.* AMSDELL.

In the matter of the estate of MAJOR MACAPES, *deceased.*

In a special proceeding instituted to procure a decree directing the disposition of the real property of a decedent for the payment of his debts, the Surrogate is bound, under Code Civ. Pro., § 2755, upon the return of the citation, to take proof of the claims of all who appear as creditors of the decedent, including those which have been presented to the executor or administrator, and rejected, or not allowed, by him. Actual creditors and those claiming to be such, have the same right to appear and establish their demands.

Matter of Glann, 2 *Redf.*, 75; Barnett v. Kincaid, 2 *Lans.*, 320—disapproved.

PETITION by the executor of decedent's will for leave to mortgage, lease or sell his real property, to pay his debts. Maurice Turner and others, infant devisees, by their guardian, objected to the proof of the claims of Matilda Amsdell and others, alleged creditors, who appeared upon the return of the citation. Further facts appear in the opinion.

J. E. WEEDEN, *executor in person.*

J. V. GOODWILL, GEO. U. LOVERIDGE *and* R. R. CROWLEY, *for creditors.*

C. D. DAVIE, *guardian ad litem.*

THE SURROGATE.—This is a proceeding instituted by the executor of the will of Major Macapes, deceased, for leave to sell the real estate of testator to pay his debts. Upon the return of the citation, a large number of creditors appear to prove their claims. A portion of these have been duly presented to the executor and formally rejected by him, while others have been presented to the executor, and no definite action has been taken by him concerning them. In either event, they are *disputed* claims (Cooper v. Felter, 6 *Lans.*, 485; Tucker v. Tucker, 4 *Keyes*, 136). The guardian ad litem, appearing on behalf of infant devisees, objects to the consideration of these disputed claims, upon the ground that the court has no jurisdiction to entertain proof in reference thereto.

The objection is an untenable one. I am aware that, ordinarily, a Surrogate's court has no jurisdiction over claims presented to an executor or administrator and rejected by him. The common law courts must pass upon the validity of such claims (Tucker v. Tucker, 4 *Keyes*, 136 *supra;* McNulty v. Hurd, 72 *N. Y.*, 518; Fiester v. Shepard, 92 *N. Y.*, 251). But in proceedings to sell real estate, the executor, if a party at all, is merely a formal one. The real parties in interest are the heirs at law, devisees and creditors; and the statutory inhibition, instead of extending to them, explicitly confers the power upon the Surrogate to hear the proof where an heir at law or devisee objects to a claim presented, or one *represented as existing against decedent* (Code Civ. Pro., § 2755).

These proceedings can be commenced, either by the representative, or by a creditor (Code Civ. Pro., § 2750). And the Code does not, otherwise than by implication, make the executor or administrator a necessary party to the citation in case the proceedings are instituted by a creditor. Again, § 2752 requires the name of each creditor, "or person *claiming* to be a creditor," to be set forth in the petition— thus giving a creditor, and one claiming to be such, an equal right to appear and establish their demands.

Section 2788 is even more broad and liberal in its terms as to the taking of proof than § 2755, and it imperatively enjoins the Surrogate to hear the allegations and proofs "respecting any demands against the decedent."

These various sections certainly give the Surrogate's court ample jurisdiction over any claim which is sought to be made a charge upon the fund arising from the sale of the land. The allowance or rejection of a claim by the executor has not the least relevancy in the matter whatever. Whether a claim presented bears the seal of his sanction, or whether it comes into court unfathered and unprotected by his magic power, it is treated the same. It must be run through the same hopper, must be *proved, established*, before the Surrogate, and that too, as I interpret the law, by common-law proof. Less proof than is necessary to justify a judgment in a justice's court, where defendant does not appear, will not suffice.

So unimportant a factor is the executor in these proceedings that, where a judgment has been taken against him by default, in his representative capacity, it is of no significance or use whatever, and is subject to contest the same as an unliquidated demand (Code, § 2755).

And even in case a judgment has been recovered against him upon the merits, it is merely *presumptive* evidence of the debt (*id.*).

To permit the Surrogate to hear proof where the claim is controverted by the real parties in interest, to wit, the heirs at law, and yet allow the mere figure head in the proceedings to oust the Surrogate of jurisdiction, would be investing the executor or administrator with altogether too much authority, inasmuch as he is only nominally a party.

I know one or two cases hold the contrary doctrine, as to jurisdiction of the Surrogate (see In re Glann, 2 *Redf.*, 75; Barnett v. Kincaid, 2 *Lans.*, 320); but the later authorities adopt and sustain the more consistent doctrine (Hopkins v. Van Valkenburg, 16 *Hun*, 3; People v. Westbrook, 61 *How. Pr.*, 138.; Kammerrer v. Ziegler, 1 *Dem.*, 177).

I will hear the proofs upon all claims presented.

Cayuga County.—Hon. J. D. TELLER, Surrogate.— February, 1885.

OLIVER *v.* FRISBIE.

In the matter of the estate of EARL T. FRISBIE, *deceased.*

Testator, by his will, appointed his son T. and one C. its executors; bequeathed sundry legacies, which he charged upon his real property; and gave to the executors a power of sale of the latter, in order to carry out his testamentary provisions. C., who performed most of the executorial duties, having found an opportunity to sell, at a fair valuation, a parcel of the real property which, both before and since testator's death, had been occupied as a residence by T., the latter refused to join in the deed upon the ground that he ought to have the property himself at less than the stipulated price, at the same time stating that it was worth more than such price to an outsider. On account of this refusal, the contract of sale was abandoned. Upon petition, by the residuary legatees, for the revocation of T.'s letters,—

Held, that T. was not a testamentary trustee within the meaning of Code Civ. Pro., § 2819; that the power to sell and distribute the proceeds of the realty was so inseparably connected with the office of executor that no distinct proceeding to remove him as trustee, or donee of a power in trust, could be had; and that, while the delinquency of which he had been guilty could not be construed as improvidence, within the meaning of Code Civ. Pro., § 2685, subd. 2, it was such misconduct in the execution of his office as rendered him unfit for the due execution thereof, within the meaning of that subdivision, and that the prayer of the petition should be granted.

PETITION for the revocation of letters testamentary. The facts appear sufficiently in the opinion.

JAMES LYON, *for petitioners.*

M. V. AUSTIN, *opposed.*

THE SURROGATE.—This is an application by Henrietta Oliver and others, residuary legatees under the will of Earl T. Frisbie (proved in this court Oct. 5th, 1883), for a decree revoking the letters testamentary, issued the same day to Theodore E. Frisbie, upon the ground of improvidently managing the property and that, by reason of misconduct in the execution of his office, he is unfit for the due execution of the office of executor.

The said Theodore E. Frisbie is the son of the decedent. He is named in the codicil to said will, with Charles H. Carpenter, the son in law of the decedent, as such executor. Both of them qualified and received letters. Charles Frisbie, the only remaining child and residuary legatee, appeared upon the hearing and gave evidence to support the petition. The testator left personal property amounting to about $6,000; real estate in the town of Throop of the value of about $800; one piece in Auburn valued at about $2,200; and another piece, of which the value was disputed, and which is situated upon Adams street in Auburn, and consists of a house and lot whereon the said Theodore E. Frisbie has resided since the death of the testator and for about three years previously.

By the will, certain legacies are made a charge upon all the testator's real estate, and the executors are empowered and authorized to sell and convey any real estate of which the testator might die seized, without undue haste and not at a sacrifice, in order to carry out the provisions of the will.

The will directs that any advancements which the testator had made to Theodore, should be charged against him and be credited to the testator's estate in the general distribution of the residuum.

The proof shows that the decedent had advanced $500 to Theodore. Before this application was made, all the debts of the estate, amounting to about $1,100, had been paid. The Throopsville property had been sold for $800, and $550 of the proceeds paid out upon a legacy. The testator's widow has been paid the legacy of $1,500. All other legacies are unpaid.

In June, 1884, Mr. Carpenter, as executor, after

having advertised several months, found a person who desired to purchase the Adams street property, and who offered $1,300 for it. A deed was made and executed by Carpenter and presented to Theodore Frisbie, the co-executor, for his signature. Frisbie refused to sign the deed, giving, as his reason, that he thought he ought to have the property himself, and that he ought to have it for $1,000; also stating that the place was worth to an outsider more than $1,300. Upon another occasion the executor Frisbie stated, in the presence of the other legatees, that he would not sign the deed, claiming that he ought to have the place for $1,000, that his wife would not let him sign, and that the place was worth $1,500. On account of his refusal to sign the deed, the contract of sale had to be abandoned.

It appears from the evidence that $1,300 was a fair valuation of the property, and that there had been no opportunity to sell it for more money. The rental value was about $10 a month. All of the legatees were in favor of the sale except Theodore, and he was occupying the house without having given any security or made any agreement with the other executor to pay rent.

It appears in evidence that he built a barn upon the lot during his father's lifetime at an expense of $226.87, but there is evidence to show that this was accepted by the father in lieu of rent, and from the will it is clear the testator did not intend Theodore should have any farther interest in the place than that indicated in the residuary clause, and that he intended the place should be sold to meet the legacies

chargeable upon it.   During his occupancy and before
his father's death, Theodore paid taxes and made
some necessary repairs.   There seems to have been
some expectation on his part that his father would
give him the property, and from all the evidence it
very conclusively appears that his refusal to sign a
deed is based upon the hope that the other parties in
interest would be prevailed upon to do in part what
the testator failed to do in this behalf.   It further
appears that the papers have been held by Mr. Carpenter, that all the moneys have passed through his
hands, and that Theodore E. Frisbie has taken but
very little part in the settlement of the estate.

Under these circumstances, the question arises
whether Theodore Frisbie has come under the con-
demnation of the statute, and should be removed as
executor.   The authority for such action must be
found in § 2685 of the Code.   The power to sell and
distribute the proceeds of the real estate is so inseparably connected with the office of executor, that it
would seem no distinct proceeding to remove him as
trustee, or donee of a power in trust, can be had.   He
is not a testamentary trustee within the meaning of
§ 2819 of the Code.   He is simply an executor with
power of sale as to the realty, which is treated by the
will as personal property.   Under the construction
given by the courts to " improvidence," it would
hardly seem that the acts or delinquency charged in
this case can come under that head (Emerson v.
Bowers, 14 *N. Y.*, 449).

It remains to inquire whether there has been shown
such misconduct in the execution of his office as

renders this executor unfit for the due execution of his office. In the case of Quackenboss v. Southwick (41 *N. Y.*, 117), it was held that the removal of a trustee was proper where the relations between him and his co-trustee are such that they will not co-operate in carrying out the trusts beneficially to those interested, and a majority of the beneficiaries ask for the removal. The statute provided that the court may remove any trustee who shall have violated his trust, or who shall be insolvent, or who, for any other cause, shall be deemed an unsuitable person to execute the trust (1 R. S., p. 730, § 70). In this case, it appeared that the relations between the trustees were such that they would probably not co-operate in closing the trust beneficially to those interested in the estate. The court held this to be a cause rendering one or the other trustee an unsuitable person, and regarded the wishes of those interested (they being *sui juris*) as to which should be removed.

In the Matter of Mechanics Bank (2 *Barb.*, 446), the Supreme Court held, under the same statute, that a trustee in a mortgage given by a railroad company, who refused to take possession of the mortgaged property upon default, and enforce the collection of the mortgage, on the request of the bondholders, and who, by his trust, sought to coerce the bondholders to afford assistance to the debtor by granting time, violated his trust and should be removed. The court says: " If he is permitted to continue in the trust, I have no assurance that he will not extend the delay, on the same pretence for years yet to come."

The case at bar is stronger for the application of

this rule than the one last cited. In this, the executor refuses to sign the deed because he thinks he
ought to have the property at a reduced price. He
is attempting to coerce the parties in interest into
compliance with his individual claim. He is setting
up his private demands in hostility to the performance
of his official duty, and it cannot be said that the
alleged inadequacy of the purchase price was the
ground of his refusal to sign the deed.

The judgment of an executor or trustee when
relied upon by a testator is conclusive, and the opinion of the court is not to control the exercise of discretion. But that judgment must be exercised in .
good faith, and not used for selfish ends.

In the case of Deraismes v. Dunham (22 *Hun*, 86),
the court held that unfriendly relations between
trustees, which endangered the execution of the trust
and prevented harmony of action, were sufficient to
justify the removal of a trustee, citing Story Eq. Jur.,
Sec. 1280. See Matter of Morgan (63 *Barb.*, 621), and
Wood v. Brown (34 *N. Y.*, 337).

In the Matter of Cohn (78 *N. Y.*, 248), the question
arose whether there was sufficient cause for the
removal of an assignee for misconduct or incompetency. It appeared, among other things, that the
assignee was counsel for a party whose interests were
adverse to those of the creditors whom he represented in his trust capacity. The court held this a
good ground for removal, and that the creditors were
entitled to an assignee who could act impartially and
without a violation of a duty which he owed to others.
The court says: "The words 'misconduct' and 'in-

competency,' as used in this statute, have no technical meaning. The two were intended to embrace all the reasons for which an assignee ought to be removed. This power (of removal) could not be less than that possessed by a court of equity, and that, upon such facts as exist here, a court of equity would have power to remove a trustee cannot be doubted (2 *Perry on Trusts*, §§ 817, 818)."

We think we are justified in a similar interpretation of § 2685 of the Code, and that the facts appearing in this case show such misconduct as has rendered Theodore E. Frisbie unfit for the due execution of his office as executor. The books contain much learning upon the subject of the injustice of parties who act in a fiduciary capacity seeking to derive advantage to themselves.

Sales made by trustees for their own benefit have repeatedly been set aside, and the courts have uniformly held that transactions, in which motives of personal convenience or interest have been subserved, are thereby tainted with fraud. It would seem to follow that a refusal on the part of such person to act, upon the ground that his personal convenience or interest would be interfered with, would be misconduct under the statute in question.

Chancellor KENT, in the case of Davoue v. Fanning (2 *Johns. Ch.*, 25), says the only way for a trustee to purchase safely is by application to the court, which will divest him of his character of trustee and prevent all the consequences of his acting both for himself and for the *cestui que trust*. The suggestion is significant, and if this executor has any equities

relating to the property which he occupies, he may
be in better position to obtain his rights if the prayer
of the petition is granted. I think he should be
removed, and findings may be prepared in accordance
with the views herein expressed.

———————

KINGS COUNTY.—HON. J. I. BERGEN, SURROGATE.—
July, 1884.

COLLINS *v.* WAYDELL.

In the matter of the estate of JOHN COLLINS, *deceased.*

Letters testamentary under decedent's will were issued in April, 1861, and
the executors, in July of that year, filed an inventory of the estate;
but their account was never judicially settled. M., a legatee, attained
majority in February, 1879, and applied in April, 1884, under Code Civ.
Pro., § 2723, for an order compelling the executors to file an account.
The latter pleaded the statute of limitations (Code Civ. Pro., § 2723,
subd. 4; id., § 396, subd. 1, and clause *ad. fin.*).—*Held,*

1. That, the object of the proceeding being manifestly to ascertain the
petitioner's share in testator's estate, the same was subject to the limitation of an action for a legacy.
2. That, by Code Civ. Pro., § 1819, the statute commencing to run against
such a cause of action only when the executor's account was judicially
settled, petitioner's remedy was not barred.
3. That petitioner's delay in instituting the special proceeding was not
such laches as would justify a dismissal.

APPLICATION to compel John H. Waydell and
Andrew G. Collins, the executors of decedent's will, to
file an intermediate account. The facts appear sufficiently in the opinion.

MAN & PARSONS, *for petitioner.*

N. B. HOXIE, *for executors.*

THE SURROGATE.— This is an application on behalf of Margaret J. Collins, one of the legatees and devisees under the will of John Collins, deceased, for an order requiring the executors of said will to render an account of their proceedings, under § 2723 of the Code of Civil Procedure.

John Collins died February 16th, 1861; letters testamentary under his will were issued April 1st, 1861; and the inventory was filed July 8th, following. Margaret Collins was born February 22nd, 1858.

The executors answer that the right to this proceeding accrued to the petitioner at the expiration of eighteen months after the issuing of letters testamentary, viz.: October 1st, 1862; and that, by §§ 388 and 396 of the Code, she was barred from commencing it at the time when she filed the petition in the proceeding.

The executors thus claim that the disability of the petitioner ceased February 22nd, 1879, the day she became of age; and that, by the final clause of § 396 of the Code, she was limited to one year after the disability ceased, in which to bring her action.

I think, however, that she is not barred by the statute of limitations. In the case of House v. Agate (3 *Redf.*, 307), it was held that a petition in the Surrogate's court must be filed within the time in which actions of a similar character are required to be commenced in courts of common law or equity. The same doctrine was maintained in Cole v. Terpenning (25 *Hun*, 482), and other cases therein cited. In Cole v. Terpenning, the petition for an accounting was denied upon the ground that it was barred by the statute of limitations, but it will be observed that § 1819 of the Code was not in force at the time the petition was filed.

That section provides : " If after the expiration of one year from the granting of letters testamentary or letters of administration, an executor or administrator refuses upon demand to pay a legacy, or distributive share, the person entitled thereto may maintain such an action against him, as the case requires. But for the purpose of computing the time within such an action must be commenced, the cause of action is deemed to accrue, when the executor's or administrator's account is judicially settled, and not before."

There is no doubt that this is a proceeding to ascertain the distributive share of the petitioner in the testator's estate.

I am, therefore, of the opinion that the last clause of § 1819 of the Code, which fixes the time when the right to an action is deemed to have accrued, namely, when the account of the executor or administrator is judicially settled (that not having been done in this case) disposes of the question of the statute of limitations.

As to the question of *laches*, I think the time which has elapsed since the disability of the petitioner ceased, is not sufficient for me to refuse to grant the prayer of the petition.

An order may be entered requiring the executors to account.

KINGS COUNTY.—HON. J. I. BERGEN, SURROGATE.—
July, 1884.

LOUNSBERY v. PARSON.

In the matter of the judicial settlement of the account of the executors of the will of JAMES H. LOUNS-BERY, deceased.

Testator, by his will, directed his executors to complete the building of his house, if unfinished at the time of his death, at an expense not exceeding $50,000 in the aggregate; and, if the same should not be furnished at that time, to pay to his wife as desired "not exceeding $15,000, as an additional specific legacy, to enable her to furnish the same." He then devised the house to his wife, and her heirs and assigns forever. The devisee sold the house unfurnished, and received from the executors $15,000, as an absolute legacy. Upon objection to such payment,—

Held, that the purpose mentioned in the legatory clause was not of the substance of the gift, which was an unconditional one; and that the payment by the executors was proper.

CONSTRUCTION of decedent's will upon the judicial settlement of the account of Anna R. Parson, and others, executrix and executors thereof. Objections were filed by Lucretia H. Lounsbery and others, legatees. The facts are stated in the opinion.

SCUDDER & CARTER, *for executors.*

D. G. WILD, *for Lucretia H. Lounsbery and others, legatees.*

LAWRENCE KNEELAND, *for adm'x of estate of H. F. Lounsbery, deceased.*

H. INGRAHAM, *special guardian.*

THE SURROGATE.—The following question relating to a legacy contained in the last will and testament of James H. Lounsbery, deceased, has been submitted to me for my decision: The fifth clause of the testator's will provides as follows : "If the house I am erecting on Clinton Avenue in said Brooklyn shall be unfinished at my death, I order and direct my trustees to finish the building thereof in accordance with the plans and specifications now made thereof, and to expend for that purpose not exceeding the sum of fifty thousand dollars, including the amount previously expended thereon. If the same is not furnished at my death, they shall pay to my said wife, at such time or times as she desires, not exceeding fifteen thousand dollars as an additional specific legacy to enable her to furnish the same."

He then gives the house to his widow, Anna R. Lounsbery, since married to Parson, and her heirs and assigns forever.

After testator's death, the house was completed and sold by the devisee unfurnished, and the executors paid to the widow the sum of $15,000, as provided by the fifth clause of the will, contending that the legacy so bequeathed was an absolute and unconditional one. The last phrase of said clause, namely, "to enable her to furnish the same," some of the legatees contend, makes the legacy a conditional one, i. e., for the furnishing of the house.

To that proposition I cannot accede, for it appears to me that the testator intended to make an absolute gift of a sum not to exceed $15,000, to his widow, which she might apply to furnishing the house or to any other purposes she desired. The expression is not equivalent to "if," or "provided," or "upon the understanding that the money be used in furnishing the house." It was simply, as the testator says, an additional specific legacy to enable her to furnish the same.

In the case of the Five Points House of Industry v. Amerman (11 *Hun*, 161), the testator gave $500 to plaintiff, to be applied to the uses of the farm in Westchester county. Judge BRADY, in writing the opinion of the General Term, says: "The language employed is—to be applied to the uses of the farm in Westchester county. The testator gave the sum, but annexed a wish or direction that it should be applied in a particular manner. There is nothing in the language adopted indicative of an intention to make a condition. The legacy is not on condition, or provided, or upon the understanding, but absolute as a gift, with a direction or wish annexed to or coupled with it."

2 Lomax on Executors, 141, says: "If a legacy be given to a person for a particular purpose, that purpose will not operate as a condition to the bequest, and though it become impossible to appropriate it to that purpose without any fault of the legatee, he will nevertheless be entitled to the legacy. It rests on the principle that, the fund being appropriated to the benefit of the legatee, the mode in which it shall be applied is but a secondary object and does not enter into the substance of the gift, and the absolute interest vests in the legatee. See, also, 1 Roper on Legacies, 645, and 2 Williams on Executors, 1293.

In Knox v. Lord Hotham (15 *Simons*, 82), it was held that the bequest to a daughter " towards purchasing a country residence" was an absolute gift.

In Skinner's Trust (1 *Johnson & Hemmings*, 102), where the testator gave his manuscripts and £1,000 towards printing them to his grandson, to assist him when he went to college, the grandson was held entitled to elect to take the £1,000, it appearing to be impossible to publish the book at a profit. See, also, Barton v. Cooke (5 *Vesey*, 461); Lewes v. Lewes (16 *Simons*, 266).

In the case at bar, the testator by his will directed that, in case of his death before the completion of his house, his trustees should finish the building thereof, and, in case the same was not furnished, his trustees should pay the above legacy to his wife to enable her to furnish the same.

I think that the testator intended that the house should be completed at an expense not to exceed the sum stated, and that the trustees should pay to testator's wife the sum of $15,000, to furnish the same. He in no way restricted her from selling both house and furniture whenever she chose.

In order to make the legacy conditional the intention must be clearly expressed, and before it will be inferred that the testator intended to make such an unreasonable condition as that his wife should expend a legacy in buying furniture which she would have the power to sell immediately afterwards, such intention must be expressed in clear and unequivocal language. I am, therefore, led to the conclusion that the direction contained in said bequest was not a condition which would defeat the gift.

KINGS COUNTY.—HON. J. I. BERGEN, SURROGATE.—
July, 1884.

JONES *v.* LE BARON.

In the matter of the estate of CALEB B. LE BARON,
deceased.

In a special proceeding instituted under Code Civ. Pro., § 2750, *et seq.*, to
procure a decree directing the disposition of a decedent's real property
for the payment of his debts, the fact that an alleged creditor's claim
has already been presented to and admitted by the personal representative throws the burden of proof upon a party objecting thereto.

The provision of Code Civ. Pro., § 829, forbidding a party to a special proceeding to be examined, upon the hearing, in his own behalf, *against
the executor or administrator* of a deceased person, concerning a personal transaction or communication between witness and the decedent,
does not apply to a special proceeding instituted, by a creditor, to dispose of decedent's real property for the payment of his debts, where
the testimony of another alleged creditor, offered in his own behalf,
concerning such a transaction or communication, is objected to by
petitioner. The rule is for the protection of the personal representative of decedent, and he alone can take advantage thereof.

A decedent's discharge in bankruptcy may be attacked collaterally, in a
special proceeding in a Surrogate's court relating to his estate, and
declared void, as against a creditor as to whom the same was fraudulently procured.

Payments made by an administrator to redeem decedent's real property
from sales for arrears of taxes, allowed to him, in a peculiar case, as a
preferred claim against the estate, with interest.

HEARING of objections upon an application, made
by William A. Jones, an alleged creditor, for a decree
directing the disposition of decedent's real property for the payment of his debts. The facts appear sufficiently in the opinion.

BLANCHARD, GAY & PHELPS, *for administrator and others.*

GEO. WILCOX, R. L. SCOTT, ADRIAN VAN SINDEREN *and* A. W.
GLEASON, *for objecting creditors.*

THE SURROGATE.—This is an application, under
§ 2750 of the Code of Civil Procedure, for a decree
directing the sale of the property of a deceased person
for the payment of his debts.   Upon the return of the
citation, a number of creditors appeared and presented their claims.   The claims of Anna G. Le Baron
for $2,405.57; Oceana H. Le Baron for $19,305.50;
Mary E. Le Baron for $23,372.53; and the adminis-
trator for the sum of $926.40, were disputed.   It ap-
pears by the evidence that the personal property is
insufficient to pay the debts of the decedent, and
therefore the creditors are compelled to resort to the
real estate of the decedent for the payment of the
same.   It also clearly appears that the debts of the
decedent are largely in excess of the value of the real
estate, and that, in no event, could the creditors receive more than a small *pro rata* amount of their
claims.   William A. Jones, who has presented and
proved his claim, objects to the claims of the Le Baron
family, to wit: Oceana H. Le Baron, Mary E. Le
Baron, and Anna G. Le Baron, who are sisters of the
decedent—first, upon the ground that the proof of the
indebtedness is too indefinite; second, that, under
§ 829 of the Code, all the evidence of these parties
concerning conversations or transactions with Caleb
B. Le Baron should be excluded; third, that the discharge in bankruptcy of Caleb B. Le Baron estops
these claimants from establishing their claims.

I have carefully reviewed all the testimony taken in
these proceedings, and am of the opinion that these
claims were sufficiently proved, unless the testimony
given by the claimants as to the conversations and

transactions with the decedent should be stricken out. It appears, from the account of the administrator on file in this office, and the evidence in these proceedings, that the administrator had admitted these claims. The petitioning creditor simply objects to the said claims, but offers no evidence to show that they are not valid.

It seems to me that the claims having been presented to the administrator and by him admitted to be valid claims against the estate establishes, *prima facie*, their validity, and puts the burden of proof upon the objector (Matter of Fraser, 92 *N. Y.*, 239). Section 828 of the Code declares that "a person shall not be excluded or excused" on account of interest except as otherwise specially provided. Nor do I think that it comes within the exception provided in § 829 of the Code, which declares "that a party or a person interested in the event . . . . . shall not be examined in his own behalf or interest . . . . . against the executor, administrator or survivor of a deceased person . . . . . concerning a personal transaction or communication between the witness and the deceased person . . . . . except where the executor, administrator or survivor . . . . . is examined in his own behalf . . . . . concerning the same transaction or communication." To exclude evidence under this section, the case must be brought strictly within the wording of the statute. It is not enough to be within its spirit (Seven v. National Bank of Troy, 18 *Hun*, 228; Lobdell v. Lobdell, 36 *N. Y.*, 327). The testimony referred to is not against the administrator or survivor, as the statute says it must be.   The administrator admits the claims, and the survivor does not object to the evidence. The objector is merely a creditor of the decedent. The statute was enacted to protect the representatives of deceased persons, and they are the only persons who can take advantage of it.

The claimants in this proceeding are the sisters, heirs and survivors of the decedent.   They loaned him a large portion of their property, and trusted implicitly in his integrity and ability to pay them.   In my opinion, they have a strong legal and moral claim upon his estate for the payment of the same.

The only question remaining to be determined is, does the discharge in bankruptcy of Caleb B. Le Baron, in 1868, operate as a discharge of these claimants' debts.

It appears from the evidence that the claim of Anna G. Le Baron arose after the discharge was granted, and therefore is not affected by it; and that the portions of the claims of Oceana H. Le Baron and Mary E. Le Baron, which arose prior to the granting of the discharge, are not barred by it, inasmuch as the proceedings in bankruptcy of Caleb B. Le Baron omitted to mention them as creditors, and they did not receive any notice of said proceedings, and had no knowledge that he had been discharged in bankruptcy.

I am of the opinion, from the evidence, that the decedent, Caleb B. Le Baron, wilfully and fraudulently omitted their names from the schedule of his debts in bankruptcy; that he never caused them to be notified of the said proceedings for his discharge;

that he knew he was in debt to these claimants, his sisters, and knew where they resided, as they frequently visited him at his office during and before the time when the proceedings in bankruptcy were in progress. He commenced in 1850, paying money on account of his indebtedness to each of his said sisters and continued so doing until within a month of his death. By omitting their names from the schedules in bankruptcy, and keeping them and each of them in entire ignorance of his proceedings therein, he deprived them of the opportunity to resist his discharge, or to participate in their share of the dividends of his assets.

In the case of Batchelder v. Low (8 *National Bankruptcy Register*, 571), it was held "that the discharge is to be pleaded in suits upon claims in courts where pending, and those courts must to some extent determine the validity and effect of the pleas. No other court could consider them and render judgment upon them in those cases. The provision in the same section, that the certificate shall be conclusive evidence of the fact and regularity, seems to relate to the mode of proof of the discharge, and not the effect of it when proved. As now understood, the provisions of the Bankrupt act do not prevent plaintiffs from contesting the validity of the discharge, as to them, in this court, by showing that it was obtained upon proceedings of which they were fraudulently deprived of notice."

In the case of Poillon v. Lawrence (77 *N. Y.*, 207), it was held that, where a bankrupt applied for a discharge in a name other than the one in which he

contracted the debt, thus depriving the creditor of
any notice of the application for his discharge, it
could be attacked in the court in which the creditor
sought to establish his claim, and that the discharge
would be held inoperative as to the debt of the creditor defrauded thereby, by reason of the failure to
make him a party to the proceeding, by proper publication or otherwise.

I am, therefore, led to the conclusion that, by reason of the bankrupt having wilfully and fraudulently
omitted the names and claims of his sisters from
his schedules of his debts, and not having given them
any notice of the application for his discharge, the
discharge can be attacked by them in this court, and
so far as the same affects said sisters it is inoperative.

In reference to the claim of the administrator for
having paid taxes upon property at East New York,
Kings county, amounting to $926.40, on November
20th, 1883, it appears from the evidence that the
same had accumulated upon the property now sought
to be sold under these proceedings, for the years
1871 to 1876, and the property was sold by the
State Comptroller for arrears of taxes of those years;
and that the administrator redeemed the same on the
day named, in order that the property might not be
charged with the additional interest of ten per cent.

While the administrator, strictly, has nothing to do
with the real estate of the decedent, and has no right
to apply the personal property in payment of claims
against the real estate, still, the only property the
decedent left of any value was this real estate in
question, and, the administrator having acted in good

faith, and for the best interests of the estate, in redeeming the property from the sale for the unpaid taxes which had been levied and confirmed as a lien upon this real estate prior to the death of the decedent, I think that the same should be allowed to him as a preferred claim against the decedent, with interest thereon from November 20th, 1883; for, if it had not been redeemed, the taxes would still remain as an existing and first lien upon this property. The administrator having paid them, he should be subrogated to the right the State had against the property for the unpaid taxes.

Decreed accordingly.

KINGS COUNTY.—HON. J. I. BERGEN, SURROGATE.— November, 1884.

BOLLES *v.* BACON.

In the matter of the judicial settlement of the account of the executor of the will of HARRIET ROGERS, *deceased.*

Testatrix, by her will, after directing her executor to pay all her debts, gave the residue of her estate, which consisted of personal property, to her niece, B., "with whom I have resided for many years last past, to have and to hold the same unto her, her heirs and assigns forever." B. died before testatrix, leaving two children who survived the latter. Upon the settlement of the executor's account, it was contended that the recital as to residence indicated that the legacy was made in satisfaction of a claim; also that the concluding words of the bequest were substitutional, under which B.'s children took by purchase, and that the court might and should supply the word "or" before "her heirs."—

Held, that these contentions were unfounded; that the recital in question
  contained merely words of identification; that the habendum operated
  as a limitation; and that the legacy lapsed under the general rule.

An executor has no right to buy off contestants of his decedent's will, and
  charge the expenditure against the estate.

CONTEST over the construction of decedent's will
upon the judicial settlement of the account of
Stephen H. Bacon, the executor thereof. Objections were filed by Enoch Bolles, and others, decedent's nephews and nieces. The facts are stated in
the opinion.

VAN WINKLE, CANDLER & JAY, *for executor.*

BRANCH & BRANCH, *for objectors.*

THE SURROGATE.—The testatrix, who died in March,
1881, by her will, after making certain specific
bequests, declares as follows: "All the rest, residue
and remainder of my estate, both real and personal,
which I may die seized or possessed of, or entitled
unto, of whatsoever kind, nature or description the
same may be, and wheresoever situate, I do hereby
give, devise and bequeath unto my niece, the said
Lucy Ann Bacon, with whom I have resided for many
years last past, to have and to hold the same unto her,
her heirs and assigns forever."

Lucy Ann Bacon, the residuary legatee, died in
March, 1880, leaving two children her surviving,
namely, Stephen H. Bacon and Daniel Bacon, the
former of whom is the accounting executor. The
testatrix never had any children. Her father and
mother died before her, and at her death she had one
brother, Thomas Owen, living, since deceased. The

testatrix lived several years after executing her will. The contestants are her brothers' and sisters' children. The estate consists of personal property.

The main question arising upon this accounting is: does the legacy given by the residuary clause of the will lapse, or do the children take it as the heirs at law of Lucy Ann Bacon, the legatee and devisee therein named?

The intention of the testator must be ascertained from the language of the will. The heirs at law of Lucy Ann Bacon insist that the words "to have and to hold to her, her heirs and assigns forever," must be construed as words of purchase.

The testatrix, by the fifth clause of her will, directs that, in case of the death of her nephew, Peter B. Rogers, or her niece, Harriet Wheeler, before her, leaving issue, such issue shall take the legacy bequeathed to the one so dying.

There is nothing in the context of the will to show that the testatrix intended that, in the case of the death of Lucy Ann Bacon, her children should take the legacy, but on the contrary, it appears to me that the fifth clause raises a strong presumption that the devise and legacy in the residuary clause were limited to the devisee and legatee, only if she survived the testatrix.

For had she intended that the heirs of the devisee and legatee should take the place of their mother, in the event of the death of the mother prior to her own decease, a similar provision would have been made as in the case of her nephew and her niece. The words "to have and to hold the same unto her, her heirs and assigns forever," are not substitutional words, but words of limitation, and could never be construed alternatively, so as to substitute the heirs in place of the deceased devisee and legatee, without violating the best established rules of construction (Armstrong v. Moran, 1 *Bradf.*, 314; Comfort v. Mather, 2 *Watts & Sergeant*, 450; Brett v. Rigden, *Plowden*, 340; Steede v. Berrier, *Freeman's K. B.*, 292; Elliott v. Davenport, 1 *Pierre Williams*, 84; Goodwright v. Wright, *id.*, 397; Thurber v. Chambers, 66 *N. Y.*, 42).

The counsel for the executor contends that the word "or" should be supplied and placed before the words "her heirs and assigns forever," in the residuary clause. That, I think, would be establishing a very bad precedent, as, practically, it would be asking the court to make a will which would be in direct conflict with the clear and express language of the testatrix.

The established rule in the construction of wills is that no word can be supplied so long as there is any fair ground to question what particular words were intended to have been used, which were not (1 Redf. on Wills, 454). Courts will supply only such words as it is clear it was the intention of the testator to use, and then only in case there is ambiguity.

The counsel for the executor urges that the words used in the residuary clause, "with whom I have lived for many years," imply that the legacy was given in satisfaction of a claim in favor of the devisee and legatee against the testatrix.

I think that these words are merely words of identification, and form no part of the disposing clause.

They simply describe the person whom she desired to make the object of her bounty, and in no way suggest that the bequest was made in satisfaction of a claim. A legacy is never held to be a payment of a debt, unless the terms of the will show this to have been the intent (Boughton v. Flint, 74 *N. Y.*, 476; Williams v. Crary, 4 *Wend.*, 443).

In the case at bar, the testatrix, in the first clause of her will, directs her executor to pay all her debts. This direction negatives any intention on her part of making this legacy in satisfaction of a debt (Fort v. Gooding, 9 *Barb.*, 371).

I am, therefore, led to the conclusion that the legacy given by the testatrix, in the sixth clause of her will, to her niece, Lucy Ann Bacon, lapsed and went to the next of kin of the testatrix.

In reference to the item, in schedule C. of the account, of $500 paid to Abraham Wakeman, Esq., I think the referee was right in disallowing it, for it appears from the testimony of Mr. Wakeman that he was not employed by the executor, but on the contrary was employed by Georgiana Pettengill and others to contest said will; and after a large amount of testimony had been taken, a settlement by way of a compromise was effected, and Mr. Pettengill paid him · for his services. And it further appears from the testimony of the executor, that he did not employ Mr. Wakeman, but that he allowed the contestants $500 for legal services and disbursements. If Mr. Bacon paid to Mr. Pettengill the amount which the latter paid his counsel for contesting the will, it is not, in my opinion, a proper item to be allowed to him.

An executor has no right to buy off contestants of a will and charge the expense against the estate.

⟨•◦•⟩

KINGS COUNTY.—HON. J. I. BERGEN, SURROGATE.—
December, 1884.

TAYLOR *v.* WARDLAW

In the matter of the probate of the will of MARY J.
TAYLOR, *deceased.*

The document propounded as decedent's will was in the handwriting of
W., one of the subscribing witnesses, who was not a lawyer, and was
written upon two pages of note paper, in three divisions, as follows :
(1) Near the end of the first page was decedent's name with the words
"her mark" under it, in the draughtsman's handwriting, and, immediately under this, decedent's signature. To the left were the signatures
of W. and R., and the date. (2) On the next page, what purported to
be a codicil to the will, dated the same day, was executed in a similar
manner. (3) And, immediately following, was the clause, "I appoint
W. my executor," similarly subscribed, and witnessed by R. and M.
The testimony, though somewhat conflicting, showed a substantial
compliance with the statutory requirements as to publication. It appeared that the draughtsman expected the decedent to make her mark,
which, however, she declined to do, writing her name, instead; and
that the codicillary matter and the executorial appointment were
originally omitted by inadvertence, and the omissions successively
supplied.—

Held, that the paper, though inartificially drawn, constituted one harmonious will—even the last execution being sufficient;—and that the same
was entitled to probate.

CONTEST over the application for probate of decedent's will. The facts are stated in the opinion.

D. & T. McMAHON, *for proponent.*

WM. D. VEEDER, *for contestant.*

THE SURROGATE.—The testatrix resided in the city of Brooklyn, and died October 17th, 1884, leaving a will dated two days previously. She left no husband and but one son, John Taylor, her only heir at law, who contests the will, alleging 1*st*, that at the time of the execution, the testatrix was not of sound mind and memory, and did not possess testamentary capacity; 2*d*, that the paper writing propounded was not executed according to law; and 3*d*, the same was not the last will and testament of deceased. The contestant offered no testimony in support of his allegations, but rested his case upon the testimony submitted by the proponents.

I am satisfied, from the evidence of the subscribing witnesses and the family physician, that the testatrix was possessed of testamentary capacity, and that she was not unduly influenced in the making and execution of her will. For while all the witnesses agree that she was in weak and feeble health, still she understood perfectly what she was doing, the nature of her property, and the claims which her relatives and friends had upon her bounty. She directed Mrs. Murphy where to get pen, ink and paper, and knew what pair of spectacles she wanted, and told Mrs. Murphy where she could find them. Also, Mrs. Murphy testified that testatrix conversed with her all the afternoon, about general matters, until the arrival of Messrs. Wardlaw and Rouss. The only question remaining to be determined is, whether the paper writing submitted for probate was executed according to law, so as to entitle it to be admitted to probate as the last will and testament of testatrix.

From the evidence it appears that the will was in the handwriting of James Wardlaw, one of the subscribing witnesses, and is all embraced on two pages of note paper. Near the end of the first page, there appear the name of Mary Jane Taylor, "her mark," in the handwriting of James Wardlaw, the draughtsman; immediately under it, the signature of the testatrix; to the left, the signatures James Wardlaw and C. B. Rouss, as subscribing witnesses, and the date, October 15th, 1884. On the next page is what purports to be a codicil to said will, dated the same day, and executed in a similar manner to the preceding one; and immediately following, on the same piece of paper, there appear these words:

"I appoint James Wardlaw my sole executor.

MARY JANE TAYLOR,
her + mark.
MARY JANE TAYLOR."

Witness—
C. B. ROUSS,
BRIDGET MURPHY."

The will was drawn by a layman not accustomed to drawing wills, but he was an intelligent man, who sufficiently understood the statutory requirements for the proper execution of a will.

While the testimony of C. B. Rouss, one of the subscribing witnesses, in reference to the order in which it was executed was somewhat conflicting, still after he heard the testimony of the other witnesses, he corrected his testimony by stating that the paper containing the three signatures of the testatrix was all signed together, after the whole document had been written. This is confirmed by Mr. Wardlaw and Mrs. Murphy, the other subscribing witnesses. It is well settled that, where one of the witnesses proving a will shows that all of the statutory requirements have been complied with, it is sufficient, even though the other one denies that such was the case (Rugg v. Rugg, 83 *N. Y.*, 592; Kinne v. Kinne, 2 *T. & C.*, 391; Matter of Bogart, 20 *N. Y. Week. Dig.*, 141).

The fact appears that Mrs. Taylor wanted to make her will, and that Mr. Wardlaw, at her request, set about drawing it. When he had finished the first page, he believed that he had provided for all of the testatrix's bequests, and then signed the name of Mary Jane Taylor, "her mark." But before its execution he ascertained that he had omitted some bequests, and then continued on the next page to provide for them, and when he had thus provided, he again signed the name of Mary Jane Taylor, "her mark," at the end thereof. Then finding that he had not provided for an executor, he asked the testatrix if he should be appointed, and she replied, "yes." Thereupon he added the clause appointing himself as executor, and again signed the name of Mary Jane Taylor, "her mark," at the end thereof; after which, he read the whole will to Mrs. Taylor and asked her to make her mark at the several places indicated. She appeared indignant, and said that she would write her name, which she proceeded to do, in the three places indicated, as fast as she could, one after the other. She then declared the whole document to be her last will and testament, and requested the subscribing witnesses to witness it.

On the first page of the document, there are two insignificant bequests to the subscribing witnesses, Wardlaw and Rouss, from which it might be argued that the testatrix had been influenced by them in making the same, but I think that the character and position of these persons, and the fact that they were intimate friends for many years, rebut the inference that any influence had been exercised by them ; and show that the testatrix in so doing desired to express her gratitude by giving them small mementos as souvenirs to them.

While the will is rather inartificially drawn, and the testimony in reference to its execution is somewhat conflicting, still, I am of the opinion, from the document propounded and the testimony in the whole case, that even the last execution is sufficient, and that the whole paper is one entire and harmonious will, and should be admitted to probate as the last will and testament of Mary Jane Taylor, deceased.

Decreed accordingly.

KINGS COUNTY.—HON. J. I. BERGEN, SURROGATE.—
December, 1884.

HOWARD *v.* HOWARD.

In the matter of the estate of SAMUEL J. HOWARD,
deceased.

Testator, by his will, gave certain property to his executor, in trust to
receive the income and apply the same to the use of E., his widow, for
life, who he also provided should be paid an annuity of $250, in lieu of
dower. The annuity and income not being duly paid, and E. having
presented a petition praying that the executor be compelled to file an
account, and for the payment of the same, respondent set up an agreement between himself and E., whereby, in consideration of an increased
allowance, she withdrew her opposition to the probate of the will, and
released her dower; which agreement, it was contended, ousted the
Surrogate's court of jurisdiction, and rendered resort to another tribunal necessary for its enforcement. The agreement contained a clause
expressly negativing a waiver by E. of her rights under the will.—
Held, that, notwithstanding the agreement mentioned, the Surrogate's
court had jurisdiction to compel the execution, in E.'s favor, of the
provisions contained in the will, and that the prayer for the filing of an
account should be granted.

PETITION by Emeline T. Howard, testator's widow,
to compel J. P. J. Howard, the executor of his will,
to file an account and pay certain income and an
annuity provided by the will in her favor.

MICHAEL GRU, *for petitioner.*

WM. COIT, *for executor.*

THE SURROGATE.—This is an application to compel
the executor to file an account and for the payment
of an annuity.·

The petition of Emeline T. Howard alleges that her
husband, Samuel J. Howard, died in July, 1883, leav-

ing a will and codicil, which were admitted to probate by this court on September 15th following, by which he gave to the petitioner a life estate in the one half of the premises No. 83 Fleet street, Brooklyn, and the other half thereof to his executor and trustee in trust, to receive the rents and apply the same to the use of the petitioner during her life, and also an annuity of $250, to commence from the death of the testator, in lieu of dower. And the petitioner further alleges that the executor has not paid to her the annuity and the income since May 23d, 1884, as provided by the will; and that more than one year has elapsed since the will was admitted to probate.

The executor, on the return day of the citation, set forth in his affidavit, that the petitioner on September 8th, 1883, executed an agreement with said executor, by which she was, in consideration of an increased allowance, to withdraw her opposition to the probate of the will, and release her dower in her husband's estate, and that, by the execution of said agreement, she was remediless in this court. I think, however, that the petitioner has a right to insist in this court upon the payment of her annuity and the income provided for her by the will. In the agreement referred to, she did nothing but release her dower in the estate of her husband, and withdraw her opposition to the probate of the will. That was done in consideration that the executor should give to her an increased allowance to the one provided for in the will.

In this application she does not seek the aid of this court to enforce the agreement, but simply to compel the executor to provide for the payment of the annuity and income to her, as provided in the will. There can be no doubt, so far as the agreement provides for an allowance in excess of that expressed in the will, that the petitioner must seek her remedy in another court. The executor has had charge of this estate for a little more than one year, and the records in this county show that he has, in that time, mortgaged and sold most of the large estate which the testator left; besides judgments to a considerable amount have been docketed against him. I very much fear that he has not provided for the payment of the petitioner's annuity, and the other annuities mentioned in the testator's will. The agreement expressly provides that the petitioner has not waived any of her rights under the provisions of the will.

I must, therefore, overrule the objection of the executor to the jurisdiction of this court, and order that he file an account of his proceedings.

An order may be entered directing the executor to render an account of his proceedings, as such, on or before January 12th, 1885.

KINGS COUNTY.—HON. J. I. BERGEN, SURROGATE.—
January, 1885.

SAW-MILL CO. v. DOCK.

In the matter of the estate of LUTHER DOCK, *deceased.*

Letters of temporary administration upon the estate of a decedent can be granted only where an application for letters in chief is pending, and under the circumstances specified in Code Civ. Pro., § 2668, subd. 1.

An original independent proceeding by a creditor to procure temporary
letters, to enable him to collect his debt, is unauthorized.

Jurisdiction over a non-resident respondent can be obtained only by voluntary appearance, or by service of a citation in the manner specified in
Code Civ. Pro., § 2524.

PETITION by the South Brooklyn Saw-Mill Company for letters of temporary administration upon
decedent's estate. The facts are stated in the opinion.

M. A. RAYMOND, *for petitioner.*

T. G. BERGEN, *for Susan V. Dock.*

THE SURROGATE.—The petitioner, in its application,
alleges that Luther Dock was a resident of the city of
Philadelphia, and died there on February 6th, 1884,
leaving a widow and two children, and leaving assets
in this State unadministered upon; that petitioner is
a creditor of the estate; that no application has been
made to any Surrogate in this State for original letters
of administration upon the estate of decedent; and
asks that letters of temporary administration be
granted to it, to enable it to collect its claim.

It is objected, by counsel for the widow, 1st, that
the service of citation is not sufficient; and 2d, that
the court has no power to grant letters of temporary
administration, where no application for letters of
administration in chief is pending. It appears, from
the papers submitted, that the only service of citation which has been made upon the next of kin of
the deceased, is one of thirteen days' notice by mail,
upon the next of kin residing in the city of Philadelphia. That, in my opinion, is not sufficient. The
only way in which the court can acquire jurisdiction
of non-residents is by the service of citation as pre-

scribed by § 2524 of the Code of Civil Procedure, or by voluntary appearance.

But in this case I think that such application cannot be sustained, as there is no proceeding nor application pending for letters of administration in chief. Subdivision 1 of § 2668 of the Code provides that, where delay necessarily occurs in the granting of letters testamentary or letters of administration, in consequence of a contest arising upon an application therefor, or for probate of a will, or in consequence of the absence from the State of an executor named in the will, or for any other cause, temporary letters of administration may issue. This section assumes that an application is pending for letters of administration in chief, before temporary letters will be issued.

Temporary letters may be granted where a delay necessarily occurs in the granting of letters in chief, in consequence of a contest arising upon the application for them. There being no application for letters in chief pending, no delay can occur in the granting of them. Therefore, the application for temporary letters must fall.

Motion denied, with $10 costs.

KINGS COUNTY.—HON. J. I. BERGEN, SURROGATE.—
February, 1885.

LYNCH *v.* PATCHEN.

In the matter of the estate of EMILY COIT, *deceased.*

Where a creditor of a decedent petitions the Surrogate's court, under Code
Civ. Pro., § 2717, for a decree directing payment of his claim, subd. 2 of
§ 2718 casts upon him the burden of proving, "to the satisfaction of
the Surrogate, that there is money or other personal property applicable to the payment or satisfaction" thereof.

A creditor of testatrix, who had recovered a judgment against the executors, having presented a petition, under Code Civ. Pro., § 2717, for a
decree directing the latter to pay the same, it appeared that there was
no personal property actually in their hands. The will, however,
devised certain real property to the executors, in trust to collect the
income, and pay the same to the children of the testatrix during the
life of her husband, W., and, upon his death, to sell the property and
divide the proceeds among said children. W. was dead. He had been
adjudged to have an estate by the curtesy in the real property in question,—which reduced the executors' rights in the premises to a power
of sale and distribution.—

Held, no assets; and that the prayer of the petition must be denied.

PETITION by Teresa Lynch, a creditor of decedent,
under Code Civ. Pro., § 2717, for a decree directing
Samuel W. Patchen, executor, and Emily L. Grey,
executrix of decedent's will, to pay her claim. The
facts appear in the opinion.

ABM. KLING, *for petitioner.*

BERGEN & DYKMAN, *for executors.*

THE SURROGATE.—The testatrix died on June 11th,
1875, leaving a last will and testament which was
duly proved before the Surrogate of Kings county,
on December 1st, 1876; and letters testamentary

were, on the same day, issued to Samuel W. Patchen and Emily L. Grey, as executor and executrix.

A judgment for $1,466.24 was recovered in the Supreme Court, on September 17th, 1879, against said executors, in favor of one Teresa Lynch, who now petitions this court for an order to compel said executors to pay said claim, pursuant to § 2717 of the Code of Civil Procedure.

The executors have interposed an answer denying the possession of any personal property, and alleging that certain real estate in Avenue B. in the city of New York, of which the testatrix died seized, was devised to them by the tenth clause of her will, in trust to collect the rents and income thereof during the life of the testatrix's husband, and pay over the same to the children of the testatrix; and, on the death of testatrix's husband, to sell the said real estate as soon as practicable, and divide the proceeds among her children.

The inventory shows that the testatrix died possessed of only $53, personal property; and an account was filed on September 12th, 1881, in this court, wherein they charged themselves with the sum of $131.80, and credited themselves with the sum of $1,238 for expenses and disbursements in the administration of the estate.

Subdivision 2 of § 2718 of the Code of Civil Procedure provides that, " where it is not proved to the satisfaction of the Surrogate that there is money or other personal property of the estate applicable to the payment or satisfaction of the petitioner's claim, and which may be so applied without injuriously affecting the rights of others entitled to priority or equality of payment or satisfaction," etc.

This section, I think, requires affirmative proof, to satisfy the court that there are sufficient assets to pay the petitioner's claim.

In this case, the petitioner has not shown any further assets than appear from the inventory and account already filed. But he relies upon the tenth clause of the will, devising the real estate in New York to the executors, in trust, for the benefit of the children, and insists that the rents and income derived from that property should be applied towards the payment of the petitioner's claim.

In an action in the Supreme Court, in which William A. Coit was plaintiff, and these executors and others were defendants, it was held that, inasmuch as the plaintiff and the testatrix were intermarried before 1848, and had issue born alive, the plaintiff had a life estate, as tenant by the curtesy, in said premises, and that the devise in trust attempted to be executed by the tenth clause of the will of said Emily Coit, during the life of William A. Coit, was plainly in conflict with the life estate, and must therefore yield to his paramount right; and this was subsequently affirmed by the general term (25 *Hun*, 444).

Therefore, the rents and profits of said real estate did not come into the hands of the trustees named in the will, as William A. Coit took the same during his life, and since his death the parties entitled to the remainder have taken the same, and the only power the executors have over the real estate, is simply a power to sell and distribute the same among the devisees upon the death of William A. Coit.

I am of the opinion that the executors have no personal estate in their hands, and further that they were not entitled to the rents and profits of said real estate, and, therefore, said motion should be denied.

KINGS COUNTY.—HON. J. I. BERGEN, SURROGATE.— February, 1885.

MORGAN *v.* PETTIT.

In the matter of the judicial settlement of the account of MARY E. MORGAN *and* STEPHEN JENNEY, JR., *as executrix and executor of the will of* JOHN LACEY, *deceased.*

Testator, by his will, provided : "On the arrival of my youngest child at lawful age, I direct that my said estate, or so much thereof as shall be remaining, be divided equally between my said wife and children." Testator left, him surviving, besides his widow, two children each of whom attained majority. Upon a judicial settlement of the executors' account, a question having arisen as to the relative rights of the three beneficiaries in the residue,—

Held, that the widow and children took, each, one third thereof.

CONSTRUCTION, upon judicial settlement of executors' account, of a clause in decedent's will directing the division of his estate equally between his wife, afterwards Mary E. Morgan, and children Isabella Pettit and Thomas Lacey. The facts appear in the opinion.

J. M. STEARNS, JR., *for executors.*

THE SURROGATE.—The testator, by his will provides as follows: "On the arrival of my youngest
child at lawful age, I direct that my said estate, or so
much thereof as shall be remaining, be divided
equally between my said wife and children."

The testator left him surviving his wife and two
children, both now of full age. On the final settlement of the executors' account, they ask for a
construction of said clause. The question to be
determined is whether the widow and children take
each an equal share, or the widow one half of the
residuum, and the two children the other half.

I think that the language used by the testator, to
wit: "be divided equally between my said wife and
children," must be construed to mean that his wife
should take the same share in the residue of his
estate as each of his said children, and no more.

In the case of Lord v. Moore (20 *Conn.*, 122), there
was a bequest "to receive the income and divide the
same equally between my said wife and children;"
and the court held that the wife was entitled to only
the same share as each of the children.

In the case of Myres v. Myres (23 *How. Pr.*, 410),
there was a devise to testator's son, M., "and the
heirs of my son N., and their heirs forever, to be
equally divided between my son M. and the heirs of
my son N.;" and the court held, that M. took the
same share as each of the children of N., and that the
words which are deemed to control the rule of construction in these cases are those which denote that
the division is to be between or among the legatees
in equal parts.

In the case of Bunner v. Storm (1 *Sandf. Ch.*, 35), there was a bequest of "one seventh of the estate, to be equally divided among testator's daughters, E., M. and C. and the heirs of a deceased daughter, H.;" and the court held that, upon the force of the words "equally divided," each child of the deceased daughter, H., took the same share as E., M. and C. The same construction was given in Collins v. Hoxie (9 *Paige*, 81); Murphy v. Harvey (4 *Edw.*, 131); Lee v. Lee (39 *Barb.*, 172); Blackler v. Webb (2 *Pierre Williams*, 384); Dowding v. Smith (3 *Beavans*, 541). I am, therefore, of the opinion that the widow and each of the children take one third of the property remaining in the hands of the executors undistributed.

Decreed accordingly.

———•━◦•━•›———

KINGS COUNTY.—HON. J. I. BERGEN, SURROGATE.— February, 1885.

CURTIS *v.* WILLIAMS.

In the matter of the estate of HUGH ALLEN, *deceased.*

Code Civ. Pro., § 2645, enacted in 1880, requires an administrator, with the will annexed, before letters are issued to him, to qualify as prescribed by law with respect to an administrator in intestacy, and makes the provisions of the article containing § 2667 applicable to his official bond. .The latter section, which was enacted in the same year, and prescribes the requisites of the bond of an administrator in intestacy, was amended in 1882, by adding a provision that, "in cases where all the next of kin to the intestate consent thereto," the penalty of the bond may be limited in a manner specified.—

Held, that the former section, and the latter *as amended*, are to be construed together, as if enacted simultaneously, and that an administrator with the will annexed may avail himself of the provisions contained in the amendment of 1882, upon obtaining the consent of the next of kin, although they may have no interest in the decedent's estate.

The existing statutory rule on this subject—criticised.

The principal decedent, A., died in 1881, leaving a will, pursuant to which letters testamentary were granted to B.; who died in 1884, not having fully administered upon A.'s estate, and leaving a will, pursuant to which letters testamentary were granted to C. and others. Letters of administration, with the will of A. annexed, having been granted to D., upon her petition and the consent of the next of kin of A., and her filing a bond in the penalty of $10,000, and she having petitioned for an accounting by B.'s executors as to property of A. received by them, the respondents denied the legality of D.'s appointment on the ground of the inadequacy of the penalty of her official bond.—

Held, that D. was duly appointed; that the grant of her letters could not be attacked collaterally in the proceeding at bar; that respondents must account as desired; and that, if the security already given should thereupon prove inadequate, petitioner should be required to file an additional bond, or deposit the excess of moneys and securities in a trust company, subject to the Surrogate's order.

PETITION by Josephine A. Curtis, administratrix with the will of decedent annexed, for an accounting by John J. Williams and others, executors of the will of decedent's executor, as to moneys, etc., of the first decedent's estate received by them. The facts are stated in the opinion.

STEARNS & CURTIS, *for petitioner*.

ROGERS, LOCKE & MILBURN, *for respondents*.

THE SURROGATE.—The testator, Hugh Allen, died in Brooklyn in 1881, leaving a will in which he appointed his brother, John Allen, Jr., his sole executor, to whom letters testamentary were granted. In March, 1880, the said John Allen, Jr., died, without having fully administered upon the estate of his father. He left a will, which has been duly admitted to probate by the Surrogate of Erie county, and letters testamentary whereunder were duly issued to William Allen, John J. Williams and Charles S. Hall, the executors and trustees therein named.

The motion now made is to require the executors of said John Allen, Jr., to render an account of the money and other property received by them belonging to the estate of Hugh Allen, deceased, and to deliver the same to Josephine A. Curtis, the administratrix with the will of Hugh Allen, deceased, annexed.

The respondents, the executors of John Allen, Jr., in their answer, do not controvert any of the allegations set forth in the petition, but simply aver that the petitioner was not duly appointed administratrix with the will of Hugh Allen, deceased, annexed, for the reason that no bond was given by the petitioner for twice the amount of the personal property of said decedent.

Section 2645 of the Code of Civil Procedure provides that, before letters can issue to an administratrix with the will annexed, she must qualify as prescribed by law with respect to an administrator upon the estate of an intestate, and that the provisions of the article relating to the bond to be given by the latter shall apply to the bond to be given pursuant to this section.

Section 2667, in the article referred to in § 2645, requires the person appointed administrator, before letters are issued to him, to " execute to the people of the State and file with the Surrogate the joint and several bond of himself and two or more sureties, in a penalty, fixed by the Surrogate, not less than twice the value of the personal property of which the deceased died possessed."

In 1882, this section was amended by re-enacting the entire section as originally adopted by the act of 1880, with the amendment of 1881 referring to limited letters, and adding thereto the following: "In cases where all the next of kin to the intestate consent thereto, the penalty of the bond required to be given shall not exceed twice the amount of the claims of creditors against the estate, presented to the Surrogate, pursuant to a notice to be published twice a week for four weeks in the State paper, and in two newspapers published in the city of New York, and once a week for four weeks in two newspapers published in the county where the intestate usually resided, and in the county where he died, reciting an intention to apply for letters under this provision, and notifying creditors to present their claims to the Surrogate on or before a day to be fixed in such notice, which shall be at least thirty days after the first publication thereof; but no bond so given shall be for a less sum than five thousand dollars, and such bond may be increased by order of the Surrogate for cause shown. Pending such application, no temporary administrator shall be appointed except on petition of such next of kin." It is contended by counsel for the respondents that, inasmuch as this amendment was adopted since the enactment of § 2645, it cannot be construed in connection therewith.

The whole section was re-enacted, and must stand from that time, as if originally enacted in that form, and I think must be construed in connection with

§ 2645, as if adopted at the same time (Dexter & Limerick P. R. Co. v. Allen, 16 *Barb.*, 15; Ely v. Horton, 15 *N. Y.*, 595; Mundy v. Excise Comm'rs, 9 *Abb. N. C.*, 117; Board of Excise of Westchester v. Curley, *id.*, 100).

If the construction contended for by the respondents' counsel is correct, then an administrator with the will annexed could not avail himself of the benefit of the amendment of 1882 by giving modified security, while an administrator in chief could. It seems to me that the legislature did not intend to make such a distinction, but rather that the amendment should apply to both.

It is true that the granting of letters of administration with the will annexed upon the consent of the next of kin might work a great injustice to the parties ultimately or contingently interested in the estate under the will.

The duties and powers of an administrator with the will annexed, as far as administration of the personal estate is concerned, are the same as those of an executor, and his conduct is governed by the terms of the will, while those of the administrator are determined by statute. It may be that the parties entitled under the will are not next of kin, and would take nothing in case of intestacy. Section 2667 might well be amended by requiring the consent of all the legatees and next of kin, before appointing an administrator with the will annexed with modified security. But I am called upon to construe the statutes as I find them, and not as I think they should be.

The petitioner, in her application for letters of

administration with the will annexed, having alleged
all the jurisdictional facts prescribed by statute to
entitle her to such letters, and a decree having been
made upon her petition upon the consent of the next
of kin of the testator, and she having executed and
filed her joint and several bond, with two sureties, in
the penalty of $10,000, I think that the letters of
administration with the will annexed on the estate of
Hugh Allen, deceased, were properly granted, and
that the respondents cannot attack them in this collateral proceeding. The Surrogate's court is now a
court of record, and its decrees made within its jurisdiction have equal force and effect with those of other
courts, and once legally made can only be set aside,
modified, or revoked on the application of parties to
these proceedings in the usual manner (Bloom v.
Burdick, 1 *Hill*, 130; Kelly v. West, 80 *N. Y.*, 139;
Harrison v. Clark, 87. *id.*, 572; Matter of Hood, 90
id., 512; Martin v. Dry Dock & E. B. R. Co., 92 *id.*,
70; Abbott v. Curran, 20 *N. Y. Week. Dig.*, 344;
Code Civ. Pro., § 2591).

I am, therefore, of the opinion that the respondents
should be required to account for all the money and
property in their hands belonging to the estate of
Hugh Allen, deceased, and if, upon such accounting,
it should appear that the property to be delivered is
much in excess of the bond already given therein,
that the petitioner should file an additional bond, or
consent that the money and securities sought to be
transferred should be deposited with the Brooklyn
Trust Company, in the name of the petitioner, as
administratrix with the will annexed of Hugh Allen,

deceased, and not to be withdrawn except upon the order of the Surrogate.

<hr>

KINGS COUNTY.—HON. J. I. BERGEN, SURROGATE.— March, 1885.

HOME INSURANCE CO. *v.* LYON.

In the matter of the judicial settlement of the account of JOHN R. HALSEY *and* JOHN ANGUS, *as executors of the will of* JOHN HALSEY, *deceased.*

The executors of decedent's will filed an intermediate account in 1882, whereupon a decree was made, pursuant to which the assets then realized were distributed among the creditors whose claims had been presented and proved. A creditor company which held a claim secured by mortgage, did not present the same, but, after the distribution, foreclosed the mortgage, obtained a judgment for over $2,000, deficiency, and, upon a judicial settlement of the executors' account, asked to be allowed, out of the assets then on hand, the same dividend to which it would have been entitled, if its claim had been presented upon the intermediate accounting, before the declaration of a second dividend. Decedent's estate was insolvent.—

Held, that the demand in question was proper and should be allowed, being justified by the provisions of 2 R. S., 87, § 28, which prohibits a preference in the payment of any debt over another of the same class.

APPLICATION by the Home Insurance company, upon the judicial settlement of executors' account, for a preferred dividend out of assets of the estate; opposed by Samuel E. Lyon and others, executors of the will of D. H. Haight, a deceased creditor.

BARNEY & COWMAN, *for the H. Ins. Co.*

THOS. L. OGDEN, *for the opposing creditors.*

THE SURROGATE.—It appears from the account that the estate of John Halsey, deceased, is insolvent, and that the executors, in June, 1882, filed an intermediate account, upon which a decree was made distributing the assets then in their hands *pro rata* among the creditors who then presented their claims.

The Home Insurance Co. held a claim secured by way of mortgage, which they did not foreclose until after the intermediate accounting. They have since foreclosed the same, and obtained a judgment for deficiency on October 14th, 1882, for $2691.72, and now ask, upon the final settlement of the executors' account, that they be paid out of the assets now in the executors' hands the same dividend they would have been entitled to receive had they presented their claim for their share of the fund distributed pursuant to the decree of June 7th, 1882.

Part 2 of the Revised Statutes, ch. 6, title 3, § 28 (3 R. S., 7th ed., 2299), provides that "no preference shall be given in the payment of any debt over other debts of the same class."

Had the Home Insurance Co., before the decree of 1882, applied to this court, upon proof that it had probable cause to apprehend a deficiency upon the foreclosure of their bond and mortgage, the court would have been justified in making an order directing the executors to retain enough of the assets then in their hands to pay the probable *pro rata* dividend on such anticipated deficiency (Williams v. Eaton, 3 *Redf.*, 503). The only effect of not applying for a reservation of assets was, that the company assumed the risk that further assets would be discovered and reduced to the possession of the executors. And, so far as the relations of the company and the other creditors are concerned, they in equity should be dealt with as reserved assets, and treated as if an order had been made to that effect.

In this case, a dividend was paid to the creditors, other than the Home Insurance Co., pursuant to the decree of 1882; and if the petitioner's claim is now denied, it would be giving to the creditors then repre- sented a dividend in excess of that proposed to be given to the petitioner. I think, however, that the assets now in the hands of the executors must be treated as if they were before the court in 1882, and had been reserved, on the application of the petitioner, to provide for the payment to it of a *pro rata* share or dividend, at the rate established by that decree; and that the decree should provide that the Home Insurance Co. be first entitled to receive, out of the assets now in the hands of the executors, a sum equal to what would have been its share of the fund distributed pursuant to the decree of June 7th, 1882, had its judgment for deficiency then existed; and secondly, that the balance of the assets shall be distributed, *pro rata*, among all of the creditors, including the Home Insurance Co.

KINGS COUNTY.—HON. J. I. BERGEN, SURROGATE.—
April, 1885.

LYENDECKER *v.* EISEMANN.

In the matter of the estate of ADAM EISEMANN,
deceased.

"Where a man having a family" dies, leaving a widow, the appraisers are
authorized to set apart for her (1) the articles of personal property
specifically enumerated in 2 R. S., 83, § 9, as amended in 1874; (2) "and
also other household furniture which shall not exceed one hundred
and fifty dollars in value" (id. subd. 4) ; and (3) "necessary household
furniture, provisions or other personal property, in the discretion of
said appraisers, to the value of not exceeding one hundred and fifty
dollars" (L. 1842, ch. 157, § 2).

Where an executor or administrator has only received, and not paid out,
funds of the estate, he should be allowed therefor commissions at one
half the legal rate.

HEARING of objections to the account of Margaret
Eisemann, a superseded administratrix of the estate
of decedent, interposed by Margaret Lyendecker, her
successor.   The facts are stated in the opinion.

LORENZO LOVEJOY, *for the accounting party.*

A. SIMIS, JR., *for objector.*

THE SURROGATE.—The decedent, Adam Eisemann,
died on October 29th, 1884.   Letters of administration were granted to his widow, Margaret Eisemann,
on November 18th, 1884, and were revoked on
February 12th, 1885.   On February 27th, 1885, Margaret Lyendecker was appointed in her stead.

It appears, from the inventory on file, that the
appraisers made an appraisement of the personal property which the decedent left at the time of his death

amounting to $2229.70, and set apart the articles therein mentioned, to the widow, not exceeding in value $50, and $150 in cash. To this item the contestant objects. I have examined the question, and find that, by chapter 157 of the Laws of 1842, the appraisers were authorized to set apart, for the use of the widow and family of the decedent, household furniture, provisions or other personal property, in the discretion of the appraisers, to the value of not exceeding $150, in addition to the articles specified in the Laws of 1824; that, subsequently, by an act passed in 1874 (ch. 470), the original act of 1824 was amended, and among other things subdivision 4 of § 1, as amended, provides that certain additional articles, and also other household furniture which shall not exceed $150, in value, shall not be deemed assets, but shall only be stated in the inventory without being appraised. This act of 1874 in nowise repeals the act of 1842, but both must be read and construed together.

I, therefore, think that, where a decedent leaves a widow or minor children, the appraisers are authorized to set apart the articles specified in chapter 157 of the Laws of 1842, or the sum of $150, and, in addition, the articles specified in chapter 470 of the Laws of 1874, and household furniture to the value of not exceeding $150. In schedule C. of the account, the administratrix credits herself with having paid $50 appraisers' fees. That I think, under the circumstances, should be reduced to $30. She testified that she had paid the appraisers' fees to her counsel, but the appraisers testified that they had never received them. In the same schedule, she credits herself with $25, counsel fee. Inasmuch as her administration of the estate had been conducted so loosely as to require her letters to be revoked within three months after the same were granted, I think the sum paid by her to her counsel should be disallowed.

On the day of her appointment, she drew from the savings bank, in which the funds of the decedent were deposited, $2205, and gave the same to her attorneys. It was not required for the use of the estate, except possibly a few dollars to pay for disbursements. I think she should be charged with interest at the rate of four per cent. upon said amount, from the time of its withdrawal from the savings bank to date—that being the rate of interest the same would have earned if permitted to remain in the bank.

In regard to the compensation claimed by the administratrix, she should be allowed commissions at one half the legal rate, for the reason that she has only received the fund, and it can only be paid out by the administratrix subsequently appointed in her stead.

KINGS COUNTY.—HON. J. I. BERGEN, SURROGATE.—
April, 1885.

WYCKOFF *v.* VAN SICLEN.

In the matter of the estate of ALBERT WYCKOFF, *deceased.*

Decedent's sole surviving executor, having instituted a special proceeding
  for the judicial settlement of his account, and omitted to charge himself, in the latter, with several items of assets set forth in the inventory,
  which was thereupon offered in evidence by objectors, for the purpose
  of charging him with the omitted items, he pleaded the statute of limitations as a bar, nearly twenty years having elapsed since the issue of
  letters testamentary, and the account never having been settled.—
Held, that the executor had waived this plea by his voluntary institution of
  the accounting proceeding.
It appeared that the accounting executor, who was a farmer, having in his
  hands $500 cash assets of the estate, handed this sum over to his
  co-executor, who was his uncle and a man of business, in good standing, in order that the latter might pay therewith the debts of decedent
  at his place of business, pursuant to advertisement. The latter having
  misappropriated the amount and died insolvent,—
Held, that the former was liable for the devastavit, and should be charged
  with the amount, but not with interest thereon.
Decedent's executor, who was appointed in 1855, voluntarily accounted in
  1865, distributed all the funds of the estate then in his hands, and
  retained about $200 as his commissions, without objection from any of
  the beneficiaries. Upon a judicial settlement of his account, had in
  1885,—
Held, that, in the absence of an allowance by the Surrogate, this sum had
  been improperly retained, and that the executor should be charged
  with the same, but, under the circumstances of the case, without
  interest.

HEARING of exceptions to report of referee, to
whom were referred the account, and objections
thereto, of J. W. Van Siclen, sole surviving executor
of decedent's will, upon an application for judicial
settlement. The referee, by his first conclusion of

law, found that the accounting party should be charged with a sum of $500, paid by him to his co-executor, by whom the same was misappropriated, less certain deductions specified; and that "no interest should be charged on this sum against said executor, J. W. Van Siclen, for the reason that he paid said sum of $500 to his co-executor in good faith, and for a proper and legitimate purpose of the estate, and at the time of said payment had no reason to suspect the integrity or solvency of his said co-executor." Further facts are stated in the opinion.

SACKETT, LANG, REED & McKEWAN, *for executor.*

EDGAR BERGEN, *for Eliza J. Wyckoff, and others, objectors.*

THE SURROGATE.—The testator, Albert Wyckoff, died on September 15th, 1855, leaving a will, by which he appointed his brother, Jacob V. D. Wyckoff, and his nephew, John Wyckoff Van Siclen, executors thereof, and which was proved November 15th, 1855, letters testamentary thereon being granted on the same day. Jacob V. D. Wyckoff died June 24th, 1857, insolvent, having made an assignment in April, 1857.

The surviving executor petitioned this court in November, 1882, for a final judicial settlement of his account as such executor. Upon filing the same, objections thereto were made by several of the persons interested in the estate. Thereupon the account with the objections was referred to Herbert C Smith, Esq., to hear and determine. The matter now comes up before me, upon exceptions filed to the confirmation of his report.

The accounting executor did not charge himself in his account with several items of assets set forth in the inventory. The contestants offered the inventory in evidence for the purpose of showing the amount of assets which came into the executor's hands. Objection was made by the executor's counsel, upon the ground that the statute of limitations was a bar to all the claims of the contestants, whereby they sought to charge him with assets in excess of those appearing in his account. If this objection is a valid one, it practically disposes of all the objections to the executor's account.

In this case, however, the executor has made a voluntary accounting, embracing some of the items mentioned in the inventory, and has caused all the parties interested in the estate to be cited to appear on such accounting, and prays that it may be judicially settled and allowed, and he be discharged as such executor.

There has never been any judicial settlement of the executor's account, and, while many years have elapsed since the death of the testator, it does not seem to me that, after making his voluntary account, he can now avail himself of the statute of limitations. He voluntarily submitted himself to the jurisdiction of this court by filing his petition and account, and he must be bound by such action and be deemed to have waived the statute of limitations (Calkins v. Isbell, 20 *N. Y.*, 147).

"If an executor upon being cited to account, instead of denying his liability cites all the parties in interest, he admits his liability to account" (Kellet

• v. Rathbun, 4 *Paige*, 102). If not, why issue the citations? If the statute is a bar in this case, then the executor could have submitted any account he chose and asked that it might be judicially settled, and he be discharged from his trust. Hence I think that the referee was right in overruling the objection of the executor to admitting the inventory in evidence, as that is the first thing with which to charge himself (In re Jones, 1 *Redf.*, 263).

The accounting executor charged himself with cash assets amounting to only $216.44, while it appears from his testimony that he found among the testator's assets $716.44; that he counted the money and retained the sum of $216.44, and gave to his co-executor, J. V. D. Wyckoff, the rest of the money. And further on he says: "We advertised for debts against the testator and my co-executor was to pay them at his place of business, and I gave him the $500 for that purpose. I don't think that he paid any of the debts."

There is no doubt that his co-executor misappropriated the $500, and I think that the fact of the accounting executor having had all the cash assets in his hands, and he having given the $500 to his co-executor with which to pay the debts of the estate, and he having misappropriated the same, the accounting executor must be charged with the said sum less the amounts collected, as found by the referee in his seventh finding of fact (Croft v. Williams, 88 *N. Y.*, 384). But I agree with the referee that he should not be charged with interest, for the reasons given by the referee in his first conclusion of law.

In reference to the item of $964.47, being money . deposited in the Long Island bank to the credit of the deceased, the testimony shows that Jacob V. D. Wyckoff drew this money without the knowledge or consent of the accounting executor, and converted the same to his own use; and that the accounting executor discovered a day or two afterwards from his co-executor, that he had drawn the same and would replace the money. He says: "I demanded this money back from Mr. Wyckoff some little time afterwards, to the best of my recollection about six months after he had it. He said he had to use some money. I am not positive as to what he wanted to use it for. He did not want it for the purposes of the estate of Albert Wyckoff, deceased."

The referee has sought to charge the accounting executor with that amount upon the ground that he had knowledge of the fact of such withdrawal and conversion, and neglected to take any proceedings whatever to recover the money for the estate until nearly two years afterwards, and not until the said Wyckoff had become insolvent.

I do not think, however, that the testimony will warrant so broad a finding of fact, namely, "that he had knowledge of the fact of such withdrawal and conversion," etc. For the testimony of Mr. Van Siclen is clear and uncontradicted, that he knew nothing of the withdrawal of the funds from the bank until after the same had been done by his co-executor, and that, when he discovered it, he went to Mr. Wyckoff and expressed surprise by saying to him, that he did not think that he could draw it without his consent, whereupon Mr. Wyckoff promised to replace the same.

Mr. Wyckoff, at that time, was a man in good financial standing, and his co-executor had no reason to apprehend that the money would be misappropriated, and I think that Mr. Van Siclen should not be charged with the amount so drawn by Mr. Wyckoff from the bank, as I do not believe that any of the funds came into his hands, or was lost by any neglect or failure on the part of Mr. Van Siclen to discharge his duties, nor by any affirmative act or acquiescence on his part, but on the contrary, that the loss resulted wholly and exclusively from the misconduct of Mr. Wyckoff. When it was discovered by Mr. Van Siclen that Mr. Wyckoff had misappropriated the fund, he took immediate steps for the recovery of the same against the assignee of his co-executor (Wilmerding v. McKesson, 28 *Hun*, 184, *and cases cited*).

     *   *   *   *   *   *   *

In relation to the item of $197.46 retained by the executor for commissions in 1864, and disallowed by the referee for the reason that no accounting had been had before the Surrogate, and no sum allowed by him for commissions, there is no doubt the general rule is, that executors should not retain, nor take out of the funds of the estate, their commissions until their accounts have been passed by the Surrogate, and their commissions fixed and allowed by him. But in this case it will be noticed that the executor had been acting as such for nearly ten years, before he had the estate in such a position as to be able to distribute it among the parties entitled thereto. It appears, according to his accounts, that he distributed all of the funds of the estate in his hands in January, 1865; that he voluntarily accounted and paid over to the beneficiaries under the said will all of the funds in his hands at that time, and retained to himself the item of $197.46 as his commissions, and no objections were made thereto. He rested his account at that time, and has only collected $345 since that time.

While I think the referee was right in disallowing the same, still I think it would be manifestly unjust to punish him by requiring him to pay interest on the same from 1865 to date.

This case is one of exceeding great hardship on the accounting executor, for it appears that the principal contestant is the widow of Wyckoff, the delinquent executor, and through whose acts all the loss has occurred to the estate.

I have discovered in the evidence no fact which would justify me in charging Mr. Van Siclen with a *devastavit* committed by his co-executor, Mr. Wyckoff, except the payment by him of the $500 to his co-executor out of the cash assets in his hands for the purpose of paying the debts of the testator, and which his co-executor misappropriated. The testator was a resident of Kings county, and by his will he made his brother, Wyckoff, who was then a merchant, doing business in the city of New York, of good reputation and financial standing, and his nephew, Van Siclen, a farmer, and then a young man, his executors and trustees. It was but natural that his brother, being a business man, and older and much

more experienced in financial matters, should have
taken upon himself the principal management of the
estate.   And Mr. Van Siclen being the younger, and
not accustomed to accounts and the management of
estates, deferred to the judgment of his uncle, until
he discovered that his uncle was insolvent, and then
he took the active management of it and saved what
he could by foreclosing mortgages, bringing suits
against the assignee of his uncle, collecting rents and
paying off mortgages, thereby saving a considerable
amount to the estate.

I have carefully reviewed all of the testimony in
this case, and am of the opinion, that the referee's
report in all other respects, except as herein modified,
should be confirmed, for the reasons set forth therein.

KINGS COUNTY.—HON. J. I. BERGEN, SURROGATE.—
April, 1885.

REYNOLDS *v.* REYNOLDS.

*In the matter of the judicial settlement of the account
of* ANN REYNOLDS, *as executrix of the will of*
THOMAS REYNOLDS, *deceased.*

While it is the general rule, that as between life tenant and remainderman, taking under a will, the expenses of administering the trust must
be borne by the former, and paid out of the income, the same is subject to exceptions, as *ex. gr.*, in the case of a disposition of the residue,
to ascertain the amount of which such expenses are necessarily
incurred.
Testator, by his will, after directing his executors to pay all his just debts

and funeral and testamentary expenses, and making certain specific bequests, gave the net residue and remainder of his estate to his executors, in trust to manage the same, collect the income, and, after deducting all proper costs, charges and expenses pertaining to the trust, to pay over the net residue of rents, etc., to his wife for life with remainder over; and appointed his wife and another, executrix and executor thereof. The widow alone qualified. Upon the judicial settlement of her account *as executrix*, had with a view to handing over the funds to a trustee,—

Held, that the expenses of administration and commissions were chargeable to the *corpus* of the estate.

Whitson v. Whitson, 53 *N. Y.*, 479; Cammann v. Cammann, 2 *Dem.*, 211— distinguished.

HEARING of objections interposed, in behalf of decedent's children, to the account filed by the executrix of his will, in proceedings for judicial settlement. The facts appear in the opinion.

S. M. & D. E. MEEKER, *for executrix.*

WALTER L. LIVINGSTON, *special guardian.*

THE SURROGATE.—The testator, Thomas Reynolds, by his will, which was duly admitted to probate by this court on June 5th, 1883, after bequeathing certain specified articles to his widow, gives the rest, residue and remainder of his estate to the executors therein named in trust, to manage, control and invest from time to time, or keep invested the same in real estate, bonds, stocks or bond and mortgage, as they, she, or he shall deem best, and collect and receive the rents, interest, dividends, issues, income and profits thereof, and after deducting all proper costs, charges and expenses pertaining to the trust, to pay over the net residue of such rents, interest, dividends, etc., to his wife during her life, and, after her death, to his son during his life.

The testator died on May 18th, 1883. His executrix now submits her accounts and asks that the same be judicially settled.

*   *   *   *   *   *

The special guardian for the infant urges that the items for expenses of administration and the executor's commissions, should be charged to the life tenant. The life tenant is the only executor who has qualified. The other executor named in the will proposes to qualify as trustee, upon the settlement of Mrs. Reynolds' accounts.

There is no doubt that the general rule is that, where the income is given to one person for life, and the principal and remainder to another party, the life tenant must bear the expenses connected with the trust, the same to be paid out of the income. But in this case the estate is in the hands of Mrs. Reynolds as executrix, and is in process of being administered; and until that is done, the rest, residue and remainder given by the third clause of the will cannot be ascertained. After her accounts shall be judicially settled in the proceedings now pending, the decree will fix an amount to be held by the trustee, pursuant to the trust imposed by the will.

I do not think that the cases, cited by the learned counsel, of Whitson v. Whitson (53 *N. Y.*, 479) and Cammann v. Cammann (2 *Dem.*, 211) go as far as to charge the executors' commissions and the expenses of the administration of the estate upon the life tenant of the rest, residue and remainder; for until the executors' accounts have been judicially settled, the amount of the rest, residue and remainder cannot be ascertained.

In the case of Whitson v. Whitson (*supra*), there was a bequest to Eliza C. Whitson of the life use of the sum of $10,000, and the executors were directed to semiannually pay to her the lawful interest of the said sum of $10,000, from the day or date of testator's death; and the question was—whether the widow (Eliza C. Whitson) was entitled to an annuity of $700 a year without an abatement for taxes, etc., or the income to be derived from the investment of $10,000, less the taxes. It was held that the legacy was not an annuity, but simply a gift of the interest of that amount.

And in the case of Cammann v. Cammann (*supra*), there had been a previous decree fixing the rest, residue and remainder of the decedent's estate in accordance with the direction of testator's will, which was set apart to his executors as trustees, and the income derived therefrom applied to the benefit of the decedent's widow during her life. I agree with the learned Surrogate in that case, for there there had been a settlement of the executors' accounts, and the rest, residue and remainder had been ascertained and fixed as trust funds in the trustees' hands. The case at bar, I think, is distinguishable from the cases above cited, and I am, therefore, of the opinion, that such expenses are not expenses connected with the trust, but expenses connected with the administration of the estate, and that the same, together with the executor's commissions should be paid out of the *corpus* of the estate. I also think that the testator, by the first clause of his will, in which he directs his executors to pay all the just debts and funeral and testamentary expenses out of his estate, intended that the same should be charged to the *corpus* of the estate and not to the life tenant.

Decreed accordingly.

KINGS COUNTY.—HON. J. I. BERGEN, SURROGATE.—
April, 1885.

TAFT *v.* TAFT.

In the matter of the estate of JONATHAN T. WELLS,
deceased.

The word "issue," in a will, where no light is thrown upon its meaning by the context or extrinsic circumstances, must be construed to denote the lineal descendants, in the first degree, of the ancestor indicated, to the exclusion of remoter kindred.

Palmer v. Horn, 88 *N. Y.*, 519—followed.

CONSTRUCTION of will upon executors' accounting. The facts are stated in the opinion.

ALMET F. JENKS, *for executors.*

A. R. DYETT, FRED'K BELTZ, and E. P. SCHELL, *for objectors.*

THE SURROGATE.—This contest arises upon the judicial settlement of the accounts of Andrew W. Kent, executor of the last will and testament of Jonathan Tremaine Wells, deceased. The items to which objections have been filed are very numerous. I will, therefore, consider them in their order and briefly dispose of them.

* * * * * * * *

The testator, by the fourth clause of his will, gave a legacy to William Taft of $5,000, and, by the tenth clause, bequeathed the residue of his estate to the legatees mentioned in his will, in the proportion that he had before bequeathed the legacies to them severally. By the ninth clause, he provides: "If any or either of the persons to whom I have hereinbefore bequeathed a legacy shall depart this life before me, then I give and bequeath the sum of money hereinbefore bequeathed to the one so dying to his or her lawful issue then surviving." William Taft, the legatee, died before the testator, leaving two children, namely, Richard V. Taft and Benjamin E. Taft; and three grandchildren — children of a deceased son, William Y. Taft, who also died before the testator.

The children of William Y. Taft now claim, under the 4th, 9th and 10th clauses of the will, to be entitled to share in the legacy of $5,000 bequeathed to their grandfather, William Taft, *per capita* with their uncles, Richard V. and Benjamin E. Taft; so that the question before the court is—does the term "lawful issue" refer to the children of William Taft solely, or include the grandchildren, that is, the children of William Y. Taft, who died prior to the testator?

In the case of Palmer v. Horn (84 *N. Y.*, 519), Judge EARL, in expressing the opinion of the court, says: ".The word 'issue' is an ambiguous term. It may mean descendants generally, or merely children, and whether in a will it should be held to mean the one or the other, depends on the intention of the testator, as derived from the context or the entire will, or such extrinsic circumstances as can be considered. In the later cases there is a strong tendency, unless restrained by the context, to hold that it has the meaning of 'children.'" See, also, 4 Kent Com., 278, *note*.

In this case, there is no extrinsic evidence to make clear the intent of the testator. I, therefore, think that the word "issue" must be construed as limited to the children of William Taft, and that the surviving children take the legacy bequeathed to their father; and that the grandchildren have no interest in it nor claim upon it.

KINGS COUNTY.—HON. J. I. BERGEN, SURROGATE.— May, 1885.

KNIGHT *v.* LIDFORD.

In the matter of the judicial settlement of the account of the executors of the will of HENRY KNIGHT, *deceased.*

The residue of testator's estate was given by the will, to his executors as trustees, in trust to collect the income and pay the same to designated beneficiaries for life, with remainders over. At the time of testator's death, a portion of the estate consisted of certain shares of the stock of a railroad corporation, whose entire capital was divided into 14,000 shares, of which only 13,052 had ever been issued, the balance, 948 shares, remaining in the treasury. Thereafter, pursuant to a resolution of the board of directors, whereby it was determined to distribute

KNIGHT V. LIDFORD.

the unissued shares ratably among the existing stockholders, the executors received, as their quota, 22 shares, which they sold, realizing by
the transaction the net amount of $1,741.25. Upon a judicial settle-
ment of their account, the question arising, whether this sum was to
be regarded as an augmentation of the capital fund, or the whole
thereof was payable to the life tenants, as income,—

Held, that the case was to be distinguished from the ordinary one of the
declaration of an extra corporate dividend, payable in stock, in that,
here, the stockholders merely received a *pro rata* distribution of what
already belonged to them, viz.: a portion of the original capital,—the
company acquiring no additional property as an equivalent; and that
the increase was to be credited to the *corpus* of the estate.

Clarkson v. Clarkson, 18 *Barb.*, 646; •Riggs v. Cragg, 26 *Hun*, 89—distinguished.

UPON the judicial settlement of the account of
Mary Ann Knight, and others, as executrix and executors of decedent's will, objections thereto were
interposed in behalf of Grace A. Lidford and Frank
H. Knight, infant beneficiaries in remainder. The
facts are stated in the opinion.

JAS. B. KEYES, *for executors.*

F. P. BELLAMY, JOS. H. BARTLETT, *and* A. W. PROCTOR, *for beneficiaries.*

WALTER L. LIVINGSTON, *special guardian.*

THE SURROGATE.—Upon the judicial settlement of
the executors' account, two objections were raised by
the special guardian of the infants.

1st. The first involves the question whether the
extra dividend of a certain number of shares of the
original capital stock of the Atlantic Avenue Railroad company, issued to its stockholders since the
death of the testator, is to be regarded as capital
belonging to the estate, the income of which is to be
paid to the life tenants, or as income, the whole of
which is to be so paid.

2d. The special guardian for the remaindermen insists that the executors should sell the Brooklyn Park bonds, and the Jersey City Water scrip and bonds, which are now selling at a very high premium, and invest the proceeds thereof for the benefit of the remaindermen.

The testator, by his will, devised and bequeathed the remainder of his estate to his executors and trustees in trust, to be divided into four equal parts, and to collect and receive the income from one fourth thereof, and pay the same to his widow, Mary Ann Knight, during her life, and after her death to pay the principal to his children, share and share alike; and to collect and receive the income from the other three fourths, and pay the same to his children during life, and after the death of each child to pay the principal of each one fourth to the issue of such child, if any; the share of any child dying without issue, to be distributed among the surviving children.

It appears, from the account and the testimony submitted in connection with it, that the capital stock of the railroad company mentioned was $700,000, divided into 14,000 shares, each of the par value of $50; of which 13,052 shares had previously been issued, leaving a balance of 948 shares in the treasury of the company unissued. At a meeting of the directors of the company after the death of the testator, held September 17th, 1884, it was resolved to issue said 948 shares as follows: to the stockholders of the company as they that day appeared of record on the books of the company, at the rate of seven and one quarter shares for each 100 shares of stock then

owned and held by each stockholder, and in like proportion for any larger or smaller amounts of stock so
owned or held. In addition, it was also resolved,
that, for the purpose of equalizing fractional parts of
shares between stockholders, the stock should be
rated at $1.50 (it was then in the market at $1.60),
and payments should be received from any stockholder whose fraction of a share should amount to a
moiety thereof, in the like manner and at the same
rate. On October 1st, 1884, the executors received
from the Atlantic Avenue Railroad company 22
shares of the capital stock of said company, paying
therefor $18.75 for equalization; and on November
22d, 1884, they sold the same at $80 per share,
amounting to $1,760. After deducting the sum of
$18.75 paid by them for equalization of shares, they
now ask to whom they shall credit the balance of said
sale of $1,741.25,—whether the same should be paid
to the executors and trustees to be held by them as
capital, or be paid by them to the life tenants as
income. In reference to the question whether an
extra stock dividend shall be deemed capital or income, the English and American decisions are very
conflicting, and the question has not been definitely
settled by the Court of Appeals of this State.

It is true, that the cases of Clarkson v. Clarkson
(18 *Barb.*, 646), and Riggs v. Cragg (26 *Hun*, 89),
hold that the same is income. But in Brander v.
Brander (4 *Ves.*, 100); Barton's Trust (*L. R.*, 5 *Eq.
Cas.*, 238); Minot v. Paine (99 *Mass.*, 101); Doland
v. Williams (101 *id.*, 571); Atkins v. Albree (12 *Allen*,

359); and Moss's Appeal (83 *Penn.*, 264), it was held to be capital.

The Court of Appeals of this State, in the case of Riggs v. Cragg (89 *N. Y.*, 487), Chief Justice AN-DREWS writing the opinion of the court, in referring to the question of capital and income of stock dividends, say that " the question has not been settled by the court of last resort, but it will be the duty of this court when occasion arises, to settle the question upon principle, and establish a practical rule for the guidance of trustees and others, which shall be just and equitable as between the beneficiaries of the two estates." I think, however, that the case at bar is distinguishable from the cases of Clarkson v. Clarkson and Riggs v. Cragg (*supra*), inasmuch as the extra dividend in stock was a part of the original capital of the company, which had not been issued, but was held in the treasury, to be issued or sold by the company at such times as it might deem proper.

When this extra dividend was declared and issued, it was simply distributing among the stockholders what then belonged to them, for the company received no additional property or equivalent in any way for the stock so issued. It was only giving to them the balance of the unissued stock, which was held in the treasury. To regard this extra dividend of stock as income, would be unjust to the remaindermen, as it would reduce the value of the original issue of the stock to the extent of the extra stock dividend.

I, therefore, think that the extra dividend in this case must be deemed an augmentation of the capital.

As to the second objection, I think that the trustees should be permitted to hold the investments now in their hands, for the reason that they were investments made by the testator in his lifetime, which by his will he authorized his trustees to hold for the purposes of the trust therein created.

A decree may be entered accordingly.

Kings County.—Hon. J. I. BERGEN, Surrogate.— June, 1885.

BIGGS *v.* ANGUS.

In the matter of the application for probate of papers severally propounded as the will of CHARLOTTE ANGUS, *deceased.*

Decedent, who died in April, 1885, executed a will in 1875; and, in 1880, executed, as and for her will, three identical instruments, making a different disposition of her property, and containing a clause expressly revoking, in general terms, "all other or former wills" made by her. The three instruments of 1880 were severally entrusted by her to three different persons, one of whom was an attorney, P. Shortly before her death, she insisted on sending for the three last mentioned papers, declaring her intention to revoke them. Accordingly, P. attended upon decedent, and wrote at the end of one, and upon the back of another of these papers, a formal revocation, each of which was read to the testatrix, who declared that it was "all right," and subscribed it in the presence of P. and another witness, who thereafter subscribed their names to an attestation clause in the usual form. The third paper, which was in P.'s possession, he omitted to cancel. Upon an application for probate of the will of 1875, and a cross application for the probate of that of 1880, it was—

Held, that both wills were effectually revoked, and that decedent died intestate.

APPLICATION having been made to the Surrogate's
court for the probate of a paper propounded as decedent's will, dated June 19th, 1875, by John Angus,
her husband, objections were interposed by Francis
A. Biggs, her son by a former marriage, who, during
the progress of the cause, produced in court an instrument dated December 2d, 1880, making a different
disposition of the property, with a petition praying
for the probate thereof as decedent's will. Thereupon
the first proponent filed objections, averring, among
other things, that said last mentioned will had been
revoked on April 3d, 1885; and the two proceedings
were consolidated and heard as one matter. It appeared that decedent died April 14th, 1885, leaving
the first mentioned paper, executed in due form, and
also another paper, dated December 2d, 1880, executed in triplicate, each purporting to be her last will.
The three triplicate originals were severally entrusted
by decedent to three different persons, one of whom
was an attorney, Oliver N. Payne. None of them
contained or exhibited any recital or minute showing
them to be intended as such triplicates, this fact
appearing solely from the identity of their form and
execution. The instrument of 1880 contained a clause
expressly "revoking all other or former wills by"
decedent "made." Each of the triplicates was
written upon both sides of several pages of legal
cap paper. On the back of one of the set appeared
the following:

"In the name of God, Amen, I, Charlotte Angus,
wife of John Angus, of the city of Brooklyn, county
of Kings, and State of New York, of the age of

seventy-three years, weak of body but of sound disposing mind and memory, do hereby revoke and annul, and declare of none effect, my foregoing last will and testament, bearing date December 2d, 1880. In testimony whereof, I have hereunto set my hand and seal this 3rd day of April, 1885.

CHARLOTTE ANGUS. [SEAL]

" The foregoing instrument (revocation of her will, dated Dec. 2d, 1880), half a page, was signed, sealed, published and declared by the said testatrix, Charlotte Angus, as and for her revocation of her will of Dec. 2d, 1880, in the presence of us, who, at her request and in her presence, and in the presence of each other, have subscribed our names as witnesses thereto.

OLIVER N. PAYNE, residence, etc.

MARY E. THURBER, residence, etc.'

On the last half page of another of the set, was written a revoking clause identical with that quoted, subscribed and sealed in like manner, and followed by these words:

" The foregoing instrument (revocation of her will, dated Dec. 2d, 1880), consisting of half page, was signed, sealed, published and declared by the testatrix, Charlotte Angus, as and for her revocation of her will of December 2d, 1880, in the presence of us, who, at her request and in her presence, and in the presence of each other, have subscribed our names as witnesses thereto.

OLIVER N. PAYNE, residence, etc.

MARY E. THURBER, residence, etc."

The third instrument of the set, entrusted to the

possession of Oliver N. Payne, was intact. Further facts appear in the opinion.

D. P. BARNARD, *and* JOHN H. CLAYTON, *for John Angus.*

H. GRAVES, *for F. A. Biggs.*

THE SURROGATE.—The testatrix died April 14th, 1885, leaving her surviving her husband, John Angus, and one son, Francis A. Biggs, by a prior husband; having executed a will dated June 19th, 1875, by which she devised all her estate absolutely to her husband, John Angus, which he propounded for probate, and which was contested by the son of the testatrix, upon the ground that she had executed a subsequent will dated November 2d, 1880, containing a revocation clause revoking all former wills made by her; and he asks that the will of 1880 be admitted to probate as the last will and testament of Charlotte Angus, deceased. It is unnecessary to discuss the question of the validity of the will of 1875, as it is disposed of by the will of 1880, which contained a provision expressly revoking all former wills made by the testatrix.

The will of 1880 was executed in triplicate; and on the 3rd day of April, 1885, testatrix executed a revocation of said will, written on the last page of two of the triplicate set thereof. The only questions to be disposed of are—whether said revocation was executed in conformity to the statutory requirements for the execution of a will; whether the testatrix at that time possessed testamentary capacity; and whether she executed it free from undue influence. It appears from the testimony that testatrix, in the

presence and hearing of the witness, Mary E. Thurber, told her husband, John Angus, to go to lawyer
Payne's after a paper of hers, and also to Mr. Stanley's, as she had made a will and had done something
and gave away something that did not belong to her,
and she wanted to have it changed. "She could
not die with it on her mind." Her husband told
her: "no, if that suited her the way things were,
let it be so." She said: "no, I can't die and let this
be so." He refused twice to go, and then insisted on
her writing an order to Mr Payne, which she did,
first directing witness, Mary E. Thurber, to get her
glasses, designating where they could be found. A
few hours afterwards, Mr. Payne came to the house
and drew the revocation of the will of 1880, writing
it in duplicate, one on the last page of two of the
triplicate set of the will of 1880, but neglecting to
write it on the third of the set, which he had in his
possession.

It further appears that, in the presence of witness,
Mary E. Thurber, Mr. Payne read the revocation so
written to the testatrix, and she declared that "it
was all right" and signed it, and then at her request,
the witnesses, Mary E. Thurber and Oliver N. Payne
signed the attestation clause. The testimony, also,
shows that testatrix executed it without being unduly
influenced by her husband, and that she was of sound
mind and memory at the time of its execution.

Upon a careful review of all the testimony, I am of
the opinion that the revocation was executed in conformity to the statutory requirements; that testatrix
at the time of its execution possessed testamentary

capacity; that she was not unduly influenced to execute the same, and that the said will of date April 3rd, 1880, was legally revoked thereby.

Therefore, I am of the opinion that the testatrix, Charlotte Angus, died intestate.

MONROE COUNTY.—HON. J. A. ADLINGTON, SURRO-GATE.—October, 1884.

GARDINER v. RAINES.

In the matter of the probate of the will of CHARLES A. GARDINER, *deceased.*

The intent of the legislature, in requiring, by 2 R. S., 63, § 40, subd. 2, a testator's subscription to his will to be "made in the presence of each of the attesting witnesses," or, etc., was not simply that the testator and witnesses should be within the same enclosure, but that the latter should either actually see the former write his name, or have their attention directed to the act of signing while the same is taking place.

The rule that a will may be subscribed by the testator in the presence of one witness, and the signature be thereafter acknowledged to the other—applied.

Evidence for and against the proposition that testator acknowledged his subscription to one of the subscribing witnesses—weighed, and the authorities relating to the subject of such an acknowledgment—collated and discussed.

PETITION for the probate of decedent's will, presented by William G. Raines, one of the executors therein named; opposed by Celeste M. Gardiner, a sister of decedent. The facts are stated in the opinion.

GEO. RAINES, *and* D. B. HILL, *for proponent.*

WM. F. COGSWELL, *for contestant.*

THE SURROGATE.—Charles A. Gardiner, the testator above named, died April 29th, 1884, at his residence in the town of Gates, Monroe county, N. Y., leaving the paper presented for probate, purporting to be his last will and testament, by which he makes distribution of his entire estate, with the exception of a trifling legacy, in a manner entirely different from that which would have been made under the statutes of this State, had he died intestate. The instrument bears the date of March 18th, 1884, and it appears to be signed by the testator at the end. The signatures of the attesting witnesses, Hannan and Hempsted, appear first at the left of the testator's and one line below, and then follows a regular attestation clause, to which their names are also affixed.

The execution of the instrument took place at the rooms of the "Ancient and Accepted Scottish Rite," a Masonic body, in the city of Rochester, N. Y. By previous appointment, the testator met Mr. William G. Raines, the draftsman of the will, and a legatee thereunder, at this place, on the evening of the day aforesaid, for the purpose of transacting this particular business; and, shortly after their arrival, Mr. Gardiner requested Mr. John W. Hannan and Mr. John Q. A. Hempsted to step into the room, stating to each that he wanted him to witness his will.

The "Throne Room," so called, was the one in which the signatures of the testator and the witnesses were affixed to the will. It was an apartment about twelve feet wide and fifteen feet long, and the desk at which the writing was done was situated at the side of the room most remote from the door. Adjoining the "Throne Room," was another known as the "Robing Room," into which retired for a brief time the persons engaged about this transaction, on account of the entrance into the "Throne Room" of several people whom the testator apparently did not wish to know what business his party were engaged in. While in the "Robing Room," a number of questions were put to the testator and answered by him in relation to the matter of the will, to which reference will hereafter be made. The "Throne Room" having been now vacated, the party then returned thither, and the witnesses signed their names under the attestation clause. The sister of the testator, his only heir at law and next of kin, opposes the probate of the will on the ground that it was not subscribed, published and attested, in conformity with the statute regulating the execution of last wills and testaments.

The statute is as follows: "Every last will and testament of real and personal property shall be executed and attested in the following manner:

1. It shall be subscribed by the testator at the end of the will;

2. Such subscription shall be made by the testator, in the presence of each of the attesting witnesses, or shall be acknowledged by him to have been so made, to each of the attesting witnesses;

3. The testator, at the time of making such subscription, or at the time of acknowledging the same, shall declare the instrument so subscribed to be his last will and testament;

4. There shall be at least two attesting witnesses, each of whom shall sign his name as a witness, at the

end of the will, at the request of the testator " (R. S., part 2, ch. 6, tit. 1, art. 3, § 40).

The evidence shows a complete compliance with the requirements of the first, third and fourth of the foregoing subdivisions, and the only question to be decided is—whether or not the alleged will was signed by the testator in the presence of each of the attesting witnesses, or the signing thereof was acknowledged by him to each of said witnesses. Mr. Hannan, one of the attesting witnesses, was present and saw Mr. Gardiner affix his signature at the end of the will. Mr. Hempsted was also in the same room, but, as I believe from the evidence, was standing at the door of the room, with his back toward the desk at which the signing was done, in conversation with some other persons, who had knocked for admission at the precise moment when the testator signed the will, and did not see the signature made, nor know that the signing was taking place. The latter fact he asserts positively, and the other witnesses, though certain that he was within the same enclosed space, are not able to say that Hempsted saw the signature affixed, or had his attention directed to the fact that the signing was taking place at the time.

There is abundant authority for sustaining the probate of a will, notwithstanding the denial, by one or both of the subscribing witnesses, of the observance of the proper legal forms, in cases where there is a regular attestation clause, and the surrounding circumstances tend to show the due execution of the will (Trustees of Theological Seminary v. Calhoun, 25

N. Y., 422; Kinne v. Kinne, 2 *T. & C.*, 391; Matter of Cottrell, 95 *N. Y.*, 329).

I see no reason, however, to doubt the testimony of Mr. Hempsted, that he did not see the execution of the will by the testator, and did not know whether it had been signed when he first affixed his name to the instrument above the attestation clause; and I have adopted the foregoing version of that part of the transaction as most consistent with all the evidence in the case; for, although there are some circumstances which would warrant the belief that he actually saw the signature affixed, yet they do not overcome his positive testimony to the contrary. The decisions are not numerous upon the precise point of what constitutes *signing in the presence of the attesting witnesses*, within the language of the statute, but it seems to me that the intention of the legislature was, not simply that the witnesses and the testator should be within the same enclosure, but that the witnesses should either actually see the testator write his name, or should have their attention directed to the act of signing while the same is taking place.

In the case of Peck v. Cary (27 *N. Y.*, 9), Emott, J. says: "signing such a paper (*i. e.* a will) in the same room with the witness, who does not see the act, and who does not know at the time that any such act is taking place, is not a signing in his presence." In Burke v. Nolan (1 *Dem.*, 436), the Surrogate discussing the question of publication of a will, says: "It may well be that if the witness was in such a position that he *could and ought* to have heard what was said, the remarks should be considered as having been made within his hearing, on the same principle that, if he was in a position to see the testator sign the will, it must be deemed to have been signed in his presence."

In Spaulding v. Gibbons (5 *Redf.*, 316), it is said that " if the witness wàs in the same room with the testator, or in the adjoining room, in such a position that he could see him sign, after his attention had been drawn to what was going on, the signing will be considered to have taken place in his presence."

In the case of Jauncey v. Thorne (2 *Barb. Ch.*, 40–70), the Chancellor says: " The attesting witnesses should see the testator, or some one for him, sign the instrument which they are called upon to witness, or the testator should either say or do something in their presence and hearing, indicating that he intends to recognize such instrument as one which has been signed by him, as a valid will."

In Mitchell v. Mitchell (16 *Hun*, 97), the court says: " There are four separate clauses in the statute, each of which has its own distinct object . . . . . The second clause is, that the subscription of the testator shall be made in the presence of each of the attesting witnesses. The principal object of this is, that the witnesses may be able to say from positive knowledge that the subscription was made by the testator." I think that, within the rule laid down by the above authorities, the signing of this will, by the testator, was not done in the presence of Hempsted; and that the said will, therefore, was not executed in his presence, within the meaning of the first clause of the above quoted second subdivision of the statute.

A will, however, may be signed in the presence of one witness, and the signature thereafter acknowledged to the other attesting witness (Matter of Tonnele, 5 *N. Y. Leg. Obs.*, 254; Hoysradt v. Kingman, 22 *N. Y.*, 372).

This, I think, was done in the case under consideration, and that the execution of the will is sufficiently proved. Mr. Hempsted states that the question was asked Mr. Gardiner in the Robing Room—whether he had signed this paper as his last will and testament, and that he replied: "Yes; certainly." Mr. Hannan testifies that while the four persons, who were engaged in and about the execution and attestation of this will, were in the Robing Room, Mr. Raines read over the attestation clause in the presence and hearing of them all, and that questions were there asked by Mr. Raines and answered by Mr. Gardiner, one of them being: "Is this your last will and testament?" and that the testator said it was. Mr. Raines then said, in the presence and hearing of both witnesses and the testator: "Now, gentlemen, step back and sign." Mr. Hannan further states that there were questions put that he does not now remember. Mr. Raines testifies that, while holding the will in front of Gardiner, after they, with the two attesting witnesses, had passed into the Robing Room and were standing near together, he asked this question: "Charlie, do you wish these two gentlemen to understand you have signed this as your last will and testament?" and that Gardiner answered: "Yes;" that the question was then asked: "Do you wish them to sign as subscribing witnesses to your last will and testament?" and that Gardiner answered: "I do." Mr. Hempsted at another point in his evidence says that Raines asked Gardiner: "Is this your last will and testament?" to which Gardiner answered: "Yes;" and that the further question was asked— if he (Gardiner) accepted Hannan and himself (Hempsted) as witnesses to his last will and testament; and that Gardiner said: "Yes, certainly." He also stated that there may have been one or two more questions put that he does not recollect. It is entirely clear from the evidence in the case, to which reference has been briefly made, that the testator's signature was duly acknowledged by him, to both of the attesting witnesses, after it had been affixed to the will.

Even if the testimony of Hempsted, that Mr. Gardiner was asked, in the Robing Room, whether he had signed the paper as his last will and testament, and that he replied: "Yes, certainly," were rejected, on account of the subsequent attempt to deny or qualify it, and the same course were pursued with the statement of Mr. Raines, that he said to the testator: "Charlie, do you wish these two gentlemen to understand that you have signed this as your last will and testament?" and that Gardiner answered: "Yes"— on the ground that Raines is an interested witness, still enough unimpeachable evidence remains to require the admission of this will to probate.

The authorities are numerous and decisive, to the effect that a much less formal observance of the different requirements of the statute is sufficient to sustain the probate of a will.

In 1 Williams on Executors (6th Am. ed., 117, 118),

it is stated that "the result of the cases appears to be that, where the testator produces the will, with his signature visibly apparent on the face of it, to the witnesses and requests them to subscribe it, this is a sufficient acknowledgment of his signature." In Morris v. Porter (52 *How. Pr.*, 1) the court says: "Had it distinctly appeared that the will, when handed to the witnesses to be attested, bore the signature of the testatrix, accompanied by the request that they should be witnesses to it as her will, that would, doubtless, have been an acknowledgment of the subscription by her, within the meaning of the statute." In Kinne v. Kinne (2 *T. & C.*, 391), it is declared not to be necessary to a due acknowledgment of the signature, that it should be referred to in words. An acknowledgment that the instrument purporting to be a will, and purporting to be signed by the testator, is his will, is a sufficient acknowledgment of the signature." In Baskin v. Baskin (36 *N. Y.*, 418), the court says that "when the testator produces a paper bearing his personal signature, requests the witnesses to attest it, and declares it to be his last will and testament, he thereby acknowledges the subscription, within the meaning of the statute.

In Peck v. Cary (27 *N. Y.*, 9–39), the court cites, with apparent approval, many cases in which certain acts and declarations, for the most part extremely informal, were held to be sufficient acknowledgments of the subscriptions of wills; and among them is the case of Mary Warden (2 *Curteis*, 334), in which the testatrix had signed the will before the witnesses came into the room; they were sent for by her, and after their arrival the draftsman of the will produced it, and told the testatrix that the witnesses had come, to which she replied: "I am very glad of it; thank God." The witnesses thereupon signed their names in her presence. It was held that the signature was sufficiently acknowledged.

In re Harder (1 *Tuck.*, 426), it was held by the Surrogate that "the words: 'Will you witness my will?' or 'I want you to witness my will,' addressed by the decedent to, and heard by both subscribing witnesses, constitute a sufficient acknowledgment."

It is not essential that the signature should be actually shown to the witness at the time the acknowledgment is made. In Willis v. Mott (36 *N. Y.*, 486), it was held that "the statute does not require that the testator shall exhibit. his subscription to the will, at the time he makes his acknowledgment," and that "it would, therefore, follow that when the subscription is acknowledged to an attesting witness it is not essential that the signature be exhibited to the witness." In Hoysradt v. Kingman (22 *N. Y.*, 372), it is stated that "an acknowledgment by the testator of his signature and execution of the will is equivalent to the actual seeing by the witnesses of the physical act of subscription." See, also, Taylor v. Brodhead (5 *Redf.*, 624); Matter of Gilman's will (38 *Barb.*, 364–369); Gamble v. Gamble (39 *Barb.*, 373).

While a failure to comply with either of the statutory requirements, in the execution of a will, is fatal (Chaffee v. Bapt. Miss. Conv., 10 *Paige*, 85; Lewis v. Lewis, 11 *N. Y.*, 220; Remsen v. Brinckerhoff, 26

Wend., 325), yet the courts in the above cited cases, and in many others of similar tenor, have authoritatively declared what is a sufficient compliance with those requirements; and within these cases, I am constrained to hold that the will of Mr. Gardiner was properly executed, with all the formalities required by law, by a competent testator, and must therefore, be admitted to probate.

MONROE COUNTY.—HON. J. A. ADLINGTON, SURROGATE.—February, 1885.

POTTER *v.* McALPINE.

In the matter of the probate of the will, and codicils thereto, of HENRY S. POTTER, deceased.

The sanity of every man, and his capacity to make a will, are to be presumed until the contrary appears, and the burden of proving mental disability is on him who asserts it.

The court, when asked to reject an alleged will, can pay no heed to such considerations as that the same is mean, unjust and inequitable; or that it withholds the absolute ownership of decedent's property from his own children, or makes unequal provisions for them; or that public sentiment and the moral sense of the community condemn the instrument and its author.

The prevailing system of presenting, in the courts, the testimony of medical experts upon the question of sanity,—criticised, as being poorly calculated to assist in arriving at the exact truth.

The sixth subdivision of decedent's will made the enjoyment, by one of his sons, of the income of a share of the estate conditional upon the beneficiary's not living with, or in any manner contributing to the support or maintenance of his wife.—

Held, that the condition was precedent, and illegal and void, being both against public policy and good morals, and one which would require a

violation of the statutes (Code Crim. Pro., §§ 899–904); and that the
gift was discharged therefrom and valid.

Testator, by a codicil to his will, provided: "Nor shall my executors and
trustees be obliged or compelled to file with the Surrogate any inventory of my estate." Upon the application for probate,—

Held, that it is against public policy to permit such interference with the
forms of procedure established by law, removing the barriers designed
to protect estates from misappropriation; and that the clause in question was invalid and of no effect.

PETITION for the probate of the will, and codicils
thereto, of decedent, presented by Byron D. McAlpine, one of the executors therein named; opposed
by Charles B. Potter and others, decedent's children.
The facts appear in the opinion.

D. D. SULLY, *for proponent.*

COGSWELL, BENTLY & COGSWELL, and J. A. STULL, *for contestants.*

THEO. BACON, *and* WM. C. ROWLEY, *special guardians.*

THE SURROGATE. — The instruments, propounded
for probate and purporting to express the testamentary intentions of the decedent, are the alleged will,
dated June 19th, 1880, and three codicils thereto,
bearing the respective dates of July 8th, 1881, September 13th, 1882, and August 17th, 1883. The
probate is contested by Alfred B. Potter and Charles
B. Potter, the sons of the decedent, and by his unmarried daughter, Miss Henrietta Potter, on the
grounds of failure to comply with the formal requirements of the statute, in the execution of the several
instruments, and also lack of testamentary capacity.
The answers of the contestants also put in issue,
under § 2624 of the Code of Civil Procedure, the
validity of the dispositions of property made by the

sixth and *ninth* subdivisions of the will, and allege
that the same are illegal and void.

Mr. Henry S. Potter died at the city of Rochester,
N. Y., January 9th, 1884, aged about eighty-six years.
He left surviving him the contestants above named,
and two married daughters, Mrs. Mary E. Hart and
Mrs. Susan P. McAlpine. His estate amounts to about
$1,250,000, of which $250,000 is in real estate.

The will, omitting the subdivisions alleged to be
invalid, gives the entire estate of the decedent to
certain persons named as executors and trustees, to
hold in trust, for the purposes set forth in the will,
during the lives of Henry N. Potter and Reynolds
P. McAlpine, two infant grandsons of the testator.
There is a specific bequest to the decedent's wife of
all household furniture, pictures and books; a like
bequest of a piano, stool, music and rack therefor, to
his daughter, Henrietta; and an annuity of two hundred dollars to his sister.

It further directs the executors to pay all debts
and the necessary expenses of the care and management of the estate; to pay to his said wife and to his
daughters, Mrs. Mary E. Hart and Mrs. Susan P.
McAlpine, each, one sixth of the net annual income
of his estate; and to his son, Alfred B. Potter, semiannually during his natural life, so much of one sixth
of the net annual income of the estate as shall be
necessary to maintain and support his family and
educate his children. The surplus of Alfred's one
sixth share of the income of the estate is directed to
be accumulated, and his proportionate part thereof
paid over to each of said Alfred's children, as they

successively arrive at the age of twenty-one years. The payment to the testator's children of their respective shares of the income of the estate, is directed to cease upon the death of the survivor of the two grandsons upon whose lives the trust estate is limited, but to each of his own children who may survive the said grandsons is bequeathed absolutely the sum of fifteen thousand dollars, except to Charles, whose right thereto is dependent upon the condition in the sixth subdivision.

The wife of the testator died before him, and the will provides that, in such case, the net annual income shall be divided into five equal parts, and each child shall have the same right in and to one fifth, as had been before given in the several one sixth shares. Upon the death of the survivor of the two grandsons aforesaid, or after the decease of all the children of the testator, though said grandsons shall still be alive, the executors are directed to close up and distribute the entire estate, share and share alike, among the grandchildren of the testator; the children of any deceased grandchildren to receive their parents' share. Power to lease and sell real estate, and to invest and manage the whole estate, is conferred upon the executors.

The codicil of July 8th, 1881, bequeathed the sum of $15,000 to various benevolent and charitable institutions in the city of Rochester. The one dated September 13th, 1882, directs the omission, from the assets of the estate, of a certain parcel of real estate conveyed to Mrs. McAlpine. The last codicil, dated August 17th, 1883, changes the number of executors, and names certain other persons who shall act as such in certain contingencies. It also contains this clause, viz: "I further order and direct that my executors and trustees, mentioned in my said will and this codicil, shall not be required to make any bond or give any security as such executors and trustees of my said will and estate, nor shall my executors and trustees be obliged or compelled to file with the Surrogate any inventory of my estate."

The last clause, relating to the non-filing of an inventory, is challenged by the answers herein as illegal and void. The material parts of the subdivisions attacked for invalidity, are as follows:

"*Sixth*—Pay to my son, Charles B. Potter, one thousand dollars of the income of my estate, annually, in semiannual payments of five hundred dollars each, if that sum, $1,000, does not exceed annually one sixth of the net annual income of my estate; if it does, then pay him only one sixth of the net annual income of my estate during his natural life . . . . . This one thousand dollars is intended for the support and education of said Charles' children, and to be deducted from his share of the income of my estate. If one sixth of the net annual income of my estate . . . . . amounts to more than one thousand dollars, invest the excess and the accumulations thereof as a separate investment, until my said son Charles shall not live with, or at any time contribute in any manner to the support or maintenance of his present wife, Jennie W. Potter; if he does not live with, or at any time, or in any way, contribute to her support or maintenance, then pay to him his full share—one

sixth of the income of my estate, and all accumulations
that may have been held as aforesaid of his one sixth
share of the income of the estate; and also from that
time pay to him one sixth of the net annual income
of my estate in semiannual payments, deducting the
rental value of" certain specified real estate.

"*Ninth*—Pay to my said daughter, Henrietta, semiannually, as much of one sixth of the net annual
income of my estate as shall be necessary to support
her respectably during her natural life . . . . . If
she marries and has a child or children, give to her
an additional amount; if there shall be enough of the
balance of said one sixth of said income sufficient to
support and educate such child or children, pay to
her, said Henrietta, as much of said balance as my
executors shall deem necessary for that purpose,
invest the balance of said one sixth of the said
income of my estate and its accumulations, and divide
and pay her child, or children, as heretofore directed
and provided in the case of my son, Alfred B. Potter's
children, whatever said surplus and its accumulations
shall amount to at her death; if she shall have no
child, or children, add the same to the assets of my
estate and treat as part of my estate."

It would be idle for me to profess to be unaware of
the fact that, in the community in which the decedent had so long dwelt and in which he was so widely
known, a public interest has been manifested in this
contest over his will and its results. Both parties
have had their adherents and advocates.

It was urged upon the argument, for the contestants,
that the will was a mean, unjust and inequitable one,

in withholding the absolute ownership of the decedent's property from his own children, and in its unequal provisions for them; and it was further said that public sentiment and the moral sense of the community condemned the instrument and its author. To this it was correctly and appropriately replied, that public sentiment may be properly urged to influence the law makers, the legislature, but that it can have no effect with those whose sole duty it is to administer the laws as they find them; and that it was not an unusual thing for men who have accumulated large fortunes, to endeavor to entail their property so far as the law permits.

It is the duty of courts of Probate to guard carefully the testamentary privileges which the law confers upon the citizens of the land, and at the same time to see to it that the rights of the heirs and next of kin of decedents, under the statutes of descent and distribution, shall not be swept away by alleged wills made by their ancestor, when so much enfeebled in intellect as to be incapable of exercising sound reason and judgment, or when so unduly influenced by another as not to be free to act according to his own inclination or desire. I shall endeavor, therefore, in the consideration of this matter, to be governed only by the evidence herein and by the law applicable to the case.

In the law of wills there are two principles firmly established by the authorities, which should be distinctly borne in mind, viz.:

First. Every man, under the conditions and in the manner prescribed by law, has the right to make a will and dispose of his property in such way and to such persons as shall be most pleasing to him, however absurd, unjust or inequitable the disposition may appear to others. He may do what he will with his own (Clapp v. Fullerton, 34 *N. Y.*, 190; Seguine v. Seguine, 3 *Keyes*, 663–671; Reynolds v. Root, 62 *Barb.*, 250; Wood v. Bishop, 1 *Dem.*, 512). For example, he may give all his property to strangers and thus disinherit his relatives. He may exclude his children or divide his estate among them unequally; and this general power of disposition he possesses down to the last hour of conscious, intelligent existence (Hollis v. Drew Theological Seminary, 95 *N. Y.*, 166; Horn v. Pullman, 72 *id.*, 269). He is not prohibited indulging, in this regard, his passions, his prejudices or his caprices, and his will is not to be disregarded by the judgment of any tribunal, whether of law or equity, because his dispositions are by them deemed unreasonable, or prompted by passion, prejudice or unworthy motive (Marvin v. Marvin, 3 *Abb. Ct. App. Dec.*, 192).

Second. The sanity of every man and his capacity to make a will are to be presumed until the contrary appears, and the burden of proving mental disability is on him who asserts it (Delafield v. Parish, 25 *N. Y.*, 9; Brown v. Taney, 24 *Barb.*, 583; Ean v. Snyder, 46 *id.*, 230; Jackson v. Van Dusen, 5 *Johns.*, 144; Miller v. White, 5 *Redf.*, 320).

I shall now take up the specific objections to the probate of these instruments in the following order:

1st. The question of the execution of the alleged will and codicils.

The due and proper execution of the several instruments presented for probate was satisfactorily proved. The alleged will and the several codicils thereto were each brought by the decedent in person to the offices of the Traders National Bank in the city of Rochester, and there signed by him in the presence of the subscribing witnesses; each instrument was duly published according to its nature, and the attesting witnesses subscribed the same in the presence of each other, and of the testator. One witness to each paper testifies positively to the observance of all the requirements of the statute in each instance, and while the other one does not recollect all of the details of the occurrence, yet he does not testify in any wise against the execution. The attestation clause in each case is full and complete. The signatures are all genuine. On some, if not all, of these occasions, the attestation clause was read over by the decedent to the witnesses. "The failure of recollection of the subscribing witness to a will, as to what occurred at the time of signing, will not defeat the probate thereof, if the attestation clause and the surrounding circumstances establish its execution" (Rugg v. Rugg, 83 *N. Y.*, 592; Matter of Will of Cottrell, 95 *id.*, 329; Lane v. Lane, *id.*, 494; Whitefield v. Whitefield, 19 *Week. Dig.*, 3-6; Kinne v. Kinne, 2 *T. & C.*, 391).

2*d*. The question of testamentary capacity.

A strenuous effort was made by the contestants to prove that the decedent was insane, and lacking in testamentary capacity, at the time of the execution of the alleged will and codicils. A number of medical experts were examined, including one or two alienists of high repute in their profession, who gave it, as their opinion, that the decedent was of unsound mind ; and considerable testimony was adduced tending to show that there had been such an enfeeblement of his mental and bodily powers, during the last three or four years of his life as to produce unsoundness of mind, which the contestants claimed took the form of melancholia, delusion and senile dementia. The sum of the evidence on this subject was that the decedent, who was an old man, had grown crabbed, irritable, morose and petulant in his manner; that he was forgetful and of failing memory ; that there was a tremulousness in his hands and head ; that at times he exhibited great and unreasonable fear of personal violence and robbery when apparently in no actual danger; that he was extremely close, stingy, niggardly and penurious in pecuniary matters ; and that he had formerly made wills disposing of his property in quite a different manner from that directed in the present will.

It is scarcely necessary to say that all the testimony, tending to support the points set forth in the foregoing summary, might be given its greatest weight, and yet fall far short of establishing unsoundness of mind in the decedent. " By a sound mind, within the meaning of the law, is not meant a mind which is perfectly balanced and free from all prejudice or passion " (Phillips v. Chater, 1 *Dem.*, 533). A will is not to be set aside merely because its maker was weak, or sometimes foolish, or lacked the average mental capacity of his neighbors, or did not dispose of his property as others, who know nothing of his reasons, might think he ought to have done (Rice v. Rice, 50 *Mich.*, 448). Failure of memory, being a natural attendant upon age, will not incapacitate an aged person from making a will (Reynolds v. Root, 62 *Barb.*, 250; Pilling v. Pilling, 45 *id.*, 86–95; nor does morbid avarice, or senility or physical weakness (Cornwell v. Riker, 2 *Dem.*, 354–395). Testamentary incapacity cannot be inferred from an enfeebled condition of mind or body (Horn v. Pullman, 72 *N. Y.*, 269; Children's Aid Society v. Loveridge, 70 *id.*, 387–410). Perverse opinion, violence of manner, ill temper, moroseness, severity, and even brutality are to be distinguished from alienation of mind (Riggs v. American Tract Society, 95 *N. Y.*, 503–513). An unequal or unjust will raises no presumption of unsoundness of mind, nor does radical change from previous testamentary dispositions (La Bau v. Vanderbilt, 3 *Redf.*, 384; Horn v. Pullman, 10 *Hun*, 471; affi'd, 72 *N. Y.*, 269; McLaughlin v. McDevitt, 63 *id.*, 213).

The importance to be attached to many of the above mentioned indications of the failure of the decedent's mental and bodily powers depends upon the extent to which these infirmities had advanced and the manner of their manifesting themselves; if the failure of memory extended to important business affairs and transactions, as well as to trivial matters; if the change of manner from cheerfulness and affability to moroseness and discourtesy was shown alike to intimate friends and ordinary acquaintance; if the penuriousness and avarice had recently supplanted open-handed generosity; if great physical strength and courage had given way to excessive timidity and feebleness, and business capacity and sagacity to folly and blundering in the management of business affairs, there would then be ample warrant for holding that the testator was no longer competent to make a will. I do not find the evidence that these hypotheses are true.

Mr. Potter, until within a week from his death, was the sole manager of his large estate. He gave personal supervision to all his affairs, made profitable investments of his funds, and retained to the last that business shrewdness which had made of the poor clerk a millionaire. He was slight of frame and of a nervous temperament, and probably had never been a man of much physical courage. He was always close and parsimonious in the extreme, and while in the latter part of his life he was less affable and courteous than formerly to some people, yet, to many others, he always showed his old-time civility and courtesy.

Many witnesses,—prominent bankers, merchants, business and professional men of Rochester, old friends and acquaintances of Mr. Potter, testified to these things, and said that the decedent, to nearly the close of his life retained all his faculties to a remarkable degree for one so old; that he was active, energetic and shrewd in business to the last; that he took an intelligent interest in public and municipal affairs, and also in social and economic questions; and that his acts and conversation were entirely rational.

Much stress was put upon the assumed change in the decedent's testamentary intentions. Some evidence was given to show that, about twenty years before his death, and again some ten years later, Mr. Potter had said that he intended his family should all share alike in his property. It is enough to say, in regard to this statement, that the decedent never seems to have entertained such an intention at any time when he actually made and executed a will. Every will of which we have any account discriminated against his son Charles, and gave little or nothing to him absolutely. The will drawn by Mr. McGuire in August, 1879 (excepting the disposition of the homestead and household furniture), gave to none of the testator's children an absolute estate in any of the property, but only an equal share in the income thereof. That will was based upon one drawn by Mr. Cochrane and, therefore, the Cochrane will probably contained similar limitations upon the rights of enjoyment, given to the decedent's children. Mr. May's recollection of the contents of the proposed will shown to him are too indefinite to afford any satisfactory evidence of its contents. It does not seem, therefore, that the will now under consideration differs so radically from any other actually executed, or from any intention previously entertained, as to arouse suspicion of aberration of mind in the maker thereof. "A change of intention is of no importance if there be a sound mind, unconstrained" (Titlow v. Titlow, 54 *Penn.*, *St.* 216). "A testator has a right to change radically and arbitrarily the manner of disposing of his property, and, in the absence of fraud, courts will sustain his action in this respect" (McLaughlin v. McDevitt, 63 *N. Y.*, 213).

The soundness of mind of the decedent and his capacity to execute a will are further assailed by medical experts who state no facts, but give their opinions upon facts already in proof, or assumed to be true for the purposes of the examination. The present system of presenting the testimony of experts, in the courts, is poorly calculated to assist in arriving at the exact truth. The expert produced as a witness has almost invariably given assurance that he will swear to an opinion favorable to the party calling him, and for this he usually receives a fee proportioned to his estimate of the value of his opinion to the side for which he testifies (Templeton v. People, 3 *Hun*, 357, 361). The experts are frequently men who never knew, or even saw the decedent. They base their opinions upon a few detached circumstances in his life, generally grouped together in the form of hypothetical questions, which magnify or exaggerate the facts and circumstances to which they call attention.

" Isolated incidents in the life of intelligent, educated and cultured people, can be so grouped together as to make the most sane of men appear to have been mentally unsound, and, in order to a wise and safe judgment, the isolated incidents usually presented to experts need to be supplemented by a statement of the general character, conduct and habits of the person " (Dickie v. Van Vleck, 5 *Redf.*, 284–299).

In the present case, while I credit the physicians, who pronounced Mr. Potter of unsound mind, with honestly entertaining that conviction, I am obliged to dissent entirely from their opinion, which, in my judgment, is founded upon wholly insufficient and inadequate data, and upon assumptions of the existence of facts which, in my opinion, were not established. Among other things, they assume that the fear exhibited by the decedent on several occasions was wholly groundless. Mr. Potter, in two instances, said that the men, who were the objects of his alarm, had threatened to kill him. We are bound to believe that he told the truth, since there is no proof of the contrary, and especially as there is corroborative evidence of the threat in each case. His fear, therefore, though excessive, was not imaginary. In the only other case in which this undue fear was shown, the decedent had a considerable sum of money with him, and there was a "big fellow" near who might have attacked him, if wicked and malicious enough so to do, though there was probably no real danger. These several exhibitions of fear the contestants' experts pronounced to be delusion; but I do not so understand the term.

"An insane delusion is one which not only is founded in error, but is without evidence of its truth, and often exists against the clearest evidence to the contrary. Its essence is that it has no basis in reason and cannot be dispelled thereby" (Merrill v. Rolston, 5 *Redf.*, 220, *and cases cited on p.* 252; Seamen's Friend Society v. Hopper, 33 *N. Y.*, 619). But even if it were conceded that in this particular the decedent was laboring under delusion, it is difficult to see how that fact could in any wise affect the validity of his will. "A person under delusion, or a monomaniac, may make a valid will, if the delusion which affects the general soundness of his mind has no relation to the subject, or object, of the will, or the persons who would otherwise be likely, ordinarily, to be the recipients of his bounty " (Lathrop v. Am. Board of Foreign Missions, 67 *Barb.*, 590–595; 1 Redf. on Wills, 79; Children's Aid Society v. Loveridge, 70 *N. Y.*, 387; Riggs v. American Tract Society, 95 *id.*, 503; Fraser v. Jennison, 42 *Mich.*, 206–238). A number of the most learned and highly respected physicians of this city, who had known Mr. Potter well for many years, testified that they did not consider him of unsound mind; and that they never saw anything singular or unusual in his manner or conduct; and with them, on this question of sanity, I agree, upon all the evidence in the case.

The formal execution of these instruments, and the competency of the testator having been established, it now remains to consider the validity of the directions for the accumulation of income contained in the foregoing sixth and ninth subdivisions of the will. The answers of the contestants expressly allege the invalidity of the accumulation therein provided for; and I am, therefore, required, by § 2624 of the Code of Civil Procedure, to determine the question raised as to the personal property.

The *sixth* subdivision of the will makes the enjoyment by Charles B. Potter of his one fifth part of the income of the estate, conditional upon his not living with, or in any manner contributing to, the support or maintenance of his wife, Jennie W. Potter. This is an attempt, on the part of the decedent, to carry out a threat made by him many years ago, to punish

Mrs. Charles B. Potter for daring to interfere in some business transactions between him and her husband. The testator was a self-willed man, intolerant of opposition, accustomed during all his life to exercise a patriarchal control over his children and their affairs. Mrs. Charles B. Potter, a refined and cultivated woman, of independent character and judgment, soon after her marriage with his son came into conflict with her father in law in various ways. He resented what he evidently considered an unwarrantable interference with his paternal sovereignty; and a mutual dislike sprang up which continued during the life of Mr. Potter, the elder, and became so strong that Mrs. Potter forbade her children to visit the house of their grandfather.

No one will justify the attitude of hostility which the testator took toward the wife of his son, nor his attempt to carry into effect his threat to punish her through his will; but it is easy to see why a man, such as this testator was, should make the endeavor to gratify his desire for revenge.

This condition is illegal and void. It requires the violation of the laws of the State, and if complied with would render Mr. Charles B. Potter liable to imprisonment in the county jail (Code Crim. Pro., §§ 899–904). It is, also, contrary to public policy and good morals. The condition is evidently precedent in its character, and while, at the common law, it would doubtless work a forfeiture of the gift, yet in equity and under the civil law, though the condition is void, yet the gift is good. "With respect to legacies out of personal estate, the civil law, which in this respect has been adopted by courts of equity, differs in some respects from the common law in its treatment of conditions precedent; the rule of the civil law being that, where a condition precedent is originally impossible . . . . . or is illegal as involving *malum prohibitum,* the bequest is absolute, just as if the condition had been subsequent" (2 Jarman on Wills, *5th Am. ed.,* 12, 13 ; 2 Williams on Ex'rs, *6th Am. ed.,* 1372). "When the illegality of the condition does not concern anything *malum in se* but is merely against a rule or the policy of the law, the condition only is void, and the bequest single and good " (1 Roper on Legacies, 757).

The law regards with favor the marital relation and frowns upon the attempts of individuals to sever or interrupt it. In Tenant v. Braies (*Tothill,* 78), there was a bequest, made to the daughter of the testator of a sum of money, " if she will be divorced from her husband." The gift was held good, but the condition void. In Brown v. Peck (1 *Eden's Ch.,* 140), a testator directed his executors to pay to his niece, Rebecca, " if she lived with her husband, £2 per month and no more, but if she lived from him and with her mother, to allow her £5 per month." The condition was held to be *contra bonos mores,* and the legacy of £5 per month simple and pure. In Conrad v. Long (33 *Mich.,* 78), one half of the testator's real estate was devised to his sister, Elizabeth, " if at any subsequent time she should conclude not to live with her present husband, Henry Long, as his wife. But if she did continue to live with him, then to the testator's brother." It was held that she took the estate clear of conditions. See, also, Cooper v. Remsen (5 *Johns. Ch.*, 459–463).

The same result is reached in another way, as suggested by the learned counsel who appeared in support of the probate, as special guardian of certain infants, viz.: The direction to accumulate is void, whether as to income of personal or real property (1 R. S., 726, §§ 37, 38; and id., 773, § 3).

The said direction, being unlawful and void, should be regarded as stricken out of the will (Williams v. Williams, 8 *N. Y.*, 525–563; Pray v. Hegeman, 92 *id.*, 508). Section 2 of 1 R. S., 773, makes § 40 of 1 R. S., 726, applicable to accumulations of personal property as well as to rents of realty; and the accumulations of income, therefore, belong to the persons entitled to the next eventual estate (Cook v. Lowry, 95 *N. Y.*, 103).

"Those who presumptively will be entitled to receive the rents and profits" (and income), "when the period of accumulation ends, are entitled to anticipate the event which is to terminate the accumulation, and to take at once what is unlawfully directed to be accumulated" (Manice v. Manice, 43 *N. Y.*, 303–389). Charles B. Potter is the person entitled to take the accumulations, and one fifth of the annual income, upon the happening of the event which terminates the accumulation, viz.: his ceasing to live with or support his wife, and he is, therefore, entitled to the same at once and absolutely, the direction to accumulate being void (Pray v. Hegeman, 92 *N. Y.*, 508).

That portion of the sixteenth subdivision of the will is also void, which in substance excludes Charles

B. Potter from the bequest of $15,000 to each child of the testator surviving the grandchildren, Henry N. Potter and Reynolds P. McAlpine, unless he shall have previously become entitled to receive his one sixth by abandoning and not supporting his wife. If he shall survive said grandchildren, he will be entitled to the said $15,000, absolutely.

The directions for the accumulation of such part of the income of one fifth of the estate as should not be expended for the support of Miss Potter, the unmarried daughter, contained in the ninth subdivision of the will, is wholly void. It is not for the benefit of any minor in being at the time of the testator's death (1 R. S., 773, § 3). So long, therefore, as Miss Potter remains unmarried and without issue, the surplus income will belong to those entitled to the next eventual estate (Cook v. Lowry, *supra*). It vests, therefore, in the grandchildren of the testator living at his death in equal shares, subject to open and let in after-born grandchildren who may come into existence before the final distribution of the estate (Monarque v. Monarque, 80 *N. Y.*, 320–326; Kilpatrick v. Johnson, 15 *N. Y.*, 322, 327).

An executor is required by law within a reasonable time after qualifying, with the aid of appraisers, to make a true and perfect inventory of all the goods, chattels and credits of his testator (2 R. S., 82, § 2). This inventory shall be filed with the Surrogate within three months after the issue of letters. If this is not done, he may be compelled, on the application of a creditor, or person interested in the estate, to perform such duty; and in case of default he may be committed to jail (Code Civ. Pro., §§ 2715, 2716). In actions and special proceedings, the inventory is presumptive evidence of the amount and value of the estate both for and against the executor. It would often be extremely difficult, if not impossible, to prove what property came into the possession of an executor if he were excused from making and returning an inventory thereof. If the executor converts to his own use, makes away with or fraudulently withholds any of the money or property of the estate, he is guilty of embezzlement (L. 1877, ch. 208). If a testator can dispense with the making of an inventory by will, many of the safeguards thus thrown around the estate which comes to the hands of the executor would be thrown down, and fraud and misappropriation of the trust property would be rendered much easier and less liable to detection than at present. It is against public policy to permit such interference with the forms of procedure established by law, or to remove the barriers designed to protect estates from misappropriation. The safety, preservation and honest distribution of decedent's estate require that provisions like the one in question should be declared invalid and of no effect.

As the testator's general plan for the distribution of his estate will be but slightly interfered with by this decision, it will not be necessary to inquire what should be done if it had been seriously broken in upon. The will and codicils, therefore, must be admitted to probate, except the parts herein declared invalid, and a decree in conformity with this opinion may be settled on two days' notice to parties interested.

MONTGOMERY COUNTY.—HON. Z. S. WESTBROOK,
SURROGATE.—April, 1885.

MATTER OF PALMER.

In the matter of the estate of JAMES M. PALMER,
deceased.

No inventory of decedent's property having been made or filed, and no proceedings having been taken to compel the return of an inventory, certain creditors cited the executors to account, with a view to the
payment of their claims; whereupon the latter filed a duly verified
account showing that no property of decedent's estate had come into
their hands.—

Held, that the burden was cast upon the creditors, of proving that the
executors were chargeable with assets.

Testator, during his lifetime, insured his life in two "benefit insurance
associations," the certificates being made payable to his mother, who,
shortly before testator's death, assigned the same to the executor and
executrix named in his will, the latter of whom was his wife, in trust
for the use of the assignor during life, the principal, upon her death,
to go to the wife. Simultaneously with this assignment, testator executed his will confirming this disposition of the moneys to become payable upon the certificates. Testator having died insolvent, and the
executors having received the benefit moneys, decedent's creditors
sought to reach the same as constituting assets of his estate.—

Held, that it was to be presumed, from the beneficial nature of the policies,
that the same were within the scope of the statutes relating to the
insurance of a man's life for the benefit of his family, and that the
moneys which the executors had received thereunder were not assets
in the hands of the executors, and could not be disposed of as such, but
should be applied in accordance with the terms of the trust, to the
exclusion of the claims of decedent's creditors.

APPLICATION by certain creditors of decedent to
compel Frederick F. Wendell, as executor, and Elizabeth Palmer, as executrix, of decedent's will, to account and pay their claims. The facts appear in the
opinion.

MATTER OF PALMER.

SUTTON & MOOREHOUSE, WELLER & MOORE, *and* W. H. VAN STEEN-
BURGH, *for creditors.*

J. D. WENDELL, *for executors.*

C. N. HEMIUP, *for Mrs. Palmer.*

THE SURROGATE.—The executor and executrix are
called upon to account by sundry creditors, who have
filed claims against the deceased, incurred by him
in his lifetime. An account, duly verified, has been
presented and filed, by which the executor and executrix represent that no property or assets have come
into their hands, for which they are liable to account.
No inventory has been made or filed, and no proceedings have been taken to compel the return of an
inventory.

The contesting creditors, however, allege that the
executor and executrix received certain moneys from
insurance upon the life of the deceased, which are
liable to be applied to the payment of debts, and for
which they should account, that the proper application thereof may be made.

It appears that the testator, James M. Palmer, died
March 10th, 1883, being at that time wholly insolvent.
In his lifetime he became a member of the " Commercial Travellers Association," and of the " Empire
Order of Mutual Aid," benefit insurance associations
of this State, and held the usual certificates of membership therein. The benefits in these companies
were made, by the testator, payable to his mother,
Mrs. C. C. Palmer, either when he originally joined
or subsequently, and she held the certificates.

On January 3rd, 1883, for the purpose of providing

for payment of the benefits in these associations to the wife and mother of deceased, and by concurrence of the parties, Mrs. C. C. Palmer duly assigned the certificates of membership in said associations to the executor and executrix (the latter being the wife of the testator), by an assignment in writing, in which it was provided that $6,000, to be realized therefrom, should be kept upon trust by the assignees, and the fund invested, and the interest be paid to the assignor during her life, and, upon her death, the principal to the wife.

The deceased, at the same time and as a contemporaneous transaction, made his will, bearing even date therewith, in which he expressed a desire and intention that the moneys realized from said certificates of insurance, should be disposed of as follows: $6,000 to be safely invested by the executor and executrix (who are the same persons named as assignees in the assignment referred to), and the income thereof paid to his mother, Mrs. C. C. Palmer, during her life, and, upon her death, the principal fund to his wife, her heirs or assigns, and " the balance of said insurance money, viz.: $1,000," to be paid to his said wife. After the testator's death, his will was duly proved, and the executor and executrix obtained the money on said insurance certificates, to wit, $5,000, from the "Commercial Travellers Association," and $2,000 from the "Empire Order of Mutual Aid." It is not claimed that there is any property liable to be applied to the payment of testator's debts, unless the said insurance moneys can be reached for that purpose.

With the account as verified and filed, showing that

no property has been realized, the burden is cast upon the contesting creditors to show that the executor and executrix have, or are chargeable with, property or assets liable to the payment of testator's debts.

The testator had the legal right to provide this insurance for the benefit of his family, and designate the beneficiaries who should receive the benefits thereof after his decease, exclusive of the claims of creditors. This has been the law of this State for many years in respect to general life insurance, aside from the special character of benefit associations (L. 1840, ch. 80; L. 1858, ch. 187; L. 1870, ch. 277; L. 1873, ch. 821). The only restriction in the insurance of a man's life for the benefit of his family, is that he shall not be allowed to expend for that purpose over $500, annually (L. 1870, ch. 277). And when the premiums paid by the husband in such case exceed the $500, annually, limited by the statute, the excess only can be reached by creditors.

Payment of an excess over the premiums allowed by the statute, by a person who is insolvent, would so far be a fraud upon his creditors; and the excess of insurance in such case, and so far, could be legally reached and applied to the claims of creditors. This question, however, does not arise in this case. To bring an insurance upon the life of a man for the benefit of his wife within the acts referred to, it is not essential that it should appear, either by the terms of the contract or policy, or by extrinsic evidence; the intention will be presumed from the beneficial nature of the policy (Brummer v. Cohn, 86 *N. Y.*, 11).

It may be that the mere assignment of the certificate by Mrs. C. C. Palmer would have been ineffectual to transfer the moneys over to the trustees (the assignees) had the testator (the assured) seen fit to change the beneficiaries before his death. But at the time of the assignment, and as a concurrent act, he made his will in confirmation of the transfer, and therein and thereby made the wife and mother the beneficiaries under the certificates, and provided for the disposition of the moneys, to be derived therefrom for their benefit, substantially the same as in the assignment. That operated as a valid and effectual designation of the wife and mother as the beneficiaries, and continued unrevoked at his death, and the associations recognized it as such. The executor and executrix of the will, as assignees under the transfer, became, by the acts of the parties, trustees of the fund to be realized from the insurance certificates, to receive and dispose of the same as provided by the assignment and will, construed together, for the exclusive benefit of the wife and mother. After the sum of $6,000 is set apart, for the income thereof to be paid to the mother, the "balance" is given to the wife absolutely, and directed to be paid to her.

The contesting creditors assert that the moneys received from the benefit associations became assets in the hands of the executor and executrix, to be accounted for as a part of the estate.

This is a mistake: the certificates were not, during the lifetime of the testator, liable to be seized by legal process to pay his debts, and the moneys realized therefrom after his death did not become assets

to be accounted for and applied to the payment of
the claims of creditors, or for distribution among the
next of kin (Brown v. The Catholic Mut. Benefit
Assoc'n, 33 *Hun*, 263).

The act of the legislature incorporating the " Empire Order of Mutual Aid " (L. 1879, ch. 189) specially provides that the benefits paid shall be exempted
from seizure, by legal or equitable process, to pay a
debt or liability of the deceased party, on account of
whose death the same shall be paid. This provision
is contained substantially in the by-laws of all benefit
associations, though the particular provisions in the
charter or by-laws of the Commercial Travellers
Association have not been made to appear.

It may be assumed, however, that they contain the
ordinary provisions for paying over the fund, provided as a benefit, to the designated beneficiaries.
In such cases the benefits are exempted from the
claims of creditors. It is the object of these associations not to benefit the estates of members during
life, or increase them after death, but to provide
funds for the benefit of their families or others specially dependent on them, after death, who may be
designated during the lifetime of the members to
receive the same (Loos v. John Hancock Life Ins.
Co., 41 *Mo.*, 538; Brown v. Catholic Mut. Benefit
Assoc'n, *supra*). It is held, in some cases, that the
fund provided as a benefit can in no event be passed
to the estate of a deceased member, and if the beneficiary named to receive the benefit, in accordance
with the by-laws of the association, dies before the
assured, the benefit fails, and cannot be collected by

the executor or administrator of the deceased (Hellenberg v. Ind. Order of B'nai B'rith, 94 *N. Y.*, 580).

In this case, it is not even shown that the testator ever contributed or paid anything towards sustaining his membership, or that his estate has ever, in any respect, been diminished by reason thereof. The creditors fail to show that they have, in any respect, been injured by reason of the insurance, or that any provision of law has been violated in providing the insurance benefits for the wife and mother of the testator. Until they do so, they have no just grounds for complaint.

They have failed, as it appears to me, to show that the insurance moneys came to the hands of the executor and executrix as assets liable for the payment of debts, and, considering the beneficial character of the moneys, every reasonable presumption should be indulged against any such conclusion, that the intention of the testator, in making a just provision for his family, may not be frustrated where no rule of law or principle of justice is contravened.

I think that the accounts of the executor and executrix, as filed, should be finally judicially settled and allowed, and the objections thereto overruled.

A decree will be entered accordingly.

NEW YORK COUNTY.—HON. D. G. ROLLINS, SURRO-
GATE.—July, 1884.

COOPER *v.* BENEDICT.

*In the matter of the application for revocation of pro-
bate of the will of* TUNIS COOPER, *deceased.*

The enactment of Code Civ. Pro., § 2622 has lent a new sanction to the
doctrine enunciated in Delafield v. Parish, 25 N. Y., 34,—that the proponent of a will is bound to prove to the satisfaction of the court that
the paper in question declares the will of the deceased, and that the
supposed testator was, at the time of execution, of sound and disposing mind and memory.

Under Code Civ. Pro., § 2652, requiring the Surrogate, if he "decides that
the will is not sufficiently proved to be the last will of the testator,"
etc., to make a decree accordingly, the same rule is applicable where
the proceeding is, in form, one to revoke a decree of probate already
granted.

APPLICATION by Tunis B. Cooper and Allen B.
Cooper, sons of decedent, for a decree revoking the
probate of his will; opposed by Eliza Cooper, widow
and executrix, and Eli Benedict, executor thereof.
The facts are stated in the opinion.

A. J. ROGERS, *for petitioner.*

AMOS G. HULL, *for respondents.*

THE SURROGATE.—"Before admitting a will to probate," says § 2622 of the Code of Civil Procedure, "the
Surrogate must inquire particularly into all the facts
and circumstances, and must be satisfied of the genuineness of the will and the validity of its execution."
The enactment of this statute has given a new sanction to a principle which has been frequently asserted

by our courts, and which, in Delafield v. Parish (25 *N. Y.*, 34), is thus enunciated :

"In all cases the party propounding the will is bound to prove to the satisfaction of the court that the paper in question declares the will of the deceased, and that the supposed testator, at the time of making and publishing the document, was of sound and disposing mind and memory. . . . . . If, upon a careful and accurate consideration of all the evidence on both sides, the conscience of the court is not judicially satisfied that the paper in question contains the last will of the deceased, the court is bound to pronounce its opinion that the instrument is not entitled to probate."

These doctrines are applicable to the case at bar, although in form this proceeding is not a proceeding *for* probate, but one to *revoke* probate already granted (Code Civ. Pro., § 2652; Collier v. Idley's Ex'rs, 1 *Bradf.*, 94).

To the voluminous testimony taken before the referee, and submitted for my consideration, I have twice given attentive reading. As a result, I am bound to declare that I am "not judicially satisfied that the paper (here) in question contains the last will of the decedent." I have grave doubts whether, at the time of its execution, Tunis Cooper was mentally competent to make a will; whether he was capable of sufficient thought, reflection and judgment to know what property he had, and intelligently decide and declare whom he would make, and whom he would refuse to make, the objects of his testamentary bounty. His bodily and mental condition on April 2d, 1881, and thenceforward for twelve days, to and including April 14th, 1881, when he executed this alleged will, has been the main topic of controversy in this proceeding. As to these matters, the evidence is very conflicting. Statements of some of the witnesses are diametrically opposed—and that, too, in important particulars—to statements of others, and the value of much of the testimony for the will, and much of that against it, is seriously impaired by the fact that it was given by witnesses whose interests and sympathies are greatly involved in the contest. Outside the region of conflict, there is one circumstance which has greatly impressed me, and, as much as any other, has excited my doubts of decedent's competency. He had three sons, Tunis, Allen and Franklin, all of whom were members of his household. Tunis was more than thirty years of age; Allen was twenty-two, and in business with his father as a wheelwright; Franklin, above ten. These sons are mentioned by name in the will, and so mentioned as necessarily to involve the notion that two of them, at least, and perhaps all three, are yet in their minority.

The fourth clause of the paper provides that, upon the death of the decedent's wife, and the consequent termination of her life estate in certain real property, that property shall be sold by the executor, and the proceeds divided into three equal parts, and paid " to my three sons, Tunis, Allen and Franklin, as they shall respectively arrive at the age of twenty-one years." The executor is subsequently instructed to " invest the share, to which either of my sons may be

entitled during his minority, on bond and mortgage,"
etc. .

The interest on this investment is directed to be
paid, semiannually, to "the lawful guardian of my
sons, for their benefit during their minority." The
eleventh clause is, in part, in these words: "I hereby
appoint my friend, Eli Benedict, testamentary guardian of my minor children during their minority."
The twelfth clause provides for the sale of certain
New Jersey realty, and for the division of the proceeds into four equal parts. One of these parts is
given to the widow, and the others "to my three
sons, Tunis, Allen and Franklin, as they shall arrive
at the age of twenty-one years."

Now, it appears, by Mr. Meyer's testimony, that
every word of this instrument was carefully read to
the testator, and afterwards carefully read again.
Some portions, indeed, seem to have been three times
called to Mr. Cooper's attention. It is certainly
strange, upon the assumption that he had sufficient
possession of his faculties to make a will, that he did
not, at one time or another, of the three readings,
make known the fact that only one of his children was under age. If the will had contained
but a single intimation that he had more than one
minor child, and if it had been read to him but
once, his silence might not be deemed specially
significant; but in at least six instances it conveys
a distinct intimation that, besides Franklin, the testator had certainly one child—perhaps two children—not yet of age; and each of these six intimations was thrust at least twice upon the decedent's

attention. His failure to suggest a change, in this regard, in the phraseology of the will, or even to make any comment upon the evident error of its draughtsman, is, in my judgment, a circumstance of the gravest importance. It indicates that the decedent's mental strength had so far abated that he had actually forgotten that all his children but Franklin had come of age; or it shows that his mind was so far away from the business of will-making as to render it unsafe to treat the paper here propounded as an embodiment of his testamentary purposes.

A decree may be entered, granting the petition for revocation of probate.

NEW YORK COUNTY.—HON. D. G. ROLLINS, SURROGATE.—August, 1884.

OAKLEY *v.* OAKLEY.

In the matter of the estate of HENRY S. OAKLEY, *an infant.*

Where the guardian of an infant's property takes the responsibility of encroaching upon the capital of a trust fund, of which his ward is entitled to the income, he must make out as clear a case, for the subsequent sanction of his course, as he would have been required to do, had he applied, in advance, for authority to adopt it.

The temporary guardian of an infant, whose estate consisted exclusively of his interest as *cestui que trust* under a will, pursuant to which a fixed annual income was regularly paid over by the trustee to the guardian, for the infant's benefit, having expended in that behalf about $400 in excess of the amount of trust moneys which had come to his hands, asked, upon the judicial settlement of his account, to be allowed the amount specified, to be paid out of future income to be received by his successor. The referee, to whom the account was referred, found that, in view of the necessities, prospects and social standing of the infant, the expenditures in question were properly made.—

Held, that the propriety of those expenditures must be judged by a different standard from that which had been applied, and that they should be disallowed, upon the ground that they were beyond the infant's means.

Upon the judicial settlement of the account of the temporary guardian of an infant, whose only estate consisted of a fixed income under a testamentary trust, it appearing that the guardian, to whom a successor had been appointed, had expended all the moneys received by him for the infant's benefit,—

Held, that the successor of the accounting party should be directed, by the decree, to reserve, out of future income, a sum sufficient to pay the legal commissions of the latter.

HEARING of exceptions to report of referee, upon judicial settlement of account of temporary general guardian of infant's property. The facts appear sufficiently in the opinion.

HENRY THOMPSON, *for accounting guardian.*

GEO. E. BLACKWELL, *for Sarah Oakley, objector.*

THE SURROGATE.—Mr. E. B. Oakley was appointed temporary guardian of Henry S. Oakley, an infant, in June, 1877. The ward reached the age of fourteen in 1879, but it is only recently that, upon his own application, his mother has been substituted as his guardian. Her predecessor in the trust is here, seeking the judicial settlement of his account. He claims that his just and proper expenditures have been in excess of his receipts, and, accordingly, asks this court to adjudicate that, to the amount of such excess, his former ward is his debtor, and that such indebtedness, as also his lawful commissions as guardian, shall be paid out of the income of the ward's estate. The account, together with certain objections thereto, was lately submitted to a referee whose report is before me.

It appears that, during the whole period of the guardianship, the infant's estate consisted solely of his interest as a beneficiary under the will of his grandfather. By that will, Mr. Samuel F. Engs was appointed trustee of a certain trust, whose income he was directed to pay over for the benefit of this infant, during his minority. No part of the principal of that fund has, at any time, been in the possession or under the control of the accounting guardian. The amount of income which has come to his hands is less, by about $390, than the amount which he has expended for the ward's benefit. The referee finds that, in view of the necessities, prospects and social standing of the infant, these expenditures were properly made.

It is not now disputed that the accounting guardian has charged himself with all moneys received by him for his ward's benefit. Nor is it disputed that he has actually expended all the moneys for which he seeks to be credited. The propriety of these expenditures, however, must be judged by another standard than that which has been applied by the referee. Even if the principal from which the income was realized for the ward's benefit had been in the hands of the accounting party, or under his control, he would not have been justified in encroaching upon it, in the least, for the maintenance, support and education of the ward, unless the income was insufficient for that purpose. Even in that event, indeed, he would not, in strictness, have been authorized to incur expense in excess of income, without the express sanction of the court. And, where he takes the responsibility of thus encroaching upon the capital, he must make out as clear a case, for the subsequent sanction of his course, as he would have been required to do, had he applied, in advance, for authority to adopt it (Holmes v. Logan, 3 *Strobh. Eq.*, 31; Bond v. Lockwood, 33 *Ill.*, 223; Jarrett v. Andrews, 7 *Bush, Ky.*, 311; Long v. Norcom, 2 *Ired. Eq.*, 354; Gott v. Culp, 45 *Mich.*, 265; Roseborough v. Roseborough, 5 *Tenn.*, 314; Kelaher v. McCahill, 26 *Hun*, 148; Smith v. Bixby, 5 *Redf.*, 196).

Now, under the circumstances appearing in the case at bar, if the accounting guardian had applied to me for leave to incur the expenses for which he seeks to be reimbursed, I should have felt obliged to deny his application; not because the support and education sought to be thus provided for the infant were out of keeping with his social standing, but because they were beyond his means. Says the court, in deciding Long v. Norcom (*supra*): "Where a guardian thinks he is promoting the ward's welfare by educating him for a higher walk in life than is suitable to his degree and circumstances, he must be benevolent at his own expense, and not at that of the ward." This doctrine is just and salutary. Applied to the facts of the case at bar, it compels the disallowance of the claim of the accounting party, to be credited with the excess of his expenditures over his receipts.

Second. Counsel for the present guardian claims that Mr. Oakley's account should be surcharged in the sums wherein, in any particular year, his expenditures exceed the ward's income for the same period.

This claim cannot be sustained (Carmichael v. Wilson, 3 *Molloy*, 83; Speer v. Tinsley, 55 *Ga.*, 80).

Third. The accounting guardian has done nothing to forfeit his commissions; and the decree to be entered in this proceeding may provide for the reservation, by the present guardian, out of any moneys of the ward's estate now in her hands, or which may come to her hands, of a sum sufficient to pay the legal commissions of her predecessor.

Fourth. The expenses of this accounting ought to be borne neither by the infant wholly, nor wholly by the guardian. The account was voluntarily rendered. The objector, in behalf of the infant, challenged nearly all the credit items, and alleged that the accounting party had failed to charge himself with a portion of the moneys he had received. The objector, therefore, has been only in part successful; and even those payments which I have felt bound to disallow were, probably, made in good faith, and for the supposed advantage of the ward.

The decree may provide that the referee's fees may be paid, one half by the guardian, and one half from the infant's estate. It will make no provision for costs or counsel fees, for either party.

NEW YORK COUNTY.—HON. D. G. ROLLINS, SURRO-
GATE.—September, October, 1884.

BUDLONG v. CLEMENS.

In the matter of the estate of CHRISTIAN WEISENBACH,
deceased.

In a special proceeding, instituted under Code Civ. Pro., § 2717, to compel
payment of a claim, the petition alleged, substantially, that decedent's
estate was indebted to petitioner in the sum of $267, without setting
forth the nature or basis of the demand ; whereto respondent interposed an answer, averring, upon information and belief, that the pretended foundation of the claim was the rendering of services and
incurring of expenses, in and about decedent's estate, and denying
that the same was done at decedent's request.—

Held, that the answer did not set "forth facts which show that it is
doubtful whether the petitioner's claim is valid and legal," etc., so as
to necessitate a dismissal of the petition under Code Civ. Pro., § 2718 ;
but that respondent was entitled to a direction, to the petitioner, to
state the nature of his claim with greater particularity.

A claim by an attorney employed by an executor, for services rendered in
conducting proceedings for the probate of decedent's will, and otherwise in the settlement of the estate, and for moneys advanced for disbursements therein, is against the executor personally, and not against
the estate of the decedent.

APPLICATION by Morris M. Budlong, an attorney,
and an alleged creditor of decedent's estate, to compel Frank Clemens, the executor of the will of decedent to pay his claim. The facts appear in the
opinion.

J. P. OSBORNE, *for petitioner.*

JOHN O'BYRNE, *for executor.*

THE SURROGATE.—The respondent is not entitled,
by reason of his answer, to a dismissal of this proceeding. Such answer does not "set forth facts

which show that it is doubtful whether the petitioner's claim is valid and legal." It undertakes to allege (though from what is, very likely, a clerical error it does *not* allege, but rather denies) that, according to the information and belief of the respondent, the pretended foundation of the plaintiff's claim is the rendering of certain services, and the incurring of certain expenses, in and about the estate of the decedent; and it undertakes to deny that these pretended services were authorized by the decedent, or that these pretended expenses were incurred at his request. Now these facts, even if they were well pleaded, would not be sufficient to justify the dismissal of the present proceeding; for the petitioner himself makes no allegation whatever as to the nature or the basis of his demand. This is, therefore, the state of the pleadings as they now stand—the petitioner says: "The estate of this decedent is lawfully indebted to me in the sum of $267." The respondent says, or undertakes to say: "I have been told, and I believe, that the petitioner claims that sum in payment for services rendered the decedent. If such be the pretended basis of the claim, I allege that it is not well founded." Manifestly, this is not enough to bring the case within the provisions of § 2718. The petition must, therefore, be granted, unless, within ten days from the entry of this order, the respondent files an amended answer, or, in order to better prepare himself for filing such answer, applies to the Surrogate for a direction, to the petitioner, to set forth the nature of his claim with greater particularity.

THE petitioner thereupon filed a petition in which he specified, as the items of his claim:

"Professional services as follows: Presenting the will to the Surrogate, attending to and securing the probate of the same, and obtaining letters testamentary; preparation of papers, applying to the Surrogate, and obtaining the release of one of the executors; counsel, advice and services, in and about various other matters of the estate; disbursements."

The following opinion was filed on October 13th, 1884:

THE SURROGATE.—The claim, for whose payment this application is made, is a claim against decedent's executor, personally, and not against decedent's estate (Austin v. Munro, 47 *N. Y.*, 360; Ferrin v. Myrick, 41 *id.*, 318; Bowman v. Tallman, 2 *Robt.*, 385). Its collection must, therefore, be sought in another tribunal. Even if it could be here enforced against the executor in his representative capacity, he has interposed an answer which attacks its validity, and for that cause · necessitates a denial of the petition (Code Civ. Pro., § 2718, subd. 1).

NEW YORK COUNTY.—HON. D. G. ROLLINS, SURRO-
GATE.—October, 1884.

KOCH *v.* ALKER.

In the matter of the estate of THADDEUS H. LANE,
deceased.

In a special proceeding, instituted under Code Civ. Pro., § 2717, to compel
payment of an alleged claim against a decedent's estate, an objection,
properly interposed, whereby it is insisted that the demand is excessive
in amount, necessitates a dismissal of the petition,—the issue so raised
being one which the Surrogate's court has no authority to determine.

PETITION by Joseph Koch to compel Henry Alker
and another, administrators of decedent's estate, to
pay his claim. The facts appear sufficiently in the
opinion.

JOSEPH KOCH, *petitioner, in person.*

HENRY ALKER, *for respondents.*

THE SURROGATE.—On the hearing of this application, the respondent's counsel, while disavowing any
purpose to question, in other respects, the claim of
the petitioner, insisted that it was excessive in
amount. If this objection shall be presented in the
form of a verified answer, the claim must necessarily
be treated as a disputed one, and, as such, one which
the Surrogate has no authority to determine. The
respondent will be afforded an opportunity to interpose such a verified answer, embodying his objection
to the petitioner's claim.

In default of such answer, an order must be entered directing payment.

NEW YORK COUNTY.—HON. D. G. ROLLINS, SURROGATE.—October, 1884.

DUSTAN v. CARTER.

In the matter of the judicial settlement of the account of WALTER CARTER, *as executor of the will of* CAROLINE A. DUSTAN, *deceased.*

Notwithstanding that, by 2 R. S., 90, § 43, legacies are, unless the will otherwise directs, not to be paid until after the expiration of one year from the time of granting letters, interest upon a general legacy, in an ordinary case, begins to run at the expiration of one year *from the death of the testator.*

Campbell v. Cowdrey, 31 *How. Pr.*, 172—followed; Bradner v. Faulkner, 12 *N. Y.*, 472—commented upon.

UPON the judicial settlement of the account of the executor of decedent's will, Matilda Dustan, a legatee named in the will, having filed a claim to be paid interest on her legacy from a date specified, the executor applied to the Surrogate for instructions in the premises.

R. E. ROBINSON, *for executor.*

GEORGE J. GREENFIELD, *for legatee.*

THE SURROGATE.—1st. The fact that the delay in the distribution of this estate has been solely due to the restrictions imposed by law upon the action of its ex-

ffect the question
the right of the
Penn. Hospital, 1
Bradf., 364).
ulated from a date
rs testamentary, or
n of a year from
question was, in
ourt, at the New
ll v. Cowdrey, 31
ld that, upon lega-
ideration, interest
one year from the
hed them. No ap-
and I cannot find
it has been over-
deed, the question
been, in no other
mination of any of
that those tribu-
en called upon to
me particular will,
tion, a legatee was
of his testator, or
in discussing that
se language broad
ly not intended to
roversy. Thus, in
), it was claimed,
at the beneficiary
under a testator's
h. This view had

been sustained by the Surrogate, and by the Supreme court; but, in holding that the judgment below must be reversed, GARDINER, Ch. J., pronouncing the opinion of the Court of Appeals, after referring to the provisions of the statute forbidding the payment of legacies "until after the expiration of one year from the time of granting letters testamentary, or of administration" (R. S., part 2, ch. 6, tit. 3, § 43; 3 *Banks*, 7*th ed.*, 2300), said: "They" (the appellants) "can rely upon the general rule, that no interest would accrue until it became, by law, the duty of the executors to pay the legacy." These words, taken in connection with the context, are fairly enough translated, in the reporter's head note, as a declaration by the court that "legacies are not payable until after the expiration of a year from the granting of letters testamentary, unless the will direct them to be sooner paid," and that, " unless the will so directs, a legacy does not draw interest before it becomes legally payable;" and yet it is plain that, in using the words just quoted from Judge GARDINER's opinion, the court simply intended to decide that the respondents were *not*, by the terms of the will, entitled to interest *from the decedent's death.* This basis for calculating interest being rejected, the one which, for aught that appears upon careful scrutiny of the case, presented itself to the minds of the counsel and the court alike, as the *only* alternative, was the allowance of interest *from the expiration of a year after the grant of letters.* There seems to have been no such contention, on the part of the respondents, as that which was afterwards successfully urged in Campbell v. Cowdrey, that in-

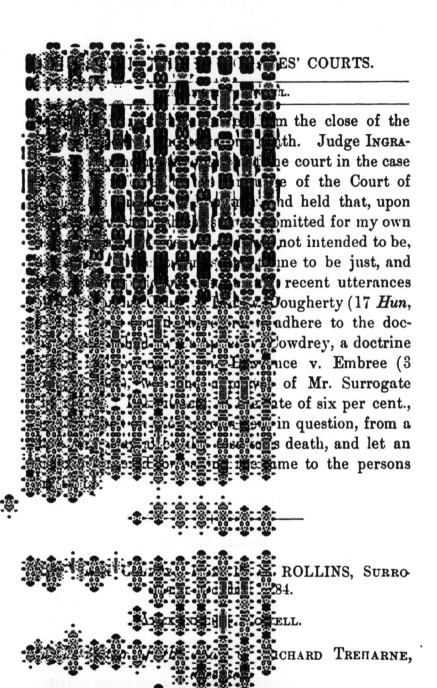

m the close of the
th. Judge INGRA-
e court in the case
e of the Court of
d held that, upon
mitted for my own
not intended to be,
me to be just, and
recent utterances
ougherty (17 *Hun*,
adhere to the doc-
owdrey, a doctrine
nce v. Embree (3
of Mr. Surrogate
ate of six per cent.,
in question, from a
s death, and let an
me to the persons

ROLLINS, SURRO-
84.

ELL.

CHARD TREHARNE,

his executors to pay, out
ortgages now being exist-
(describing them), to the
nd discharged from mort-

gage liens, as soon as practicable after my decease;" and further gave his real property, and the residue of his personal property, to the executors, in trust "to pay over the entire net annual rents of said real estate, after payment of all taxes, assessments, insurance, and repairs of and upon said real estate, and the interest" of the personal property, to his wife, for the maintenance and education of his minor children, with remainder over. The mortgages fell due after the death of the testator. A referee reported that the interest on the mortgages, accruing after testator's death, had been improperly charged to the *corpus* of the personalty.—

Held, that the will contained an "express direction," within the meaning of 1 R. S., 749, § 4, requiring the mortgages to be satisfied, both as to principal and interest, out of the personal property.

HEARING of exceptions to report of referee, to whom the account of Thomas C. Powell and another, as executors of decedent's will, and objections thereto filed by Caroline A. Alexander, decedent's daughter, were referred, in proceedings for judicial settlement. The facts are stated in the opinion.

RICHARD J. LEWIS, *and* T. J. RUSH, *for executors.*

GEORGE F. MARTENS, *for objector.*

CHARLES E. DAVISON, *for special guardian.*

THE SURROGATE.—This testator provided as follows, in the fifth article of his will: "I direct my executors . . . . . to pay, out of the residue of my personal estate, the mortgages now being existing liens upon the two dwelling houses" (describing certain pieces of real property which, at the time of his decease, and at the time of the execution of his will, were owned by him, subject to such mortgages), " to the end that said dwelling houses may be free and discharged from mortgage liens as soon as practicable after my decease."

r the death of the
re discharged, prin-
sonal estate. For
tors, in the settle-
k to be credited.
objection thereto,
who, by his report
est which, after the
mortgage, has been
us of the personal
is justified by some
direction of dece-
; for, if both the
on the subject, the
with the interest
ance with the doc-
argeable, like other

he Revised Statutes
the provision fol-
state, subject to a
or or testator, shall
evisee, such heir or
such mortgage out
orting to the execu-
tor, *unless there be*
such testator that

at bar, seems to me
ection, and thus to
by the mortgages
He gives his real

estate, and his residuary personal estate, to his executors, in trust, " to pay over the entire net annual rents of said real estate, after payment of all *taxes, assessments, insurance and repairs,* of and upon said real estate, and the interest, income and profits and dividends of said personal estate," to his wife, in quarterly payments, for the support and maintenance of the family, and the care and education of her children, until the survivor of his two youngest children shall attain his majority; when the entire residuary estate, real and personal, is directed to be distributed in equal parts to his wife and children.

The specification of the burdens to which the rents of the real estate are subjected does not include either the discharge of mortgages or that of interest on mortgages. It does not, therefore, in the least abate, but rather augments, the force of the fifth article, as an express direction, by the testator, that the mortgages, principal and interest, be satisfied out of the personalty. This interpretation, too, better than any other, seems to me to accord with the fact that the income, which is sought to be charged with the burden of interest, was given by the testator to his widow, for the maintenance of his family, and the care and education of his children.

The referee's report is sustained, with modifications above noted, and a decree may be entered accordingly.

ROLLINS, Surro-...884.

...ERT.

...ULIA O'BRIEN, *de-*

...n one who, if not by some ...iority, under the statute, is ...disqualification is declared

...tters of administration shall ...amous crime . . . . . nor to ...petent, by the Surrogate, to ...n of drunkenness, improvi-

...statutory prohibition, the ...ithin the definition of the ...with death, or by imprison- ...*iction* must have been had ...st the laws thereof ; ...te, of the crime of larceny, ...part of the convict, which ...rogate, of incompetence to

...en, a son, and by ...f decedent, for let- ...estate. The facts

...o persons who are ...ation on this estate, ...r a grandson, the ...riority, unless he is for some cause disqualified.   Evidence has been submitted tending to show that he has been convicted, in the state of New Jersey, of the crime of larceny; and it is insisted that, by such conviction, he has become incapacitated from receiving letters.   The statute, which is claimed to create such disqualification, is in words following: "No letters of administration shall be granted to a person convicted of an infamous crime, nor to any one incapable by law of making a contract, ... nor to any person who shall be adjudged incompetent by the Surrogate to execute the duties of such trust by reason of drunkenness, improvidence, or want of understanding" (§ 32, tit. 2, ch. 6, part 2, R. S.; 3 *Banks*, 7th ed., 2291).

Upon the facts here presented, two questions arise for determination:

First. Does one, by reason of his conviction of an offense against the laws of a foreign state, ever become "a person convicted of an infamous crime," within the meaning of the statute above quoted?

The signification of the term "infamous crime," wherever that expression occurs in our statutes, is absolutely fixed by § 31, ch. 1, tit. 7, part 4, R. S.; 3 *Banks*, 7th ed., 2539. It is there declared that "whenever the term *infamous crime* is used in any statute, it shall be construed as including every offense punishable with death, or by imprisonment in a State prison, and no other." It follows, therefore, that the first clause of § 31, which prescribes the qualifications of administrators, must be construed precisely as if it were thus worded: "No letters of administration shall be granted to a person convicted of a crime

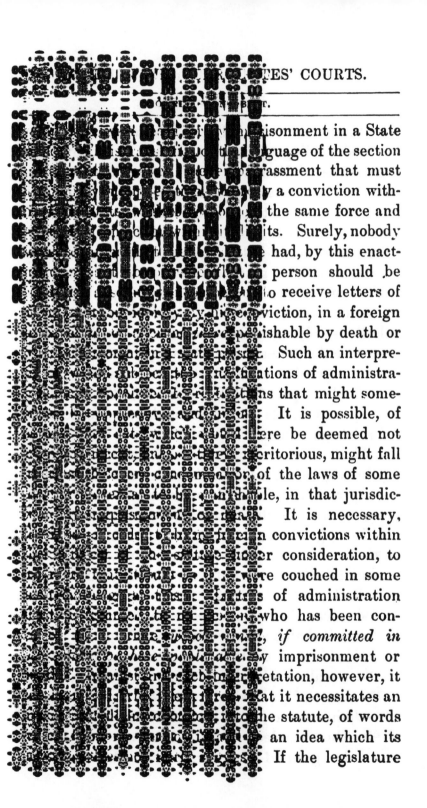

isonment in a State
guage of the section
assment that must
a conviction with-
the same force and
its. Surely, nobody
had, by this enact-
person should be
o receive letters of
viction, in a foreign
ishable by death or
Such an interpre-
ations of administra-
ns that might some-
It is possible, of
ere be deemed not
ritorious, might fall
of the laws of some
le, in that jurisdic-
It is necessary,
convictions within
r consideration, to
re couched in some
of administration
who has been con-
if committed in
imprisonment or
etation, however, it
at it necessitates an
he statute, of words
an idea which its
If the legislature

had intended to give to foreign convictions the force
and effect of convictions within the State, it would not
have been difficult to make that intention clear and
unequivocal. In the very Revision, of which the section now under consideration forms a part, a careful
discrimination in this regard was made by the legislature, in defining criminal offenses, and prescribing
punishment therefor. Section 8, tit. 7, ch. 1, part 4,
R. S. (3 *Banks, 7th ed.*, 2536), declares : " *If any person convicted of any offense punishable by imprisonment in a State prison shall* . . . . . subsequently be
convicted of any offense . . . . . he shall be punished as follows," etc. That this provision was
deemed too narrow to include extra-territorial con-
victs is evidenced by the contemporaneous enactment
of § 10 of the same title (3 *Banks, 7th ed.*, 2537),
which declares that " every person who shall have
been convicted, in any of the United States, or in any
district or territory thereof, or in any foreign country, of an offense which, if committed within this
State, would be punishable by the laws of this State
by imprisonment in a State prison, shall, upon conviction for any subsequent offense committed within
this State, be subject to the punishment herein prescribed upon subsequent convictions, in the same
manner and to the same extent as if such first conviction had taken place in a court of this State."

Upon comparing § 8, above quoted, with that which
prescribes the qualifications of administrators (bearing in mind the statutory definition of " infamous
crime "), it will appear that the two provisions are
substantially identical. If, therefore, the legislature

rritorial conviction
of an administra-
at the provisions of
cation would have
enactment as § 10,
from other grounds
lusion, I should, for
hold that the mere
ever, *ipso facto*, in-
an administrator,
ad in the courts of

ion is emphasized by
ause of the statute
clause provides that
ue to no one "inca-
t." Manifestly, this
under the laws in
construction would
of reasoning, inca-
crime may well be
s under and by the

ourt of Appeals, in
N. Y., 466), subse-
rust Co. v. Gleason
it bearing upon the
it should not be re-
termination of those
of § 23, tit. 7, ch. 1,
94). "No person,"
on a conviction for

felony shall be competent to testify in any cause, matter or proceeding, civil or criminal, unless he be pardoned," etc. It was held by the Court of Appeals, Judge RAPALLO pronouncing its opinion, that the disqualification to testify, which was created by that statute, was restricted in its operations to persons convicted and sentenced under the laws of the State of New York. Some of the reasons by which that conclusion is supported are not strictly applicable here, but there are others which have exact application, and all in all there is a very close analogy, between the statute reviewed in Sims v. Sims, and the one which prescribes the qualifications of administrators.

For these reasons, I feel bound to hold that Daniel O'Brien's conviction, in New Jersey, of the crime of larceny does not necessarily disqualify him from becoming an administrator in New York.

Second. There remains to be considered the question whether the Surrogate has discretionary power, even though the New Jersey conviction does not, as of course, work a disqualification, to refuse, because of such conviction, the issuance, to O'Brien, of letters of administration. It has been repeatedly determined by the courts of this State that the withholding of letters from a person who, if not by some cause incapacitated, would be entitled in priority under the statute, is never justifiable, save in cases where such person is declared to be disqualified by the statute itself (Coope v. Lowerre, 1 *Barb. Ch.*, 45; Emerson v. Bowers, 14 *N. Y.*, 449).

The only statutory provision which can possibly be

which forbids the
all be adjudged, by
ecute the duties of
ce." This presents
tion of larceny can
evidence of his in-
dence,—a question
than once by our
Coope v. Lowerre
eviewing a decision
nty:

uilt or delinquency
from administration
reference given by
been actually con-
. . . . (This excep-
only includes persons
improvidence which
tes had in contem-
is that want of care
of property which
ate and effects un-
inished in value, in
d be committed to
rinciple of exclusion,
ased upon the well
areless and improvi-
ry care and forecast
ion of property for
usted with the man-
property of others.
and seeks to obtain

the possession of the property of others by theft, robbery or fraud, is not evidence either of. his providence or improvidence. The dishonest man, who preys upon the rights of others, and deprives them of their property by unlawful means, may be, and frequently is, not only careless but reckless in squandering the property which he has thus acquired. Or he may, on the other hand, preserve and hoard up his ill-gotten gains with all a miser's care."

The decision of the Court of Appeals, in McMahon v. Harrison (6 *N. Y.*, 443), is not in conflict with the decision just quoted. In the trial below, the Surrogate had decided, upon the authority of Coope v. Lowerre (*supra*), that a professional gambler was not, as such, *improvident*, within the meaning of the statutes declaring the qualifications of administrators. This judgment was subsequently reversed by the Supreme Court (McMahon v. Harrison, 10 *Barb.*, 659). That court announced its adherence to the proposition that, under the provisions of the statute, "vices and moral delinquency can not, of themselves, disqualify a person to act as administrator;" but it decided, nevertheless, that a professional gambler, whose habitual occupation it was to put large sums of money at hazard upon games of chance, was, in the nature of things, an improvident person.

This view was subsequently approved by the Court of Appeals (6 *N. Y.*, 443). The pursuit of gambling was pronounced as, in itself, a token of improvidence, but the general doctrine of Coope v. Lowerre was unhesitatingly approved. See also Emerson v. Bowers (14 *N. Y.*, 449).

cannot, upon the
rien is incompetent,
come administrator

ROLLINS, SURRO-
1884.

EZ.

BENITA CARRIO DE
ceased.

of executor may resign, but
can he retract a renuncia-

rs testamentary, performed,
ice, and procured, upon his
ers, he becomes a stranger
ege previously belonging to
tator's will.

f Code Civ. Pro., § 2039,—
appointment to be retracted
to sanction the doctrine of
not only declined to under-
lemnly declared his refusal
at any time before the estate
ntative, or thereafter, when

J. as its executors, and let-
in June, and to J. in Sep-
same year, filed a petition
d appointment as executor
ry," and embodied, in the
had renounced the same;
ng the acceptance of M.'s

renunciation and revoking his letters. J., who thereafter entered upon the execution of the duties of the trust, having died in 1884, leaving assets unadministered, M. applied for letters testamentary, filing what purported to be a retraction of renunciation.—

Held, that the case was one for the grant of letters of administration with the will annexed, pursuant to the provision of Code Civ. Pro., § 2643, which requires such letters to be issued where the office of legal representative is vacant by reason of the revocation of letters; and that the petition of M. should be denied.

APPLICATION for a decree granting letters testamentary under decedent's will. The facts appear sufficiently in the opinion.

WEEKES & FORSTER, *for the application.*

THE SURROGATE.—Miguel Garcia, who was appointed by this decedent one of the executors of his will, received, as such, his letters testamentary in June, 1878. In October of the same year, he filed in this court a petition, setting forth his wish "to renounce the said appointment as executor, and all right and claim to letters testamentary," and to render a final account of all his proceedings in the administration of his trust. Such account was subsequently filed. Its "schedule G" contained the following statement:

"I have renounced the executorship and all claims to letters testamentary, and wish to have such letters revoked. This accounting is had, that the charge of the estate may be transferred to John Garcia, of the city of New York, who is one of the executors named in the will, and who qualified as such on September 30th, 1878.   MIGUEL GARCIA."

Upon this accounting, a decree was entered, in November, 1878, by which, among other things, it

king of certain pay-
ia, " the said renun-
his appointment as
y is accepted, and
s aforesaid granted,
revoked."

trust, and, in May
inistered upon the
ner executor, now
mentary ; and, hav-
instrument in the
unciation, he claims
in the executorship.
e Code of Civil Pro-
writing, signed by
may renounce an
renunciation," the
y be retracted by a
letters testamentary
e will annexed have
n his place, or after
have been revoked,
issued has died or
other acting execu-

traction of a renun-
he statute book as a
vil Procedure. Its
lative sanction to a
dly asserted by the
doctrine that one
upon himself any

of the duties of an executor, but who had even made solemn declaration of his refusal to act in that capacity, might, nevertheless, retract such refusal at any time before the estate should be put in charge of a legal representative, or at any time thereafter, when it should, for any cause, have ceased to be in such charge.

I am very clear that it is not the design of the statute to allow this privilege of retraction to persons who have actually received letters testamentary, performed for a time the duties of the executorial office and procured, upon their own application, the revocation of letters. Such persons become, upon such revocation, strangers to the estate, so far as regards any right or privilege, which previously belonged to them, by reason of their appointment under the testator's will.

It will appear, upon examination, that, in no reported case, has the right to retract a renunciation been recognized by the courts, save where the retractor had renounced absolutely; that is, had rejected his title of executor and refused to take and receive letters (Judson v. Gibbons, 5 *Wend.*, 224; Robertson v. McGeoch, 11 *Paige*, 640).

In such cases, it was the theory of the common law that, as an executor's right to administer sprang from his testator's will, he could claim the exercise of that right, despite previous renunciation, whenever his testator's estate was without any lawful representative (House v. Lord Petre, 1 *Salk.*, 311); that he was not, by virtue of such renunciation, divested of his interest nor discharged from his trust.

at any time exer-
intermeddled with
been repeatedly
Jackson v. White-
Prenderghast, 3
e of things, could
to *retract* a renun-

How. Pr., 214),
present in many
Testator appointed
of them qualified
ed to this court for
the same were
urrogate an instru-
and acknowledged,
executor. B. con-
til his death, when
non, with the will
ry legatee entitled

ght by A., for the
Van Vorst, J.,
urt, held that such
and dismissed the
that the reasons
an intimation that
his renunciation
ed, but for the fact
had been already

ot, I think, convey

any such notion.   The two prominent facts which there thrust themselves upon the attention were: 1st., that no attempt had been made by the plaintiff to retract his renunciation ; and 2d., that the estate was then actually in charge · of a duly appointed administrator.

In view of the latter circumstance, the decision that the plaintiff could not retract his renunciation, because, after the appointment of an administrator, it was too late for him to do so, by no means involves an intimation that, at any time before such appointment, he was in a position to have made a retraction effective.

The letters of the present applicant were revoked in pursuance of authority conferred upon the Surrogate of this county by L. 1870, ch. 359, § 3.   A general provision, giving similar power to Surrogates throughout the State, now appears in §§ 2689 and 2690 of the Code of Civil Procedure.   Section 2693 of that Code declares that, " Where all the executors, or all the administrators to whom letters have been issued, die or become incapable, ... or the letters are revoked as to all of them, the Surrogate must grant letters of administration to one or more persons as their successors, in like manner as if the former letters had not been issued."

So, too, it is provided by § 2643 that " if, at any time, by reason of death, incompetency, ... renunciation or . . . . . *revocation of letters*, there is no executor or administrator with the will annexed, qualified to act, the Surrogate must, upon the application, etc., ... issue letters of administration

" (specifying the

oner has no claim

must be denied.

ROLLINS, Surro-

84.

RGE W. M. Nutt,

hod of procedure for com-
turn an inventory. The
ng the respondent to make
e attached, is one of those
It of a judicial determina-
ued, as of course, by the
ed upon the delinquent.
ppear is improper.

arine P. White, as
creditor of dece-
Lewis, administra-
e to file an inven-
in the opinion.

that the order of
his respondent was

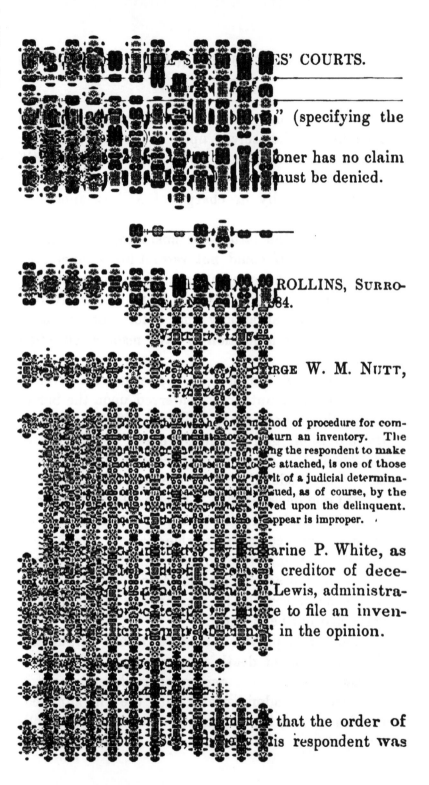

directed, within one week thereafter, to file an inventory as administrator of this estate, was not personally served.

It is claimed by respondent's counsel that, because of this fact, the proceeding for attachment must fail. It is insisted, on the other hand, in behalf of the petitioner, that the respondent became liable to immediate attachment by his failure to obey the order of December 18th, 1883, directing him to return an inventory, or show cause, etc., which order appears to have been served personally. Without reciting the various steps which have been taken in these proceedings, since they were first instituted, I hold, with the petitioner, that personal service of the order of September 25th is not essential to the validity of this attachment, if, by any prior order, whereof the petitioner *had* or *waived* personal service, he was lawfully directed to file an inventory. All that has taken place since the early stages of these proceedings has simply served to extend the time for compliance with the original direction, and to suspend, in the interval, the issuing of the attachment.

But, upon careful review of this whole matter, I am convinced that, at the beginning of the proceedings, there was, in the petitioner's practice, an irregularity which was, perhaps, so far waived as to justify the entry of the order of September 25th, 1884; so far waived, indeed, as to have made this respondent, in case he had been personally served with that order, attachable for failure to comply with its provisions; but which, in view of the absence of such personal

must be held to

es the procedure,
pelling an execu-
entory. He must
neglect. There-
fied that the ex-
, must make an
turn the inven-
cause," etc. It
this section pro-
h must be issued
tion, and not one
of course, by the
Hawley, 2 *Dem.*,

upon which these
een that they do
retend to comply
They seek rather
of the Revised
seded, and which
t. 3, ch. 6, part 2
ed., 92). Those
or administrator
inventory within
ogate shall issue
etc.

personally served
on its face, pur-
not by the Sur-
gate's court, and

no order seems to have been entered, directing its issuance.

In view of this state of facts, I must, therefore, vacate the attachment.

———————

NEW YORK COUNTY.—HON. D. G. ROLLINS, SURRO-GATE.—November, 1884.

MARSHALL *v.* WYSONG.

In the matter of the estate of JOHN R. MARSHALL, *deceased.*

Where there are two reasonable and consistent interpretations of a testamentary provision, by one of which an executor would be debarred from receiving any compensation for the rendition of official service, while the other would effect no such inhibition, the court is bound to adopt the latter.

Testator, who left an estate of the value of more than $100,000, above all debts, nominated his wife and two other persons as executrix and executors of his will, which contained an article as follows : "It is my request that the persons herein named as executors will consent to act as such executors and trustees, and that each executor and trustee, *other than my wife,* do also take and receive the full rate of commissions provided by law for each executor, intending thus to provide suitable compensation for their services in, and attention to the duties devolved upon them." The statute, in force at the time of the execution of the will, allowed to each of three executors, in the case of such an estate, the full commissions awardable to a sole executor. Letters testamentary were issued to all the nominees. Upon a judicial settlement of the representatives' account, the widow's right to compensation being questioned,—

Held, that the intent, evinced by the italicized words, was to exclude the wife of testator, not from the category of those who should take and receive compensation for the performance of official duty, but from that of those to whom he preferred the request to take and receive the same ; that, accordingly, the will containing no denial of compensation

f three full commissions,
ro., § 2736, upon proof of
she had rendered.

in proceedings for
ount of James P.
, as executors of
ted in the opinion.

ial guardians.

dated June 20th,
wife, Eveline G.
P. Kernochan and
He subsequently
executed February
Vysong.   On April
Between that date
g, the Surrogate
h of the four per-

determining the
bout to be entered,
y provision should
ommissions to Mrs.
tains a statement,
cutors, to the effect
ely participated in
This allegation is
d is pronounced to

be "incorrect and misleading." The referee, to whom were submitted the various issues of the accounting, found, by his report, that none of Mrs. Marshall's objections were well taken. He did not refer specifically to that one which relates to the character and extent of her services as executrix, and, for that reason, perhaps, none of her exceptions to the report make any reference to such objection. Under these circumstances, it is insisted that the Surrogate, in deciding, as he did decide, several months since, to confirm, in all things, the referee's report, has already passed adversely upon the very claim which is here set up, in behalf of Mrs. Marshall. This position may, perhaps, be technically correct, though, upon several grounds, even its technical correctness may well be doubted. But, in view of the fact that the Surrogate did not discover, until after announcing his decision, that the question of Mrs. Marshall's right to commissions was involved, or was claimed to be involved, in the proceedings before the referee, and did not intend, in declaring his approval of the referee's report, to determine that question, it will be treated as if it were now, for the first time, presented for his consideration.

If this executrix has any just claim to commissions, her title rests upon § 2736 of the Code of Civil Procedure, as amended by L. 1881, ch. 535, § 23. The section, as thus amended, contains the following provision: "Where the value of the personal estate of the decedent amounts to one hundred thousand dollars or more, over all his debts, each executor or administrator is entitled to the full compensation al-

r or administrator,
e, in which case the
ld be entitled shall
rding to the services

uted that the value
of his indebtedness,
absence, therefore,
ill, this executrix is
ee full commissions
quantum of service
this estate. It is
rms of the will, she
commissions, or any

expressed in Secor v.
r of Gerard (1 *Dem.*,
ally forbid the pay-
mpensation for their
therefore, to exam-
cle in the will which
utrix of rights that
bsence of such arti-
te above quoted.
of the will: "It is
ein named as execu-
ecutors and trustees,
stee, *other than my*
he full rate of com-
ch executor, intend-
mpensation for their

services in and attention to the duties devolved upon them."

Now, what is the significance of the expression "other than my wife," as it is used in the foregoing sentence? Of course, the wife is shut out from *some* category, in which the two other executors are included. But from what? The testator does not, it will be observed, expressly *give* the compensation indicated by his will to all the executors except his wife. He "requests" that such executors, other than his wife, shall "receive and take" such compensation. Now, with what is the idea of exclusion, involved in the exception "other than my wife," here associated? Is it associated with the word "request," or with the words "receive and take?" This is an important inquiry; for, while either construction would be sensible enough, only one of them could operate to deprive the executrix of the statutory compensation. Has the testator, in effect, said: "I request that all my executors, except my wife, *shall receive and take* full commissions, etc., and I request that my wife *shall not receive and take* such commissions;" or has he simply said: "*I request* that all the executors, except my wife, shall receive and take full commissions, but, as to my wife, *I do not make such request?*" For aught that is disclosed by the terms of the will itself, and I have nothing else to guide me to its correct interpretation, the somewhat unusual circumstance that this testator chose to supplement the clause appointing his executors with another, requesting them all to serve, and saw fit, also, to request the Messrs. Kernochan to "receive

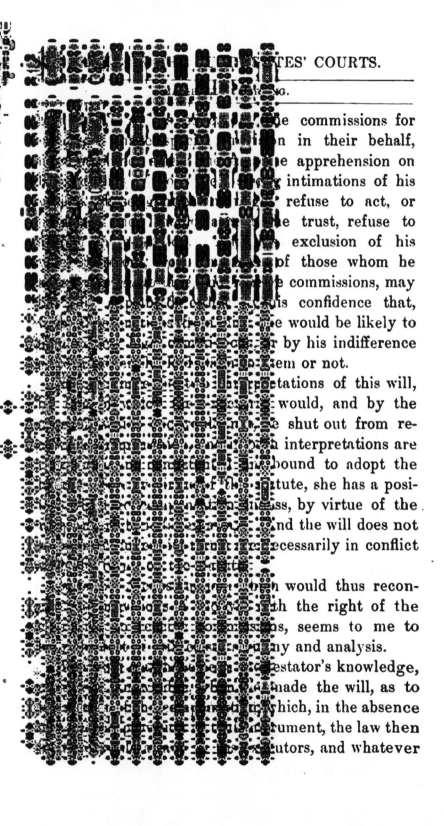

e commissions for
n in their behalf,
e apprehension on
intimations of his
refuse to act, or
trust, refuse to
exclusion of his
of those whom he
commissions, may
is confidence that,
e would be likely to
r by his indifference
em or not.

tations of this will,
would, and by the
shut out from re-
interpretations are
bound to adopt the
tute, she has a posi-
ss, by virtue of the
nd the will does not
ecessarily in conflict

would thus recon-
th the right of the
s, seems to me to
ny and analysis.
estator's knowledge,
made the will, as to
hich, in the absence
rument, the law then
utors, and whatever

standard, concordant with that fixed by statute, or variant from it, he may have supposed that he was establishing, as regarded the two Messrs. Kernochan, the fact remains that the amount of commissions, to which those executors would have been entitled under the law then in force, was, in no respect, either restricted or enlarged by the directions of the will. As regarded the rate of commissions upon estates whose value, above debts and liabilities, was not less than $100,000, the law then in operation was L. 1863, ch. 362, § 8, which declared that, where there were several executors, their commissions should not be apportioned according to their services, but that each executor should be entitled to the commissions of a sole executor, unless the number of executors should exceed three, in which event they should each take an equal share of three full commissions.

What the testator says, therefore, is this, and nothing more,—that the two Messrs. Kernochan shall each have, as executor, the same compensation that he could lawfully claim, if remitted to his rights under existing laws. And yet, in spite of the fact that the language of the will, in this regard, is quite free from ambiguity, I think it clear that the testator must have supposed that he was providing for the Messrs. Kernochan other and larger compensation than that established by statute. The last clause, in the above quotation from the will, seems inexplicable upon any other hypothesis. The testator there assigns his reason for giving the direction contained in the clause preceding. He declares that, by that direction, he has aimed to *"provide suitable compensation"* for the

is it at all likely that
rovision which, as we
ary and ineffective in
ccompanied by these
*provision had been
ffective by the testator*
nable to suppose that
d with the statutory
f executors' commis-
s committed to their
100,000 in value, and
that, unless he made
pensation, the execu-
gether, entitled to no
and that he, accord-
now under interpre-
that he was providing,
rnochan, as " suitable
es which he should
e amount which those
utory standard, *as the*
ntitle him to receive.
ed article is not only
uction, but is hardly
is difficult to believe
object, as, upon any
f the executrix, it is
ffect, to deprive Mrs.
executrix. If the
constitute, and were
spirit and essence of
estator, certainly, took

a very roundabout and intricate course for accomplishing a very simple and definite purpose. " My wife shall receive no commissions for acting as my executrix"—are words, for example, which would have effectually served his purpose, and would have utterly cut away the ground on which rests the present contention. These words of explanation furnish, therefore, a cogent argument in support of the claim that the exception regarding the wife, whatever may be its true import, was not the sole object, and probably not the principal object, of the provision here in question. For, it is a significant circumstance that those words of explanation have no bearing whatever upon the words " other than my wife ; " they relate exclusively to the clause respecting the Messrs. Kernochan, and their employment by the testator affords, therefore, strong indication that, in his estimation, that clause had some positive force and effect, and was, accordingly, worth explaining.

If this be the case—if the testator supposed that the provision for which he saw fit to assign a reason, entitled the Messrs. Kernochan, as executors, to a larger compensation than that established by law—it is clear that the words " other than my wife " contain no necessary implication, and, indeed, convey no special suggestion that, for executorial service which the wife might thereafter render, she should go wholly unrewarded. For nobody would think of claiming that those words indicated a disposition, on the testator's part, to deprive his widow of whatever commissions the law might allow her, were it not for the fact that it is just such commissions as were

when the will was
her—that the testa-
xcepted persons.

B. and C. as his
ensation for " each
following methods :
um,—whether just
y commissions, or
short thereof, it
without allusion to
to the subject; or,
in lieu of statutory
uch specified sum in
; or, (d) By giving
some specified ratio
ommissions, as, for
uch commissions, or
cases, and, indeed,
testamentary com-
B. and C. was not,
recisely that which
the will had been
words of exception,
missions would be in
would exclude A.
cular reward which
executors, and from

present case, the
be construed pre-
cessary to construe
le of the will where-

in they appear, had, *in fact provided*, as in my judgment he plainly *intended to provide*, and *supposed that he was providing*, a special rate of compensation for the Messrs. Kernochan.

If this be the true interpretation of the disputed article, then the rights of the executrix are precisely what they would have been, if the will had said nothing whatever respecting the compensation of any of the persons to whose care the testator committed the posthumous estate. She is entitled to a portion of three full commissions—such portion to be ascertained, as has been already stated, by instituting a comparison between the value of services she has rendered in this administration, and the value of the whole service rendered up to the present time.

A reference will be requisite for taking testimony upon this question of fact, unless, by agreement of the parties interested, it shall become unnecessary.

NEW YORK COUNTY.—HON. D. G. ROLLINS, SURROGATE.—November, 1884.

SHEPARD v. PATTERSON.

In the matter of the estate of JOHN SHEPARD, *deceased.*

An executor cannot be allowed for advances made by him, without authority from the court, to infant *cestuis que trustent*, out of the earnings of a fund directed by the will to be accumulated for their benefit until the termination of their minority.

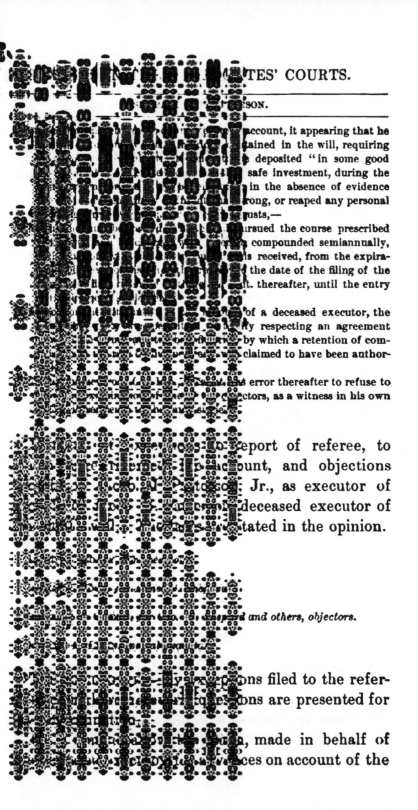

account, it appearing that he
tained in the will, requiring
deposited "in some good
safe investment, during the
in the absence of evidence
rong, or reaped any personal
usts,—

rsued the course prescribed
compounded semiannually,
s received, from the expira-
the date of the filing of the
t. thereafter, until the entry

of a deceased executor, the
ty respecting an agreement
by which a retention of com-
claimed to have been author-

error thereafter to refuse to
ctors, as a witness in his own

report of referee, to
ount, and objections
Jr., as executor of
deceased executor of
tated in the opinion.

and others, objectors.

ons filed to the refer-
ons are presented for

n, made in behalf of
ces on account of the

infants Malnette F. Seaman and Clara E. Shepard. The testator directed, by one of the provisions in his will, that the income of a certain portion of his estate, ordered to be invested for these infants' benefit, should be accumulated until they should respectively come of age. However praiseworthy may have been the executor's motives in advancing moneys for the use of these minors during their minority, he cannot be credited therefor upon this accounting. Such advances were made without authority of law.

2d. The will directs that the income of the share of these infants in the testator's estate, as well as the income of the share of Jessie Allen, should be deposited "in some good savings bank," or devoted to some other safe investment during their respective minorities, and that the accumulations thereon, together with the income itself, should be paid over to them upon their severally attaining their majorities. It is not claimed that the executor made investments in accordance with these instructions. He is charged in the account, as filed, with interest upon all sums received by him on behalf of the infants, from the dates when the same, respectively, came to his hands, until August 1st, 1883. The referee has reported that interest is also chargeable up to December 15th, 1883, the date at or about which this account was placed on file. It is clear that the testator's directions, respecting the disposition of the income in question, should have been obeyed, and that such income should have been deposited in some good savings bank, if, as seems to have been the case, no more desirable investment were attainable. Under all the circumstances, as the

…een guilty of inten-
…ny personal advan-
…is trust, he must be
…ctually pursued the
… follow. He must,
…terest, compounded
… per cent., upon all
… infants, from a rea-
…—after such sums
… of the filing of this
…rty accounting may
…visable to have the
… be in the hands of
…their prompt trans-
…rom December 15th,
…the decree judicially
…ccount, therefore, I
…three per cent. only.
…efore me, I cannot
…ions, withheld from
…eficiaries, should be
…ccounting. The account-
…to testify respecting
…been made between
…parties in interest,
… cent. commissions
…zed. To controvert
…the question of the
…nderstood to be re-
…mination, one of the
…ss. His testimony
…ected, as it seems to

me, in view of the fact that the accounting party had himself been examined on the same subject (Code Civ. Pro., § 829). As to this matter, therefore, I must again submit the case to a reference for further inquiry.

With such modifications as are above indicated, the report of the referee is confirmed.

New York County.—Hon. D. G. ROLLINS, Surrogate.—November, 1884.

Tappen *v.* M. E. Church.

In the matter of the estate of Joshua York, *deceased.*

Notwithstanding the limitations apparently implied in Code Civ. Pro., § 2743,—which provides that, "Where an account is judicially settled . . . . . and . . . . . the validity of a debt, claim or distributive share *is not disputed or has been established,* the decree must determine to whom it is payable, the sum to be paid by reason thereof, and all other questions concerning the same,"—a Surrogate's court has jurisdiction, upon the judicial settlement of an executor's account, to *decide all questions* necessary to determine a dispute on the part of the executor, as to the validity of the claim of one asserting a right as legatee under the will, and to construe the will for the purpose of making such determination. So—

Held, where the will bequeathed $500 to the trustees of the S. A. church, "towards paying off the debt of the church," and $500 to the managers or trustees of the M. C. Mission ; and the executor, seeking to procure the entry of a decree judicially settling his account, contended that the former bequest was ineffective by reason of the fact that the church designated was, neither then nor when the testator died, in a state of indebtedness ; and the latter, void on the ground that there was no existing person or institution bearing the name of the "M. C. Mission," and none competent to take the bequest whereof the will made the M. C. Mission the beneficiary.

Fraenznick v. Miller, 1 *Dem.,* 136—overruled.

RCH.

he claims of certain
will, upon the judi-
Thomas B. Tappen,
appear sufficiently

or, by one of the
his will, gives $500
venue M. E. church,
enth street, towards
rch." By the same
nagers or trustees of
0." His executor,
administration, now
judicial settlement;
th the above named
rrogate, for lack of
estions thus raised,
rty to retain in his
demands growing
successfully prose-

st named is ineffec-
church in one hun-
now in debt, and
died. He claims,
erson or institution
City Mission," and

none which is competent to take the bequest whereof the will makes the Methodist City Mission the beneficiary.

It is insisted, in behalf of the parties respectively claiming as legatees, that the Surrogate is fully authorized, by the Code of Civil Procedure, to determine these disputed questions.

Section 2743 of that Code provides that, "Where an account is judicially settled as prescribed in this article, and any part of the estate remains and is ready to be distributed to the creditors, legatees, next of kin, husband or wife of the decedent, or their assigns, the decree must direct the payment and distribution thereof to the persons so entitled, according to their respective rights."

The section further declares that, "Where the validity of a debt, claim or distributive share is not disputed or has been established, the decree must determine to whom it is payable, the sum to be paid by reason thereof, and all other questions concerning the same."

In the case of Fraenznick v. Miller (1 *Dem.*, 136–154), I contrasted the section just quoted from the Code with the statutory provision which it had superseded, namely, § 71, tit. 3, ch. 6, part 2 of the R. S. (3 *Banks*, 6th *ed.*, 104).

I referred to the fact that, while by the earlier provision the right of determining *all* questions concerning *any* debt, claim, legacy, bequest or distributive share had been conferred upon the Surrogate, the authority of that officer to make such determination is limited, by the later statute, to "debts, claims or distributive shares *whose validity is not disputed, or has been established.*

Because of this fact, and because of the fact that Mr. Commissioner THROOP had declared in his edition of the Code, by a note to the very section under consideration, that it was the purpose of the codifiers to bring the letter of the new enactment into unmistakable conformity with the construction that the courts had put upon the old, I felt bound to hold, in Fraenznick v. Miller, that, whenever an executor or administrator should dispute the validity of a demand against his decedent's estate, whether such demand should be made in behalf of one claiming as creditor, or as legatee, or in any other capacity whatsoever, the authority of the Surrogate in the premises would be straightway suspended, and would remain suspended until the validity of such demand should have been passed upon by some tribunal of competent jurisdiction, and by some other tribunal, of course, than the court of the Surrogate.

While this interpretation was, in my judgment, unavoidable, I adopted it with no little reluctance, and am glad to find what seems to me abundant warrant for abandoning it, in certain recent decisions of the Court of Appeals.

In Matter of Verplanck's Estate (91 *N. Y.*, 439), where questions similar to those here presented were under consideration, EARL, J., pronouncing the unanimous opinion of that court, declared that Surrogates "must have jurisdiction to construe wills, so far at least as is needful to determine to whom legacies shall be paid." Referring to the then recent decision in Riggs v. Cragg (89 *N. Y.*, 479), he added: "We were unanimously of the opinion that they possessed such a power under the Revised Statutes, before the Code of Civil Procedure, *and it was clearly not the intention of the Code to narrow or diminish the jurisdiction of Surrogates, but rather to enlarge it.*" By the words italicised, taken in connection with their context, I understand that the propositions declared in Riggs v. Cragg, respecting the jurisdiction of Surrogates upon final accountings, though those propositions in terms relate only to cases arising under the Revised Statutes, are pronounced to be equally applicable to cases arising under the Code.

In Riggs v. Cragg, a person claiming as legatee sought to enforce, from his testator's executors, the payment of a disputed legacy. There were divers persons interested in the estate, whose rights would be affected by the enforcement of a decree in the petitioner's favor. None of these persons were cited, or had appeared as parties to the proceeding. Commenting upon this fact, ANDREWS, J., pronouncing the opinion of the court, said: "When the Surrogate can see that other persons claim, or may claim, the same thing as the petitioner, and that a real question is presented, as to the right of several persons to the legacy or fund, natural justice requires that he should not proceed to a determination, without the presence of all the parties who may be affected by the adjudication. The statute provides for bringing in all the parties in interest on the final accounting, *and in that proceeding jurisdiction is conferred to settle and adjust conflicting rights and interests.*"

The learned Judge subsequently referred to the oft cited decision in Bevan v. Cooper (72 *N. Y.*, 317), and, after suggesting that, upon the reported facts of that case, there seemed to have been no necessity, *as incident to the accounting or distribution*, for the Surrogate to assume the power of interpreting the testator's will, added: " It is doubtless true that a Surrogate has no general jurisdiction in the construction of wills, but where the right to a legacy depends upon a question of construction, it must be determined before a decree for distribution can be made. *The Surrogate has, we think, jurisdiction . . . . . upon a final accounting, where all parties interested are before the court, to determine such construction as incident to the authority to make distribution."*

In Matter of Verplanck (*supra*), the Court of Appeals recently upheld a Surrogate's authority to determine, upon an executor's accounting, whether a provision in a testator's will should be deemed invalid, as involving a suspension of the power of alienation, and whether, by another provision, directing distribution of a portion of his estate, the testator intended a distribution *per stirpes* or one *per capita*.

The opinion of RUGER, Ch. J., in Fiester v. Shepard (92 *N. Y.*, 251), contains certain intimations that are not, perhaps, in thorough harmony with the doctrine of the two cases last cited, but that doctrine has been still more recently reasserted by the court of last resort, ANDREWS, J., pronouncing its opinion, in Purdy v. Hayt (92 *N. Y.*, 446).

Upon the authority of these decisions, I must deny the motion of counsel for the executor, and, in the decree about to be entered, must settle and determine the rights of all who claim as legatees under the will. A reference will be ordered for that purpose.

New York County.—Hon. D. G. ROLLINS, Surrogate.—December, 1884.

Nicholson *v.* Myers.

In the matter of the probate of the will of Rhomelia M. Myers, *deceased.*

Upon an application, made more than thirty years after the date of its alleged execution, for the probate of decedent's will, F., one of the subscribing witnesses, testified that he signed it as such, and saw it signed by the decedent and by the other witness, since deceased; that, according to his best recollection, which, however, he admitted was indistinct, decedent signed while seated at a stand in a room of her residence, thereafter yielding her seat to F., who, after signing, gave place in like manner to the second witness. The only other evidence was that afforded by an attestation clause, which lacked the usual completeness of form, being to the following effect: "Signed and acknowledged by said (decedent) as her last will and testament in our presence; and signed by us in her presence."—

Held, though with some hesitation, that there was sufficient evidence of a virtual acknowledgment, by decedent, of the testamentary character of the instrument, and request to the witnesses to sign as such; and that the petition for probate must be granted.

Application for the probate of decedent's will, made by Mary H. Myers, widow of decedent's deceased husband; opposed by Mary E. Nicholson, and others, decedent's children.

Geo. R. Brown, *for proponent.*

Edward Fitch, *for contestants.*

THE SURROGATE.—I find, though with some hesitation, that the paper here propounded for probate, was duly executed by this decedent as her will. Mr. A. W. French swears that he signed it as an attesting witness; that he saw the testatrix sign it, and saw it signed also by his fellow subscribing witness, who is now dead. This was more than thirty years ago. It is not singular, therefore, that the particular circumstances surrounding the transaction no longer remain in Mr. French's memory. As to whether the decedent declared the paper to be her last will, or was silent on that subject; and as to whether she formally requested the witnesses to act as such or failed to do so, he has no recollection whatever. Upon this state of facts, there being no cause for suspecting the validity of the paper propounded, I should unhesitatingly admit it to probate, if it contained a full attestation clause, reciting that it had been signed by the witnesses upon the decedent's invitation, and that it had been declared by her to be her last will (see Rolla v. Wright, 2 *Dem.*, 482; *and cases cited*).

The attestation clause falls short, however, of this completeness. It is in the following words: "Signed and acknowledged by said Rhomelia M. Myers as her last will and testament in our presence; *and signed by us in her presence.*"

The words italicised, when read in the light of certain portions of the testimony of Mr. French, justify me in holding that, when he and the other subscribing witness signed the attestation clause, they must have acted in compliance with a virtual request of the decedent, that they should thus participate in the execution of her will. Mr. French testifies that, according to the best of his recollection (though he admits his recollection is indistinct), Mrs. Myers signed this disputed paper while seated at a stand between the windows of a room in her residence; that, when she affixed her signature, she arose and yielded her seat to one of the witnesses; that he thereupon placed his name upon the paper, and then surrendered it to the other witness, who followed his example. Now, if the statements of the attestation clause be taken as true, these acts of the witnesses were performed in the immediate presence of the decedent, with her evident acquiescence and approval, and, indeed, by her actual procurement; and they were performed, too, in connection with a paper which she, *then and there*, acknowledged to be her will. The circumstances involve, it seems to me, a substantial " request," on her part, which fully answers the requirements of our statute of wills.

Unless, therefore, the contestant wishes to urge some objections to the validity of this paper, other than those which relate to the validity of its execution, it must be admitted to probate.

NEW YORK COUNTY.—HON. D. G. ROLLINS, SURRO-
GATE.—December, 1884.

HALSEY *v.* HALSEY.

In the matter of the estate of WILLIAM HALSEY,
deceased.

An order of the Surrogate's court, directing an executor to file an official
bond within twenty days after service of a copy of the order, provided,
in case of his failure so to do, as follows: "it is hereby ordered that
the letters testamentary be revoked and annulled." The executor perfected an appeal from the order within the time specified; after the
expiration of which, an application was made for an absolute decree
of revocation.—

Held, that the application must be denied; on the ground that, either the
order in question was itself a decree revoking letters, in which case a
further decree was unnecessary,—or it was not such a decree, in which
event it was not within Code Civ. Pro., § 2583, and the appeal operated
as a stay.

APPLICATION by Maria Halsey, decedent's widow,
for entry of decree revoking letters testamentary
issued to William Halsey as executor of decedent's
will. The facts appear in the opinion.

JACKSON & BURR, *for petitioner.*

B. C. LEVERIDGE, *for executor.*

THE SURROGATE. — By order of the Surrogate,
dated September 26th, 1884, this executor was
directed to file a bond because of his non-residence
within the State. The order contained this provision :
"If the said executor fail to execute and file said
bond within twenty days after the service of a copy
of this order upon himself or his attorney, it is

hereby ordered that the letters testamentary . . . . .
be revoked and annulled."

Before the expiration of these twenty days the
executor perfected an appeal to the Supreme court.
I am now asked to enter a decree absolute, revoking
his letters testamentary, the twenty days having
long since elapsed, and no bond having been, as yet,
placed on file. To this the executor objects. His
argument in opposition takes the form of this dilem-
ma: Either the decree of revocation for which
the petitioner now asks is unnecessary, because the
executor's letters have already been revoked by the
order of September 26th last, or the executor's appeal from that order, within the twenty days it
allowed him for filing a bond, operates as a stay of
proceedings, and forbids the entry of the decree now
sought to be entered.

The petitioner insists in opposition that, despite
the appeal, he is entitled to the relief prayed for, in
view of the provisions of § 2583 of the Code of Civil
Procedure, which expressly declares that " an appeal
from a decree revoking letters testamentary does not
stay the execution of the decree appealed from."
This, however, does not answer the executor's objection. The order or decree already entered was
" a decree revoking letters," or it was not. If it
was such a decree, no further decree is necessary.

If it was not, then, despite § 2583, the appeal has
operated as a stay.

Motion denied.

NEW YORK COUNTY.—HON. D. G. ROLLINS, SURRO-
GATE.—December, 1884.

KILFOY *v.* POWERS.

In the matter of the estate of THOMAS POWERS,
deceased.

Alienage is not a bar to heirship.

Under the provision of Code Civ. Pro., § 2615, requiring the heirs of a
decedent to be cited upon an application for the probate of a paper
propounded as his will, where the same relates to real property, a
non-resident alien brother and sister of a deceased citizen of the
United States, if among his next of kin, are entitled to citation ; the
latter inheriting, in case of intestacy, as if a citizen, and the former in
like manner, subject to a conditional defeasance, enforceable at the
instance of the State.

UPON application by John Powers, a brother of
decedent, for the probate of the latter's will, a
question arose as to the necessity for citing Bridget
Kilfoy and David Powers, decedent's non-resident
alien brother and sister.

WILLIAM A. HAGGERTY, *for proponent.*

THE SURROGATE.—The decedent, who, at the time
of his death, was a citizen of the United States,
owning real estate in this county, died here in July
last. Among his surviving next of kin are a sister
and a brother, both non-resident aliens. A paper
purporting to be his last will, and to devise to his
wife and to a brother residing in the United States
certain real property, having been offered for probate, the question has arisen as to the necessity of
issuing citations to this alien brother and sister.

Section 2615 of the Code of Civil Procedure directs that, upon an application for the probate of a will affecting real estate, all the "heirs" of the testator must be cited. Are the alien brother and sister of this decedent to be deemed his "heirs," within the meaning of this section? "An heir," says Blackstone, "is he upon whom the law casts the estate immediately on the death of the ancestor" (2 Blacks. Comm., ch. 14, p. 201). At common law, aliens were incapable of taking by descent, and they were formerly under the same incapacity in the State of New York (2 Kent's Comm., 53; Lynch v. Clarke, 1 *Sandf. Ch.*, 640). This disability was removed by the act of 1845. That act (L. 1845, ch. 115, § 4; as am'd, L. 1874, ch. 261, and L. 1875, ch. 38 [3 *Banks*, 7*th ed.*, 2170]), recognizes the right of alien kin of a person deceased, who was, at the time of his death, a resident alien, or a citizen of the United States, to take, *as his heirs*, the lands which would have descended to them in that capacity, had they been citizens of the United States. The title of an alien male of full age is, however, made defeasable by the State, upon his failure to file an affirmation or deposition respecting his intended citizenship, in the manner provided by § 1 of the act. That, under the provisions of this statute, non-resident aliens can take by descent seems too plain to be doubted, and has been often expressly asserted by our courts (Goodrich v. Russell, 42 *N. Y.*, 177; Luhrs v. Eimer, 80 *N. Y.*, 171; Hall v. Hall, 81 *N. Y.*, 131).

I hold, therefore, that this decedent's sister, though a non-resident alien, is entitled, if he shall be found to have died intestate, to the same interest in his real estate that she could take, were she a citizen of the United States, and that his alien brother is entitled to a like interest, subject to be defeated by the State, and only by the State, in case he should neglect to make and file the deposition or affirmation that the statute requires.

Both brother and sister must, therefore, be cited.

New York County.—Hon. D. G. ROLLINS, Surro-
GATE.—December, 1884.

Geissler v. Werner.

In the matter of the estate of Frederic Autenreith, *deceased.*

It is the duty of a testamentary trustee to defend any actions whereby the trust estate is attacked; for which purpose he may lawfully employ counsel ; and, on the settlement of his account, he will be allowed credit for such reasonable and necessary sums as he has, in good faith, expended for the protection of the estate.

Upon an application, by the beneficiary of a trust, to compel the trustee to pay to her alleged arrears of income, the respondent answered that he had expended nearly $350 for counsel fees, in defending an action brought by the petitioner for the purpose of extinguishing the trust, and wherein he had recovered a judgment for costs, which his attorney claimed was a lien on any sum to which petitioner might be entitled under the will,—such sum being less than the amount for which credit was asked by the respondent.—

Held, that the application must be denied without prejudice.

Petition by Amalie Geissler, a beneficiary under decedent's will, for an order compelling John F.

Werner, executor thereof of and trustee thereunder, to pay over the income of trust moneys. The facts are stated in the opinion.

HENRY F. LIPPOLD, *for petitioner.*

WEHLE & JORDAN, *for respondent.*

THE SURROGATE.—The respondent in this proceeding was appointed testamentary trustee by the will of this decedent, and was directed to pay to the petitioner, during her lifetime, the interest of a certain sum to be invested for her benefit. She now applies for an order, compelling the trustee to pay over such income as has accrued since March, 1883. It is alleged by the respondent, in his answer, that he has expended nearly $350 for counsel fees, in defending an action brought by this petitioner for extinguishing the trust for her benefit, and that, in such action, he has recovered against her a judgment for costs, amounting to $159.54, which latter amount is claimed by his attorney as a lien upon any sum to which the petitioner may be, or may become, entitled, under the provisions of the testator's will. The law is clearly settled, that it is the duty of a trustee to defend any actions whereby the trust estate is attacked; that, for conducting such defense, he may lawfully employ counsel; and that, on the settlement of his account, he will be allowed credit for such reasonable and necessary sums as he has, in good faith, expended for the protection of the estate (Noyes v. Blakeman, 3 *Sandf.*, 543; affi'd, 6 *N. Y.*, 584; Downing v. Marshall, 37 *N. Y.*, 380). The propriety and reasonableness of the expenses incurred by the respondent can be inquired into upon his accounting, when all persons interested in the fund can have an opportunity to be heard. As the amount of the income that could, in any event, be claimed by the petitioner is less than the amount for which the respondent asks credit, I must direct that her application be denied, without prejudice to its renewal, and without costs to either party.

NEW YORK COUNTY.—HON. D. G. ROLLINS, SURRO-GATE.—December, 1884.

WALSH v. DOWNS.

In the matter of the estate of CATHERINE WALSH, *deceased.*

In a special proceeding, brought by an executor or administrator under Code Civ. Pro., § 2706, to discover property of the decedent withheld from the petitioner, the allegations on the part of the latter may be exclusively on information and belief, without disclosing the sources or grounds thereof. The only pre-requisite to the issuing of a citation, is the satisfaction of the Surrogate that there are reasonable grounds for the inquiry.

PETITION by Michael Walsh, executor of decedent's will, for the examination of John Downs and another, under Code Civ. Pro., § 2706, relating to proceedings to discover property of a decedent withheld from his representative. The facts appear sufficiently in the opinion.

L. W. EMERSON, *for petitioner.*

JOHN A. FOSTER, *for respondent.*

THE SURROGATE. — Counsel for the respondent, Downs, claims that this petition is insufficient, because its allegations, which are wholly upon information and belief, do not state the sources of the petitioner's information, or the grounds of his belief. In proceedings of this character, I think that such averments are unnecessary. The Surrogate may direct a citation to issue, and parties cited to be examined, whenever he is satisfied that there are reasonable grounds for the inquiry; and he may properly be satisfied of that fact by allegations, on the part of the petitioner, of any circumstances which tend to show that property of a decedent's estate is in the possession or under the control of the respondent, and that too, whether the petitioner positively alleges the existence of such facts, or merely avows his belief of their existence because of information received by him from sources that he fails to reveal.

The citation has properly issued, and the respondents must appear for examination.

NEW YORK COUNTY.—HON. D. G. ROLLINS, SURROGATE.—December, 1884.

MORGAN *v.* DARDEN.

In the matter of the estate of ELIZABETH W. COLE, *deceased.*

By the terms of a trust created by the will of testatrix, the trustees were directed, upon the respective deaths of two life beneficiaries, A. and B., to divide one half of the principal fund equally among the children of the one so dying, each of such children to receive his or her share on becoming 21 years of age; it being further provided as follows: "Should the said A. decease before arriving at the age of 21 years, leaving no issue, then on her death I direct her share to be divided among the issue of B. . . . . . Should B. decease leaving no issue, then I direct that her share be divided among the surviving issue of A." B. having died leaving C., her only child, her surviving, and A. having died *at the age of* 37 *years*, leaving no issue, C. received one half of the fund, as the child of B., and claimed the other half under the clause of substitution.—

Held, that the half primarily given to the children of A. was diverted to B.'s children only upon the happening of three contingencies, one of which—the death of A. *during minority*—having become forever impossible, the gift over was ineffective, and the amount thereof fell into the residue.

UPON the judicial settlement of the account of Alexander P. Irvin, as executor of, and trustee under, the will of decedent, a contest arose between Estelle B. Darden, and Edith Morgan and others, infant residuary legatees, over the disposition of a legacy. The facts appear in the opinion.

HOWARD R. BAYNE, *for Mrs. Darden:*

The intent of testatrix is to prevail over the particular words which she has used. That one of two possible constructions is to be preferred which avoids intestacy, or a residuum not contemplated by the testatrix; and one which harmonizes with the general scheme of disposition, rather than another which is at variance therewith. The court should lay aside the strict criticism of inexorable logic, and adopt that opinion which a man of ordinary intelligence would adopt in reading the will. The will is perhaps peculiar in the design of testatrix that the objects of her bounty, who were most nearly related in blood, should have the usufruct only, while their children should enjoy the fee. In the second paragraph, her sister was a life tenant, her niece and great niece were succeeding life tenants, with remainder in fee to the children of this niece and great niece, respectively, with cross limitations. . . . . .

The will contains a perfect system of cross limitations, which is sustained throughout, except in the second paragraph, where the language employed is susceptible of two constructions; one of which mars, while the other preserves the symmetry and uniqueness of this method of disposition which testatrix has clearly adopted. . . . . .

The first part of the clause, "Should the said Medora Yerby decease," etc., contains three conditions : (1) death, (2) under 21 years, (3) leaving no issue. The second part—"then, on her death"—contains only two: (1) "then," whatever that may mean, (2) "on her death." "Then, on her death," was substituted for "decease before arriving at the age of 21 years;" being broader and more unlimited than the original for which it stands. . . . . .

The clause, "*then, on her death*," if any effect is to be given to it, at all, is a substitution of the instance or condition, on which the limitation over to Mrs. Young's issue occurs. This substitution is to be adopted because it is *the last*, because it avoids a residuum which the testatrix did not contemplate as possible, because it means equality between persons equally deserving in the testator's mind, and because it preserves the unique and symmetrical character of the will. Cites 2 Jarm. on Wills, 487 ; Shepperd v. Lessingham (*Amb.*, 122). . . . . . Perhaps the most salient confirmation of this construction is that the testatrix did not provide for the failure of any part of the $3,000 legacy, disposed of in the second paragraph, and for its passing into the residuary estate, as she did carefully, in every other case.

WM. B. CROSBY, *special guardian for residuary legatees:*

No intention that the legacy shall go over to Mrs. Darden can be presumed (1 Redf. on Wills, 430, 432). Even if there is ground for believing that there was an accidental omission to complete the provision for Mrs. Darden, the court cannot supply the omission (1 id., 440, 441; Madison v. Chapman, (5 *Jur.*, *N. S.*, 277; Boodle v. Scarisbrick, 1 *H. of L. Cas.*, 188). The legacy must go to the residue.

LORD, DAY & LORD, *for executor.*

THE SURROGATE.—The will of this decedent contains the provision following: " I give to my executors the sum of $3,000 . . . . . in trust to invest, ... and to pay over the net income to the use of Louise E. White during her natural life, and from and after her death, and also in case said Louise E. White shall decease before me, I direct said income to be paid, one half to her daughter, Martha B. Young, and the other half to the use of Medora Yerby, granddaughter of Louise E. White, during natural life. Upon the death of said Martha B. Young, I direct said executors to divide one half of said $3,000, among the children of said Martha B. Young, and upon the death of said Medora Yerby I direct my executors to pay over the other half of said $3,000 to and among the children of said Medora Yerby, and I direct that the children of Martha B. Young and of Medora Yerby shall each receive his or her share when they become 21 years of age. *Should the said Medora Yerby decease before arriving at the age of* 21 *years leaving no issue, then on her death* I direct her share to be divided among the issue of Martha B. Young, said issue taking *per stirpes* and not *per capita*.   Should Martha B. Young decease leaving no issue, then I direct that her share be divided among the surviving issue of Medora Yerby *per stirpes* and not *per capita.*"

Louise E. White and Martha B. Young having died, one half of the above named legacy has been paid to Mrs. Estelle B. Darden, the only child of Martha B. Young.   In July last, Medora Yerby died at the age of 37 years.   Mrs. Darden now claims the remaining half of the legacy.   It is claimed, in opposition, by the special guardian of the infants interested in the residuary estate, that such remaining half passed into the residuum by reason of the decease of Medora Yerby without issue *after* she had arrived at the age of 21 years.

I have examined with great interest the ingenious argument of counsel for Mrs. Darden, but it has not persuaded me that I am at liberty to substitute other words, in place of what seems to me to be the very plain and unequivocable language of this will.   The gift over is to take effect only upon the happening of these three events: 1*st*, the death of Medora Yerby;   2*d*, her dying without issue; and, 3*d*, *her dying during her minority.*

To saddle the gift over with these conditions may or may not have been a judicious provision for the testatrix to make, but it is a very intelligible one, and is couched in words which are free from ambiguity. As one of the three contingencies has not happened, and as its happening has now become impossible, I hold that the gift over has become ineffective, and that the $1,500 must, therefore, go to the residuary legatees.

NEW YORK COUNTY.—HON. D. G. ROLLINS, SURRO-GATE.—December, 1884.

WARNER v. KNOWER.

In the matter of the estate of JOHN F. GRAY, *deceased.*

An executor cannot show to himself, in his capacity as a debtor to his testator's estate, any greater favor than would be proper in the case of another debtor.

The statute, 2 R. S., 84, § 13,—providing that "the naming of any person executor in a will shall not operate as a discharge or bequest of any claim which the testator had against such executor, but such claim shall be included . . . . . in an inventory, and such executor shall be liable for the same as for so much money in his hands at the time such debt or demand becomes due," etc.,—must receive a restricted interpretation, made in view of the mischief designed to be thereby remedied : it was not its purpose to place a debtor-executor in a position more favorable than that of other debtors of the estate.

Decker v. Miller, 2 *Paige*, 149 ; Baucus v. Stover, 89 *N. Y.*, 1—followed ; King v. Talbot, 40 *N. Y.*, 76—distinguished.

At the time of testator's death, K., who was appointed executor, held moneys belonging to the former, amounting to nearly $170,000. Several months previously, the parties had made an agreement, indefinite as to time, that K. should be chargeable with interest on such moneys in his hands at the rate of four per cent., per annum. The will gave the executors full and absolute discretion as to the form, manner and extent of any and all investments of the estate. Upon the judicial settlement of his account as executor, K. contended that he was not bound to discharge his debt immediately upon receiving letters, but was at liberty to exercise his discretion as to the time of payment. A referee reported that the executor must be treated as if principal and interest, due when he qualified, had been moneys of the estate then in his hands, which he failed to invest ; and that he was chargeable with interest at one per cent. less than the statute rate, commencing to run six months after the issue of his letters.—

Held, that the executor's contention must be overruled, unless the will could be construed as giving him power to make new loans of the estate funds, at four per cent., without security—which it could not ; that, however, the statutory provision declaring an executor liable for his own debt "as for so much money in his hands at the time such debt or demand becomes due," etc., had not the literal application implied by the report ; and that K. should be charged with interest on the principal of his indebtedness, at the rate of four per cent. until his qualification, and six per cent. thereafter, until he actually collected or set apart the amount of the same for the benefit of the estate.

HEARING of exceptions taken by Mary E. Warner and another, testamentary guardians of Louise Warner, one of the infant next of kin of decedent, to report of referee, to whom were referred the account, and objections thereto, of Benjamin Knower as executor of decedent's will, in proceedings for a judicial settlement. The facts appear sufficiently in the opinion.

JOHN N. WHITING, *for executor.*

GEO. H. STARR, *for exceptants.*

H. B. B. STAPLER, *special guardian.*

THE SURROGATE.—Dr. John F. Gray died June 5th, 1882, leaving a will, wherein he named Augustus G. Hull and Benjamin Knower as his executors. Letters testamentary were issued to the latter on the 15th of

August, following. Mr. Hull has never qualified. The questions now presented for my determination arise upon exceptions to the report of the referee, to whom Mr. Knower's account, as executor, together with the objections thereto, was lately submitted by the Surrogate.

It is an undisputed fact that, several months before Dr. Gray's death, and at a time when large sums of money belonging to him were held by Mr. Knower, it was agreed that the holder should be chargeable with interest thereon at the rate of four per cent., per annum. It appears also that, when the testator died, this indebtedness of Mr. Knower amounted to nearly $170,000. His duty, as executor, respecting the collection of this sum and the nature and extent of his liability for interest thereon, between the date of the testator's death and the date of its actual payment into the estate, or its investment for the estate's benefit, are the most important matters here in controversy.

In one of the codicils to the testator's will are the words following: "I desire and direct that the executors of my said will shall have full and absolute discretion, as to the form and manner and extent of any and all investments of my estate." It is contended, on behalf of Mr. Knower, that, in view of the provision just quoted, he was not bound as executor to collect the amount of his indebtedness immediately upon his reception of letters testamentary, but that he was, on the contrary, at liberty to exercise his sound discretion, as to when he should insist upon its payment into the estate. This contention was unsuccessfully urged by the executor's counsel before the referee. It cannot, it seems to me, be upheld, unless the provision above quoted can be fairly construed as giving the executor discretionary authority, even after the testator's death, to make new loans of the estate funds to private individuals, at four per cent. interest, and without security.

I do not forget that the discretion, which an executor may properly exercise in making investments of trust funds, is essentially different from the discretion that he may properly exercise in temporarily continuing investments made by his testator; that, even in cases where one has given in his will no special direction as to investments, and has conferred no extraordinary powers upon his executor, the courts have, nevertheless, afforded such executor reasonable opportunity for converting the assets of the estate into investments sanctioned by law, and have held him not accountable for losses resulting from reasonable delay in effecting such conversion.

The facts of the case at bar do not, however, call for the application of any such principle. If this executor, when he entered upon his duties, had found, among the assets of the estate, an unsecured debt of a private individual other than himself, it would have been his duty, under the same circumstances, *mutatis mutandis*, as are here disclosed, to make immediate demand for its payment.

For I take it that the agreement between the decedent and Mr. Knower was revocable at the pleasure of either. The latter was at liberty, at any time, to relieve himself from the burden of interest, by surrendering the principal, and the former would, at any time, upon demand, have been entitled to the return of his money. The debtor would, thereupon, have become liable for interest, at the legal rate, thenceforward until his indebtedness should be discharged.

Now, an executor cannot show to himself, in his capacity as a debtor to his testator's estate, any greater favor than he can properly show to other debtors. It is a familiar legal doctrine, well stated in Benchley v. Chapin (10 *Cush.*, 175), that, when the same person is bound to pay money in one capacity, and to recover it in another, the law presumes that he has done what it was his duty and in his power to do, and holds him chargeable, as if it had been actually done. To similar effect, see, also, Commonwealth v. Gould (118 *Mass.*, 307); Hazleton v. Valentine (113 *Mass.*, 480); Winship v. Bass (12 *Mass.*, 198); Hall v. Pratt (5 *Ohio*, 72); Norris v. Towle (54 *N. H.*, 290); Soverhill v. Suydam (2 *T. & C.*, 464); Stevens v. Gaylord (11 *Mass.*, 269).

It is upon this principle that, in localities where one's appointment as executor has not served, as it served at the common law, to absolve him from indebtedness to his testator, he has been held liable for the amount of such debt, as for so much moneys actually in his hands.

In passing adversely upon the contention of the accounting party in the present case, the referee has reported that, not only as to the moneys due the testator at the time the executor qualified, but also as to the interest thereupon, the executor must be treated precisely as if such moneys had, ever since he entered upon his duties, been actually in his hands, and must, therefore, account for the same, with interest thereon, precisely as if, so being in his hands, he had failed to invest them, or to invest them properly for the benefit of the estate. The referee has accordingly applied, to the case at bar, the rule in King v. Talbot (40 *N. Y.*, 76), and has held that the executor is chargeable with interest, at one per cent. less than the statutory rate, for a period, commencing six months after the issue of letters testamentary.

While the referee does not expressly state the grounds upon which he bases this conclusion, it evidently rests upon his construction of a statutory provision whose correct interpretation was the subject of dispute at the trial, and has since been discussed in the argument before the Surrogate.

The words of that provision are as follows: "The naming of any person executor in a will shall not operate as a discharge or bequest of any claim which the testator had against such executor, but such claim shall be included among the credits and effects of the deceased in an inventory, and such executor shall be liable for the same as for so much money in his hands at the time such debt or demand becomes due, and he shall apply and distribute the same in the payment of debts and legacies, and among the next of kin as a part of the personal estate of the deceased" (§ 13, tit. 3, ch. 6, part 2, R. S.; 3 *Banks*, 7th ed., 2295).

Now, in advance of the inquiry as to the origin of this statute, and as to the mischiefs it was designed to remedy, it seems evident, upon its face, that it

was intended, not to create a substantial distinction
between the liability of a debtor-executor and that of
other debtors of a decedent, but rather to assimilate
the liability of one to that of the other; and that it does
not undertake to declare that, under all circumstances
and in all respects, and for all purposes, an executor's
debt to his testator should be treated as if it were so
much money actually in the executor's hands, but
only that it should be so deemed for a particular purpose, and for the avoidance of a particular embarrassment. While the bearing of this statute upon the
precise question under consideration seems never to
have been judicially determined, there are two decisions of our Court of Appeals, distinctly recognizing
that the provision above quoted should receive a
restricted interpretation. In Soverhill v. Suydam
(2 *T. & C.*, 464), a proceeding for the distribution of
surplus moneys, it was claimed by certain judgment
creditors of one who had been appointed the executor
of a will of another and earlier judgment creditor,
that such appointment, by virtue of the section in
question, operated to extinguish the judgment that
had been recovered by the testator, and the lien
thereof, and to make an indebtedness represented by
it as, in effect, money then in the hands of the executor. But the Supreme Court held that neither the
debt of the executor nor the lien of the judgment
was discharged by the appointment. MILLER, P. J.,
in delivering the opinion of the court, said: "It
is not discharged, unless the executor applies the
amount of his indebtedness in payment of claims
against his debtor, in due course of administration.

If he refuses, or is unable to pay, the debt he owes
the testator still exists, and may be sued for and its
payment enforced, and any security held therefor
may be applied to the payment of such debt."

Judge RAPALLO, who pronounced the opinion of the
Court of Appeals affirming the judgment below in the
case just cited, declared that the purpose of the section
under consideration was the abolition of the common-
law rule exonerating an executor from his indebtedness to his testator, and that the provision, directing
that the debt should be included in the inventory,
and that the executor should be liable for it, as so
much money, etc., was inserted for obviating the
incongruity of requiring the executor to proceed
against himself for the collection of such debt.   In
the course of his opinion, the learned Judge said:
"When an executor. has, in the performance of his
trust, paid out for these purposes (the payment of
debts and legacies and claims of next of kin) the
amount due from him to the estate, his debt and all
liens on his individual property by which the debt
may have been secured, will of course be discharged.
But before this is done, it was not, in our judgment,
the intention of the legislature, while preserving the
debt, to discharge liens by which it might be secured.
Subjecting the executor, as between him and those
interested in the estate, to liability for his debt, as for
so much money in his hands, does not necessarily
discharge a lien on real estate by which the debt may
be secured.   That provision merely superadds to his
original obligation a liability to account, as executor,
for the amount of the debt, and was intended to

facilitate the administration, and for the benefit of
the estate, and not for that of the executor or of his
individual creditors, who may have subsequent liens
upon his property."

To similar effect is the decision in Baucus v. Stover
(89 *N. Y.*, 1). "While the debt must be regarded,"
the court says in that case, "as money in his (the
executor's) hands for the purpose of administration,
it will not, for all purposes, stand on the same footing
as if he had actually received so much money. If
wholly unable to pay the money in pursuance of the
order or decree of the Surrogate, on account of his
insolvency, he cannot be attached and punished for
contempt, as he could be if the money had been
actually received from some other debtor."

The two cases just cited clearly establish that the
statute, to which the referee seems to attach so much
significance, must not receive a strict and literal
interpretation; else the lien would not have been
sustained in Soverhill v. Suydam, and it would have
been held, in Baucus v. Stover, that the claim of the
estate against its executor was enforceable by attachment.

That the legislature, by its enactment of the statutory provision here in question, did not intend to
effect the result that the learned referee thinks it
has accomplished is discovered, also, by an examination of the notes of the Revisers.

"The debt of an executor," they say (3 R. S., 2d
ed., 640), "is now liable to creditors, and in some
cases to legatees; but, when not required for these
purposes, it is discharged or belongs to the executors,

and is not to be distributed among the next of kin, unless it appear, on the face of the will, that the testator did not intend to discharge the debt. Few persons are aware of this; and, as well to avoid the disputes that arise, as to establish what is believed to be a just rule, this section is copied substantially from the laws of Maryland. Since an allowance is made to executors for their services, the reason of the old rule has ceased."

It was the avowed object of the provision in the Maryland law to abrogate the old doctrine, whereby the bare appointment of an executor worked an extinguishment of his indebtedness to his testator, and to furnish a simple method of making such indebtedness available as an asset of the estate. To do this, the Maryland statute provided that the executor should include any such claim in his list or inventory of debts due the estate, and it provided also for the enforcement of his liability in the event of his failure so to do. In case of his voluntary recognition of the claim, or of its establishment upon a trial, the statute declared that the executor should "account for the sum due in the same manner as if it were so much money in his hands" (2 Maxcy's Laws of Maryland, 479).

It clearly appears, upon examining the provisions just referred to, that it was no part of their purpose to place a debtor who chanced to be an executor in any more favorable situation than could be occupied by other debtors of the estate. It seems equally plain that such was not the purpose of our own statute.

Even at the common law, whenever, because of special circumstances, a debt due from the representative of an estate to his decedent was held to survive his appointment as such representative, the debtor seems to have been held liable, like any other debtor, for interest on the amount of his indebtedness, until that amount had been realized for the estate (Turner v. Cox, 8 *Moore's P. C. C.*, 288, 309, 315; Ingle v. Richards, 28 *Beav.*, 366 ; Styles v. Guy, 1 *Macn. & G.*, 422).

I can see no reason why that rule should not be adopted in the case at bar, and, therefore, hold that this executor must be charged with interest on his indebtedness, at the rate of six per cent., per annum, from the time when he received letters testamentary until he actually collected, or set apart for the benefit of the estate, the amount of such indebtedness. He must be charged with interest at four per cent., up to the date of his qualifying as executor. This course is countenanced by Baucus v. Stover (*supra*), and by Decker v. Miller (2 *Paige*, 149). In the former case, the inventory disclosed a specified balance due from the executor at the time of its date. The court held that he was chargeable with the balance due upon his debt, and with the interest thereon as so much money in his hands.

Decker v. Miller was an action by an executor to compel his fellow executor to account for a debt owed by him to the testator during his lifetime. The Chancellor charged the defendant with interest, at the legal rate, down to the time the amount of the debt was paid into court.

With such modifications as are made necessary by the foregoing decision, the report of the referee is confirmed.

NEW YORK COUNTY.—HON. D. G. ROLLINS, SURRO-GATE.—December, 1884.

FARMERS LOAN & TRUST CO. *v.* MCKENNA.

In the matter of the estate of WILLIAM KENNELLY, *deceased.*

Although Code Civ. Pro., § 2531 recognizes the authority of the Surrogate to appoint a special guardian for an infant at the latter's instance, that section must be construed, in connection with id., § 2530, as authorizing such appointment only where the general guardian does not appear, or the Surrogate is satisfied that the latter is disqualified to adequately protect the interests of his ward.

Where, therefore, an infant having a general guardian applies to a Surrogate's court for the appointment of a special guardian, to represent him in a proceeding therein, he must give to the former notice of the application.

APPLICATION for appointment of guardian ad litem of infant next of kin of testator, upon accounting of executor of his will. The facts are stated in the opinion.

DAVID MCCLURE, *for general guardian.*

J. MCKENNA, *special guardian.*

THE SURROGATE.—The executor of this estate is now accounting before the Surrogate. Upon the application of two of the testator's minor children, an order has been entered, appointing a special guardian to protect, not only their own interests, but those also of two other infants, sisters of the petitioners. Of all these infants, the Farmers Loan and Trust company is general guardian, and, as such, is entitled to represent its wards, unless their interests require that they should be represented by a special guardian (Code Civ. Pro., § 2530).

Now, it nowhere appears, in the papers upon which the order of appointment herein was grounded, that the general guardian cannot fully represent the infants in the proceeding for the settlement of the executor's accounts. Although § 2531 recognizes the authority of the Surrogate to appoint a special guardian for an infant at the infant's instance, that section must be construed, when read in connection with § 2530, as authorizing such appointment only in cases where there is no appearance of the general guardian, or where it is shown, to the satisfaction of the Surrogate, that the general guardian is, for some reason, disqualified from affording to the interests of his wards adequate protection.

In cases where an infant has a general guardian, it is, therefore, an irregular practice to appoint a special guardian upon the application of such infant, without notice of such application having first been given to the general guardian. No such notice was given in the case at bar.

It is now claimed, however, that, in an action brought against these infants for the partition of lands in which they are interested, the attorneys for this general guardian acted as attorneys for the plaintiff, and that such action was commenced against the wishes of two of the infants, who have expressed a wish that said attorneys shall not appear for them on this accounting. It does not appear, however, that the commencement or prosecution of the action for partition is detrimental to the interests of these infants, or that their general guardian is unable or unwilling or unlikely to protect their interests to the full.

The order appointing the special guardian must be set aside, and the general guardian permitted to appear.

NEW YORK COUNTY. — HON. D. G. ROLLINS, SURRO-GATE. — December, 1884.

BEEKMAN v. VANDERVEER.

In the matter of the estate of BENJAMIN F. BEEKMAN, *deceased.*

Code Civ. Pro., § 2718, relating to an application to compel *an executor* to pay a legacy, and id., § 2806, containing a similar provision in reference to *a testamentary trustee*, have essentially the same purpose. They establish modes of procedure whereby a beneficiary under a will may obtain prompt relief, where it is plain that the rights of other persons cannot be thereby prejudiced; while, on the other hand, where the grant of such relief may prove prejudicial to others, the latter are required to be allowed an opportunity to be heard.

Testator, by his will, directed the executors to invest $100,000, and pay the income to his wife B., during her life or widowhood. This provision, which was declared to be in lieu of dower, was accepted by the widow, who for a time received interest upon the amount mentioned ; but no sum was ever invested as required.   B. having filed a petition with the Surrogate, alleging that the value of the estate had deprecia-

ted far below its appraised and estimated value, and praying that the
executors be directed to pay to her an amount equal to her dower
interest, as a purchaser for value, it appeared that there were several
alleged creditors of the estate, whose aggregate claims exceeded the
estimated value of the latter, and none of whom had been cited.—

Held, that, whether the testamentary provision in petitioner's favor called
into exercise the functions of the executors as such, or as trustees,
those claiming as creditors must be brought in as parties, unless petitioner chose to discontinue and institute a proceeding for the judicial
settlement of the executors' account.

Riggs v. Cragg, 89 N. Y., 479—followed.

PETITION by Catharine A. Beekman, widow of decedent, for a decree directing John R. Vanderveer, and
another, executors of decedent's will, to pay to her
"a sum not exceeding the value of the unpaid balance of her dower in the real estate of her husband."
The facts are stated in the opinion.

JOHN A. MAPES, *for petitioner.*

FRANK F. VANDERVEER, *for executor.*

THE SURROGATE.—By the will of this testator, his
executors were directed to invest, for the benefit of
his wife, the sum of $100,000, and to pay her the
income of such investment so long as she should live
and remain his widow, such bequest, if received and
accepted by her, to be in lieu of all rights of dower.
In her petition, filed with the Surrogate on the 11th
inst., she alleges that, at the time of her husband's
death, the appraised value of his personal property
was nearly $500,000, and that the value of his real
estate exceeded, by at least $150,000, the aggregate
of the mortgages by which it was encumbered. Her
petition further avers that, with the knowledge of
these facts, she accepted the provision made for her

in the will, and for a time received the interest on $100,000, but that the condition of the estate has never been such as to enable the executors to invest that sum for her benefit; that personal assets of the estate, once supposed to be valuable, have proved to be utterly worthless, and that the value of the real property left by the testator has shrunk so far below the encumbrances upon it that proceedings for foreclosure have, in some instances, resulted in deficiency judgments.

Under these circumstances, the petitioner claims that, to the extent of her dower interest, which has become part of the assets of the estate, she must be deemed a purchaser for value, and that, as such, she is entitled to receive from the executors an amount equal to such interest. It appears that there are several persons who hold claims against this estate. Some of these claims are undisputed, and are secured by judgments. The largest is of a contingent character. Taken together, they involve a sum larger than the present estimated value of the entire estate. None of those creditors, or alleged creditors, have been cited to attend this proceeding. Whether the testamentary direction for the benefit of the petitioner is one which only calls into exercise the functions of the executors, as such, or whether, on the other hand, it invokes their action as trustees, is perhaps not entirely clear. In the one case, this proceeding rests upon § 2717 of the Code of Civil Procedure; in the other, it must be treated as brought under § 2806. Section 2806 declares that, "Where it appears, upon the presentation of a petition . . . . . that a decree made pursuant to the prayer thereof might affect the rights of other persons, with respect to the estate or fund held by the testamentary trustee, the citation must, also, be directed to those persons. When that fact appears upon the return of the citation or upon the hearing, and it also appears, presumptively, that the petitioner is entitled to a decree, all the persons whose rights may be so affected must be brought in by a supplemental citation, before a decree is made." Now, it is obvious that the entry of a decree granting the prayer of this petitioner might affect the rights of such persons as claim to be creditors of this estate. If, therefore, the respondents are to be deemed testamentary trustees, such claimants must doubtless be cited.

Section 2718 requires that a petition for an order directing an executor to pay legacies must be dismissed without prejudice, "where it is not proved, to the satisfaction of the Surrogate, that there is money or other personal property of the estate applicable to the payment or satisfaction of the petitioner's claim, and which may be so applied without injuriously affecting the rights of others entitled to priority of payment or satisfaction." While the language of this section differs from that of § 2806, the purpose of the two provisions is, I think, essentially the same. They aim to establish modes of procedure, whereby a beneficiary under a will may obtain prompt relief, whenever it is plain that the rights of other persons cannot thereby be prejudiced: but where, upon the other hand, it appears that such prejudice to others may result from the granting of such relief, they forbid its granting until such others have been afforded opportunity to be heard.

Before considering upon its merits, therefore, the claim so skillfully presented by counsel for the petitioner, all who claim as creditors must be brought in, unless the petitioner shall choose to abandon the present proceeding, and to institute another for the judicial settlement of the executor's accounts (Riggs v. Cragg, 89 *N. Y.*, 479).

NEW YORK COUNTY.—HON. D. G. ROLLINS, SURROGATE.—December, 1884.

ST. FRANCES HOSPITAL *v.* SCHRECK.

In the matter of the estate of ANTON MUSSIG, *deceased.*

An act was passed by the legislature, in 1866 (L. 1886, ch. 201, §7), declaring that the corporation thereby created should be "subject to the provisions of title seven, part first, of chapter eighteen of the Revised Statutes, in relation to devises or bequests by will." The R. S. contain no such title ; but, in a compilation, published as the fifth edition of the R. S., in 1859, a so-called seventh title was appended to the chapter in question, consisting of Laws of 1848, chap. 319, the sixth section whereof contains a restriction upon devises and bequests contained in a will not made and executed at least two months before the death of the testator.—

Held, that the reference in the act of 1866 was to the act of 1848, appearing as the added title in the compilation referred to.

The designation of "St. Frances Hospital," as a legatee, *held* a curable misnomer for the "Sisters of the Poor of St. Frances."

CONSTRUCTION of decedent's will upon application for the probate thereof, made by Frank Schreck, the executor therein named.   The facts are stated in the opinion.

GEO. F. ROESCH, *for petitioner.*

A. SIMIS, Jr., *special guardian.*

THE SURROGATE.—The paper propounded as the will of this decedent is entitled to probate. A decree may be entered, accordingly. It makes two bequests which I am asked to pronounce void: one to "St. Nicholas German Roman Catholic church," the other to "St. Frances Hospital in Fifth street." The testator died ten days after he executed his will. Because of this fact, it is claimed that both the bequests in question are invalidated by the restrictive provisions of L. 1848, ch. 319, § 6, which declares that testamentary gifts to certain corporations shall not take effect, unless the execution of the will whereby they are granted precedes, by at least two months, the death of its maker.

The St. Nicholas German Roman Catholic church was incorporated under L. 1813, ch. 60, and is, accordingly, empowered, by L. 1863, ch. 45, to take devises and bequests without such restrictions as are established by the act of 1848 (Riley v. Diggs, 2 *Dem.*, 184). The objection to the legacy in its behalf cannot be sustained.

There is no doubt that, by his bequest to "St. Frances Hospital," the testator intended to benefit the "Sisters of the Poor of St. Frances," a corporation organized under L. 1866, ch. 201. Section 6 of that act contains a provision which would prevent a mistake, in naming this institution as legatee in a will, from defeating the testator's intention. Besides, even in the absence of such provision, the error would not be fatal (Riley v. Diggs, *supra*).

This bequest must, however, be pronounced invalid. By § 7 of the act of 1866 (*supra*), this corporation is made "subject to the provisions of title 7, part 1, of chapter eighteen of the Revised Statutes."

The 5th edition of the compilation, "arranged in the manner of the Revised Statutes," was published in 1859 by Banks & Bros. Section 6 of the act of 1848 there appears as part of title 7 (2 Banks, 5th ed., p. 624). It was, doubtless, this arrangement of the statutes to which the legislature referred. The act of 1848 never, in fact, formed part of the Revised Statutes, but I have no doubt that the reference, in the act of 1866, to the provisions of title 7 subjected this corporation to the restrictions which the act of 1848 established (People v. Clute, 50 *N. Y.*, 451).

NEW YORK COUNTY.—HON. D. G. ROLLINS, SURROGATE.—December, 1884.

MATTER OF WHITEHEAD.

In the matter of the estate of JOHN WHITEHEAD, *deceased.*

Where there is manifestly a *casus omissus* in the statute, respecting practice, owing to inadvertence in amendment, it is the duty of a Surrogate's court to adopt the practice formerly pursued in similar cases by the Court of Chancery, and more recently by the Supreme Court, in its exercise of equity power.

Tompkins v. Moseman, 5 *Redf.*, 402—approved.

Notwithstanding the definition contained in Code Civ. Pro., § 2514, whereby the term "testamentary trustee" is declared to include a person designated by a will, *or by any competent authority*, to execute a trust created by will, the provision of id., § 2815, allowing a Surrogate to require security from a testamentary trustee, in the cases therein specified, applies only to one named in a will; this exceptional meaning being "plainly apparent from the context."

From the provision of Code Civ. Pro., § 2818, requiring a testamentary trustee, appointed as successor to one who has resigned or been removed, to qualify in the same manner as an administrator with the will annexed, no inference is to be drawn, of an intent to relieve the successor of a deceased or insane trustee from the like necessity.

The trustees designated in testator's will having died, leaving the trust unexecuted, and application having been made to the Surrogate's court for the appointment of a successor; on granting the application,—

Held, that the appointee must give security for the faithful discharge of the duties of his trust, in like manner as an administrator with a will annexed.

APPLICATION by Margaret E. Whitehead, decedent's widow, for the appointment of a successor to deceased testamentary trustees. The facts are stated in the opinion.

JAMES PARKER, *for petitioner.*

THE SURROGATE.—One of the trusts created by this testator's will is still unexecuted, and the trustees whom he selected for its execution are dead. The Surrogate is now asked to appoint their successor, and to decide whether such successor should be required to give bonds for the faithful discharge of his duties. If there were any statutory answer to this question, one would naturally expect to find it in § 2818 of the Code of Civil Procedure. That section authorizes the Surrogate, in the event of the death, lunacy, resigna-

tion or removal of a testamentary trustee, to appoint
a successor. It provides, also, that, under certain
circumstances, such successor shall be required to
qualify in the same manner as an administrator with
the will annexed, and, among other things, to give,
like him, security for the proper performance of his
trust. But this statutory requirement extends only
to cases where the vacancy in the office of trustee has
been brought about by resignation or removal, and
does not include cases where it has been caused by
lunacy or death. I agree, however, with Surrogate
COFFIN (see Tompkins v. Moseman, 5 *Redf.*, 402),
that, from this circumstance, no reference can be
justly drawn that the legislature designed to relieve
the successors of deceased or insane testamentary
trustees from any burdens that it imposed upon the
successors of testamentary trustees inmoved from
office or permitted to resign. With the exception
that will presently be noted, § 2818, as it stood before
the amendment of 1884 (and that amendment has no
bearing upon the question now under consideration),
was, word for word, like § 2587 of the first draft of the
Code as prepared by the Commissioners to revise the
Statutes. When thus prepared, it read as follows:

"Where a sole testamentary trustee has, by a
decree of the Surrogate's court, been removed or
allowed to resign, and the trust has not been fully
executed, the same court may appoint his successor,
unless such an appointment would contravene the
express terms of the will. Where a decree removing
the trustee or discharging him upon his resignation
does not designate his successor, or the person desig-

nated therein does not qualify, the successor must be appointed and must qualify as prescribed by law for the appointment and qualification of an administrator with the will annexed."

It will be observed that the Surrogate's authority to appoint successors to original testamentary trustees, was proposed to be limited to cases where such trustees had resigned, or had been removed, and that it was proposed, also, to require, from the successor of every such trustee, the security of a bond. The Commissioners attached to this section a note, declaring that its object was to extend to the Surrogates of all counties the authority conferred upon the Surrogate of this county by L. 1870, ch. 359, § 3, and added these words: "We are not disposed to recommend the extension of the power, as to vacancies created by death, insanity," etc.

The section quoted was, before its adoption, so amended in its first clause as to effect the very enlargement of authority that the commissioners deprecated. But, evidently by inadvertence, the corresponding change was not made in the clause relating to qualification. Under these circumstances, and in the absence of any express direction of statute, it is the Surrogate's duty to adopt the practice formerly pursued in such cases by the Court of Chancery, and more recently by the Supreme Court in its exercise of equity power (Tompkins v. Moseman, *supra*).

There are many cases which recognize the propriety and legality of requiring a bond from the successors of testamentary trustees (see Matter of Robinson, 37 *N. Y.*, 264; People v. Norton, 9 *id.*, 176; Milbank

v. Crane, 25 *How. Pr.*, 193; Matter of Stuyvesant, 3 *Edw. Ch.*, 299; Ex parte Jones, 4 *Sandf. Ch.*, 615).

Counsel for the petitioner opposes this view of the Surrogate's duty, and authority, by reference to § 2815 of the Code. " Any person beneficially in-. terested in the execution of the trust," says that section, "may present to the Surrogate's court a petition setting forth . . . . . any fact respecting a testamentary trustee, the existence of which, if it was interposed as an objection to granting letters testamentary to a person named as executor in a will, would make it necessary for such a person to give security in order to entitle himself to letters, and praying for a decree directing the testamentary trustee to give security for the performance of his trust, and that he may be cited to show cause why such a decree should not be made. . . . . . Upon the return of the citation, a decree requiring the testamentary trustee to give such security may be made, in a case where a person so named as executor can entitle himself to letters testamentary only by giving a bond; but not otherwise."

Now, it seems to be claimed by petitioner's counsel that, only in cases expressly specified in § 2818, already discussed, and in cases covered by § 2815, can a "testamentary trustee" be required by the Surrogate to give bonds, and it is insisted that the term "testamentary trustee," as used in the latter section, is not limited in its meaning to trustees appointed by the will of a testator, but includes, also, any successor to such trustees who may be appointed by the Surrogate. In support of the latter contention, counsel refers to § 2514, which declares that, with certain exceptions, the expression "testamentary trustee," wherever it is used in the 18th chapter of the Code, shall be held to include "every person who is designated by a will, or by any competent authority, to execute a trust created by a will." The same section, however, provides that such rule of interpretation shall not be observed "where a contrary intent is expressly declared in the provision to be construed, or is plainly apparent from the context thereof."

From a careful examination of the context, it is, I think, "plainly apparent" that the term testamentary trustee, as used in § 2815, means a trustee named in the will, and no other. This is strongly indicated by the close similarity which exists, throughout the 18th chapter, between the provisions that relate to executors and those that relate to testamentary trustees. That policy of the law which, only under special circumstances, permits the exaction of a bond from executors before granting them letters testamentary, would naturally require that similar restrictions be placed upon the Surrogate's authority to impose, upon testamentary trustees selected by the testator himself, the burden of giving security.

That policy, on the other hand, could not be extended to the successors of such trustees with any more propriety than to administrators with the will annexed, which latter class of officers have always been required to give bonds. The Code says, in effect, considering its various provisions as a whole, that persons named as executors in a will are entitled to letters testamentary without giving bond, unless, when their right thereto is challenged, it appears that they reside out of the State, or that their circumstances do not afford adequate security for their due administration of the estate (§§ 2685, 2686, 2687). And it substantially says, also, that persons named as trustees in a will are entitled to exercise the functions of their office without security, subject only to the same limitations that are established in the case of executors (§§ 2815, 2816, 2817).

As to the successors of such trustees, however, I am convinced that the Surrogate, may, in all cases, lawfully require security at the time of their appointment. It must be furnished in the case at bar.

NEW YORK COUNTY.—HON. D. G. ROLLINS, SURROGATE.—December, 1884.

KEATING *v.* BRUNS.

In the matter of the estate of ANTHONY DELEYER, *deceased.*

Testator, by his will, gave all his property to his executors, in trust, to reduce the personalty to cash and sell the realty, and of the proceeds to invest $15,000, the income whereof they were directed to collect and pay to his minor adopted daughter, M., then living with him, for life ; with remainder over. The personal property was of insignificant value. The will made no other provision for M. Upon the executors' accounting, it appearing that they had in their hands only about $16,000, proceeds of a sale of the real property, which, after payment of commissions and expenses, would not suffice for the investment directed in the will; the court was asked to determine from what date interest, payable to the life beneficiary before the permanent establishment of the fund, was to be calculated—whether (1) from the testator's death, or (2) the end of a year thereafter, or (3) the time when the proceeds of sale of the real property were realized.—

Held, that the real property became personal at the death of testator ; and that M. was entitled, as one to whom the testator stood *in loco parentis*, to interest from the date of that event.

Brown v. Knapp, 79 *N. Y.*, 136—followed.

CONSTRUCTION of decedent's will, upon the judicial settlement of the account of William D. Bruns, and another, executors thereof. The facts are stated in the opinion.

GEO. F. MARTENS, *for executors.*

WM. H. FIELD, *for Margaretta A. Keating, formerly Goerck.*

L. W. EMERSON, *special guardian.*

THE SURROGATE.—The first article of this testator's will directs the payment of his debts. The second (omitting such parts as are foreign to the present inquiry) is as follows: "I give to my executors my real and personal estate upon the following trusts: As soon after my decease as may be done, to reduce my personal estate into cash, to collect the rents and income of my real and personal estate, and to sell all my real estate at public or private sale, and, from the proceeds, in the first place to invest and keep invested $15,000, and to collect the interest and income thereof, and to pay over the same as received to my adopted daughter Margaretta Atelia Goerck, now living with me, for the term of her natural life." The will then provides for the disposition of the principal fund, upon the death of the life beneficiary.

For this adopted daughter, decedent made no other testamentary provision than the one above specified. The personal property which he owned at the time of his death was of insignificant value. As the net proceeds of the sale of all the real estate, the executors received about $21,000. It appears that there is now in their hands the sum of $16,145.92, and that, after the payment of their commissions and of the expenses of this accounting, the remaining assets will not suffice for the investment of the full amount of $15,000, directed by the second article of the will.

Under these circumstances, I am asked to determine whether, in ascertaining the amount that should be paid to the life beneficiary before the permanent establishment of the fund, she should be allowed interest from the death of the testator, or from a year later, or from the time when the proceeds of the sale of the real property were actually realized. The direction to the executors to make that sale was absolute; it was made to depend upon no contingency, and involved the exercise of no discretionary authority. In theory of equity, the land was money from the testator's death. Treating the question of interest, therefore, as if the entire estate had always been personal property in the executor's hands, I am of the opinion that this case falls within the rule promulgated in Brown v. Knapp (79 *N. Y.*, 136). It is a bequest to a minor toward whom the testator stood *in loco parentis*, and for whom he made no provision for support or maintenance, for the year succeeding his death. It is, therefore, a case where he must be presumed to have intended that the legatee should, during that year, be maintained at the expense of his estate (see, also, Lupton v. Lupton, 2 *Johns. Ch.*, 614; Cooke v. Meeker, 36 *N. Y.*, 18; Lowndes v. Lowndes, 15 *Vesey*, 301; Williamson v. Williamson, 6 *Paige*, 298; King v. Talbot, 40 *N. Y.*, 76; Loder v. Hatfield, 71 *N. Y.*, 92).

A decree may be entered accordingly.

New York County.—Hon. D. G. ROLLINS, Surro-gate.—December, 1884.

Herbert *v.* Stevenson.

In the matter of the estate of WASHINGTON M. SMITH, *deceased.*

Since the amendment of Code Civ. Pro., § 2606, made in 1884, a Surrogate's court may require an accounting from the representative of a deceased executor or administrator, in like manner as it might have, from the latter during his lifetime, after revocation of his letters.

Under Code Civ. Pro., § 765, forbidding the entry of a judgment against a party (to an action) who dies before a verdict, report or decision is actually rendered against him,—made applicable to a Surrogate's court by id., § 3347, subd. 6—a contested accounting proceeding abates, abso-lutely, by the death of the accounting party before the matters at issue have been substantially decided.

Leavy v. Gardner, 63 *N. Y.*, 624—followed.

The administrator of a decedent's estate having instituted a special pro-ceeding for the judicial settlement of his account, and a hearing having been had upon exceptions to the report of the referee to whom the account and objections had been referred, the Surrogate, by a written memorandum, announced his conclusions as to certain exceptions, and, as to others, granted leave to the administrator to offer additional evidence, which was introduced. Thereafter the administrator died, before the undetermined issues had been passed upon, and before any decree of settlement had been entered; whereupon contestants sought to revive the special proceeding against the administratrix of his estate.—

Held, that the same had abated by the administrator's death ; that no decree could ever be entered therein ; and that the application for revival must be denied.

APPLICATION by Ella S. Herbert, and others, children of decedent, for the revival of a special proceeding, instituted for the judicial settlement of the account of the administrator of the decedent's estate, against Anna L. Stevenson, the widow and administratrix of the estate of such representative. The facts appear sufficiently in the opinion.

R. W. TOWNSEND, *for petitioners.*

HUGH STEVENSON, *for Anna L. Stevenson.*

THE SURROGATE.—Vernon K. Stevenson, now deceased, was, in his lifetime, administrator of this estate. An accounting proceeding, instituted by him as such administrator, was pending in this court at the time of his death. In December, 1883, the Surrogate, by a written memorandum for counsel, announced the conclusion he had reached in regard to certain exceptions that had been taken to the report of a referee, to whom the account and the objections thereto had been submitted.

As to one of the matters in controversy, leave was given the accounting party to offer additional evidence. Such evidence was afterward, and in Mr. Stevenson's lifetime, introduced; but the issue upon which it bears has not been passed upon by the Surrogate, and no decree has been entered, settling, in whole or in part, the administrator's account. The petitioners, who are children of the decedent Smith, now pray that the accounting proceeding be revived and continued against the widow of Mr. Stevenson, who has lately been appointed his administratrix.

It is admitted that, prior to the recent amendment of § 2606 of the Code of Civil Procedure (see L. 1884, ch. 399), the Surrogate had no jurisdiction to cite A., as executor or administrator of B., to account for B.'s dealings, as executor or administrator of C., with C.'s estate; except for such assets of C. as had come into A.'s possession (Dakin v. Demming, 6 *Paige*, 95; Montross v. Wheeler, 4 *Lans.*, 99; Farnsworth v. Oliphant, 19 *Barb.*, 30; Le Count v. Le Count, 1 *Dem.*, 29; Bunnell v. Ranney, 2 *id.*, 327).

But by § 2606, as it now reads, the Surrogate can require an accounting from a representative of a deceased executor or administrator, just as he might require it from the deceased executor or administrator himself, after the revocation of his letters. There is no doubt, therefore, that, in a new proceeding, this administratrix can be directed to render a full account of her husband's management of decedent's estate. I am convinced, however, that the proceeding, which has abated by Mr. Stevenson's death, cannot be revived.

In Leavy v. Gardner the Special Term of the Court of Common Pleas permitted an action to foreclose a mechanic's lien to be continued, after the death of the defendant, against the defendant's executor. Its action was reversed at General Term, and the reversal affirmed by the Court of Appeals (63 *N. Y.*, 624), upon the ground that the proceeding thus allowed to be continued was not an *action*, within the meaning of the Code, but was a *special proceeding*, to which the Code provisions, respecting the revival of actions, had no application.

I am unable to find any reason for upholding, in the case at bar, the contention of this petitioner's counsel, that might not, in the case of Leavy v. Gardner, have been urged with equal or greater pertinency in behalf of the plaintiff Leavy. Section 755, which provides that actions shall not abate if the cause of action survives, does not apply to Surrogates' courts, but § 765 is expressly made applicable thereto by subdivision 6 of § 3347. This section 765 forms part of title 4 of chapter 8 (the title that treats of "Proceedings upon the death of a party"), and declares that nothing in the title contained shall authorize the entry of a judgment against a party who dies before a verdict, report or decision is actually rendered against him, but that, in such case, the verdict, report or decision is absolutely void.

No "decision," within the meaning of that word in the section just quoted, has been rendered, as to any of the matters at issue in the accounting proceeding (Adams v. Nellis, 59 *How. Pr.*, 385; Weyman v. Bank, *id.*, 331); therefore no decree can ever be entered.

NEW YORK COUNTY.—HON. D. G. ROLLINS, SURRO-
GATE.—December, 1884.

TILDEN *v.* DOWS.

In the matter of the estate of WILLIAM TILDEN,
deceased.

The language of Code Civ. Pro., § 2804,—which allows a person who "is
entitled, by the terms of the will," to the payment of money or delivery of property, to proceed against a testamentary trustee for satisfaction,—indicates, even more strongly than that of id., § 2717, relating
to executors, etc., a purpose to postpone, until a judicial settlement of
the accounts, proceedings to enforce claims made against a testator's
estate by persons holding *assignments* of legacies.
Peyser v. Wendt, 2 *Dem.*, 224—compared.

PETITION by Milano C. Tilden, in his own right,
and Edward P. Kennard, as assignee, for a decree
directing David Dows, and others, executors of
decedent's will, to pay a legacy. The petitioner
alleged that, "by an assignment dated September
6th, 1884, he assigned to said E. P. Kennard his distributive share in the monies, securities and property
in the hands of the executors and trustees under the
will of his late father, and all his right, title and
interest therein."

J. H. CHOATE, *and* C. E. TRACY, *for executors.*

W. S. McFARLANE, *for petitioner.*

THE SURROGATE.—If the petition of Milano C.
Tilden is founded upon § 2717 of the Code of Civil
Procedure it must be denied for the reasons stated
in Peyser v. Wendt (2 *Dem.*, 224).   And the like

reasons compel me to deny it, if it is based upon § 2804.

The only persons, who can be granted the relief which that section provides, are persons "entitled *by the terms* of the will." This language indicates, even more strongly than does that of § 2717, the purpose of the legislature to postpone, until the executor's or trustee's accounting, any proceedings to enforce claims made against a testator's estate by persons holding assignments of legacies. To hold that the assignee of a legacy is entitled thereto "*by the terms* of the will*" would involve a very forced construction of very plain language. The fact that § 2743, which, by § 2811, is made applicable to testamentary trustees, expressly provides that, in a proceeding for judicial settlement of accounts, the claims of assignees can be considered and determined by the Surrogate is, it seems to me, a circumstance of much significance. It justifies the inference that, if the legislature had designed to extend to assignees the privileges of §§ 2717 and 2804, its intention would have been made manifest, and not hidden in words that certainly *seem* to convey a contrary meaning.

There are reasons, that readily suggest themselves, why it may have seemed advisable to afford, to the immediate objects of a testator's bounty, summary relief which no persons else, except creditors, are permitted to enjoy. And the fact that, in proceedings under §§ 2717 and 2804, a petitioner is required to cite nobody but the executor or testamentary trustee, and that the Code makes no provision whatever for bringing in any other parties, is a strong argument in support of the restricted construction that I have put upon those sections. In proceedings thereunder, it seems to have been the intention of the legislature that no persons should participate, except the applicant himself on the one side, and the legal representative of the estate on the other. Now, if the right to make the application is confined to those who, in strict sense, are "entitled under the will," to use the language of § 2717, or "entitled by the terms of the will," in the words of § 2804, this limitation in respect to parties is just and reasonable. But it is very unreasonable and unjust, if the expressions above quoted are accorded an interpretation broad enough to include the assignees of a person so entitled.

The case of Beverly B. Tilden does not essentially differ from that just considered. The instrument creating the trust has in effect constituted Mr. Kennard assignee of Beverly's interest in the estate.

Both petitions must, therefore, be denied.

New York County.—Hon. D. G. ROLLINS, Surrogate.—December, 1884.

Kirk v. Cashman.

In the matter of the estate of Charles Cashman, *deceased.*

The word "children," in a testamentary paper, must be taken in its accustomed sense, and limited to offspring in the first degree, in the absence of indications that the testator intended to give it some other meaning.

Prowitt v. Rodman, 87 *N. Y.*, 42; Beebe v. Estabrook, 79 *id.*, 246—distinguished.

Testator, by his will, gave a share, in remainder, of his residuary estate, after the death or marriage of his widow, "to his sister M., if living, and if not living then to her children." At the widow's death, M. had died leaving, her surviving, sons and daughters and certain grandchildren—children of a son who had died before his mother. Upon the judicial settlement of the executor's account, the context furnishing no evidence favoring an exceptional construction,—

Held, that the surviving sons and daughters of M. took their parent's legacy in equal shares, to the exclusion of the children of their deceased brother.

CONSTRUCTION of decedent's will, upon judicial settlement of the account of Michael H. Cashman, surviving executor thereof.

GRAY & DAVENPORT, *for Mary Walsh and others.*

TOWNSEND WANDELL, *for executor.*

DUDLEY F. PHELPS, *special guardian*

THE SURROGATE.—By the will of this testator, who died in 1847, his residuary estate was given to his executors, to receive the income thereof, and pay the same to his wife while she should live and remain his widow. The will further provided that, upon her death or marriage, such estate should be converted into money, out of which should be paid to his brother Richard, if living, and if not living then to his children, in equal parts, the sum of one thousand dollars; to his sister, Mary Kirk, if living, and if not living then to her children, the sum of three thousand dollars; and a like sum to the children of his deceased brother James.

The testator's widow, who never remarried, recently died. His sister, Mary Kirk, died in 1864, leaving her surviving five children and several remoter descendants, the children and grandchildren of certain of her own children whom she had survived. A decree, settling the accounts of decedent's executor, is about to be entered; and I am asked to decide whether certain children of Thomas Kirk (a son of Mary Kirk) are entitled to share in the second of the above named legacies, Thomas Kirk, their father, having died five years before the death of his mother, the sister of the testator.

It is urged, in their behalf, that they fairly come within the category of "children," as that word is used by the testator. To this proposition I cannot assent. The word "children," like any other word in a testamentary paper, must be taken in its accustomed sense, in the absence of indications that, when the testator used it, he meant to give it some other meaning. I find no such indications in the will now before me, and, upon the authorities below cited, feel bound to hold that the term "children" must here receive its strict construction (Mowatt v. Carow, 7 *Paige*, 328; Sherman v. Sherman, 3 *Barb.*, 387; Lawrence v. Hebbard, 1 *Bradf.*, 255; Hone v. Van Schaick, 3 *N. Y.*, 540; Guernsey v. Guernsey, 36 *id.*, 272; Feit's Executors v. Vannatta, 21 *N. J. Eq.*, 84; Magow v. Field, 48 *N. Y.*, 668; Palmer v. Horn, 84 *id.*, 516; Wylie v. Lockwood, 86 *id.*, 291).

A provision for children was held, in Prowitt v. Rodman (37 *N. Y.*, 42), to include grandchildren and great grandchildren, but in that case the will furnished numerous and striking indications that such was the intention of its maker.

Beebe v. Estabrook (79 *N. Y.*, 246) is cited, in support of the claim that the word "children" ought not to be limited to offspring in the first degree, but the decision in that case is not applicable to the case at bar. The broad signification was there made necessary by a due regard to the spirit and purpose of the statute of advancements.

The surviving sons and daughters of the testator's sister, Mary Kirk, are entitled to equal shares of the legacy in dispute. The decree may provide accordingly.

NEW YORK COUNTY.—HON. D. G. ROLLINS, SURROGATE.—December, 1884.

ANDREWS *v.* GOODRICH.

In the matter of the estate of JOHN W. SCHMIDT, *deceased.*

The doctrine reasserted that, as regards the mode of computing commissions of testamentary trustees, the principal and income of the trust estate are to be treated as one fund, and that, where trustees have already received the statutory allowance of five per cent. upon one thousand dollars, and two and one half per cent. upon nine thousand, one per cent. must thenceforward be the full measure of their compensation.

Slosson v. Naylor, 2 *Dem.*, 257—followed; Hancox v. Meeker, 95 *N. Y.*, 528—distinguished, and commented upon at length.

The only matter determined in Hancox v. Meeker (95 *N. Y.*, 528) declared to be—that the right of a testamentary trustee to make periodical rests in his accounts, and at such times, even without presenting such accounts for settlement, to withhold his lawful commissions, is not limited to cases where by statute, or by general rule, or special order of court, such periodical rests are required or permitted, but extends, also, to cases where, by the direction of his testator's will, or for the proper administration of his testator's estate, he is required to, and does, make periodical payments.

HEARING of objections filed by Emily S. Andrews, a daughter of decedent, and a legatee named in his will, to the account of Ella D. Goodrich, sole surviving executrix of, and trustee under the will, in proceedings for judicial settlement. The facts are stated in the opinion.

BARTLETT, WILSON & HAYDEN, *for objector.*

CRANE & LOCKWOOD, *for executrix.*

THOMAS HAVILAND, *special guardian.*

THE SURROGATE.—In Slosson v. Naylor (2 *Dem.*, 257), a proceeding wherein testamentary trustees were accounting before the Surrogate under circumstances somewhat similar to those that here appear, I decided that, as regarded the mode of computing commissions, the principal and income of the estate should be treated as one fund, and that, as the trustees had been allowed, upon a previous accounting, five per cent. upon one thousand dollars, and two and one half per cent. upon nine thousand dollars, one per cent. must thenceforward be the full measure of their compensation. This doctrine is claimed, by counsel for the accounting party in the case at bar, to have been disapproved by the Court of Appeals, MILLER, J., pronouncing its opinion, in Hancox v. Meeker (95 *N. Y.*, 528).

I have carefully examined the evidence in that

case, the will there under review, the account of the trustees, the briefs of counsel and the decision itself. As a result, I am convinced that the Court of Appeals did not determine the question here at issue, and cannot fairly be claimed to have expressed or intimated an opinion concerning it ; and that, therefore, certain detached phrases which have been quoted from the language of MILLER, J., as decisive of that question, should not be regarded as authoritative.

In Hancox v. Meeker, the trustees annually, at the time of paying to the various *cestuis que trust* their respective shares of income, retained certain sums by way of commissions. Years elapsed before their first accounting. At such accounting, it was claimed, in their behalf, that their several retentions of the amounts withheld should be sanctioned by the Surrogate as just and proper at the time of such retentions respectively. The contestant, on the other hand, objected " to all the items in said account charged as commissions to the executors," upon the ground that they were unlawfully charged, and could not be allowed "until a final settlement of the account."

A referee, to whom the accounts were submitted, having overruled this objection, the contestant excepted, partly upon the ground that no commissions could be allowed, until a final settlement, " and also because said executors had improperly and unlawfully made annual rests, in each year, in the month of April, since the death of the testator, no account having ever been rendered prior to the present one, and in each of said rests he has charged the full commission allowed by law for a single accounting—to wit: at the rate of five, two and one half, and one per cent., respectively." In support of this complaint, that the accounting party had annually deducted commissions at the rate of five, two and one half, and one per cent., there was no evidence whatever, nor was there any pretence of evidence. This was substantially admitted in the brief of appellant's counsel; indeed, the fact that commissions had not been calculated at those rates is apparent from an examination of the account itself. The executors had never received commissions upon the principal of the estate, or upon any part thereof, and it does not appear that, at any one of their so called " annual rests," the entire sum theretofore retained by them as commissions amounted to so much as five per cent. upon the first $1,000, two and one half per cent. upon the next $9,000, and one per cent. upon the balance of the aggregate amount of all income that, up to that time, they had received and paid out. It is evidently in recognition of this state of things that, at page 538 of his opinion, Judge MILLER says: "The trustees retained no commissions on the principal, and it is not made to appear that the amount retained exceeded the amount of their legal commissions, or was in any respect illegal. It is claimed that the amount retained was less than that to which they were entitled, and the contrary is not established." Now, it is evident, from what has been stated already, that, as regards the rate of commissions allowable to trustees upon income that they receive and distribute, no question was before the court in Hancox v. Meeker.

The parties there accounting had, for several years, without judicial sanction but with the knowledge and consent of the *cestuis que trust*, kept for themselves a certain share of the annual income of their testator's estate, as and for their commissions. Their action in this regard had been disapproved by the General Term of the Supreme Court, which had held, upon appeal, that "charges for commissions must be deferred until the final settlement of the accounts." It was with the correctness of that proposition and of that proposition only, that, so far as relates to the matter of commissions, the Court of Appeals concerned itself, in deciding Hancox v. Meeker. And it seems to me that the only matter there determined is this:—that the right of a testamentary trustee to make periodical rests in his accounts, and, at such times, even without presenting such accounts for settlement, to withhold his lawful commissions, is not limited to cases where, by statute, or by general rule, or special order of court, such periodical rests are required or permitted, but extends also, to cases, where by the direction of his testator's will or for the proper administration of his testator's estate, he is required to make and does make periodical payments.

It has not escaped my notice that, in thus enlarging the sphere in which executors and trustees are allowed, in advance of a formal accounting, to retain their commissions, the Court of Appeals has approvingly referred to certain reported cases where the retention or allowance, at stated periods, of full commissions (that is, of commissions at the rate of five, two and one half, and one per cent.) seems to have been sanctioned. But to one who keeps in mind the matters really in controversy, in Hancox v. Meeker, it is evident that, in citing and criticising the various decisions upon which comment is there made, it was simply the purpose of the court to justify the action of the accounting trustees in annually withholding commissions upon income received and distributed; it was not its intention to determine the mode of computing such commissions, nor even, as it seems to me, to intimate an opinion *obiter* upon that subject. I must, therefore, in the case at bar, adhere to the rule laid down in Slosson v. Naylor (*supra*). This I do with the less hesitation because, in other particulars than have yet been specified, the facts here appearing widely differ from those presented in Hancox v. Meeker.

1*st*. As already stated, the trustees had not, in the latter case, received or demanded any commissions upon the *corpus* of the estate; and had apparently retained no more than five, two and one half, and one per cent. upon the aggregate income.

2*d*. There had been accountings out of court between the parties in interest, and the commissions in dispute had been retained by the trustees with the consent of all the beneficiaries, the contestant not excepted.

Giving the decision of the Court of Appeals, therefore, the broadest and most comprehensive effect which can, in any view, be claimed for it, it cannot fairly be regarded as decisive of the matter here in dispute. But for the non-receipt, by the accounting trustees, of commissions on the *corpus*, their annual settlements with the parties beneficiary, and their unopposed retention, at such times, of their compensation, the court might very likely have reached a different conclusion from that which I am asked to accept as decisive of the case at bar.

NEW YORK COUNTY.—HON. D. G. ROLLINS, SURROGATE.—January, 1885.

BRESLIN *v.* SMYTH.

In the matter of the estate of MARGARET B. DUFFY, *deceased.*

After the letters of an executor or administrator have been revoked, a Surrogate's court cannot compel him to account, upon petition of a creditor of the decedent; its authority, in this respect, being limited by Code Civ. Pro., § 2605, to a case where proceedings are instituted by a successor, or a former co-representative.

Such a court is equally without power to issue an injunction against an executor or administrator so removed, or to direct him to pay the claim of an alleged creditor of the decedent, under Code Civ..Pro., § 2717.

Whether a judgment entered against an executor or administrator after the revocation of his letters can be enforced against the decedent's estate, *quære*. If it can, the method is by application, under Code Civ. Pro., § 2609, for leave to sue upon the judgment debtor's official bond.

PETITION by Michael P. Breslin, an alleged creditor of decedent, for an order directing Thomas Smyth, late administrator with the will of decedent annexed, to deposit moneys with the court, and for payment of his claim, and for an accounting, and an injunction. The facts appear in the opinion.

W. J. FANNING, *for petitioner.*

THE SURROGATE.—This petitioner alleges that, on October 13th, 1884, he recovered a judgment in the Superior court against Thomas Smyth, administrator, *c. t. a.*, of this decedent's estate. It appears that, by an order of the Surrogate, entered twenty days before the recovery of such judgment, Smyth's letters as such administrator were revoked. This order of revocation contained no provision for the accounting of the deposed administrator, or for his delivery into this court, or to his successor, of the money or property of the estate in his hands.

The petitioner now asks for relief in various forms: —that Smyth be directed to account, and to make deposit of the property of this estate, and to pay the petitioner the amount of the aforesaid judgment, and that he be restrained from using, until the further order of this court, any funds of the estate still in his possession. Without discussing the propriety of thus including in one petition an application so multifarious, I am clear that such application must, in all its parts, be denied. Section 2603 of the Code of Civil Procedure gives the Surrogate discretionary authority to provide, in a decree revoking the letters of an executor or administrator, for an accounting and for the deposit of such property of the estate as such executor or administrator may have in his hands; but, as has been stated already, the order whereby this respondent was removed from office contains no such provision. Section 2605 specifies the persons who may enforce such an accounting and deposit, and among them such as occupy the attitude of this petitioner are not included.

The fact that the respondent is no longer in office necessitates my denial of this application, so far as it seeks an injunction (§ 2481, subd. 4), and also so far as it asks for an order directing payment of petitioner's claim (§ 2717). It may be doubtful whether, under the circumstances here disclosed, his judgment can be enforced against the estate (§§ 2603, 2604); but if he has a valid claim because of it, or of the demands upon which it is founded, § 2609 points out a method by which its collection may be enforced, in case no successor has been appointed to the deceased administrator.

Petition dismissed.

NEW YORK COUNTY.—HON. D. G. ROLLINS, SURROGATE.—January, 1885.

CLUFF v. TOWER.

In the matter of the estate of BURGESS CLUFF, *deceased.*

Under Code Civ. Pro., § 2481, subd. 6, which authorizes the Surrogate, in a proper case, to vacate a decree of his court, and provides that the powers thus granted "must be exercised . . . . . *in the same manner* as a court of record and of general jurisdiction exercises the same," the manner indicated is that sanctioned by a court of the character mentioned, in proceedings to set aside or open a judgment; the same being properly initiated by a notice of motion or order to show cause.

MOTION by Mary Cluff, decedent's widow, to set aside an order referring issues presented in her petition for the removal of Edward E. Tower, executor of decedent's will.

ROBERT OWEN, *for the motion.*

OLCOTT & MESTRE, *opposed.*

THE SURROGATE.—1*st*. I have already allowed the widow of this decedent to abandon a proceeding that she recently instituted, reserving until now the question what terms, if any, should be exacted as the condition of the discontinuance. The moving party must pay to her adversary $10 costs.

2*d*. Upon careful review of the various provisions of the Code bearing upon the subject, I am persuaded that the moving party has pursued the proper practice, in her proceeding to set aside the order which directed the submission to a referee of the issues presented in her petition for the removal of the executor, and for his accounting. Section 2481, subd. 6 authorizes the Surrogate, in a proper case, to vacate a decree of his court, and provides that the powers thus granted "must be exercised . . . . . in the same manner as a court of record and of general jurisdiction exercises the same powers." That manner is indicated by the practice which, in such courts, is customarily sanctioned in proceedings to set aside or open a judgment. Such proceedings may be begun by a notice of motion, or by an order to show cause.

NEW YORK COUNTY.—HON. D. G. ROLLINS, SURRO-
GATE.—January, 1885.

RICHARDSON *v.* KIDDER.

In the matter of the estate of RICHARD H. BOWNE,
deceased.

It seems, that a surety, who has engaged himself for the whole of a debt,
cannot, by paying part of it, become entitled to stand in the creditor's
shoes, and cannot successfully prosecute his claim against his principal
until such creditor has been fully paid.

Where a creditor receives, from the estate of his debtor, dividends upon a
debt partly secured by the guaranty of a third person, such dividends
should not be appropriated exclusively to the *excess* of the debt, above
the sum guaranteed, but should be applied ratably to the whole indebtedness, thus relieving the surety from liability, to the extent of the
dividend on the part secured.

Decedent who, in his lifetime, was appointed guardian of K., then an infant, and filed an official bond, in a penalty of $60,000, upon which R.
was a surety, died insolvent, and indebted to K. in a large amount.
The latter, having recovered a judgment for more than $70,000 against
decedent's executors, commenced an action against R. which was compromised, R. paying $33,000 and obtaining a release from further
liability. The appropriate dividend upon the whole amount of the
judgment having been paid into court, by the executors, out of the
insolvent estate, K. claimed the entire dividend, while R. contended
that he was entitled to a share thereof proportioned to his payment.—

Held, that the dividend must be divided between the claimants, in the
proportion of the paid to the unpaid portion of the judgment.

PETITION of William F. Kidder, a creditor of decedent, for an order directing payment of his claim.
The facts appear in the opinion.

ALEX. THAIN, *for petitioner.*

DE FORREST & WEEKS, *for executors.*

THE SURROGATE.—This decedent was, many years
since, appointed guardian of William F. Kidder, then

an infant, and, as such guardian, executed and filed with the Surrogate a bond in the sum of $60,000. Upon that bond Joseph Richardson was one of the sureties. Bowne died insolvent in 1881, being indebted to Kidder in a large amount. Kidder soon afterward recovered judgment against Bowne's executors for over $70,000, and then commenced an action against Richardson, the surety. During the pendency of that action, a settlement was effected, by which Richardson paid $33,000, and obtained a release from further liability. Kidder then applied to Bowne's executors for his *pro rata* share of the insolvent estate. The appropriate dividend upon the whole amount of the judgment (about $2,500) has been deposited with the Surrogate, for such person or persons as shall be found entitled thereto.

Richardson insists that, immediately upon his payment of the $33,000, he became a creditor, in that amount, of this decedent's estate, entitled, no less than Kidder, to a dividend. He insists, also, that Kidder's dividend should be calculated, not with reference to the entire amount of his judgment, but with reference, rather, to the amount of such judgment less $33,000; and that, as regards the dividend upon the sum of $33,000, he is himself entitled thereto. Kidder claims, on the other hand, that, as against Richardson, he should receive the entire amount now deposited with the Surrogate.

As a general rule, it is doubtless true that a surety, who has engaged himself for the whole of a debt, cannot, by paying part of it, become entitled to stand in the creditor's shoes, and cannot successfully prosecute his claim against his principal until such creditor has been fully paid. I have found many cases upholding that doctrine; but there is another doctrine, more applicable to the present situation, that seems to be no less firmly established. It has been repeatedly held that, if a creditor receive from the estate of his debtor dividends upon a debt *partly* secured by the guaranty of a third person, such dividends should not be exclusively appropriated to the *excess* of the debt above the sum guaranteed, but should be applied ratably to the total indebtedness, thus relieving the surety from liability, to the extent of the dividend on the part secured (Raikes v. Todd, 8 *Adol. & Ell.*, 846; Thornton v. McKewan, 1 *Hem. & M.*, 525; Midland Banking Co. v. Chambers, *L. R.*, 4 *Ch. App.*, 398).

Now, in the present case, Richardson, having been fully exonerated from liability for such part of his original obligation as he has not paid, stands, as it seems to me, as to the part he has paid, in precisely the same attitude that he would occupy if, from the very beginning, he had been under the partial obligation only. The decisions in Ewart v. Latta (4 *Macq.*, 983), Ex parte Hope (3 *Mont., D. & D.*, 720), and Midland Banking Co. v. Chambers (*supra*) are cited in opposition to this view. Those cases are clearly distinguishable from the case at bar. In the first, the surety had not discharged himself from his liability by the partial payment, and in both the others the surety had, by agreement, relinquished to the creditor all claims to dividend from his principal's estate.

Let a decree be entered in conformity with this opinion.

New York County.—Hon. D. G. ROLLINS, Surro-GATE.—January, April, 1885.

TILBY v. TILBY.

In the matter of the application for probate of a paper propounded as the will of JAMES TILBY, deceased.

Although Code Civ. Pro., § 1023 has no application to a Surrogate's court, which, therefore, cannot be required to determine particular questions before rendering its decision,—its authority to pass upon proposed findings, after such rendition, is expressly recognized by id., § 2545.

Gormerly v. McGlynn, 84 *N. Y.*, 285—distinguished.

The provisions of Code Civ. Pro., limiting the time for taking an appeal from a Surrogate's court to thirty days from the time of service of a copy of the decree or order complained of (§ 2572), and declaring that, to render an appeal effectual for any purpose, the appellant must give an undertaking to the effect specified (§ 2577); and General Rules of Practice 32 and 33, requiring a *case* to be made and served within ten days after service of a copy of the decree or order, but permitting the Surrogate to allow further time, etc.; are to be construed independently of each other: under these regulations, the Surrogate may enlarge the time for making and serving a *case* before the appeal is perfected by filing security, if the time for perfecting the same has not expired.

SUBMISSION, by James Tilby, and another, decedent's heirs at law, and contestants of his alleged will, of requests for findings, after decision rejecting the paper propounded as such will by Sara C. W. Tilby, as decedent's widow.

D. S. RIDDLE, *for proponent.*

J. F. MALCOLM, *for contestants.*

THE SURROGATE.—Counsel for contestants herein has submitted certain proposed findings, upon the various questions involved in the controversy recently decided by the Surrogate, touching the genuineness and validity of the paper propounded as this decedent's will. It is objected, by proponent's counsel, that, at this stage of the proceedings, the Surrogate, having rendered his decision, has no authority to pass upon proposed findings. This objection is not well taken, and finds no support in the decision of the Court of Appeals in Gormerly v. McGlynn (84 *N. Y.*, 285), cited by proponent's counsel. That cause was tried at special term of the Supreme court, one of the tribunals to which § 1023 of the Code of Civil Procedure has undisputed application. This section provides that requests to find shall be presented before a cause is finally submitted to a judge or referee; and, according to the decision in Gormerly v. McGlynn, it has done away with the proceedings, in that regard, prescribed by the thirty-second of the General Rules of Practice, before its recent amendment. But with § 1023 Surrogates' courts have no concern (see Code Civ. Pro., § 3347, subd. 7). By § 2545, however, it is expressly declared that, upon the settlement of a case, either party may request a finding upon any question of fact, or a ruling upon any question of law (Hartwell v. McMaster, 4 *Redf.*, 389; Matter of Chauncey, 32 *Hun*, 430).

PROPONENT having made an application for an extension of time to make, and serve a copy of, a

case upon appeal from the decree rejecting the
alleged will, the following opinion was filed, April
14th, 1885 :

THE SURROGATE.—This is an application for an extension of time, within which to make a case on
appeal.   It is urged, in opposition, that the Surrogate
is powerless to grant it, because of the fact that the
security required by § 2577 of the Code of Civil Procedure has not been filed, and that, accordingly, the
appeal is for no purpose effectual.   It is true that,
for the reason specified, the appeal is as yet incomplete, but the time within which it may be perfected
has not yet expired.

Rule 32 of the General Rules of Practice provides
that, on appeal from this court, a case must be made
and served within ten days after service of a copy of
the decree or order appealed from ; but it also provides that further time may be allowed by the Surrogate.   Rule 33 declares that, if a party omits to make
a case within the time limited by rule 32 (that is,
within ten days, plus such further time, if any, as
may have been allowed), he shall be deemed to have
waived his right thereto.

Now, if the opposition to this application is well
founded, and the time for making a case cannot be
enlarged while the appeal is still unperfected, it follows that the appellant .must, at the peril of utterly
losing his right to a review of such alleged errors as
took place at the trial, but are not part of the record,
either prepare and serve a case within precisely ten
days, or within the ten days file security.   No such

result can have been contemplated by the statute regulating the procedure on appeal, or by the Rules of Practice above cited.

Section 2572 of the Code provides that an appeal by a party must be taken within thirty days after service of a copy of the decree or order from which the appeal is taken. Section 2577, as has been stated already, requires that an undertaking shall be given, before such appeal can be made effectual.

I think that these requirements and the requirements of the Rules are entirely independent of each other, and that the Surrogate may, at any time after the entry of the decree or order sought to be reviewed, extend the time for making and serving a case, even though the appeal has not been perfected, provided that the time for perfecting it is as yet unexpired (Salls v. Butler, 27 *How. Pr.*, 133).

Application granted.

NEW YORK COUNTY.—HON. D. G. ROLLINS, SURROGATE.—January, 1885.

PENDLE *v.* WAITE.

In the matter of the estate of CHARLES WAITE, *deceased.*

In order to entitle one to proceed, under Code Civ. Pro., § 2715. as a creditor of a decedent, against the executor or administrator of the latter, to compel the filing of an inventory, he must either distinctly declare himself to be such a creditor, or set forth facts showing that he is entitled in that capacity (id., § 2514, subd. 11).

APPLICATION by George Pendle, to compel Mary G. Waite, executrix of decedent's will, to file an inventory.

PAYSON MERRILL, *for the application.*

WM. BLAKIE, *for executrix.*

THE SURROGATE.—George Pendle has applied for an order· compelling the executrix of this decedent's will to file an inventory. He alleged, in his affidavit, that he was, for some time prior to February, 1882, engaged in business with one Charles Waite, a son of the decedent, under the firm name of Pendle & Waite; that, during the said month of February, without his knowledge or consent, his partner paid this decedent, out of the firm assets, the sum of $10,000; that the firm was not, at that time, indebted to decedent in a larger sum than $100; that, as against himself (Pendle) and the creditors of the firm, such payment was fraudulent and void; that the decedent never repaid that sum or any portion thereof, and that, therefore, "the said firm *or* its legal representative" has a valid claim against this estate for the said sum of $10,000. I think that counsel for the executrix is correct in claiming that the moving party does not show himself entitled to the relief for which he asks.

Section 2715 of the Code of Civil Procedure gives "a creditor or person interested in the estate" of a decedent the right of enforcing the filing of an inventory by such decedent's executor or administrator. Within the meaning of that section Mr. Pendle is not "interested in the estate" (see definition of that term in § 2514 subd. 11). If, therefore, he can justly insist upon the entry of an order directing that an inventory be filed, it is because he is a "creditor" of this estate. Now, it is true as counsel for the executrix insists, that he does not distinctly *declare* himself to be such creditor, nor allege facts which show him to be entitled as such.

It is not enough for him to aver that some person other than himself is a creditor, even though the allegation to that effect be undisputed. Nor is it sufficient for him to declare, as he does, that "*either* the said firm *or* its legal representative" has a valid claim, etc. His application must, therefore, be denied.

NEW YORK COUNTY.—HON. D. G. ROLLINS, SURROGATE.—January, 1885.

MATTER OF BERRIEN.

In the matter of the estate of PETER B. BERRIEN, *deceased.*

Old age and physical infirmity are not, *per se*, disqualifications for the office of administrator of the estate of an intestate.

APPLICATION for letters of administration, in intestacy.

FRANKLIN B. LORD, *for widow.*

THE SURROGATE.—Old age and bodily ailments and infirmities do not, of themselves, disqualify one from appointment to the office of administrator. The evidence that has been submitted, respecting the physical and mental condition of this decedent's widow, has not satisfied me that she is, within the meaning of R. S., part 2, ch. 6, tit. 2, § 32, as amended, "incompetent" to execute the duties of administratrix, "by reason of want of understanding."

Letters may, therefore, issue to Rachel Berrien, in conjunction with Alonzo Baker. •

New York County.—Hon. D. G. ROLLINS, Surrogate.—January, 1885.

Sayre v. Sayre.

In the matter of the estate of Rachel Sayre, *deceased.*

Upon an application, by the personal representative of a deceased legatee under decedent's will, to compel the executor thereof to account, the latter filed an affidavit alleging that he, petitioner's intestate, and another were the only "heirs at law" of their mother, the decedent, and that they had "divided and settled the estate of their mother, and passed and received releases to each other, and to deponent individually and as executor;" without setting forth the so-called releases or disclosing their character.—

Held, that such affidavit showed no cause why petitioner's application should not be granted.

Petition by Delia A. Sayre, to compel Henry D. Sayre, executor of decedent's will, to "make and render a judicial settlement of his accounts and proceedings," as such executor.

Jonathan Marshall, *for petitioner.*

Wm. C. Traphagen, *for executor.*

THE SURROGATE.—The petitioner, as the administratrix of the late John J. R. Sayre, who was a legatee under this decedent's will, seeks to compel an accounting from decedent's executor. The executor has filed an affidavit, wherein he alleges that petitioner's husband, Elizabeth A. Greer, and himself were the "only heirs at law" of their mother, the decedent, and that they "divided and settled the estate of their mother, and passed and received releases to each other, and to this deponent, individually and as executor." The respondent claims, accordingly, that the petitioner has no interest in the estate. It is insisted, in opposition, that the affidavit, assuming its contents to be true, fails to establish such lack of interest in the petitioner. The contents of the so called releases are not set forth, nor are their nature and character in anywise disclosed. The antecedent statement, that the three children of decedent "divided and settled" their mother's estate, does not justify the inference that the "releases" were of such sort as to have precluded the petitioner's intestate in his lifetime, or herself since his death, from demanding an accounting.

As matters now stand, I must grant the application, but shall delay for ten days the entry of any order. Within that time, the respondent is permitted to file any release or releases referred to in his affidavit, or to file an additional affidavit, containing more definite allegations in the premises.

NEW YORK COUNTY.—HON. D. G. ROLLINS, SURRO-
GATE.—January, 1885.

ZAPP *v.* MILLER.

In the matter of the estate of ADAM MULLER, *deceased.*

Decedent, during his lifetime, assigned a certain leasehold to Z., who, to
secure a part of the consideration, gave back a bond, and mortgage
thereof, conditioned for the payment of $3,700, in semiannual instal-
ments " until the whole principal sum is fully paid, and interest on the
amount from time to time remaining unpaid . . . . . at the rate of
seven per cent., per annum." Z. assigned the lease, subject to the
mortgage, which the assignee assumed and agreed to pay, to M., who
assigned to another without mentioning the mortgage. Thereafter M.,
having been appointed executor of decedent's will, which disposed of the
estate for life, with remainder over, caused the mortgage to be satisfied
of record, and filed an account charging himself with no indebtedness
in the premises. Upon a judicial settlement of M.'s account, had
after the death of the life tenant, and to which the latter's representative was not a party, no evidence was given of the payment of any
part of the principal of the mortgage, or interest thereon.—

Held, that M., by his assumption, became decedent's debtor in the amount
of the mortgage, and was chargeable therewith, in favor of the remaindermen, with interest at the rate of seven per cent., from the date of
the instrument, save for the period between the death of the decedent
and that of the life tenant.

Warner v. Knower, *ante,* 208—compared.

Where a will gave to testator's widow the income of all his estate, " after
deducting taxes, assessments, interest on mortgages, if any, *and other
charges and expenses,* for and during her natural life,"—

Held, under the doctrine of *ejusdem generis,* that disbursements for funeral expenses, transportation of decedent's remains, and services of his
attending physician, were chargeable to the *corpus* of the estate, and
not to income.

HEARING of exceptions to the report of referee, to
whom were referred the account of Charles J. Miller,
the executor of decedent's will, and the objections
thereto, filed by Catharine Zapp, a legatee, in proceedings for judicial settlement.

F. H. RODENBURGH, *for executor.*

BLISS & SCHLEY, *for objector.*

THE SURROGATE.—To the account of this testator's executor, filed in October, 1883, various objections were interposed on behalf of Catharine Zapp, a legatee. The issues thus raised were submitted to a referee, whose report is before me for review. Such of its findings as have been excepted to by the executor I shall now proceed to consider.

In October, 1871, one Jacob Zapp mortgaged to this decedent, for the sum of $3,700, certain leasehold property in the city of New York. The mortgage was given to secure the payment of a part of the consideration for decedent's assigning the lease of such property to the mortgagor. In February, 1875, this lease was assigned by Zapp to Charles J. Miller, the person here accounting as executor, "subject," as was in the assignment set forth, " to a certain mortgage . . . . . to secure the sum of $3,700, which said Charles J. Miller hereby assumes and agrees to pay." In March, 1879, Miller assigned the lease to another, by an instrument that made no mention of the mortgage. In November of the same year, he became this decedent's executor, and, in January, 1882, as such executor, caused the mortgage to be satisfied of record.

In his account on file, he has charged himself with no indebtedness in connection with the transactions above described, and at the trial before the referee no evidence was offered tending to show that any sum, either as principal or interest, had been paid upon the bond whose payment the mortgage was given to secure.   I concur with the referee in holding that Miller, by assuming this mortgage, became decedent's debtor, and, as such, subject to precisely the same liability as that to which his assignor had been subject theretofore (Fleishhauer v. Doellner, 9 *Abb. N. C.*, 372 ; Burr v. Beers, 24 *N. Y.*, 178 ; Comstock v. Drohan, 71 *id.*, 9).

The referee finds that there should be charged, against this executor, interest at the rate of seven per cent., from the date of the mortgage until now, save for the period between the decedent's death and the death of the life tenant.   He finds that, during that interval, such life tenant was alone entitled to interest on the mortgage in question, and that the executor is not called upon to account therefor in this proceeding, to which the representatives of such life tenant are not parties.   I sustain the referee's conclusions, both as to the time for which interest should be charged, and as to the rate at which it should be computed.   The mortgage is conditioned for the payment of " $3,700, in instalments and manner following, viz.: the sum of $500 on the first day of July, 1873, and a further sum of $500, or more, every succeeding six months thereafter, viz.: every first day of January and July thereafter, *until the whole principal sum is fully paid, and interest on the amount from time to time remaining unpaid*, to be computed from November 1st, 1871, at and after the rate of seven per cent., per annum, to be paid half-yearly on the first day of January and July of each and every year." ·

Under the decision of the Court of Appeals, in O'Brien v. Young (95 *N. Y.*, 428), I hold that the interest on the mortgage here in question is still running against this executor at 7 per cent.   There is nothing in the recent opinion of the Surrogate, in Warner v. Knower (*ante*, 208), that is in conflict with this notion.   It was there held that, despite the statute declaring that, for certain purposes, an executor's indebtedness to his decedent's estate must be regarded as so much money in his hands, assets of such estate, a debtor-executor is, nevertheless, chargeable with legal interest upon the amount of his debt until such debt has in fact been paid, and that the obligation of such debtor-executor, in that regard, is precisely like the obligation of any other debtor under like circumstances.   Now, in the present case, this executor is chargeable with the same amount of interest that the original mortgagor would be bound to pay, if the lease had never been signed by him, and if the executor had never assumed any liability on the mortgage.

I sustain the exception respecting the disbursement of $618 for funeral expenses, including expenses for transportation of decedent's body, and for services of his attending physician.   The referee does not question the reasonableness and propriety of these expenditures, but holds that, by the terms of the will, they are properly chargeable against the income, and not against the *corpus* of the estate.   The will provides that the testator's widow shall have the interest and income of all his estate, real and personal, "after deducting taxes, assessments, interest on mortgages, if any, and other charges and expenses, for and during

her natural life." I have no doubt that the signification of the general words "other charges and expenses" is narrowed by their association with the words
preceding (Stephens v. Taprell, 2 *Curt.*, 458; Newman v. Newman, 26 *Beav.*, 220; Cook v. Oakley,
1 *P. Wms.*, 302; Barnaby v. Tassell, *L. R.*, 11 *Eq.*,
363; Roberts v. Kuffin, 2 *Atk.*, 112; Minor's Executor v. Dabney, 3 *Rand.*, *Va.*, 191).

The doctrine of *ejusdem generis* is not always one
of easy application, but it can be here applied without
difficulty. The "other charges and expenses," that
are to be deducted from the interest and income, are
charges and expenses which, *like* taxes, assessments
and interest on mortgages, are ordinarily charged
upon a life tenant.

NEW YORK COUNTY.—HON. D. G. ROLLINS, SURRO-
GATE.—January, 1885.

LARKIN *v.* SALMON.

In the matter of the estate of WILLIAM SALMON,
deceased.

A gift, by will, of "all the money left in the W. S. Bank, after carrying
out" (certain prior directions contained in the will), is a specific legacy
of a chose in action, which the legatee is entitled to receive *in specie*,
together only with such increment as may have attached thereto. No
claim will lie, under any circumstances, against the executors, for
interest, *eo nomine*, thereon; nor are they bound to make the same
productive.

Platt v. Moore, 1 *Dem.*, 191—followed.

HEARING of exceptions to report of referee, to whom were referred the account of Patrick Salmon and another, as executors of decedent's will, and the objections thereto, filed by Mary Larkin and another, decedent's sisters, upon proceedings for judicial settlement.

DEVELIN & MILLER, *for executors.*

M. S. THOMPSON, *for objectors.*

THE SURROGATE.—The first three clauses of the will of this testator contain directions for paying two legacies of $1,000 each, and for fencing a plot in Calvary Cemetery.   The fourth clause is unimportant for present purposes.   The fifth is in .words following: "All the money left in the West Side Bank, after carrying out the directions in the first three clauses of this my will, I direct to be divided between my wife, my three sisters and my brother, share and share alike."

As one of the results of an examination, before a referee, of the accounts of this decedent's executors, it appears that, after such executors had made certain payments out of moneys left by decedent in the West Side Bank, there remained on deposit in such bank, and applicable to the discharge of the bequest contained in the fifth clause of the will, the sum of $3,861.22.   Upon this amount, less $500, the referee finds that the executors are chargeable with interest at 3 per cent., from July 1st, 1883, about one year after the testator's death, until December 1st, 1884, six months after the executors had filed their account.

To this finding the accounting parties have excepted. Their exception must be sustained.

The legacy given by the fifth article of the will is a "specific legacy," as it seems to me, within the definition of that expression sanctioned by the highest judicial tribunals (Bothamley v. Sherson, *L. R.*; 20 *Eq.*, 304 ; Fontaine v. Tyler, 9 *Price*, 94 ; Stephenson ·v. Dowson, 3 *Beav.*, 342 ; Kirby v. Potter, 4 *Ves.*, 748 ; Mayo v. Bland, 4 *Md. Ch.*, 484 ; Walton v. Walton, 7 *Johns. Ch.*, 256 ; Towle v. Swaysey, 106 *Mass.*, 100). As such specific legacy, it does not draw interest, *eo nomine*. The legatee is entitled to receive it *in specie*, together with such increment as may actually have attached to it,—nothing more and nothing less (Murphy v. Marcellus, 1 *Dem.*, 288 ; Platt v. Moore, *id.*, 191, *and cases cited*).

Now, it is not claimed, in the case at bar, that the legacy under consideration has actually earned any interest. On the contrary, it is for the very reason that the executors have failed to make such legacy productive that the referee finds them accountable. I have been referred to no reported case, in which an executor has been held chargeable with interest for neglecting to convert into money the thing given as a specific legacy, and to invest the proceeds for the benefit of the legatee. And I see no reason for abandoning the doctrine asserted in Platt v. Moore (*supra*), where it was held that the executors of a testator who had bequeathed certain insurance policies as a specific legacy were not bound to collect the policies, but would perform their full duty by merely delivering and assigning them to the beneficiary.

It would scarcely have been claimed, if the bequest here in dispute had been a bequest of books or jewels or household furniture, that the executors would have been bound, or would, indeed, have been authorized, to sell the things bequeathed, and make investment of the proceeds for the benefit of the legatees. And I know of no rule of law, applicable in such a case, that is not equally applicable in a case like the present, where there is a legacy of a chose in action.

The exception to the referee's report is, therefore, sustained.

New York County.—Hon. D. G. ROLLINS, Surrogate.—January, 1885.

BLISS *v.* OLMSTEAD.

In the matter of the estate of Eliza A. Stebbins, *deceased.*

Testatrix, by her will, after bequeathing, absolutely and in trust, divers preferred pecuniary legacies, amounting to $51,300, directed the executor, in order to satisfy them, to use any bonds or securities she might leave, having a market value not less than par, reckoning the same at par (including accrued interest), without regard to the ruling premium, as if they had been specific legacies, so that all the legatees should receive the same proportional amounts out of her estate; and authorized the executor to retain any securities as trust funds or to sell any thereof for the purposes of distribution. She left municipal bonds of different cities, commanding a premium in the market, of the par value of $38,500, which the executors sold, and also other securities.—
Held, that the preferred legatees were entitled, *pro rata,* to the proceeds of the sales of the $38,500 bonds, with the accrued interest, and the premium realized, and also whatever increase had attached thereto, but not to interest, *eo nomine,* on the proceeds; and that the deficiency,

ascertainable by deducting the par value of such bonds from the aggregate amount of such legacies, was payable as general legacies, with interest, in the respective cases, from the death of testatrix, or from the expiration of one year thereafter, under the ordinary rules.

UPON the judicial settlement of the account of Dwight H. Olmstead, as executor of the will of decedent, he asked the court for an interpretation of the will, in relation to the distribution of the residue. The facts appear in the opinion.

L. D. OLMSTEAD, *for executor.*

THEO. W. DWIGHT, *special guardian of Henry L. Bliss and others, infant legatees.*

THE SURROGATE.—By the clauses in her last will that are numbered from 3 to 13 inclusive, this decedent bequeaths divers legacies. By clauses 13 and 14 she establishes a scheme for discharging those legacies in terms following :

" I direct that all the foregoing bequests shall be paid and satisfied in full in the manner herein provided, and prior to the subsequent bequests made by this will, and to allowances and expenses of administration, which subsequent bequests are to be paid *pro rata* in case of a deficiency of assets to pay them in full. In paying the foregoing legacies, and in setting apart the above mentioned trust funds, my executor shall use any bonds or securities I may leave, the market value whereof is not less than par, together with the accrued interest thereon, reckoning such bonds and securities at their par value (including accrued interest), without regard to the premium on or market value of said bonds and securities, in the

same manner as if they had been specific legacies;
that is to say, in case of a bequest to any legatee
above named equal to the par value of one or more
bonds, said bonds, with the interest accrued thereon,
shall be turned over and given to such legatee in
satisfaction of such bequest, and the distribution of
bonds and payments shall be such that all my aforesaid nephews and nieces and *cestuis que trust* shall
receive the same proportionate amounts out of my
estate, according to the foregoing bequests to them
or for their benefit respectively, and my said executor shall be at liberty to retain any such bonds or
securities as he may select for the trust funds until
the termination of said trust, or to sell any bonds for
the purpose of making such distribution."

It seems clear to me that, by virtue of the provisions just quoted, the executor of this estate is authorized—if, indeed, he is not absolutely required—to
discharge, so far as may be, all legacies bequeathed
in clauses preceding clause 14, by one or the other
of two methods: 1*st*, by the actual turning over to
the beneficiaries of bonds that have a market value
at or above par; or, 2*d*, by turning over the proceeds
of such bonds, in the event that the executor may
have seen fit to convert them into money for convenience of distribution.

The preferred legatees, to the extent that their
bequests can be satisfied by the direct use of such
securities as are applicable to their satisfaction, or by
using the proceeds of such securities are, in effect,
legatees of specific legacies, and are entitled, as such,
to whatever, by way of increment, may have become

attached to such legacies at the time of their discharge. As I read this will, the testatrix substantially says to her executor: "If you shall find in my estate bonds or securities worth their par value or more than that, apply them, as far as they will reach, in satisfaction of the preferred legacies, or, if you choose, sell them and apply their proceeds. Do this, however, in such fashion that no one of the preferred legatees shall fare better than his fellows; and that the employment of securities, or proceeds of securities, in satisfaction of the preferred legacies as a class, shall operate to discharge such legacies to the extent of the par value of such securities only, however largely in excess of such par value their real or market value may chance to be."

Now, it appears that decedent left, at her death, certain bonds of municipal and railroad corporations, and certain promissory notes secured by mortgages. Of those bonds a portion were worth less than par. They are not, therefore, "such bonds or securities" as are referred to in clauses 13 and 14. Nor do the promissory notes fall within that category. The total value of all the bonds and securities specially applicable to the discharge of the preferred legacies is $38,500, made up of the items following: New York city bonds, $24,500; Holyoke and Westfield bonds, $10,000; New Haven and Northampton bonds, $4,000.

The bequests to the preferred legatees are, in the aggregate, $51,300. In partial satisfaction of this last named sum, i. e., to the amount of $38,500, I hold that the proceeds realized by the executor, from the sale of the bonds above enumerated, may properly be applied.

The preferred legatees are entitled, *pro rata*, to all such proceeds, including not only the income that had accrued upon the bonds when sold, but also the liberal premium that they then commanded, in the same manner and with the same effect as if the legacies had been, in the strictest sense, specific legacies of the bonds themselves. And I further hold that, as to this $38,500, the preferred legatees are not entitled to interest, *eo nomine*. They have no better claim, it seems to me, than they could have maintained, in case such bonds had, in terms, been specifically bequeathed, and it has been repeatedly decided that the legatee of a specific bequest is not entitled to interest as such. Whatever produce may have actually accrued upon his legacy belongs to him ; no more and no less (Murphy v. Marcellus, 1 *Dem.*, 288 ; Platt v. Moore, *id.*, 191, *and cases cited*).

It has been stated already that the total amount of the preferred legacies is $51,300. A deduction therefrom of the par value of the bonds applicable to their discharge ($38,500) leaves remaining the sum of $12,800.   To the extent of this $12,800, the bequests in question are simply general legacies, differing from those that follow the 14th clause in this circumstance alone, that they command priority of payment. Such of them as are given in trust for the support and maintenance of *cestuis que trust* are entitled to interest from the death of the testatrix (Nahmens v. Copely, 2 *Dem.*, 253).   The others are entitled from a year later, and so, too, are all the unpreferred

legacies, except the trust provision for the benefit of
Cloe Bates Sackett, which is allowed interest from
decedent's death.

NEW YORK COUNTY.—HON. D. G. ROLLINS, SURRO-
GATE.—February, June, 1885.

RANK *v.* CAMP.

In the matter of the estate of FREDERIC GROTE,
deceased.

Upon an application for an order directing a temporary administrator to
pay to the applicant a sum of money on account of a legacy or distributive share to which he is entitled, a citation is properly addressed to
and served upon the administrator alone.

The force and effect of a testamentary provision cannot be finally determined upon an application for an advance upon a legacy, made under
Code Civ. Pro., § 2717.

During the pendency of a special proceeding, instituted to procure a decree
admitting to probate a paper propounded as the will of decedent, one
of the latter's next of kin, who was named as legatee in the disputed
instrument, having applied for a decree directing the payment to her of
a sum of money, to be reckoned as part of her distributive share, or of
her legacy, according to the event, the executor filed an answer setting
forth that the applicant was opposing the admission to probate of the
alleged will, which contained a clause declaring that, in case any
legatee should contest the validity of the instrument, the provision in
his favor should cease, and fall into the residue.—

Held, that the facts set forth showed that the applicant had rendered
"doubtful" her claims as legatee, and that, under Code Civ. Pro.,
§ 2718, subd. 1, the petition must be dismissed.

PETITION by Mary C. Rank, decedent's daughter,
to compel Hugh N. Camp, temporary administrator
of decedent's estate, to pay her a sum of money as
legatee or distributee.

REDFIELD & LYDECKER, *for petitioner.*

G. W. COTTERILL, *for proponents.*

THE SURROGATE.—This estate is now in the hands of a temporary administrator pending a controversy over the probate of a paper propounded as decedent's will. The contestant in that proceeding has presented a petition, whereby she asks that such temporary administrator be directed to pay her, out of the first moneys that shall come into his hands, some sum of money on account of her legacy or distributive share. The citation issued upon this petition is addressed to the temporary administrator only, and upon him alone has it been served. In this respect, however, the petitioner seems to have complied with the requirements of the Code (§§ 2672, 2717, 2718).

No answer has been interposed by the temporary administrator, but, on the return day of the citation, counsel for the proponents asked leave to file an affidavit or affidavits in response to the allegations of the petition, in the event that the Surrogate should hold that, upon its face, it entitles the petitioner to relief.

I so hold, and give leave to proponents' counsel to file affidavits on or before Monday, the 9th inst.

THE proponents having interposed an answer disputing the petitioner's claim, the following opinion was filed June 11th, 1885:

THE SURROGATE.— The daughter of this testator is opposing the probate of the paper propounded as his

will. Pending the controversy, she asks that, out of
the assets of the estate, there be paid to her a sum of
money, to be reckoned as part of her distributive
share as next of kin, in case her contest shall prove
successful, and, in case it shall fail, to be reckoned as
part of her legacy. The proponents dispute the petitioner's claim, and set forth facts that, as they contend, make its validity and legality doubtful. It is
insisted in their behalf that, under these circumstances,
the Surrogate should dismiss the proceeding, in accordance with the express directions of § 2718 of the
Code of Civil Procedure. The grounds upon which
the proponents attack the contestant's right to take
any benefit from her father's will are these:

The paper in controversy contains the following
provision:

(Article 34): "Should any legatee or devisee contest the validity hereof, or any of the provisions
herein contained, then any bequest or disposition
herein made in favor of any such contestant shall
thereupon cease, and be immediately revoked, can-
celed and annulled, and all gifts, bequests," etc.,
"herein given to any such contestant shall thereupon
immediately become and form a part of the rest,
residue and remainder of my estate," etc.

Now, if the provision just quoted is valid and effectual, the proponents are obviously correct in claiming
that, in case the paper of which it forms a part shall
be established as the testator's will, the contestant
will be discovered to have no interest whatever in the
estate.

The force and effect of Article 34 cannot of course

be finally determined upon this application, but the matter must, nevertheless, be provisionally considered for the purpose of ascertaining whether the contestant's action in opposing probate has rendered "doubtful" her claim as legatee. The validity of such a condition as burdens the dispositions of the paper before me has not, so far as I am advised, been passed upon by the Court of Appeals of this State, or by any of our appellate tribunals.

In Jackson v. Westerfield (61 *How. Pr.*, 399), an action for the construction of a will, it was held by VAN VORST, J., that a clause in the disputed paper, which imposed restraints upon proper inquiry into testamentary capacity and the legality and validity of dispositions of property, should not be favored. The learned Justice cited, in support of that proposition, several English cases, holding that such conditions were to be treated, so far as regards bequests of personalty, *and in cases where there was no gift over*, as not obligatory but as *in terrorem* only, and he held that non-compliance with the conditions would not work a forfeiture where there was *probabilis causa litigandi.*

It has already appeared that, in the present case, there is an express direction that any forfeited bequest or devise shall go to the residuary legatees and devisees. Now, there are many decisions in the English courts which sustain the right of a testator to provide that, for unsuccessful opposition to the probate of his will, one named as a beneficiary shall forfeit his devise or legacy, and this especially when the testator has provided for a gift over. Aside from other and earlier cases that support this proposition, may be cited Cooke v. Turner (15 *M. & W.*, 727), Stevenson v. Abington (11 *W. R.*, 935), and Evanturel v. Evanturel (*L. R.*, 6 *P. C.*, 1).

The validity of such conditions as are here under discussion was maintained by the Supreme Court of Ohio, in Bradford v. Bradford (19 *Ohio State*, 546), and was denied by the Supreme Court of Pennsylvania, in Chew's Appeal (45 *Penn. St.*, 228).

It is unnecessary to pursue the subject further. I certainly should not feel justified, in the present state of the law, in holding that the question, whether the contestant has forfeited all claim as legatee under the will, is entirely free from doubt, and must, therefore, in obedience to § 2718, as interpreted by the Court of Appeals, in Hurlburt v. Durant (88 *N. Y.*, 121), dismiss this petition, without prejudice to any claim that the contestant may hereafter make, after the probate proceedings have terminated.

NEW YORK COUNTY. — HON. D. G. ROLLINS, SURROGATE. — February, 1885.

KOCH *v.* WOEHR.

In the matter of the estate of GEORGE KOCH, *deceased.*

The direction—which, it is provided by Code Civ. Pro., § 2748, must be inserted in a decree for the distribution of a decedent's assets—to the executor or administrator to pay to the county treasurer a legacy or share which is not paid *to the person entitled* thereto, within a time specified, is generally of no practical importance, and may in most cases with propriety be omitted.

Testator, by his will, gave the residue to "my (his) brothers and sisters now living, and the descendants of any deceased brothers and sisters." Upon the judicial settlement of the executor's account, it appeared that decedent once had a sister, A., of whom nothing further was known.—

Held, that the share of A., if living, or of her descendants, if any, could not properly be left in the executor's hands, subject to a direction, in the decree, to pay the same to the county treasurer, at the expiration of two years, in the contingency specified in Code Civ. Pro., § 2748, but that a reference must be had to determine who was *the person entitled* thereto.

SETTLEMENT of decree upon judicial settlement of account of Frederick Woehr, as executor of decedent's will. Christian Koch and others of decedent's next of kin appeared in the proceedings.

KURZMAN & YEAMAN, *for executor.*

VON BRANDENSTEIN & BRUNO, *for Christian Koch.*

THE SURROGATE.—It is provided, by § 2748 of the Code of Civil Procedure, that a decree for distribution of the assets of a decedent's estate shall "direct the executor or administrator to pay to the county treasurer a legacy or distributive share, which is not paid to the person entitled thereto at the expiration of two years from the time when the decree is made, or when the legacy or distributive share is payable by the terms of the decree."

Though the direction for inserting this provision in decrees of distribution is, in terms, one of universal application, such insertion is generally of no practical importance, and, in most cases, may with propriety be omitted. Where, however, there are good grounds for doubting whether a person to whom a legacy or distributive share is ordered to be paid, will, within two years thereafter, be within the reach of the executor or administrator, so as to receive payment of his share in the funds of the estate, the procedure established by § 2748 may wisely be adopted. The executor of this decedent suggests its adoption, in the decree about to be entered in the case at bar. These are the facts:

The fourth clause in decedent's will is in words following: "I give all the rest, residue and remainder of my estate unto my brothers and sisters now living, and the descendants of any deceased brothers or sisters." Now, the decedent once had a sister named Anna K. Koch. Whether she is now living or dead, and whether she was alive when the testator died, or had pre-deceased him without leaving descendants her surviving, are questions whose answers are admittedly involved in doubt. It is manifestly improper, therefore, to enter such a decree as the executor proposes—viz.: a decree *directing payment to Anna K. Koch herself* of the one eleventh share to which decedent's brothers and sisters are respectively entitled, and further directing the payment of that sum to the Chamberlain (as the county treasurer of New York county), in the event that, after two years shall have elapsed, *said sum shall not have been already paid to Anna K. Koch.* It is justly claimed by counsel for certain of the legatees that such a provision involves the unwarranted assumption that Anna K. Koch is the "person entitled" to the legacy in question, whereas it may be ascertained, upon inquiry, that she died childless in the testator's life-time, and that her brothers and sisters who survived the testator, and the descendants of her brothers and sisters who did not, are themselves the "persons entitled" to the share that would, under other circumstances, have been hers.

Before I direct any disposition of that share, therefore, an inquiry must be instituted into the circumstances that are supposed to justify the presumption of Anna K. Koch's death, and the belief that she left no descendants who were living at the death of the testator. A reference will be ordered for taking proof upon these questions.

NEW YORK COUNTY.—HON. D. G. ROLLINS, SURRO-GATE.—February, 1885.

MASON *v.* WILLIAMS.

In the matter of the estate of LOUIS C. HAMERSLEY, *deceased.*

The Code of Civil Procedure makes no provision for the trial of issues raised by means of objections filed, by parties opposing the probate of a will, upon an application by the temporary administrator of decedent's estate for leave to discharge certain items of alleged indebtedness.

Under Code Civ. Pro., § 2674, providing that "the Surrogate may, upon the application of the temporary administrator, and upon proof to his satisfaction that the assets exceed the debts, make an order permitting the applicant to pay the whole or any part of a debt due to a creditor of the decedent," the only limitation upon the authority of such a representative to pay debts, in his own discretion, as if he were an administrator in chief, is the necessity for satisfying the Surrogate that the total value of the assets exceeds the amount of all the debts ; this requirement being satisfied, the Surrogate should grant permission to discharge a debt whose validity is attested by the administrator's oath, and which bears no indication of mistake, exorbitance or fraud, subject to such objections as any person interested may interpose upon a subsequent accounting.

APPLICATION by George G. Williams, temporary administrator of decedent's estate, for an order permitting him to pay certain debts and expenses of administration ; opposed by Henry Mason and others, contestants of the will

GEO. G. DEWITT, JR., *for administrator.*

F. & C. A. H. BARTLETT, *for objectors.*

THE SURROGATE.—The temporary administrator of this estate, who has been acting as such since December 20th, 1883, asks for an order authorizing and directing him to withdraw, from the funds deposited by him in the Union Trust company, an amount sufficient to pay certain debts and expenses of administration, which are specified in his application and in the several schedules thereto attached. In obedience to the directions of the order by which he was granted letters, notice of this application has been given to the proctors for parties contesting the probate of the paper propounded as this decedent's will. They oppose the payment of several items of alleged indebtedness which the petitioner asks leave to pay, and have indicated the nature of their opposition by filing written objections.

The Code makes no provision for the trial of such

issues as are thus sought to be raised. It provides
(§ 2674) that, after the lapse of a year from the grant
of letters, "the Surrogate may, upon the application
of the temporary administrator, and upon proof to
his satisfaction that the assets exceed the debts, make
an order permitting the applicant to pay the whole or
any part of a debt due to a creditor of the decedent."
It will be observed that, while the validity of any
debt that the applicant may ask leave to discharge is
not, by the terms of the section, required to be established to the satisfaction of the Surrogate, it is,
nevertheless, distinctly provided that, before making
the desired order, that officer *must* require proof that
the total indebtedness of the estate is less than its
total assets.

I cannot believe that this apparent discrimination,
between things required to be proved and things not
required, is accidental and without real and positive
significance. Is not this, indeed, the scheme of the
fifth article, of which § 2674 forms a part—that
a temporary administrator must furnish security
for the due performance of his trust precisely as if
he were administrator in chief; that he may then
exercise, under certain prescribed limitations, the
same authority that could be exercised by such an
administrator; that his authority to pay debts is
subject to this restraint, and this alone, that it cannot
be made effective until it is demonstrated, to the satisfaction of the Surrogate, that the value of the total
assets left by the decedent is greater than the amount
of all his debts; and that, when this has been established, he will be permitted, as he would, of course, be

permitted were he administrator in chief, to use his own discretion respecting payment of persons claiming to be creditors, subject to such objections as any persons interested may see fit to interpose upon his subsequent accounting?

I am disposed to think that this interpretation of the statute is a true one, and in any event I am very clear that the Surrogate should not, except under special circumstances, withhold from a temporary administrator the permission to discharge debts whose validity has been attested by the oath of that officer, and which bear no indications of mistake, exorbitance or fraud. For the reasons suggested upon the argument of this motion, payment of the claim in behalf of the Chemical National bank may properly be postponed. The other claims to which objection is made amount, in all, to little more than $5,000. Even if they shall ultimately prove to be baseless, the administrator's bond will afford ample security for any error he may make in treating them as meritorious.

An order may be entered granting the prayer of his application, with the modification above indicated, and with the reservation of the right of these contestants to dispute upon the accounting, any items to which they now object (Stokes v. Dale, 1 *Dem.*, 260).

NEW YORK COUNTY.—HON. D. G. ROLLINS, SURRO-
GATE.—February, 1885.

ROWLAND *v.* MORGAN.

In the matter of the estate of EDWIN D. MORGAN,
deceased.

The provision of the Revised Statutes (2 R. S., 93, § 58), concerning the
commissions of executors and administrators, which directs the allowance thereof for receiving and paying out *sums of money*, is to be so
construed as to treat the reception of every variety of assets as a
receiving of money, and the application of such assets to the discharge
of debts and legacies, and to the establishment of trusts, etc., as a
pecuniary disbursement.

A result of the adjudicated cases is a recognition of the divisibility of the
commissions of executors and administrators, for receiving and for
paying out moneys, and of the propriety of an allowance, in many
instances, of half-commissions, for receiving, in advance of any paying
out whatever.

Upon the judicial settlement of the account of executors, a question having arisen as to the mode of computing commissions upon certain
securities which, forming part of the assets of testator's estate, had
been retained by the former under authority conferred by the will, and
were about to be delivered to testamentary trustees,—*Held,*

1. That the market value of such securities, at the time when they came
into the executors' hands, should be taken as the basis for half-commissions, for receiving; and

2. That the half-commissions, for paying out, must be computed upon
their value at the time of entering the decree directing their transfer
to the trustees.

SETTLEMENT of decree upon judicial settlement
of account of Edwin D. Morgan and others, as executors of decedent's will. William F. Rowland, an infant
nephew of decedent, and others, appeared in the proceedings. The facts are stated in the opinion.

DANIEL LORD, *for executors.*

JOHN H. PARSONS, *special guardian.*

THE SURROGATE.—Among the assets of this decedent's estate, at the time of his death, were certain
corporate securities whose market value is subject to
great fluctuations.   Some of those securities are still
in the hands of the executors who are here accounting, and the decree to be entered in this proceeding
will direct their delivery to the testamentary trustees.
Their present market value is less than the value
which was put upon them at the time the executors
filed their inventory.   Under these circumstances, how
must they be rated, in the computation of commissions ?

The statutory provision regarding commissions
(§ 58, tit. 3, ch. 6, part 2, R. S.; 3 *Banks, 7th ed.*,
2303) is in the following words :   " On the settlement
of the account of an executor or administrator, the
Surrogate shall allow to him, for his services . . . . .
for receiving and paying out all sums of money," etc.,
" at the rate," etc.

A strict interpretation of the language just quoted
would not authorize the award of commissions upon
any assets of a decedent's estate, except such as had
been theretofore actually reduced to money ; but it
has been repeatedly held that the provision should be
so construed as to treat the reception of every variety
of assets as a reception of money, and the application
of such assets to the discharge of debts and legacies,
to the establishment of trusts, etc., etc., as a paying
out of moneys, within the meaning of that expression
in the statute (Cairns v. Chabert, 3 *Edw. Ch.*, 312 ;
Matter of De Peyster, 4 *Sandf. Ch.*, 511 ; Wagstaff v.
Lowerre, 23 *Barb.*, 209 ; Ogden v. Murray, 39 N. Y.,

202; Ward v. Ford, 4 *Redf.*, 34; Matter of Roosevelt, 5 *Redf.*, 601).

In still another particular, the statute above quoted has been liberally construed. Though, in terms, it seems to provide for the allowance of five, two and one half, and one per cent., commissions, upon such amounts, and such only, as have been both received and paid out, the courts have frequently sanctioned the allowance of half commissions for receiving, in advance of any paying out whatever. This practice seems to have obtained before the enactment of the present statute, and under the rule in Chancery established in conformity with the act of April 15th, 1817. That act authorized the Court of Chancery, in the settlement of the accounts of guardians, executors and administrators, to make them a reasonable allowance for their services, and provided that, when the rate of such allowance should be fixed by the Chancellor, it should be conformed to in the settlement of such accounts.

This rate was subsequently established by an order of the Court of Chancery (3 *Johns. Ch.*, 631). It is in these words: "Ordered, that the allowance settled by the Chancellor as a compensation for guardians, executors and administrators in the settlement of their accounts . . . . . for receiving and paying money shall be five per cent., on all sums not exceeding $1,000 *for receiving and paying out the same,*" etc.

In 1838, after the enactment of the existing law, a report of one of the Vice Chancellors came before Chancellor WALWORTH for confirmation (Matter of Kellogg, 7 *Paige*, 265). A guardian had received a legacy bequeathed to his ward, and, after expending therefrom a small sum in the ward's behalf, had invested the remainder upon bond and mortgage. The report of the Vice Chancellor had allowed the guardian, on his first annual accounting, commissions upon the entire estate, both for receiving and for paying out. This report was modified by the Chancellor so as to allow the guardian one half commissions for receiving the sum in question, and to disallow commissions upon the trust fund that still remained in the hands of the guardian. "The statute," said the Chancellor, "gives a certain allowance by way of commissions, for receiving and paying out moneys by executors, guardians, etc., without specifying how much is to be allowed for receiving and how much for paying out the same. And it may sometimes happen, upon a loss of the fund without any fault on the part of the guardian or other trustee, or upon a change of trustees, that the guardian or trustee may be entitled to compensation for one service and not for the other. In such cases, the language of the statute must be construed with reference to the decision of Chancellor KENT, in Matter of Roberts (3 *Johns. Ch.*, 42), where he first established the allowance, to be made in conformity with the directions of the act of April, 1817 ; that is, one half commissions for receiving, and one half for paying out the trust money." There are many reported cases which similarly recognize the divisibility of the statutory allowance of commissions, and the propriety of awarding, upon the settlement of accounts, commissions for receiving assets that still remain in the hands of the accounting party (Ward v. Ford, *supra;* Howes v. Davis, 4 *Abb.*, 71; Laytin v. Davidson, 95 *N. Y.*, 263).

For an *express* determination of the precise question here presented, I have vainly ransacked the law reports of this State; but several of the decisions above cited seem to involve of necessity an *implied* determination, that, in computing the one half commissions for receiving, such assets as formed a part of a decedent's estate at the day of his death, and continue to form a part of it at the time of the accounting, must be valued at the price they were worth in the market when they first came into the hands of the executor or trustee. For, in the cases above cited two propositions are clearly established:

1st. That commissions for the receiving and paying out of moneys may justly be claimed by executors, guardians, trustees, etc., who have received and paid out assets never actually converted into money.

2d. That an accounting executor, guardian, trustee, etc., may lawfully be granted commissions for receiving such property, even when the property so received remains in his hands precisely as it reached them.

It is a necessary corollary from these propositions that, whenever, upon assets other than moneys, courts have allowed one half commissions for receiving, in advance of any paying out, such commissions have been computed upon estimated values that must, in many instances, have differed greatly from the values of such assets, as subsequently ascertained by actual sale, or as subsequently estimated in fixing the basis for computation of the one half commissions for paying out. It is evident, indeed, that, when the trustees of this decedent's estate shall hereafter account for the very securities that are now the subject of consideration, if it shall chance that such securities still remain in their possession, and if they shall ask to be allowed commissions for receiving the same, in advance of any paying out, it will be necessary, for the purpose of computing such commissions, to treat such securities as worth the exact amount of their market value at the time of their reception by the trustees. What may ultimately prove to be their actual worth to the beneficiaries cannot now be determined. At some future day they may be converted into money. They may then have a value even higher than has been assigned to them in the inventory. On the other hand, the proceeds of their sale may fall far short of the sum that could be obtained for them if they were to-day thrust upon the market.

It would seem, therefore, upon grounds quite apart from those that are furnished by the decisions to which I have referred, that the present value of the securities about to be delivered to the trustees is not the proper sum upon which to compute one half commissions for receiving. Indeed, there seems to be no more reason for computing, upon such a basis, the commissions for receiving than there is for computing commissions for paying out upon the basis of the value of these securities when they first came into the hands of the executors. In adjusting commissions for receiving and paying out, such assets of a decedent's estate as its executor has actually sold and converted into money, before his accounting, should be valued at the precise amount realized by their sale. When there has been a literal receiving and paying out of moneys, a literal obedience to the statute can be and should be observed. But assets that, at the time of the accounting, remain unsold, and that have not been applied to the discharge of debts or legacies, or otherwise used in the course of administration, may justly be taken, in the reckoning of what are sometimes called "receiving commissions," at their market value when received. And, analogously, whenever such assets shall have been "paid out," within the meaning of that expression in the statute, their value at the time of such paying out will afford the correct basis for calculating the remaining one half commissions, to which the representative of the estate will then have become entitled.

I have examined at random several accounts which, for one cause or another, have occasioned controversy in our appellate courts, respecting the proper adjustment of the commissions of the representatives of decedents' estats. Each of those accounts seems to have been prepared upon the theory that I have here approved, and none of them were, for that cause, subjected to adverse criticism.

For the foregoing reason, I hold that, in computing commissions upon the securities which formed a part of this estate when it came into the hands of the executors—which have since been retained by them in the exercise of the discretionary authority given them by the testator's will and which they are now

about to pass over to the trustees—the market value
of such securities, at the time they came into the
hands of the executors, must be taken as the basis
for the one half "receiving" commissions; and the
one half commissions for "paying out" must be
computed upon the value of those securities at the
time the decree shall be entered upon this accounting.

NEW YORK COUNTY.—HON. D. G. ROLLINS, SURRO-
GATE.—February, 1885.

SHIELDS *v.* SULLIVAN.

*In the matter of the judicial settlement of the account
of* ALGERNON S. SULLIVAN, *public administrator, as administrator of the estate of* RICHARD
HEATHER, *deceased.*

2 R. S., 87, § 28, forbidding preference to be given in the payment of any
debt of a decedent over other debts of the same class, and declaring
that the obtaining a judgment against the executor or administrator
shall not "entitle such debt to any preference over others of the same
class," does not undertake to provide respecting *the costs* of an action
for the collection of such debt, the same not being one of the "debts
of the deceased" (§ 27).

The administrator of decedent's estate, which was insolvent, was ordered
to pay to various creditors a *pro rata* dividend of forty per cent., and
to retain other assets, amounting to more than $900, "to abide the
result of the claims of" a creditor, S., who thereafter recovered a
judgment against the administrator, for a sum, of which about $100
constituted the costs of the action wherein the judgment was rendered.
The administrator contended that S. was only entitled to forty per
cent. of the total amount of the judgment.—

Held, that the costs of S. must be paid in full, and the dividend of forty per cent. be calculated upon the residue of the amount for which the judgment was recovered.

A Surrogate's court cannot make any allowance to an executor or administrator, as counsel fees in litigation, in other courts, concerning the estate, until he has paid his counsel and applies for reimbursement.

APPLICATION by Denis Shields, a creditor of decedent, for an order directing the payment to him of certain costs, and a dividend upon the principal of his claim.   The facts are stated in the opinion.

JAS. B. LOCKWOOD, *for D. Shields.*

JOSEPH F. MOSHER, *for administrator.*

THE SURROGATE. — This estate is insolvent.   In December last, its administrator was directed to pay various creditors a dividend of forty per cent. upon the amount of their respective claims, and to retain in his hands the remaining assets, amounting in all to $904, " to abide the result of the claims of Denis Shields."   Shields subsequently recovered judgment against this administrator for the sum of $1,849.76, together with $121.55, as costs and disbursements, making in all the sum of $1,971.31.   He now claims that, in addition to forty per cent. of the $1,849.76, he is entitled to payment *in full* of his costs and disbursements, out of the assets of the estate.   This claim is opposed by the administrator, who insists that, as respects costs, no less than as respects other elements which, taken together, make up the amount of the judgment, the judgment creditor must content himself with a dividend of forty per cent.

Section 27, tit. 3, ch. 6, part 2 of the R. S. (3 *Banks, 7th ed.,* 2298), prescribes the order in which an executor or administrator must discharge his decedent's debts. That order is as follows:

1st. Such debts as are preferentially entitled under the laws of the United States.

2d. Taxes assessed against the decedent in his lifetime.

3rd. Judgments and decrees against him according to their priority.

4th. "All recognizances, bonds, sealed instruments, notes, bills and unliquidated demands and accounts."

Section 28 of the same title declares that "no preference shall be given in the payment of any debt over other debts of the same class, except those specified in the third class . . . . . *nor shall the obtaining of a judgment against the executor or administrator entitle such debt to any preference over others of the same class.*" In view of these statutory provisions, is the creditor Shields entitled to 100 per cent., upon so much of the whole amount of his judgment as relates to costs, despite the fact that, upon the remainder, he can justly lay claim to 40 per cent., only?

In Columbia Insurance Co. v. Stevens (37 *N. Y.*, 536), the Court of Appeals held that one who had successfully defended an action, brought against him by the receiver of an insolvent corporation, was not bound to accept, with the general creditors, a *pro rata* dividend for his costs, but was entitled to be paid in full, out of the funds in the receiver's hands. In opposing that doctrine, counsel for the receiver, as I have discovered upon examination of his brief in the Court of Appeals, cited certain statutory provisions closely analogous to those that are relied upon by decedent's administrator in the case at bar. He referred to § 79, tit. 4, ch. 8, part 3, of the Revised Statutes, the section that establishes the order in which moneys in the hands of the receiver of a corporation must be distributed among its creditors. Debts entitled to preference under the laws of the United States have priority; next follow judgments obtained against the corporation, to the extent of the value of the real estate on which they are liens; all other creditors are entitled to be paid, *pro rata*, according to their respective demands. It was forcibly argued, in behalf of the receiver, that this forbade any preference of judgments, except so far as they were liens upon real estate, and that a judgment for costs, not being included among the excepted or preferred claims, was entitled, in case of deficiency of funds, to its *pro rata* dividend only. In commenting upon this phase of the controversy, Judge WOODRUFF, pronouncing the opinion of the court, said: "To the suggestion that the statute will not permit the preference sought, it must suffice to say that it is not sought to give a preference to the defendants in the payment of a *debt of the company as such;* it is to require the fund to bear and pay an expense incurred for its benefit or increase."

This language is very apposite, in its application to the case at bar. The statute whose provisions are invoked by counsel for this administrator establishes the order for payment, not of claims against a decedent's estate, but of "debts of the deceased." And when it declares (§ 28) that the obtaining of a judgment against an executor or administrator for a debt of his decedent "shall not entitle *such debt* to any preference over others of the same class," it does not provide and does not undertake to make provision respecting *the costs of an action for the collection of such debt.* The administrator's successful defense of the suit brought by the creditor Shields would have secured, for the undisputed creditors of this estate, an additional dividend out of the fund reserved, and it is but just that, out of that fund, the prevailing party should receive in full the costs that have been awarded him by the Supreme Court.

Upon the argument of this motion, it was suggested, by counsel who represented the administrator in the Supreme Court action, and who was successful to the extent of cutting down plaintiff's claim from $1,900 to $1,300, that the administrator should be granted, for counsel fees in that litigation, an allowance out of the fund in his hands, and that such allowance, as an expense of administration, is entitled in priority over the claims of creditors. I cannot sustain this contention, and for these reasons:

1st. In no event could such allowance be made, until the administrator had paid his counsel and applied for reimbursement.

2d. The order directing the reservation of funds in the hands of the administrator must be construed, in view of the circumstances under which it was entered, as directing the application of those funds in the first instance to the satisfaction of the Shields judgment.

3rd. Even were it otherwise, it is evident that, while

the expenses incurred by the administrator in the defense of the action in the Supreme Court might properly have been deducted from the total assets before
the payment of dividends to creditors, they cannot
now be saddled upon one creditor alone.   He could
only be liable for his *pro rata* share, and, for the
reasons I have indicated, he should not be held
answerable even for that.

Let an order be entered, directing the administrator to pay to Dennis Shields or his attorney the costs
and disbursements awarded him by the Supreme
Court, together with forty per cent. of the whole
amount of the judgment, exclusive of such costs.

NEW YORK COUNTY.—HON. D. G. ROLLINS, SURRO-
GATE.—February, 1885.

VISSCHER *v.* WESLEY.

*In the matter of the judicial settlement of the account
of* BENJAMIN H. KENDRICK, *as administrator of
the estate of* EDWARD E. KENDRICK, *deceased.*

The death of a judgment debtor within the State does not defeat the
operation of the statute regulating the presumption of payment of the
judgment ; nor does it affect the rights or remedies of the judgment
creditor, except that the personal representative of decedent is substituted as the person whose recognition of the validity of the judgment may serve to take the case out of the statute, and except, also,
that one year and six months are added to the twenty years, within
which the creditor is bound to enforce his rights or be treated as having abandoned them.

An allegation, in an administrator's answer to a creditor's petition for payment of his claim, that one not a party to the proceeding recovered a judgment against decedent, during his lifetime, for a sum specified, and that the same is entitled to priority over petitioner's claim, is not an acknowledgment of indebtedness, of which the judgment creditor can avail himself, under Code Civ. Pro., § 376, in order to repel the presumption of payment of the judgment.

Decedent, a judgment debtor, died within this State, and an administrator of his estate was appointed, within twenty years after the date when the creditor was first entitled to a mandate to enforce the judgment. Upon a judicial settlement of the administrator's account, the creditor, who sought payment of his judgment, failed to prove a partial payment or written acknowledgment of indebtedness, made by decedent in his lifetime, or by the administrator before the expiration of twenty-one years and six months after the date mentioned.—*Held,* under Code Civ. Pro. §§ 376, 403,

1. That the question as to the statutory bar could be raised by any other creditor, or any of the next of kin, even without the administrator's co-operation, and against his wishes ;

2. That the judgment in question had lost its priority, and its validity as against other persons interested in decedent's estate and could not be revived by the administrator.

UPON the judicial settlement of the account of the administrator of decedent's estate, Edward Visscher and others, creditors of decedent, objected to the payment of a claim made by Edward Wesley, under a judgment recovered against decedent in his lifetime. The facts are stated in the opinion.

JAMES HENDERSON, *for administrator.*

H. G. ATWATER, *for objector.*

THE SURROGATE.—A decree is about to be entered, whereby the accounts of this decedent's administrator will be judicially settled and determined. The assets of the estate are insufficient to pay creditors in full, and if a certain judgment recovered against the decedent in his lifetime, at the suit of Edward B. Wesley, is still a valid and subsisting claim against this estate, it is entitled to preference over the claim of any other creditor, and its payment will exhaust the entire fund applicable to the discharge of debts. It is contended, however, by counsel for other judgment creditors, that, in the distribution of the assets of this estate, the Wesley judgment should be wholly disregarded, because of the neglect to enforce it within the period prescribed by § 376 of the Code of Civil Procedure. The dates of the occurrences that need to be considered in passing upon the matter here in dispute are as follows:

1st. The judgment was recovered on May 29th, 1863.

2d. On January 9th, 1883, the decedent died.

3rd. His administrator qualified as such on February 9th, 1883.

4th. The Wesley claim was submitted to him on March 27th, 1884. He received and retained it, and orally promised to include it in his final account, so that it " could be paid if entitled to priority."

5th. On March 28th, 1884, the administrator filed with the Surrogate his answer to a petition presented on behalf of a creditor for the payment of his claim. To that proceeding Wesley was not a party. The administrator alleged in such answer that Wesley had recovered against the deceased, in his lifetime, a judgment for the sum of $1,997.87, which judgment was dated May 29th, 1863, and was entitled to priority of payment over the claim of the petitioner in that proceeding.

6th. On November 28th, 1884, the administrator filed with the Surrogate his petition for the citation of divers persons to attend the judicial settlement of his account. Among the persons thus sought to be cited was Edward B. Wesley, who was described in the petition as a "judgment creditor," but without specification of the amount of his judgment or of the date of its recovery, or of any other circumstance relating thereto."

7th. On the day last named (Nov. 28th, 1884) citation was issued as prayed for in the petition, and Edward B. Wesley, by his attorney, admitted due service thereof. Such petition was made returnable on December 12th, 1884.

8th. On December 15th, 1884, more than 21 years and 6 months after the recovery of the Wesley judgment, the administrator filed his account, wherein he included, in a schedule of "claims presented and unpaid," the following item: "Claim of Edward B. Wesley for a judgment obtained by him May 29th, 1863, ... against the deceased, Edward K. Kendrick, for the sum of $1,997.87 and interest."

Under these circumstances, is the Wesley claim still entitled to preference over the claims of other creditors?

It is provided, by § 376 of the Code of Civil Procedure, that a final judgment or decree for a sum of money "is presumed to be paid and satisfied after the expiration of twenty years from the time when the party recovering it was first entitled to a mandate to enforce it." "This presumption," the statute proceeds to declare, "is conclusive, except as against a person who, within twenty years from that time, makes a payment, or acknowledges an indebtedness

of some part of the amount recovered by the judgment or decree, or his heir or personal representative
or a person whom he otherwise represents.   Such an
acknowledgment must be in writing and signed by
the person to be charged thereby." By § 403 it is
provided that "the term of eighteen months after
the death, within the State, of a person against whom
a cause of action exists is not a part of the time limited for the commencement of an action against his
executor or administrator."

Unless, therefore, in the present case, this decedent
in his lifetime, or his administrator, between the date
of his decedent's death and November 30th, 1884,
made some payment on account of this judgment, or
acknowledged, in writing under his own signature,
the whole or a part of the indebtedness which it
represented, the presumption of its payment has
become absolute, and it has not only lost its priority,
but, as against the claims of other persons interested
in this estate, has practically lost its validity, and cannot now be revived by the administrator (McLaren v.
McMartin, 36 *N. Y.*, 88).   The provisions of the
statute are clear and unequivocal.   Its operation has
not been defeated by the decedent's death, nor have
the rights and remedies of the judgment creditor
been in any wise affected thereby, except that the
administrator has been substituted in place of his
decedent, as the person whose recognition of the
validity of the judgment, either by partial payment
or by written and signed acknowledgment, would
serve to take the case out of the statute, and except,
also, that one year and six months have been added

to the twenty years, within which the creditor was bound to enforce his rights or be treated as having abandoned them.

Section 415 of the Code explicitly declares that " the periods of limitation prescribed by this chapter . . . . . must be computed from the time of the accruing of the right to relief by action, special proceeding, defense or otherwise, *to the time when the claim to that relief is actually interposed by the party as a plaintiff or a defendant in the particular action or special proceeding*." The presentation, therefore, of the creditor's claim to this administrator, the demand for its payment and the oral promise of the administrator to include it in the accounting have put the creditor in no better position than he would have occupied, if he had made similar demand of the decedent himself in his lifetime, and had obtained from him verbal acknowledgment of his continued indebtedness. Such acknowledgment would not have availed him (Cotter v. Quinlan, 2 *Dem.*, 29; Warren v. Pfaff, 4 *Bradf.*, 260; Shapley v. Abbott, 42 *N. Y.*, 443).

I am very clear, also, that the reference to the Wesley judgment, in the answer of March 28th, 1884, was not such an acknowledgment of that judgment as to give it new vitality. In Wakeman v. Sherman (9 *N. Y.*, 85), the Court of Appeals held that, in order to be effective, such an acknowledgment " must be made to the creditor or to some one acting for him, or if made to a third person, must be calculated and intended to influence the action of the creditor." To the same effect, see, also, Winterton

v. Winterton (7 *Hun,* 230); Fletcher v. Updike (67 *Barb.,* 364); Bloodgood v. Bruen (8 *N. Y.,* 362).

In the case last cited, it was distinctly held that the recognition of a debt as a subsisting obligation did not suffice to interrupt the operation of the statute of limitations, when such recognition was made by the debtor in a sworn answer in a legal proceeding to which the disputed creditor was not a party.

Some doubts were expressed, upon the recent argument, whether any person other than the administrator was in a situation to attack the Wesley judgment for the cause above considered. I hold that any person interested in the estate as creditor or next of kin is entitled to raise this question, even without the administrator's co-operation and against his wishes (Shewen v. Vanderhorst, 1 *Russ. & M.,* 347; Ex parte Dewney, 15 *Vesey,* 479; Partridge v. Mitchell, 3 *Edw. Ch.,* 180; Moodie v. Bannister, 4 *Drewry,* 432).

New York County.—Hon. D. G. ROLLINS, Surrogate.—February, June, 1885.

SOLOMONS v. KURSHEEDT.

In the matter of the judicial settlement of the account of MANUEL A. KURSHEEDT, *as executor of the will of* MOSES SOLOMONS, *deceased.*

The statute does not prescribe any special form to be adopted by an executor in making up his account. Such a paper should contain a clear

and definite statement of his dealings with his testator's estate, so that
it can be made the subject of intelligent objections.

An inventory, made and filed by an executor, of the assets of his decedent's estate, has not the effect of binding, even presumptively, his
successor in office.

K., who, at one time, qualified as executor of the will of each of two decedents, whose respective testamentary provisions were in direct
antagonism, cited all persons interested in either of the estates to
attend the judicial settlement of his account as representative of one
thereof, and applied to the court for instructions as to the proper mode
of presenting the account.—

Held, that such instructions should not be given, but that the executor
should, in the first instance, solve for himself the problem which confronted him, leaving it to those interested to raise desired issues by the
interposition of suitable objections.

Testator, by his will, executed in 1881, appointed his mother, S., executrix, and two others, F. and M., executors of his will, giving them the
residue of his estate, in trust to retain the same, or convert it and invest the proceeds, and pay the income of all or any part thereof to S. for
life, with remainder over; further directing his executors, at any time,
upon his mother's written request, "unless declared by her family
physician and two other trustworthy doctors to be mentally unsound,"
to pay and deliver to her any part, not exceeding one half, of the principal, in absolute ownership. This latter provision was, by a codicil,
extended to include the entire estate. S., who alone qualified as executrix, shortly after receiving letters executed, with the knowledge of
F. and M., a written instrument, declaring her election, in pursuance
of the power vested in her, to take and hold in absolute ownership, all
testator's estate, with certain exceptions, delivered the same to M.,
and thereafter died, leaving a will of which she appointed M. executor. M. having qualified as executor of the will of S. and also of that
of testator, and rendered his account in the latter capacity, in which
he recognized the instrument executed by S. as a transfer to her of the
estate of testator, the residuary legatees under the will of the latter,
objected that the acts of S. were ineffectual as an appropriation of
such estate.—

Held, that the testator could not have intended that the failure of F. and
M. to qualify should deprive the chief object of his bounty of the privilege accorded to her by his will; that S., by executing the instrument
in question, became invested with title to the property, though M. at
the time of its delivery was not executor,—provided she was then of
sound mind; that it was not yet too late to determine the question of
her competency; and that the entry of a decree upon the accounting
should be deferred, to permit such determination to be had.

Hull v. Hull, 24 *N. Y.*, 647—compared.

HEARING of objections interposed by Hannah M. Solomons, claiming to be interested in decedent's estate, to the account of the executor of the will of the latter, in proceedings for judicial settlement. The facts appear in the opinion.

M. A. KURSHEEDT, *executor.*

G. W. LYON, *for objector.*

THE SURROGATE.—The will of this testator designated three persons to execute its provisions. One of those three was the testator's mother, Selina Solomons, who qualified as executrix in April, 1883. At that time she took possession of this estate, and continued to hold it in her exclusive charge until her decease. One of the clauses of the will which she was called upon to execute contained the provision following: "I order that my executors hereinafter named as trustees with and for my said mother shall, at any time, upon my mother's written request . . . . . pay and deliver to her, in absolute ownership, any part or portion of the principal or capital of the trust estate in their hands, not exceeding one half thereof." This direction the testator subsequently modified by a codicil wherein he empowered his executors to pay over any part or the whole of his estate "in the same way, manner and form" that he had by his will authorized them to adopt in the paying over of one half.

In May, 1883, Selina Solomons executed an instrument, wherein she assumed to exercise the power which is claimed to have been vested in her by her son's will and codicil, and elected " to take and hold in absolute ownership all the personal estate of said testator, and all proceeds of his real estate, in excess of the amount required to pay his debts and funeral and testamentary expenses and certain monetary legacies, amounting in all to $9,100." She had previously filed an inventory of the assets of the estate wherein she had charged herself as executrix with the sum of $93,047.62. It will not be disputed that, if the provisions in her behalf in the will and codicil of Moses Solomons are valid, and if she could lawfully exercise, and did in fact exercise, the authority conferred by such will and codicil upon his executors, then there were no assets of Moses Solomons' estate at the time of her death, except such sums as might be necessary for satisfying the legacies above referred to, and for the payment of debts and funeral and testamentary expenses.

After the death of Selina Solomons, Manuel A. Kursheedt, who was named as executor in Moses Solomons' will, duly qualified as such, and at the same time qualified as executor of the will of Selina Solomons. He is now accounting under somewhat peculiar circumstances. The claims of persons who are entitled to take under Moses Solomons' will, in case its provisions to Selina Solomons shall for any cause fail to take effect, are in direct antagonism to the claims of those who will take under the will of Selina Solomons, in case such provisions shall be ultimately upheld. The executor has very properly, therefore, cited all persons interested in either of the two estates to attend the judicial settlement of his account (Fisher v. Banta, 66 *N. Y.*, 481). Upon the return of the citation, he asked instructions from the Surrogate as to the proper mode of presenting his account. The Surrogate, upon objection by counsel for Hannah M. Solomons, who claims to be interested in this decedent's estate, declined to give such instruction, and held that the executor should, in the first instance, solve for himself the problem which confronted him, and should, accordingly as he might be advised, ignore the pretended operation of this decedent's will and codicil and the instrument executed by Selina Solomons appropriating to herself the assets of this estate, or should, on the other hand, treat the testamentary provision of Moses Solomons and instrument executed by his mother as effecting a valid transfer of the property to which they related.

After this decision had been rendered, the executor filed an account wherein he set forth that the only assets that had come to his hands, as this decedent's executor, were certain moneys that amounted in the aggregate to $6,662, and that that entire sum had been applied by him to the payment of the legacies which he enumerated. He accordingly charged himself with said sum of $6,662 and credited himself with the same amount. The form of this account is criticised by counsel for said Hannah M. Solomons, who moves that it be stricken from the files as incomplete and inconsistent on its face.

Upon the oral argument of this motion, I intimated that there was a seeming variance between certain statements in the account proper, and other statements in Schedule B. which is appended thereto. Upon closer examination, however, of the paper as a whole, these statements do not seem to me incongruous. The accounting executor substantially takes the position that the property whose ownership is likely to be the chief subject of controversy, belongs to Selina Solomons' estate. His position in this regard can, of course, be attacked by any persons who may seek to surcharge the account. But to hold, at the very threshold of the accounting, that the executor is bound to surcharge himself with all the assets of this estate that ever came to the hands of Selina Solomons, including such assets as she assumed to appropriate to her own use in pursuance of the authority claimed to have been conferred upon her by the testator's will, would be to determine, in advance of any hearing upon the merits, the most important matter that is likely to arise in the controversy over this account. It seems to me that counsel for Hannah M. Solomons practically asks the court to do the very thing which, under objection of such counsel, the court has already declined to do.

The statutes do not prescribe any special form to be adopted by an executor in making up his account. Of course, every such account should contain a clear and definite statement of the executor's dealings with his testator's estate, so that it can be made the subject of intelligent objections. It is true, as counsel for Hannah M. Solomons says, that ordinarily, where an executor has made an inventory, the natural and orderly mode of accounting is for such executor to charge himself with the amount of such inventory, and with any increase of assets he may have since received, crediting himself in detail with sums paid out for the discharge of debts, etc., etc., and with any loss or depreciation not occasioned by his own fault. But this course need not always be pursued, and under the circumstances here disclosed may properly enough be departed from. This executor has as yet filed no inventory, and no application seems to have been made to compel him to file one. As executor of Moses Solomons, the inventory made by his predecessor in office does not bind him even presumptively; he is only called upon to account for such property as has come to his hands, and for such other, if any there be, as might have come to his hands if he had exercised proper care and diligence in recovering it.

It may appear, in the course of this investigation, that he is justly chargeable with all the assets that belonged to this estate at the testator's death. But the question, whether or not he is so chargeable, is a question which can in no other way be more promptly or more satisfactorily determined than by trial of issues that can be raised by the interposition of objections to the account as filed.

ON June 24th, 1885, the following opinion was filed in the same matter:

THE SURROGATE.—Two testamentary papers, both written by decedent's own hand, have since his death been admitted to probate, as together constituting his last will and testament. By the earlier of these two papers, which is dated November 10th, 1881, the testator appoints his mother, Selina Solomons, his executrix, and Frederick A. Kursheedt and Manuel A. Kursheedt his executors. To such executrix and executors he gives *in trust* his entire residuary estate, real and personal. He authorizes them to retain the same or to convert it and invest the proceeds, and to pay any part or the whole of all interest, rents and income therefrom, to Selina Solomons during her natural life, " at such times and in such manner and in such sums as she may desire the same."

The will then provides as follows; "And I further order that my executors hereinafter named as trustees with and for my said mother shall, at any time upon my mother's written request (unless declared by her family physician and two other trustworthy doctors to be mentally unsound), pay and deliver to her in absolute ownership any part or portion of the principal or capital of the trust estate in their hands not exceeding one half thereof; and in the event of her becoming physically unable to sign such written request, then such payment is to be made to her on her verbal request, made in the presence of a witness to be chosen by my mother, and the said witness shall sign and give proper receipts for the same."

The will further directs the distribution of the residue of the estate after the death of the testator's mother, and the payment of her debts and funeral expenses.

The codicil is dated November 20th, 1881, ten days after the execution of the will. It begins with a preamble, reciting that the testator had empowered his executors, the Messrs. Kursheedt, to deliver or pay over to his mother any part of the principal or capital of the estate, to the extent of one half thereof, "in certain ways, forms and contingencies." It then proceeds in these words: "In view of unforeseen and possible depreciation or loss of any portion of my real and personal estate, and with the intent of insuring my mother ample and luxurious support and maintenance, *or for any other purposes by her desired*, I hereby authorize and empower my aforesaid executors to pay over any part or the whole of my real or personal estate, in the same way, form and manner as stated and directed in my will."

The testator died in February, 1883. His will and codicil were admitted to probate in April following. Selina Solomons at once qualified as executrix, and, four weeks later, executed an instrument in writing in words following:

"To all to whom these presents shall come, greeting: Know ye that I, Selina Solomons, of the city of New York, widow of Lucius Solomons, and sole acting executrix of and trustee under the last will and testament of Moses Solomons deceased, pursuant to the power vested in me by said will and the codicil thereto, do hereby elect to take and hold in absolute ownership all of the personal estate of said testator and all proceeds of his real estate over and above the amount that may be required to pay his debts and funeral expenses and the several legacies bequeathed by the second, third, fourth, fifth and sixth clauses of said will, said legacies amounting in all to the sum of $9,100.

Dated N. Y., May 6th, 1883.

[Signed]   SELINA SOLOMONS.

In the presence of

ISABEL DE SOLA MENDEZ.

H. L. COHEN."

At the time of the execution of this paper, which was drawn with the knowledge of both Manuel and Frederick Kursheedt, and was delivered to the latter, neither of those gentlemen had qualified as executor of this estate; nor at any time thereafter, while Selina Solomons was alive, did either of them receive or apply for letters. It was not until February, 1884, after her death and after her own will had been admitted to probate, that Manuel A. Kursheedt, who qualified as her executor, qualified also as executor of this testator. In the latter capacity he has filed, for judicial settlement, the account here in controversy. He charges himself with $6,662, being the aggregate amount of the pecuniary legacies satisfied by him, and he credits himself with a like sum expended for their satisfaction.

The testator's nephews, to whom, upon the death of his mother, the "residue and remainder" are given by his will, object to this account, claiming that the execution by Selina Solomons of the instrument above set forth, whereby she assumed to take to herself absolutely the bulk of her deceased son's estate, did not operate as an effectual transfer of that property, and that the accounting party should accordingly be charged therewith.

The testator provided that the request of his mother for "payment and delivery to her in absolute ownership," etc., etc., should be obeyed by the executors *unless*, at the time of making such request, she should be "declared by her family physician and two other trustworthy doctors to be mentally unsound."

The will and codicil of this testator clearly manifest his solicitude for his mother's welfare, and his purpose to provide for her in the most bounteous manner, even though it might involve the devotion of his entire estate to her absolute use and dominion. Her right, however, to secure the possession and ownership of all or part of that estate was made subject to the single condition above specified. In the contingency of her mental unsoundness, it was evidently the testator's purpose that his estate should be held in trust by his executors, and applied in their discretion for his mother's "ample and luxurious support."

But with this limitation, the direction to the executors was imperative. If they had qualified, and if Mrs. Solomons had presented to them her "written request," being at the time of such presentation a person of sound mind, the executors would have possessed no discretionary power to deny it. It is evident that the testator intended that his mother should, in any event, save in the event of her mental incapacity, have the right to take to herself the whole residuary estate, and to enjoy and possess it absolutely.

The testator could not have intended that the death

of the two male executors, or their refusal or neglect
to take out letters or to perform their official duties,
should operate to deprive the chief object of his
bounty of the privilege accorded to her by his will.
Under all the circumstances, I think that, by her execution of the instrument heretofore quoted, she became invested with the title of the property to which
that instrument relates—with this proviso, that, when
it was executed, she was not of unsound mind.

In case any question should now be made respecting her mental condition at that time, an issue of fact
will be presented for determination. In this regard,
there is a close analogy between the case at bar and
that of Hull v. Hull (24 *N. Y.*, 647). The will there
construed by the Court of Appeals provided that the
character and amount of a legacy, to be paid the testator's son upon his arrival at the age of thirty years,
should be ascertained with reference to the son's solvency or insolvency at that period. If, " in the
opinion of the executors," he should be then " insolvent and unable to pay all his just debts and liabilities," his full enjoyment of his father's bounty was
directed to be postponed. The executors having
renounced, letters of administration with the will
annexed were issued to the person entitled, who
thereupon commenced a suit for the construction
of the will. It was insisted that the testator had
submitted the determination of the fact of solvency
to the personal discretion of the executors, and that,
as they had voluntarily renounced, compliance with
the testator's directions had become impossible, and
the provision in question inoperative.

The court said (WRIGHT, J., pronouncing its opinion): "It may be conceded that, when a matter or thing is to be determined or decided entirely by the personal discretion of one or more parties, and they die or refuse to exercise this discretion, there is no way by which any determination or decision can be made; but where a direction in a will is that the executors or trustees are to do or to determine upon any particular thing, and a rule is given, based upon facts readily ascertainable in the usual manner of legal determination of facts, then it is not a case of pure personal discretion, and the courts will uphold the will, and order the facts, if disputed, to be determined in the usual way."

The question of Selina Solomons' mental capacity might have arisen for judicial determination in her lifetime, if the Messrs. Kursheedt had qualified as executors, and had refused to comply with her "request." In that case, she could have invoked the authority of the courts, for ascertaining the fact of her competency, and determining her rights under the decedent's will. If, at the time of the execution of the paper here in controversy, she was, in fact, mentally competent to execute it, I am inclined to think that what she did may be regarded as such a substantial compliance with the directions of the testator as to have perfected her title to his whole residuary estate. And if such has not been the effect of her action, I hold that her representative, or the persons interested in her estate, are now at liberty to take steps, as they may be advised, for determining the question of her competency, and for curing any defect in the execution of the power conferred on her by the will of this testator.

The entry of a decree upon this accounting will be deferred, until the parties have had reasonable opportunity to avail themselves of the suggestions of this memorandum.

NEW YORK COUNTY.—HON. D. G. ROLLINS, SURROGATE.—February, 1885.

PEASE *v.* EGAN.

In the matter of the judicial settlement of the account of CLARA M. EGAN, *as executrix of the will of* JOHN EGAN, *deceased.*

The denial of an application to open a decree is properly incorporated in an order, and not in a decree; and the maximum allowance of costs thereupon is $10 and the necessary disbursements, as prescribed in Code Civ. Pro., § 2556.

APPLICATION by Clara E. Pease to vacate decree entered in proceedings for judicial settlement of executrix's account.

JONAS H. GOODMAN, *for Clara E. Pease.*

FRANK F. VANDERVEER, *for executrix.*

THE SURROGATE.—The petitioner's application for an order setting aside the decree entered·upon the accounting of this decedent's executrix, and permitting the interposition of objections to her accounting, was submitted to a reference, and, upon the coming in of the referee's report, was denied by the Surrogate. The executrix now asks for costs against the petitioner, and claims that such costs should be taxed as upon the rendition of a decree, pursuant to § 2561 of the Code of Civil Procedure. The petitioner insists, on the other hand, that the denial of the application will culminate in an *order* and not in a *decree*, and that the costs which, under such circumstances, the Surrogate should award are such as are indicated by § 2556.

The latter contention must be sustained. The decree sought to be vacated was a final determination, within the meaning of § 2550; but the refusal to disturb it must be incorporated in an order (§ 2556). Section 2481, subd. 6, prescribes the mode of exercise of the power that the petitioner here invoked. The procedure to be adopted is that which is, in like cases, pursued in courts of record of general jurisdiction, and in such courts a proceeding to open a judgment is ordinarily instituted by motion (2 Till. & Shear., 722). The Code declares that the decision of the court denying such an application is an order, and that the application for the order is a motion (Code Civ. Pro., §§ 757, 768). The costs that may be awarded on a motion cannot exceed $10 and the necessary disbursements (§ 3251, subd. 3; Stokes v. Dale, 1 *Dem.*, 264). Such, therefore, must be the allowance here.

NEW YORK COUNTY.—HON. D. G. ROLLINS, SURRO-
GATE.—February, 1885.

HENRY *v.* HENRY.

In the matter of the estate of JAMES G. HENRY, *deceased.*

A petition for the revocation of probate of a will should not differ essentially, in its statement of the grounds of objection, from an answer to a
petition for probate. Upon the principle embodied in Rule No. 4, in
force in New York county, which regulates the contents of such an
answer, averments of matters of evidence are generally out of place in
a petition for such revocation, and may be stricken out, on motion.

MOTION by Sarah M. Henry, executrix of decedent's
will, to strike out allegations contained in a petition
of Evan J. Henry, sole next of kin of decedent, for
the revocation of probate of the will, as irrelevant,
redundant and scandalous.

CHARLES G. CRONIN, *for the motion.*

FRANCIS N. BANGS, *opposed.*

THE SURROGATE.—Section 2533 of the Code of
Civil Procedure declares that " the Surrogate may at
any time require a party to file a written petition or
answer containing a plain and concise statement of
the facts constituting his claim, objection or defense,
and a demand of the decree, order or other relief to
which he supposes himself to be entitled."

The fourth rule of this court establishes the procedure for initiating the contest over the probate of a
will, and requires that the contestant shall file a

verified answer containing a *concise* statement of the
grounds of his objections to probate, and of any facts
that he may allege tending to show a lack of jurisdiction in the Surrogate's court.   I see no reason why
a petition for *revoking* probate should, in this respect,
differ essentially from an answer to a petition for the
granting of probate.   There are obviously many cases
in which the Surrogate, in the just exercise of the discretionary authority conferred upon him by § 2533,
would not only permit, but would feel bound to require, a petitioner or objector to make a full and
detailed statement of the facts and circumstances
upon which his claim or defense might depend.   But,
in general, a probate proceeding is of such a character that its issues may be clearly and distinctly presented without resort to any such particularity of
detail as appears in the petition for revocation which
is here attacked.

The averments, that the moving party seeks to
eliminate from the petition, concern circumstances
and occurrences that must be regarded rather as
matters of evidence bearing upon the issues to be
tried, than as necessary allegations making or tender-
ing such issues.

The whole case is presented in sufficient detail by
such portions of the petition as have not been objected
to.   The remaining portions must, therefore, be
stricken out, but with the exception following . . . .

Let an order be entered accordingly.

NEW YORK COUNTY.—HON. D. G. ROLLINS, SURRO-
GATE.—March, 1885.

CADMUS v. OAKLEY.

*In the matter of the application for probate of a
paper propounded as the will of ANN VOORHIS,
deceased.*

In Code Civ. Pro., § 829, forbidding a person, in certain specified cases, to
be examined as a witness in his own behalf or interest, against *any
person deriving his title or interest* from, through or under a deceased
person, concerning a personal transaction or communication between
the witness and the deceased person, the italicized words should be
construed as being equivalent to "any person *claiming to* derive,"
etc., and so to include the contestant of a will, upon the hearing of a
special proceeding for its probate.

Upon the hearing of a contested application for the probate of a will, a
person named as legatee in the paper propounded is incompetent,
under Code Civ. Pro., § 829, to testify in his own behalf or interest
(*i. e.*, in general, in support of the application), concerning a personal
transaction or communication between himself and the decedent.
Section 2544 of that Code, declaring that "a person is not disqualified
or excused from testifying respecting the execution of a will by a provision therein, whether it is beneficial to him or otherwise," conveys
no intimation that a person within its description is not, in like
manner as others, subject to the limitations contained in the former
section.

DURING the pendency of the controversy over the
admission to probate of the alleged will of decedent,
previous phases of which are reported in 2 *Dem.*,
298, a question arose as to the competency of the
testimony of a witness who had been examined under
a commission. The facts appear sufficiently in the
opinion.

D. M. HELM, D. N. ROWAN, and W. J. DAVIS, *for executors and proponents.*

CHAS. E. TRACY, *for residuary legatee.*

L. H. ROWAN, and GEO. W. LYON, *for contestants.*

TOWNSEND WANDELL, *special guardian.*

THE SURROGATE.—Section 911 of the Code of Civil Procedure provides that a deposition taken without the State, pursuant to article 2, title 3, chapter 9, may be read in evidence by either party at the trial, subject to such objections to the competency of the witness, or of the testimony, as might be made if the witness were then under oral examination.

Certain portions of the testimony of Ann E. Blake, whose deposition was lately taken in this proceeding by order of the Surrogate, are objected to, upon the ground that they concern matters about which the witness is made, by § 829 of the Code, incompetent to testify.

She is named as legatee in an instrument whose title to probate is still the subject of controversy, and the testimony which is here challenged relates to personal transactions and communications between herself and the decedent. The language of § 829, omitting such portions as are foreign to the present inquiry, is as follows: " Upon the hearing, upon the merits, of a special proceeding, a person interested in the event . . . . . shall not be examined as a witness in his own behalf or interest . . . . . against any person deriving his title or interest from, through or under a deceased person concerning a personal transaction or communication between the witness and the deceased person."

Now, is Mrs. Blake "a person interested in the event" of this probate proceeding, and has she been "examined in her own interest," and is the contestant "a person deriving title or interest from, through or under" this decedent?

The first two of these questions it is not difficult to answer. Mrs. Blake is named as a legatee in the very instrument that is sought to be proved by her testimony. If that instrument shall be admitted to probate, she will become entitled to her legacy; on the other hand, should Mrs. Voorhis be discovered to have died intestate, Mrs. Blake will take no portion of this estate. It is very clear, therefore, that, within the meaning of § 829, the witness is interested in the event of this proceeding, and that, when she gave the testimony objected to, she was under examination in her own interest.

. But does this contestant fall within the category of persons deriving title or interest from, through or under decedent? Strictly speaking, it is only by the result of the very probate controversy in which this disputed evidence is offered that it can be ascertained whether the contestant has any title or interest whatever in this estate; but I think that the expression "deriving title or interest" should be construed as if it read "claiming to derive title or interest." Such an interpretation is quite in harmony with that which the courts have sanctioned, in construing other parts of the same section. For example, there is included, in the class of testimony whose introduction the sec-

tion disallows, testimony "against executors" and it
has been held that this word, "executors," is broad
enough to embrace persons named as such in a disputed will, even in advance of the admission of such
will to probate, and even for the purposes of the trial
of the very proceeding brought for obtaining such
probate (Schoonmaker v. Wolford, 20 *Hun*, 166).
The case just cited is applicable to another phase of
the present contention, and upon its authority alone,
I should be inclined to exclude the testimony of Mrs.
Blake, so far as it relates to any personal communications and transactions between herself and the
decedent (see, also, Snyder v. Sherman, 23 *Hun*,
139; Lee v. Dill, 39 *Barb.*, 516; and Matter of Smith,
95 *N. Y.*, 516).

The case last cited was a proceeding for the probate
of a paper purporting to be a decedent's will. The
instrument named, as executor and as principal legatee, the person who afterwards became its proponent.
Its validity was contested by a legatee under other
testamentary papers bearing an earlier date. At the
trial before the Surrogate, the proponent had been
permitted to testify in regard to certain personal
transactions and communications between himself and
the decedent. To this testimony the contestant had
objected, upon the ground that it fell under the ban
of § 829. The overruling of this objection, and the
reception of the testimony, were held, by the Court
of Appeals, to have been erroneous. Says ANDREWS,
J., pronouncing the opinion of the court: "We think
the contestant was a person deriving an interest under the deceased within the meaning of this section

(*i. e.*, § 829). It is true, the interest was not fixed or certain. If the will propounded for probate is valid, she has no interest, and, if it should be set aside, it does not follow that the will under which she claims will be established. . . . . . Her interest, though contingent and uncertain, was derived under the deceased. Her position, though not precisely analogous, is similar to that of heirs or next of kin contesting the will of their ancestor, *and it can scarcely be doubted that they would be within the protection of the section.*"

It is claimed by counsel for certain residuary legatees, at whose instance this witness was examined, that, so far as relates to probate controversies, § 829 has been repealed or modified by § 2544. The latter section is as follows: " A person is not disqualified or excused from testifying respecting the execution of a will by a provision therein, whether it is beneficial to him or otherwise." I do not regard these words as conveying any intimation that such a person shall not, in the same manner and to the same extent as other persons, be subject to the limitations of § 829.

So far as the deposition of Mrs. Blake relates to personal communications or transactions between herself and the decedent, it cannot, therefore, be received in evidence.

NEW YORK COUNTY.—HON. D. G. ROLLINS, SURRO-
GATE.—March, 1885.

NESBIT *v.* NESBIT.

In the matter of the estate of JOHN NESBIT, *deceased.*

The presumption of the continuance of life shown to have once existed
must yield, in case of conflict, to that of innocence of crime.

Upon an application, made in 1885, for a decree granting to petitioner, as
decedent's widow, letters of administration on his estate, it appeared
that petitioner had been married in 1874 to one D., with whom she
afterwards lived as his wife, and whom she last saw in 1875. There
was no evidence that D. had been seen by any one since 1878. In
1883, petitioner was married to decedent, who was cognizant of her
prior marriage to and relations with D.—

Held, that there was better warrant in the law and in the evidence, for
holding that D. was dead than for holding that decedent and petitioner
were guilty of a bigamous marriage; and that the prayer of the petition should be granted.

Rex v. Twyning, 2 *Barn. & Ald.,* 386—followed.

The provision contained in 2 R. S., 139, § 6, relating to the avoidance of a
second marriage contracted by a person whose former husband or wife
has been absent for five years, without being known to such person to
be alive during that time, has application only in a case where the
absentee has been discovered to be still alive.

APPLICATION by Catherine Nesbit, for the grant to
her, as the widow of decedent, of letters of administration upon the estate of the latter; opposed by
Franklin P. Nesbit and others, decedent's sons.

SULLIVAN & CROMWELL, *for petitioner.*

MAN & PARSONS, *for objectors.*

THE SURROGATE.—This petitioner claims to be the
widow of John Nesbit, deceased, and to be entitled,

as such, to administer upon his estate. Her claim to letters is disputed by Mr. Nesbit's three sons, his children by a deceased wife, who died in 1879.

On January 4th, 1883, I find, by the evidence, that there was celebrated a ceremonial marriage between John Nesbit and this petitioner. I also find that the two thereafter cohabited as husband and wife, until Mr. Nesbit's death. It is insisted, on behalf of the next of kin, that, at the time when such marriage was solemnized, the petitioner was the lawful wife of one Oscar Decker, and was, for that cause, incapacitated from becoming the wife of John Nesbit. That she was married to Decker in the year 1874, and that thereafter the two lived together, at first in England and afterwards in this city, is not disputed.

According to the testimony of the petitioner herself, she last saw Decker at the city of Indianapolis, in the state of Indiana, in the year 1875. There is no evidence that she has ever seen him since. He was then under arrest upon a criminal charge. Of this charge he was subsequently tried and convicted. In December, 1875, he was sentenced to imprisonment in the state prison at Michigan city, where he remained in confinement until September, 1878. On or before the 3rd of October of that year, he returned to this city, and on that day, under the name of George Mason, he was arrested by policeman Erwin for the crime of burglary. After giving bail for his appearance to answer that charge, he seems to have speedily taken his departure from New York, and to have henceforth avoided making it another visit. There is no legal and satisfactory evidence that, at any time or in any place, he has since been seen by any human being.

The testimony in this proceeding was taken out of court, and subject to such objections as might thereafter be insisted upon. by the respective parties, when the cause should be submitted to the Surrogate. I must strike out, on motion of petitioner's counsel, those portions of the testimony of Henry G. Julian to which objections have been noted on petitioner's behalf, as shown by the stenographer's minutes. The evidence then remaining does not satisfy me that, since the autumn of 1878, Decker has ever given actual demonstration that he was still alive. In this state of the evidence, what is to be presumed, as to his existence or non-existence on January 4th, 1883, when the petitioner was married to John Nesbit? Is it to be presumed, in favor of the next of kin, that, because he was alive in October, 1878, he continued to live in January, 1883 ; or, on the other hand, is the petitioner entitled to the benefit of a contrary presumption, and is the burden of proof upon the next of kin, to show that her marriage with decedent was unlawful, and that in contracting it she was guilty of bigamy? Which presumption must yield to the other, that of the continuance of Oscar Decker's life, or that of this petitioner's innocence of crime?

This is an interesting question, but not a novel one. It does not appear to have been distinctly answered by the courts of New York, but it has been answered by the courts of several of our sister states in many reported decisions.

The doctrine that ordinarily prevails, as to the presumption of continuance of life, is well stated by Surrogate BRADFORD: "Whenever the law is invoked as to rights depending upon the life or death of an absent party, he is to be deemed to be living until seven years have expired, and after that he is to be deemed as dead; not that the law finds, as a matter of fact, that he died on the last day of the seven years, but that rights depending upon his life or death are to be administered as if he died on that day" (Eagle v. Emmet, 4 *Bradf.*, 117).

This presumption in favor of seven years continuance of life has been repeatedly held, however, to be inferior in force to the presumption of innocence, where the two have come into conflict; and the doctrine is now firmly established, that one who enters into a second marriage, the validity of which is attacked upon the grounds urged by the respondents in the present contention, must be presumed legally competent to contract such marriage until positive proof has been furnished that his or her former wife or husband was living at the time of such second marriage (Dixon v. People, 18 *Mich.*, 84; Klein v. Laudman, 29 *Mo.*, 259; Sharp v. Johnson, 22 *Ark.*, 79; Greensborough v. Underhill, 12 *Vt.*, 604; Hull v. Rawls, 27 *Miss.*, 471; Cochrane v. Libby, 18 *Maine*, 39; Spears v. Burton, 31 *Miss.*, 547; Gibson v. State, 38 *id.*, 313; Yates v. Houston, 3 *Tex.*, 433; Lockhart v. White, 18 *id.*, 102; Canady v. George, 6 *Rich. Eq.*, *S. C.*, 103; Loring v. Steineman, 1 *Metc.*, 204; Kelly v. Drew, 12 *Allen*, 107; Blanchard v. Lambert, 43 *Iowa*, 228; Matter of Edwards, 58 *id.*,

431; Senser v. Bower, 1 *Penrose & Watts* [Pa.], 450).

The doctrine of the cases just cited seems to be approved in Clayton v. Wardell (4 *N. Y.*, 230); and in O'Gara v. Eisenlohr (38 *N. Y.*, 296), it is recognized by MASON, J., pronouncing the opinion of the Court of Appeals, though he proceeds to show why the presumption of innocence should not, upon the facts of the case, be allowed to prevail.

Upon the foregoing authorities, I feel bound to hold (in the absence of evidence establishing that, at any time between the winter of 1878 and January, 1883, Oscar Decker was living) that, when John Nesbit died, this petitioner was his lawful wife. Even if I make a far less rigid application than the authorities above cited seem to require of the presumption of innocence, as conflicting with the presumption of life, I can come to no other conclusion than that which has just been declared.

Many of those authorities approvingly refer to the decision in Rex v. Inhabitants of Twyning (2 *Barn. & Ald.*, 386). The facts of that case, which was a controversy as to the settlement of a pauper, were these : A. intermarried with B. B. absented himself, and, for the space of a year, there were no tidings of him. A. then married C. It was insisted, by one of the parties to the action, that, in the absence of evidence to the contrary, it should be presumed that B. was living at the time of A.'s second marriage. But the court (BAILEY and BEST, JJ.) held otherwise. "The presumption of law," they said, "is that he (B.) was not alive, when the consequence of his being so is that another person has committed a criminal act. We think, therefore, that the sessions were right in holding the second marriage to have been valid, unless proof had been given that the first husband was alive at that time."

This decision was rendered by the Court of King's Bench in 1819. Sixteen years later, the same court held that the validity of the second marriage of a man, whose first wife was shown to have been alive twenty-five days before such second marriage was solemnized, was not necessarily to be presumed, from the mere absence of proof that such first wife did not die in that brief interval (Rex v. Inhabitants of Harborne, 2 *Ad. & Ell.*, 540). Upon these two cases, Mr. BEST (Principles of the Law of Evidence, § 334) makes the following comment: "There is no conflict whatever between the decisions, ... nor does the principle involved in either of them present any real difficulty. The presumption of innocence is a *presumptio juris* and, as such, is good until disproved. Rex v. Twyning decides that the presumption of the fact of the continuance of life, derived from the first husband's having been shown to be alive about a year previous to the second marriage, ought not to outweigh the former presumption in the estimation of the sessions or the jury; while R. v. Harborne determines that, if the period be reduced from twelve months to twenty-five days, it would be otherwise, and that the sessions or a jury might, in their discretion, presume the first husband to be still living."

Manifestly, the doctrine of Rex v. Twyning was not intended to be diametrically reversed by Rex v.

Harborne; in other words, it is not asserted, by the later decision, that, where the validity of a marriage is attacked upon the grounds urged by the next of kin in the case at bar, the presumption of life outweighs the presumption of innocence. Upon the evidence as it stands in the case at bar, with the two presumptions *in equilibrio*, I do not feel warranted in finding that Decker was alive in January, 1883.

The circumstance, that the petitioner seems to have given some sort of encouragement to the institution of a proceeding for obtaining a divorce from her first husband, is relied upon by contestant, as indicative of her lack of good faith in contracting the second marriage. That circumstance gives little help toward the solution of the question whether, at the time the second marriage was solemnized, Decker was alive or dead. Even if she had fully sanctioned the bringing of an action for divorce, and such an action had been actually begun by her direction (and the evidence falls far short of establishing that state of facts), her conduct would not have involved of necessity a conviction or belief, on her part, that her first husband was still living; much less would it have established the fact of his continued existence. It would merely have indicated a lack of certainty that he was dead.

Upon all the evidence, I see no reason for doubting that the decedent was fully advised of the petitioner's first marriage, and of her subsequent relations with Decker, and that his knowledge or lack of knowledge as to Decker's being alive or dead was of a piece with her own. If, therefore, Decker was living when Nesbit took this woman to wife, he became amenable, no less than she herself, to the penalties of the criminal law. The presumption of innocence, by which she is shielded, extends also to this decedent. I am glad to find better warrant, in the law and the evidence, for holding that Decker is dead, than for holding that Nesbit was a guilty party to a bigamous marriage.

It is, of course, unnecessary, in view of the grounds upon which I have based the decision of this controversy, to consider a question which was the chief subject of discussion upon the argument, namely, the question whether the petitioner's second marriage should not be deemed valid because of Decker's absenting himself from her for five successive years, without being known by her to be living during that time.

Sec. 6, tit. 1, ch. 8, part 2, of the Revised Statutes (3 *Banks*, *7th ed.*, 2332) declares that, under such circumstances, "the second marriage shall be void only from the time that its nullity shall be pronounced by a court of competent authority."

But manifestly it is only when the person " absenting himself" has been discovered to be still living that occasion can arise for invoking the provisions of this statute.

Letters may issue to Catherine Nesbit. The cross-petition of the next of kin is denied.

NEW YORK COUNTY.—HON. D. G. ROLLINS, SURRO-
GATE.—March, 1885.

TOLER *v.* LANDON.

In the matter of the judicial settlement of the account
of CHARLES G. LANDON *and another, as executors*
of the will of EMMA STRECKER, *deceased.*

Upon the failure of the general guardian of an infant to give the security
required as a condition of the payment to him of a legacy bequeathed
to his ward, the executors should be directed to pay the same into the
Surrogate's court, as if there were no guardian.

The statute does not contemplate the assumption, by a Surrogate, of
responsibility as custodian of *chattels* bequeathed to an infant. He
can be called on to receive a legacy so bequeathed, only where its subject-matter renders it capable of investment for the infant's benefit.

APPLICATION by the executors of the decedent's
will, for an order directing them to deposit certain
moneys, etc., in the Surrogate's court. A cross-
motion for relief was made by Hugh K. Toler, as administrator of the estate of Laura M. Toler, a legatee.

GEORGE DEWITT, JR., *for executor.*

ROOT & MARTIN, *for H. K. Toler.*

THE SURROGATE.—Sections 46 to 51 of tit. 3, ch. 6,
part 2, of the R. S. (3 *Banks, 7th ed.*, 2301) provide
that a legacy to a minor, in case it is of the value of
fifty dollars or more, must be paid to the general
guardian of such minor, upon the giving of security,
to be approved by the Surrogate; and that, "if there
be no such guardian, or the Surrogate do not direct
such payment," the legacy shall be invested, under

VOL. III—22.

the direction of the Surrogate, in permanent securities, in the name and for the benefit of such minor, which securities shall be kept in the Surrogate's custody. It was held, in McLoskey v. Reid (3 *Bradf.*, 329), that, in case the general guardian of an infant legatee should fail to give the bond required to be given upon the receipt of the ward's legacy, the Surrogate should proceed as if the ward were without a guardian, and should direct the fund to be paid into court and invested for the minor's benefit. In the case at bar, it appears that the executors of this testatrix have failed to comply with the provisions of the decree of April 8th, 1884, directing them to pay to Laura Thébeaud, as general guardian of the infants Isabella, Josephine, Pauline, Jules and Marie Thébeaud, certain legacies bequeathed to them respectively by this testatrix, and that the reason for such failure is the fact that the general guardian has neglected to give the required security. The executors now ask that an order be entered, directing them to deposit the legacies in question in the Surrogate's court. This application is granted.

Second.—The executors also ask that such order may provide for the delivery, into the Surrogate's custody, of a certificate of deposit of certain watches, jewelry, etc., which certificate is now in their hands. By the will of the testatrix, these articles were bequeathed as a specific legacy to certain designated persons, among whom are some of the minors above named. The embarrassment under which the executors labor, in respect to this property, is one from which they cannot obtain relief by surrendering it into the charge of the Surrogate. The statute does not contemplate that that officer shall take such charge of any other bequests than bequests to an infant legatee, and even as regards those, he is called upon to take that responsibility, only when the thing bequeathed is capable of investment for the infant's benefit. As regards, therefore, the watches, jewelry, etc., which are the subject of the specific legacy, the executors' petition must be denied.

I also deny the counter application of the administrator of the estate of Laura M. Toler, deceased. He must seek relief in another tribunal.

————— ‹•••› —————

NEW YORK COUNTY.—HON. D. G. ROLLINS, SURROGATE.—March, 1885.

PRIVÉ *v.* FOUCHER.

In the matter of the probate of the will of ADRIEN PRIVÉ, *deceased.*

A Surrogate's court has no jurisdiction to determine the validity, construction or effect of a testamentary disposition of *real* property, upon an application for probate.

The statutory restrictions upon the validity of bequests to corporations, conditioned upon the survival of certain relatives of the testator, are not obviated or modified by the fact that the testamentary provisions are of a contingent nature, and only to be enjoyed in the event of the death of such relatives.

APPLICATION for the probate of decedent's will, made by Victor Foucher, the executor therein named; opposed by decedent's widow.

PRIVÉ V. FOUCHER.

E. HUERSTEL, *for executor.*

L. RINDSKOPF, *for contestant.*

CARLTON C. RANDALL, *special guardian.*

THE SURROGATE. — Section 2624 of the Code of Civil Procedure empowers the Surrogate to determine the validity, construction and effect of any disposition of personal property contained in the will of a resident of this State, and executed within the State. The Surrogate has no jurisdiction to make such determination respecting a testamentary disposition of real property. Whether the decedent left any personalty does not clearly appear. Assuming that he did, I hòld that his bequest to the French Benevolent Society is not subject to the limitations of L. 1848, ch. 319, § 6. That section declares that testamentary gifts to certain corporations shall fail to take effect, unless the execution of the instrument that bestows them shall have preceded, by at least two months, the death of its maker. The society in question was not, however, incorporated under the act of 1848, and is not within the restraints of that statute.

Second.—The testator left a wife and child, him surviving. It follows from this circumstance, by virtue of L. 1860, ch. 360, § 1 (made applicable to the French Benevolent Society by the act of March 13th, 1868), that the bequest to that corporation is effectual only to the extent of one half of this estate, after payment of debts. By the terms of the said act of 1868, this society is subjected to another restraint. It is prevented from taking, by devise or bequest, more than one fourth of this decedent's estate, by the fact that he left him surviving a lineal descendant, to wit, the daughter already mentioned. Although the interest that the society can take is of a contingent character, and can only be enjoyed in the event of the death of the daughter in the lifetime of the mother, or if the daughter shall survive the mother, then in the event of her dying before she shall attain thirty years of age,—that fact does not prevent or modify the operation of the statute. The *existence* of the wife and daughter is the circumstance under the act of 1860, and the *existence* of the daughter is the circumstance under the act of 1868, by which is determined the interest that a beneficiary is permitted, under the restrictions of those statutory provisions, to take in this estate.

Until a contingency shall arise, which will necessitate the practical application of this decision, the methods by which the interest of the French Benevolent Society can be practically ascertained need not be considered.

New York County.— Hon. D. G. ROLLINS, Surrogate.—March, 1885.

PRICE *v.* FENN.

In the matter of the estate of John D. Fenn, *deceased.*

In a special proceeding instituted for the disposition of decedent's real property for the payment of his debts, the citation having been duly served upon certain infants, interested in the estate, who were under the age of fourteen years and resided within the State of New York, and a special guardian having been, before the hearing, appointed for each, upon his parent's application, without the notice to the infant required by Code Civ. Pro., § 2531, the purchasers at the sale under the Surrogate's decree objected to the title upon the ground of the omission of such notice.—

Held, under Code Civ. Pro., § 2784, subd. 1, that the omission in question was not of such a character as that it "would affect the title of a purchaser at a sale made pursuant to the directions contained in a judgment rendered by the Supreme Court in an action," and that the objection taken must be overruled.

It is the proper practice, in proceedings in a Surrogate's court to which an infant is a party, where no application is made, upon the return of the citation, for the appointment of a special guardian, for the Surrogate to appoint such a guardian upon his own motion.

The practice of inserting, in citations to infants, a clause advising them that, in the event of their not appearing by general guardian, and failing to ask for the appointment of a special guardian, a special guardian will, upon the return of the citation, be appointed by the Surrogate—commended.

SARAH FENN, widow and sole executrix of the will of decedent, having instituted a special proceeding for the disposition of his real property, for the payment of his debts, James K. Price, and another, two of the purchasers at the sale had in the proceeding, declined to take title, upon grounds stated in the opinion. Thereupon an order was granted directing those purchasers to show cause why they should not be compelled to complete their purchase, or said property be sold at their risk and expense; and, after a hearing, it was "ordered, adjudged and decreed that" said purchasers "complete the purchase of the property so purchased by them at the freeholder's sale herein, in accordance with the terms of sale signed by them at the time of such sale, by paying the balance of the purchase money of said premises to said freeholder, but without interest or costs, and accepting his deed of said premises.

W. R. BROWN, *and* C. R. WATERBURY, *for freeholder.*

F. SMYTH, *for purchasers.*

THE SURROGATE.—In the course of the proceedings looking to the disposition of this decedent's real property for the payment of his debts, certain of such property has been sold pursuant to a decree of the Surrogate.   The purchasers refuse to take title, upon the ground that five infants interested in the estate have not been properly represented in the proceedings.   These infants are severally under the age of fourteen years, and reside within the State of New York.   Each of them was duly served with a citation, and, before the hearing of the application for the sale of the property in question, there was appointed for each a special guardian, who seems to have protected the interests committed to his care. It is claimed, in behalf of the purchasers (no persons else joining in the contention), that the order appointing the special guardian of these infants is of no effect, inasmuch as his appointment was, in each instance, made upon the application of a person other than the infant (to wit, the father of the infant), without personal service upon the infant of a notice that such application would be made.

Section 2531 of the Code of Civil Procedure declares that, "where a person other than the infant applies for the appointment of a special guardian, at least eight days' notice of the application must be personally served upon the infant, if he is within the State, in like manner as a citation is required by law to be served."   Does the fact that the notice, for which this section provides, was not given in the case at bar afford a sufficient excuse to these objectors for refusing to accept title to the premises that they have purchased?

Section 2530 of the Code declares that, " where an infant does not appear by his general guardian . . . . . the Surrogate must appoint a competent and responsible person to appear as special guardian." Neither that section nor any other statutory provision limits the authority of the Surrogate, in making such an appointment, to cases in which an application for such appointment has been previously made, or declares who shall be permitted to present such an application, or indicates whether the application should be general in its character, asking simply for the appointment of some competent and responsible person, or particular, asking for the selection of some designated individual. Nor does the statute book throw any light upon the question whether, in case of such an application as I have styled " particular," the Surrogate would be bound to appoint the person specified, in the event that such person should not seem to be incompetent or irresponsible.

Surrogate COFFIN of Westchester county held, in Matter of Ludlow (3 *Redf.*, 391), that, on the return day of the citation issued in a proceeding to which infants are parties, if no person had applied for the appointment of a special guardian for such infants, the Surrogate should appoint of his own motion. Such has been the constant practice in this county, a practice that seems very sensible and proper; one that would not have been open to criticism before the Code was enacted, and is not in conflict with any of the provisions of that instrument.

The Surrogate is powerless to compel the making of an application for the appointment of a special guardian, and, unless, in the absence of such application, he can lawfully appoint, a proceeding in which an infant is a party must come to a standstill, or must be prosecuted to the end, without any binding effect upon such infant.

If, therefore, the respective fathers of the several infant parties in the case at bar had not asked for the appointment of a special guardian, and if the Surrogate *ex mero motu,* had appointed the very person who has in fact guarded the interests of these infants, I think that his action in that regard would have been strictly regular.

It is, however, the better practice to insert in citations to infants a clause advising them that, in the event of their not appearing by general guardian, and of their failing to ask for the appointment of a special guardian, a special guardian will, upon the return of the citation, be appointed by the Surrogate. By this means the infants have the same notice of the purpose of the Surrogate to *make* the appointment as by § 2531 they are required to have, of the purpose of some party to the proceeding to *apply* for such appointment.

Now, in the present case there has, doubtless, been an irregularity in the neglect to give these infants, by citation, or otherwise, the notice for which § 2531 provides. But does that irregularity so vitiate these proceedings as to impair the title which these objectors could take to the property purchased, and to relieve them accordingly from fulfilling their contract?

The Surrogate obtained jurisdiction of these infants when they were served with the citation issued upon a petition that set forth the jurisdictional facts prescribed by the statute (Code Civ. Pro., § 2474; Matter of Becker, 28 *Hun*, 207; Sibley v. Waffle, 16 *N. Y.*, 180; McMurray v. McMurray, 66 *N. Y.*, 175; Ingersoll v. Mangam, 84 *N. Y.*, 622). Now, § 2784 of the Code declares that the title of a purchaser in good faith, at a sale pursuant to a decree made in a proceeding like the present, "is not affected by any of the following omissions, errors, defects or irregularities, except so far as the same would affect the title of a purchaser at a sale made pursuant to the directions contained in a judgment rendered by the Supreme Court in an action—"1st., Where a petition was presented, and the proper persons were duly cited, and a decree for a sale and an order directing the execution thereof were made, ... by any omission, error, defect or irregularity occurring between the return of the citation and the making of the decree or order directing the execution of the decree."

The petition herein was duly presented, the infants as well as the other parties were regularly cited, and the decree directing the sale, and the order confirming the sale and directing the execution of the same, were properly entered. Under these circumstances, I hold that the error, omission or defect complained of is not of such a character that it would, in an action in the Supreme Court, affect the title of a purchaser of property at a sale made pursuant to the judgment in such action (Alvord v. Beach, 5 *Abb. Pr.*, 451; Gaskin v. Anderson, 7 *Abb., N. S.*, 1; Herbert v. Smith, 6 *Lans.*, 493; De Forest v. Farley, 62 *N. Y.*, 628; Darvin v. Hatfield, 4 *Sandf.*, 468; Holden v. Sackett, 12 *Abb., Pr.*, 473; Blakeley v. Calder, 15 *N. Y.*, 617; Jordan v. Van Epps, 19 *Hun*, 526; Coit v. Reynolds, 2 *Robt.*, 655; Graham v. Bleakie, 2 *Daly*, 55; Matter of Dolan, 88 *N. Y.*, 309; Silleck v. Heydrick, 2 *Abb. N. S.*, 57; Matter of Luce, 17 *Week. Dig.*, 35; Minor v. Betts, 7 *Paige*, 596).

In the case last cited, approvingly referred to in Varian v. Stevens (2 *Duer*, 635), Chancellor WAL-WORTH decided a question that arose under L. 1833, ch. 227. The act provided that, upon the filing of a bill for the partition of lands, if any of the defendants should be minors, it would, under certain circumstances, become the duty of the court to appoint a guardian for such minors without exacting security, " provided, however, that a copy of the said petition and notice in writing, signed by the solicitor of the complainants, specifying the time and place, when and where the said petition will be presented, shall be served, at least ten days before the presentation of such petition, upon the general guardian of the minor or minors, in case there be such guardian, *or upon the minor, if there be none.*"

The act drew no distinction between resident and non-resident infants, in its requirements respecting service of notice, though, in the particular case in which the question of its construction arose, the infants lived out of the State. The Chancellor directed that, the general notice to appear and answer having been duly published, the appointment of guardian *ad litem* might be made at once, without further notice to the infants.

In view of the decisions above cited, I hold that, in the case at bar, the neglect to give the infant parties notice of the application for the appointment of their special guardians, does not excuse these objectors from taking title.

NEW YORK COUNTY.—HON. D. G. ROLLINS, SURROGATE.—March, 1885.

MATTER OF COMBS.

In the matter of the judicial settlement of the account of FRANK COMBS *and others, as executors of the will of* CHARLES U. COMBS, *deceased.*

A legacy to a testator's widow in lieu of dower carries interest from the testator's death, although its value exceeds that of the dower interest.

DETERMINATION of question as to interest on legacy, on executors' accounting.

ROBT. A. DAVIDSON, *for executors.*

THOS. B. SEAMAN, *special guardian.*

THE SURROGATE.—All that the will of this testator gives to his widow is given to her in lieu of dower.

Under the decision of the New York courts this circumstance, alone, entitles her to interest on the seven thousand dollar legacy from her husband's death (Hepburn v. Hepburn, 2 *Bradf.*, 76; Parkinson v. Parkinson, *id.*, 77; Seymour v. Butler, 3 *id.*, 193; Williamson v. Williamson, 6 *Paige*, 298; Bullard v. Benson, 1 *Dem.*, 493). The fact, that the total value of the ·provisions in her favor exceeds her dower interest, does not affect the question.

NEW YORK COUNTY.—HON. D. G. ROLLINS, SURROGATE.—March, 1885.

VERNET *v.* WILLIAMS.

In the matter of the estate of MORGAN L. SAVAGE, *deceased.*

Testator, by his will, gave a legacy to his daughter, V., a married woman, directing his executors to pay it "as soon as practicable" after his death; and, by a later clause, provided that, "after the payment" of V.'s legacy, and "as soon as possible" after his death, the executors should invest a specified sum, and pay to his widow the interest and increase "commencing from my (his) decease."—

Held, that no feature of the case took the bequest to V. out of the operation of the general rule, that interest does not begin to run on a legacy, until the expiration of a year after the death of the testator, in the absence of an express or implied direction of the will to the contrary.

PETITION of Hester E. Vernet, legatee, for a decree directing Thomas H. Williams, executor, to pay her legacy. The facts are stated in the opinion.

D. G. WILD, *for petitioner.*

O. A. SANDERSON, *for executor.*

THE SURROGATE.—I am asked to determine from what period interest should be computed upon a certain legacy bequeathed by the will of this testator to his daughter, Mrs. Vernet. It is not claimed, by counsel for the legatee, that there is any feature in this case which takes it out of the operation of the general rule, that interest does not begin to run on a legacy until a year after the death of the testator, unless he has given, by his will, an express or implied direction for an earlier payment of such interest, or of the legacy itself. But it is insisted that such a direction has here been given, and that, because of it, Mrs. Vernet is entitled to interest from her father's death. The only direction immediately associated with the bequest is that the executors shall pay it "as soon as practicable" after testator's death. Now have these quoted words any real importance? It is the policy of our law that legacies shall not ordinarily be paid until a year from the testator's death. And in this State, and in other localities where the same policy prevails, it has been held that such words as are here relied upon cannot be regarded as a direction that that policy be departed from.

Said Chancellor ELDON, in Gibson v. Bott (7 *Vesey*, 89), commenting upon the words "as soon as conveniently may be:" "Where those words occur as to legacies, interest is never given until the end of the year. The court is obliged to take the general rule, as it is impossible to make the inquiry in every particular case. Suppose a testator directed his executor to convert the property with all convenient speed, to pay certain legacies, and then gave the interest of the residue for life, remainder over; the legatee could make no complaint until the end of the year."

In the earlier case of Sitwell v. Bernard (6 *Vesey*, 520), the same Chancellor, in commenting upon the inequalities attending the application of this doctrine, said : "Upon the principle that the inquiry as to the condition of the personal estate, when each and every part could be got in and made productive, is endless and immeasurable, the court cuts the knot by doing what, in general cases, is convenient, though in particular cases both convenience and justice may be disappointed."

Benson v. Maude (1 *Madd. & Geld.*, 15) was a case in which a testator had directed his executors to set up a certain trust " as soon as they should think proper." In the opinion of the Vice Chancellor, this direction "amounted to the same thing as a direction to raise and pay a legacy as soon as the executors should find it convenient; and, as the court has adopted a year as the rule of convenience, the legacy could not be raised until the end of the year."

In the cases cited below, it was held that the legatee was not entitled to interest for the first year, though there was in each of them a testamentary direction substantially like that in the case at the bar, and, in some instances, even more stringent in its terms :   Williamson v. Williamson (6 *Paige*, 298); Hoagland v. Schenck's Ex'rs (16 *N. J. Law*, 370); Kent v. Dunham (106 *Mass.*, 586); Rogers v. Rogers (2 *Redf.*, 24); Bradner v. Faulkner (12 *N. Y.*, 472);

Kerr v. Dougherty (17 *Hun*, 341); Sullivan v. Winthrop (1 *Sumner*, 1); Webster v. Hale (8 *Ves.*, 410).

These cases must be taken as decisive of the present contention, unless the claim of the legatee finds support, in some clauses of the will that have not yet been considered. It does not. The testator gives instructions regarding the payment of certain other beneficiaries, in terms similar to those which he adopts in his bequest to Mrs. Vernet, and, by a later provision, he directs that, " after the payment " of certain legacies including the one to Mrs. Vernet, and " as soon as possible " after his decease, his executors shall invest the sum of $20,000, and pay to his wife, during her life, the interest and income, " commencing," as he says, " from my decease."

It is argued that the testator's use of the phrase " as soon as possible " indicates his wish that the $20,000 trust should be speedily set up, and that, therefore, the direction that it should not be established until *after* the payment of Mrs. Vernet's legacy, implies an emphatic wish that that legacy should be discharged at once. At first blush, there seems to be some force in this suggestion; but on more careful consideration it will appear that this clause opposes, more than it assists, the contention of the legatee— for by it the testator explicitly declares that his wife shall receive interest from his death on the $20,000, and by one of the earlier clauses of his will he provides that his wife shall be paid $500 " immediately " after his death. Those express and positive directions enhance the significance of his failure to give special direction respecting interest on Mrs. Vernet's legacy, and make it plain that his injunction to his executors, to discharge that legacy as soon as practicable, did not call upon them to do so until after the lapse of a year.

Decreed accordingly.

◄◄◄●►►►

NEW YORK COUNTY.—HON. D. G. ROLLINS, SURROGATE.—April, 1885.

BUCHAN *v.* RINTOUL.

In the matter of the judicial settlement of the account of JAMES RINTOUL, *as trustee under the will of* THOMAS B. RICH, *deceased.*

As to what is the proper judicial interpretation of the expression "legal heirs of the estate," occurring in a will, *quære.*

Testator, by his will, bequeathed to O. the sum of $5,000, gave to his wife a life interest in the residue of his estate, and established a scheme for the distribution of the remainder after her death. A codicil to the will contained the following clause: "In the second article of my will of the bequest to Rachel Oliver my wife's sister the sum of $5,000 I revoke and instead bequeath unto her the sum of $300 to be paid to her annually in equal quarterly payments during her natural life at which time will cease and go to the legal heirs of the estate in equal sums to be paid by my acting executrix and executors." The widow died after O., who had received her annuity of $300, though no fund to produce it had been specially set apart. The estate being about to be distributed, decedent's next of kin claimed to be entitled to $5,000 by virtue of the clause quoted.—

Held, that so much of this clause as followed the word "cease" was void for uncertainty, and that the estate should be distributed as if the codicil ended with that word.

CONSTRUCTION of decedent's will upon judicial settlement of account of trustee thereunder. Robert C.

Buchan and others, next of kin of the decedent, appeared in the proceedings. The facts are stated in the opinion.

DAVENPORT & LEEDS, *for trustee.*

COUDERT BROS., *for R. C. Buchan and others.*

R. S. CLARK, *for Ann McClure.*

W. R. BARBOUR, *for Jane Rich and others.*

THE SURROGATE.—This decedent left several testamentary papers that, taken together, constitute his last will. The earliest of these papers contains a provision, not revoked or modified by any of later date, whereby he gave his wife a life interest in his residuary estate, and established the scheme for the distribution of the remainder after her death. By another article in the same instrument, he bequeathed to his wife's sister, Rachel Oliver, the sum of $5,000. This bequest was afterwards revoked by a codicillary provision, and in its place was substituted a life annuity of $300, which sum was statedly paid to her until she died. Resort was had, for such payment, to the income of the estate generally, and no particular fund was ever set apart for producing the interest or income to feed the annuity. The testator's widow outlived Rachel Oliver, but is now deceased, and as the estate is about to be distributed the question arises, what force and effect, if any, can and should be given to certain obscure language in that clause of the third codicil which makes provision for the Rachel Oliver annuity.

Counsel for the residuary legatees claims that this

language is utterly meaningless; but, on behalf of the next of kin, it is insisted that it should be construed as giving to themselves an interest in decedent's estate to the amount of $5,000. Their counsel has undertaken to show how, by certain omissions, transpositions, interpolations and substitutions of words and phrases, the provision in dispute can be transformed into an intelligible and definite bequest to his clients. There are difficulties in the way of adopting the interpretation for which he contends; difficulties that cannot be better illustrated than by juxtapositing the codicil as it is with the codicil as he translates it, and thus observing how many and how serious are the changes that are admittedly necessary, before the provision in question can appear in the guise of a bequest of five thousand dollars to the next of kin.

Below is set forth, in the left hand column, the actual codicil; in the column at the right, the words that I am asked to reject are in brackets, and those that I am asked to insert are in italics.

"In the second article of my will of the bequest to Rachel Oliver my wife's sister the sum of $5,000 I revoke and instead bequeath unto her the sum of $300 to be paid to her annually in equal quarterly payments during her natural life at which time will cease and go to the legal heirs of the estate in equal sums to be paid by my acting executrix and executors."

In the second article of my will [of] the bequest to Rachel Oliver, my wife's sister, *of* the sum of $5,000 I revoke and instead bequeath unto her, *from the income of said amount*, the sum of $300 to be paid to her annually in equal quarterly payments [during her natural life] *until the time of her death*, at which time *the annuity* will cease, and *the said principal sum of five thousand dollars* go to the legal heirs of the estate in equal sums to be paid by my acting executrix and executors.

I should have grave doubts, even if the testator had used the very language which is thus sought to be substituted for his own words, whether the gift over would not be void for the uncertainty of its description of the persons included in the term "heirs of the estate." Had the testator used the word "heirs" simply, that word might fairly enough be treated as substantially synonymous with the term "next of kin." This expression, "heirs of the estate," is one that, so far as I am advised, has never received judicial interpretation; but it is not infrequent in common parlance for people to speak of the beneficiaries under a will as the "heirs" of the testator, even though such beneficiaries are strangers to his blood. That this decedent meant to indicate, by the phrase "heirs of the estate," his residuary legatees seems to me quite as reasonable a conjecture as any other that could be suggested.

The difficulty of interpreting these words is not, however, the most serious one that must be compassed before the codicil here in dispute can be made intelligible. The chief obstacle lies in this: the testator says that he bequeaths an annuity of $300 to be paid to Rachel Oliver annually "during her natural life, at which time will cease and go to the legal heirs," etc. Now, assuming that the phrase "during her natural life" may fairly be construed, in the light of the context, as meaning "until her death," what is it that was then to "cease?" "Cease" is here a predicate without a subject. But if, in spite of this grammatical inaccuracy, the clause can be treated as having any meaning at all, is it not clear that the thing that the testator directed to "cease" with Rachel Oliver's life is the annuity of $300? And is it not equally clear that the thing that was to "cease" is the very thing that, upon Rachel's death, was to "go to the legal heirs of the estate?" It would scarcely be contended that such an indefinite and indeterminate gift of the annuity could be held valid; but if the legal heirs were not at Rachel's death, to take the annuity, what is it that they were to take? Counsel for the next of kin answers: "five thousand dollars." He insists that, by comparing the provision for Rachel Oliver's benefit in the will proper with the substituted provision in the codicil, it will appear that the testator's purpose in changing the form of his bequest was, first, to provide for payment to the beneficiary, during her life, of $300, annually, *from the income of the five thousand dollars* that he had originally bequeathed to her outright, and, secondly, to divert the principal sum of $5,000 into the hands of his next of kin after such beneficiary should die.

This interpretation of the disputed provision involves the notion that the executors would not have been warranted in setting apart a larger sum than $5,000 for producing the annuity, and that Rachel Oliver's right to receive as much as $300 annually was dependent on the contingency that a sum as large as $300 should be annually obtained from investment of the $5,000. I find no sufficient warrant for this theory in any of decedent's testamentary papers. For aught that they disclose, it may have been his chief and possibly his sole design, in making the amended provision, to insure the enjoyment by the beneficiary of the full annual sum of $300, even though an amount much larger than $5,000 might be required for producing it. Whether he intended that result or not, there can be little doubt that he actually accomplished it; and if Rachel Oliver had outlived the decedent's widow, and the executors had then set apart, say $7,500, in government bonds at four per cent., for producing the annuity, it might plausibly enough have been claimed, upon her death, that the whole fund of $7,500 passed under the codicil to the "heirs of the estate;" and such a claim would have had quite as substantial foundation as the one now interposed. All in all, I confess my inability to penetrate the obscurity in which the testator has veiled his intentions. I hold that all that follows the word "cease," in the third codicil, is void for uncertainty, and that the estate should be distributed as if the codicil ended with that word.

NEW YORK COUNTY.—HON. D. G. ROLLINS, SURROGATE.—April, 1885.

LOESCHE v. GRIFFIN.

In the matter of the estate of CHARLES H. F. AHRENS, *deceased.*

An unverified list of a decedent's assets cannot be treated as an inventory thereof, within the meaning of the statute relating to such instrument.

A Surrogate's court has no authority to require a party to a special proceeding therein to furnish security for the payment of his adversary's costs.

APPLICATION by Gottfried Loesche and others, residuary legatees under the decedent's will, to compel Hobart R. Griffin, the executor, to file an inventory, etc.

T. F. HASCALL, *for the application.*

R. B. GWILLIM, *for executor.*

THE SURROGATE. — The inventory filed by this decedent's executor in November, 1883, is still missing from the files. When I vacated the order of April, 1884, that directed the filing of an inventory to supply the place of the one that had been mislaid, it was with the understanding that a copy of the inventory filed would be served upon the adverse party. This does not seem to have been done, the executor having contented himself with furnishing a list, not under oath, of the assets left by this decedent.

The present application for an inventory is, therefore, granted. The fact that the property cannot now be submitted for inspection is no bar to it (see Silverbrandt v. Widmayer, 2 *Dem.*, 263); and as the property is said to consist of but four items whereof each is an item of money, this direction can not occasion the executor any serious inconvenience.

The motion to require the executor to furnish security for costs must be denied. I have no power to grant it. The provisions of chapter 21, tit. 3, of the Code of Civil Procedure are not applicable to special proceedings in Surrogates' courts (see § 3347, subd. 13).

NEW YORK COUNTY.—HON. D. G. ROLLINS, SURRO-
GATE.—April, 1885.

PFALER v. RABERG.

In the matter of the probate of the will of MARY
KIEDAISCH, *deceased.*

Testator's will contained the following clause : "All the rest, residue and
remainder of my estate I bequeath to my executrix, *to remain with her
forever,* upon the following trust, however : to be devoted and applied
in such sums and amounts as she may see fit, to preserve and keep in
order my burial place or plot in B. cemetery."—

Held, that the trust attempted to be created was for a purpose for which
the law recognizes the right of a testator to make provision ; and that
since, by its terms, the entire residue might be at once consumed, the
bequest was not open to objection as involving an unlawful suspension
of absolute ownership, or of the power of alienation.

CONSTRUCTION of decedent's will upon an application for the probate thereof, made by Louisa Raberg,
the executrix therein named ; and opposed by George
F. Pfaler and another, decedent's next of kin. The
facts are stated in the opinion.

CHARLES GOELLER, *for proponent.*

BROWN & RABE, *for contestants.*

THE SURROGATE.—It is conceded that the paper
propounded as the will of this decedent was properly
executed. I find upon the evidence that, at the time
of its execution, its maker was possessed of testamentary capacity, and was not swayed by any such in-
fluences as the law deems undue. The instrument is,
therefore, entitled to probate.

I am asked, in accordance with the provision of

§ 2624 of the Code of Civil Procedure, to pass upon the validity of the fourth clause. That clause is in words following: "All the rest, residue and remainder of my estate I bequeath to my said executrix, to remain with her forever upon the following trust, however: to be devoted and applied in such sums and amounts as she may see fit, to preserve and keep in order my burial place or plot in Brooklyn cemetery."

This is not a direction, it will be observed, to apply the income of a fund, but a direction to devote the fund itself to the purpose prescribed by the testatrix. The fact that the bequest is given to the executrix "to remain with her forever," when it is considered in connection, on the one hand, with the limitations under which she is placed as regards the purpose to which she may apply it, and, on the other hand, with the discretion allowed her as regards the time of its expenditure, affords no justification for the claim that the testatrix contemplated the preservation and investment of the principal and the expenditure of income alone. As the executrix is empowered to consume the entire residue at once, or to draw upon it from time to time, as in her judgment may seem advisable, the bequest is not open to the objection that it involves an unlawful suspension of the power of alienation (Robert v. Corning, 89 *N. Y.*, 225). The object for which the trust is created is one for which the law recognizes the right of a testator to make provision (Matter of Frazer's accounting, 92 *N. Y.*, 239; Emans v. Hickman, 12 *Hun*, 425; Gilman v. McArdle, 12 *Abb., N. C.*, 414; Matter of Hagenmayer's Will, *id.*, 432). There are no grounds on which I can pronounce this provision invalid.

A decree may be entered admitting the will to probate, and adjudging its fourth clause to contain an effectual disposition of the residuary estate.

NEW YORK COUNTY.—HON. D. G. ROLLINS, SURRO-GATE.—April, 1885.

BENEDICT *v.* COOPER.

In the matter of the application for revocation of probate of the will of TUNIS COOPER, *deceased.*

The stenographer of a Surrogate's court is not within the scope of Code Civ. Pro., § 90, which prohibits the appointment of a clerk, deputy-clerk, etc., of a court of record to act as referee, or in other specified capacities, except upon the consent of parties not in default; nor of id., § 2511, which contains a similar prohibition as to a clerk or other employe in a Surrogate's office.

Under the rule of construction established by § 3355 of that Code, §§ 90 and 2511 are to be read together, the prohibition of the last named section being subject to the exception contained in § 90.

In a special proceeding instituted for the revocation of probate of a will, the citation was duly served upon all the necessary parties, including decedent's infant son, a special guardian for whom was, however, neither applied for nor appointed. By the consent of all the parties who appeared and took part in the subsequent hearing, a referee was appointed to take testimony and report the same to the Surrogate; who decided, upon the testimony reported, to revoke the decree of probate. The executors, respondents, opposed the entry of a decree, contending that, because of a failure to appoint a special guardian for the infant party, the order of reference and all subsequent proceedings were unauthorized.—*Held*,

1. That, by the service of the citation upon all the necessary parties, including the infant, the court had acquired jurisdiction of the proceeding and of all the parties thereto;

2. That the testimony taken in pursuance of the consent of parties should not be tossed aside as worthless at the instance of those so consenting;

3. That a special guardian should be appointed for the infant, to ascertain

and report whether it would be for the best interests of the latter to set aside the order of reference and the proceedings subsequent thereto, or that the same should stand, and a decree be entered in conformity with the decision already made.

PETITION by Eli Benedict, executor, and Eliza Cooper, executrix, of decedent's will, for an order to all parties interested to show cause why an order of reference made in a special proceeding for revocation of probate of decedent's will, and all proceedings had thereunder, should not be set aside as void, upon grounds stated in the opinion.

HULL & MEYERS, *for petitioners.*

A. J. ROGERS, *for Tunis B. Cooper and another, contestants.*

THE SURROGATE.—A paper, purporting to be the will of this decedent, was admitted to probate as such in May, 1881. In April, 1882, a proceeding was commenced for revocation of such probate. Citations were duly issued, and duly served upon all necessary parties, and, with the consent of all who appeared and took part in the subsequent trial, Edward F. Underhill, Esq., was appointed referee to take testimony and report the same to the Surrogate. Mr. Underhill proceeded with the examination of such witnesses as were brought before him by the contending parties, and a large volume of evidence was subsequently submitted for my consideration. In July of last year, I rendered a decision granting the petition for revocation. No decree, however, has as yet been entered. My attention is now called to the fact that decedent's infant son has hitherto had no special guardian to represent him and protect his interests. The

alleged will names his mother, the widow of the decedent, as its executrix and also as one of its chief
beneficiaries. The widow and her co-executor protest
that no decree should be entered, and that, because
of the failure to appoint a special guardian for the
infant, the order of reference and all subsequent proceedings were unauthorized and should now be set
aside. Such a course would involve much expense
and long delay in settling the affairs of this estate.
It is, for that reason, greatly to be deprecated, and
should not be pursued unless it is absolutely unavoidable. May it not be avoided?

It is clear that, by the service of citation upon all
the necessary parties to this proceeding, including
the infant, this court acquired jurisdiction of the proceeding and of all parties thereto (Price v. Fenn,
ante, 341, *and cases cited*); any decree, therefore,
that might be entered, even while the infant was still
unrepresented, would not be absolutely void, but
would merely be voidable at the infant's instance
(McMurray v. McMurray, 41 *How. Pr.*, 41; 66 *N. Y.*,
175; Matter of Becker, 28 *Hun*, 207; Boylen v.
McAvoy, 29 *How. Pr.*, 278). Nevertheless, these
petitioners, being named as executors in the disputed
paper, and having duly qualified as such, are justified
in insisting upon such a disposition of this controversy as shall be conclusive upon all persons interested therein.

Now, I do not think that, to accomplish this result,
it is essential that I should at once, and without ascertaining whether or not such a course would be advantageous for the infant, set aside all the proceedings

since and including the entry of the order of reference. If, upon inquiry properly instituted for that
purpose, it shall appear that the best interests of the
infant demand that these proceedings shall stand, it
will, in my judgment, be the duty of the Surrogate
to make decree in conformity with his recent decision.

It is insisted by counsel for the respondents that
the entry of the order of reference herein was
unauthorized, in view of the limitations upon the Surrogate's authority that are established by § 2546 of
the Code of Civil Procedure. That section declares
that an appointment of a referee may be made " on
the written consent of all the parties appearing."
Such consent, in the present case, was given by the
petitioners and the respondents, and I must certainly
refuse to toss aside as worthless the testimony taken
in pursuance of that consent, until I am asked to do
so by somebody who was not a party to it (Musgrove
v. Lusk, 2 *Tenn. Ch.*, 576). If the special guardian
whom I shall appoint to represent the infant shall see
fit to raise this objection, it will be again considered.

It is also urged, by counsel for the respondents,
that the referee herein was disqualified from holding
that office by reason of his being the stenographer of
the Surrogate's court. This objection is somewhat
ungracious, for counsel does not claim that, at the
time he consented to Mr. Underhill's appointment, he
was ignorant, either of the fact that the appointee
was the court stenographer, or of the statute which
is claimed to work the disqualification. But it is no
more ungracious than it is unsound. In view of
§ 3355 of the Code, sections 90 and 2511 must be

construed as if they had simultaneously become law ;
and, so construed, they simply forbid the appointment of "a clerk or other person employed," etc.,
except upon the written consent of all the parties
(Estate of Thorn, 4 Monthly Law Bulletin, 48).
And besides I am of the opinion that the stenographer does not have such a relation to the Surrogate's court or office as to bring him within the scope
of either § 90 or § 2511.   See §§ 2508 and 2512.

All in all, the disposition which the court shall
make of this whole matter must be governed entirely
by what, upon investigation, shall appear to be most
advantageous for the infant (Bowen v. Idley, 1 *Edw.
Ch.*, 148; Croghan v. Livingston, 17 *N. Y.*, 218;
Fulton v. Roosevelt, 1 *Paige*, 178; Levy v. Levy,
3 *Madd.*, 245).   If it shall appear that the infant's
share in his father's estate is greater in the contingency of his father's intestacy than in that of the
final establishment of the disputed paper as his will—
and I am inclined to think that such is the case—
then further litigation may be wisely avoided.

A special guardian will be appointed to ascertain
and protect the interests of the infant; and, as his
interests and those of his mother are or may be
adverse, the Surrogate will appoint such special guardian of his own motion after due notice to the infant
(Price v. Fenn, *supra*).

NEW YORK COUNTY.—HON. D. G. ROLLINS, SURRO-
GATE.—May, 1885.

TOWNSEND v. PELL.

In the matter of the estate of ALEXANDER G. MERCER,
deceased.

Where a non-resident of the State died without its limits, leaving personal
property in New York county, which was taken into actual custody by
a domiciliary executrix before the filing of a petition in the Surrogate's
court of that county, in pursuance whereof the will was admitted to
probate here,—

Held, that the court had no judisdiction in the premises, and that the
decree must be set aside, and the letters issued to the petitioner
revoked.

APPLICATION to set aside decree admitting will to
probate, etc.   The facts are stated in the opinion.

JAMES STIKEMAN, *for J. J. Townsend.*

SCUDDER & CARTER, *for Anna Pell.*

THE SURROGATE.—This testator executed his will
at Newport, R. I., in 1870, and thereafter resided in
that city until November, 1882, when he died.   He
named Anna Pell as his executrix, and Edward King
and Frederick W. Rhinelander as his executors, and
directed that John J. Townsend should be substituted
in place of any one of the three who should fail to
qualify.   At the time of his death he was possessed of
no real estate in this county, and had no personal
property here except moneys on deposit in certain
banks and trust companies, and stocks and bonds in
the custody of bankers.   The will was proved in the

probate court at Newport, Rhode Island, and letters testamentary were subsequently issued by that court to Mrs. Pell. Mr. Townsend made application for letters, as Mr. King had predeceased the testator; but, as the security required in such cases by the law of Rhode Island was not furnished, Mr. Townsend's application was continued until the further order of the probate court; and no further order has as yet been made.

On August 29th, 1884, Mr. Townsend filed with the Surrogate of this county an exemplified copy of the testator's will and a decree of the probate court at Newport admitting it to probate, together with his petition praying for the probate thereof in this court and for issuance to him of letters testamentary. A decree was entered upon such petition in accordance with its prayer, and, on September 12th, 1884, letters testamentary were granted to Mr. Townsend. No citation was issued in that proceeding, and none was applied for, and no notice was given to Mrs. Pell, or to any other person, that such proceeding had been instituted. Mrs. Pell now seeks to set it aside. She alleges—and her allegation is not disputed—that soon after she had qualified as executrix, and before Mr. Townsend filed his petition with the Surrogate, she came to New York and reduced to her possession, as executrix, all the assets of her testator's estate that were within this county, collecting all sums of money here held upon deposit for his account, and taking into actual manual custody all bonds and certificates of stock belonging to the estate.

There is nothing in the averments of Mr. Towns-

end's affidavit respecting the action of the executrix
in subsequently placing these assets, or a portion of
them, in the custody of Mr. Griswold, inconsistent
with Mrs. Pell's claim, that, at the time of the filing
of Mr. Townsend's petition, there were no unadministered assets, and that there are now no unadministered assets, belonging to the testator's estate
within the jurisdiction of this court. I am, therefore, of the opinion that, at the time of entering the
decree herein, and of the granting of letters testamentary, the Surrogate was without authority in the
premises (Evans v. Schoonmaker, 2 *Dem.*, 289; affi'd
on appeal, Matter of Schoonmaker, 31 *Hun*, 638).

The application of Mrs. Pell is, therefore, granted,
and that of Mr. Townsend, denied.

NEW YORK COUNTY.—HON. D. G. ROLLINS, SURRO-
GATE.—May, 1885.

MATTER OF NOYES.

In the matter of the estate of FREDERICK B. NOYES,
deceased.

A tax or assessment upon a decedent's real property, which has been levied
and confirmed before his death, being one of the "debts of the deceased" which his personal representative is, by statute (2 R. S., 87,
§ 27), required to proceed with diligence to pay, a devisee of the
property is entitled to have the incumbrance discharged out of the
decedent's personal estate, unless the will contain directions to the
contrary.

DETERMINATION of question as to payment of taxes upon real property devised by decedent's will.

JOHN A. FOLEY, *executor, in person.*

THE SURROGATE.—This testator left a will and codicil. By the first clause of the former instrument, he directed his executors to pay his just debts; by the fifth clause of the latter, he gave to one of those executors "two lots of ground situate in One Hundred and Thirty-fifth street, near Eighth avenue, in the city of New York." Upon the property devised in the terms just quoted, certain taxes and assessments were due and unpaid at the time of the testator's death. I am asked to determine whether the devisee takes the land clear of these taxes and assessments, or takes it *cum onere*.

It was the rule of the common law that the devisee of real property, upon which subsisted any encumbrance that had been put upon it during the testator's lifetime, was entitled to have such encumbrance satisfied out of the personal assets of the testator's estate. This rule was broad enough to include a mortgage, and, only in cases where an intention to make the devised estate the primary fund for the payment of encumbrances was plainly manifested, did the devisee take his devise *cum onere* (Roper on Legacies, 732; Mosely v. Marshall, 27 *Barb.*, 45; Wright v. Holbrook, 32 *N. Y.*, 587).

So far as regards mortgage debts, the rule of the common law was abrogated in this State by § 4, tit. 5, ch. 1, part 2 of the Revised Statutes (3 *Banks*, 7th ed., 2205), which declares that the devisee of real estate, subject to a mortgage executed by his testator, shall satisfy and discharge such mortgage out of his own property, without resorting to the testator's executor, unless there be an express direction in the will that such mortgage be otherwise paid.

But so far as regards the burden of taxes and assessments levied and confirmed before the death of the testator, the rule of the common law remains unchanged. They are "debts" which the executor is required by law "to proceed with diligence to pay" (§ 27, tit. 3, ch. 6, part 2, R. S.; 3 *Banks, 7th ed.,* 2298; Seabury v. Bowen, 3 *Bradf.,* 207; Griswold v. Griswold, 4 *id.,* 216; Bates v. Underhill, 3 *Redf.,* 372; Hone v. Lockman, 4 *id.,* 64; Coleman v. Coleman, 5 *id.,* 524).

NEW YORK COUNTY.—HON. D. G. ROLLINS, SURRO-
GATE.—May, 1885.

SIMPKINS *v.* SCUDDER.

In the matter of the judicial settlement of the account of HENRY J. SCUDDER, *as executor of the will of* NATHANIEL S. SIMPKINS, JR., *deceased.*

It seems, that inability on the part of a legatee to take a legacy, at the time when it has become due, and when the executor is ready to pay it, will ordinarily prevent the running of interest thereon during the continuance of the inability.

But where the father of an infant legatee, during the year succeeding the testator's death, advised the executor of his intention to procure the appointment of a general guardian who would be entitled, as such, to receive the legacy, and, in consequence of delay in applying for letters of guardianship, an appointment was not made until after the expiration of that year, the executor continuing to hold the fund in his hands,—

Held, that the legacy should have been invested for the infant's benefit, pursuant to 2 R. S., 91, § 48; and that, though the executor was exonerated from personal liability, the infant was entitled to interest at the rate of six per cent., commencing at the end of a year from the death of the testator.

Hoffman v. Penn. Hospital, 1 *Dem.*, 118—distinguished.

DETERMINATION of question, arising upon judicial settlement of executor's account, as to allowance and rate of interest on legacies bequeathed by decedent's will to Allen T. Simpkins and others, infants. The facts are stated in the opinion.

PAYSON MERRILL, *for guardian.*

L. C. LEDYARD, *for executor.*

THE SURROGATE.—By the will of this testator, who died in October, 1883, five nephews and nieces, all infants in law, were severally bequeathed a legacy of $25,000. Prior to the expiration of the year succeeding the testator's death, the father of these infants advised the executor of his purpose to procure the appointment of some person as their general guardian, who would be entitled as such to receive their legacies. There was some delay in applying for letters of guardianship, and when such letters were issued, more than a year had elapsed from the testator's death. A decree is now about to be entered, settling the executor's accounts and directing general distribution of the estate; and I am asked to determine whether these infant beneficiaries are entitled to interest upon their legacies, and, if so entitled, then at what rate and for what time.

In the case of Hoffman v. Penn. Hospital (1 *Dem.*, 118), I held that, whenever in contemplation of law a legacy is due, interest at the legal rate begins to run upon it, even though the condition of the estate is such that its payment is then impossible; and that, until such legacy is finally paid, such interest continues to run at the same rate, though its amount may exceed the income that the funds of the estate have yielded during the same period. I did not, in Hoffman v. Penn. Hospital, consider the question, whether an inability on the part of a legatee to take a legacy, at the time when it had become due, and when the testator's executor was ready to pay it, would or would not prevent the running of interest during the continuance of the inability. I think that, under some circumstances, it certainly would, and that it would under the circumstances disclosed in the case at bar, if, in the interval that has elapsed since the expiration of a year from the testator's death, no other course had been open to the executor, except to hold the legacies in question in his hands until the appointment of a guardian.

But it is provided by §§ 48 and 49 of title 3, ch. 6, part 2 of the Revised Statutes (3 *Banks*, *7th ed.*, 2301), that, in case a legatee is a minor and has no guardian, or the Surrogate does not direct payment of a legacy to such guardian, the legacy shall be invested in permanent securities, in the name and for the benefit of such minor, and that the interest thereon shall be applied, under the direction of the Surrogate, to such minor's education and support. Now, in the present case, it is not claimed that the executor is at fault because of his failure to comply with the requirements of this statute; but, while he is admittedly exonerated from personal liability, I think that the infants, in view of the fact that no investment has in fact been made for their benefit, are entitled to interest at six per cent., from the expiration of a year after the testator's death.

This conclusion is in accordance with the decision of the Supreme Court of Massachusetts in Kent v. Dunham (106 *Mass.*, 586), and with that of the Court of Appeals of Virginia, in Lyon's Adm'rs v. Magagno's Adm'rs (7 *Gratt.*, 377).

NEW YORK COUNTY.—HON. D. G. ROLLINS, SURRO-
GATE.—May, 1885.

WATERS *v.* COLLINS.

In the matter of the judicial settlement of the account of JOHN D. COLLINS *and another, as executors of the will of* RHINALDO M. WATERS, *deceased.*

Unless a testator distinctly indicates that one or more of his beneficiaries is to be preferred to others, or one or more of his bequests is founded upon a consideration, and is not, therefore, a mere bestowal of bounty, the courts will presume an intent that all should be paid alike, and, in case of a deficiency of assets, will direct a ratable abatement.

Testator, by his will, directed the establishment of a trust fund of $50,000, for the use of his daughter G., for life; and, by a codicil, bequeathed to C., one of the persons named as executors, $700, which sum, he declared, "is to be over and above any and all commissions that he may be entitled to receive as one of the executors," and was given upon condition that C. qualified and acted as executor, which he did. There being a deficiency of assets, it was contended, on the one hand, that the trust provision in G.'s favor took precedence, as being made for the support and maintenance of a daughter; and, on the other, that the legacy to C. was not mere bounty, but was in the nature of a compensation for services expected from and actually rendered by the legatee.—

Held, that the two legacies must abate proportionally.

CONSTRUCTION of will, and codicil thereto, of decedent, upon judicial settlement of executor's account. The facts appear in the opinion.

JOHN D. COLLINS, *executor, in person.*

W. A. W. STEWART, *for U. S. Trust Co., trustee.*

THE SURROGATE.—This testator left a will and a codicil. The will directs his executors to pay over to the United States Trust company the sum of $50,000, for the use of his daughter Gertrude for life. By the codicil, John D. Collins, one of his executors, is bequeathed the sum of $700, " which said sum," to use the language of the testator, " is to be over and above any and all commissions that he may be entitled to receive as one of the executors of my said will, and is to be paid out of real or personal estate; but this legacy is limited upon the condition that said Collins shall accept, qualify and act as executor hereunder." The executors are now accounting, and have credited themselves with $630, advanced to Mr. Collins in part payment of his legacy. It seems that the assets of the estate are not likely to be adequate to satisfy, in full, the trust for the daughter and the Collins legacy.

The question arises, therefore, which of these two provisions, if either, is entitled to priority over the other. Such priority is claimed for the former, because it is primarily a provision for the support and maintenance of testator's daughter. In behalf of Mr. Collins, on the other hand, it is urged that the bequest for his benefit is not mere bounty, but is in the nature of compensation for services that the testator expected him to render, and that, since testator's death, he has in fact rendered in the management of this estate; that such legacy is for that cause entitled to precedence, as well as for the additional reason that it is given by the codicil, which is a later expression of testator's purposes than is afforded by the will.

If there were any repugnance or inconsistency between the two papers, the latter would prevail; but there is not. The will and codicil must, therefore, be construed precisely as if the provisions of both were contained in one instrument. The executor's claim to priority because of the supposed consideration for the legacy in his behalf is not well founded.

In Heron v. Heron (2 *Atk.*, 171), it was held by Lord HARDWICKE that bequests to executors, even though given expressly for " care and pains," did not differ from general legacies so as to take them out of the ordinary rule in respect to abatement for deficiency of assets. The same doctrine was asserted in Attorney General v. Robins (2 *P. Wms.*, 24); in Fretwell v. Stacy (2 *Ver.*, 434); and in Duncan v. Watts (16 *Beav.*, 204).

As to the $50,000 provision, the fact that it is a bequest for maintenance does not give it priority (Wood v. Vandenburgh, 6 *Paige*, 277). The testator provided that, if its full amount could not be raised out of the personal estate, the executors should sell the real estate, all or part, so as to produce it, but in this respect it has no advantage over the Collins legacy, which is expressly ordered to be satisfied "out of real or personal estate."

It is probable that, so far from intending to give either of these two provisions precedence over the other, the testator expected that both would be paid in full, and that his estate would be sufficient, indeed, to answer all his testamentary dispositions. I hold that, in case of a deficiency of assets, the two legacies must abate *pro rata* (Blower v. Morret, 2 *Ves. Sen.*, 419; Beeston v. Booth, 4 *Madd.*, 161; Thwaites v. Foreman, 1 *Coll. C.*, 409; Wood v. Vandenburgh, *supra*).

NEW YORK COUNTY.—HON. D. G. ROLLINS, SURRO-GATE.—May, 1885.

MATTER OF RUSSELL.

In the matter of the judicial settlement of the account of ALGERNON S. SULLIVAN, *public administrator, as administrator of the estate of* JOHN RUSSELL, *deceased.*

A referee appointed by a Surrogate, pursuant to the authority conferred by Code Civ. Pro., § 2546, having, by the terms of that section, the same power "as a referee appointed by the Supreme Court for the trial of an issue of fact in an action," the procedure before him is governed by the provisions of General Rule of Practice 30, which excepts testimony, taken upon the trial of the issues in an action, from its requirement that testimony taken before a referee shall be signed by the witness giving the same.

MOTION to compel witnesses to sign minutes of testimony given by them before referee, in proceedings for judicial settlement of administrator's account.

WM. B. TULLIS, *for the motion.*

RUFUS P. LIVERMORE, *opposed.*

THE SURROGATE.—With two exceptions, none of the numerous witnesses examined before the referee in these proceedings has signed his testimony. In advance of the argument of the pending motion for the confirmation of the referee's report, it is insisted, by one of the parties to this controversy, that no testimony ought to be considered by the Surrogate until it has been signed by the witness who gave it. Is this objection well founded?

The Surrogate's authority to direct a reference, under such circumstances as appear in the case at bar, is derived from § 2546 of the Code of Civil Procedure. That section provides that, "in a special proceeding, other than one instituted for probate or revocation of probate of a will, the Surrogate may, in his discretion, appoint a referee to take and report the evidence upon the facts, or upon a specific question of fact; to examine an account rendered, to hear and determine all questions arising upon the settlement of such an account, which the Surrogate has power to determine; and to make a report thereon, subject, however, to a confirmation by the Surrogate. *Such a referee* (that is, any referee authorized to be appointed by § 2546) has the same power," says the Code, " as a referee appointed by the Supreme Court, for the trial of an issue of fact in an action; and the provisions of this act, applicable to a reference by the Supreme Court, apply to a reference made as prescribed in this section, so far as they can be applied in substance, without regard to the form of the proceeding."

Now, what are the *"powers of a referee appointed by the Supreme Court for the trial of an issue of fact in an action,"* and what is the course of procedure before such a referee, so far as concerns this question of the signing of testimony? Rule 30 of the General Rules of Practice gives the answer to these questions. From its requirement that testimony taken before a referee shall be signed, testimony so taken *upon the trial of the issues in an action* is expressly excepted.

It follows that testimony taken in references ordered by the Surrogate under § 2546 falls within the same exception, and that it does not, therefore, need to be signed.

NEW YORK COUNTY.—HON. D. G. ROLLINS, SURRO-
GATE.—May, 1885.

McKIE *v.* CLARK.

*In the matter of the judicial settlement of the account
of* JOHN M. CLARK *and another, as executors of
the will of* THOMAS McKIE, *deceased.*

Testator's will, besides bequeathing various specific and pecuniary legacies,
directed the executors to pay cash, or assign securities, to a trust company to the amount of $200,000, for the benefit of his widow for life,
after whose death the fund was to be *repaid to the executors* : it further gave the net income of the remainder of his estate, during the
widow's life, to his children equally, providing that such remainder
should be held by and in charge of the executors, the rents and income
bo collected by them, the personal estate kept invested, and the said
net income paid over semiannually, or as often as practicable ; and
directed the executors, upon the widow's death, to divide the entire
estate, including the $200,000, into equal parts, and pay over or assign
the same to the children.

Upon an accounting in 1878, the executors were each allowed half commissions on all assets received by them, and the same upon all sums
paid out, as well as upon the balance directed by the decree to be
retained in their hands until a final distribution. That decree provided "that they" (the executors) "retain to themselves, in their
capacity of trustees, all the remainder of said moneys," etc., "to be
held and accounted for by them as such trustees, upon the trusts and
in accordance with the provisions and directions" in the will. The
widow having died, the executors, upon a judicial settlement of their
account, had with a view to a final distribution, claimed full commissions upon the entire amount undistributed at the time of the former
accounting.—

Held, that the will required, from the persons to whom the estate was committed, the employment of no other than purely executorial functions ;
that the decree of 1878, in conferring upon them the new name of trustees, did not change their real character, or confer upon them any new
rights or privileges ; and, that as to such funds as had been in the
executors' hands since their former accounting, their claim to commissions should be disallowed.

Johnson v. Lawrence, 95 *N. Y.*, 154—compared; Laytin v. Davidson, *id.*,
263—distinguished.

DETERMINATION of question as to executors' commissions, arising upon the judicial settlement of their account. The facts are stated in the opinion.

JACOB F. MILLER, *for executors.*

EMMET & ROBINSON, *for N. Y. L. Ins. & T. Co., trustee.*

COUDERT BROS., *for Chas. McKie.*

R. E. ROBINSON, *special guardian for Thomas McKie.*

THE SURROGATE.—A decree is about to be entered, settling the accounts of this testator's executors. What commissions shall it direct the accounting parties to retain? The provisions of the testator's will are substantially as follows: 　　　　·

By the first article, certain specific legacies and $10,000 in cash are given to his wife. By the second, his executors are instructed to pay over to the N. Y. Life Insurance & Trust Co. the sum of $200,000 in cash, or to assign and transfer to such company securities of that value. The company is directed to keep such fund invested, so that it shall produce interest or income, and to pay such interest or income to the testator's widow during her lifetime. The second article further provides that, at the death of the widow, the fund shall be repaid to the executors. Article third gives, to each of the testator's seven children, the sum of $10,000.

Article fourth is as follows: " After satisfying the foregoing provisions, I give and bequeath the net income of the remainder of my estate, during the lifetime of my wife, to my children above named, in equal shares, the said remainder of my estate to be held by and in charge of my executors, the rents and income collected by them, the personal estate kept invested, and the said net income paid to my children half yearly, or as often as practicable."

Then follows article five, in these words: "Upon the death of my said wife, I direct my executors to divide all my estate then remaining, including the said $200,000 of which she had the income, in equal parts or shares, one in respect to each of my children, and to pay over or assign," etc., etc.

In accordance with the directions of article second, the executors long since paid to the New York Life Insurance and Trust Company the sum of $200,000 for the widow's benefit. She is now dead, and the fund has been returned to the executors. The entire estate remaining in their hands is, therefore, ready for distribution. Upon a former accounting, in 1878, the executors were each allowed full commissions, at the rate of two and one half, one and one quarter, and one half per cent., upon the value of all assets received by them, and at the same rate, also, upon all sums they had paid out, and upon the balance directed by the decree to be retained in their hands to await the death of the widow and the final distribution which would thereupon ensue. It is now claimed, among other things, by the accounting parties, that they are entitled to full commissions as trustees, at the rate of five, two and one half, and one per cent., upon the entire amount undistributed at the time of the former accounting. That claim is based, in large measure, upon one of the provisions of the decree

which was entered upon the judicial settlement of
their accounts in 1878. The provision referred to is
the following :

" That they " (the executors) " retain to themselves,
in their capacity as trustees . . . . . all the remainder
of the said moneys and property in their hands, as
shown by the said account, and such other moneys
and property, if any, as shall be received by them, ·
or to which they shall be entitled, as such executors
or trustees, to be held and accounted for by them as
such trustees, upon the trusts and in accordance with
the provisions and directions in the .said will contained."

If the decree of 1878 did not contain the above
quoted provision, I should have no hesitation whatever, in rejecting the claim of these accounting
parties for commissions upon the residuary funds in
their hands. It seems to me that the will requires,
from the persons to whom the testator commits his
estate, the employment of no other than purely executorial functions. It nowhere refers to them as
" trustees," or gives to them any part of the estate
in " trust," and it assigns to them no duties that could
not be performed by administrators with the will
annexed. As to the payment of the seven legacies;
of $10,000 each, and the delivery of the $200,000 to
the trust company, these acts called for ordinary
executorial service, and for nothing more. It is true
that the accounting parties were directed to hold the
residue of the estate in their hands during the widow's
life, to keep the same invested, and to pay over the
income to certain beneficiaries. But, in this respect,

the terms of the will are not essentially different from those that appear in the testamentary paper that was the subject of discussion by the Court of Appeals, in Hall v. Hall (78 *N. Y.*, 535), or in the will that that court has more recently had under review, in Johnson v. Lawrence (95 *N. Y.*, 154). I think that the case at bar bears a much closer analogy to that last cited than it bears to the case of Laytin v. Davidson (95 *N. Y.*, 263), with which it has been compared by counsel for these executors. I mean no reflection upon any of the parties to the 1878 accounting, or upon any persons concerned in it, when I say that the language of FINCH, J., in Johnson v. Lawrence, seems to me to be very apposite to the situation of the affairs of this estate at the time of the entry of the 1878 decree: "The attempted change of capacity at that moment was purely constructive; not warranted by the will; needed for no purpose except as a foundation for double commissions."

And, to quote again from Judge FINCH'S opinion, the point of time had not arrived when, "within the provisions of the will, and in the contemplation of the testator, it had become the duty of the executors to pay over to themselves as trustees the funds of the estate." At the date of the former decree herein, there was no reason why the executors, as such, should not have been directed to do precisely what they were enjoined to do by the will, namely, to continue their possession as executors of the residue in their hands, to pay thereout, from time to time, the accumulating income, until the return of the $200,000, and then to make complete and final distribution of the whole estate. I feel bound to hold that the decree of 1878, which dubbed the executors with the new name of trustees, did not change their real character or confer upon them any new rights or privileges. For this proposition I find abundant warrant in the criticisms ·of Judge FINCH, respecting the decree which was relied upon to support the contention of the accounting parties, in Johnson v. Lawrence.

As 'to such funds, therefore, as have been in the hands of the executors since their former accounting, their claim to commissions is disallowed.

⬥⬥⬥⬥

NEW YORK COUNTY.—HON. D. G. ROLLINS, SURRO‍GATE.—June, 1885.

ASINARI *v.* BANGS.

In the matter of the application for probate of a paper propounded as the will of AUGUSTA GIL‍LENDER, *deceased.*

Upon a petition for probate of a will executed in duplicate, one of the two originals being shown to have been destroyed by the maker, *animo revocandi,* and there being no proof that the other was in her possession at any time after its execution, though it did not appear but that it was still intact,—

Held, that a decree might be entered denying the application.

APPLICATION for the probate of decedent's alleged will, made by Francis N. Bangs; opposed by Helena L. G. Asinari, decedent's daughter.

VOL. III.—25

ROOT & STRONG. *for proponents.*

VAN SCHAICK, GILLENDER & STOIBER, *for contestant*

THE SURROGATE.—Upon the evidence submitted in this proceeding, I find that one of the duplicate wills proved to have been executed by Mrs. Gillender was torn in pieces by her, *animo revocandi.* There is no proof that the other is not still intact, but it is not shown to have been, at any time after its execution, in the decedent's possession. It must, therefore, be presumed, in the absence of evidence to the contrary, that the destruction of that one of the two papers which was within her reach was intended to nullify the other. A decree denying probate may, therefore, be entered.

Before I can pass upon claims for costs and allowances, affidavits, showing what time has been devoted to the controversy, must be submitted to the clerk.

NEW YORK COUNTY.—HON. D. G. ROLLINS, SURROGATE.—June, 1885.

WEST *v.* GUNTHER.

In the matter of the estate of MARY E. GUNTHER, *deceased.*

A foreign general guardian is not entitled to recognition by the courts of this State. He should apply for ancillary letters, under Code Civ. Pro., § 2838.

PETITION of William C. West, as the general guardian of the property of George H. Buckner, an infant eleven years of age, and legatee under decedent's will, to compel Francis F. Gunther, executor thereof, to pay to petitioner the legacy bequeathed to the infant.

COURSEN & COURSEN, *for executor.*

SCOTT LORD, Jr., *for petitioner.*

THE SURROGATE.—By the will of this testatrix, a legacy was bequeathed to George H. Buckner, an infant. I am asked to direct that such legacy be paid to William C. West, who holds letters of guardianship issued by the probate court of Monroe county, in the state of Michigan. This application must be denied. The power of a guardian is derived from the court that appoints him, and the fact that one has received such appointment from a foreign jurisdiction does not entitle him to recognition in the courts of New York (Morrell v. Dickey, 1 *Johns. Ch.*, 153; Williams v. Storrs, 6 *Johns. Ch.*, 353; Ex parte Dawson, 3 *Bradf.*, 130; McLoskey v. Reid, 4 *Bradf.*, 334; Matter of Neally, 26 *How. Pr.*, 402; Biolley's Estate, 1 *Tucker*, 422; Matter of Hosford, 2 *Redf.*, 168; Trimble v. Dzieduzyiki, 57 *How. Pr.*, 208; Weller v. Suggett, 3 *Redf.*, 249). Section 2838 of the Code of Civil Procedure provides for the issuance of ancillary letters, in case infants who reside in the United States, but without the State of New York, are entitled to property within the State. Such proceedings should be instituted as that section points out.

NEW YORK COUNTY.—HON. D. G. ROLLINS, SURRO-
GATE.—June, 1885.

HOYT *v.* JACKSON.

*In the matter of the application for revocation of
probate of the will of* JESSE HOYT, *deceased.*

Under ordinary circumstances, where a witness, in obedience to the command of a subpœna *duces tecum*, attends in court, and produces papers
which contain matter relevant and material to the pending controversy,
the same are admissible in evidence, not only upon the offer of the
party at whose instance the subpœna was issued, but also upon that of
his adversary.

The provision of Code Civ. Pro., § 837, to the effect that the rule compelling *parties* to answer relevant questions "does not require a witness
to give an answer which will tend to . . . . . expose himself to a
penalty or forfeiture," cannot be invoked to justify the contestant of a
will in refusing to furnish testimony which would establish the fact of
the validity of the disputed document.

Where a witness, in obedience to a subpœna *duces tecum*, attends in court
and, after being sworn, produces papers which he thereupon places in
the custody of the court, either party has thereafter the same right,
which he had when the witness was present, to insist that the papers
shall be placed at his disposal, for use as evidence in the cause.

The privilege established by Code Civ. Pro., § 835, which declares that
"an attorney or counsellor at law shall not be allowed to disclose a
communication made by his client to him . . . . . in the course of his
professional employment," is that of the client and not of the attorney; and, where the former is a party to a litigation, this privilege
exists, notwithstanding the abrogation of the rule which rendered
parties incompetent as witnesses.

Mitchell's Case, 12 *Abb. Pr.*, 249—dissented from.

But where a party to a pending controversy subpœnaes his own attorney
to produce papers at the trial, which, upon their production, he omits
to offer in evidence, he is to be treated as thereby giving the right to
his adversary to introduce them, if discovered to be pertinent to the
issue.

APPLICATION by decedent's daughter, Mary J. Hoyt,
for the revocation of probate of decedent's will;

opposed by James W. Jackson and others, executors.
A previous phase of the controversy was reported in
2 *Dem.*, 443. During the progress of the case upon
the part of the contestant, a subpœna *duces tecum*
was issued at the request of the contestant, and was
served upon Mr. Conkling, former counsel for the
contestant, to produce certain papers therein described. In obedience to the subpœna, Mr. Conkling
attended in court, and requested that he be sworn as a
witness, and, on being sworn, he produced to the Surrogate the papers mentioned and described in the
subpœna, and, taking the court's direction, he delivered them to the Surrogate.

Before resting their case, the contestant's counsel
moved that the papers deposited with the court " by
Mr. Conkling be placed in the custody of counsel for
contestant." The court said : " For the present I
deny your motion." Thereupon Mr. Evarts, of counsel for proponents, asked the court to put at their
disposition, for use as evidence in the cause, the
papers produced under the subpœna issued by the
other side.

Wm. M. Evarts, and Elihu Root, *for the motion.*

B. F. Butler, and Roger A. Pryor, *opposed.*

The Surrogate.—Assuming that the papers lately
produced by Mr. Conkling, at the instance of contestant's attorney, but not offered in evidence by him,
are material and relevant to the issues of this proceeding, have the proponents, under the circumstances
here appearing, the present right to introduce them

in evidence in face of the contestant's protest? I have never had occasion to deal with so important a question of practice, upon which so little light has been thrown by decided cases. I have been unable, indeed, even with the assistance afforded me by counsel, and after thorough ransacking of the text books and reports, to find any judicial decisions which could clearly guide me to the solution of the comparatively simple question that would be here presented, if the witness who produced these papers, in obedience to the writ of subpœna *duces tecum*, had never been counsel for the contestant, and if, therefore, the question of a client's privilege were in no wise involved.

There are numerous cases, English and American, touching the right of one of the parties in a litigation to put in evidence papers and documents that he has brought into court, in pursuance of a notice for their production from his adversary. But those decisions are based upon a principle that is manifestly inapplicable to the present situation, and to any situation indeed where there has been a production of papers, not by one of the parties in a cause at the demand of the other, but by a third person at the instance of one of the parties.

A subpœna *duces tecum* is a process whereby a court, at the instance of a suitor, commands a person, who has, in his possession or control, some document or paper that is pertinent to the issues of the pending controversy, to produce it for use at the trial. Now, it seems to me that, under ordinary circumstances, when a witness has appeared in response to such a subpœna, and has produced papers and documents by such subpœna directed to be produced, such papers and documents, if they contain relevant and material matter, are admissible in evidence upon the offer, not only of the party at whose instance the subpœna has been issued, but also upon the offer of his adversary. It was held by CRESWELL, J., in Snelgrove v. Stevens (1 *Car. & Mar.*, 508), that a witness being in court, and having a material document in his possession, was bound to produce it if required, though he had not received notice to produce it, and had not been served with a subpœna *duces tecum*.

Whether, as between the witness and the court, that doctrine should be approved or disapproved, it is plain that, under ordinary circumstances, its enforcement in the conduct of a trial would not be an error of which either of the contending parties could take advantage. If the witness himself should not protest against the disclosure, for the purposes of evidence, of documents that he had brought to the court room, not at the instance of the party offering them, but either at the instance of the opposite party, or without the summons of either, it is plain that such opposite party could make no objection. But how does the case stand, when the person subpœnaed is or has been counsel for one of the litigants?

Unless the doctrine of the common law, respecting privileged communications between an attorney and client, has been abrogated, in whole or in part, by the change in our system of jurisprudence, whereby parties have been made competent and compellable witnesses, it is very clear that Mr. Conkling, had he brought these papers into court pursuant to a subpœna from the proponents, could not have been compelled, and indeed could not have been permitted, to disclose them without the contestant's consent (Jackson v. Burtis, 14 *Johns.*, 391; Jackson v. Denison, 4 *Wend.*, 558; McPherson v. Rathbone, 7 *id.*, 216; Coveney v. Tannahill, 1 *Hill*, 33; Kellogg v. Kellogg, 6 *Barb.*, 116; Mallory v. Benjamin, 9 *How. Pr.*, 419).

Now, the statement of that proposition suggests three subjects of inquiry:

1st. If these papers were now in the possession or under the control of the contestant herself, could she be required to produce them by a subpœna *duces tecum*, issued at the instance of the proponents?

If this question be answered in the affirmative, then

2d. Does the fact that she could be so required empower the court to enforce their production by her counsel, if the papers chance to be in his possession, and thus make ineffectual the client's claim of privilege? And if not, then

3rd. Has the contestant, by the fact that she has herself brought about the production of the papers, waived the right, that she might else have maintained, to protest against their disclosure to the proponents, and against the proponents' use of them for purposes of evidence?

The first question of the three it is not difficult to answer. With certain exceptions, that need not here be noticed, a party is now examinable as a witness for any purpose, in any manner and at any stage of the cause, and may, like any other witness, be required to produce books and papers (Bonesteel v. Lynde, 8

How. Pr., 226; Commercial Bank v. Dunham, 13 *id.*, 541; Brett v. Bucknam, 32 *Barb.*, 655; People v. Dyckman, 24 *How. Pr.*, 222: Central Nat. Bank v. Arthur, 2 *Sweeny*, 194; Smith v. McDonald, 50 *How. Pr.*, 519; McGuffin v. Dinsmore, 4 *Abb.*, *N. C.*, 241).

It is claimed by contestant's counsel that their client is protected, from producing the papers sought to be put in evidence against her, by the doctrine of the law that is now embodied in § 837 of the Code. "This provision," says that section (that is the provision requiring parties to answer relevant questions), "does not require a witness to give an answer which will tend to accuse himself of a crime or misdemeanor, or to expose himself to a penalty or forfeiture." If the application that counsel for the contestant seeks to make of this section, and of the decision of Judge PECKHAM, in Anable v. Anable, is correct, then any person interested in the result of a probate controversy may refuse absolutely to give testimony in the cause. The contestant stands in no other attitude to the matter than either of the proponents. It is true, as counsel argues, that this estate, pending the controversy, is not *in nubibus*. It has vested in somebody, and when this controversy shall terminate, it will be ascertained in whom it has vested. At present it does not appear that the contestant has any estate other than that given her by the will, and if her testimony would establish the fact that the will is valid, then she could not lawfully refuse to furnish that testimony by reason of any protection afforded her by § 837.

The second of the three questions I have suggested is more difficult of solution.

It was held by DALY, Ch. J., in Mitchell's Case (12 *Abb. Pr.*, 249), that the enactment of the law making a party compellable to testify as a witness operated as an abrogation of the doctrine, that had theretofore prevailed, respecting the inviolability of the confidence between attorney and client. This decision is put upon the ground that the exemption of the attorney from the necessity of testifying was never regarded as his personal privilege, but as existing purely for the protection of his client; that he was, in this respect, considered as one and the same person with his client. "When the Code," says the learned Judge, "declares that a party to an action may be compelled to testify in the same manner, and subject to the same rules of examination as other witnesses, it is obvious that the meaning is that whatever may be required of other witnesses may be required of him. If they must produce books and papers, so must he, and if he has placed them in the possession of his attorney, agent, or any other person, the one who has them in actual custody may be compelled to bring them before the court, to be used as evidence. In courts of equity the principle of protection was never extended to all papers belonging to a client which he may have put in the hands of his solicitor; but the general rule was that whatever the client was bound to produce, for the benefit of a third person, his solicitor, if the document or paper was in his possession, was also bound to produce."

In support of this proposition several cases are

cited by Judge DALY. The list could be considerably enlarged (see Fenwick v. Reed, 1 *Mer.*, 114; Furlong v. Howard, 2 *Schoales & Lef.*, 115; Busk v. Lewis, 6 *Madd.*, 29; Vawter v. Ohio & Miss. R. R. Co., 14 *Ind.*, 174; Egrement v. Langdon, 12 *Ad. & Ell.*, *N. S.*, 711).

The case of Courtail v. Thomas (9 *Barn. & Cr.*, 288) is much to the purpose. By an order of court, in a suit pending between a lessor and a lessee, the lease was put in possession of the lessor's attorney. An action was subsequently brought by the lessee against the tenant in possession, and the lessor's attorney was served with a subpœna *duces tecum* to produce the lease that he had received in his professional capacity. It was held by the trial court that he was not bound to produce it; but Lord TENTERDEN said, on review of the proceedings: "It appears clearly that the lessor might have been subpœnaed at the trial, and compelled to produce the lease, because it is not part of his title; and if he could be compelled to produce it, then the attorney (who stands in the situation in which plaintiff did) was bound to produce it.

This doctrine seems to be sanctioned by Cowen & Hill's notes to Phillipps on Evidence (*5th Am. ed.*). In note 62, it is declared that "the privilege of the attorney seems to be co-extensive with that of the client;" and in note 578, the rule is stated thus: "Attorneys and solicitors who hold the papers of their clients cannot be compelled, under a subpœna *duces tecum*, to produce them in a controversy between third persons, except where their clients would be compelled."

The whole theory of the protection of a party against his attorney's voluntary or enforced production of documents confidentially entrusted to him seems to have been this—that a party ought not, in consequence of having put such document in his attorney's hands, to be placed in a more unfavorable situation than he would have occupied, if they had remained in his own possession.

Now, if the decision in Mitchell's Case is to be followed, the claim of these proponents must be sustained; for, if that decision be authoritative, Mr. Conkling, were he now upon the witness stand with these disputed papers in his hands, could be required to produce them at the call of the proponents (Snellgrove v. Stevens, *supra;* Field v. Zemansky, 3 *Bradf.*, 111, 479); and, manifestly, whatever right the proponents had to require their production when the witness was present has been in no respect affected by the fact that the papers have been lodged with the Surrogate, for such disposition as may seem to him just and lawful. In other words, if the proponents would have had a right, when the witness was present, to insist upon the use of any material and relevant documentary evidence that he had produced and put in the custody of the Surrogate, they have a right to insist that the Surrogate shall now place that evidence at their disposal. But I am convinced that, whatever might have been the law applicable to this subject between the passage of the act permitting parties to be witnesses and the enactment of the present Code of Civil Procedure, the privilege under discussion now exists substantially as it did when the decisions were rendered upon which contestant's counsel rely.

"An attorney or counsellor at law," says the Code, "shall not be allowed to disclose a communication made by his client to him in the course of his professional employment." If, therefore, Mr. Conkling had brought these papers into court, in obedience to a subpœna issued upon the call of the proponents, I should not have directed their production, except with the contestant's consent.

There remains to be considered the question whether the contestant, by the acts of her present counsel, has waived her privilege to protest against the introduction of these papers in evidence. That this privilege may be waived, is, of course, not open to dispute (Southard v. Rexford, 6 *Cow.*, 254). Indeed, it is squarely asserted by § 836 of the Code. Now it is contended by the proponents that the privilege has in fact been waived in the case at bar. It was always the law that, if a party availed himself of the testimony of his own attorney, the opposite party became entitled to cross-examination (Vaillant v. Dodemead, 2 *Atk.*, 524). A party was never permitted, after opening the door of inquiry wide enough to get what he wanted from his attorney, to slam it in the face of a cross-examiner.

By a parity of reasoning, a party who has subpœnaed his own attorney to produce papers, may fairly enough be treated as having thereby given the right to his adversary, in case such papers should be produced pursuant to the subpœna, and should be discovered to be pertinent to the issue of the controversy, to put the same in evidence. I am so strongly disposed to believe that this proposition is sound that, if a denial of the proponents' motion would put it utterly out of their power to command thereafter the production of these papers, I should feel bound to afford them at once the opportunity of putting the papers in evidence. But, under all the circumstances, I have concluded to take another course—the course that, on the day this matter was argued, I intimated that I might decide to adopt. I shall direct the return of the papers to the witness who produced them, thus placing all persons interested, as far as may be, in the situation that they occupied before this discussion arose, and leaving with the proponents and the contestant to take further action, accordingly as they may be advised.

I think it proper to add that nothing has yet occurred in the history of this matter, so far as it has revealed itself to the court, that calls for animadversions upon the conduct of any of the counsel now or heretofore concerned in these proceedings. The fact that one who is brought into court under a subpœna *duces tecum* has formerly been of counsel for one of the contending parties affords no excuse for refusing to comply with the direction of the writ, even when it has been procured by his former client's adversary.

The law is well stated by Chief Justice SHAW, in Bull v. Loveland (10 *Pick.*, 9). " There seems to be no difference in principle, between compelling a

witness to produce a document in his possession
under a subpœna *duces tecum,* in a case where the
party calling the witness has a right to the use of
such document, and compelling him to give testimony
when the facts lie in his own knowledge. A subpœna
duces tecum is a writ of compulsory obligation which
the court has power to issue, and which the witness is
bound to obey, and which will be enforced by proper
process to compel the production of the papers when
the witness has no reasonable or lawful excuse for
withholding it; and of such lawful or reasonable
excuse the court and not the witness is to judge.
When the witness has the paper ready to produce in
obedience to the summons, it is a question of the
discretion of the court, under the circumstances of
the case, whether the witness ought to produce or is
entitled to withhold the paper." It seems to me that,
in the present case, the witness adopted a course
which was at once consistent with his relations with
his former client, and with his duty to the court, and
which may, perhaps, have been essential for the
proper protection of his own interests.

In the case of Foster v. Hall (12 *Pick.,* 89), an
attorney at law, who had received from the grantee
of property confidential communications on the subject of its transfer, submitted to the court whether
he should be examined respecting the matter. In
commenting upon this course, Chief Justice SHAW
says: " Mr. Robinson very properly submitted it to
the court upon the facts disclosed whether he should
answer or not, having no wish to either volunteer or
withhold his testimony."

The rule in such a case is that the privilege is the privilege of the client and not of the attorney, and therefore, whether the facts shall be disclosed or not must depend upon the just application of the rule of law, and not upon the will of the witness.

The stenographer will be directed to return to Mr. Conkling the papers produced by him and not as yet offered in evidence.

NEW YORK COUNTY.—HON. D. G. ROLLINS, SURROGATE.—June, 1885.

ABBEY v. AYMAR.

In the matter of the probate of the will of WILLIAM AYMAR, *deceased.*

In the construction of testamentary papers, language which, tested by strict grammatical rules, refers to the happening of events in the future may be held to include past occurrences of a similar character, including those transpiring before the execution.

Testator, by his will, directed that, upon the death of his sister, J., his estate should be divided into fourteen parts, one of which parts, it was provided, "is hereby given to and shall be vested in the children of my deceased niece, H., in equal shares. And in case either of the children of said H. *shall die* before my said sister, J., leaving lawful issue surviving, such issue shall take the share which would have been taken by such deceased child of H., if living." H. had left her surviving eight children; of whom seven survived the testator, and one had died before the execution of the will leaving a son, F., who survived the testator. Upon the application for probate of the will, a question having arisen as to the construction of the clause quoted, it was contended, on the part of the seven children of H., that the bequest in dispute was primarily given to a class in which no person other than themselves was included, and that F. could not take under the substitutionary clause, not having been a member of that class, at its creation; while it was argued, in behalf of F., that the primary benefits of the bequest were extended to a class consisting of (1) such children of H. as survived J. and (2) the issue of others *at any time* dying, leaving issue surviving.—

Held, that F. took the share to which his parent would be entitled, if living.

Christopherson v. Naylor, 1 *Meriv.*, 320—dissented from; Lawrence v. Hebbard, 1 *Bradf.*, 252—compared.

UPON the application for probate of decedent's will, a question arose as to the interest thereunder of Frank R. Abbey, an infant grandson of Hannah Talmage, decedent's niece. The facts are stated in the opinion.

GEORGE C. BLANKE, *for proponent.*

B. A. SANDS, *special guardian of Louisa Aymar and others, infants.*

GEORGE G. DUTCHER, *special guardian for Frank R. Abbey.*

THE SURROGATE.—Upon the probate of this will, a question has arisen touching the true construction of the twelfth paragraph of its seventh article. That article directs that, upon the death of the testator's sister Judith, his estate shall be divided into fourteen parts, and distributed according to a scheme in such article specified. The paragraph that has given rise to the present contention is as follows: "One other fourteenth part of my said estate is hereby given to and shall be vested in the children of my deceased niece, Hannah Talmage, in equal shares. And in case either of the children of said Hannah Talmage shall die before my said sister Judith, leaving lawful issue surviving, such issue shall take the share which would have been taken by such deceased child of Hannah Talmage if living."

It appears that Hannah Talmage left her surviving

eight children. One of them, a daughter, died before the making of this will, leaving one child, an infant, who is now living. Is this infant entitled to the share in the estate that his mother would take were she still alive?

It is obvious that a testator, in selecting a class of persons—for example, the children of A.—as objects of his bounty, and providing for the issue of A.'s children deceased, may or may not wish to include the issue of such children of A. as have died before the date of the will. In directing that issue shall stand in place of their deceased parents, and take the share which their parents would have taken, if living, he may intend to limit this secondary gift, if I may so term it, to the issue of such "parents" only as shall die after the execution of his will and before his own death, or before some other indicated period of distribution; or he may wish, on the other hand, to include among his beneficiaries the issue of "parents" who are already dead. Which of the two is meant is sometimes plainly indicated by the testator himself. It is very far, however, from being plainly indicated in the case at bar. It has accordingly been necessary to make exhaustive examination of adjudged cases, in which language similar to that which has occasioned the present controversy has been judicially interpreted. The result of that examination will presently appear.

It is insisted, on behalf of the seven children of Hannah Talmage who were living at the date of testator's will, and all of whom are still alive, that the words—"in case *either* (that is *any*) of the children

shall die "—refer to the contingency of the death of
such children as were alive at the date of the will,
and of such children only, and that those words have,
therefore, no application whatever to any child or
children then dead.   If the testator's language must
be rigidly interpreted according to its grammatical
construction, this proposition is obviously correct.
"Shall die" literally imports death in the future,
and it was not possible, in December, 1883, that the
mother of this infant should thereafter die, seeing
that she was already dead.

But in the construction of testamentary papers, it
has often been the case that language, which by
strict grammatical tests has referred to the happening of events in the future, has been held to include
past events of a similar character.   Thus, in Doe d.
James v. Hallett (1 *Maule & Sel.*, 124), a son of
J. S., born before the date of a testator's will, was
held entitled to take an estate that such testator had
devised to the sons of J. S., "to be begotten."   The
same doctrine is declared in Hewet v. Ireland (1 *P.
Wms.*, 426). So in Wilkinson v. Adam (1 *Ves. &
Bea.*, 422) a devise "to the children I may have by
A., and living at my decease," was held to include
the devisor's children by A., who were in existence
at the date of his will.

In other reported cases, even more closely analogous
to the case at bar than those above cited, the words
"shall die," and kindred expressions occurring in
testamentary papers, have been held to have the
force of the words "shall be dead" or "shall have
died"—the idea of futurity suggested by the word

"shall" being thus specially associated, not with the
period of death but with the period of distribution, and
with the fact of death *in the past*, as at that period
in the future affecting the respective rights of persons interested as beneficiaries.

Among the adjudged cases wherein this liberal.
construction has been sanctioned, are : [*a*] Sheppard's
Trust (1 *K. & J.*, 269); [*b*] Chapman's Will (32
Beav., 382); [*c*] Parsons v. Gulliford (10 *Jur.*, *N. S.*,
231); [*d*] Loring v. Thomas (1 *Dr. & Sm.*, 497);
[*e*] Hannam v. Sims (2 *De G. & J.*, 151); [*f*] Harris
v. Harris (*L. R.*, 11 *Ch. Div.*, 663); [*g*] Jarvis v.
Pond (9 *Sim.*, 549); [*h*] Adams v. Adams (*L. R.*, 14
Eq., 246). The expressions construed in the foregoing decisions were respectively as follows, viz.:
a– "Shall depart this life;" *b*, *c* and *d*– "Shall die in
my lifetime;" *e*– "Shall happen to die;" *f*– "Shall
die;" *g*– "In case of the decease of," etc., etc.;
h– "Should any die." I am clear, therefore, that
the infant claimant in the case at bar is not to be excluded from sharing in the benefits of the legacy here
in question, merely because, in choosing his words
for bequeathing it, the testator has said "shall die,"
instead of "shall be dead."

Even in Christopherson v. Naylor (*infra*) which, as
will presently appear, is the leading case in support
of the position that the issue of that child of Hannah
Talmage who died before the date of this will can
take nothing under it, the court said: "The question in this case does not depend upon the words
'shall happen to die in my lifetime.' Though according to strict construction those words import futurity,

they might have been understood as speaking of the event at whatever time it happened." I shall, accordingly, treat the provision that is here to be construed, as if it were thus expressed: " The issue of such children of said Hannah Talmage [(as shall have died before)" or "(as shall be dead at the death of) my said sister Judith] shall take," etc.

It is next claimed, in behalf of the surviving children of Hannah Talmage, that the bequest in dispute, even as its terms are above paraphrased, is primarily given to a class in which no other persons than themselves are included, and that the infant who claims the share of his deceased mother can take nothing under what they term the substitutionary clause, because, at the time the original class was created, his mother was not a member of it.

The counsel who makes this contention greatly relies upon the decision of Sir WILLIAM GRANT, in Christopherson v. Naylor (1 *Mer.*, 320). By the will there under review, a testator made a bequest " to each and every the child and children of my brother and sisters which shall be living at the time of my decease; but if any child or children of my said brother and sisters shall happen to die in my lifetime and leave any issue . . . . . living at his decease . . . . . then and in such case the legacies hereby intended for such child or children so dying . . . . . are given and bequeathed to his, her or their issue, such issue taking only the legacies which his, her or their parent or parents would have been entitled to, if living." It was held that, under the provision above quoted, the nephews and nieces of the testator were

primary legatees; that to the issue of nephews or
nieces nothing whatever was given, except by way
of substitution; that no person, therefore, could be
treated as a substituted legatee, unless there was
some original legatee in whose place he was entitled
to stand; and that, as none of the testator's nephews
and nieces could have taken under the will except
those who were living at its date, the issue of those
who were already dead could not take by substitution.

The theory of interpretation which is invoked in
the case at bar, in behalf of Hannah Talmage's
grandchild, is very fully and emphatically enunciated
by Vice Chancellor KINDERSLEY, in Loring v. Thomas
(1 *Dr. & Sm.*, 497).

The special guardian insists that the testator has
not made an original bequest to Hannah Talmage's
children as a class, and then supplemented it by a
substitutional bequest to the issue of members of that
class who should thereafter die, but that he has extended the primary benefits of his bequest to a more
comprehensive class, which consists of such children
of Hannah Talmage as shall be living at Judith's
death, together with the issue of such others of her
children as at any time theretofore shall have died
leaving issue surviving, such issue to take a parent's
share, etc.

While the question here presented has been frequently discussed in the judicial tribunals of England, almost from the beginning of the century, it
seems to have been submitted in but a single instance
for the determination of a New York court. A testator, whose will was construed in Lawrence v. Hebbard

(1 *Bradf.*, 252), had disposed of the residue of his estate in these words: "The remainder of my property is to be equally divided among my eleven children, and in case of the death of any of my children, their portion shall be divided among their children if they have any." A daughter of the testator had died before the execution of the will, leaving a son her surviving. Surrogate BRADFORD held that such son was entitled to the share that his mother would have received, had she lived to claim it. The decision, however, was in part founded upon the fact that, at the date of the testator's will, there were but ten of his children living, and that his direction that the residue should be divided into eleven parts was, therefore, a plain intimation of his purpose to extend the benefits of the disputed bequest to the issue of the deceased daughter.

Long v. Labor (8 *Penn. St.*, 229), May's Appeal (41 *Penn. St.*, 512), and Wheeler v. Allen (53 *Me.*, 232), are the only other American decisions that have fallen under my observation. They favor the broad rather than the narrow construction of such words as are here submitted for interpretation.

The English reports abound in cases very similar to the one at bar, many of them, indeed, almost identical with it. Some of those decisions strongly support, while others no less strongly discountenance, such a claim as is here urged by the special guardian. Very many of them turn upon the question whether the disputed gift is strictly substitutional in its character, or is, on the other hand, an original substantive gift to issue. The principle of the distinction is a

plain one, but its application has given rise to all
sorts of subtleties and refinements of construction,
and to decisions that are utterly irreconcilable.　To
review those decisions would be a profitless task.
They are grouped below in the order of their dates.

The exclusion of the infant from the benefits of
Mr. Aymar's will seems to be demanded by [1816]
Christopherson v. Naylor (1 *Meriv.*, 320); [1827] But-
ter v. Ommany (4 *Russ.*, 70); [1833] Waugh v.
Waugh (2 *Myl. & K.*, 41); [1838] Peel v. Catlow
(9 *Sim.*, 372); [1843] Gray v. Garman (2 *Hare*,
268); [1852] Coulthurst v. Carter (15 *Beav.*, 421);
[1853] Congreve v. Palmer (16 *Beav.*, 435); [1854]
Thompson's Trust (5 *De G., M. & G.*, 280); [1859]
Stewart v. Jones (3 *De G. & J.*, 532); [1859] Smith
v. Pepper (27 *Beav.*, 86); [1869] Hotchkiss' Trust
(*L. R.*, 8 *Eq.*, 643); [1871] Atkinson v. Atkinson
(6 *Ir. Rep., Eq.*, 184); [1873] Hunter v. Cheshire
(*L. R.*, 8 *Ch. App. Cas.*, 751); [1876] West v. Orr
(*L. R.*, 8 *Ch. Div.*, 60); [1883] Widgen v. Mello (*L.
R.*, 23 *Ch. D.*, 737).

On the other hand, the infant's claim as a beneficiary has the apparent sanction of [1835] Tytherleigh
v. Harbin (6 *Sim.*, 329); [1837] Giles v. Giles (8 *id.*,
360); [1837] Rust v. Baker (*id.*, 443); [1839] Bebb
v. Beckwith (2 *Beav.*, 308); [1839] Jarvis v. Pond (9
Sim., 549); [1844] Gaskell v. Holmes (3 *Hare*, 438);
[1856] Etches v. Etches (3 *Dr.*, 441); [1858] Hannam v. Sims (2 *De G. & J.*, 151); [1858] Faulding's
trust (26 *Beav.*, 263); [1861] Loring v. Thomas (1
Dr. & Sm., 497); [1863] Chapman's will (32 *Beav.*,
382); [1863] Jordan's Trust, (2 *New.*, 57); [1864]

Parsons v. Gulliford (10 *Jur.*, *N. S.*, 231); [1866] Attwood v. Alford (*L. R.*, 2 *Eq.*, 479); [1868] Gowling v. Thompson (19 *Law T. Rep.*, *N. S.*, 242); [1869] Philp's will (*L. R.*, 7 *Eq.*, 151); [1869] Potter's trust (*L. R.*, 8 *Eq.*, 52; [1870] Barnaby v. Tassell (*L. R.*, 11 *Eq.*, 363); [1872] Adams v. Adams (*L. R.*, 14 *Eq.*, 246); [1877] Sibley's trust (*L. R.*, 5 *Ch. Div.*, 494); [1877] Smith's trust (*id.*, 497, *note*); [1878] Wingfield v. Wingfield (*L. R.*, 9 *Ch. Div.*, 658); [1879] Harris v. Harris (*L. R.*, 11 *Ch. Div.*, 663); [1881] Lucas's will (*L. R.*, 17 *Ch. Div.*, 788).

I have extricated myself from this tangle of conflicting authorities in a state of mind such as Sir JAMES BACON, V. C., found himself to be in, when he pronounced his opinion in Barnaby v. Tassell (*supra*). He sustained the claim of the issue of a predeceased child, but declared that he did so " with the greatest hesitation and the least possible confidence in the soundness of the result." I shall follow his example.

Decreed accordingly.

NEW YORK COUNTY.—HON. D. G. ROLLINS, SURROGATE.—June, 1885.

THOMPSON *v.* THOMPSON.

In the matter of the estate of SAMUEL C. THOMPSON, *deceased.*

A *residuum* of a testator's estate is nothing more nor less than what is *left*, after satisfaction of all express or prior dispositions.

Testator, by his will, gave all his property to his executors, in trust (1) to discharge his debts; (2) to pay to his widow, for life and in lieu of dower, the interest or income from one third of all his property; (3) to pay to his mother $100,000; and (4) to dispose of the residue as directed. The condition of the estate was such as to leave a large residue, in excess of the mother's legacy, and after setting apart one third of the entire estate for the widow.—

Held, that the widow was entitled to the interest or income of one third of all the property, after payment of debts, without a deduction of the amount of the mother's legacy.

As to whether, in case an assignment, to the life beneficiary, of one third of the estate, after payment of debts, left less than the specified amount of the mother's legacy, the provisions contained in clauses (2) and (3) would abate equally—*quære*.

Waters v. Collins, *ante*, 374—compared.

CONSTRUCTION of will, upon judicial settlement of account of Abby S. Thompson, decedent's widow, as executrix, and F. G. Adams and another, as executors of decedent's will. Ferris S. Thompson, an infant son of decedent, appeared in the proceedings.

MORE, APLINGTON & MORE, *for executors.*

JOHN P. MORRIS, *special guardian.*

THE SURROGATE.—This testator devised and bequeathed to his executors all his property, real and personal, upon the following trusts:

1st. To discharge his debts.

2d. To pay to his widow, for life and in lieu of dower, "the interest or income from one third of all my [his] property, real and personal."

3rd. To pay to his mother $100,000.

[The fourth provision is unimportant for the present discussion.]

5th. To pay, deliver over and transfer, subject to the above directions, all the rest and residue of his property, etc., etc.

A decree is about to be entered, settling the accounts of testator's executors, and the question arises whether, in ascertaining the principal sum upon which is to be allowed interest or income to the widow, the legacy of $100,000 must be first deducted; or whether, on the other hand, the widow must be held entitled to the interest or income of one third of the entire property, in excess of the amount required for payment of debts. The solution of this question may, perhaps, be somewhat simplified by considering what would be the fair interpretation of this will if, instead of providing for payment to his widow of interest and income, the testator had given her outright one third part of the entire estate. The will, if in all other respects unchanged, would then have contained directions as follows, and in order following: 1st. For the satisfaction of debts; 2d. For the delivery to the widow of one third of all the testator's property, real and personal; 3rd. For the payment to his mother of $100,000; 4th. For the disposition of the residue.

It seems to me that, in the construction of such a will as that, it would be absurd to claim that any portion of the legacy bequeathed by the third clause would be deductible from the one third of the entire estate which is disposed of by clause second, save, perhaps, in the contingency of the inadequacy of assets to discharge the former legacy in full.

Any scheme of distribution under such a will, that would assign a penny to the residuary legatee, would be unjust to the beneficiary named in the second clause, if it involved the slightest deduction from her one third of the entire estate, as a contribution to the

$100,000 legacy. For the legatee or devisee of a residue can take nothing, until all other devises and bequests have been fully satisfied. Law and lexicons thoroughly accord in pronouncing a *residuum* to be nothing more nor less than what is left. If the value of an estate thus disposed of should prove to be precisely $150,000, after payment of debts, with what show of reason could it be claimed that the widow would be entitled to but one third part of $50,000, and that the remaining two thirds would go to the beneficiaries of the residue? There cannot, it seems to me, be room for doubt that, in such a case, the widow would take $50,000 and the mother $100,000, a scheme of distribution that would leave no residue whatever.

Now, the case at bar only differs from the case suppositionally stated in this — that the testator's widow is here made the beneficiary, not of one third of his property, but of the interest or income of one third. It is obvious, however, that the interest or income to which she is entitled is interest or income upon the very same capital or *corpus* that she could justly have demanded in the case supposed. When it has been ascertained what she would have taken, if she had been given one third of the whole estate, there has been an ascertainment of the principal sum upon which she is entitled, by this will, to interest and income.

A different question might, perhaps, be presented if an assignment to the widow of one third of the entire estate, after payment of debts, left less than $100,000 applicable to the bequest to the mother.

It may be that, in such a case, the dispositions under the second and third clauses would abate equally, though the fact that the former contains the sole provision in favor of the testator's widow, and that such provision is in lieu of dower, might, even in case of a deficiency of assets, entitle it to a preference. It would not, however, be so entitled from the mere circumstance that it precedes the others in order of statement.

Unless a testator distinctly indicates that one or more of his beneficiaries is to be preferred to the others, or unless one or more of his bequests is founded upon a consideration, and is not, therefore, a mere bestowal of bounty, the courts will presume that he intended that all his beneficiaries should alike be paid, and in case of a deficiency of assets will direct a ratable abatement (Waters v. Collins, *ante*, 374). But, in the present case, there is no question of abatement, as there is a large residue, in excess of the $100,000 and the sum which, under an interpretation most favorable to the widow, is disposed of by the second clause of the will.

Let a decree be entered, in accordance with the suggestion of counsel for Mrs. Thompson.

New York County.—Hon. D. G. ROLLINS, Surrogate.—June, 1885.

Wetmore *v.* Wetmore.

In the matter of the estate of Apollos R. Wetmore,
deceased.

After an executor's account has once been judicially settled, the mere fact
that, since the entry of the decree, assets have come into his possession for which the decree made no provision does not, of itself,
afford sufficient grounds for compelling another accounting. Considerations of economy may indicate the propriety of the postponement
of another settlement, until it can embrace the results of a completed
administration.

Application by William Wetmore, a legatee named
in decedent's will, to compel George C. Wetmore and
Charles E. Carryl, executors thereof, to render and
settle their account. The petition alleged that more
than four years had elapsed since the executors'
appointment, and that they had not rendered any
account since February, 1884, subsequent to which
time they had collected at least thirty-nine thousand
dollars.

A. T. Ackert, *for petitioner.*

B. F. Edsall, *for executrix.*

The Surrogate.—The account of the testator's
executors, showing their dealings with his estate
from the date of their appointment until February,
1884, was judicially settled and determined by a
decree entered in October last. The present pro-

ceeding has been instituted by one of the legatees for the purpose of procuring from the respondents an account of their subsequent administration. They allege in answering affidavits that, upon the decision of an action now pending in the Supreme Court, and upon the sale or partition of certain real estate in St. Louis, they will be able to give final account of their stewardship, and that such decision is likely to be reached, and such sale or partition to be made, in the course of a few months.

They insist, therefore, that any accounting that should now be ordered would involve unnecessary expense to the estate. The Code of Civil Procedure (§§ 2724–2727) provides that, after the lapse of eighteen months from the issue of letters testamentary or letters of administration, a creditor or person interested is entitled, upon due application, to an order from the Surrogate, requiring the holder of such letters to file his account for judicial settlement. As to the time in which subsequent accountings can be enforced, the statutes are silent. It was held by the Court of Appeals, in Matter of Hood (90 *N. Y.*, 512), that, when the accounts of an executor or administrator have once been judicially determined, mere lapse of time will not justify an order directing him to account again, and that a petition for such further accounting should be denied, unless it sets forth facts that explain its necessity. The petition in the case at bar alleges that the executors have come into possession of assets, in regard to which the decree of October last made no adjudication. But this circumstance does not, of itself, afford sufficient ground for granting the relief prayed for. The respondents have presented urgent reasons why, upon considerations of economy, no accounting should now be ordered. Besides, one of the executors, Mr. Carryl, has filed a somewhat detailed statement, showing the nature and value of the assets, and the disposition of the moneys disbursed since the last accounting. I must, for the present at least, deny the petition, but with leave to the petitioner, if he wishes to do so, to examine Mr. Carryl in respect to the statement above referred to. Such an examination may disclose, to the satisfaction of the petitioner, that the formal accounting may well be postponed until it can embrace the results of a completed administration (Geer v. Ransom, 5 *Redf.*, 578).

NEW YORK COUNTY.—HON. D. G. ROLLINS, SURROGATE.—June, 1885.

BOOTH *v.* TIMONEY.

In the matter of the probate of the will of CECILIA
L. BOOTH, *deceased.*

Under Code Civ. Pro., § 2476, subd. 3, prescribing the jurisdiction of
Surrogates' courts to take the proof of a will in certain cases, and id.,
§ 2611, providing that a will of personal property executed, without the
State and within the United States, as prescribed by the laws of the
place of execution may be proved here, a Surrogate's court may grant
probate to a will executed, in and according to the laws of another

state, by a resident thereof who dies therein, leaving personal property in its county, without waiting until the instrument has been submitted to the proper judicial tribunal of the decedent's domicil.

The paper propounded as the will of the personal property of decedent, who was a resident of the state of New Jersey, where she died in 1884. and where the same was executed, was in decedent's handwriting. and embraced upon one page of a half sheet of note paper, upon which her name appeared only in the opening clause: "If I, Cecilia L. Booth, should die within the year 1884, I leave," etc. The paper was subscribed, at decedent's request, by two witnesses, who attended for the purpose of attesting it, and in whose joint presence decedent declared it to be her will, intentionally placing it before them so that her name stood revealed, though it did not clearly appear but that one of them was in an adjoining room, when that name was written. Decedent left personal property in the county of New York, where the instrument was presented for probate.—*Held*,

1. That the Surrogate's court of New York county had jurisdiction to take proof of the will, in the first instance.

2. That the validity of the execution depended on the law of decedent's domicil.

3. That the instrument was duly executed, according to the provisions of the New Jersey statute of 1851, which required a will to be "signed by the testator," and the signature to be made, or by him acknowledged, in the presence of two witnesses present at the same time.

APPLICATION for the probate of decedent's will, made by Geraldine J. Timoney, a legatee therein named; opposed by Joseph A. Booth, decedent's husband. The paper propounded was an informal document written upon one page of a half sheet of note paper. Further facts appear in the opinion.

ALFRED T. ACKERT, *for petitioner*:

Any instrument that is designed not to take effect until the maker's decease is testamentary (1 Jarm. on Wills, 24). A will in the handwriting of a party proves itself (Bacon's Abridgment, vol. 7, p. 388). A will may be made so as to take effect only on a contingency (Cowley v. Knapp, 42 *N. J. L.*, 297). The particular order of the several requests to the

valid execution of a testament is not at all material
(Munday v. Munday, 15 *N. J. Eq.*, 293; Allaire v.
Allaire, 10 *Vroom*, 113). The declaration was sufficient, as well as the publication; whatever would
amount to a publication would answer the requirement that it should be declared to be the testatrix's
will (Munday v. Munday, *supra*). The statute of New
Jersey does not require signing in the presence of
the witnesses. The testatrix declared the writing to
be her will, in presence of two witnesses present at
the time, which was a compliance with the statute
(Errickson v. Fields, 3 *Stewart*, 634). A construction, as to the mode of execution of a will, should be
avoided, which will make the statute a snare instead
of a protection (Gilbert v. Knox, 52 *N. Y.*, 125). The
Statute of Wills is not to be construed strictly, except
as to the evils it was designed to prevent (Rieben v.
Hicks, 3 *Bradf.*, 353). The evidence shows that the
instrument is in the handwriting of the testatrix;
and where the testatrix declares the paper to be her
will without signing her name at the end, it will be
presumed she thereby intends to adopt her name
written in any other portion of the will as the final
act of signing, *and that is sufficient* (Ellis v. Smith, 1
Vesey Jr., 11; Adams v. Field, 21 *Vermont*, 256;
Redf. Am. Cases on Wills, 613; Lemayne v. Stanley,
3 *Lev.*, 1; Armstrong v. Armstrong, 29 *Ala.*, 538;
Hilton v. King, 3 *Lev.*, 86; Grayson v. Atkinson,
2 *Ves.*, 454; Selden v. Coalter, 2 *Virginia Cases*,
533; Allen v. Everett, 12 *B. Mon.*, 379; Sally Miles'
Will, 4 *Dana*, 1; Smith v. Evans, 1 *Wil.*, 313; Green-
leaf on Ev., part 2, § 674; 2 Chitty Blackst., 377;

Toler's Exec., 2). This instrument relates entirely to personal property. The will of a non-resident, without regard to the place of its execution or the place of testator's death, may be admitted to probate in a county where part of the personal estate was situated, if the same be executed in pursuance of the laws of the testator's residence (Supm. Ct., 1884, Matter of Seabra, 18 *Week. Dig.*, 428; Code Civ. Pro., §§ 2476, 2611).

STANLEY, CLARK & SMITH, *for contestant.*

THE SURROGATE.—On the 10th of August, 1884, this decedent died at Long Branch, N. J., where she had resided for several years. A paper purporting to be her last will was propounded in this court on August 16th, 1884, and a petition was filed, praying for its admission to probate. Objections were duly interposed, and the issues thus raised were afterwards brought to a trial which is now concluded. The instrument in controversy is in words following:

"If I, Cecilia L. Booth, should die within the year 1884, I leave to my sister, Geraldine Josephine Timoney, all the money due me from my late father's deceased will, also my wearing apparel and furniture, and I also leave to my little nephew, Albert Philip Timoney, all money deposited in the Emigrant Savings Bank, in my maiden name, Cecilia L. Hatfield.

"Witnessed by Amelia Kurrus, Mamie Clifford, June 16, 1884."

It appears in evidence that the whole of this instrument, except the names of the two attesting witnesses, is in the handwriting of the decedent; that those

names were written by Amelia Kurrus and Mamie
Clifford, respectively, at decedent's express request;
and that, while these two witnesses were together in
her presence, she declared the paper to be her will.
Its admission to probate is resisted upon the following
grounds:

First.—It is claimed that, as the decedent, at the
time of her death, was domiciled in New Jersey, there
executed the disputed paper and there died, the Surrogate of this county has no jurisdiction to grant
probate to such paper, in the first instance, and before
it has been submitted to the proper judicial tribunal
of decedent's domicil.

Whatever authority the Surrogate has in the premises is derived from the Code of Civil Procedure.
Section 2611 of that Code declares, among other
things, that a will executed without the State of New
York, and within the United States, in accordance
with the laws of the place of its execution, may be
proved in the State of New York. Section 2476
confers upon the Surrogate's court of this county
jurisdiction to take proof of the will of a non-resident
testator who has died without the State, leaving personal property within such county. That the decedent,
in the case at bar, left personal property in the county
of New York is alleged in the petition, and is not
denied. The respondent's contention as regards jurisdiction is therefore overruled (see Russell v. Hartt,
87 *N. Y.*, 19).

Second.—It is insisted that the evidence fails to
show the due execution of the paper which has occasioned the present controversy. The strength of this

objection must be tested, not by the laws of New York, but by the laws of New Jersey (see Moultrie v. Hunt, 23 *N. Y.*, 394 ; Dupuy v. Wurtz, 53 *id.*, 556).

The act entitled " A supplement to the act entitled An act concerning wills" was passed by the New Jersey Legislature in 1851, and has been in force ever since (Nixon's Digest, 1032). Its first section is as follows : "All wills and testaments . . . . . shall be in writing and shall be signed by the testator, which signature shall be made by the testator, or the making thereof acknowledged by him, and such writing be declared to be his last will in presence of two witnesses present at the same time, who shall subscribe their names thereto as witnesses in the presence of the testator."

The contestant insists that the paper here in controversy fails to conform to the requirements of the foregoing statute in two particulars : 1*st*, because it does not bear the " signature " of the alleged testatrix, and 2*d*, because the name of Cecilia L. Booth, which appears in the body of the instrument, and which is relied upon as the decedent's signature, is not satisfactorily shown to have been written by her in the presence of the two subscribing witnesses or in their presence to have been acknowledged as her signature.

The reports of judicial decisions in the state of New Jersey are silent, with respect to the meaning of the words " signed " and " signature," in the statute of 1851, of the word " signed " in the statute of 1850, and of the same word in the statute of 1714. The last named act (1 Laws of New Jersey, 7) provided that wills should be in writing and should be "signed" by the testator. When that act went into operation, the Statute of Frauds (29 Charles II., ch. 3) was nearly forty years old. That statute had prescribed, by its fifth section, that all devises and bequests of lands should be "in writing and *signed* by the parties so devising the same" . . . . . and should be "attested and *subscribed* by three or four credible witnesses." As early as 1680, the Court of King's Bench decided that, within the meaning of § 5, the position of the testator's signature was immaterial (Lemayne v. Stanley, 3 *Lev.*, 1). It was held by all the Judges that the words "I, John Stanley," written by John Stanley himself in the exordium of his will, constituted a valid signature "within the statute, which does not appoint where the will shall be signed, in the top, bottom or margin, and, therefore, a signing in any part is sufficient."

This decision has been adversely criticised by writers of legal treatises; but the interpretation which it fastened upon the Statute of Frauds was stoutly upheld in the English courts for more than a century and a half, and, until the enactment of the statute of 1 Victoria, ch. 26, a subscription by the testator at the foot or end of his will was never deemed essential to its validity (see Cook v. Parsons, *Finch's Prec. in Ch.*, 185; Coles v. Trecothick, 9 *Ves.*, 234; Morrison v. Turnour, 18 *id.*, 174; Trott v. Skidmore, 6 *Jur.*, *N. S.*, 760).

The American courts have generally followed in the path of these decisions, though at times somewhat grudgingly. It was declared by the General

Court of Virginia, in 1815 (Selden v. Coalter, 2 *Va. Cas.*, 553), that, in interpreting the Statute of Wills of that State (a statute which was admittedly borrowed from 29 Charles II., ch. 3), the doctrine of Lemayne v. Stanley (*supra*), should be accepted as authoritative. PARKER, J., pronouncing the opinion of the court, said that the word "signed," as used in the Virginia Wills act, must be taken as having the legal sense that had been stamped upon it by the English courts, and declared it to be settled law that the insertion of a testator's name in the beginning of a holographic will constituted a sufficient signing.   To similar effect see, also, Matter of Sarah Miles (4 *Dana* [*Ky.*], 1; Adams v. Field, 21 *Vt.*, 256; Allen v. Everett, 12 *B. Monroe*, 371; Armstrong v. Armstrong, 29 *Ala., N. S.*, 538).

These cases fully establish the proposition that, where the testator's signature is made one of the essential features of the valid execution of a will, his name need not be subscribed at the foot or end of such will, but if written in any part of the instrument, will constitute a sufficient signature, provided that such instrument is in the handwriting of the testator himself, and that, by inserting his name, he has designed to authenticate such instrument without further signature, and provided also that such insertion of his name has been made by the testator in the presence of the attesting witnesses, or has in their presence been duly acknowledged.

Several of the cases above cited go much further than this; few have fallen under my observation that do not go as far.

In Catlett v. Catlett (55 *Mo.*, 340), cited by the contestant, the so-called will was not in the handwriting of the testator, and was not put upon paper in his presence. Besides, the *testimonium* clause clearly indicated that the introduction of his name at the beginning of the instrument was not intended to take the place of a more formal signature. In Waller v. Waller (1 *Gratt.*, 454), also cited by contestant, the paper in dispute was holographic, but, though it concluded with an unfilled attestation clause, it bore the names of no witnesses. From these facts the court inferred that the instrument was deliberative merely, and that, in its unfinished state, its maker could never have intended it as a completed will.

Ramsey v. Ramsey (13 *Gratt.*, 664) and Roy v. Roy's Ex'rs (16 *Gratt.*, 418) are decisions interpretative of the Virginia Wills act of 1849. That act required, not only that a will should be *signed* by the testator, but that it should be signed " in such a manner as to make it manifest that the name was intended as a signature." In view of the exactions of this statute, the courts held, in the two cases just cited, that the act of a testator in writing his name at the commencement of a holographic will was an equivocal act, and would not constitute a sufficient signing, unless the testator's intention to give it effect as a signature was somehow made apparent on the face of the paper. Whatever construction I might give to the words " signed " and " signature " in the New Jersey statute of 1851, if the question of their meaning were now *res integra*, the weight of authority fully sustains the proponent's claim that Mrs. Booth's insertion of her name, in the opening sentence of the paper before me, constituted, when taken in connection with the attendant circumstances, a valid and sufficient signing.

In Hoysradt v. Kingman (22 *N. Y.*, 372), DENIO, J., referring to the re-enactment in this State, of the Statute of Frauds and to the decisions of the English courts interpreting that statute, declared that those decisions were "authority with us, to the same extent as in the English courts." In Davis v. Shields (26 *Wend.*, 352–358) our Court of Errors clearly recognized the technical distinction between the word "sign" and the word "subscribe." So, also, did our Court of Appeals, in James v. Patten (6 *N. Y.*, 9). So did the legislature of this State when, in 1830, the existing Wills act was placed upon the statute book. The express direction in that act contained, that a testator's name must thenceforth be *subscribed* at the end of his will, was avowedly inserted to prevent the recurrence of the mischiefs that were supposed to have resulted from the loose interpretation of the word *sign* in the Statute of Frauds.

Similar restrictive provisions were enacted in Pennsylvania three years later, and by the British Parliament in 1837. It was after these conspicuous events that the legislature of New Jersey addressed itself, in 1861, to the modification of the statute of 1714, respecting the execution of wills. The word "signed" had then a precise technical meaning, which had been firmly established by a long line of adjudications. Surely, that much construed word would not have been made to do duty in the amended statute if the legislature had intended to prescribe more stringent rules than had theretofore existed, respecting the place of a testator's signature.

Third.—The evidence does not distinctly show that the witness Mamie Clifford saw the name of Cecilia L. Booth written by the decedent; and it is possible that, at the time it was written, Miss Clifford was not in the same room with the decedent, but in the room adjoining. Under all the circumstances, however, the signature was probably made in her presence within the decisions of Compton v. Mitton (7 *Halst.*, 70), Mickle v. Matlack (17 *N. J. Law*, 88) and Ludlow v. Ludlow (35 *N. J. Eq.*, 489). Besides, there can be no doubt that, when Mrs. Booth was writing the will, both the witnesses were at hand, for the purpose of attesting it; and that, when in their presence she declared it to be her will, she intentionally placed it before them, so that her name stood revealed. This was a substantial acknowledgment of the signature (Beckett v. Howe, 39 *L. J. R.*, *N. S.*, *Prob. & M.*, 1; In the goods of Janaway, 44 *L. J.*, *P. & M.*, 6; Ilott v. Genge, 3 *Curt.*, 172; Keigwin v. Keigwin, 3 *Curt.*, 611; In the goods of Bosanquet, 2 *Rob.*, 577; Gwillim v. Gwillim, 3 *Sw. & Tr.*, 200; Baskin v. Baskin, 36 *N. Y.*, 416).

Petition granted.

NEW YORK COUNTY.—HON. D. G. ROLLINS, SURRO-
GATE.—June, 1885.

KNAPP *v.* REILLY.

*In the matter of the application for revocation of
probate of the will of* PATRICK J. O'NEILL, *deceased.*

Where, upon an application to revoke a decree admitting a will to probate,
the court finds *grave reason to doubt* whether, at the date of the
alleged execution, decedent was physically and mentally capable of
participating in the essential formalities, and whether he subscribed
the instrument according to law, the prayer of the petition should be
granted.

The signatures of attesting witnesses are effectual, in this State, only
where preceded, in point of time, by the signature of the testator.

It appeared that decedent, at the time of the alleged execution of his will,
was, from long continued sickness, in a state of chronic stupor, from
which he could be awakened, but into which he would speedily relapse,
the interval of lucidity being too brief for any considerable mental
exertion ; that, of the subscription to the instrument,—which was in
the following form : "Patrick [his + mark] J. O'Neill,"—decedent
wrote only the first three letters, and then dropped the pen, saying he
could go no further ; whereupon R. proceeded to make the mark and
complete the signature. There was no evidence of a request by decedent to R., so to do, nor of a subsequent indication of knowledge or
approbation, on the part of the former, of what had been done.—

Held, that the act of R. did not constitute a subscription of decedent's
name, and that the fragmentary signature written by the latter was
not sufficient as an authentication of his will.

PETITION for the revocation of probate of decedent's will, presented by Mary Knapp, one of his
next of kin, and a legatee under the will ; opposed
by James A. Reilly, the executor thereof. The facts
appear sufficiently in the opinion.

I. GRAY BOYD, *for petitioner.*

JAMES F. HIGGINS, *for respondent.*

THE SURROGATE.—This is a proceeding for revocation of the probate of a paper that was lately adjudged to be the will of Patrick J. O'Neill. As was held in Hoyt v. Jackson (2 *Dem.*, 446), the decree heretofore entered must stand or fall, accordingly as this respondent has established or failed to establish to the satisfaction of the Surrogate that, within the meaning of § 2623 of the Code of Civil Procedure, the paper in dispute was duly executed, and that, at the time of executing it, its maker was in all respects competent to make a will, and was free from undue influence and restraint. In a proceeding for revocation, no less than in a proceeding for the grant of probate, the burden of proof is upon the party who seeks to uphold the will. If, therefore, upon all the testimony the *factum* is left in a state of uncertainty, probate should always be denied, or, if it has been theretofore accorded, should be set aside (Howland v. Taylor, 53 *N. Y.*, 627).

In the case at bar, I find grave reason to doubt

1st. Whether on January 16th, 1885, the date of the instrument here in controversy, this decedent was physically and mentally able to participate in the essential formalities of its execution; and

2d. Whether such instrument was subscribed by him according to law.

First.—Was the decedent, when this paper is claimed to have become a will, able to execute it? The disability under which he suffered, if he suffered under any disability at all, was not in the nature of insanity, as that word is commonly understood in trials of testamentary causes; it was simply an inability, by reason of long continued disease, in which his brain had at last become involved, to exert certain faculties without which one cannot be deemed, in the eye of the law, a person of sound disposing mind, memory and understanding. His condition is thus described by one of the attesting witnesses: "He was in a doze . . . . . in a kind of sleepy, comatose state all the time. If you were talking to him, he would fall off to sleep. . . . . . The day before (meaning the day before the execution), I went for the priest for him, for I thought he was going then." Said another witness, a sister of decedent: "He was sleepy . . . . . in a dazed condition . . . . . sometimes he did not even know his child—while I was giving medicine to him he was going to sleep, and did not know that I had given it to him."

Still another witness testified that, about the time the will purports to have. been executed, the testator "seemed stupid; he would look at you with a kind of look, and would not appear to recognize you; he did not seem to understand anything that people were talking to him about; he was in a dazed and drowsy condition, and incapable of transacting business." The progress of the disease, which resulted in decedent's death, was detailed by his attending physician, Dr. Buck, who visited him daily during the last two months of his life. From Dr. Buck's testimony, it is apparent that his patient, for about a week prior to his death, including the two days when the will is claimed to have been prepared and authenticated, was incapable of sufficient thought, reflection and judgment to project or execute a testamentary paper. He was in a state of stupor, from which he could at times be awakened, but into which he would speedily relapse, the interval of lucidity being too brief for any considerable mental exertion. "By shaking him and rousing him," said the doctor, "I could make him look up and recognize me; but if I asked him a question, I could not get a satisfactory answer."

The only testimony at variance with that above summarized was given by Reilly, the proponent. It is of a negative character, and it by no means serves to remove my doubts as to the decedent's competency. Of the two questions, therefore, that I have set myself to answer, the first must be answered in the negative.

Second.—Even if the evidence satisfactorily established O'Neill's testamentary capacity, I should feel bound to revoke the probate of his alleged will, on account of irregularities in its execution. The writing, which is claimed to constitute the "subscription" required by law, is in its proper place, at the end of the *testimonium* clause, and is as follows: "Patrick [his + mark] J. O'Neill." A portion of this name, and a portion only, was written by the decedent himself. The witness Murray says that, when Patrick had finished the letter "t," the pen dropped from his hand, and he said he could not go any further. Murray testified that Reilly then proceeded to make the "+" mark, and to finish the signature. The other attesting witness confirms Murray, as to the dropping of the pen from decedent's hand, but says nothing as to who made the mark. Reilly's version of the incident is in these words: "He (meaning the decedent) attempted to sign and failed, but he made his mark, and I wrote the balance of the name."

The conflict between these statements must, in my judgment, be settled in favor of Murray, upon the corroborative evidence afforded by the paper itself; for the mark in question has very noticeable characteristics of Reilly's handwriting, and is conspicuously unlike the decedent's. This, however, is not of itself a fatal defect; for, even though made by Reilly, the mark would suffice as the subscription of the decedent, if it appeared that, in making it, Reilly acted under decedent's directions, and that, in the presence of the attesting witnesses, the decedent acknowledged it as his signature (Chaffee v. Bapt. Miss. Conv., 10 *Paige*, 85; Van Hanswyck v. Wiese, 44 *Barb.*, 494; Robins v. Coryell, 27 *Barb.*, 556); but the case is barren of evidence tending to show that the decedent requested Reilly to take up the pen that had fallen from his own grasp, or that, after Reilly had made the mark and completed the signature, the decedent indicated to the attesting witnesses that what had been done had been done with his knowledge and approbation. In view of this fact, can it be said that the paper was duly subscribed? I think not. Reilly's act did not constitute a subscription, and such portion of the word "Patrick" as was written by decedent himself does not serve for a sufficient signature; for his relinquishing of the pen before he had completed the task he had undertaken was evidently due to physical weakness, and not to a purpose on his part to treat, and to have the witnesses treat, the fragmentary signature already written as the authentication of his will.

I feel bound to find, also, that the names of the attesting witnesses, as they now appear on this paper, were written before the decedent made the abortive effort to attach his signature. Both those witnesses profess to have a distinct recollection that such is the case. The proponent swears to the contrary. Now, if he were a lawyer, and experienced in the matter of the execution of wills, and if it appeared that, on the 16th of January, he knew that the signatures of attesting witnesses are only effectual in this State, when preceded in point of time by the signature of the testator (Jackson v. Jackson, 39 *N. Y.*, 153; Sisters of Charity v. Kelly, 67 *N. Y.*, 409), I might accept his story of the sequence of events, in preference to that of the other witnesses; but, in the absence of these reasons for crediting him with special accuracy of recollection, I accept the statements of Murray and O'Neill, as to the order of signing.

While I have decided upon the grounds above stated, to revoke probate, I think it but fair to proponent to say that the allegations of the petition which charge him with fraudulent practices are not sustained. I greatly doubt whether the decedent, on either the 15th or 16th of January, understood that his interviews with Reilly related to the preparation or execution of a will. I believe that, so far as he had any notion at all as to why Reilly had been summoned to his sick room, he supposed that it was for

the adjustment of the dispute about furniture which
is fully described in the evidence.   On the other
hand, I can well understand how Reilly might naturally have understood, from what he saw and heard
upon his first visit to the decedent, that he was expected to prepare a will.   He and the O'Neills were
evidently acting at cross purposes, and, though there
is some conflict in the testimony which can scarcely
be reconciled with a disposition on the part of all the
witnesses to reveal the truth, the facts that I accept
as proved call for no adverse criticism upon the
motives or the conduct of any persons interested in
these proceedings.

Probate revoked.

ONONDAGA COUNTY.—HON. G. R. COOK, SURROGATE.—
February, 1885.

CARR *v.* BENNETT.

In the matter of the estate of WILLIAM CHURCHILL,
deceased.

Testator, by his will, after providing for the payment of his debts, funeral
expenses, etc., gave to his adopted daughter, J., an adult married
woman living with her husband, the farm on which testator resided,
and the household furniture, absolutely, and further directed his executor to invest $4,000 in a specified manner, and to pay the interest,
after deducting commissions, annually to said daughter ; the principal,
at her death, to go to her children.   The estate was adequate for the
payment of all debts and legacies ; more than $4,000 thereof being, at
the time of testator's death, and continuously thereafter remaining
invested as specified, and drawing interest.   The life legatee asked for
interest on said sum from testator's death; the residuary legatees, on

the other hand, contending that interest did not begin to run upon the legacy until all decedent's debts were paid.—

Held, that the life provision for J. was a general legacy, not falling within any of the exceptions to the general rule, whereby interest on such legacies begins to run only at the expiration of a year from the testator's death.

Authorities upon the subject of payment of interest on legacies—collated; and the rules governing the same—stated.

Lynch v. Mahony, 2 *Redf.*, 434; and Pierce v. Chamberlain, 41 *How. Pr.*, 501—doubted.

APPLICATION by Jennette Carr, an adopted daughter of testator, for a decree directing the payment of interest on a legacy.

KNAPP, NOTTINGHAM & ANDREWS, *for executor.*

JASPER N. HAMMOND, *for Mrs. Carr.*

THE SURROGATE.—This is a proceeding by petition, on the part of Jennette Carr, a legatee and devisee named in the last will and testament of William Churchill, deceased, praying that Lyman C. Bennett, the executor of the will of said deceased, be cited to show cause why a decree should not be made, requiring him to pay to the petitioner the interest on $4,000 from the time of the decease of the testator. The testator died August 15th, 1882, leaving a will which was proved December 15th, 1882; and, on the same day, letters testamentary were issued to Lyman C. Bennett, the executor therein named. On the return day of the citation, the executor presented his petition praying for a final judicial settlement of his accounts, and for permission to resign his trust as executor and trustee under said will; and the matter was adjourned to the return day of the citation for final settlement.

The provisions of the will, in favor of Mrs. Carr, are as follows: "After paying the debts I may be owing at my decease, together with my funeral expenses, and after the erection of a suitable monument over the spot where my remains may be deposited, I give and bequeath to my adopted daughter, Jennette, now the wife of Sullivan Carr, the farm upon which I now reside, together with all the household furniture of every description, to have and to hold the same for her own use and benefit her heirs and assigns forever. I also order and direct that my executor hereinafter appointed shall invest the sum of $4,000 of my estate in bonds and mortgages, upon unincumbered real estate, or government bonds, and the interest thereof, after paying said executor a suitable fee for looking after said fund, shall be paid annually to said Jennette Carr, and at the death of said Jennette Carr the whole of the above bequest shall be equally divided between the children of said Jennette, to have and to hold the same for their use and benefit their heirs forever."

On settlement, it was conceded that the estate of said deceased was ample to pay all debts and legacies; that, when the testator died, more than $4,000 of his estate was invested in bonds and mortgages, and from the time of his decease to the present time, more than that amount has been continuously invested in such securities; and that Mrs. Carr was a married woman, living with her husband, was an adopted daughter of the testator, and forty-two years of age. Under the provisions of this will, she claims interest on her legacy from the death of the testator. The residuary legatees, through the executor, contend that, under the provisions of said will, interest did not begin to run until after all debts were paid, which have but recently been settled, on account of a disputed claim. The only question submitted to the Surrogate to determine, was from what time interest should be allowed on this legacy—whether from the death of the testator, or from one year after his decease, or one year from the date of letters testamentary, or from the time the last debt was paid.

By statute, legacies are not payable until one year from the issuing of letters testamentary. The common law doctrine was that general legacies drew interest from and after one year from the death of the testator, when no time was indicated or fixed by the will, as to when interest was to commence. This rule has been strenuously adhered to, both in England in this country, where no statutory act contravened, with few exceptions. There are, however, certain exceptions to this rule, to which I shall hereafter refer.

In 2 Williams on Ex'rs, 878, the following doctrine is laid down: "When no time of payment is fixed, the executor is allowed, by law, one year from the testator's death, to ascertain and settle his affairs; at the end of which time, the court, for the sake of general convenience, presumes the personal estate to have been reduced into possession. Upon that ground, interest is payable from that time, unless some other period is fixed by the will. Nor will interest be payable from an earlier date, although there is a direction in the will to pay the legacy 'as soon as possible.' If, indeed, the legacy is decreed to be a satisfaction

·rest from the
:piration of the
·r, the legacy will
ne, from the condi-
·. and although the
·. The general rule
in Pearson v. Pearson :
:terest or not is totally
pecuniary legacies. I
ning v. Barker, where the
disposable for the payment
·y years after the death of the
·gacies were held to bear inter-
·r the testator's death; and the
. opinion that it was a general,
rule that pecuniary legacies bear
·e expiration of twelve months, if
: any time be a fund for the payment
that, in case the fund was productive
·elve months, all the intermediate profits
·.ie residuary legatee. The executor may
·gacy within the twelve months, but is not
d to do so. He is not to pay interest for any
thin the twelve months, although, during that
he may have received interest. But if he has
·, he is to pay interest from the end of the twelve
:iths, whether the assets have been productive or
·t.' "

At page 856, the following doctrine is enunciated :
" If an annuity be given by will, it shall commence
immediately from the testator's death, and consequently the first payment shall be made at the expira-

tion of a year next after that event. A distinction was taken by Lord ELDON, in Gibson v. Bott, between an annuity and a legacy for life. 'If an annuity,' said his lordship, 'is given, the first payment is paid at the end of the year from the death; but if a legacy is given for life, with remainder over, no interest is due till the end of two years. It is only interest of the legacy; and till the legacy is payable, there is no fund to produce interest.' However, a different doctrine prevails with respect to a bequest of a *residue* of personal estate for life, with remainder over. For the later decisions have established that the person taking the residue for life is entitled to the income, in some shape or other, from the death of the testator."

At page 880, in treating of general legacies, it is said: "This rule is subject to an exception in case of the testator being the parent (or *in loco parentis*) of the legatee. For there, whether the legacy be vested or contingent, if the legatee be not an adult, interest on the legacy shall be allowed, as a maintenance, from the time of the death of the testator, if there is no other provision for that purpose. The court will determine the *quantum* of allowance, either the whole of the usual interest allowed by the court, or less, according to circumstances. Where the legatee is the child of the testator, and a specific sum is given by the will for maintenance, no greater allowance can be claimed for that purpose, although it be less than the usual rate of interest upon the legacy."

This exception is not extended in favor of a wife, nor of natural children, nor of nieces and nephews, nor of grandchildren, unless the testator was *in loco parentis.*

Roper on Legacies (vol. 2, pp. 1245, 1246), says: " Specific legacies are considered as severed from the bulk of the testator's property, by the operation of the will, from the death of the testator, and as specifically appropriated, with their increase and emolument, for the benefit of the legatee, from that period; so that interest is computed on them from the death of the testator; and it is immaterial whether the enjoyment of the principal is postponed by the testator to a future period or not. With respect to general legacies, the law, for convenience, has prescribed the general rule that, where no time of payment is named by the testator, and in the absence of any intention to be inferred from the will itself, such general legacies shall be raised and satisfied out of the testator's personal estate at the expiration of one year next after his death; from which period the legatees will be entitled to interest, though actual payment within that time may be impracticable.* But where the court has decreed a legacy to be in satisfaction of a debt, the court gives interest always from the testator's death. Annuities, as before stated, in the absence of any direction in the will to the contrary, commence from the death of the testator, and the first payment becomes due, unless otherwise directed, at the end of the year from that event. The rule is otherwise with respect to a general legacy bequeathed for life; for, that not being payable out of the assets before the end of the year from the death, no interest will be due thereon until the expiration of the second year.

But the case is otherwise where the residue is given for life."

" In the case of Hutchin v. Mannington (1 *Ves. Jr.*, 366), Lord THURLOW spoke of the known practice of the court to compute interest upon legacies from the year's end after the testator's death " (id., p. 1250). " Where a general legacy is given to one for life, with remainder over to another, the case is otherwise. For, the interest not being payable out of the assets until the end of the year from the death of the testator, no interest will be due until the end of the second year " (id., p. 1252). " Where the legatee is a child of the testator (or one to whom he has placed himself *in loco parentis*), interest shall be allowed to such legatee, from the time of the death of the testator " (id., p. 1256). " We may here observe that the exception in favor of children of the testator, and those to whom he had placed himself *in loco parentis*, does not extend to adults " [citing Raven v. Waite, 1 *Swanst.*, 553 ; Wall v. Wall, 11 *Jur.*, 403] (id., p. 1270).

In Raven v. Waite (*supra*), Sir THOMAS PLUMER remarked that all the cases decided were cases of infants ; that no case had been produced in which it was ever extended to a legacy in favor of an adult.

Redfield on Wills lays down substantially the same doctrine, as to interest on legacies as is laid down by Williams on Executors and by Roper on Legacies. In vol. 3, p. 312, he says : " Pecuniary legacies carry interest after one year from the decease of the testator, unless the payment is further delayed by the terms of the will." " As far as we have been able to examine the American cases, they profess to go upon the principles already stated in this section, both as to the time a legacy becomes payable, and the right of the legatee to demand interest,—that legacies are payable in one year from the decease of the testator, even where directed to be paid as soon as convenient" (id., p. 371). "The distinction between annuities and legacies of the interest or income of a sum of money, as to the time when it becomes payable, is thus defined by Lord Eldon, in Gibson v. Bott (7 *Ves.*, 89, 96): 'If an annuity is given, the first payment is paid at the end of the year from the death. But if a legacy is given for life, with remainder over, no interest is due till the end of two years. It is only interest of the legacy, and till the legacy is payable, there is no fund to produce interest'" (id., p. 473).

Dayton on Surrogates (3rd, ed., pp. 464, 465) lays down the following rules in regard to legacies and interest thereon: "When no time of payment is fixed, the executor is by law allowed one year from the testator's death, to ascertain and settle his affairs; at the end of which time the court, for the sake of general convenience, presumes the personal estate to have been reduced into possession. Upon that ground, interest is payable from that time, unless some earlier period is fixed by the will. If, indeed, a legacy is given in lieu of dower, or is decreed to be in satisfaction of a debt, the court always allows interest from the death of the testator. A further exception to the rule exists, in case of a legacy given to a child by a parent, whether by way of portion or not, in which instance the court will give interest from death, to create a provision for its maintenance. This exception is confined to legacies in favor of infants, and has never been extended to a legacy given to an adult, nor does it apply to the case of a wife. Again, a legacy to a child whose support and maintenance are otherwise provided for by the bounty of the testator, like a legacy to a more distant relative, or to a stranger, is not payable and does not draw interest until one year after the death of the testator, where no time of payment is prescribed by the will. After the expiration of the year from the death of the testator, the legacy will carry interest. The provisions of the Revised Statutes relative to the payment of debts and legacies have not changed the rules as to the payment of interest on legacies. The object of the statute was only to allow a specified time to the executor or administrator after taking out letters to settle the estate. And it was not designed to affect or modify the rights of the parties interested in claims or legacies. An annuity bestowed by will, without mentioning any time of payment, is considered as commencing from the death of the testator, and the first payment as due at the expiration of one year, from which latter period interest may be claimed in cases where it is allowable at all."

"There is a distinction between income and an annuity. The former embraces only the net profits, after deducting all necessary expenses and charges. The latter is a fixed amount, directed to be paid absolutely and without contingency. A further distinction has been taken between an annuity and a legacy for life. If an annuity is given, the first payment is made at the end of the year from the death. But if a legacy is given for life, with remainder over, it is laid down that no interest is due till the end of two years. It is only interest of the legacy, and till the legacy is payable, there is no fund to produce interest. However, a different doctrine prevails with respect to a bequest of the residue of the personal estate for life with remainder over; for it seems now to be established that the person taking the residue for life is entitled to the proceeds from the death of the testator" (id., p. 449).

Thus we see that text writers, and authors of works pertaining to legacies and the settlement of estates, agree as to the general doctrine in relation to the payment of legacies and the interest thereon; and these rules, practice and doctrine have been adopted and followed, both in England and this country, for more than one hundred years.

In Wheeler v. Ruthven (74 *N. Y.*, 431), ANDREWS, J., says: "The general rule is well settled that, where a general legacy is given without assigning any time for payment, it bears interest from the expiration of a year after the death of the testator."

In Williamson v. Williamson (6 *Paige*, 298), Chancellor WALWORTH holds that, where the interest or income of a residuary estate is given to a legatee for life, and no time is named for the commencement of such enjoyment, the legatee is entitled to the income of the clear residue, as afterwards ascertained, to be computed from the death of the testator; and that a legacy to a child, whose support is otherwise provided for by the bounty of the testator, is not to draw interest until one year from the decease of the testator, where no time of payment is named by the will.

In Eichhold v. Greenebaum (1 *Chicago Legal News*, 210), it was held that a legacy to a widow did not draw interest until one year from the decease of the testator, there being no estate of which she was dowable, and nothing in the will indicating that it should be sooner paid.

In Miles v. Wister (5 *Binn.*, 479), TILGHMAN, Ch. J., says: "Where a legacy is given to a child, payable at the age of twenty-one, without mention of interest, the rule is that interest shall be allowed from the death of the parent, because it must be supposed that the parent intended to do his duty, and not leave the child without a maintenance; but this rule does not extend to legacies given to strangers or distant relatives, because none but a parent is bound to provide for a child. Courts of equity have gone great lengths to provide a maintenance for infants who are entitled to legacies payable at a future time."

The case of Weld v. Putnam (70 *Maine*, 209), was one where a life use of the residue of her estate, both real and personal, was given by testatrix in trust for the benefit of her sister, and Chief Justice APPLETON very properly held that she was entitled to the use from the death of the testatrix.

This is the general rule where the residue, or any aliquot part thereof, is given for life, with remainder over (see Williamson v. Williamson, *supra*).

Ayer v. Ayer (128 *Mass.*, 575), was a case where the testator gave to his brother Frederick the use of $100,000 during life, and on his decease to his children. Justice MORTON held that Frederick was entitled to interest from the death of the testator. By the general statutes of Massachusetts (ch. 97, § 23), it is declared that, when by a will an annuity or the rent, use, income or interest of any property, or the income of any fund is given to or in trust for the benefit of a person for life, he shall be entitled to receive the same from and after the decease of the testator. This decision is entirely in harmony with the decisions of that state. In some states there are statutes giving interest on life estates from the death of the testator. Where such laws exist, they are controlling, and the general rules of law do not apply.

In Bradner v. Faulkner (12 *N. Y.*, 472), the testator gave his daughter $16,000. The will was silent as to when interest should commence, and the rules of law were to govern. The Surrogate of Livingston county allowed Mrs. Faulkner interest on her legacy from the death of her father. This decision was affirmed at the General Term, and reversed by the Court of Appeals. The legatee was not an infant, was devised other property, and did not come within the exception to the general rule.

In Cooke v. Meeker (36 *N. Y.*, 15), the plaintiff was an infant, and, under the exception to the general rule, the court very properly allowed her interest from the testator's death. DAVIES, Ch. J., says: " By the Revised Statutes, no legacies are to be paid until the expiration of one year from the time of granting letters testamentary unless the same are by the will directed to be sooner paid (2 R. S., 91, § 43). This is an affirmance of the doctrine of the common law and has not changed the rule as to the time when interest on legacies begins to run (3 *Bradf.*, 364). At common law the general rule was that interest upon a legacy is payable only at the expiration of a year from the testator's death (Toler on Ex., 324). If, however, an annuity be given, or if, by implication from the terms of the instrument, the legacy be given for maintenance and support, it shall commence immediately from the death of the testator, and consequently the first payment shall be made at the expiration of the year next after that event."

BOCKES, J., in the same case, says: "At common law, when a legacy was given without specifying any time of payment, it vested in the legatee on the death of the testator, though not payable until one year afterwards."

In the case of Mary A. Fish (1 *Tucker*, 122; s. c. 19 *Abb.*, 209), Surrogate TUCKER held that interest on a general legacy did not commence until one year from the granting of letters, unless the will directed otherwise. Upon an appeal to the general term, the Surrogate's decree was reversed (31 *How. Pr.*, 172). INGRAHAM, P. J., says: "I concur in holding that the legatee was not entitled to interest until one year after the death of the testatrix. I see nothing in the statute nor in the case of Bradner v. Faulkner (12 *N. Y.*, 472), to the contrary. In Williamson v. Williamson (6 *Paige*, 298), the Chancellor states the rule to be that the legatees are not entitled to interest until one year after the death of the testatrix. In Bradner v. Faulkner (*supra*), the question was whether interest was chargeable on the legacy from the death of the testator. It is evident that the attention of the court was not directed to a case of a residuary legatee, contesting a will for years, where the legacies were large, and where, if the views of the court below are sustained, the residuary estate is increased by litigation. I concur with BRADFORD, Surrogate, in Lawrence v. Embree (3 *Bradf.*, 364), that the object of the statute was only to allow a specific time for the executor to settle the estate, and it was not designed to affect or modify the rights of parties interested in claims or legacies, and that the old rule in equity governing the payment of interest whereby a legatee is entitled to interest after one year from the death of the testator is still in force. The plaintiff is entitled to interest after one year from the death of the testator."

In Lynch's Estate (2 *Redf.*, 434), and Lynch v. Mahony (52 *How. Pr.*, 367), the legacy in question was as follows: "I give to the executors of this my will the sum of $1,500, in trust to invest the same and pay the income thereof to my sister Ann, wife of Martin Mahony, of Saratoga Springs, during her life and, upon her death, to pay said sum to her children surviving her in equal shares." The case of Fish (*supra*), which was overruled at General Term; Cooke v. Meeker (*supra*), which was a case of an infant; Bradner v. Faulkner (*supra*), where it was held that interest did not commence at the death of the testator, and some other authorities, are cited. The learned Surrogate says: "I do not feel at liberty to disregard the plain and emphatic language of the learned Chief Justice, in Cooke v. Meeker, which may be presumed to have received the attention and scrutiny of the other judges of the court, though it may not have been necessary to the decision of this case. The two Pennsylvania cases, above cited, are also directly involved in this case upon this point; and, therefore, I am not able to resist the force of the argument to the contrary above suggested. I feel constrained to respect the above authorities, and to hold that the interest upon the legacy in question began to run from the decease of the testator, and that the executor be directed to pay accordingly."

In Pierce v. Chamberlain (41 *How. Pr.*, 501), the testator, by his will, required his executor to pay to Truman R. Coleman $4,000 (there was, at the testator's death, $40,000 on deposit with Coleman, drawing interest), to be invested by Coleman in the best manner, and the interest and income to be paid by him semiannually to the plaintiff (who was the testator's adopted daughter), during her life, and at her decease to pay the principal to her heirs, and directed his executors to pay the legacies mentioned in his will as fast as they might be able to do so, without sacrificing his estate. The testator died February 10th, 1868. On August 15th, 1868, $4,000 of the money on deposit with Coleman was formally transferred by the executors to Coleman, but the interest accruing intermediate those periods was withheld. The action by the plaintiff was to recover such interest; and DANIELS, J., at special term, held that the plaintiff was entitled to interest from the date of the testator's death. The case of Cooke v. Meeker (*supra*) is cited, wherein the plaintiff was an infant; and it does not appear but that the plaintiff in this case was an infant. The last two cases mentioned are about the only cases I have been able to find and examine, which would seem to sustain the doctrine claimed by Mrs. Carr, herein.

In Lawrence v. Embree (3 *Bradf.*, 364), which is very much like the case now before me, the testatrix gave to her nephew and his wife and the survivor of them, the interest, dividends or other income of $2,500, for and during their joint lives and the life of the survivor of them, and then the principal to their living children. BRADFORD, Surrogate, says: "Generally, when no time of payment is fixed, legacies are not due until the lapse of a year from the death of the testator, and do not, of course, begin to earn interest until they become due. But annuities are considered as commencing from the death of the testator, and the first payment due at the expiration of the year (Gibson v. Bott (7 *Ves.*, 96, 97; Fearns v. Young, 9 *id.*, 553; Stamper v. Pickering, 9 *Sim.*, 176). There may be some ground for applying the reason of this rule to the legacies of the interest and income of certain specified sums. But, in examining the cases, I do not perceive any distinction has been recognized between bequests of income and general legacies. This will contains a clause authorizing the executors to invest the trust moneys, the interest whereof is payable during the lifetime of several of the before named legatees, and the principal to others upon their respective deaths, either in bonds and mortgages, or stocks, and there is no specified time when to make these investments, so that the general rule of allowing a year to make the investment would seem applicable. Taking this bequest and this provision together, it would amount to a legacy of $2,500 to the executors in trust to invest and pay the income for life to the first takers, and the principal on their decease to their children, and in such case the sum given would not begin to draw interest until the expiration of the year. The provision of the Revised Statutes, relative to the payment of debts and legacies, have not changed the rule as to the payment of interest. The object of the statute was only to allow a specified time for the executor or administrator, after taking out letters, to settle the estate. And it was not designed to affect or modify the rights of parties interested in claims or legacies. If a delay in the probate is to deprive legatees of interest on their legacies, because the executor cannot be compelled by the Surrogate to pay before a certain time has elapsed after letters issued, a premium for delay and contention would be awarded, and great injustice sanctioned by law. I am quite clear that the rules governing the payment of interest on testamentary bequests remain as they ever were, according to the established principles of the courts of law and equity."

Welsh v. Brown (2 *Am. Prob. R.*, 221; s. c., 43 *N. J. Law R.*, 37) is also a case almost precisely like this. In that case, the testatrix made to the plaintiff the following bequest: "I do give and bequeath to my niece, Aletta Brown, my gold watch, my melodeon, my black ear-rings, my black furs, one set of silver teaspoons (second choice), my cashmere shawl, my brown silk dress, and the interest of $2,500, to be paid to her annually by my executor; and at her death, the said sum of $2,500 shall be paid or divided equally among any child or children of hers that may then be living." The action was brought by Miss Brown, the legatee, against the executor, to recover $175, one year's interest on said sum of $2,500, accruing between April 22d, 1874, the time of the death of the testatrix, and April 22d, 1875. The court below decided in favor of the plaintiff.

On appeal, the decision was reversed. DEPUE, J., in his very able and learned opinion, says: "With respect to general legacies, the law, for convenience, has prescribed a general rule that, where no time is named by the testator, and in the absence of any intention derived from the will itself, such general legacies shall be raised and satisfied out of the testator's estate at the expiration of one year after his death (2 Roper on Legacies, 1245; 2 Lead. Cas. in Eq., 639; notes to Ashburner v. MacGuire). On a legacy coming within the class of general legacies, if the legacy be not paid at the expiration of the year, interest from that time will be allowed as damages, and interest on a legacy will not be computed from a period prior to that time, unless there be a clear expression of intention that interest shall be reckoned from an antecedent time or event. In that case, the interest is regarded as the substance of the gift, and is not recoverable as such unless there be a clear intention apparent on the face of the will that interest shall be payable from a period prior to the expiration of the year. The gift to the plaintiff is of the interest on a gross sum of $2,500, to be paid to her annually by the executor, and after the plaintiff's death the principal sum is payable to other parties. The will provides that the executor, after putting out at interest a sum sufficient to pay the interest and legacies bequeathed, shall divide the residue among the heirs of the testatrix. It further directs that all taxes on the money or interest bequeathed shall first be deducted, and the balance only paid, and that the said money or interest should be subject to the taxes, as long as it remains in the hands or under the control of the executor. In substance, the bequest is to the executor to invest and pay over the net income or interest after deducting taxes, to the life tenant during her natural life, and after her death to pay the principal to the legatees in remainder. The executor, in the administration of the estate as executor, was under no obligations to set apart the principal sum on which interest was to be allowed until the end of the first year, and until the separation was made there was no fund to produce interest for the life tenant. In legal effect, the bequest is analogous to those in Lowndes v. Lowndes (15 *Ves.*, 301) and Raven v. Waite (1 *Swanst.*, 553), upon which interest was allowed only from the expiration of the year. In my examination of the English cases, I have not found a single decision in which a bequest similar to that under consideration has been considered as excluded from the general rule that the legacy shall, for such purposes, take effect after the lapse of a year. The distinction between an annuity, pure and simple, which is to be paid at all events out of the testator's estate, at the expense of the residuary legatee, and the interest or income for life of a certain sum set apart by the testator for that purpose, and given over in gross to another after the death of the life tenant has been quite uniformly adhered to. Baker v. Baker (6 *H. of L. Cas.*, 623) was decided upon that distinction. Lord CRANSWORTH, in delivering his opinion, said: 'In all these cases, arising upon the construction of wills, the real question is whether what is given is given as an annuity or is given as interest on a fund; and where that question is to be considered, what you must look to is this—whether the language of the testator imports that a sum at all events is annually to be paid out of his general estate, or only the interest, or a portion of the interest of a capital sum, which is to be set apart. This distinction is recognized by Lord Justice ROLT, in Birch v. Sherratt (*L. R.*, 2 *Ch. App.*, 649). The principle upon which it rests is that a bequest of a specific sum of money is one gift, one legacy, the benefit of which the testator has apportioned between the donee for life and the remainderman. To the life tenant he has given the interest or produce of the fund during life, and the capital sum to the remainderman after the death of the former. Such a legacy is, therefore, subject to the rule that general legacies are to take effect and be payable at the expiration of one year from the testator's death.

The executor is not bound to set apart the legacy for investment, before the end of the year, and until that be done, there is no fund to produce the interest that is payable to the life tenant.'"

The authorities which I have cited and so extensively quoted from would seem to determine the general rule in regard to legacies and the interest thereon, and by which this case should be decided. These authorities are substantially in harmony, each with the other, with the exception of Lynch v. Mahony and Pierce v. Chamberlain (*supra*), the former a decision made by the Surrogate of New York, the latter a special term decision made by Judge DANIELS, both able judicial officers. No appeal seems to have been taken in either case, and they were perhaps decided without much investigation as to the general rule.

In this case, the testator, by his will, after absolutely devising and bequeathing to Mrs. Carr his farm and household furniture, directs his executors to invest the sum of $4,000 in bonds and mortgages upon unincumbered real estate or government bonds, and, after paying the executor a suitable compensation for taking care of the funds, directs the balance of the interest to be paid to her annually, during life, and on her death the principal to her children. No time is indicated by the will from which interest is to commence.

This legacy is not like an annuity of a certain amount, payable absolutely and without contingency from the residuary estate, or from a certain portion of the estate specially appropriated for that purpose, and payable out of the *corpus* of the estate, if the income of the fund is insufficient for the purpose. Neither does it come within the exception to the general rule. For the legatee is not an infant; and if she were, other provisions are made for her maintenance; and for that reason her legacy would not draw interest until after one year from the death of the testator.

This legacy seems to come within the rule of general legacies,—which draw interest from one year after the death of the testator when no time is fixed or indicated by the will. Such has long been the fixed and settled rule and practice on the settlement of estates.

By statute, legacies are not payable until one year from the granting of letters testamentary. The object of this statute is, first, to give the executor ample time to reduce the estate into money; second, to allow him time to publish for six months notices to the creditors of the testator to present their claims, which notice cannot be published until six months after the issuing of letters; and, third, one year is allowed after the recording of a decree admitting a will to probate for persons interested in the estate of the decedent to present a petition praying that the probate thereof be revoked. It was evidently not the intention of the legislature, in postponing the payment of legacies, to change the old and well settled rule as to the interest thereon.

It has been contended that legacies do not draw interest until they become payable, which would be one year from the issuing of letters testamentary, where no time is fixed by the will. If such a rule were to prevail, a residuary legatee of a large estate, who was intended to be given only a small or nominal sum, might, by causing a delay in the application for probate, by contesting the will, or inducing some one interested to contest the same, or by initiating a contest over the issuing of letters testamentary, delay the issuing of the latter for years, and create for himself a fortune at the expense of other legatees, and defeat the real intent of the testator under the apparent sanction of the law. The same rule would apply where the will was not found for many years after the testator's death. Such a rule is not favored, and has not, to any great extent, been followed on the settlement of estates.

A legacy of the residuum of an estate, or any aliquot part thereof, for life, with remainder over, gives to the legatee for life whatever interest or income the estate may earn, after the payment of debts and other legacies, from the death of the testator. A legacy in lieu of dower, or in satisfaction of a debt, also draws interest from the testator's death.

What is given by this legacy is $4,000 to one for life, with remainder over. No greater amount is given or attempted to be given. If no life estate were attached, no interest would or could be claimed, under any rule of law, until one year after the testator's death.

A life estate in a general legacy of a specified amount neither increases nor decreases it. The executor is not compelled to invest the amount until the twelve months have elapsed, and the earnings of it for the first year, if invested, belong to the residuary legatee. What the testator has done is to apportion the legacy. To Mrs. Carr he has given what it may earn from and after one year from the time of his decease, and to her children he has given the principal, on the happening of that event.

If the testator had intended that the legacy should draw interest from the time of his decease, he could easily have indicated such intention in and by his will. In the absence of any mention or indication in his will, it must be presumed that he intended to apply the . general rule, which gives interest from and after one year from his decease, payable at the expiration of two years from that event.

The mere mention by the testator, in his will, that, after his debts and funeral expenses are paid, he gives, bequeaths, etc., does not postpone the payment of legacies and interest thereon until after the actual payment of all debts, provided the estate is ample to pay both debts and legacies. It is the usual expression, and amounts to nothing. Debts, funeral expenses, etc., have to be first paid or provided for, before legacies are paid, whether any such expression occurs in the will or not.

After a thorough examination of the authorities, I reach the conclusion that the legacy to Mrs. Carr for life, and then to her children, is a general legacy; that she is entitled to interest thereon from and after one year from the decease of the testator; and that interest thereon became due and payable at the expiration of two years from such decease.

The general rules, in regard to the payment of legacies, where no time is fixed or indicated by the will, together with the interest thereon, may be stated thus:

1st. Specific legacies are considered as severed from the bulk of the testator's property, by the operation of the will, from the death of the testator, and as specifically appropriated, with the income and increase thereof, for the benefit of the legatee, from that period; and interest is computed thereon from the death of the testator.

2d. By statute, general legacies are not payable until one year from the issuing of letters testamentary, but draw interest from the expiration of one year after the testator's death, as at common law.

3rd. A legacy given to a widow, in lieu of dower, where the testator died seized of real estate of which she was dowable, draws interest from the death of the testator.

4th. A legacy given in satisfaction of a debt, draws interest from the testator's death.

5th. A legacy given to a child of the testator, or one to whom the testator has placed himself in loco parentis, will, if such child is an infant, and is not otherwise provided for by the testator's bounty, or in some other way, draw interest from the testator's death, to provide means for the support and maintenance of such infant child; the amount of interest for the first year to be fixed by the court according to circumstances, not, however, to exceed the amount necessary for the proper support, education and maintenance of such infant during the year succeeding the testator's death.

6th. An annuity draws interest from the death of

the testator, in the absence of any direction contained in the will, to the contrary.

7th. A general legacy of a specific amount, bequeathed to one for life, with remainder over, on the death of the life tenant, will begin to draw interest at the end of twelve months from the death of the testator; and the first payment of interest will become due thereon at the expiration of the second year.

8th. A life tenant of the residue of the testator's estate will be entitled to the net earnings of such residue from the testator's death, after providing for the payment of debts and other legacies.

ONONDAGA COUNTY.—HON. G. R. COOK, SURROGATE.— November, 1883.

LYMAN *v.* PHILLIPS.*

In the matter of the application for revocation of probate of the will of LEWIS S. PHILLIPS, *deceased.*

A substantial compliance with the statute, 2 R. S., 63, § 40, in the execution of a will, is all that is required. An acknowledgment of the execution by the testator, made to a witness after the latter has signed, is sufficient, where the two acts are performed on the same occasion. The several independent requirements of the statute may be joint in their execution.

Decedent, having written and subscribed the paper purporting to be his will apart from witnesses, took it to the place of business of S., made formal publication in his presence and procured his signature in

---

* Surrogate's decree affirmed at Gen. Term and in Ct. of Appeals.

attestation. He then went, with the document, to the office of B., an attorney, told him that it was his will, or his last will and testament, and requested him to sign as a witness, which B. did, the signature of decedent being, at the time, plainly visible. The evidence showed that decedent's acknowledgment of the character of the instrument was made after B. had signed, and that the latter thereafter told decedent that it was very informally drawn, specifying various objections as to its form and the manner of execution, and advised him to go to some attorney and have a will regularly drawn up; from which views, however, decedent dissented. B., who omitted to add to his signature a statement of his place of residence, testified that such omission was owing to an impression on his part that, when decedent left the office, he did so with the purpose of having the paper redrawn, and did not regard it as an executed will. Upon an application to revoke probate, it was contended that the execution was invalid by reason of the failure of decedent to acknowledge it until after B. had completed his signature; and, also, that the latter could not be regarded as an attesting witness.—

Held, that the will was duly published in the presence of B., whose signanature, as the second witness, gave to it legality and validity; and that the petition for revocation should be denied.

APPLICATION by Mary J. Lyman and another, next of kin of decedent, for a decree revoking the probate of his will; opposed by Mary B. Phillips, executrix thereof. The facts appear sufficiently in the opinion.

FRANK HISCOCK, *and* FREDERICK A. LYMAN, *for petitioners.*

A. L. JOHNSON, *and* I. D. GARFIELD, *for respondent.*

THE SURROGATE.—This is an application under § 2647 of the Code of Civil Procedure, on the part of Erastus B. Phillips and Mary J. Lyman, a brother and sister of Lewis S. Phillips, late of the town of Geddes, in the county of Onondaga, deceased, for the revocation of the probate of his last will and testament.

The testator died January 9th, 1883, leaving a will, of which the following is a copy:

" *To whom it may concern*:—Considering the uncertainty of life, I hereby make my last will by which I give and bequeathe all my property and effects, both personal and real, to my wife, Mary Bigelow Phillips, and I hereby appoint her executrix of this my will. If she should always find it convenient to pay my sister, Caroline Buck, the sum of three hundred ($300) dollars a year during her life, and also to give my brother, Edwin W. Phillips, during his life the interest on ten thousand dollars, (or seven hundred dollars per year,) I wish it to be done.

Dated this 26th day of February, 1879.

LEWIS S. PHILLIPS.

JAMES A. SKINNER,
WM. A. BEACH,   } Witnesses.
JOHN B. STRAUB.

J. B. Straub is clerk in our store."

The will was duly proved in the Surrogate's court of the county of Onondaga, as a will of real and personal estate, on February 21st, 1883, as alleged in the petition herein for revocation of probate of the same. The testator left him surviving Mary Bigelow Phillips, his widow, Erastus B. Phillips, Edwin W. Phillips, Mary J. Lyman and Caroline Buck, his brothers and sisters, and Stellie Phillips, a daughter of Addison B. Phillips, a deceased brother, his only heirs at law and next of kin, severally of full age. The value of the personal estate of the testator is $100,000. It was conceded, on the argument, that the testator was sixty-four years of age at the time of his death.

The will of the testator was drawn and signed by him apart from the witnesses, and they signed their names as witnesses to the same in the presence of the testator, but not in the presence of each other. Every word and letter upon the will is in the handwriting of the testator except the names of the three subscribing witnesses thereto. The will is written on one side of a sheet of letter paper, and covers nearly the whole of the same. Upon the trial, no question was raised by the contestants, as to the competency of the testator to make a will; and it appeared, from the evidence of the subscribing witnesses that were sworn, that he was fully competent to make and execute such an instrument, and there was no evidence of fraud or undue influence or coercion.

James A. Skinner and William A. Beach, two of the subscribing witnesses to said will, were called on the part of the proponent, and no witnesses were called on the part of the contestants. The other subscribing witness to said will was not called, and it did not appear, on the trial, whether he was dead or alive. If alive, and he could have recalled any important fact that took place at the time of the execution of the will, he would very likely have been found and called by the proponents or contestants in so important a matter.

There was no conflict of evidence or dispute as to how the will was executed. The only question raised upon the trial and argument was as to whether the testator had complied, in the execution of his will, with § 40, 2 R. S., 63, which is as follows.*

---

* See the section in question quoted on page 100, *ante.*

The statute must be observed and complied with in its several provisions in the execution of a will, and a failure to comply therewith renders the instrument invalid. A substantial compliance therewith, however, is all that is required. It would seem that, after the testator had drawn and signed his will, he took it to the store of the witness Skinner, told him that he wanted him to witness his will, took it from his pocket and laid it in front of Mr. Skinner and said: "this is my last will and testament;" he acknowledged the execution of it, and that that was his signature, and said to Mr. Skinner: "I want you to witness it." Mr. Skinner thought that the testator told him to sign to the left of his signature, and then Mr. Skinner signed his name as a witness to the will. Mr. Skinner, who was the first witness to the will, says the testator's name was signed to the will when it was brought to his store.

It would seem that the testator then took the will to the law office of the witness William A. Beach laid the will in front of him on the table, told Mr. Beach that it was his last will and testament and that he wanted him to sign it as a witness; that, while the testator was talking, Mr. Beach was writing his name to the will; and that the testator finished talking just as Mr. Beach wrote "h," the last letter of his name. Mr. Beach says that he then told the testator that he thought the paper was very informally drawn, to trust an estate to after he was out of the way, and that, if he were the testator, he would go to some attorney, and have it drawn up in regular form. Mr. Beach says that the testator asked him in what respect it was informal; and that he told him he thought it was all informal. The testator said he had no fears of it; that he had copied it from a will of somebody that had been contested and stood the test, and that he had no question about it. Mr. Beach says that he then told Mr. Phillips that that might be so, but that the attestation clause was not right; that he had no attestation clause; that the witnessing of it, in his mind, was informal; that he ought to have that part of it redrawn at least and have it witnessed regularly; that the testator then wanted to know what was necessary. Mr. Beach said he told him that, in his opinion, the two witnesses should be there together, and that the testator should sign in their presence, and that they should sign in his presence.

The testator told Mr. Beach that he did not think that he was right upon that. Mr. Beach then told him that he did not know that he was, but that he would avoid all trouble by having it redrawn. The testator then said that he was satisfied that it was done according to law, that he had drawn it in his own handwriting for reasons of his own, and that he had executed it. Mr. Beach then remarked to the testator that it would be better to sign before the witnesses. The testator said it would make no difference, that he had signed it and that it was all right. Mr. Beach then stated to the testator that he would avoid the possibility of any difficulty if it were he. The testator replied that he was sure in his own mind that it was right, but that he would see about it. The testator then took the will and put it in his pocket, they had some little talk about politics, and

the testator left.   Mr. Beach says he finished his signature after the testator told him what the instrument
was; that the testator's name was signed to the will at
the time.   The testator then told Mr. Beach that he
had made it just as he wanted it; that it expressed
his idea of what he wanted done with his estate; that
he had drawn it himself, and he cautioned Mr. Beach
about saying that he had made a will.   Mr. Beach says
that the testator acknowledged that he had executed
it.   The testator said that he had copied it from a
form, and that it was right, and that he did not think
that it was necessary for the witnesses to be together.
Mr. Beach said he thought the testator was there
fifteen or twenty minutes.   Mr. Beach on his cross-
examination says that the reason why he did not sign
his residence was that he had so strongly criticised
the will, and recommended that it be redrawn, that,
when the testator left his office, he supposed he had
left to have it redrawn; that it left that impression
on his mind, and that he thought that the testator
did not regard it as an executed will.   Mr. Beach
said he could hardly have any understanding upon
that subject, but that he had an impression, coming
from his own criticism, that the testator would have
the will or attestation clause redrawn.

The right to dispose of property by will is an
ancient privilege that has been extended to the citizens of all countries.   It is very evident, in this case,
that the testator intended to avail himself of such
privilege, and make a will disposing of his property
in such manner as he thought proper; and, to make
it more evident to the world as to what his intention

was, he wrote it with his own hand and used his own language (for reasons of his own, as he told Mr. Beach, and it expressed just his idea of what he wanted done with his estate). If he had desired that his estate should pass to his widow and next of kin in such proportions as the law directs, he would have died intestate. There would have been no necessity of his making a will. That he died, supposing he had left behind him a valid instrument disposing of his estate, there can be no doubt, for it would seem that he made every effort within the reach of man to execute such an instrument.

He drew the will himself, signed it, and then went personally about the city for the express purpose of procuring attesting witnesses to the execution of it.

The evidence of the two subscribing witnesses, sworn upon the trial of this matter, leads me to believe that the testator had, in some way, made himself familiar with the law in relation to wills and the execution of the same, for by his will he clearly points out the channel in which he desires his estate to go, in a short and precise manner, and in the execution of his will he seems posted on all the requirements of the law in relation thereto.

Mr. Skinner testified that he knew nothing about the law in relation to the execution of wills, but it would appear that, so far as he was concerned in the execution of this instrument, the statute was observed and literally complied with. The will was signed at the end by the testator. The testator acknowledged his signature, or the execution of the will (either of which was sufficient), said it was his last will and testament (which was a publication of it), requested Mr. Skinner to sign his name as a witness, told him where to sign to the left of his signature, and Mr. Skinner so signed his name as a witness.

It is claimed, on the part of contestants, (1) that the testator did not acknowledge the execution of this instrument to the witness Beach until after Beach had signed his name to the will, and that the execution is, therefore, invalid; and (2) that the witness Beach cannot be held to be an attesting witness to the will. In England as well as in this country, where the testator signs his name to a will in the absence of the witnesses, he must acknowledge his signature or the execution of the instrument to each of the attesting witnesses, who must be present at the same time, and, in some states and countries, the testator must acknowledge the execution of the instrument to each of the witnesses, even if he does sign in their presence.

Since the decision of the Court of Appeals in Hoysradt v. Kingman (22 *N. Y.*, 372), there cannot be any doubt, if there was any before, that, under our statute, it is not necessary to the due attestation of a will that the witnesses should sign in the presence of each other.

The English law (1 Vict., ch. 26, sec. 9) is somewhat different from our law, and is as follows: "No will shall be valid unless it shall be in writing and executed in the following manner, viz.: It shall be signed at the foot or end thereof by the testator, or some other person in his presence, and by his direction. Such signature shall be made or acknowledged by the testator in the presence of two or more witnesses present at the same time. Such witnesses shall attest and shall subscribe the will in the presence of the testator."

The question arises as to what is a sufficient acknowledgment by a testator of the execution of his will where an acknowledgment is required. What constitutes such an acknowledgment should be the same in all countries and states. That question has frequently been before the courts in England and in this country, and decisions made and rendered thereon, as appears from the reports.

In Ellis v. Smith (1 *Ves. Jr.*, 11), decided in 1754, the precise point in the case was as to what was a sufficient acknowledgment by the testator of the execution of his will; whether the testator's declaration before the witnesses that the paper was his will was equivalent to signing before them, and Lord Chancellor HARDWICKE, assisted by Sir JOHN STRANGE, Master of the Rolls, and by the Chief Baron of the Exchequer decided that it was. In Ilott v. Genge (3 *Curteis*, 172, 175), Sir HERBERT JENNER FUST says: "It is not necessary that a testator should state to the witnesses that it is his signature. The production of a will by a testator, it having his name upon it, and a request to the witnesses to attest it would be a sufficient acknowledgment."

In Gaze v. Gaze (3 *Curteis*, 457), the testator himself produced the will to the witnesses signed and sealed, and directed them to put their names to it as witnesses. It did not exactly appear whether he used the words—"put your names below mine," or pointed out the place where their names were to be signed. The witnesses did subscribe the will in the presence of the testator and of each other. Sir HERBERT JENNER FUST says: "There can be no doubt of the intention of the deceased that this paper should operate and take effect as his will." And he held that it was a sufficient acknowledgment.

In Blake v. Knight (3 *Curteis*, 547, 564), Sir HERRERT JENNER FUST says: "I am quite satisfied that the name of the testator was signed to the paper before the witnesses subscribed, and I think that his acknowledging this to be his will, it being all in his own handwriting and his name, as I hold, being then signed to it, amounts to a sufficient acknowledgment of his signature." And he admitted the will to probate. In Inglesant v. Inglesant (*L. R.*, 3 *Prob. & Div.*, 172), the signature of the testatrix was put to the will before one of the witnesses, came into the room. Mrs. Lee, in whose house the testatrix resided, in the presence of the testatrix upon the second witness coming into the room requested him to put his name under the name of the testatrix. The testatrix did not say anything or do anything in reference to the will after the two witnesses were there, and the question was whether the words used by Mrs. Lee could be taken to be the words of the testatrix. Sir JAMES HANNEN says: "The authorities abound, which show that, if the words used by Mrs. Lee had been spoken by testatrix namely an invitation to the witnesses to put their names under the signature of the testatrix, that would have been an acknowledgment sufficient to render the execution valid. Therefore, the question is whether the invitation given by Mrs. Lee in the presence of the testatrix was equivalent to an invitation by, and, therefore, an act of the testatrix herself." And he held that he must accept the words of Mrs. Lee as the words of the testatrix, and established the will.

In Nickerson v. Buck (12 *Cush.*, 343) [In Mass., the law requires three subscribing witnesses, but the witnesses do not have to see the testator sign nor need they attest in the presence of each other], the testator signed by making his mark, and the two subscribing witnesses did not see him sign. Judge DEWEY held that, "if the witness be requested by the testator to sign his name to an instrument as an attesting witness, and the testator declares to the witness that the signature to the will is his, that is abundantly sufficient. But," he says, " the adjudicated cases go further, and hold that the actual signature of the testator may be made known to the witnesses in other modes than an express declaration to the witnesses that the will is his. Any act or declaration that carries by implication an averment of such fact is equally effectual. Hence it has been repeatedly held that a declaration by the testator to the witness that the instrument is his will, or even a request by him to the witness to attest the will, or other varied form of expression implying that the same had been signed by the testator, are, either of them, quite sufficient."

In Ela v. Edwards (16 *Gray*, 92), the will was drawn by the testatrix, and her name signed thereto, and borne thereupon, in the proper place for attesting witnesses, the names of three persons were duly writ-

ten. The two that were living testified that the testatrix sought them as witnesses, took the paper from
her custody, asked each to sign as a witness, pointed
them to the proper place on the left hand side to put
their names, had them sign their names in her presence, and then took the paper into her custody.
Held, that the will was properly attested.

In Allison v. Allison (46 *Illinois*, 61) [In Ill., two
witnesses are required; their statute is similar to
ours], the testator signed in the absence of the witnesses and then went out and called Hoyt and Walsh,
the subscribing witnesses, to come in and sign a paper.
They went in where the testator was; the draftsman
of the will read over the attestation clause, the testator sitting in the room within hearing distance, the
testator then handed the pen to Hoyt, who having
signed his name, handed it to Walsh, who also signed.
The testator said nothing the witnesses could remember. The chief objection taken to the proof was that
the testator did not sign the will in the presence of
the witnesses, or acknowledge it to be his act or deed as
required by law. Justice LAWRENCE says: "It is true
the testimony shows no formal acknowledgment, in
set terms or by words to that effect, and yet the
entire transaction amounts to an acknowledgment,
as distinct and satisfactory as language could have
made it. The statute does not require the acknowledgment to be in language; any act which indicates
the same thing with unmistakable certainty will answer as well. Although he uttered not a word, he
really acknowledged the instrument to be his will as
satisfactorily as if he had said: ' I, Daniel Allison, do

acknowledge this instrument to be my last will and testament.'" Also see Peck v. Cary (27 *N. Y.*, 9), and Nelson v. McGiffert (3 *Barb. Ch.*, 158).

In Brown v. McAlister (34 *Indiana*, 377), Judge WORDEN, quoting from elementary writers, says: "The mere fact that one calls upon a witness to subscribe a paper as a witness of its execution is, no doubt, abundant evidence of his acknowledgment that he executed it." Judge DOWNEY, in the same case, says: "But as it is shown by the facts that the testatrix went to the persons who were chosen by her to be the witnesses, produced the paper already written, told them that she desired them to witness her signature, and thereupon signed the paper in the presence of the witnesses, who then and there wrote their names to it as witnesses, the question in the case is whether or not it is necessary that she should have *stated* to the witnesses that it was her will. I decide that it was not necessary that she should have made such *statement;*" and the will was sustained.

In Randebaugh v. Shelley (6 *Ohio State*, 314, 315) [the statute of Ohio, in relation to the execution of wills, is similar to that of New York], BARTLEY, Ch. J., says: "It was not necessary that the witnesses should attest the instrument in the presence of each other. Neither of the witnesses saw the testator subscribe his name to the paper; one of them, however, heard him expressly acknowledge the same, but the other did not. And the question is presented as to whether the will is to be invalidated because the testator, having subscribed the will in the absence of the witnesses, did not, in express and direct language say to the witnesses that he had executed it or signed it as his last will and testament. It appears that the witnesses were called in to attest the paper without being informed expressly that the instrument was a will, and upon the paper being presented to him by the testator, with his (the testator's) name written at the end of it, he subscribed his name as a witness at the testator's request. It was not essential to the attestation that the witnesses should have been made acquainted with the particular contents of the instrument. Where an attesting witness does not see the testator subscribe his name to the will, the law requires that he should hear the testator acknowledge the fact of his having subscribed it. This acknowledgment is not required to be made in any particular words or in any particular manner. If by signs, motions, conduct or attending circumstances, the attesting witness was given to understand that the testator had already subscribed the paper as his will, it was a sufficient acknowledgment."

In Robinson v. Smith (13 *Abb. Pr.*, 360, 361), the will was in the handwriting of the testator. Both of the witnesses subscribed their names at the testator's request, in his presence, and in the presence of each other, and the testator declared the instrument to be his last will and testament. The witnesses did not see the testator sign, nor did he, by words, acknowledge it to be his last will and testament. The court says: "Did he in substance do so? Had he subscribed his name before the subscribing witnesses signed? Did the testator and the witnesses know that it was a testamentary instrument? Was the testator's name visible to it when he laid it on the table in front of the witnesses? I am satisfied that the testator had then signed it, and that the testator and the subscribing witnesses understood that it was a testamentary instrument." The Judge said: "I can hardly conceive how a person could more forcibly and effectually acknowledge the execution of an instrument than by laying it down on a table, with his name to it, saying: ' I declare this to be my last will and testament, and I have sent for you as witnesses, and wish you to sign it as such.' "

In Jauncey v. Thorne (2 *Barb. Ch.*, 40, 65), Chancellor WALWORTH says: "But the production of the will with the testator's name subscribed to it, and in such a way that the signature could be seen by the attesting witnesses, and the request of the testator that they should witness the execution of the instrument as his will, would of itself be a sufficient acknowledgment of his signature, to render the will valid under the provisions of the act which was in force when this will was made.

In Nelson v. McGiffert (3 *Barb. Ch.*, 163), Chancellor WALWORTH says: " Not only the witnesses, but the testator himself, must therefore have understood that they were witnesses to the execution of a will, in conformity to his desire and wish; although he may not have said in terms: ' I request you and each of you to subscribe your names as witnesses to this my will.' If such a formal request were necessary to be proved in all cases, and the witnesses were required to recollect the fact so as to be able to swear to it after any considerable length of time, not one will in ten would be adjudged valid.   In the execution of wills, the statute does not require any particular form of words to be used by the testator, either in the admission of his signature, in the publication of the instrument as his will, or in the communication to the witnesses of his request or desire that they should subscribe their names to the will, as attesting witnesses to the fact of its due execution by him.   But it is sufficient if the formalities required by the statute are complied with in substance."

In Coffin v. Coffin (23 *N. Y.*, 10), the witnesses were present at the testator's, on the day the will was executed, by the procurement of the testator, and for the purpose of witnessing his will.   When the instrument was ready for execution, they were called into the room where the will was executed. They came there, saw the testator subscribe his name to the will, and signed their names as witnesses. Before doing so, one of the witnesses asked the testator if he requested him to sign as a witness, to which he answered in the affirmative, and both witnesses then signed.   COMSTOCK, Ch. J., says: "We apprehend it is clear that no precise form of words addressed to each of the witnesses at the very time of the attestation is required.   Any communication importing such request, addressed to one of the witnesses in the presence of the other, and which, by a just construction of all the circumstances, is intended for both, is, we think, sufficient.   The statute, in separate and independent clauses, besides the subscription of the testator, requires that he shall declare the instrument to be his last will, and shall request the witnesses to sign it. In this case, the publication and request that the witnesses should sign it as such are both included in the testator's answer, when asked if he wished to have the paper attested as his will. But this objection we think is not fatal. All that the statute requires is that the act of publication and the act requesting the witnesses to sign shall both be performed. The acts are distinct in their nature and quality, but their performance may be joint or connected. If a testator should say to the witnesses: 'I desire you to attest this instrument as my last will and testament,' the language would not only be a request but a clear publication of the will."

In Baskin v. Baskin (36 *N. Y.*, 418), the will was drawn by the witness Smith, signed by the testator in his presence, and then Smith at the testator's request signed his name as a witness. Wilsey, the other witness, was then called in from an adjoining room. The will was in sight on the stand. The testator said to Wilsey that he wanted him to sign his will. Smith then handed the testator his will, and, as he held it in his hand, Smith asked him if he acknowledged that to be his last will and testament, and the testator said that he did acknowledge it to be his last will and testament. Wilsey then signed his name as a witness. The Surrogate held that that was not a sufficient acknowledgment of the subscription in the presence of Wilsey, within the meaning of the statute in relation to wills, and refused probate. The General Term reversed the decision of the Surrogate, and the decision of the General Term was affirmed in the Court of Appeals. The attestation clause stated that the will was signed and published in the presence of the attesting witnesses (which was not true as to Wilsey), as it was not signed by the testator in his presence. Judge PORTER, in his opinion, says: "It is clear the testator intended a complete execution of the instrument; that with this view he signed it; that he supposed he was acknowledging that he had done so when he requested Wilsey to attest the truth of the facts stated in the certificate; and that Wilsey so supposed when he certified that he was a witness to the signature as well as to the publication."

In Willis v. Mott (36 *N. Y.*, 486), the head note says: "If the testator presents the will already subscribed by him to the witnesses, acknowledge that he has executed it as such will, that the same is his will, and request him to sign as a witness, and he signs in the presence of the testator, it is sufficient."

In re Harder (1 *Tucker*, 429, 430), Surrogate TUCKER says: "Although this case has been so ably and thoroughly reviewed and argued by the learned counsel retained in it, I cannot see any doubt in the testimony; the simple question is whether the words addressed by the decedent to, and heard by both of the subscribing witnesses, 'will you witness my will,' or 'I want you to witness my will,' constitute a sufficient acknowledgment, declaration and rogation. The rulings of our courts on this subject have been quite uniform and very liberal. It has been held that any communication of the idea, that the instrument is his will, will meet the object of the statute. This knowledge of the nature of the transaction must be evinced with reasonable definiteness by the party executing the will, so that the testamentary character of the instrument is shown to have been communicated by the testator to the witness. It has been held in many cases in our courts, and appears to be settled law, that a separate acknowledgment of the signature of the testator is not necessary, where the instrument is already signed by him when he acknowledges the instrument to be his will. The greater includes the less, and his acknowledgment that this instrument is his will is held to include and dispense with the acknowledgment that the signature appended to it is his signature."

I have reviewed, to some extent, the decisions of the courts, both in this country and England, as to what constitutes a sufficient acknowledgment by a testator of the instrument as his will, where an acknowledgment is required, and find that the decisions of the various courts upon that subject have been in substantial harmony for more than a century last passed. It seems to be pretty well settled now that almost any word, expression or definite act of a testator said, made or done by him, indicating that he acknowledged or thereby intended to acknowledge, by such word or act, the instrument signed by him as his will, is a sufficient acknowledgment of the instrument as his will.

*　　*　　*　　*　　*　　*

In this case, the testator, having drawn and signed his will and had it attested by one witness, took it to Mr. Beach for the sole purpose of having him attest it as a subscribing witness thereto, told him that it was his will or his last will and testament, and requested him to sign his name as a witness, and Mr. Beach did so sign his name; the signature of the testator was visible on the face of the will, about two inches to the right and nearly opposite to where Mr. Beach signed. This I hold is a sufficient acknowledgment of the testator's signature, and of the execution of the will, a publication of the same and request to sign, and just as effectual as if the testator had said: " I acknowledge this to be my signature, I acknowledge the execution of this instrument as my will, declare it to be my will, and request you to sign as a witness thereto."

These several independent requirements of the statute may be joint in their execution.

If a person who was about to become a subscribing witness to a will should say to the testator who had signed his will: "Do you acknowledge and declare this to be your last will and testament, and request me to become a subscribing witness thereto;" and the testator should say: "yes," or nod, or bow his assent thereto (for an acknowledgment is but an admission, declaration, assent or confession), it would be a sufficient acknowledgment, publication and request to sign as a witness.

In Baskin v. Baskin (*supra*), the Court of Appeals say: " When, however, the testator produces a paper to which he has personally affixed his signature, requests the witnesses to attest it, and declares it to be his last will and testament, he does all the law requires. It is enough that he verifies the subscription as authentic, without reference to the form in which the acknowledgment is made, and there can be no more unequivocal acknowledgment of a signature thus affixed than presenting it to the witnesses for attestation and publishing the paper so subscribed to be his will." See Willis v. Mott (*supra*); Jauncey v. Thorne (*supra*); Robinson v. Smith (*supra*); Ilott v. Genge (*supra*); and Matter of Harder (*supra*). I find all these authorities to be in harmony with the doctrine laid down in Baskin v. Baskin. These decisions are not in conflict with that made in Mitchell v. Mitchell (16 *Hun*, 97). In that case, the testator went to the store where the two witnesses were, took out a paper, and said to the witnesses: "I have a paper I want you to sign." One of the witnesses took the paper, partly opened it, saw what it was, and might perhaps have seen the testator's signature. It did not appear that the other witness saw the signature of the testator at all. The testator then said: "This is my will, I want you to witness it;" the two witnesses signed the paper under the attestation clause; the testator then took the paper and said: "I declare this to be my last will and testament." Under the facts of the case, the court very properly held there was, at least as to one witness, if not as to both, no presenting of the signature for attestation, which is essential.

But Mr. Beach testified that the testator did acknowledge that he executed the will. It does not particularly appear, by the evidence, at what period of time during the execution of the will, or conversation in relation to it with Mr. Beach, such acknowledgment was made, and it is claimed by the contestants that such acknowledgment was made after the signing by Mr. Beach, and, as a matter of fact, I conclude such was the case, and for this reason the contestants claim that the will is invalid. In Doe v. Roe (2 *Barb.*, 200), Van Alstyne, the testator, had procured John Wood to draw his will; two witnesses were sent for, and when they came into the room they were told by Doctor Root, in the testator's presence, that they had been called in to witness the will. Doctor Root then read the will to the testator, and asked him if that was his last will and testament, to which he replied in the affirmative; he then signed the will and the three witnesses subscribed their names to the attestation clause in his presence. HARRIS, P. J., says: "I cannot doubt, then, that when the testator was asked by Doctor Root, after the instrument had been read to him, whether it was his last will and testament, his reply in the affirmative was a sufficient publication of the will to answer the requirement of the statute."

Nor do I regard it as at all material in what order the various steps necessary to constitute a due execution of a will take place. The publication is required to be at the time of signing. The clear intent of the statute is that the testator shall not sign the will at one time and one occasion, and at another time and upon another occasion declare it to be his will; both shall be done at the same time and on the same occasion. But which shall be done first in the order of time,—whether the testator shall declare the instrument he is about to sign his last will and testament or shall first subscribe the paper and then make the declaration of his purpose is immaterial. It is enough that the two things are not done at different times.

In Leaycraft v. Simmons (3 *Bradf.*, 38), and in Vaughan v. Burford (*id.*, 78), the same doctrine is laid down. In O'Brien v. Galagher (25 *Conn.*, 231), WAITE, Ch. J., says: "So far as the question has been noticed in the American courts, the inclination seems to have been to consider the order in which the testator and the witnesses put their names to the will as immaterial, providing the instrument is in all other respects legally executed." Therefore, it would seem that, under the decisions of the courts, the acknowledgment of the execution of the will by the testator, after the same had been signed by the witness Beach, was sufficient, it having been done on the same occasion of his signing.

The remaining question claimed on the part of the contestants is that the witness Beach cannot be said or held to be a subscribing witness to the will. The evidence of Mr. Beach shows that he signed the will at the end thereof, as a witness thereto, at the request of the testator and in his presence; that, after so signing his name, he commenced criticising the will, told the testator that it was very informally drawn to trust an estate to after he was out of the way, and that he had better go to some attorney and have it drawn up in regular form. The testator then asked Mr. Beach in what respect it was informal, and Mr. Beach told him that it was all informal, and the testator said he had no fears of it.

Mr. Beach told him there was no attestation clause, and the witnessing of it was informal. The testator wanted to know what was necessary. Mr. Beach replied that, in his opinion, the two witnesses should be there together, and that he should sign in their presence, and they in his presence. The testator then said to Mr. Beach that he did not think he (Mr. Beach) was right upon that, and that he was satisfied it was done according to law; that he had drawn it in his own handwriting for reasons of his own, and that he executed it. Mr. Beach answered that it would be better to sign before the witnesses. The testator said it made no difference, he had signed it and it was all right; that he was sure in his own mind it was all right, but he would see about it.

What did the testator mean when he told Mr. Beach he would see about it? He meant he would see if the will was informally drawn, if it was necessary to have an attesting clause, if the witnessing of it was informal, and if it was necessary for the two witnesses to be together, and he sign in their presence, and they in his. He had told Mr. Beach he had no fears of it, that he was satisfied it was done according to law, that it was not necessary to have the two witnesses together when he executed it, and he was sure in his own mind it was all right. But he would see about it. Inasmuch as he, a lawyer, had raised all these questions, he would see if it had been executed according to law. The testator probably again consulted some law book, or advised with some counsellor, as to whether the will was sufficiently formal and legally executed.

These recommendations made by Mr. Beach to the testator were very appropriate, and, if acceded to by

the testator, would probably have avoided this litigation. They were such recommendations as Surrogates and lawyers frequently make, when consulted
for advice by those who have made wills and want to
know if they are in proper form and shape.

But such recommendations and criticisms never
have the effect of revoking or annulling such instruments after they have been executed. The criticisms
and recommendation of Mr. Beach to the testator,
that the will be redrawn, were not to make the provisions of the will more favorable to the contestants
and next of kin, nor to vary the channel in which
the testator had directed his estate should go upon
his decease, but simply to save the executrix of the
will trouble, when she offered the instrument for probate, from any question being raised as to the formal
execution of the will.

It was not that Mr. Beach objected to be a subscribing witness to the will or would be benefited by
its being redrawn; it was simply a friendly criticism
from an old friend of the testator, for the benefit of
those named in the will. Mr. Beach was satisfied that
the reason he did not write his place of residence was
that immediately after writing "h," the last letter in
his name (and which letter was written after the testator had got through talking, after telling him it was
his last will and testament and asking him to sign his
name as a witness to the will), he so strongly criticised the will, and recommended that it be redrawn,
that, when the testator left the office, he supposed he
had left to have it redrawn; that it left that impression upon his mind, so that he did not write his place

of residence and he thought the testator did not regard
it as an executed will.

To the question put to Mr. Beach by Mr. Hiscock:
" Did you understand, at that time, that it was a completed transaction, that he was to come back again
or that something else was to be done ? " Mr. Beach
said he could hardly say he had any understanding
upon the question. He had an impression, coming
from his own criticisms, that the testator would have
that part (the attestation clause) of the will at least
changed; but that it did not amount to an understanding. There does not seem to be a particle of
evidence in this case tending to show that the testator
did not regard it as an executed instrument, except
that Mr. Beach says he thought the testator did not
regard it as an executed will. On the contrary, the
evidence of Mr. Beach seems to show very clearly
that the testator did regard it as a completely executed instrument, and thereafter procured the name of
another subscribing witness thereto; for when Mr.
Beach told him it was informal, the testator said he
had no fears of it. When Mr. Beach told him he
would avoid all trouble by having it redrawn, the testator said he was satisfied it was done according to
law, he had drawn it in his own hand for reasons of
his own, and had executed it (the testator and two
witnesses had previously signed, which made it a complete instrument), and he was sure in his own mind
it was all right. This shows that the testator did
regard it as an executed will. But what was the
effect of what was done ? Did the testator go to Mr.
Beach's office and ask him to sign his name as a wit-

ness to the instrument for the sole purpose of becoming an attesting witness to his will, and did Mr. Beach subscribe his name thereto at the request of testator, and for the sole purpose of becoming a subscribing witness thereto? There can be no doubt but that was the intention of the testator and the sole object of his visit, and there is no more doubt but that Mr. Beach signed his name for the sole and only purpose of becoming a subscribing witness thereto, and did thereby become such witness within the meaning of the law. His having commenced writing his name before the testator finished talking was of no consequence, it did not affect the validity of the instrument. His signature as the second witness to the will gave to it life, and made it a legal and valid instrument. Having once become a legal and valid instrument, it remained such at the death of the testator, it never having been revoked by him.

A decree should be made confirming the probate of said will.

<hr />

ORANGE COUNTY. — HON. R. C. COLEMAN, SURROGATE.—October, 1884.

HULSE *v.* REEVS.[*]

In the matter of the estate of JESSE S. HULSE, *deceased.*

Testator, who died in 1844, by his will, directed his executors to sell his real property, place the proceeds at interest, and dispose of the same as follows: his widow, S., to have them during her natural life; if she

[*] Surrogate's decree affirmed at Brooklyn Gen. Term, February, 1885.

should have heirs of his body, they to be supported and educated out of the fund, and, at majority, to have one half thereof, and, at the death of S., the remainder; if, at the death of S., there should be no heirs of his body living, the proceeds to go in equal shares to two nephews, N. and C. There was a posthumous son of testator, H., who died after attaining majority and before S. N. died after testator, and before H. The net proceeds of the sale of the real property, viz.: $3,000, were retained by the widow, who died in April, 1884. Upon an application to compel the distribution of a portion of the proceeds,—
Held,

1. That the will effected an equitable conversion of the real into personal property.
2. That the taking by H. was not absolute but dependent on his surviving the death of S.; and was, therefore, defeated by the happening of a condition subsequent.
3. That N.'s legacy lapsed by his dying before S., and that, therefore, as to one half of the fund in question, decedent died intestate.
4. That the other half was payable to C.

JESSE S. HULSE died May 15th, 1884, leaving a will which was admitted to probate August 20th of the same year, and contained the following provisions: "I give and bequeath unto my beloved wife, Sarah J. Hulse, all my personal property for her own benefit. . . . . . I further direct that the executors to this will may at their discretion and they are hereby empowered to dispose of the farm on which the tavern and store house is situated; also the house, lot and tannery adjoining; also a lot of 13 acres known as the Neely lot, all situated in Smith village, town of Minnisink, county of Orange—the proceeds to be placed at interest and disposed of as follows, viz.:

My beloved wife, Sarah J., to have the proceeds during her natural life. If she should have heirs of my body, they to be supported and educated out of it, and at the age of twenty-one years to have one half of the property, and at the death of the said Sarah

J., the remainder. And I further direct that if at the death of my wife, Sarah J., there should be no heirs of my body living that I bequeath the proceeds of the real estate to Nathan E. Hulse and Charles S. Hulse (equally), sons of my brother, Silas Hulse." The will appointed the widow executrix, and Benjamin Horton and John E. DuBois, executors thereof.

On June 13th, 1844, Sarah J. Hulse, the widow, gave birth to a son, the child of the decedent, named Smith Hulse. There were no other children. Smith Hulse died June 21st, 1865, leaving his mother his sole heir at law and next of kin. Nathan E. died July 17th, 1864. The executors and executrix of the will of Jesse procured a judicial settlement of their account by a decree of the Surrogate's court of Orange county, made February 7th, 1866, whereby it appeared that the sum of $3,000 remained, as the net proceeds of the sale of the real property mentioned in the will. Of this sum, that decree directed $750 to be paid to Charles S. Hulse at the death of Sarah, and authorized Sarah to retain the balance, to her own use. She, in fact, retained also, as executrix, the $750 referred to. Charles S. was a party to the settlement. Nathan E. was not represented. No appeal was taken from the decree. Sarah died April 29th, 1884.

The present special proceeding was instituted by Charles S. Hulse, the administrator of the estate of Nathan, to compel Floyd H. Reevs, the administrator of the estate of Sarah, to pay over to the surviving executor of the will of Jesse one quarter of said $3,000, as the share of Nathan, in said proceeds, and to compel said executor to pay over the same to the petitioner.

NAUNY & MEAD, *for petitioner.*

B. R. CHAMPION, *for respondent.*

H. A. WADSWORTH, *for executrix of Jesse S. Hulse.*

THE SURROGATE.—The first thing to be determined is whether the fund is to be treated as real or personal property. It was derived from sales of real estate, made, in pursuance of the provisions of the will. The real estate was not devised to the executors, nor was the legal title vested in them by operation of law; it, therefore, descended to the heirs at law, subject, however, to the power of sale, which, when executed, divested the legal title of the heirs, and the purchase money became assets in the hands of the executors. The object of the testator to have his real estate converted into money is obvious, for, the only disposition made by him of this part of his estate is a disposition of the proceeds. The conversion was directed for the convenience of division, and those to whom it is given take an interest in the money and not in the land. These principles are well settled, and the fund must be regarded as personal estate, whoever may be entitled to it.

I next proceed to consider the nature of the interest which the son, Smith Hulse, took under the will. The following is the provision of the will: " The proceeds to be placed at interest and disposed of as follows: My beloved wife, Sarah J., to have the proceeds during her natural life. If she should have heirs of my body, they to be supported and educated out of it, and, at the age of twenty-one years, to have one half of the property, and, at the death of the said Sarah J., the remainder; and I further direct that if, at the death of my wife, Sarah J., there should be no heirs of my body living, that (so, in original) I bequeath the proceeds of the real estate to Nathan Emmet Hulse and Charles S. Hulse (equally), sons of my brother, Silas Hulse."

There are here several provisions for different people, connected together both grammatically and in sense, which have to be considered separately, but construed in connection with each other. So much of it as relates to the time of payment to the heirs of his body, when taken alone, is of such a character that the testator's intention cannot to a certainty be known, as to whether he intended to vest the legacy in them before the times mentioned; but the words, *"at* the age," and "*at* the death," the courts have held, bring the gift within the class of cases where time is essential to the vesting of the legacy. Where, however, a contrary intention is indicated by other parts of the will, effect will be given to such intention. This part, as to time, when taken in connection with the preceding part of the sentence, shows to my mind that the testator meant to make the having of heirs of his body the essential condition of the gift to such heirs, the payment only being deferred till the times indicated. This view is strengthened when we allow the force which is given by the courts to the further provision for their support and education (Paterson v. Ellis, 11 *Wend.*, 259; Weyman v.

Ringold, 1 *Bradf.*, 42).   In this view of the case, if there were no other provisions of the will to be considered, the legacy to the heirs of his body, on the birth of the son, related back to the death of the testator, and vested at that time in the son, payment of one half being deferred until he arrived at twenty-one years of age, and of the other half until the death of his mother.

There is, however, a further provision of the will to be considered, and its proper effect to be given it, which is: "that, if, at the death of my wife, Sarah J., there should be no heirs of my body living, *that* (to be read as *then*) I give and bequeath the proceeds of the real estate," etc.   This was intended, either as a provision for the disposition of these proceeds in the event of his wife's death, never having had heirs of his body, or, having had heirs, to impose a condition upon the gift to such heirs after they had come into existence, and as well to dispose of the same in that event.   The first can hardly have been intended, for the expression is: "if there should be no heirs of my body *living*," which, while it might include either situation,—that there had been heirs, who had died, or that there never had been any,—more properly implies the fact that there had been such heirs.   I, therefore, conclude that this provision relates to, and imposes a condition upon, the gift to the testator's heirs, and that the taking by them should not be absolute but dependent upon the event of being living at the death of testator's wife, and thus belonged " to that fluctuating class of devises which are liable to be defeated by the occurrence of some subsequent event (Delavergne v. Dean, 45 *How. Pr.*, 206).

The son lived to take the one half given him on arriving at the age of twenty-one years, but died before his mother, and thereby this last clause became operative. This brings us to the consideration of the nature of the interest given by this last clause to the nephews. As I have shown, if the son had survived his mother, he would have taken absolutely, and the nephews would have had no interest in the estate. The gift to the nephews, therefore, depended upon a condition precedent, *i. e.*, the death of the heirs of the body of the testator before his widow. Nathan survived the testator, but died before the happening of the contingency upon which his interest depended. Did the gift to him thereby lapse? Usually a lapse occurs by reason of the death of the legatee before the death of the testator; but, as Vice Chancellor McCoun says, in Marsh v. Wheeler (2 *Edw.*, *Ch.* 162), "still, there are cases of a lapse when the party interested dies after the testator, provided it happened before the legacy is payable; and yet, to have this effect, it must clearly appear that the time of payment is made the substance of the gift, and that the testator meant the time of payment to be the period when the legacy should vest; and, in such a case, if the legatee die before the time arrives, although after the testator's decease, the legacy necessarily fails." And, as stated by Chief Judge Folger, in Loder v. Hatfield (71 *N. Y.*, 98), " it is a general rule that the postponement of the time of payment will not, of itself, make a legacy contingent, unless it be annexed to the substance of the gift; or, as it is sometimes put, unless it be upon an event of such a nature that it is to be presumed that the testator meant to make no gift unless that event happened" (*Redf. Surr. Prac.*, 575.; Orph. As. v. Emmons; 3 *Bradf.*, 148; Williams v. Seaman, 3 *Redf.*, 148).

There can be no question but that the testator intended that there should be no gift to the nephews, unless his wife died without heirs of his body living. The gift was to the nephews as tenants in common, to them equally. There was, therefore, no survivorship; but the share of Nathan, by reason of his death before the widow, lapsed; and, as there is no disposition made by the will, it passed to the next of kin of the testator, his son and widow, and not to the representatives of the deceased Nathan. Charles, being living, is entitled to an equal half of the fund, which the administrator of the estate of Mrs. Hulse is willing to pay him.

The administrator of Nathan Emmet Hulse, deceased, having no interest in the fund, his proceedings are dismissed.

ORANGE COUNTY.—HON. R. C. COLEMAN, SURRO-
GATE.—February, 1885.

RUMSEY *v.* GOLDSMITH.

*In the matter of the application for probate of a
paper propounded as the will of* LUTHER H.
RUMSEY, *deceased.*

Upon an application, made in January, 1885, for the probate of a paper
propounded as decedent's will, dated November 14th, 1884, it appeared
that, at the time of the alleged execution, decedent was confined to
his bed by his last illness; that the paper, which had been prepared by
one D., who was not a lawyer, at decedent's request, was read to the
latter by the draftsman, and, its contents being approved, signed in
the presence of D. alone; that D. then summoned from an adjoining
room the two persons whose names appeared as those of subscribing
witnesses, who, when they entered decedent's apartment, found him
bolstered up in bed, and the paper lying, at his side, upon a stand
whereon they wrote; that decedent was then asked by D. whether he
acknowledged that to be his last will and testament, whereto he assented by nodding or bowing his head; whereupon D. said to the
witnesses, successively, "you will please sign your name here," indicating the place, with which request they each complied. There was
no conversation between decedent and the subscribing witnesses. The
paper was not sealed, and was written entirely upon one page, which
lay open before the witnesses, so that they could have seen the decedent's subscription. The witnesses' signatures were preceded by an
attestation clause in the ordinary form, reciting that the document
was "signed, sealed, published and declared," etc., in the witnesses'
presence.—

Held, that, in view of the false recitals in the attestation clause, and the
brevity of the period which elapsed between the signing and the
examination of the witnesses, this clause could not be resorted to, for
the purpose of raising any presumption of due execution; that the
question addressed to the decedent, by the draftsman, in the witnesses'
presence, called for nothing more than an acknowledgment of the
nature of the instrument; and that probate must be refused on the
ground of non-compliance with the requirement of the statute (2 R.
S., 63, § 40), that the testator's *subscription,* if not made in their
presence, "shall be acknowledged by him to have been [so] made to
each of the attesting witnesses."

It seems, that an affirmative answer to the question, "do you acknowledge in the presence of these witnesses, that you signed this paper, as your last will and testament, knowing fully its contents?" is not an acknowledgment of subscription, within the meaning of the statute of wills.

Baskin v. Baskin, 36 *N. Y.*, 416—doubted.

PETITION for the probate of decedent's will, presented by Rienzi A. Goldsmith, the executor therein named; opposed by Warren G. Rumsey, decedent's son. The facts are stated in the opinion.

GEORGE N. GREENE, *for executor.*

H. A. WADSWORTH, *special guardian.*

THE SURROGATE.—The only question presented for determination, is whether the paper, purporting to be the last will and testament of the deceased, was executed with the formalities required by the statute; and it is conceded that the only one about which there is any question, is whether the testator, not having executed the will in the presence of the attesting witnesses, acknowledged his subscription to each of them. The provisions of the statute are: "1*st*. It shall be subscribed by the testator at the end of the will; 2*d*. Such subscription shall be made by the testator in the presence of each of the attesting witnesses, *or shall be acknowledged by him to have been so made, to each of the attesting witnesses* (2 R. S., 63, § 40).

Upon this point, three witnesses have been sworn and testified,—the two attesting witnesses, and the person who prepared the will and undertook the direction of its execution. The witnesses all agree that the will was not signed in the presence of the attesting witnesses. It appears from the testimony of Mr. Denniston, the person who prepared the will, that the will was signed by the deceased in his presence, while they were alone together, and that, while the testator was in the act of signing the will, Mrs. Giles, one of the attesting witnesses, opened the door of the room in which they were engaged, and looked in, but immediately closed the door again, without coming in; she testifies that, when she looked in, she saw the deceased writing, and that, when she was afterwards asked to be one of the witnesses, she supposed, from the size and color of the paper of the will, that it was the same paper she saw him writing on. The deceased was, at this time, very ill, and died during the next week. After the will was signed by the deceased, the two witnesses were called from the adjoining room, and Wilbur F. Giles testifies as to what occurred after that, as follows: "After we got in there, I think in about five minutes, Mr. Denniston asked Mr. Rumsey if he acknowledged that (the will) as his last will and testament; he (Mr. Rumsey) nodded his head, and after that Mr. Denniston said to me: 'You will please sign your name here'—showed me where to sign, and then my wife—he said the same thing to her, and she signed it." Q. "Was there anything said to him, Mr. Rumsey, about it?" Ans. "No, nothing else said; we went right out; we wasn't in there but a few minutes." Q. "Did Mr. Rumsey hold any conversation with you, or talk with you?" Ans. "No, sir; he didn't say a word."

Mary A. Giles, the wife of the last witness, testifies:

Q. "Did you see Mr. Rumsey sign it (the will), or not?" Ans. "No, sir." Q. "After you got there, what was done?" Ans. "Mr. Denniston asked Mr. Rumsey if he acknowledged that that (the will) was his last will and testament, and Mr. Rumsey bowed his head." Q. "What did you then—you and your husband—sign your names?" Ans. "Yes, sir; my husband first." Q. "How did you come to sign it?" Ans. "Mr. Denniston asked us." Q. "In the presence of Mr. Rumsey?" Ans. "Yes, sir." On the cross-examination, she says that, at this time, Mr. Rumsey was bolstered up, half sitting and half lying in bed; that the stand upon which they signed their names was near the head of his bed. "When Mr. Denniston asked us to sign, he stood just a little way from the bed, quite near the stand." Q. "Where Mr. Rumsey could hear?" Ans. "He couldn't help hear him." And, when asked if Mr. Rumsey did anything to show whether he heard Mr. Denniston ask them to sign, she said: "He didn't say anything; he looked towards us."

At a subsequent hearing of this case, Mr. Denniston was produced as a witness for the proponent. He testified that, at the request of the testator, he prepared the will offered for probate, and, after it was written, read it over to the deceased, who said it expressed his wish, and then signed it at the foot, in his (Denniston's) presence, and then the witnesses were called in. "They came into the room; they stood near the door where they entered, and I told them that the will was all ready for their signatures." Q. "Did they come up near to you then?" Ans.

" They came up behind me then; the testator had got back in bed before they got in, and the bed clothes were drawn over him; the stand, on which the paper lay that he had signed his name to, was there at the bed side, and the witnesses stood in the rear, a little to one side. I was standing up in front of the stand. I placed my hand upon the paper and took the acknowledgment of the testator." Q. "State what you said." Ans. "Do you acknowledge, in the presence of these witnesses, that you signed this paper, as your last will and testament, knowing its contents, or knowing fully its contents?" Q. "What did he say?" Ans. "He nodded his head, and said, 'I do'—that was the response that he made." Q. "Did anything else take place then— what did they do?" Ans. "After he had made his acknowledgment, Mr. Giles signed his name, and Mrs. Giles also." Mrs. Giles, who was present and heard the testimony of the last witness, was then recalled, and, when asked if she had any recollection as to whether there was anything more said or done than what she had already testified to, answered: " No."

The attestation clause is as follows : "Signed, sealed, published and declared by the above named testator at the date thereof, to be his last will and testament in our presence, who, at his request, in his presence, and in the presence of each other, hereto set our hands as subscribing witnesses.

" WILBUR F. GILES,
MARY ANNA GILES."

There is no evidence that this clause was read by either of the witnesses, or by any one else to them, before signing; the will is not sealed; the will bears date November 14th, 1884, and the subscribing witnesses were examined on January 12th, 1885. The force of a presumption in their favor has, in many instances, been given by the courts to the recitals of those facts stated in attestation clauses, where there has been such a lapse of time, between the act and the time when the witness is called upon to testify concerning it, as to justify the inference that his recollection of the circumstances may be imperfect, or where the witness is a person unfamiliar with the legal formalities necessary to a proper execution of a will. But a formal execution of a will cannot be presumed in opposition to positive testimony merely upon the ground that the attestation clause is in due form (Lewis v. Lewis, 11 *N. Y.*, 220). In this case, there is nothing which warrants any presumption in favor of anything contained in the attestation clause. We know that two facts there stated are not true. The will was not signed or sealed in the presence of the witnesses; nor has there been any such lapse of time as will justify the inference that the recollection of the witnesses is imperfect. We must, therefore, ascertain the facts from the evidence offered, without depending upon the attestation clause to aid us.

Unquestionably the will was not signed in the presence of Mr. Giles; nor do I think that what Mrs. Giles witnessed at the time she stood at the opened door, while the testator was signing, can be the signing in her presence contemplated by the statute:

she had not at that time been called upon to witness its execution, nor was it then communicated to her what it was that was being signed. So far as she can say, it might have been any other paper of that color, that he was then signing. But whether this may be call a signing in her presence, required by the statute, or not, the will was not signed in the presence of Mr. Giles; and, therefore, we still have to determine whether the testator acknowledged his subscription of the will to the subscribing witnesses (to each of them in my opinion, but) at least to Mr. Giles. If he did so to Mr. Giles, he did to Mrs. Giles, for both were present at the time when it occurred, if it occurred at all. If it was done, it was done in the question asked the deceased by the witness, Denniston, when he did what he calls "taking the testator's acknowledgment."

Upon this point, we have the testimony of Mr. and Mrs. Giles that the question asked Mr. Rumsey was—if he acknowledged that that was his last will and testament; to which question they say Mr. Rumsey simply nodded his head. The witness, Denniston, says the question asked by him was: "Do you acknowledge, in the presence of these witnesses, that *you signed this paper* as your last will and testament?" Even if the evidence of the witness, Denniston, is to be taken as conclusive, as to the form of the inquiry made by him of the deceased—that it was: "Do you acknowledge, in the presence of these witnesses, *that you signed this paper* as your last will and testament?" it is doubtful if it called for more than an acknowledgment of the nature of the instrument.

A testator's answer to the inquiry made by one of the witnesses: "Do you request me to sign the will as a witness?" has been held to be both a publication and a request to sign as a witness (Coffin v. Coffin, 23 *N. Y.*, 9; Rieben v. Hicks, 3 *Bradf.*, 353). But in those cases, the nature of the question directed the mind of the witness to both facts,—the nature of the instrument, and the desire of the testator to have them sign as witnesses.

Judge ALLEN, in Lewis v. Lewis (11 *N. Y.*, 220), says: "If the party does not subscribe in their presence, then the signature must be shown to them, and identified and recognized by the party, and in some apt and proper manner acknowledged by him as his signature. The statute is explicit, and will not be satisfied with any thing short of a substantial compliance with its terms." The question asked by Mr. Denniston directs the mind to the nature of the paper signed, and not to the genuineness of the signature; and so these witnesses understood it, as is plain to be seen from what they say Mr. Denniston asked Mr. Rumsey.

This case does not, however, have to rest upon this conclusion, as to the force to be given to the publication in the form testified to by the witness, Denniston; for I am satisfied that his is not the correct version of what he asked the deceased. Mr. Denniston is not a lawyer; and there is no evidence, except the mere fact that he was asked to draw this will, that he had any knowledge of the legal formalities necessary to a proper execution of a will. From their appearance upon the stand, Mr. and Mrs. Giles appeared to be intelligent people, with a clear recollection of what had transpired; fully as much so as the witness, Denniston. Mrs. Giles, after hearing Denniston's testimony, still insisted that she had no different recollection. If the Gileses manifested any bias, it was in favor of the will. There is, therefore, no reason why more weight should be given to his version of the question than to theirs. It may very well be that the witness, Denniston, is influenced by a desire to make a success of what he undertook, or his memory may be influenced by a knowledge of the usual form of acknowledgment of legal documents for record, and an intention to use that form. This supposition is strengthened by the witness's own statement that he took the testator's acknowledgment. The form of the question, as given by Mr. and Mrs. Giles, would have been the natural one to be used, if the will *had been signed* in the presence of the witnesses; and the form of the attestation clause shows that it was Mr. Denniston's intention to have it done in that way. I, therefore, conclude that the witness, Denniston, asked the deceased if he acknowledged that that (the paper on the stand) was his last will and testament.

The whole instrument was written upon one page, and was open before the witnesses upon the stand where they signed it; they could have seen the testator's signature, if they looked at it; but no mention or reference was made of or to it in expressed words. Was the answer made by the testator under these circumstances a substantial compliance with the statute requiring him to acknowledge the subscription which he had made to each of the subscribing witnesses? In Mitchell v. Mitchell (16 *Hun*, 97; affi'd, 77 *N. Y.*, 596), it was held that "the testator must acknowledge that that which purports to be his subscription was in fact made by him. This, too, is quite distinct from the testator's declaration of the nature of the instrument, which is necessary in either case. . . . . . Acknowledgment of the signature must include the same identification of *the written words* as necessarily exists when the witnesses see the testator write." In this case, the declaration was: "This is my will; I want you to witness it;" and, after the witnesses had signed it, the testator said: "I declare this to be my last will and testament." Here the will was folded, but was partly opened by one of the witnesses, so that he probably saw the signature. The other did not see the signature; and Judge LEARNED says: "No act was done which was more than the declaration that the instrument was his will." This exposition of the law is in accordance with the decision of the courts of this State since the adoption of the Revised Statutes. See Chaffee v. Bapt. Miss. Conv. (10 *Paige*, 85); Lewis v. Lewis (11 *N. Y.*, 220); Sisters of Charity v. Kelly (67 *N. Y.*, 409); Woolley v. Woolley (95 *N. Y.*, 231).

Baskin v. Baskin (36 *N. Y.*, 415), while declaring the law to be that the testator must verify the subscription of his name as authentic, would seem to be an authority that the production of the instrument, accompanied by the declaration that the paper was his last will, is an implied acknowledgment of his signature sufficient to meet the statutory requirements. This view of the law is not sustained by subsequent decisions. It is probable that the deceased intended to comply with the statute, and make a valid will, but that is not sufficient. The formalities prescribed by the statute must all be observed. He failed to acknowledge his subscription, previously made while not in the presence of the witnesses.

There is nothing in this case to warrant any supposition that the paper signed by the testator was a different one from that signed by the witnesses; nor is there anything to show that the deceased in any way identified the paper or signature as his will and signature. He simply assented by a nod, without looking at it so as to recognize it, that the paper indicated by Denniston was his will. The statute is too explicit to be satisfied with such an implied acknowledgment, and, in the words of Judge ALLEN (in Lewis v. Lewis, *supra*), "although it may operate with apparent harshness in this case, it is a beneficent and wise statute, and the public interest will be best subserved by a strict adherence to its provisions."

A decree will, therefore, be entered, refusing to admit the will to probate.

ORANGE COUNTY.—HON. R. C. COLEMAN, SURRO-
GATE.—February, 1885.

WOODRUFF *v.* WOODRUFF.

In the matter of the estate of DAVID J. WOODRUFF,
deceased.

A Surrogate's court has no jurisdiction to try and determine the question
of the validity of an assignment, procured by the administrator of an
intestate's estate, from one interested therein, of the interest of the
latter, where the same is attacked on the ground of alleged fraud in
its procurement.

A special proceeding instituted, under Code Civ. Pro., § 2685, to procure a
decree revoking letters of administration, is entirely distinct, in its
nature from those referred to in id., § 2514, subd. 11 (second sentence)
which declares that, "where a provision of this chapter prescribes
that a person interested may object to an appointment, or may apply
for an inventory, an account, or increased security, an allegation of
his interest duly verified, suffices, although his interest is disputed ;
unless," etc.   Hence, where such a decree of revocation is sought by
a widow of the intestate, who has assigned her interest in the estate as
widow, by the procurement of the administrator, though she alleges
fraud in such procurement, her proceedings will be dismissed,—the
Surrogate's court being unable to set aside the instrument for fraud ;
until which is done, the petitioner is excluded from the class of persons
interested in the estate, as defined in the first sentence of Code Civ.
Pro., § 2514.

APPLICATION by Susan M. Woodruff, decedent's
widow, for the revocation of letters of administration
issued upon the estate of decedent, who died October
26th, 1884, to William H. Woodruff, his brother,
after citation to the widow to show cause why the
appointment should not be made.

The petition alleged that the administrator, after
his appointment, by means of misrepresentations as
to the amount of the personal estate, and outstanding

claims against the deceased, induced petitioner to execute an assignment, in blank, of her interest in the personal estate, for a sum which he then paid her; that he afterwards filled in the blank with the name of his wife, and caused the assignment to be recorded in the office of the clerk of Orange county; that petitioner had retained counsel to institute proceedings to set aside the assignment; and prayed that, for this misconduct and dishonesty, the administrator be removed, and his letters revoked.

UPON the return of the citation, the administrator moved to dismiss the proceedings, upon the petition itself, on the ground that, by her own showing, petitioner had no interest in the estate.

N. FOWLER, *for petitioner.*

B. R. CHAMPION, *for respondent.*

THE SURROGATE.—This motion to dismiss is made upon the petition itself, before answer, upon the ground that the petitioner, by her own showing, is not a person interested in the estate, within the meaning of the statute, Code Civ. Pro., § 2685. By the petition, it appears that the petitioner is the widow of the deceased. She would, as such, be entitled to a distributive share of the estate. It, however, also appears that she has executed a release or assignment of this interest, whereby the defendant claims that all her interest in the estate was divested, and therefore she cannot institute these proceedings.

Now, this motion is made upon the petition, which must be taken as a whole and not in parts. The allegation showing the execution of the release is coupled with allegations which show that its execution was procured by fraud and was therefore void; being void, the petitioner still has her interest as widow in the estate. This court is of limited jurisdiction, and could not try the question of fraud, if controverted; but if conceded, and for the purposes of this motion we must take the allegations of the petition as they stand, the principles of law operate without the intervention of the court. There is a difficulty which suggests itself at this point, which is that the grantee in the assignment is not a party to these proceedings, but, as these proceedings would in no way affect that party's rights, I suppose the administrator may, so far as he is concerned, concede the fraud, and submit the matter to the determination of the court.

I am, therefore, of opinion that the motion cannot prevail, while the allegations in the petition remain uncontroverted.

THIS motion being denied, the respondent filed his answer, in which he denied ever having made any representations in regard to the estate of the deceased which were false, and alleged that all representations by him at any time made to the petitioner were fairly and honestly made, and were made without any attempt to mislead or deceive her; and asked that the proceedings be dismissed, the petitioner not being a creditor or having any interest in the estate of the deceased. Whereupon the Surrogate filed the following opinion, February 12th, 1885:

THE SURROGATE.—This proceeding was brought by the widow of the deceased, to remove the administrator of her late husband's estate, upon the ground of alleged fraudulent and dishonest acts of said administrator, in procuring from her an assignment and transfer of her interest in the estate of the deceased. The administrator, a brother of the deceased, was appointed after default by the widow to show cause. He has filed an answer, in which he denies the fraudulent and dishonest acts charged, and asks that the proceeding be dismissed, because the petitioner is not a person who may institute the proceeding, not being a creditor or person interested in the estate of the deceased (Code Civ. Pro., § 2685).

As widow, the petitioner is entitled to a distributive share in the estate, and would therefore, be a person within the meaning of this section; but the petition shows that she has executed an assignment of this interest, which she, however, claims, by reason of fraud, to be void. If this is a valid instrument, then the petitioner can have no interest whatever in the estate of the deceased. Whether or not it is a valid instrument, this court, being of limited jurisdiction, cannot try and determine (Harris v. Meyer, 3 *Redf.*, 450; Riggs v. Cragg, 89 *N. Y.*, 479), and that question must be determined before we can know whether the petitioner has an interest in the estate. The petitioner, however, urges that she does not wish to try the question of the validity of this assignment in these proceedings, but simply to try the question whether the administrator, by reason of dishonesty (§ 2685, subd. 2), in having, by means of the fraud and deceit charged, procured the said assignment should be removed from office; and that the petitioner, whose petition contains a verified allegation of interest, is an interested person within the meaning of the latter clause of § 2514, subd. 11, which is as follows: "Where a provision of this chapter prescribes that a person interested may object to an appointment, or may apply for an inventory, an account, or increased security, an allegation of his interest, duly verified, suffices, although his interest is disputed; unless he has been excluded by a judgment, decree, or other final determination, and no appeal therefrom is pending."

Each of these proceedings, in which a verified statement of interest is sufficient, is a perfectly defined and well understood proceeding, about which there is no ambiguity as to what proceedings are intended. A proceeding to remove an administrator is an entirely distinct proceeding from either of them; and can only be instituted by a creditor, or person interested in the estate (§ 2685). Who is an interested person, must be ascertained by the first clause of the eleventh subdivision of § 2514, defining the expression, "person interested," which is: "The expression, 'person interested,' where it is used in connection with an estate or fund, includes every person entitled, either absolutely or contingently, to share in the estate, or the proceeds thereof, or in the fund, as husband, wife, legatee, next of kin, heir, devisee, assignee, grantee, or otherwise, except as a creditor."

The only class, of the persons enumerated, to

which this petitioner can claim to belong, is that of a
wife, or a person contingently interested. Her interest, as a wife, she has assigned. A person, to be
contingently interested, in the legal sense in which
that word is used, is one who has an interest depending upon the happening of some defined contingency;
—as where a testator gives a legacy to A., provided
he shall attain the age of twenty-one years; but, failing to do so, the legacy is given to B. B. is a person
contingently interested in the estate of the testator.
"Contingently interested" cannot be understood to
mean *any possible*, but uncertain event, upon the
happening of which a person may become interested;
for instance, a father is not, in a legal sense, contingently interested in a legacy given his son, because
of the fact that the son might die, and the father
inherit the legacy from him; nor do I think that one
is contingently interested, who claims to be able to
have an instrument, by which his interest in an
estate has been assigned, set aside by reason of fraud.

So that, although this court could hear and determine the character of the acts complained of by the
petitioner, for the purpose of ascertaining whether
the administrator is such a dishonest person as should
be removed from his office, still I am of the opinion
that the petitioner is not a person who may institute
proceedings for that purpose.

An order will, therefore, be made, dismissing these
proceedings.

ORANGE COUNTY.—HON. R. C. COLEMAN, SURRO-
GATE.—February, 1885.

WELLING *v.* WELLING.

In the matter of the estate of WILLIAM R. WELLING,
deceased.

Although executors' and administrators' commissions are allowed only by
order of a Surrogate's court, the latter cannot withhold them; except
in certain cases, as where a will denies compensation, or provides
specifically therefor.

Under Code Civ. Pro., § 2736, relating to the commissions of executors,
etc., in cases where the decedent's personal estate amounts to $100,000,
or more, over all his debts, the only conditions necessary to entitle
executors to three full commissions, are that the estate should be of
the requisite value, and that three or more representatives should
qualify and act.

Accordingly where testator, who left an estate of the value of $400,000,
appointed three executors, each of whom qualified, but one of whom
died at the expiration of six months after the grant of letters, having
acted up to that time,—

Held, upon an accounting by the survivors, that three full commissions
should be allowed, to be apportioned among the accounting parties and
the representative of the deceased executor, although, by this means,
each of the surviving executors would receive compensation in excess
of full commissions, by reason merely of the death of their associate.

ON January 14th, 1884, letters testamentary were
issued to Thomas Welling, Sarah Welling and John
H. Butts. Butts died July 15th, 1884, after having
acted up to that time. On the accounting, it was
claimed that three full commissions should be allowed
and apportioned, the manner of the apportionment
being agreed upon between the two survivors and the
executrix of the deceased.

The special guardian of Elizabeth Welling and
others, residuary legatees, objected to more than two

full commissions being allowed the survivors, and such an amount to the representative of the deceased as would be proportionate to the services rendered by him. This estate amounted to nearly $400,000.

GEORGE W. McELROY, *for executor, Thomas Welling.*

H. W. BOOKSTAVER, *for executrix, Sarah Welling.*

L. V. BOORAEM, *for executrix of deceased executor.*

M. N. KANE, *special guardian.*

THE SURROGATE.—Commissions, at the rates fixed by the statute, are allowed only by an order of the court, on the settlement of the executor's account (Red. Surr. Prac., 3rd ed., 725; *and cases cited*). The right to such commissions, however, cannot be withheld by the court except in certain cases, as where specific compensation is provided (id., 720; *and cases cited*). The doubt here is occasioned by the death of one of the executors before settlement, and by the fact that the section (2736) allows each executor the full compensation allowed by law to a sole executor; thereby, possibly, raising the implication that each executor must, at least nominally, participate in the administration until the time of settlement of the estate, to entitle him to his full commissions, so that they may be added to the commissions of the others, and apportioned among all, as required by the last clause of the section.

"§ 2736. Where the value of the personal estate of the decedent amounts to one hundred thousand dollars or more, over all his debts, each executor or

administrator is entitled to the full compensation
allowed by law to a sole executor or administrator,
unless there are more than three, in which case the
compensation to which three would be entitled shall
be apportioned among them, according to the services rendered by them respectively; and a like
apportionment shall be made in all cases where there
shall be more than one executor or administrator."
The provisions of this section only require, where
there are three or more executors, to entitle them to
three full commissions—1st., a personal estate exceeding $100,000; 2d., three or more executors.   No
reference is made to the extent of the services required to be rendered by each, to become entitled to a
full commission, except that which is implied by the
provision for apportionment; and this provision for
apportionment is an implied recognition that one may
render less than a fair proportion of the services, and
yet be entitled to full commissions for the purpose of
apportionment.   The provision giving full commissions to each is limited and qualified by the latter
clause, directing the apportionment—only, however,
as to the manner and not as to the amount; for the
wording is that, where there are more than three,
"the compensation to which three would be entitled
shall be apportioned," etc., and " a like apportionment
shall be made in all cases where there shall be more
than one;" that is, a like apportionment shall be
made, in the case of two, of the compensation to
which two would be entitled; and, in the case of
three, of the compensation to which three would be
entitled.

An apportionment of the compensation to which all would be entitled, "according to the services rendered," implies a taking from one and giving to another, and, therefore, one will receive more than a full commission, and another less than a full commission; otherwise there is no need of an apportionment among them. If, then, a full commission is allowed for each executor, to be apportioned if all are living at the settlement, although one has rendered less than a fair proportionate share of the services, was it the intention of the legislature that it should be otherwise where an executor dies before the settlement? It is my opinion that it was not; for, if the foregoing reasoning be correct, then the legislature intended, by the expression, "the compensation to which three would be entitled," to speak of it as one sum or amount,—that amount to be ascertained by multiplying the commissions of a sole executor by the number of executors up to three; and in apportioning that amount, when ascertained, the same law should apply as would be the case in an estate of less than $100,000, where there were several executors, and one had died before settlement, i. e., according to the services rendered by each.

This seems to me to be the only sensible conclusion; for, otherwise, a different rule would prevail in cases where no real difference existed; as where one executor, after having taken an active part in the administration of the estate, say for three months, voluntarily took no further part in such administration until the settlement, or was unable to do so by reason of death.

Although, as I have said, this seems to be the only sensible conclusion, still I have been at some pains to state the reasoning which led me to it, for the reason that several lawyers of large experience, to whom I have mentioned the subject, were quite decidedly of the contrary opinion. It seemed to them anomalous that full commissions should be allowed in the case of an executor who had died before settlement, a part of which was to be apportioned among the survivors. It is evident that the legislature, for some reason, intended to allow more commissions where the estate exceeds $100,000; and it is, also, evident that we can-not adopt the amount of the commissions allowed, as a valuation of the services rendered, for the reason that twice or three times as much commissions are allowed for administering estates of $100,000 and upwards, depending only upon the number of executors acting; or, in other words, an executor is allowed just as much for rendering one third of the services, when he is one of the three executors, as he would receive for rendering all the services, if he were the sole executor, notwithstanding the fact that a sole execu-tor is required to administer the estate just as fully as would be required of three executors; on the other hand, if he had a co-executor, who did very little of the work, he would be entitled to nearly two whole commissions. So, we have all sorts of anomalies under this law, and we need not be surprised at find-ing another.

However, the testator is presumed to know the law, and he has it in his power to determine the amount of expense to which his estate shall be subjected, by way of commissions, by selecting one, two, three or more executors.   He may even provide that they shall not be allowed any commissions (Secor v. Sentis, 5 *Redf.*, 570; Matter of Gerard, I *Dem.*, 244), or he may fix the sum to be received by the executors in lieu of commissions (§ 2737).

Here, three full commissions allowed by law to a sole executor should be apportioned, and, as those entitled to such commissions have agreed as to the manner of the apportionment, the decree will be made accordingly.

ORLEANS COUNTY.—HON. I. S. SIGNOR, SURROGATE.— August, 1884.

BOARD OF MISSIONS *v.* SCOVELL.

In the matter of the judicial settlement of the account of the executor of the will of LAURA ENSIGN, *deceased.*

Upon the judicial settlement of an executor's account, a Surrogate's court has jurisdiction to try and determine a question as to the meaning of the provisions of the decedent's will, so far as necessary to enable it to direct the distribution of the entire estate.

Testatrix, by her will, directed two fourths of the residue of her estate "to be divided equally between the home and foreign missions." The context furnishing no evidence tending to identify the intended recipients of this charity, the next of kin objected, upon the executor's accounting, that the provision in question was void for uncertainty.—

Held, that the case presented was one of latent ambiguity explicable by extrinsic evidence, including declarations of testatrix made after the execution of the will; and that, upon such evidence, the legacies belonged to the Boards of Home and Foreign Missions, respectively, of the Presbyterian church in the U. S. of America.

CONSTRUCTION of decedent's will, upon judicial settlement of the account of Thomas Scovell, the executor thereof.   The facts appear in the opinion.

E. W. TAYLOR, *for executor.*

JOHN G. SAWYER, *for claimants.*

C. J. CHURCH, *for Wm. Southworth.*

THE SURROGATE.—The testatrix, after giving certain legacies and making certain bequests, disposes of the rest and residue of her estate as follows: "I also direct the money above mentioned, rest and residue of my estate, both real and personal, to be divided into four equal parts; one fourth to go to the Home for the Friendless in the city of Lockport, also one fourth to go to the Home for the Friendless in the city of Rochester; the other two fourths to be divided equally between the home and foreign missions."

One of the next of kin of deceased appears upon this accounting, and claims that the bequest of two fourths of said residue to the "home and foreign missions" is void for uncertainty, and descends to the next of kin.   The bequest is claimed by "the Board of Home Missions of the Presbyterian church in the United States of America," and "The Board of Foreign Missions of the Presbyterian Church in the United States of America," as the corporations intended by the testatrix, in the expression, "home and foreign missions."

That the question of the meaning of the testatrix, and the construction of the will, so far as necessary to direct the distribution of the entire estate, is properly raised at this time, and is one which this court has jurisdiction to determine, is, I think, fully established (Matter of Brown, 65 *How. Pr.*, 387; Riggs v. Cragg, 89 *N. Y.*, 479; Code Civ. Pro., § 2472, *subd.* 3; § 2481, *subd.* 11).

In order to establish the claims of the two societies represented, to the legacies given to the "home and foreign missions," it was shown, upon the hearing, that the deceased was, and had been for a long time a member of the Presbyterian church of Holley, N. Y., where she resided, and that she attended that church; that there were yearly collections taken in that church for the societies represented, and for no others, and when collections were taken for these societies their claims were presented by the pastor; and that she was in the habit of contributing to these societies. It also appears that there was a woman's auxiliary society connected with this church, and that she was at one time solicited to make her contributions through this society rather than through the regular church channels, but refused so to do. By the will, the testatrix also gave $1,000 to the Presbyterian church at Holley, and her house at that place for a parsonage, subject to the life estate of a niece. Thomas Scovell, executor of the will, was called as a witness, and by consent his testimony was taken, the question of its competency being reserved. He testified that, after the execution of the will, and shortly before the death of the testatrix, he read the whole will to her, and that, at that time, she gave him the key to the drawer and asked him to get the will and read it; that he read it

aloud in her hearing. The will was in her own handwriting; and when he came to the clause "home and
foreign missions," he said: "You should have designated the Presbyterian Board." She asked if she
could not put it in at that time. He told her: "No,"
it could not be done. She replied: "You know
that I am a Presbyterian and have given a thousand
dollars to the Presbyterian church at Holley, and my
house for a parsonage, after Fidelia is through, and I
want you to see that it goes to the home and foreign
missions of the Presbyterian church." No other
society or organization than those herein named have
appeared or made any claim to the legacies, nor is
there any evidence offered of the existence of any
other home or foreign mission society connected with
the Presbyterian church. The general rule that parol
evidence is inadmissible to explain or vary any
written instrument is applicable to wills as well as
other instruments. This rule is, however, subject to
certain exceptions. Where the object of the evidence
is to contradict the plain expression contained in the
will by showing that, though the testator named one
person or corporation, he did so by mistake supposing
that to be the correct name, as where the testator
gave a legacy to "The Seaman's Aid society in the
city of Boston" by mistake, intending the legacy for
"The Seaman's Friend society," supposing the name
of the former society to be the name of the latter,—
it was held that parol evidence could not be received
to correct the mistake (Tucker v. Seaman's Aid
Soc. (7 *Met.*, 188).

As stated in 1 Redf. on Wills, § 41, this case was

decided on the ground that, "although the intent of the testator is to govern in the construction, it must be the intent expressed by the will, and not the actual intent as shown by extraneous circumstances and proof;" and, as is there stated, I think the rule to be that "had there been but one society, and in attempting to describe that, some departure from the name had occurred, it might have been corrected by construction, since there was nothing else to answer the words of the will; but the case is otherwise where another person's name than the one intended is inserted in the will. That cannot be set right, but must prevail, the force of the written instrument being of paramount weight;" and, at § 39, page 565: "If there is anything in the words of the will which renders the bequest obviously more applicable to one object or subject than to any other, that must prevail, and no case for the admission of extrinsic evidence exists."

It has been repeatedly held that, where the name of a person or corporation is imperfectly stated, it may be aided by parol. In the case of the Domestic and Foreign Missionary Society's Appeal (30 *Penn. St.*, 425), the bequest was to the missions and schools of the Episcopal church about to be established at or near Point Cresson. The bequest was shown to have been intended for the Domestic and Foreign Missionary society of the Protestant Episcopal church of the United States. To the same effect is the well considered case, Lefevre v. Lefevre (2 *T. & C.*, 330; on app., 59 *N. Y.*, 434), where a bequest was made to "the American Home Mission Tract society for our western missions;" and it appeared that there was no society of that name, but that the terms in the will applied in part to two existing societies—the American Tract society, and the American Home Missionary society—it was held that testimony that the testator was acquainted with the objects and operations of the American Tract society, and that their operations were carried on extensively in the western states through the agencies of colporteurs, and that the testator took a lively interest in the operations of the society, and contributed to its funds, and expressed a preference for this society— was admissible; and, on such evidence, it was held that those two societies were entitled to the bequest · (1 Redf. on Wills, § 40, p. 587; *citing* Button v. Am. Tract Soc., 23 *Vt.*, 336).

Applying the rules thus laid down to the case under consideration, it seems clear that this is a proper one for the admission of extrinsic evidence to ascertain what the testatrix meant by the expression, "the home and foreign missions." Evidently, she meant two separate organizations or societies, as she gives two fourths of the rest and residue, to be divided equally between the home and foreign missions; and it seems clearly a case of latent ambiguity which may be explained by parol. The case of Leonard v. Davenport is a case similar in many respects to the one under consideration. The Board of Home Missions of the Presbyterian church in the United States of America was allowed to take a legacy bequeathed to "the Home Missionary society," and against the claim of the American Home

Missionary society, an unincorporated body, upon parol evidence that the testator was in the habit of contributing to the Presbyterian committee of Home Missions, was a member of the Presbyterian church with which that society was connected, that the claims of the society were presented in the church of which the testator was a member, and that he had spoken kindly of the efforts of that society (Leonard v. Davenport, 58 *How. Pr.*, 384). It is claimed, however, that the declarations of the testator can only be received where they are made prior to, or contemporaneously with, the execution of the will, and that declarations made afterward cannot be received, as the result might be to make a will entirely different from that which the testator intended. Redfield lays down the rule, after a consideration of many English and American cases, that, where there is a latent ambiguity, "any degree of latitude in regard to the admissibility of evidence to show the testator's intention either by his acts or declarations before, at the time of, and after the execution of the instrument is admissible" (§ 40, p. 591), and that, in such cases, such evidence is received merely in aid of the construction.

It is a general rule, sustained by the cases examined, that extrinsic evidence of the character offered in this case, and of declarations, made before the execution of the instrument, of the testator's intention to give a legacy to an individual or corporation, or a like declaration made at the time of execution, or a statement made by the testator after its execution, of the disposition he has made of his property, may be received where it may aid in the interpretation of what is in the will, but not where it is offered as direct evidence of intent independent of the instrument. Here, the evidence is offered and received, not to show that the testatrix did not mean to give her property to "the home and foreign missions," or that she meant to give it to other corporations of different names, where there were corporations of the names used, actually in existence, but, it not appearing that there were any of the name mentioned, to explain what she meant by the terms used; to what bodies she applied the names "the home and foreign missions." The question is not one of intent outside the will, but of what was meant by expressions used in the will. From all the evidence, I think the testatrix clearly intended to give the legacies to the claimants, the Board of Foreign Missions of the Presbyterian church in the United States of America, and the Board of Home Missions of the Presbyterian church in the United States of America; and that, in the distribution of the estate, the executor should pay to each of the above named societies, respectively, one half of the amount directed to be paid to the home and foreign missions.

Ordered accordingly.

ORLEANS COUNTY.—HON. I. S. SIGNOR, SURROGATE.—
December, 1884.

ALLEN *v.* ALLEN.

In the matter of the estate of ALFRED ALLEN, deceased.

It being the almost universal practice for the family of a deceased person to wear mourning ; and a change of wearing apparel being thus rendered necessary as a part of the preparation for the funeral, and as a mark of proper respect for the dead ; this expense, when reasonably incurred by those for whom he was bound, in his lifetime, to provide, should be borne by his estate.

Upon the judicial settlement of the account of the administratrix of decedent's estate, objection was made by certain of the next of kin to an item of $56, expended for mourning goods for the widow, who was the accounting party, as excessive, and not properly chargeable against the estate. It appeared that the decedent left no children, and that the condition of the estate was such as that a surplus of several thousand dollars would remain after the payment of all debts.—

Held, that the charge should be allowed, as a part of the necessary, or, at least, proper funeral expenses.

Held, also, upon the same accounting, against a similar objection, that the widow should be allowed a reasonable expenditure ($10) for the disinterment and re-burial of decedent's remains,—the place where they were first deposited having been discovered to be undesirable ; also $175 for a mortuary monument ; and $40, the purchase price of a lot in a well kept cemetery, the title to which she was allowed to take and hold in her individual name.

HEARING of objections interposed by David Allen and others, decedent's nephews, to the account filed by Harriet Allen, the administratrix of his estate, in proceedings for judicial settlement. The facts are stated in the opinion.

THOMPSON & SPENCER, *for administratrix.*

E. R. REYNOLDS, *and* H. S. GOFF, *for objectors.*

THE SURROGATE.—The administratrix is the widow of Alfred Allen, deceased, who left no descendant, but left a mother and several nephews, some of whom appear by counsel, and object to certain items of the account presented. The first item objected to is one of $56.09, charged as paid for mourning goods for the widow, on the ground that it is excessive, and in no event a proper charge against the estate as part of the funeral expenses, or for any other estate expense. I am referred to no authorities in this State, nor have I been able to find any holding for or against this proposition. It seems that, in other states, and in the English courts, this question has been raised, and it has been held that a moderate allowance for mourning goods may be sustained as a part of the funeral expenses, where the rights of creditors do not interfere. Redfield (Surr. Prac., *3rd ed.*, 468) says: "Mourning for the family of the testator is not a funeral charge strictly speaking, although charges therefor have been allowed in some of the states;" citing a number of cases. McClellan on Ex'rs (*2d ed.*, 459) says: "Moderate expenses for mourning, for the widow and family, may be allowed as part of the funeral expenses." The rule has been long established that it is the duty of the administrator or executor to bury the deceased according to the rank he occupied in life, and according to the estate he left; the rule being that, when the rights of creditors are not interfered with thereby, he shall be allowed from the estate he may have accumulated a burial suitable and proper for one who has occupied his position in society, before his next of kin or heirs at law shall be allowed to come in and claim his estate.

What constitutes legitimate and proper expenses has been variously determined. It has been repeatedly held that a monument or headstone should be allowed as a part of the funeral expenses (Wood v. Vandenburgh, 6 *Paige*, 277; Ferrin v. Myrick, 41 *N. Y.*, 315). In the case of McCue v. Garvey, the items of funeral expenses included $47 for a wake; all of the charges were held by the Surrogate to be reasonable as funeral charges; he held, however, that the husband, and not the wife's estate, was liable therefor, and on that ground refused to allow the entire charge. The General Term, on appeal (see 14 *Hun*, 562), held that the Surrogate erred in not sustaining the charge against the estate. The Code of Civil Procedure, § 2749, says that the expression "funeral expenses," as used in that title, includes a reasonable charge for a suitable headstone. Thus, it will be seen that the funeral expenses of a decedent are not necessarily confined to the mere interment of the remains, but may, when the circumstances of the estate warrant it, include the expenses of a funeral according to the religion of the deceased, and such expenses as may be necessary to designate his resting place by a suitable monument or headstone.

The funeral could be conducted without a hearse, yet no one thinks of objecting to such an item of expense; though not absolutely necessary, the custom of society requires it; and it seems that, where custom requires and it is the almost universal practice for the family of the deceased to wear mourning, and a change of wearing apparel is thus rendered necessary as a part of the preparation for the funeral, and as a mark of proper respect for the dead, this expense, when reasonably incurred by those for whom he was bound to provide in his lifetime, should be borne by his estate. In this case, the entire expense for mourning goods is charged at $56.09, and includes a bonnet, dresses, gloves, a veil, cloak, etc. The estate is apparently ample to pay all debts, and have several thousand dollars left. One half of this expense will, in any event, come out of the share of the administratrix, which comes to her as the widow of the deceased. I think this charge is a proper item, and must be allowed as a part of the necessary, or at least, as a part of the proper funeral expenses.

The administratrix at first buried her deceased husband in the cemetery at Waterport, near which they resided, and where it was claimed she had stated that her husband had expressed a willingness to be buried, saying that, if it was good enough for his brethren in the church to be buried in, it was good enough for him. The administratrix denies this statement, and says that what she did state was that her husband said he had lived in Waterport long enough to gain a resting place there. It appears in evidence that they owned no lot where he was first buried, and that, on inquiry, she was informed that she could obtain no good title to the lot. The ground was very much neglected, and, as one witness testifies, the fences were from one third to one half down, gates off the hinges, and the ground growing up to briars which covered nearly one half of it; woodchucks, or some other animals, were digging into the ground; he saw half a dozen holes, one day, right into a grave. Under these circumstances, the administratrix determined to remove her husband's remains to Mount Albion cemetery, some nine miles distant, where she could purchase a lot in a well kept cemetery. The expense of taking up, removing and re-interring the body was $19, very little of which would have been incurred, had the burial first taken place there, in addition to the expenses of the first interment. This may be regarded as additional expense, and this it is claimed the administratrix should pay entirely from her share in the estate, or from her own private funds, if she has any, and relieve contestants from paying any portion thereof.

The item of $40 for a lot at Mount Albion is also objected to as improper. It does not appear how much a lot at Waterport would have cost, if one could have been purchased; so it cannot be said how much could have been saved the estate if one could have been purchased there; but the administratrix testifies that she purchased only half a lot at Mount Albion, and that that was as cheap as she could buy a lot in a desirable location. She also erected a monument at a cost of $175, on the lot purchased. The title to the lot was taken in the name of the widow, and it is claimed that both the item for the monument and the item for the lot should be disallowed. It appears in evidence that, for thirty-five years, the administratrix and her husband had lived together, and for more than thirty years on the same farm, and had together accumulated the property left by him. The estate, after paying all debts, would, including real estate, leave a surplus of several thousand dollars. I think that, under all these circumstances, the administratrix had a right to select a place for the burial of her husband where not only he would be willing to be buried, but she would prefer to be buried, provided she did not incur unreasonable expense in so doing; and in this case I consider that she did right in removing the body, purchasing the lot and erecting the monument.

People living in her vicinity were accustomed to purchase lots in Mount Albion, and bury their dead there; and, had the first interment been made there, I do not see how any one could have questioned the propriety of it, nor do I think her course in expending the extra amount necessary to accomplish her desire in this respect at all open to criticism. The title to the lot was in my opinion properly taken in her own name; it was for the burial of the *family of the deceased*, which consisted only of himself and wife, and she, as sole survivor of the family, was the proper one to hold the deed. None of the next of kin or heirs at law had any interest in this lot. In this much of the estate, at least, the wife should have as much interest as her husband, viz.: the right to be buried on it and to exclude any not of the immediate family.

The charges objected to are, for these reasons, allowed, and a decree may be entered accordingly.

ORLEANS COUNTY.—HON. ISAAC S. SIGNOR, SURRO-
GATE.—June, 1885.

KELSEY *v.* VAN CAMP.

In the matter of the estate of AMOS KELSEY, *deceased.*

A Surrogate's court may construe a decedent's will *in any proceeding
where* it becomes necessary in order to enable it to exercise powers
expressly conferred upon it.

A Surrogate's court, in the exercise of its power to require from a testamentary trustee security for the performance of his duties, is not confined to proceedings instituted by a petition filed under Code Civ. Pro.,
§ 2815, but may make an order to such effect, where objection is duly
taken, on a motion to open a decree rendered upon an accounting and
modify it by delivering property to the applicant, who occupies the
position of trustee under a will.

Testator, by his will, after making certain specific dispositions, gave the
remainder of his farm, and all his other real estate, and all his personal estate not otherwise disposed of, to his wife, S., to have and to
hold during her natural life ; providing that she might use and employ
the property so devised and given to her as she might see fit, for her
own benefit, and might dispose of such part of said personal estate,
from time to time, as she might see fit, or as might be proper for the
best management thereof, for the benefit of those concerned, as she
should direct ; and ordering his executors, at his wife's death, to sell
all his real estate, and all his personal estate, or the produce thereof
that should then remain, not disposed of by him in said will, or by or
under the direction of his wife, and distribute the proceeds of sale,
after paying his debts and those of his wife, in a manner specified.
S. claimed the right to expend the personal property for her own
benefit, and that the executor should be directed, from time to time,
to pay over to her, without notice or application to the court, such
part of the principal fund as she might desire to use.—

Held, that S. had the right to the life use, only, of the personal property,
and that the executor was bound to turn over to her all such property
in his hands, to be held and managed by her as a testamentary trustee
for the remaindermen.

Campbell v. Beaumont, 91 *N. Y.*, 464—distinguished.

PETITION by Sally Kelsey, decedent's widow, for the opening and modification of a decree made December 21st, 1883, judicially settling the account of Benjamin F. Van Camp, as executor of decedent's will. The facts are stated in the opinion.

JOHN CUNNEEN, *for petitioner.*

JONES, KEELER & SALISBURY, *for executor.*

W. C. RAMSDALE, *special guardian.*

THE SURROGATE.—Amos Kelsey, the husband of the petitioner, left a will, in and by which, after certain specific devises and bequests, he makes the following provisions : " The remainder of my farm . . . . . I give and devise, together with all other real estate of which I may die seized and owner, and all my personal estate of every description, not otherwise disposed of in this will, I give, devise and bequeath to my wife Sally Kelsey, to have and to hold during her natural life, to receive and have for her own use and benefit all not in this will otherwise disposed of, the rents and profits, income, produce, increase, possession and enjoyment during her natural life, requiring her to pay the taxes, and keep the buildings and fences in ordinary and proper repair, so that their value may not be decreased by neglect during said term, and my said wife may use and employ the property so devised and given to her as she may see fit for her benefit ; and she may dispose of such part of said personal estate, from time to time, as she may see fit, or as may be proper for the best management thereof, for the benefit of those concerned, as she shall direct. At the death of my said wife, I will and direct that my executors of this will sell and dispose of, and reduce into money, as soon as can be done, without too much loss or sacrifice of property, all my real estate and all my personal estate, or the produce, thereof that shall then remain not disposed of by me in this will, or by or under the direction of my wife, and from the amount to be so ascertained let all my remaining debts, if any, and all just debts, if any, then found owing by my wife, and all expenses of administration be paid, and all the residue and remainder I give and bequeath to be divided into ten equal shares." The testator then provides for the distribution of these ten shares.

The General Term of this department have decided that, by the clear provisions of this clause of the will, the petitioner is entitled to the possession of this property. By a decree made by a former Surrogate, it was ordered that the executor should retain this property in his hands, "subject to the further order of this court."

The petitioner now asks that the executor be directed to pay over to her a portion of the principal fund now in his hands, that she may expend the same for her own benefit; and that the executor may also be directed, from time to time, to pay over to her, without notice or application to the court, such of said principal fund as she may desire to use. Counsel for the residuary legatees and for the executor ask to be allowed to show that, by reason of advanced years and hostility to certain legatees, the petitioner should be required to give bonds for the return of the principal of the personal property to be turned over to her. Counsel for the petitioner objects, on the ground that, by the terms of the will, the petitioner has not only the right to the use of the personal property, but the right to expend for her own benefit any or all of the principal as she may see fit, or to make any disposition she may see fit to make of it; by gift, sale or in any other manner.

The jurisdiction of this court to construe the will on this proceeding is also questioned. It was held in Fiester v. Shepard (92 *N. Y.*, 251), and the cases cited by the learned Judge who wrote the opinion in that case, that Surrogates' courts possessed only the jurisdiction expressly conferred by law, and such powers as were incidentally conferred, or as were incidentally necessary to carry out powers expressly conferred. The only *express* jurisdiction to construe a will is by § 2624 of the Code of Civil Procedure, which provides for determining the construction, or effect of any disposition of personal property contained in a will of a resident of the State, executed in the State, on proceedings for probate. It is quite clear that, if the Surrogate's court has any jurisdiction in this matter to construe this will, it is by reason of its being incidental to a power given him to compel the petitioner, as a testamentary trustee, to give bonds, her incompetency or want of understanding being established. The petitioner is not named as executrix, and if she holds this property in trust, must do so by reason of being created a testamentary trustee by the will.

The first question, then, to be considered is—what

power has been conferred on this court, to compel a testamentary trustee to give bonds for the performance of the trust? Section 2815 of the Code provides that such security as may be required of an executor may, for like cause, be required of a testamentary trustee, upon a petition filed, and prescribes the proceedings that shall thereupon be taken; but, the parties in interest being all in court in this proceeding, and the objections being taken on a motion to open the decree, and direct the executor to pay over the funds, or a portion of them, I think the objections may be considered, if the petitioner be a testamentary trustee, and that, for the purpose of determining that question, this court may, so far as necessary and incidental thereto, construe the provisions of the will pertaining to the personal property (Code Civ. Pro., § 2481, *subd.* 11). In Tappen v. M. E. Church (*ante*, 187), it was held, reviewing several authorities, that, on a final accounting, a Surrogate's court could construe a will as incidental to his power to distribute an estate. If he may for that reason construe a will on a final accounting, he may construe it in any proceeding where it may become necessary in order to enable him to carry out powers expressly conferred on him.

The next question to be considered is—what interest does the petitioner take in the personal property under the will? Counsel for the petitioner claims, on the authority of Campbell v. Beaumont (91 *N. Y.*, 464), and cases there cited, that the petitioner is the absolute owner of the personal property, and consequently there is no trust, for the execution of which she may be held responsible. In Campbell v. Beaumont (*supra*), there could be no question, from the plain reading of the will, that the testator intended to give his wife the right to use any or all of the principal for her own benefit, should she desire so to do. The will, after giving her the property absolutely, contained the express desire that, should any of the estate remain, his son Charles should receive and enjoy the same. It was held that the widow took an absolute title, and, that, if a limitation was intended, it was inconsistent with the absolute gift, and therefore void. The provisions of the will under consideration are not equally clear, but to my mind taken together, show that the testator meant to give his wife only a life estate in the personal property, but intended to give her the right to possess it, and manage it as she should see fit, change and convert one kind of property into another, or into cash, or make any other change she might deem best, for the management of the estate, or the benefit of herself and the other legatees. He gives to his wife all his personal estate, not otherwise disposed of, to have and to hold during her natural life; clearly only a life estate, if the will stopped here. The next clause is: "to receive and have for her own use and benefit, all not in this will otherwise disposed of" (a repetition, so far, of the former clause), " the rents and profits, income, increase, possession and enjoyment." How long? "During her natural life," not absolutely without qualification, as in Campbell v. Beaumont. After requiring her to keep buildings and fences in repair, "during said term," follows this provision:

"and my said wife may use and employ the property *so devised and given* to her as she may see fit for her benefit." This clause refers to the preceding portions of the will for the nature of the gift; which by the preceding clauses is clearly a life estate only. The testator evidently meant that she should use it as she thought best and as she desired, but evidently meant such a use as would be consistent with the estate conveyed; else why so particular, in two preceding clauses, the only ones by which the estate is conveyed, to limit the term to her natural life.

But it is claimed that the subsequent clause, which gives her the right to "dispose of such part of said personal estate, from time to time, as she may see fit, or as may be proper *for the best management thereof, for the benefit of those concerned*, as she may direct," permits her not only to dispose of any part, or the whole of the estate of which she shall deem it best to dispose, for the management of the estate, but for her own use or for any other purpose. I do not think the language warrants such a construction. The power to dispose of this property seems to be clearly limited to such disposal as may be proper to manage the estate, not for herself alone but for the benefit of all concerned, her own benefit so far as the life use is concerned, and also for the benefit of those who are to receive the *corpus* of the estate after her life estate terminates. From the inventory filed in the estate, as well as from the proceeding in which the decree was made, which it is now sought to open, it appears that quite a considerable part of the personal property consisted of farming stock, tools, etc.,

which, from their nature, would occasionally require
to be sold, replaced or converted into money or other
property, and I think this was the power intended to
given, and which was given by the will; hence
. other provision, that, at the death of his wife, the
executor should take and dispose of such property as
had not been disposed of, and convert it into money.
Such as she had already disposed of and converted
into money could be distributed with the avails of
such as he should dispose of. The testator disposed
of all his property by will, and the expression, "not
disposed of by me in this will" must mean not disposed of by the other provisions of his will than the
one under consideration. The testator also makes
any debts he or his wife may owe at the death of his
wife a charge on his estate; but I find in this provision nothing to convince me that he intended anything more than a life estate. He evidently intended,
whatever the legal effect may be, to include any produce of the personal estate, not used by his wife in
the residue of his estate to be divided, and so provides that her debts, if any, shall be paid out of the
general fund. The expression is, that the executor
shall sell, etc., "my personal estate *or the produce
thereof* that shall then remain."

In the able brief of the special guardian, my attention is called to several cases, in which provisions of
wills not wholly unlike this have been construed. In
Brant v. Virginia Coal & Iron Co. (93 *U. S.*, 326),
the language of the will was: "to have and to hold
during her life, and to do with as she sees proper
before her death." The court held that these words

only conferred a life estate, that the disposal must be consistent with the estate conferred, and that "whatsoever power of disposal the words confer, is limited, by the estate with which they are connected." In Boyd v. Strahan (36 *Ill.*, 355), the personal property not otherwise disposed of was given to the wife, " to be at her own disposal, and for her own proper use and benefit during her natural life;" and the court held that the words "during her natural life" so qualified the power of disposal, as to make it mean such disposal as a tenant for life could make. In Bradley v. Wescott (13 *Vesey*, 444), the testator gave property to his wife, Elizabeth Swanbeck, for and during her natural life; to be at her full, free and absolute disposal, and disposition during her natural life; without being in any wise liable to be called to any account of or concerning the amount, value or particulars thereof, by any person or persons whosoever; and gave certain of his said property to such person as his said wife should direct, the same to be given to them, after her death, and in case she failed to designate any one, said property was to fall into the residuum which should remain undisposed of by said wife at the time of her death. Sir WILLIAM GRANT, Master of the Rolls, said: " the first question to be disposed of is—what interest Mrs. Swanbeck took under the will . . . . . As the testator has given in express terms an interest for life, I cannot, under the ambiguous words afterward thrown in, extend that interest to an absolute property. I must construe the subsequent words, with reference to the express interest for life previously given, that she is to have as full, free and absolute disposition as a tenant for life can have." In the case of Smith v. Van Ostrand (64 *N. Y.*, 278), RAPALLO, J., makes a distinction between such power of disposal as does, and such as does not give an absolute estate. He says: "It is contended, on the part of the respondent, that the gift of the remainder to the children is repugnant to the prior gift to the wife, and therefore void, and in support of this proposition the cases of Patterson v. Ellis (11 *Wend.*, 259); Hill v. Hill (4 *Barb.*, 419); Tyson v. Blake (22 *N. Y.*, 558); and Norris v. Beyea (3 *Kern.*, 286), are cited. These cases sustain the proposition that, where an absolute power of disposal is given to the first legatee, a remainder over is void for repugnancy . . . . . In the other cases cited, the remainders were held valid, but they recognized the proposition that, if the power of disposition of the first taker is absolute, the remainder is repugnant. But they also recognize that if the *jus disponendi* is conditional, the remainder is not repugnant." In that case, a sum was given to a widow, for her support during her natural life. The court held that she had a power of disposal, but only for her own support, and hence the gift was not absolute. In the case under consideration, by transposing a few words the clause giving the *jus disponendi* is: "She may dispose of such part of said personal estate, from time to time as she may see fit, or as may be proper as she shall direct, for the best management thereof for the benefit of those concerned." The power or right of disposal here is (while as to the *manner* thereof unlimited, and left entirely to her discretion) limited as to the *purpose* for which she may dispose of it, viz.: the best management thereof as trustee for herself and the residuary legatees.

It is a general rule, in the construction of wills, that all parts of a will are to be construed in relation to each other, and so, if possible, to form one consistent whole; and it seems to me this is accomplished by this construction. In Quinn v. Hardenbrook (54 *N. Y.*, 83), GRAY, C., says that, when the contest is between the heir and a stranger to the blood of the testator, whose only claim, except for the will, would be her dower interest, the claim of the heir has the advantage; in this—that, when there are two equally probable constructions of a will, that one is to be adopted which prefers the kin of the testator to strangers. But it is not necessary to approve or apply that rule in this case. I think that this case is distinguishable from Campbell v. Beaumont (91 *N. Y.*, 464), and the cases holding similarly to that, in this— that, in these cases, there was an unquestionable right given the legatee to use and dispose of any or all of the property in question for her own sole use and benefit, and in so doing to decrease or entirely use up the principal, while in the present case, I think it is only the power of management and disposition given, which she may, *as trustee* deem best, *in managing* the estate for the beneficiaries or *cestuis que trust*, including herself as a life tenant, or one entitled to the life estate. FINCH, J., in Bliven v. Seymour (88 *N. Y.*, 478), citing Smith v. Van Ostrand (*supra*), says, in reference to executors delivering over personal property to the legatee for life: "The correct rule was declared to be that, unless otherwise directed by the will, it was the duty of the executors either to invest the money and pay over the income, preserving the principal for the remaindermen, or, if they paid it to a legatee for life, exact security which would perfectly protect the principal."

In this case, the testator, by his will, directed that his wife should have the possession, and entire control of the personal property, and the General Term so stated, in a memorandum dismissing an action brought by the executor for the construction of the will, in which he specially asks instructions in regard to paying over the funds in his hands. The decree made by the former Surrogate seems to have been incomplete, as it makes no final order as to the custody of the property, but leaves it in the hands of the executors until the further order of this court, I think that, under § 2481, subd. 6, of the Code of Civil Procedure, I can and should open the decree, and make a final order directing the executor to turn over all the personal property in his hands to the petitioner, to be held and managed by her as a testamentary trustee, unless it should be shown that some of the objections contemplated by § 2638 of the Code, or by 2 R. S., 70, ch. 6, tit. 2, art. 1, § 3 (am'd L. 1883, ch. 79) exist, or that, for any other reason, she is incompetent to manage the estate; in which case, security may and should be required, or the property withheld; and for the purpose of determining that question, the court will hear such evidence as may be presented.

SCHUYLER COUNTY.—HON. M. J. SUNDERLIN, SURRO-
GATE.—January, 1885.

FLEET *v.* SIMMONS.

In the matter of the estate of HENRY S. FLEET
deceased.

The will of decedent contained a clause, whereby his executors were fully
empowered, authorized and directed, at any time after his decease to
sell any or all of his real or personal estate, not specifically devised or
bequeathed, with a certain exception ; also giving unto them full
power and authority to execute and acknowledge all necessary conveyances to carry the will into effect. The surviving executor having
been required to give security for the faithful performance of his
duties, filed an official bond in a penalty of $11,000, with two sureties,
to whom, for the purpose of indemnifying them against loss by reason
of their recognizance, he at once conveyed a farm, and assigned a contract for the purchase of another farm, both belonging to his decedent's estate. Upon an application, by persons interested, for the
revocation of the executor's letters, on the ground of misconduct in
the execution of his office, within the meaning of Code Civ. Pro.,
§ 2685,—

Held, that, the indemnification of the sureties in the executor's bond not
being one of the purposes contemplated by the power of sale contained
in the will, the act of the executor was illegal and improper ; to
uphold which would be to subvert the very principles upon which
such a bond is required ; that the act complained of was clearly
within the spirit of the section cited, and that the prayer of the petition should be granted.

Rogers v. Squires, 26 *Hun,* 388—distinguished.

APPLICATION, by the widow and daughter of decedent, for revocation of letters testamentary issued
to George Simmons, as executor of decedent's will.
The facts are stated in the opinion.

O. P. HURD, *for petitioners.*

G. L. SMITH, *for executor.*

THE SURROGATE.—This is an application by the widow and daughter of Henry S. Fleet, deceased, to have the letters testamentary issued out of this court on July 25th, 1879, to George Simmons, one of the executors named in the will of the deceased, revoked. Albert H. Fleet, one of the executors named in the will of the deceased, and to whom, also, letters were issued, died previously to this application.

After the decease of the said Albert, upon the application of the widow (the surviving executor, Simmons, having been shown to be insolvent), an order was made by the Surrogate, requiring Simmons to give a bond in the penal sum of $22,000, for the faithful performance of his trust. This order was modified or superseded by a further order allowing said executor to give a bond in the penal sum of $11,000, and deposit a portion of the assets of the estate, pursuant to § 2595 of the Code of Civil Procedure. In pursuance of said last named order, the executor gave a bond in the penal sum of $11,000, which was executed by himself, and one Charles W. Barnes and one William Pellett as his sureties, which bond was accepted and approved by the Surrogate.

One of the grounds upon which the revocation of the letters is asked is that, at the time of giving said bond, the executor conveyed by deed, to Barnes and Pellett, his sureties, a farm of sixty acres belonging to the Fleet estate, and also assigned to them a certain contract belonging to said estate for the purchase of a certain other farm; that the executor received no consideration for such deed or assignment, but that the same was made solely to secure the said Barnes and Pellett against their liability as sureties.

There is no dispute about these facts. In fact, the executor concedes them to be true, but claims that he had the legal right so to do, and that such act was within the proper discharge of his duties in the administration of the estate, and cites the case of Rogers v. Squires (26 *Hun*, 388), as an authority to sustain his act in so doing.

In the case cited, the administrator transferred certain promissory notes belonging to the estate to his sureties, to secure them for their liability on the bond they had signed for him as administrator; and the only question in that case was—whether, by such transfer, the sureties became vested with a sufficient interest in the notes, to enable them to maintain an action upon them against the maker. The court held that, by such transfer, the sureties did obtain a sufficient interest in the notes so transferred to enable them to maintain the action, but OSBORN, J., in delivering the opinion of the court, says: "He (the administrator) probably had no legal right to divert them from this purpose (*i. e.*, as assets to be collected and disposed of according to law) by any transfer of the same for his own benefit, like turning them out as security for his own personal benefit to secure his own debts, or to indemnify his friends, who had seen fit to become sureties upon the bond which the law required for his faithful performance of his duty as such administrator."

The will of the deceased contained the following clause: "*Fifth*. My executors hereinafter named are hereby fully empowered, authorized and directed, at any time after my decease, to sell any or all of my real or personal estate, not hereinbefore specifically devised or bequeathed, except the brick house and lot where I now reside, and the household furniture therein, and convert the same into money . . . . . also giving and granting unto my said executors full power and authority to execute and acknowledge all necessary conveyances and writings to carry my will into effect."

The power of sale contained in this provision of the will must be held to have been given for the benefit of the estate; and the conveying of the farm by the executor to his sureties, to secure them for their liability in signing his bond, was not "selling and converting into money for the benefit of the estate." He obtained the right and power of sale only from the will. Without such right and power having been thus delegated to him, he could not legally sell and convey the real estate for any purpose; and, a conveyance by the executor for the purpose of securing the sureties on his bond not being one of the purposes contemplated by such provision of the will, the act was an illegal and improper one in the discharge of his duty to the estate, and one which may greatly tend to embarrass the estate and plunge it into litigation, as the surety Barnes has since died, and the title conveyed to him has now descended to his heirs. To uphold transactions of this character, in the administration of estates, would be to subvert the very principles upon which bonds are required of executors and administrators, for the faithful performance of their trusts.

My idea of the principle upon which those having in charge the settlement of estates of deceased persons are required to give security for the faithful performance of the trust reposed in them is that the law contemplates that they are to be persons possessed, either of sufficient financial ability, or of such known integrity of character, or both, as that their friends will not hesitate to *pledge their own property* as security for the faithful and proper discharge of the trust committed to their hands.

To adopt the principle contended for by the executor's counsel would subvert this principle, and virtually compel the estate to be administered to furnish security for its executor or administrator; or, in other words, the estate would be compelled to secure itself. Upon the principle contended for, an administrator may make an agreement with his sureties that, in case they will sign his bonds, the moment his letters are granted, he will execute to them a chattel mortgage or bill of sale of every dollar of the assets of the estate, to secure them for their liability. Upon this agreement they sign his bonds, the letters are granted to him, and, as administrator, he executes and delivers the chattel mortgage or bill of sale, and virtually the entire control of and title to the assets have passed from him. He is powerless to pay debts and funeral expenses; the personal property may be compelled to lie idle and depreciate in value, and interest to accumulate upon debts owing by the estate. And when the administrator is brought to account, his excuse for not converting the assets into money and paying off the claims against the estate, as the law requires him to do, is that, in order to give the required bond to obtain his letters, he was obliged to secure his sureties with the assets of the estate, and they have held them as security, and thus paralyzed his powers to act. It cannot be that the law will allow manipulations of an estate, so paralyzing in their effects to the interests of estates, and yet, if it can be allowed in the present case, *it must be* permitted in the case supposed.

I am aware that the executor claims that these transfers were made under the advice of counsel, and that, having acted under legal advice, it would be doing him great injustice to revoke his letters; but whether done under legal advice or of his own volition, the effect upon the estate is the same. The principle to be established is the same; and, as I am unable to find any adjudicated case to sustain an act of this kind, if such a precedent is to be established, so mischievous and dangerous to the interests of estates, it should come from a court of higher authority, after a full consideration of all the principles involved. I am satisfied, after the careful consideration I have given to this case, that the act complained of (and which act is conceded by the executor) comes clearly within the spirit, if not the letter, of § 2685 of the Code of Civil Procedure.

Section 2687 then provides that, if the objections or any of them are established to the satisfaction of the Surrogate, *he must* make a decree revoking the letters complained of.

In the view I have taken of this case, it becomes imperative upon the Surrogate to revoke the letters issued to the executor upon this ground alone, and it is rendered unnecessary to consider any of the other grounds urged for removal.

A decree must be entered, revoking the letters.

WESTCHESTER COUNTY.—HON. OWEN T. COFFIN, SURROGATE.—September, 1884.

PECK *v.* PECK.

In the matter of the estate of MARY P. PECK, *deceased.*

The statutory provisions regulating the form of the official bond of an executor or administrator, and prescribing, as its minimum penalty, twice the value of the decedent's personal property (see Code Civ. Pro., §§ 2645, 2667), embrace property personally possessed, as well as choses in action, and all other property to the actual possession of which the decedent was entitled as the legal owner thereof ; but cannot be intended to cover any property of which he, in his lifetime, had divested himself of the legal title, whether the transfer were procured by fraud or otherwise.

J., a brother of the intestate, having been appointed administrator of her estate upon giving a bond in a penalty of $500, being double the value of the property of which she was represented to have died possessed, petitioner, another of her next of kin, applied for an order compelling J. to give an additional bond in a penalty of $150,000, alleging that the intestate was entitled to a distributive share, amounting to $75,000, in the estate of one M., which, at the time of her death, was in the hands of J., as the administrator of the estate of the latter. J. filed an answer, setting up an assignment by intestate, in her lifetime, to himself, of her share in M.'s estate, and produced the assignment upon the hearing ; whereupon petitioner offered evidence to impeach the assignment, viz.: proof of mental incapacity, coercion and undue influence. Upon objection,—

Held, that the evidence was incompetent, the Surrogate's court having no jurisdiction to determine the question at issue, and that petitioner's application could not be entertained until the same had been submitted to the adjudication of a proper tribunal.

JARED V. PECK, a brother of the intestate, Mary P. Peck, within a year past, had made application to be appointed administrator, etc., of the intestate, representing, in his application, that the personal property of which she died possessed did not exceed, in value, the sum of $250. On giving a bond, with two sureties, in a penalty of $500, and on taking the usual oath, letters of administration were issued to him. James H. Peck, another of the next of kin of the intestate, now made application for an order compelling the administrator to give a new bond in a penalty of $150,000, alleging, as a reason therefor, that the intestate was entitled to a distributive share of the estate of the late John A. Merritt, amounting to about $75,000, which, at the time of her death, was in the hands of Jared V. Peck, as administrator, etc., of said Merritt. The administrator filed an answer, admitting that such a sum came into his hands as Merritt's administrator, as the share of the intestate, but alleging that she, in her lifetime, duly assigned it to him. On the hearing, he produced such an assignment, and put the same in evidence; whereupon a witness was called on behalf of James H. Peck, who proposed to show that said Mary P. Peck, at the time of the date of the assignment, was of unsound mind, and incapable, by reason thereof, of making a valid contract; that she was coerced to execute the same; and that she was under the dominion of undue influence on the part of said J. V. Peck. This was objected to by the counsel for the administrator.

JOHN H. CLAPP, *for petitioner.*

C. FROST, *for administrator.*

THE SURROGATE.—I think the objection to the evidence must be sustained. In the case of Grummon v. Beekman, referred to by the counsel for the petitioner, and in which he was engaged, and which is unreported, decided by this court in 1878, and which, in its main features, was almost identical with facts claimed to exist here, no objection was taken to the proof offered to impeach the validity of the assignment, such as is here interposed. The chief objection there made was that the inventory filed could not be thus impeached. The objection was overruled on the ground that the proceeding was instituted for that purpose. Without further objection, testimony was given tending to impeach the validity of the assignment on the one hand, and to sustain it on the other. My recollection is that counsel argued the matter upon the merits, not questioning the power of the court to determine accordingly. In considering it, however, it was held that the court had no power to decide the question, but that it might look into the facts far enough to enable it to see whether there was any just ground for doubt in reference to it, and if there were, to require a bond large enough in amount to cover the sum involved in the controversy. Had the question then arisen, and attention been called to it by counsel, as it has here, it would, doubtless, not have been reached.

The statute requires a bond in double the value of the personal property of which the intestate died possessed. This embraces property personally possessed, as well as choses in action and all other property, to the actual possession of which the intestate was entitled, as the legal owner thereof; but it cannot be intended to cover any property of which the intestate, in his lifetime, has divested himself of the legal title, whether such transfer were procured by fraud, or otherwise. This court being unable to try such question, when it shall have been determined by the proper tribunal in favor of the petitioner, if such should be the result, then the application can be entertained, and the order sought be granted.

WESTCHESTER COUNTY.—HON. OWEN T. COFFIN, SURROGATE.—October, 1884.

MEAD v. JENKINS.

In the matter of the estate of JOHN P. JENKINS, *deceased.*

A creditor of a decedent cannot, at his own option, divide up his claim, placing a portion as a demand against the personal, and the remainder as against the real property. An administrator of a decedent's estate, having no power over the realty, an arrangement to such an effect, entered into by a creditor with him, would be void as against the heir. Where the claim of a creditor of a decedent has been fixed in amount by the decree of a Surrogate's court, rendered upon an accounting to which he was a party, he is concluded thereby, in a proceeding subsequently instituted by him for the sale of decedent's real property, in order to procure the payment of an unpaid balance of the claim.

THE claim of the petitioner was rejected by this court in an earlier stage of the matter (4 *Redf.*, 369), as being barred by the statute of limitations. That decision was finally reversed (95 *N. Y.*, 31), and the matter remitted to this court. It appears that, on the accounting of the administrators, Mary E. Jenkins and Stephen W. Sherwood, it was stated, in the account of proceedings, in regard to this claim, as follows: "George W. Mead's claim $1,000 and interest; he has some collateral security, and has compromised as to his demand against the personal estate at $500, reserving his right to go against the real estate, if his collateral security should fail to pay his demand in full."

The claim was fixed by the decree at $500. Other facts are sufficiently stated in the opinion.

M. L. COBB, *for widow and infant heirs :*

Insists that the applicant's claim should be rejected, because he has been guilty of an unreasonable delay in attempting the recovery of it, as against the realty; and cites Ferguson v. Broome (1 *Bradf.*, 10).

J. H. GOODMAN, *for R. C. Jenkins, adult heir :*

Insists that the applicant is entitled to recover, only on the basis of the amount fixed by the decree on accounting; and cites Skidmore v. Romaine (2

Bradf., 122); Estate of James Burke (1 *Parson's Select Cas.* [*Penn. R.*], 470).

J. T. MABEAN, *for petitioner.*

THE SURROGATE.—I think the fact that a decree was made on accounting in October, 1877, fixing the amount due to Mead at $500, and according to him a *pro rata* share of the personal estate, on that basis, and which was paid to and receipted for by him, precludes him, in this proceeding, from the recovery of a larger sum. It is true, the administrators stated, in their account of proceedings, that he had presented a claim for $1,000 and interest, but had some collateral security, and had compromised as to his demand against the personal estate at $500, reserving his right to go against the real estate, if his collateral security should fail to pay his demand in full. With whom did he make this compromise ? The administrators could make no arrangement affecting the realty, and there were two minor heirs, who could not bargain or be bound by any like agreement. It seems to me his plain duty was to have presented his whole claim then, and, if there were sufficient funds to pay it, to have thereupon surrendered his collaterals ; and, if not, then to have held them, in order to secure the deficiency. He cannot thus, at his own option, divide up his claim and place so much as a demand against the personalty, and so much as against the realty. The rule is that personalty is to be first applied to the payment of debts, and when that is insufficient and shall have been applied *pro rata*, then, and not until then, the real estate may be resorted to. The personalty, on the accounting, with his claim fixed at $500, paid a dividend of 71 per cent., or $355 on this $500, leaving a deficiency of $145. Had his claim been fixed at $1,000, the dividend would have been 50 per cent., or $500 of this $1,000. If he had a right to so divide his claim, it will result in charging the real estate with $145 more of it than if this had not been done.

The amount divided among creditors on the accounting was $995.36, and the amount of the claims was $1,401.92. Aside from the deficiency of $145, on Mead's claim of $500, it left a further deficiency of $361.56 on the other claims established, none of which have been presented before me in this proceeding. If the other creditors have been paid their claims for deficiency, or abandoned them, then this debt, if allowed, as against the realty, would be $645, and interest, instead of $500, and interest. But it was held, when this case was formerly before me (4 *Redf.*, 352), that it was unnecessary for the petitioner to set forth the outstanding debts, as they were determined by the decree on the accounting, which must precede his application. That decree having fixed the amount of the outstanding debts, they cannot now be adjudged larger than they were then, although they may be fixed at less, as having been reduced by payments, or the like. The applicant bases this proceeding upon the fact that there had been an accounting, and he must abide by its result.

In Skidmore v. Romaine (2 *Bradf.*, 122), Surrogate BRADFORD well said: "It would be an anomaly to allow a greater debt against the real estate than can be demanded or has been established against the personal representatives. The personal estate is the primary fund, and the measure of recovering against the realty cannot exceed that against the personalty, though it may be less."

It is insisted by counsel for the heirs at law that, in a case like this, the application should be made within a reasonable time, without regard to the question of the statute of limitations; that the applicant's claim should be rejected, because of his unreasonable delay in making an attempt to enforce its recovery. The Court of Appeals held, in this case (95 *N. Y.*, 31), in substance, that the running of the statute was suspended until the account was actually rendered by the administrators, under the provisions of § 406 of the Code, which, in terms, applies only to " actions ;" and that the neglect of the creditor, after the lapse of eighteen months from the date of the letters, to exercise his right to an accounting, would not affect such suspension. It does not become me to question or criticise the correctness of the position ; but if the statute of limitations cannot be successfully interposed against the claim, then it could not be properly resisted on the ground that an effort to recover it, had not been made within a reasonable time.

The claim of the applicant is fixed at $145, together with interest thereon from the date of the decree on the accounting, October 17th, 1877. Of course, if he shall be paid the amount so fixed as due to him, there can be no reason on his part for further prosecuting this proceeding. No costs are allowed.

Decreed accordingly.

WESTCHESTER COUNTY.—HON. OWEN T. COFFIN,
SURROGATE.—November, 1884.

SMITH *v.* SMITH.

In the matter of the estate of REBECCA WELLS,
deceased.

Testatrix, by her will, proved in 1869, gave to her executors $3,000, in trust to invest and keep invested until M., a female infant, attained majority, and then to pay to the latter the principal, "with the accumulation of interest made thereon during her minority, should not the same have been required for her support and maintenance ;" with a disposition over, in case of the death of M. before arriving at full age. In 1878, the father of M. was appointed administrator with the will of testatrix annexed, and received a bond and mortgage for $3,000, representing the above mentioned bequest to his daughter.

M. having reached majority, the administrator filed an account which included claims, as a credit against the trust fund, for board, articles of dress, etc., furnished to the infant, to an amount which exhausted the principal and interest, with the exception of about $450. It appeared that M. was the chief beneficiary in the will of her grandfather, who died in 1876, with whom she had resided since early infancy, and whose will made generous provision for her maintenance and support; and that in 1877, she went to live with her father, and remained with him until 1882, during which period she received from her grandfather's estate from $60 to $80 per month; nearly one half of which, according to her testimony she gave to her father.—

Held, that, by the terms of the trust created by the will of testatrix, a discretion was given as to the application of interest only, and not principal, to the infant's maintenance and support ; that her receipts from her grandfather's estate were ample for that purpose, unless squandered, and that it was the father's duty to have taken measures to prevent any such misapplication by her ; that, therefore, the expenditure by him of even the interest of the trust fund was unjustifiable ; and that all the credits, claimed by him against the trust fund, must be disallowed.

THE administrator, with the will annexed, became
such in 1878. By her will, proved in October, 1869,

Rebecca Wells, the testatrix, among other things, provided as follows:

"*Eleventh.*—I give and bequeath unto my executors hereinafter named, the sum of three thousand dollars to and for the uses and purposes following, that is to say, to invest and keep the same invested on bond and mortgage on real estate, or in the public funds of the United States or State of New York, whichever may, in their opinion, be most safe and productive, until my dear baby, Mary Rebecca Smith, granddaughter, of my cousin, Henry R. Morgan, shall arrive at lawful age, and then to pay to the said Mary Rebecca the said principal sum of three thousand dollars ($3,000) with the accumulation of interest made thereon during her minority, should not the same have been required for her support and maintenance. And upon the further trust, in case of the decease of said Mary Rebecca before arriving at lawful age, then to pay and divide the same equally to and among her children living at the time of her decease, and, in case of the decease of the said Mary Rebecca before arriving at lawful age without leaving issue her surviving, then to pay the same to Benjamin R. Morgan, son of the said Henry R. Morgan."

The administrator was the father of said Mary R. Smith. On May 20th, 1878, he received from the executors of Henry R. Morgan, who had died in 1876, a bond and mortgage for $3,000 and interest from February 1st, 1876, as representing the amount so bequeathed by Rebecca Wells. At the time of Mr. Morgan's death, Mary R. Smith was about thirteen years old, and had lived with him from early infancy, her mother having died shortly after her birth. In the winter of 1876–7, she was away at school, and in February of the latter year she went to reside with her father, and continued to live with him, with the exception of about five months, until January, 1882, when she left permanently.

Henry R. Morgan, the grandfather of Mary R. Smith, left a last will and testament, in and by which she was made the chief beneficiary of his estate, and wherein provision was made for her education, maintenance and support. The executor of Mr. Morgan's will paid her school bills, and after she left school and down to the time she became sixteen years old (February 26th, 1879), he paid to her $66.66 per month, and after that period $80 per month, for her maintenance and support.

The administrator, in his account filed herein, claimed a credit, as against the fund and interest, of $478.49, for articles of dress, etc., purchased by him for his daughter, between August 14th, 1876, and February 22d, 1878, before he became administrator; and $72, paid for piano rent thereafter. He also claimed a credit, for her board from August 15th, 1876, to December 15th, 1880, at the rate of $10 per week, in the sum of $2,250; and also, for like board from May 1st, 1881, to January 23rd, 1883, at $9 per week, in the sum of $342. The account, as filed, showed the whole fund exhausted with the exception of $451. Objections to the account were filed.

G. M. MACKELLAR, *for contestant:*

Cited Wood v. Wood (5 *Paige,* 596); Matter of

Davison (6 *id.*, 136); Matter of Ryder (11 *id.*, 185); Matter of Turner (10 *Barb.*, 552); Perry on Trusts, §§ 616, 617, 618; Walker v. Wetherell (6 *Vesey*, 474); Matter of Bostwick (4 *Johns. Ch.*, 100; Lee v. Brown (4 *Vesey, Jr.*, 362); Errat v. Barlow (14 *id.*, 202).

A. B. CHALMERS, *for administrator.*

THE SURROGATE.—The contestant resided with Henry R. Morgan, her grandfather, almost from the period of her birth until his death, when she was about thirteen years old. Hence, he stood *in loco parentis* to her, and the provisions in his will for her support became operative at once. She received, or was entitled to have applied to her support, etc., about $800 per year, from the time of his death until she attained to the age of sixteen, and from that time forward nearly $1,000 per year. These sums were amply sufficient for her proper maintenance, education and support; and yet, while she was receiving the former sum, the administrator, her father, claims for past maintenance, etc., before he was entitled to receive the fund in controversy, a sum nearly equal to one half of the amount of the original fund. It is true that, in some cases, an allowance for past maintenance will be granted. Admitting the element of the father's inability, I cannot regard this as such a case, for the simple reason that the daughter had ample means for a generous support, had they been properly applied to that purpose. If they were not, the father neglected his duty as parent in not seeing that it was done. The daughter had no general guardian, and he was her natural one. Mr. Wells, the executor of Mr. Morgan's will, whose duty it was to apply this money to its destined purpose, seems to have considered that he discharged it by simply handing the money to her in order to pay her bills; while she testifies that a large portion of her annuity went into her father's hands, to relieve his pressing needs. At all events, if she, a young girl of from fifteen to eighteen years, squandered or misapplied the money, of which, by the way, there is no evidence, then, clearly, it was her father's duty to have taken such measures as were within his reach to have prevented it. If she did not squander it, there was an abundance for her comfortable maintenance; if she did squander it, the fault is his. No case, therefore, is established for an allowance for past maintenance, even if this court had the power, under the circumstances, to award it. But the whole matter depends upon other considerations.

This sum of $3,000 was bequeathed to the executors, in trust, to invest and keep invested until the contestant became twenty-one, and then to pay it to her, with the accumulated interest made during her minority, should not the same have been required for her support and maintenance. The case has been argued upon the assumption that the provision, as to what might be required for support, has reference only to the interest on the fund. This I deem a correct interpretation of the clause. The executors, then, were clothed with a discretion as to the application of the interest. Then, in case she died under twenty-one, without issue, they were directed to pay it to Benjamin R. Morgan. She is now of age and is, consequently, entitled to whatever of the fund and interest legally remains. Neither the executors, nor the administrator who succeeds them, had any right to use a dollar of the sum bequeathed, for the support of the minor, nor of the interest, unless it was required for that purpose. That they could not so encroach upon the principal, is too well settled by numerous well adjudged cases, to warrant a discussion here of the reasons upon which the rule rests. In Deen v. Cozzens (7 *Robt.*, 178), it was held, upon the authority of Matter of Davison (6 *Paige*, 136), and Matter of Ryder (11 *id.*, 185), that, where a fund or estate is given to an infant, with a valid limitation over upon the death of such infant, the court has no power to break in on the *corpus* of the gift, for the support, maintenance or advancement of the infant; and that, where it has no such authority, it has no right to ratify the act of the trustee in so doing. If, however, the minor, after coming of age, ratify such breaking in upon the fund, it shall conclude him (Lee v. Brown, 4 *Vesey, Jr.*, 362). In the case just cited, the testatrix gave £100 in trust to her executors, to place it at interest during the minority of her great nephew, John Lee, and to apply the interest toward his maintenance and education, and when he should attain the age of twenty-one, then to pay the £300 to him; but in case he should die before that, then the same was given to his brothers and sisters, equally. He attained the age of twenty-one, and subsequently brought an action to recover the £100. It was claimed, in defense, that much more than the

interest of the legacy had been expended in main-
taining and educating him at school; and it was
also claimed that the legacy was satisfied. The court,
however, assuming that the legacy had all been expended for the benefit of the legatee, nevertheless,
gave judgment in his favor, declaring that it found
no evidence of his having, after he became of age,
ratified such expenditure of it. It is not pretended
that any such ratification was made in this case.
The authorities cited preclude the possibility of
my awarding to the administrator any portion of the
corpus of the fund he claims to have used or applied
for the benefit of the legatee. As to whether he did
actually so employ or apply any of it, or not, it is unnecessary to examine or discuss.

The only remaining question to be considered is
whether, under the circumstances, the administrator,
in the exercise of a sound discretion, was justified in
using for like purposes, and other than for expenses
of administration, any part of the interest of the
fund. The language of the testatrix is that the
accumulated interest should be paid to her "should
not the same have been *required* for her support and
maintenance." In view of the fact that, during the
period when it might otherwise have been required
for such purposes, she was receiving $80, per month,
on those very accounts, from the estate of Henry R.
Morgan, nearly half of which, according to her testimony, she gave to her father, no good reason is
discovered why any allowance should be made to the
administrator therefor. The claim is for board at an
exorbitant rate, considering the relation of the parties;

he was well aware of the sum she received monthly; and must have known that none of the interest of the fund in question, could, in any reasonable or discreet manner, be "required" to pay it.

The conclusion reached, therefore, is that all of the administrator's claims are disallowed, except that for the expenses of administration, amounting to $247.95. Of course, as a matter between father and daughter, the latter will consult her own sense of filial duty in exacting or forbearing to exact the whole amount to which she is thus adjudged to be legally entitled.

No costs of this proceeding are allowed to the administrator, he being already allowed $75, therefor in the above sum of $247.95. Under the circumstances, I think the contestant's costs, including stenographer's fees, so far as unpaid, should come out of the fund.

WESTCHESTER COUNTY.—HON. OWEN T. COFFIN, SURROGATE.—November, 1884.

MATTER OF VALENTINE.

In the matter of the estate of ABRAHAM VALENTINE, *deceased.*

Under L. 1882, ch. 185, entitled "an act in relation to trustees of personal estates," and L. 1884, ch. 408, re-enacting Code Civ. Pro., § 2818, the Supreme Court and Surrogates' courts have concurrent jurisdiction over the appointment of a successor to a deceased sole testamentary trustee.

Where application for such an appointment is made to a Surrogate's court, a notice of eight days may properly be given to all the beneficiaries of the trust; but the executor of a will of the deceased trustee is not a proper party to the proceeding.

A PETITION was presented by Jane Valentine, from which it appeared that, by the will of Abraham Valentine, deceased, certain trusts were created; that Samuel M. Valentine, who was sole trustee named in said will, had died leaving certain of said trusts unexecuted; and praying for the appointment of a trustee in his place, as to one of the trusts. Only the persons interested in that trust were thereupon cited. On the return day of the citation, it was objected that the trustee to be appointed should be trustee of all the unexecuted trusts, and that the persons interested in certain other trusts should also have been cited in the proceeding. This objection was made on behalf of the executors of the deceased trustee, and also on behalf of persons claiming to be assignees of the interest of Charles E. Valentine, one of the beneficiaries of one of the trusts.

WM. G. VALENTINE, *for petitioner.*

MORRIS S. THOMPSON, *for executors of S. M. Valentine, dec'd.*

THOS. M. WHEELER, *for assignees of Chas. E. Valentine.*

THE SURROGATE.—Formerly, and prior to the Code of 1880, the Supreme Court had exclusive jurisdiction over the subject of the removal and appointment of trustees; but by that Code, § 2818, power was conferred upon Surrogates to appoint a successor where a sole testamentary trustee dies, becomes a lunatic, has been removed, or been allowed to resign. This, in terms, covers the cases of all trusts, whether express or otherwise. By § 68, 1 R. S., 730, it was provided that, where the surviving trustee of an express trust died, the trust should not descend to his heirs, nor pass to his personal representatives, but that the trust, if then unexecuted, should vest in the Court of Chancery, to be executed by some person to be appointed for that purpose. After the Code went into effect, and in 1882 (ch. 185, p. 223), the legislature passed an act, the title of which is "An act in relation to trustees of personal estates." With a slight alteration and addition, that act is a transcript of § 68 of the R. S. It provides that, "upon the death of a surviving trustee of an express trust, the trust estate shall not descend to his *next of kin* or personal representatives, but the trust, if unexecuted, shall vest in the Supreme Court," and shall be executed by some person appointed for that purpose, under the direction of the court. I take it that the term "express trust" means such an express trust as is authorized to be created by § 55 of the statute of Uses and Trusts. There is nothing in the body of the act of 1882 to indicate that a trust of personal property was the subject of the enactment, except the substitution, in that act, of the words "next of kin," in place of the word "heirs," in § 68. Without stopping to consider whether personal property can be regarded as the subject of what is known in law as an express trust, or only of a power in trust, I simply desire to call attention to the fact that a legislative attempt has been made to cause the trust, as to both species of property, to vest, in case of the death of a sole trustee, in the Supreme Court, and to be executed by some person to be appointed by that court. It would seem, therefore, but for what follows, that the Supreme Court had exclusive jurisdiction over the matter. But again, in 1884 (ch. 408, p. 486) said § 2818 of the Code was re-enacted, with certain amendments. None of these various provisions are expressly repealed, and as repeal by implication is not favored, I must hold that this court has power, concurrent with the Supreme Court, to appoint a successor to a deceased sole trustee.

I had occasion, in the case of Tompkins v. Moseman (5 *Redf.*, 402), to point out that the section failed to prescribe the mode of procedure for the appointment of a new trustee, where the sole trustee died or became a lunatic, and to hold, that in such a case, the practice of the late Court of Chancery should be followed, which was largely discretionary as to the persons who should have notice of the application. But since the act of 1882, above referred to, provides that "no person shall be appointed to execute said trust until the beneficiary thereof shall be brought into court by such notice and in such manner as the court may direct," it may be well, although the act is not, in terms, made applicable here, to give a notice of at least eight days to all beneficiaries. It will be observed that the last named act provides only for the bringing into court of the beneficiary of the trust, and not of any person interested in the remainder, nor of any assignees of the beneficiary; but as, in this case, the latter are here by counsel, I will receive any suggestion as to the person proposed as the successor to the deceased trustee, which may be made in their behalf.

The executors of the will of the deceased trustee are not proper parties to this proceeding.

———————◄•◦•►———————

WESTCHESTER COUNTY.—HON. OWEN T. COFFIN, SURROGATE.—December, 1884.

SMITH *v.* BAYLIS.

In the matter of the estate of ANNE SMITH, *deceased.*

Upon a judicial settlement of the account of the administrator of intestate's estate, a decree was rendered in July, 1884, whereby the distributive share therein of J., a son of the intestate, against whom proceedings supplementary to execution were then pending, was fixed at $212, which the administrator was ordered to retain until the disposition thereof should be directed by a court of competent jurisdiction. Thereafter the wife of J. applied to the Surrogate's court to open the decree so rendered, and amend the same by directing said share to be paid to herself, alleging, substantially, that J., during the lifetime of his mother, had conveyed to the latter all personal property to come to him from the grantee's estate, or from any other source whatever; and that said grantee had forthwith conveyed the same to petitioner.—

Held, that it was not in the power of any person, by any such process as that described, to introduce himself into the category of the next of kin of another; that petitioner, being neither a creditor nor one of the next of kin of intestate, nor the assignee of a distributive share in her estate, had no standing in court; and that her application for the opening of the decree should be denied.

THIS was an application made by Julia C. Smith, the wife of John B. Smith, to open a decree made in July, 1884, settling the accounts of Theodore Baylis as administrator of the intestate, who died in March, 1874, and directing distribution of the fund. On that accounting, it appeared that a judgment had been obtained against said John B. Smith, who was a son of the intestate, and that proceedings supplemental to execution had been taken and were pending. The distributive share of said John B. was, by the decree, fixed at $212.27, and the administrator was directed to retain the same until the further order of some court having jurisdiction in the premises should lawfully direct the disposition thereof. The petitioner stated that, on December 23rd, 1863, her husband conveyed to the said intestate all his right, title and interest of, in and to all his real and personal property then owned or possessed by him, or to come to him from the estate of Martin Smith (his father) or Anne Smith (his said mother), or from any other source whatsoever; and that, on the next day, said Anne Smith conveyed the same to the petitioner; and she, therefore, alleged that she was the owner of and entitled to said distributive share, and asked that the decree be altered and amended accordingly.

JAMES L. BAXTER, *for petitioner.*

WM. F. PURDY, *for administrator.*

THE SURROGATE.—It is not usual, to say the least of it, for a person to sell or assign what he does not own. True, in 2 Thos. Coke, 486 (*note* L.), it is said: "Leases by estoppel are such as are made by persons who have no interest at the time, or at least no vested estate, but are to operate on their ownership, when they shall acquire the same. Thus, if an heir apparent, or a person having a contingent remainder, or an interest under an executory devise, or who has no title whatever at the time, makes a lease by indenture, or by a *fine sur concessit*, and afterwards an estate vests in him, this indenture or fine will operate by way of estoppel, to entitle the lessee to hold the lands for the term granted to him; and this estoppel, when it becomes efficient, and can operate on the interest, will be fed by the interest; and the lease will be deemed as a lease derived out of an actual ownership."

There, the subject of the lease is fixed and certain, although the heir apparent may never become the heir in fact, by reason of a devise to others, in which case there would be nothing taken under the lease. It is possible that such a rule might be made applicable to a sale made by an apparent next of kin, of an expectant title to the goods of an intestate, but I have never heard of its being done. If it were, it could only operate as an estoppel against the vendor. It is generally understood that, in a sale of chattels, there is an implied warranty of title by the vendor. True, this implication may be repelled by the terms of the sale. The conveyances, in this matter, have not been submitted, nor are their contents stated further than has been recited.

The petitioner virtually claims that her husband, in 1863, sold and assigned to his mother personal property which he did not own, but which then belonged to the mother, who then assigned it to the petitioner. This, if true, was a very remarkable transaction.

Suppose the property to have consisted of the parlor furniture which belonged to the mother, and in which the son might, on her death, have an interest, as one of her next of kin, provided she died intestate and he survived her, what interest had he in it to assign during her life, that did not already belong to her? The mother then assigns the intangible interest so conveyed to her by her son, to the petitioner, still retaining the property. A stranger cannot thus be be substituted for, and transformed into, a next of kin. If the parties really designed to accomplish the alleged transfer, it could only have been effected, as it seems to me, by a will of the owner of the property. If, on the contrary, the alleged transaction operated the transfer, then the petitioner's claim would be, not that of a next of kin, but that of a creditor of the intestate. But she is neither such creditor, next of kin, or assignee of the distributive share of a next of kin, and, hence, has no interest in the estate such as to enable me to recognize her as possessed of any interest sufficient to permit her to make this application.

Having reached the conclusion indicated, upon another ground, it becomes unnecessary to determine whether the facts presented would authorize the opening of the decree.

Application denied.

WESTCHESTER COUNTY.—HON. OWEN T. COFFIN,
SURROGATE.—December, 1884.

SINGER *v.* HAWLEY.

In the matter of the estate of ISAAC M. SINGER,
deceased.

Where an intelligent and competent person is appointed special guardian
for an infant in a special proceeding in a Surrogate's court, the decree
binds him as much as it would an adult.

Before the enactment of the Code of Civil Procedure, a Surrogate's court
possessed no power to open a decree and grant a hearing, on the ground
of an error in law; and no such power has been conferred by that act,
the words "or other sufficient cause," newly introduced by § 2481,
subd. 6, being properly referable to causes *ejusdem generis,* only.

A beneficiary under decedent's will, who had recently arrived of age,
applied to the Surrogate's court for the opening of a decree rendered
in 1877, judicially settling the account of the executor of said will;
and for the like relief in respect to two decrees rendered on subsequent
accountings by the same party, as trustee and testamentary guardian
of the applicant; so far as to permit him to contest the allowance of
commissions made to said executor, as such, and as trustee and guardian, by said several decrees, alleging that the same exceeded the
amounts allowable under the statute, and that some portion thereof
were illegal by reason of being based upon the estimated value of
certain shares of stock claimed to have been specifically bequeathed;
and also to permit him to contest certain items of expenditure, allowed
for law expenses, and legal and other services, and also to contest the
direction in said decree contained, as to said stock, and the distribution
of the proceeds of certain realty. On each accounting a special guardian was appointed for the applicant, then a minor.—

Held, that the errors alleged were errors of law; and that the application
must be denied, for want of power.

DAVID HAWLEY, the testamentary guardian and
trustee of Adam M. Singer, recently cited the ward
and *cestui.que trust,* who had attained lawful age, to
attend a settlement of his accounts as such guardian,
etc. Pending this proceeding, and before the filing

of the account, Mr. Singer made an application, praying that a decree, made on the accounting of said Hawley as executor of the will of the deceased, and entered in 1877, and that two decrees on accounting by him as trustee and guardian entered, respectively, in 1878 and 1881, might be opened, vacated, modified or set aside, so far as to permit him to contest the allowance of commissions made to him as such, and as trustee and guardian, by said several decrees; alleging that the same exceeded the amounts allowable under the statute, and that some portion thereof were illegal by reason of being based upon the estimated value of certain shares of stock in the Singer Manufacturing company, claimed to be specifically bequeathed; and also to permit him to contest certain items of expenditure allowed for law expenses and legal and other services; and also to contest the direction in said decrees contained as to said stock, and the distribution of the proceeds of certain realty. On each accounting, a special guardian was appointed for the applicant, then a minor.

C. E. TRACY, *for the petitioner:*

The Surrogate has ample power to grant the relief sought (Code, § 2481). In such proceedings courts of record and general jurisdiction are governed by the Code, §§ 1282, 1283, 1291. Where an infant is concerned, and it is manifest, from an inspection of the record, that injustice has been done by clerical error or otherwise, the relief is always granted (Story v. Dayton, 22 *Hun,* 450; In re Tilden, *N. Y. Gen. Term* [not yet reported]; In re Scribner, 19 *Daily*

Register, *No.* 32, 1881; Tucker v. McDermott, 2 *Redf.*, 312).

F. N. BANGS, *for guardian and trustee:*

Section 2481 does not apply, as the last accounting proceeding was commenced before the section took effect; but if it does apply, it does not authorize the opening of a decree on the ground that the applicant thinks an error of law has been committed. The cases below cited sustain the proposition that discretion has never gone in the direction of opening judgments for any cause other than fraud, collusion, or a kindred cause; or of opening them upon a mere suggestion that errors of law have occurred. An appeal is the remedy against errors of law. And in the case of an infant, the court does its whole duty when it appoints an intelligent and competent person to be his special guardian. That being done, the decree binds him as much as it would an adult (Brick's Estate, 15 *Abb. Pr.*, 12; Daniels Ch. Pr., 5th ed., 164; Shotwell v. Murray, 1 *Johns. Ch.*, 512; Phillips v. Dusenberry, 8 *Hun*, 348; Champlin v. Laytin, 18 *Wend.*, 417).

THE SURROGATE.—There can be no doubt that subd. 6 of § 2481 of the Code is inapplicable to this case. The proceeding for the last of the series of accountings was commenced before chapter 18 went into effect; and § 3347, subd. 11, does not make it apply to such a proceeding. Nevertheless, that section was partly based upon former decisions of the courts, and was extended also, so as to embrace a broader field of jurisdiction. Before the Code, a Surrogate had power to open decrees for an excusable default resulting injuriously to the defaulting party, for clerical error, for fraud in procuring the decree, and for other like causes. The only additional power conferred is to grant a new trial or hearing " for newly discovered evidence." Hence, I regard it as wholly immaterial, in this case, whether subd. 6 is, or is not, applicable.

This brings us at once to the question, such as it is, whether this court can grant a re-hearing for an error in law. This case, certainly, presents no features resembling fraud, error in placing or adding figures, procuring a signature to an important voucher by fraudulent representation, by means of which a credit is obtained, presenting a forged voucher and the like. The facts in the memorandum of the case of Story v. Dayton (22 *Hun*, 450), cited by petitioner's counsel, are not very fully stated. It would seem that one ground of complaint was the appointment of an improper person—a clerk in the office of the administrator's attorney—as the guardian *ad litem* for the minors. The case reported discloses no particular errors of fact, or mistakes, justifying the decision to the effect that the order of the Surrogate be reversed "unless the respondent will stipulate that the decree on final settlement may be amended in the particulars specified in the opinion herein," none of which are specified in so much of the opinion as is published. Apparently, errors in fact are the subject of the allusion. Tucker v. McDermott (2 *Redf.*, 312) has no application, as a motion to open a decree was not the subject of consideration. In re Tilden (*Daily Reg.*, *Mch.* 17, 1884), no special guardian for the minor was appointed on the first accounting, which occurred in 1872, before the passage of any act requiring the appointment of such on an accounting. But, at that time, it was proper, as a matter of practice, to do so, and was then the actual practice of this court; and it had the effect of concluding him (Dayton's Surr., 3rd ed., 505–507; Kellett v. Rathbun, 4 *Paige*, 102). This fact, alone, warranted the opening of the first decree, and any alteration of that necessarily affected, and involved the correction of, other and subsequent accountings, where special guardians had been appointed. But, in that case, the question here presented does not seem to have been raised, discussed, or considered. It is thus shown that the authorities cited by the learned counsel for the petitioner furnish but a feeble support to the proposition he urges.

If there were any such errors committed in the decrees as are complained of, and as to which I am not now in a position to determine, they were purely and simply errors of law. The question as to the proper amount of commissions to be allowed is not, in many cases, easy of solution, as is evidenced by many recent and conflicting decisions in various courts. Hence, the erroneous fixing of them in the decree, or the refusal by the court to allow any at all (of which I have heard) cannot be characterized as a fraud, a mistake, a clerical error, or the like. It is simply an error in law, however ignorant, corrupt, or negligent the court may have been in the discharge of its duty; and the only remedy, if the court, on attention being called to it *dum fervet opus*, fail to correct it, is by appeal. The decree embodies the deliberate and solemn, even if reprehensible, judgment of the court. This court, before the Code, possessed no power to open such a decree and grant a rehearing in such a case; and none has been conferred upon it since, as the phrase "for other sufficient cause," is to be construed as applying to causes *ejusdem generis*, only.

It will, I think, be conceded that questions relating to the allowance of commissions on specific bequests have arisen, mainly, as matters of law, concerning the nature of the subject of the bequest, as being specific or otherwise. Their allowance or rejection is still a question of law. And, whatever the adjudication may have been, it can only be remedied, if erroneous, by appeal, and not by a motion of this character. The other errors complained of, belong to the same category, no errors of fact being assigned, and must be disposed of accordingly.

The authorities cited by the counsel for the trustee abundantly establish the principle that, where an intelligent and competent person is appointed the special guardian for the minor, the decree binds him as much as it would an adult. No allegation is made as to any want of intelligence or competency of the several persons who acted as such, on the several accountings; nor is there any suggestion of fraudulent conduct on their part.

Whether errors were committed on any, or all of the accountings, it is, therefore, needless to inquire.

In any event, the petitioner having been represented by special guardian, on each occasion, and the time to appeal having expired, I cannot but regard him as concluded.

Motion denied.

WESTCHESTER COUNTY. — HON. OWEN T. COFFIN, SURROGATE.—December, 1884.

MEAD *v.* MILLER.

In the matter of the estate of CATHARINE S. MORELL, *deceased.*

Upon an accounting by the executors of the will of decedent, the citation was served upon one of the next of kin of the latter, who was a resident of the county, but was at the time absent in England, by leaving a copy at her residence, with a person entrusted by her with its charge, of the age of about sixty years, on the 5th day of August. The citation was returnable on the 22d day of September, following, and a decree was not entered until the expiration of two months from the return day.—

Held, that the service was made "under such circumstances that the Surrogate had good reason to believe that the copy came to her knowledge in time for her to attend at the return day," as required by Code Civ. Pro., § 2520, and that the decree rendered in the proceedings, wherein the party so served failed to appear, was binding upon her.

CATHARINE S. MORELL left a will, by which, among other things, she gave to her husband, General George W. Morell, the use of a mortgage of $25,000, and the use of the proceeds, if paid in, during his life. At his death, $5,000 of the sum was given to St.

Mary's church, at Beechwood, Westchester county. This church, it is now alleged, was not then incorporated, but became so in July, 1883, under the corporate name of "The rector, churchwardens and vestrymen of St. Mary's church, Beechwood, in the town of Mt. Pleasant and county of Westchester." General Morell and George M. Miller were the executors of the will, and, December 22d, 1882, filed their account of proceedings in this court, on which a decree was then entered, directing the executors, among other things, to pay the interest of said bond and mortgage, or of the proceeds thereof, to said General Morell, during his life, and at his death to pay $5,000 thereof to said "St. Mary's Protestant Episcopal church." Jane C. Mead, one of the next of kin of the deceased, who had a home and residence in said town of Mt. Pleasant, near said Beechwood, but who was then, and for some time had been, in Europe with her children, was, in August, 1882, cited to attend the accounting; the citation being served on her by delivering a copy of it to a person of suitable age and discretion, at her said dwelling house, of which due proof was furnished. George V. N. Baldwin, a lawyer in the city of New York, was the attorney in charge of all of Mrs. Mead's business during her absence. He and Mr. Miller, one of the executors, had frequent conversations and communications, in regard to the accounting proceedings, while they were pending, and before the decree was entered. Subsequently, General Morell having died, the surviving executor commenced an action in the Supreme Court, for the construction of the will, in so far as the validity of the bequest to the church was concerned. Judge VAN VORST dismissed the complaint on the ground that the matter had been adjudicated by this court, whose decree stood unreversed. Mrs. Mead, under these circumstances, made an application to this court to open the decree, in order to the reconsidering of the question, as to the validity of the bequest.

GEO. V. N. BALDWIN, *for petitioner.*

GEORGE M. MILLER, *executor, in person.*

F. LARKIN, *for St. Mary's church.*

THE SURROGATE.—The chief question for consideration is, whether the service of the citation upon Mrs. Mead was so made as to render the decree binding upon her. Section 2520 of the Code provides for the service of the citation by leaving a copy at the residence of the party to be cited, with a person of suitable age and discretion, if he be absent, under such circumstances that the Surrogate has good reason to believe that the copy came to his knowledge, in time for him to attend at the return day. In this case, it appears, by the proof of service, that, in the absence of Mrs. Mead, a copy was left at her residence, with a person entrusted by her with its charge, of the age of about sixty years, on August 5th, 1882, which citation was returnable on September 22d, following; there being about seven weeks between the date of service and the return day. It is said Mrs. Mead was, at the time, in England. Suppose the petition had shown that she was then domiciled in that country; then, as prescribed by statute, service would have been made upon her by publication of the citation for six weeks and mailing to her a copy. Under these circumstances, there was good reason to believe that the copy came to her knowledge in time for her to attend personally, or by counsel, on the return day. But the decree complained of was not actually entered until two months from the return day had elapsed. Thus, there was ample time afforded for the protection of her interests. The facts disclosed by the affidavits presented on this motion confirm and justify the belief entertained by the court on the return day, that the copy came to her knowledge in due time. The affidavit of Mr. Baldwin states that it was well known to both of the executors of Mrs. Morell that he, Mr. Baldwin, was the attorney for Mrs. Mead and had entire control of her estate during her absence, and that he, representing Mrs. Mead, and the executors had many conferences relating to the estate of Mrs. Morell. It follows that he must have been in communication with Mr. Beck, who had charge of Mrs. Mead's property at Scarborough, near Beechwood, and with whom the copy of the citation was left. It further appears, from the affidavits, that Mr. Miller, the surviving executor, and Mr. Baldwin, the attorney for Mrs. Mead, pending the accounting proceeding, had frequent conferences in regard thereto, and frequently exchanged written communications on the subject of the adjournment of the same, from time to time.

The decree is, therefore, binding upon Mrs. Mead, unless some error of fact, fraud or mistake were committed, entitling her to relief. But none such are alleged, nor is the motion based upon any such ground. The allegation is that the decree contained a direction to pay a legacy to a religious society which was not then incorporated, and which was not, therefore, competent to take it. If that be true, it was an error of law, which this court has no power to rehear, or review. As Judge VAN VORST well says, in his opinion dismissing the complaint in the action to obtain a construction of the will, "the decree still stands unreversed. It cannot be questioned here, as the Surrogate has jurisdiction. If dissatisfied with the decree, the complaining parties should have appealed."

In the similar case of Singer v. Hawley (*ante*, 571), I have just held that I cannot open a decree on account of the commission of alleged errors of law.

Motion denied.

WESTCHESTER COUNTY.—HON. OWEN T. COFFIN, SURROGATE.—February, 1885.

LONG *v.* OLMSTED.

In the matter of the disposition of the real property of CHARLES OLMSTED, *deceased, for the payment of his debts.*

The Surrogate's court from which letters have been issued to an executor or administrator has jurisdiction, under Code Civ. Pro., ch. 18, tit. 5, to decree the disposition of his decedent's real property wherever the

same may be situated, within the limits of the State, and is not confined to that found within its own county.

In a special proceeding for the disposition of a decedent's real property for
the payment of his debts, a creditor other than the petitioner, whose
claim has been contested and allowed cannot be awarded costs under
Code Civ. Pro., § 2561, notwithstanding the *general* character of that
section, inasmuch as no provision for the payment of such an award
is made by § 2798; after compliance with the directions of which section, the entire proceeds of the disposition will have been exhausted.

In such a special proceeding, no costs or allowances can be granted to a
petitioning creditor, the right to an award thereof, being confined, by
§ 2563, to the executor or administrator, and a freeholder appointed to
execute the decree.

In such a special proceeding, the costs of none of the parties can be fixed
or adjusted so as to be embraced in the decree directing a sale, mortgage or lease. This can be done only at the time of the entry of the
supplementary decree described in § 2798.

APPLICATION by Edward B. Long, a creditor of
decedent, for a decree directing the disposition of
decedent's real property for the payment of his debts.
The facts appear sufficiently in the opinion.

M. M. SILLIMAN, *for petitioner.*

G. R. PHŒBUS, *for Miles W. Olmsted, grantee.*

J. S. MILLARD, *for R. B. Burton, mortgagee.*

JOHN C. GULICK, *for Excelsior savings bank, mortgagee.*

GUY C. H. CORLISS, *for C. K. Corliss, creditor.*

CALVIN FROST, *for J. & E. Bird, mortgagees.*

THE SURROGATE.—No objection has been taken to
the regularity of the proceedings in this matter. The
applicant, it appears, had on May 3rd, 1884, obtained
a judgment after a trial at law on the merits, in the
Supreme Court, against Rachel Olmsted, the administratrix of Charles Olmsted, deceased, intestate, for

the sum of $4,253.23 damages, exclusive of costs. This amount consisted of a balance of a larger claim, to wit, $3,093.26, and interest thereon, $1,159.97. The petitioner having presented proper evidence of the judgment, the same became, *prima facie*, proof of his claim (Code, § 2756). The burthen was thus cast upon the contestants to show, if they could, that there should have been no recovery, that the amount was too large, that payments had been made thereon, or that there were counterclaims against the same. Considerable testimony was taken, on both sides, in relation to the amount of it, without objection, but I am unable to find, on the whole, any reason to diminish the sum. It is, therefore, allowed, with interest, but without it upon the amount of interest included in the judgment.

A part of the real estate of the decedent, described in the petition, is situated in the city and county of New York, and a part in this county. Counsel for the Excelsior savings bank, which holds a mortgage on the former, executed since the intestate's death, objects that this court has no jurisdiction to order a sale of real estate for the payment of decedent's debts, where it is situated beyond the limits of this county. This objection is not tenable. The Code (§ 2752) requires the 'petition to set forth a description of all decedent's real estate situated in this State, and further provisions require this court, in a proper case, to direct a sale thereof. If this objection were valid, and this were the only real estate of which he died seized, the Surrogate of New York having no jurisdiction, it would be impossible for simple contract creditors to reach it in any proceeding of this character. Where this court has jurisdiction of the parties and subject matter, it draws to it the power to manage and control the real and personal estate of the decedent, wherever it may be situated, within the limits of the State. As that real estate is in the immediate possession of the descendants of the deceased, as it is most likely to produce the sum requisite to pay the debts established, and for other reasons unnecessary to state, I think it should be first sold or mortgaged. It appearing that the money necessary to pay the costs, expenses and debts established can be raised, advantageously to the persons interested in the real property, by a mortgage on that part of it situated in the city of New York, the decree will so provide.

The claim of Cyrus K. Corliss, of $740, for referee's fees is allowed, with interest. This last claim was disputed, and briefs in relation thereto were submitted. It being allowed, counsel for Mr. Corliss insists that he is entitled to costs under the provisions of § 2561 of the Code of Civil Procedure, in the discretion of the Surrogate. Although that section is general in its character, apparently extending to all cases, yet it would seem to be impracticable, in view of some subsequent sections, to enforce payment if such costs were granted. Section 2563 makes provision for allowances to be made to the executor, administrator or freeholder for his expenditures and services in a proceeding of this nature, and also for " such a further sum as the Surrogate thinks reasonable, for the necessary services of his attorney and counsel therein." Costs, when allowed, must be awarded by the decree (§ 2559). Subd. 1 of § 2793 provides for the payment, out of the proceeds of sale, of thĕ charges, expenses and disbursements attending the proceeding; and subd. 4 directs that, out of the remainder of the money, "must be paid the costs of the special proceeding, awarded to the petitioner in the decree." This last section prescribes minutely how the whole proceeds of sale, or the amount raised by mortgage or lease, shall be disposed of. However successful a contest may have been waged by any other person, or however he may fairly be considered entitled to be rewarded for his services, no provision is found entitling him to costs out of the proceeds. It would seem that he must be content with the joy, alone, which a successful achievement inspires. If this result were not intended, then the learned framers of the Code failed to make provision for such a case. If, therefore, costs were to be awarded to Mr. Corliss under § 2561, there is no mode of paying them pointed out by § 2793. When its directions shall have been fully complied with, the whole proceeds will have been otherwise disposed of. I must, therefore, decline to allow him costs, as such allowance does not seem to be within the purview of the statutes on the subject.

There remains a novel question, as to whether the petitioning creditor, who instituted these proceedings and has conducted them to this point, is entitled to allowances under § 2563, especially at this stage of the proceeding. He is neither an executor, administrator or freeholder contemplated and provided for in

that section. The "petitioner" is not there mentioned. A freeholder can only be appointed, after
the decree to mortgage, etc., has been made, and the
executor or administrator shall refuse to give the
bond, to secure the payment into court of the proceeds. The administratrix in this case has, in no
way, appeared in this proceeding. Can allowances
be now granted to her for services performed, not by
her, but by the petitioning creditor? And yet, if
allowed at all, it is contended it must be done by the
decree about to be entered. She may come in and
execute the decree, and then might claim the allowance, as authorized to be made to her by the section
referred to. If she refuse to give the bond, to enable
her to execute the decree, a freeholder must be appointed. As such an event cannot now be anticipated, and such appointment cannot precede the
entry of the decree in which, it is claimed, the allowance must be fixed, I do not see how, by this decree
to mortgage, etc., it can be made to a freeholder, at
all; and as the decree must direct the administratrix
to mortgage, sell, etc., must not the allowance, if any,
be made to her? I think it must, if done at this
time. Ordinarily, she would, therefore, be entitled to
any sum fixed; and would be in this case, were it not
for the provisions of § 2793. Under subd. 4 of that
section, already referred to, costs are to be paid only
to the petitioner; and she is not the petitioner, but
then as the section stands, it would seem that they
must be paid as awarded by the decree, and by it, as
has been shown, they could now only be awarded to
the executor, or administrator. So that, apparently,

in order to their allowance and recovery the executor or administrator must also be the petitioner, and in such a case as this, no one could recover costs. Such a result could hardly have been intended. By a slight transposition of the words of the sentence, so that it should have read: "must be paid to the petitioner the costs of the special proceeding awarded in the decree," every case would have been included, whether commenced by an executor, administrator or creditor. The proceedings, up to the decree of sale, are substantially the same, and involve the same amount of labor, whether instituted by the legal representative or a creditor, and where done by the latter, no reason is discovered why he should not have the same compensation for like services as the former.

But I think the counsel for the creditor is mistaken in supposing that the costs must be inserted in the decree directing the sale or mortgaging of the premises. Down to the entry of that decree, only a part of the work will have been done, and the allowance for services of an attorney throughout the proceeding could not then be understandingly made. But after the necessary amount shall have been raised, by the execution of that decree, then by § 2791, the Surrogate must, by a supplementary decree, determine the rights of the creditors and other persons interested, to share in the proceeds, and direct the distribution thereof accordingly. By the next section it is provided that each supplementary decree must fix the sums to be paid or invested as prescribed in the following sections. The next section (2793, above re-

ferred to), in subd. 1, directs the payment of the
charges and expenses, etc., and in subd. 4, directs
the payment of the costs awarded to the petitioner in
the decree.   Hence the amount of those costs can only
be fixed by the supplementary decree, and they must
be directed, by that decree, to be paid to the petitioner.   Therefore, whether the first decree be executed by the administrator or by a freeholder, the
costs belong to the petitioner, while the person executing it will be entitled to the charges and disbursements provided for in the first subdivision of that
section.   Mr. THROOP, in a note to the fourth subdivision, remarks as follows: "No express provision
was made, in the former statute, for the payment of
the petitioner's costs, and this appears to be the place
where they should, in fairness, be provided for."
This cannot properly be regarded as in conflict with
the provisions of § 2563, which says the executor,
administrator or freeholder "may" be allowed a sum
for services of counsel.   Such allowance is left to the
discretion of the Surrogate, and it is not probable
that any would be made to either of those persons,
unless he were the petitioner in the proceeding.
That section is merely permissive, while §§ 2791,
2792 and 2793 are imperative in their language.

Although the costs cannot now be adjusted and
entered in the decree to mortgage, and, therefore, the
precise amount which must be raised by the mortgage
cannot be determined with mathematical accuracy,
yet a sufficiently close approximation can be made to
enable the sum to be fixed.

The costs, to be adjusted, will, therefore, be inserted

only in the supplementary decree, and, should there
remain a surplus, it will be disposed of by that decree,
as directed by the sections last mentioned.

Westchester County. — Hon. OWEN T. COFFIN,
Surrogate.—February, 1885.

HAWLEY v. SINGER.

*In the matter of the judicial settlement of the account
of* David Hawley, *as guardian and trustee,
under the will of* Isaac M. Singer, *deceased, of*
Adam M. Singer.

A trustee, *durante minore ætate*, is entitled to commissions on amounts
received by him after the *cestui que trust* has arrived at full age and
become entitled to the possession of the fund, until his duties are
terminated by a final judicial settlement of his accounts.
Estate of Pirnie, *Tucker*, 119—disapproved.
Cowing v. Howard, 46 *Barb.*, 579—distinguished.
A statute establishing a rate of commissions allowable to trustees is not in
the nature of a contract, so as to remain in force, notwithstanding the
repeal thereof, as to one who assumed the duties of a trust before such
repeal.
It seems, that no commissions are allowable to an executor upon the value
of articles specifically bequeathed.
While a Surrogate's court has not power to open and reconsider, on the
ground of legal error, an adjudication already made, still where full
commissions have been inadvertently awarded on a fund as received
and paid out, when in truth it had been received and not paid out,
such a tribunal may, in a subsequent accounting, take cognizance of
the fact, and decline to award half commissions again for paying out.
Where the accounts of executors or administrators are subjected to successive judicial settlements, they are entitled, on the first accounting,
to full commissions on all moneys received and paid out, and half
commissions only on moneys received and not paid out; on the second,

they are allowed the other half on moneys since paid out, and full
commissions on the increase received and paid out, or directed by the
decree to be paid; taking care, however, that the total award shall not
exceed what would have been full commissions, had the whole estate
been finally settled, on one accounting.

The executor of decedent's will, who was also trustee of a trust thereby
created for the benefit of an infant during his minority, had an
accounting in 1877, in the former capacity, on which he was allowed
full commissions upon the entire amount of the estate, which was then
more than $9,000,000. In 1881, he accounted as trustee, and was
allowed full commissions upon the amount of the trust fund, which
was one sixth of the residue. The *cestui que trust* having reached his
majority, and proceedings having been instituted for the judicial
settlement of the trustee's account, with a view to the transfer of the
fund, now about $1,500,000, to the beneficiary,—

Held, that the only compensation allowable to the accounting party was
commissions at the rate of one per cent. on the amount of increase
since the last accounting.

AFTER bequeathing certain legacies, and making
some other provisions, Isaac M. Singer, deceased, by
his will, directed the residue of his estate to be divided into sixty parts, ten of which were given to his
son, Adam Mortimer Singer, then a minor, but who
recently attained his majority. The will contained
this clause :

'*Eighth.* I hereby nominate and appoint my said
executors guardians and trustees of the estate of
such of the above named legatees as are under the
age of twenty-one years at the time of my decease,
to continue such guardians and trustees until said
legatees shall respectively arrive at that age."

There were two executors named, but one died
before the will was proved, leaving David Hawley
the sole survivor. The share of said Adam M. Singer
was now payable to him, and this was an accounting
in reference thereto. The chief question arising was
in regard to the amount of commissions to which Mr.

Hawley was entitled. He rendered and settled his account as executor in 1877, when he received full commissions on the whole fund, which then amounted to between $9,000,000 and $10,000,000. Again there was an accounting, as to the share in question, in 1881, on which occasion he received, substantially, full commissions thereon as trustee. It was insisted that he could not be permitted to have them again. The proceeding on the accounting of 1881 was commenced in June, 1880, before the repeal of the act of 1866 (ch. 115).

Objection was made to certain charges for clerk hire, office rent, etc., amounting to some $330 per annum; also to certain items of charges for fees paid to counsel for services rendered, or to be rendered, in this proceeding.

F. N. BANGS, *for executor.*

C. E. TRACY, *for objector.*

THE SURROGATE.—In view of the fact that the Court of Appeals held, in the case of Hood v. Hood (85 *N. Y.,* 561), that the person named to execute the will of the deceased, who was a non-resident, and, as such, gave the bond required by the statute, in such case, was, for the purpose of fixing the liability of his sureties, simply an executor and not a trustee; and that the same Court, in 90 *N. Y.,* 512, intimated that the same person might be a trustee; that the Supreme Court, in 19 *Hun,* 300, decided that the same individual was not a trustee under the will, and again, in 33 *Hun,* 338, that he was; and also in view of the case of Johnson v. Lawrence (95 *N. Y.*, 154) reversing the judgment below on the same point; and of numerous other cases upon the subject, it is not an easy matter, amid all this apparent confusion and conflict, to determine, with any degree of assured accuracy, whether a person named to execute the provisions of a will continues to be an executor until the final closing up of the estate, or whether, at a certain point, his duties as executor have ceased and he becomes clothed with the office of trustee. This will, doubtless, continue to be a vexed question, unless legislative wisdom shall interpose, and declare no one to be a trustee under a last will and testament, unless appointed to execute one of the trusts allowed to be created by the statute of Uses and Trusts, and that, in all other cases, he shall be merely an executor. I made an unsuccessful attempt to establish some such rule in the case of Meeker v. Crawford (5 *Redf.*, 450). All that can now be done in this regard, by an inferior tribunal, is to follow the latest decision of the court of last resort.

The executor had an accounting, as such, in 1877, when he was allowed full commissions on the whole amount of the estate; again, in 1881, he had another accounting as trustee, and received full commissions on the whole of the contestant's fund, and is now, as it seems to me, entitled to them on the increase, only, since the last accounting. This leads to a consideration of the question, as to whether full commissions can again be allowed under the act of 1866 (chap. 115); the language being that "on *all* such accountings of such trustees, the Surrogate, before whom such accounting may be had, shall allow to the trustee or trustees, the same compensation for his or their services, by way of commissions, as are allowed by law to executors and administrators." The statute, if now applicable, would authorize an allowance to him of only such commissions as could be granted to an executor or administrator. The latter frequently have a second and a third accounting. In such cases, they are entitled, on the first accounting, to full commissions on all moneys received and paid out, and half commissions only on moneys received and not paid out. On the second accounting, they are allowed the other half, on money since paid out, and full commissions on the increase received and paid out, or directed by the decree to be paid; taking care, however, that all of such commissions shall not exceed what would have been the full commissions had the whole estate been settled on one final accounting. That is the mode in which commissions are allowed on "all accountings" of executors and administrators; and it seems to me that is all which is contemplated, in reference to the compensation of trustees, by the act of 1866. I therefore, reach a conclusion different from that arrived at in the Estate of Pirnie (*Tucker*, 119). That act, however, was repealed in 1880; but, notwithstanding such repeal, the question remains whether, the trustee having assumed the duties of the trust while it was in force, his rate of compensation can legally be diminished; whether it was not in the nature of a contract between himself and the deceased, which cannot be disregarded without doing violence to a provision of fundamental law. I think not. Before there was a provision to the contrary, a public elective officer, entering upon the discharge of his duties at a certain rate of compensation, could not successfully resist a legislative enactment reducing it, upon the ground that there was an implied contract, between him and those who elected him, to the effect that he was to have the usual salary theretofore pertaining to the office (see People v. Burrows, 27 *Barb.*, 89). It is well settled that costs shall be allowed to a party at the rate fixed by the law in force at the time the verdict or decision is rendered, whether such rate shall have been increased or diminished since the action was commenced. The law allowing commissions to executors was enacted in 1817. One who entered upon his duties prior to that date, but rendered his account after it, would undoubtedly have been entitled to his commissions under that act. But this is immaterial to the decision of this case, if the view above expressed, that a trustee can have only such commissions as an executor, be sound.

It is objected that the executor should not have commissions on the shares of stock in the Singer Manufacturing company bequeathed to the contestant by the testator. The ground of the objection is that an executor cannot be permitted to receive them on the value of articles specifically bequeathed. The objection would be good, if there were such specific bequest. But I think there was not. The question, however, strikes me as also immaterial. The executor, as such, having already had full commissions on it in 1877, and also as trustee in 1881, cannot, under the views above expressed, be suffered to have them again. While this court may not have the power to open and reconsider an adjudication already made, still, where full commissions have been inadvertently awarded on a fund as received and paid out, when in truth it had been received and not paid out, it possesses the power, in a subsequent accounting, to take cognizance of the fact, and to decline to award half commissions again for paying out. It cannot compel a refunding in any other way, of any excess he may have received, nor deprive him of his right to them on the increase. All, therefore, that can be properly awarded here, in this regard, are commissions, at the rate of one per cent., on the amount of increase since the last accounting.

The contestant, however, objects that commissions should not be allowed on amounts received by the executor since he became of age, and entitled to the possession of the stock and other property. To sustain this objection, he refers to the case of Cowing v. Howard (46 *Barb.*, 579). The views embraced in the opinion were given with reference to the fact that the defendant was an involuntary trustee, stress being laid upon the further fact that he was not a voluntary trustee, as the executor is here. Although the result of the opinion was that an involuntary trustee was not entitled to commissions, yet the majority of the court held otherwise, and they were allowed. There can be no doubt that the executor should continue to discharge his duties until they are terminated by a final judicial settlement of his accounts. Take the ordinary case of several general legacies which are payable at the end of one year, after which they draw interest. At the end of the year, the executor, having the fund invested, for some reason fails to have his accounting, but continues to collect and receive the interest on the securities in which the fund is so invested; when he does render his account voluntarily or by coercion, he will be entitled to commissions on the amount of increase that has accumulated since the legacies became due.

Items for money paid by the executor to counsel, as a retainer or otherwise, for services in this proceeding, must be disallowed. The only compensation he can be granted, as against the estate or fund, is such as the statute permits to be taxed as costs; and to those he is entitled.

I think the items for clerk hire, office rent, etc., objected to by the contestant, should also be allowed. Considering the magnitude of the fund, amounting now, owing to the prudent management of the executor, to about $1,500,000, and the necessity of accuracy in the accounts kept in relation to it, the expenditures seem to have been justifiable and for the benefit of the estate.

Costs are awarded to both parties out of the fund.

Decreed accordingly.

WESTCHESTER COUNTY.—HON. OWEN T. COFFIN,
SURROGATE.—March, 1885.

VALENTINE v. VALENTINE.

*In the matter of the judicial settlement of the account
of* SAMUEL H. VALENTINE, *and another, as executors of the will of* SAMUEL M. VALENTINE,
deceased executor of the will of ABRAHAM VAL-
ENTINE, *deceased.*

The courts cannot take judicial notice of the aptitude of bonds and mortgages to escape the vigilance of the taxing officer.

Testator's will authorized the executor, as trustee, to invest funds in bonds
and mortgages on real estate in the State of New York, at the best
available interest, or in the public stocks of the State of New York, or
of the United States. The trustee accordingly purchased, from time
to time, at a premium, U. S. bonds of a par value of over $40,000,
which being paid off, the premium disappeared and a shrinkage in
value occurred, between 1870 and 1885, of more than $6,000. It was
contended that the trustee was liable for the loss, by reason of mis-
management, and that, under the will, he could lawfully invest in the
stocks named, only on failing to find suitable investments in bonds
secured by mortgage on real property.—

Held, that the terms of the will did not indicate the preference contended
for; and that the trustee was not liable for the decrease in the value
of the fund, especially as it appeared that the shrinkage in the principal was more than offset by advantages secured in point of income.

The burden of impeaching the justness of disbursements, made by a trustee for expenses of administration, is upon the party objecting thereto.

ABRAHAM VALENTINE died leaving a will of which
Samuel M. Valentine, his son, became sole executor.
Among other things, the will devised a life estate in
a dwelling house in the city of New York to Jane
Valentine, the widow of a deceased son, which the
executor was directed, out of certain funds, to keep

in repair, and to pay the taxes and insurance premiums thereon. He also gave to said Jane Valentine an annuity of $2,000, to be secured out of funds ultimately given to her children. In the year 1870, an accounting was had before the then Surrogate of Westchester county, which resulted in the payment, to each of her children, of about $15,000, and the setting apart of a certain amount in securities then deemed sufficient to produce an income that would pay the annuity, and also the taxes, insurance and the cost of repairs to the dwelling house so devised. This fund consisted of $40,000, par value, U. S. bonds, which cost $42,975, and a bond and mortgage of $7,536. The latter was subsequently paid off, and the amount invested in U. S. bonds. As the bonds matured, they were paid off at their face value, the premium paid for them being thus lost. The proceeds were again invested in like bonds commanding a premium, and when paid off by the government, the premium paid was, in like manner lost. During much of the period, the gold, in which the interest was paid, was at a fluctuating premium. The account filed shows the present amount of the fund to be $44,100.

The will authorized the executor to invest the funds of the estate in bonds and mortgages on real estate in the State of New York, at the best available interest, or in the public stocks of the State of New York, or of the United States.

The executor and trustee having died in 1884, Abraham B. Valentine was appointed in his place, and this accounting was had at his instance. Among other things, it was insisted on his behalf that the executor of the deceased trustee should be compelled to pay $6,411, being the difference between the original amount of the fund and the amount now on hand. Other questions are indicated in the opinion.

The greater part of the estate was situated in the city of New York, where the deceased executor resided.

WM. G. VALENTINE, *and* EDWARD WELLS, *for trustee.*

M. S. THOMPSON, *for ex'rs of S. M. Valentine, deceased.*

THE SURROGATE. — At the date of the decree in 1870, the executor had in his hands $40,000 of 5-20 U. S. bonds—

Which cost	$42,975
He also had a bond and mortgage for . . .	7,536
Amounting to	$50,511

Which sum he was directed to retain and keep invested, and to pay from the income the annuity of $2,000, to Jane Valentine, and the taxes, insurance and repairs on a house devised to her. The mode of investment at the date of that decree does not appear to have been objected to, and was sanctioned by the court. Of the above sum of $50,511, there remains now, and is accounted for, only $44,100, being a shrinkage of $6,411. It is claimed that the executor should restore this amount, it being alleged that he has mismanaged the estate by investing in U. S. bonds, instead of in bonds and mortgages, the shrinkage being caused by investing in such bonds at a premium, and ultimately receiving their par value only. The executor charges himself with the sum of $39,911, for interest received. If he had steadily received interest at legal rates on the fund invested on bond and mortgage, it would have amounted to about $47,500; from which would be deducted taxes at the rate of two and one quarter per cent., equal to about $14,973, and there would have remained $32,507 of income, instead of $39,911.64; leaving a difference, so far as income is concerned, of $7,404.64, in favor of the mode in which the fund was invested. Thus the executor was enabled to pay the widow her annuity, the taxes, insurance and repairs on her house, and also to pay over, as surplus income, nearly $4,000, to the remaindermen; whereas, if it had been kept invested on bond and mortgage, under the most favorable circumstances, the income would have been insufficient to pay the annuity, taxes, etc., and an encroachment upon the principal would have been necessary, to the extent of the sum of $3,514; thus reducing the principal to about $47,000. If we deduct from this the $4,000 paid to the remaindermen, the fund would have been further reduced to about $43,000. Hence, the amount of the shrinkage is apparently more than compensated by the manner in which the investments were made and managed. It is claimed, however, that we should lay out of consideration the fact that bonds and mortgages were subject to taxation, as that species of property is apt to escape the vigilance of those upon whom the duty of imposing the tax rests. This, I think, we are not at liberty to do. It must be presumed that public officers will properly perform their duty, and cause all taxable property to pay its just share of the expenses of government.

The will authorized the executor to invest the fund on bond and mortgage on real estate, at the best attainable interest, or in the public stocks of the State of New York, or of the United States. It is claimed that, because the testator named the investment on bond and mortgage first, he thus indicated that as the course which should have been adopted by the executor, if practicable, and that he could only resort to the other modes, in the order named, on failing to find suitable investments under the first. I think, however, that the duty of the executor was to adopt either, alternatively, which, in the exercise of a sound discretion, he deemed to be best calculated to produce the most favorable results to the beneficiaries. As it seems to me, the deceased executor pursued just that course. Had he invested on bond and mortgage solely, the deduction of taxes would have rendered it necessary to resort to the principal of the fund, for moneys to pay the annuity, and the taxes, insurance and repairs on the house devised to Mrs. Jane Valentine; whereas the actual result now is that, while the original amount of the fund has been apparently diminished by legitimate causes, yet the charges upon it have been fully met by income, of which there was a surplus of nearly $4,000, which went into the pockets of those ultimately entitled to the fund, after paying the sum of over $6,000, for taxes, insurance and repairs. As far as can be discovered, no result more favorable to the beneficiaries could have been attained by the adoption of any of the other modes of investment authorized by the will. The account must, therefore, stand, in this respect, as rendered.

I think the credit claimed for $100, paid to counsel, should be allowed. A proper voucher is filed therefor, and no evidence to impeach it has been offered. It is simply an expense of administration, and is to be treated as any similar expense—such as for witnesses' fees, appraisers' fees, travelling expenses, copies of documents, payment of taxes, for insurance, and the like. The burthen of impeaching the justness of such expenditures is upon the contestant. It was so held in the case of Fowler v. Lockwood (3 *Redf.*, 465).

An item of credit for $162.80, for taxes paid, is objected to, on the ground that it was a tax against the individual property of the deceased executor. Of that, however, there is no evidence. The item is stated as the amount paid for taxes on personal property in 1871. As the bond and mortgage of $7,536 was then outstanding, it was, doubtless, the amount of the tax on it, at the rate of a fraction over two and one quarter per cent.

It is also insisted that the deceased executor's estate is chargeable with interest, at the rate of six per cent., on $44,100 from October 1st, 1882, when the bonds in which it was theretofore invested were called in and paid, and the amount deposited in trust companies, which paid three and one half per cent. interest, only. This disposition of the fund, it is urged by contestant, was not an investment of it at all, nor in compliance with the provisions of the will on the subject. However that may be,—however a trustee may be chargeable with a breach of duty, he cannot be held accountable therefor, unless some injury or loss has resulted therefrom. The amount of the principal has not been diminished thereby, and the income produced has been as great as if it had been invested on bond and mortgage. During the period it was so deposited, the evidence shows that the rate of interest on loans on mortgage was five per cent. If we deduct two per cent. for taxes, there would be an income of three per cent., only, thus showing an advantage of the half of one per cent., in favor of the course adopted.

The executors of the deceased trustee are, according to the tenor of recent decisions, entitled to full commissions.

Costs, to be taxed, are allowed to both parties, out of the fund.

WESTCHESTER COUNTY.—HON. OWEN T. COFFIN, SURROGATE.—March, 1885.

MITCHELL v. PRESB. CHURCH.

In the matter of the judicial settlement of the account of WILLIAM R. J. MITCHELL, *as administrator with the will of* PETER P. REID, *deceased, annexed.*

The *cy pres* power is not exercised by any court of this State.

Testator's will contained the following clause: "And I also reserve five hundred dollars for an *arbor vitæ* hedge around the plot in burying ground, and for other things necessary about the plot, and what is remaining of the above (500) five hundred to be given to some Sunday school Rye Presbyterian or charitable institution."—

Held, that the testator intended to make a bequest for a religious or charitable use; but that, he having failed to point out any corporate or natural person who could maintain an action to recover the legacy, the court could not supply the defect; and that the residue of the $500 fell into the residue of the estate.

THE testator, by his will, provided as follows : " And I also reserve five hundred dollars for an *arbor vitœ* hedge around the plot in burying ground, and for other things necessary about the plot, and what is remaining of the above (500) five hundred to be given to some Sunday School, Rye Presbyterian or charitable institution."

Only twenty-five dollars was expended for the hedge, and in doing other necessary things about the plot, and there remains four hundred and seventy-five dollars, which is claimed by a religious corporation known, as incorporated, as "The trustees of the Presbyterian church of the town of Rye, in Westchester County." There is no other Presbyterian church in that town, and the testator, in his lifetime attended that church. He appointed Thomas M. Mitchell executor of his will, who entered upon his duties, but never designated any object as the donee of the residue of said five hundred dollars. He died, and the present accounting party was appointed administrator with the will annexed.

D. HAIGHT, *for administrator.*

C. P. COWLES, *for Presbyterian church.*

THE SURROGATE.—It is now well settled that an incorporated school, society or body, is incompetent to take a legacy. There must be an incorporation, to enable the courts to enforce the payment, and the execution of the trust by a proper application of the money. True, the will does not declare the purpose for which the bequest was made, but it was, undoubtedly, for a religious or charitable one. The executor took the money, but he was not appointed the trustee to apply it to any use, nor was he, in terms, authorized to make a selection of the beneficiary to which it should be paid, and he made no such selection. If he ever had the power to do that, it did not devolve on the administrator with the will annexed. That seems to be conceded. The court is here virtually asked to do it, but the *cy pres* power is not now exercised by any court of this State. It cannot designate " some Sunday School " with the option of selecting, among others, " the Rye Presbyterian; " nor any charitable institution. The testator should have done that. He failed to point out any person or corporate body as legatee who can maintain an action for the recovery of the legacy. The amount of it will, therefore, fall into the residuum, and pass to the legal representative of the deceased executor, Thomas M. Mitchell, who is named in the will as residuary legatee.

Decreed accordingly.

WESTCHESTER COUNTY.—HON. OWEN T. COFFIN,
SURROGATE.—April, 1885.

COBB v. McCORMICK.

In the matter of the judicial settlement of the account of LYMAN COBB, JR., *as executor of, and testamentary trustee under the will of* JOHN McCORMICK, *deceased.*

Testator, who died in 1869, leaving a small estate consisting exclusively of real property, by his will, bequeathed $1,000 to his son M. ; devised the residue to his widow for life, with remainder to his children ; and devised his real property to his executors in trust to pay debts and legacies, with power of sale. The widow and all the children except M. resided on the real property until 1884, when, the former having died, the executor made a sale of the property which yielded $2,000, whereof M. claimed about $1,900 for the principal of his legacy, and interest thereon.—

Held, that the will would have been properly performed, if the executors had made a sale within a year from the grant of letters, paid M.'s legacy, and invested the balance for the widow ; that M.'s omission to enforce his rights having been tantamount to an agreement to waive the use of the legacy in favor of his mother, he could not now recover from his brothers and sisters what he had given to her ; and that his legacy was payable without interest.

THE testator died in the fall of 1869, leaving a last will and testament, which was admitted to probate in December of the same year. He left a widow and five children, two sons and three daughters, the youngest of whom is Martin McCormick. All of the property left by him consisted of real estate. The will directed the payment of his debts, and then, among other things, provided as follows :

"*Second.*—I give and bequeath to my son, Martin,

in addition to the bequest hereinafter mentioned, the sum of one thousand dollars.

"*Third.*—I give and devise all the rest, residue and remainder of all my real and personal estate, to my wife Catherine, to be used and enjoyed by her during the term of her natural life; and should the income of my said estate be insufficient for the proper maintenance and support of my said wife, then and in such case so much of the principal thereof as may be necessary, shall be used and applied to such support and maintenance. And from and immediately after the decease of my said wife, I give and devise the. said residue and remainder of my real and personal estate to my children, her surviving, to be divided equally between them, share and share alike . . . . .

"*Fourth.*—I give and devise all of my real and personal estate to Levi W. Flagg and Lyman Cobb, Jr., the executors of this my last will and testament hereinafter nominated and appointed, *in trust,* for the payment of my just debts and the legacies above specified, with power to sell and dispose of the same at public or private sale, at such time or times, and upon such terms and in such manner as to them shall seem meet."

The executor Flagg was dead.

R. E. PRIME, *for surviving executor.*

A. J. HYATT,,*for Patrick McCormick and other legatees.*

THE SURROGATE.—No testimony has been taken in this matter, but it is conceded that the widow and all of the children, except Martin, continued to reside on the real estate devised after the death of the testator, until the death of the widow, which occurred in April, 1884, the others still remaining there.   The property was sold by the surviving executor in February last. Martin McCormick, who had resided since his father's death in the city of New York, purchased the property for $2,250, from which were deducted taxes and assessments, which reduced the amount to $2,126.46. The account filed shows the whole sum on hand for distribution, without the deduction of commissions and expenses of accounting, etc., to be $2,178.01, and after such deduction, $1,995.30.   Of this sum, Martin claims there should be paid to him $1,915, being the amount of his legacy of $1,000 and interest thereon, leaving a balance of $80.30, to be divided equally among all the children.   The contestants contend that he should not be allowed interest.   This is the only question presented for consideration.

It would seem that the will operates an equitable conversion of the land into money, especially when viewed in the light of the fact that the testator left no personal estate.   The language used may be interpreted by the aid of surrounding circumstances.   That is a fact, taken in connection with the bequest of a legacy of $1,000 to Martin, which goes to show that a conversion was contemplated by the testator. 'How else was that legacy to be paid?   If this view be correct, then during all these years he, by acquiescing in the occupation of the premises by his mother, permitted her to enjoy what was equivalent to the interest of his legacy.   If, on the other hand, the will operated no equitable conversion, then his legacy was charged upon the real estate. It became due and payable one year from the date of the letters, and he could then have taken measures to enforce its payment. It must be assumed that he was cognizant of the situation of the estate, and that his father left no assets. He, therefore, knew that the real estate was the only source from which his legacy could be realized, and yet he permitted his mother, during her life, to enjoy the whole without question. This was tantamount to an agreement on his part to waive his use of the legacy in favor of his mother. And she had it. If she so had it with his consent, how can he now be entitled to it again, as against his brother and sisters? He cannot be permitted to recover from them what he had thus given away. The will would have been properly executed if the trustees had sold the real estate within the year, paid the debts and Martin's legacy out of the proceeds, and invested the residue for the benefit of the widow; and then, at her death, to have distributed what remained among all the children. But Martin took no steps, during all this time, to compel such execution. Probably it was by general consent of all, and if so, to their credit, that the mother was permitted to enjoy the whole of the little property. If he were now to bring an action against the executor to recover his legacy, under the circumstances, I think he would not be allowed the interest claimed, because he would be estopped by his acquiescence in the enjoyment of the whole estate, in which his legacy was embraced, by others.

For these reasons, I think the decree should direct the payment of the principal of the legacy only.

WESTCHESTER COUNTY.—HON. OWEN T. COFFIN, SURROGATE.—July, 1885.

BURKHALTER v. NORTON.

In the matter of the judicial settlement of the account of JOHN NORTON, *as administrator of the estate of* MARY D. HOYT, *deceased.*

The Surrogate's court is the only forum where even the question of the individual liability of a sole administrator, upon an alleged indebtedness to the intestate, can be determined.

One N., who was indebted to decedent, at the time of his death, in the amount of a promissory note for $222.50, and interest, was appointed administrator of his estate, and omitted this item of indebtedness from the inventory and from the account filed by him as such administrator. Upon a judicial settlement, certain creditors objecting to the omission, it appeared that the debt had not been discharged, and that N. was totally insolvent.—

Held, that the administrator stood in the same position as any other debtor; that the amount of the claim should be added to the sum of the inventory; and that, in case he subsequently became possessed of means, he might be compelled to account for, and pay over the amount, in the same manner as if he had, after an accounting, recovered, from a third person, a doubtful claim, for which he had received credit thereupon.

ON the accounting in this matter, it appeared that the assets of the intestate were insufficient to pay her debts. Some of the creditors objected that the administrator had omitted, from the inventory and from the account, the amount of a promissory note for

$222.50, which the deceased held against the administrator, together with interest thereon. The latter alleged that the note had been paid by him to the deceased, during her life time. The question thus raised was tried, and, upon the proofs taken, it was determined that the administrator was indebted, in the amount of the note, to the deceased, at the time of her death. It was proved, during the controversy, that the administrator was a man of no pecuniary means, and was unable to pay anything.

FRANCIS LARKIN, *for administrator.*

RALPH E. PRIME, *for Stephen Burkhalter and others, creditors.*

THE SURROGATE.—It appears to be an undisputed fact that the administrator was and is insolvent, and that the debt established against him is uncollectible. It is, therefore, claimed on his behalf that, although his indebtedness is established, yet he should be credited with the amount thereof, as in the case of any other uncollected and uncollectible claim. To prove his inability to collect it by legal process was impossible, as he could not sue himself, and this is the only forum where even the question of his liability could be determined (Churchill v. Prescott, 3 *Bradf.*, 233). He now stands in the same position as any other debtor to the deceased, the amount of whose indebtedness was omitted from the inventory, and his liability therefor, as administrator, is to be determined in the same manner. The amount of the claim should be added to the sum of the inventory, and then the same, if the debtor proved to be insolvent, should be credited to the administrator.

The administrator stands, too, in the same position as any other debtor, in this respect. Should he become possessed of means to pay his indebtedness, he may be compelled, by the parties in interest, to account for, and pay over the amount thereof, in the same manner as if he had, after an accounting, recovered a doubtful claim from a third person, for which he had received credit on such accounting.

The decree will be entered in accordance with these views.

NEW YORK COUNTY.— HON. D. G. ROLLINS, SURROGATE.—July, 1885.

MORGAN *v.* MORGAN.

In the matter of the estate of LUCINDA L. MORGAN, *deceased.*

Neither "poverty" nor "insolvency" being specified, in Code Civ. Pro.. § 2817, as grounds for the removal of a testamentary trustee, the entry of an order, requiring the giving of the security prescribed by id., §§ 2638, 2815, and neglect or refusal to comply with such order, are essential preliminaries to the Surrogate's removal of such a trustee upon the ground of insolvency.

In order to justify the removal of a testamentary trustee, upon the ground that, by an improper application of trust moneys, or an investment in securities unauthorized by law, he has demonstrated his unfitness for the due execution of his trust, within the meaning of Code Civ. Pro., § 2817, it must appear that his acts have been such as to endanger the trust property, or to show a want of honesty, or of proper capacity, or of reasonable fidelity.

M., one of two trustees under decedent's will, being the owner of an undivided interest in certain real property in the city of New York, conveyed the same to one P., who thereupon executed a first mortgage thereof to the trustees to secure a loan of $35,000, the proceeds of which came to the hands of M., and were subsequently used in the business of a firm of which the trustees were members. The mortgage afforded adequate protection for the repayment of the loan, and, for aught that the evidence disclosed, yielded a rate of interest as large as was obtainable at the time when the loan was effected. Upon an application to remove the trustees for a breach of trust, by reason of the premises,—

Held, that though they might have become amenable to some of the consequences which follow from a trustee's acting in any manner for his own benefit, in regard to the subject of his trust, the trustees had not been guilty of any such palpable breach of trust as to demonstrate their unfitness, under Code Civ. Pro., § 2817, to be continued in office, and that the application must, accordingly, be denied.

PETITION of Matthew Morgan, an infant beneficiary under decedent's will, by James N. Platt, his guardian *ad litem,* for the removal of Henry Morgan and another, from office as testamentary trustees under said will. The facts appear sufficiently in the opinion.

PLATT & BOWERS, *for special guardian.*

EVARTS, CHOATE & BEAMAN, *for trustees.*

THE SURROGATE.—This is an application for the removal of Henry Morgan and Edward Morgan as testamentary trustees of several trusts created by the will of Lucinda L. Morgan, deceased. The petitioner, a grandson of the testatrix, is entitled, so long as his uncle, Matthew Morgan, shall live, to one twenty-fourth part of the income of a certain fund of $125,000. Upon the death of Matthew Morgan, the principal of that fund is to go to his children, if any shall survive him, and to the issue of any children deceased; in case there shall be no such children or issue, then to a class in which this petitioner, if living, will be included.

The securities in which the funds of this trust are invested are not in the hands of either of the persons whose removal is here sought, but are in the sole possession of their co-trustee, Mr. Charles E. Butler. The respondents allege, and the petitioner does not deny, that these funds are intact, and that Mr. Butler's pecuniary responsibility is abundantly assured. The petitioner has, moreover, a contingent interest in certain other trusts created by decedent's will, the funds of which trusts are now under the control of the respondents, and are contained in the vaults of safe deposit and trust companies.

The alleged grounds upon which this application for removal chiefly rests, and the only ones that seem to me worthy of consideration, are these:

1st. That in June, 1884, these respondents failed in business, and have ever since been hopelessly insolvent.

2nd. That they have applied to their own use certain moneys belonging to the trusts above specified.

First.—The fact of the insolvency of these respondents is admitted by their answer. Does that fact of itself call for their removal? There are English decisions which recognize the bankruptcy or insolvency of a testamentary trustee as, *ipso facto,* a just cause for depriving him of his trust. The rigor of this rule has of late been somewhat relaxed, and the question of removal or non-removal for such a cause is now, in any given case, determined according to its peculiar facts and circumstances.

In the courts of this country, insolvency seems to

have been generally regarded as insufficient ground for the removal of a trustee, unless by reason of it the trust funds have been brought into jeopardy. Within the limitations of the Code of Civil Procedure, I greatly doubt whether a testamentary trustee can lawfully be removed by the Surrogate, on account of the precariousness of his pecuniary circumstances, until he has first neglected or refused to comply with an order requiring him to give security for the protection of his *cestuis que trustent*. Neither poverty nor insolvency is named in § 2817, as one of the grounds for which a removal may be made; but among those grounds the failure of a trustee to give bond as required by a decree of the Surrogate, made in pursuance of § 2815, is distinctly specified.

Section 2815 declares that, upon the disclosure of any facts respecting a testamentary trustee which, if shown to exist in the case of an executor, would justify an order requiring him to furnish security as a condition of receiving letters testamentary, such security may be in like manner exacted from such testamentary trustee. This refers, of course, to § 2638, which provides, among other things, for the giving of a bond by an executor, when "his circumstances are such that they do not afford adequate security" for the due administration of his trust.

I hold, therefore, that the entry of an order requiring the giving of security, and neglect or refusal to comply with such order, are essential preliminaries to the Surrogate's removal of a trustee upon the ground of insolvency. Those preliminaries are here wanting.

Second.—Should this petition be granted on account of the action of the respondents in investing $35,000 of the funds in their hands in the New York hotel mortgage? Was that investment, within the meaning of § 2817, "an improper application" of trust moneys, or an investment in "securities unauthorized by law?" And if it was, does the act of the trustees in relation to it show them to be, within the meaning of such section, "unfit for the due execution of their trust?"

It seems to me that the words last quoted must be regarded as a legislative sanction of a familiar doctrine of equity jurisprudence which is expressed by Judge STORY (2 Eq. Jur., § 1289), in these words:

"It is not every mistake or neglect of duty or inaccuracy of conduct which will induce courts of equity" to remove a trustee. "The acts or omissions must be such as to endanger the trust property, or to show a want of honesty or of proper capacity or of reasonable fidelity" (see, also, Thompson v. Thompson, 2 *B. Mon.*, 245; Lathrop v. Smalley, 23 *N. J. Eq.*, 192; Matthews v. Murchison, 17 *Fed. Rep.*, 760).

Now, there is little or no controversy as to the facts connected with the investment in question. Henry Morgan, being the owner of an undivided fourteenth part of the New York Hotel property, conveyed the same, in May, 1884, to Joseph B. Pigot, who thereupon executed a mortgage to these trustees to secure a loan of $35,000. The proceeds of this loan came to the hands of Henry Morgan, and were subsequently used in the business of M. Morgan's

Sons, a firm whereof both these respondents were members. Apart from the fact that they themselves were in effect the borrowers of funds held by them as trustees, their conduct in this transaction is not assailed and is apparently not assailable. The investment was such an one as is approved by the courts of this State, to wit, a first mortgage upon real property. The mortgage seems to afford adequate protection for the repayment of the loan, and, for aught that is disclosed in the papers before me, the rate of interest which was agreed upon between the parties was as large as was obtainable at the time such loan was effected.

Whatever adverse criticism may properly be made upon the course of the respondents in this matter of the Pigot loan, they are deserving of less severe censure than they would have merited if they had exposed the trust funds to the hazards of any speculative enterprise, or had applied them to their own use upon their mere personal security. It is true that the proceeds of the loan were employed in ways that they presumably expected would lead to their private advantage, and they may, accordingly, have become amenable to some of the consequences which follow from a trustee's acting or contracting in any manner for his own benefit in regard to the subject of his trust. To recognize the right of a trustee to lend to himself, directly or indirectly, and even upon undoubted security, the funds committed to his care, would be to open a door to many and palpable mischiefs.

This petitioner claims that the moneys loaned upon the seeurity of the Pigot mortgage have never lost their character as trust funds, and that the *cestuis que trustent* may now insist, at their option, upon charging the respondents with interest thereon at a high rate, or upon claiming all profits and advantages that such respondents may have derived from the transaction. Whether this contention is sound or not, need not here be determined. In the settlement of the respondents' accounts, it may be hereafter the subject of consideration. But, assuming that they have transgressed the strict line of their duty, they have not, in my judgment, been guilty of any such palpable breach of trust as to demonstrate their "unfitness," under § 2817, to be continued in office. The remedy which the law affords a *cestui que trust*, of bringing about, in a proper case, the removal of his trustee is prospective in its character, and has for its chief, if not indeed for its exclusive object, the future security and good management of the trust estate (Hill on Trustees, 190). Such a remedy is not needed in the case at bar, for there is no cause for apprehension that the retention in office of these respondents, until the termination of the proceeding pending in the Supreme Court for their accounting and discharge, is likely to put in the slightest jeopardy the rights of this petitioner or of the other *cestuis que trustent* whose combined interests are much larger than his own, and who favor the retention rather than the removal of the offending trustees.

My resolution to deny this petition is confirmed by

a fact to which I have already adverted. Before the day of its filing, the respondents evinced their purpose of voluntarily surrendering these trusts, and, to that end, instituted proceedings in the Supreme Court. Those proceedings may be pushed to a speedy termination, and the petitioner may thus obtain in substance the very relief for which he here prays.

Petition denied.

NEW YORK COUNTY.—HON. D. G. ROLLINS, SURRO-GATE.—July, 1885.

BEEKMAN *v.* VANDERVEER.

[No. 2]

In the matter of the estate of BENJAMIN F. BEEKMAN, *deceased.*

The widow of a decedent, who has accepted under her husband's will a legacy bequeathed to her in lieu of dower, is not entitled, as against creditors, even to the extent of the value of her dower interest, to priority of payment. Her claims are superior to those of voluntary legatees, but her husband's debts must be satisfied before any property of his estate can be lawfully applied to the discharge of her legacy.

Babcock v. Stoddard, 3 *T. & C.*, 207; Sanford v. Sanford, 4 *Hun*, 753—followed.

A PREVIOUS phase of this case is reported on page 221, *ante.* The facts are stated in the opinion.

JOHN A. MAPES, *for widow.*

R. J. MOSES, A. P. WHITEHEAD, *and* TREMAIN & TYLER, *for creditors.*

FRANK F. VANDERVEER, *for executor.*

THE SURROGATE.—In conformity with the suggestion in my memorandum of December 22d last, the
creditors of the estate of this decedent have been
made parties to the present proceeding, whereby his
widow applies for an order directing the executors
" to pay to her, on account of the legacy or provision
for her benefit or support, a sum not exceeding the
unpaid value of her dower in the real estate of her
late husband."

It appears that, since Mr. Beekman's death in
1875, the petitioner has never formally elected to
take the testamentary provision for her benefit. Nor
has she, on the other hand, ever asserted a claim
for dower.   Prior to December 1st, 1877, she received and accepted from the executors the sum of
$16,500, as interest on the $100,000 trust fund,
directed to be set apart for her enjoyment during
her life or widowhood, and since that date other
moneys have been paid to her on the same account.
It follows from this state of facts that, unless she is
for some cause entitled to be relieved from the
operation of §§ 13 and 14, tit. 8, ch. 1, part 2 of the
Revised Statutes (3 *Banks, 7th ed.*, 2198), she must
be deemed to have long since accepted her legacy
under the will.   Whether any facts and circumstances exist, which would justify a court of general
equitable jurisdiction in permitting her to renounce

her election, and to be now endowed of the lands of her late husband's estate, or, if such lands have been sold with her concurrence, to be now in her capacity as dowager, compensated out of the proceeds of such sales, need not be here considered. No such relief is asked in the present proceeding, nor is it suggested that this court is competent to grant it.

But the petitioner claims that, even without revoking her election, she is entitled under the will, as a purchaser for value, to receive out of this estate, notwithstanding its property may be inadequate to satisfy in full the demands of creditors, such sum as, taken together with the payments already made to her, shall equal the actual value of her dower interest.

It is insisted, on the other hand, by counsel for the various creditors who have appeared in this proceeding, that the petitioner, by accepting in lieu of dower the bequest made for her by the testator, is precluded, not only from recalling that election, but from avoiding the unfortunate consequences it has probably occasioned in depriving her of any further benefits under the will. They admit that, by her relinquishment of what the law gave her the option to claim, she became a purchaser of whatever interest she acquired as legatee, and that, accordingly, as between herself and those entitled to mere voluntary legacies, that interest is not liable to abatement or contribution for payment of debts; but they insist, nevertheless, that, when all other property applicable to such payment has been exhausted, they may justly look to her for contribution, even to the

extent of the entire extinguishment of her interest
in the estate.

A thorough examination of the authorities bearing
upon this question has led me to the unwelcome conclusion that the prayer of the petitioner must be
denied.   The superior claim of creditors, under similar circumstances to those that exist in the case at
bar, was upheld in Isenhart v. Brown (1 *Edw. Ch.*,
411); Chambers v. Davis (15 *B. Mon.*, 526); Brant's
Will (40 *Mo.*, 226); Steele v. Steele (64 *Ala.*, 462);
Warren v. Morris (4 *Del. Ch.*, 289, 306); Bray v.
Neill's Ex'rs (21 *N. J. Eq.*, 350); Hanna v. Palmer
(6 *Col.*, 156).

The recent decision of the Supreme Court in Babcock v. Stoddard (3 *T. & C.*, 207), and Sanford v.
Sanford (4 *Hun*, 753), the former of which arose in
the Fourth Department and the latter in the Third,
lend strong support to the contention here made in
behalf of the creditors.   By the will under interpretation in Babcock v. Stoddard, the testator gave to his
wife a legacy of $1,000, which, among other bequests,
was declared to be in lieu of dower.   He gave to a
granddaughter a small legacy, and to other grandchildren all the remainder of his estate.   The personal property proved insufficient to pay the debts
and legacies in full.   On application of a creditor,
the Surrogate directed the sale of the real estate of
which the testator died seized, and, as a result of such
sale, there was realized a sum sufficient to pay the
debts, and to leave a balance of over $1,200.   The
widow had previously died without making an election between her dower and the testamentary pro-

vision in her favor. Her executor prayed for the application of the surplus proceeds of the real estate to the $1,000 legacy bequeathed to her by the will, claiming that such bequest, being in lieu of dower, was equitably a charge upon the entire estate. The Surrogate so held, and an order was entered accordingly. On appeal this order was reversed. The court, MULLIN, J., pronouncing the opinion, declared that the only preference allowed to a bequest in lieu of dower was a right of priority over other legacies. The learned Justice expressed his regret, in view of all the facts, that the claim of the widow's representative, which seemed to be founded in reason, was discountenanced by the authorities that he felt bound to follow.

The doctrine of Babcock v. Stoddard was reasserted under somewhat similar circumstances in Sanford v. Sanford (*supra*), and, though JAMES, J., dissented, he did so upon grounds foreign to the present discussion.

If it is the law of this State, as seems to be maintained in the two cases last cited, that, where a testator's estate is inadequate to discharge the debts and satisfy also a bequest to his widow in lieu of dower, mere voluntary devisees, to whom no preference is given by the terms of the will, can avail themselves of the relinquishment of dower and be nevertheless protected against any contribution to pay the consideration for such relinquishment, then, *a fortiori* are the rights of creditors entitled to like protection.

I confess my regret that the conclusion which finds

support in the authority of this long line of cases is not seriously shaken by the decisions relied upon by petitioner's counsel. So far as Thompson v. Egbert (2 *Har.*, *N. J.*, 460) can be regarded as helpful to his contention, it is practically overruled by the later New Jersey case of Bray v. Neill's Ex'rs (*supra*).

Hall's Case (1 *Bland's Ch.*, 203); Gibson v. McCormick (10 *Gil. & J.*, 113); Thomas v. Wood (1 *Md. Ch.*, 300); and Durham v. Rhodes (23 *Md.*, 242), all turn upon the interpretation of a statute which provided that a widow, electing to accept a testamentary provision in lieu of dower, was " to be regarded as a purchaser with a fair consideration."

The Maryland courts have construed this language as putting a widow, to the extent of the dower interest which she has waived by such an election, in the category of a preferred creditor.

Thompson v. McGaw (1 *Met.* [Mass.], 166); Tevis' Ex'rs v. McCreary (3 *Met.* [Ky.], 135); and Hastings v. Clifford (32 *Me.*, 132),—cases not cited by petitioner's counsel,—are based upon statutory enactments which expressly declare that, " if a woman is deprived of the provision made for her, by will or otherwise, in lieu of dower, she may be endowed anew, in like manner as if such provision had not been made." The quotation is from the statute of Massachusetts, which does not essentially differ from that of Kentucky or from that of Maine.

The cases below cited go to the length of asserting that a testamentary provision to a widow in lieu of dower is not subject to abatement, in the first instance, and before other legacies have been exhausted, for the satisfaction of her husband's debts; but they go no further (Heath v. Dendy, 1 *Russ.*, 543; Burridge v. Bradyl, 1 *P. Wms.*, 127; Blower v. Merret, 2 *Ves. Sr.*, 420; Norcott v. Gordon, 14 *Sim.*, 258; Davenhill v. Fletcher, *Ambl.*, 244; Reed v. Reed, 9 *Watts*, 263; Hubbard v. Hubbard, 6 *Met.*, 50; Pollard v. Pollard, 1 *Allen*, 490; Gaw v. Hoffman, 12 *Gratt.*, 628; Howard v. Frances, 30 *N. J. Eq.*, 444; Potter v. Brown, 11 *R. I.*, 232; Lord v. Lord, 23 *Ct.*, 327; Loocock v. Clarkson, 1 *Dess.*, 471; Williamson v. Williamson, 6 *Paige*, 298; Stuart v. Carson, 1 *Dess.*, 500).

In the last case, the opinion of the court contains a single sentence which seems to exalt the claim of the widow to a provision in lieu of dower, even above the claims of creditors. But, as there was no such deficiency of assets as to make impracticable the full satisfaction of debts, the ambiguous words, even if used in the broad sense claimed for them by this petitioner, are merely *obiter dicta*. It is not likely, however, that the decision in Stuart v. Carson was intended to enlarge in the least the doctrine of Loocock v. Clarkson (*supra*), decided by the same court only two months before.

If the weight of authority did not forbid my adopting such a theory, I might regard the situation of this petitioner as fairly entitling her, in her capacity as purchaser of the legacy in her favor, to be treated as a creditor of the estate to the extent of the value of her dower interest, and, as such, to share, *pro rata*, with all the other creditors in all the property to which they are at liberty to resort, the value of her dower interest being taken as the sum upon which her dividend should be calculated. But it would be presumptuous for me to act upon that theory, in the face of the decisions of the Court of Chancery, and of the Supreme Court, in Isenhart v. Brown, Sanford v. Sanford, and Babcock v. Stoddard.

Petition denied.

INDEX.

ABATEMENT.

1. Under Code Civ. Pro., § 765, forbidding the entry of a judgment against a party (to an action) who dies before a verdict, report or decision is actually rendered against him,—made applicable to a Surrogate's court by id., § 3347, subd. 6—a contested accounting proceeding abates, absolutely, by the death of the accounting party before the matters at issue have been substantially decided. *Herbert* v. *Stevenson*, 236.

2. The administrator of a decedent's estate having instituted a special proceeding for the judicial settlement of his account, and a hearing having been had upon exceptions to the report of the referee to whom the account and objections had been referred, the Surrogate, by a written memorandum, announced his conclusions as to certain exceptions, and, as to others, granted leave to the administrator to offer additional evidence, which was introduced. Thereafter the administrator died, before the undetermined issues had been passed upon, and before any decree of settlement had been entered ; whereupon contestants sought to revive the special proceeding against the administratrix of his estate.—*Held*, that the same had abated by the administrator's death ; that no decree could ever be entered therein ; and that the application for revival must be denied. *Id.*

ABATEMENT OF LEGACY.

See Legacy, 4, 5.

ABSENCE.

The provision contained in 2 R. S., 139, § 6, relating to the avoidance of a second marriage contracted by a person whose former husband or wife has been absent for five years, without being known to such person to be alive during that time, has application only in a case where the absentee has been discovered to be still alive. *Nesbit* v. *Nesbit*, 329.

ACCOUNT.

1. No inventory of decedent's property having been made or filed, and no proceedings having been taken to compel the return of an inventory, certain creditors cited the executors to account, with a view to the payment of their claims; whereupon the latter filed a duly verified account showing that no property of decedent's estate had come into their hands.—*Held*, that the burden was cast upon the creditors, of proving that the executors were chargeable with assets. *Matter of Palmer*, 129.

2. The statute does not prescribe any special form to be adopted by an executor in making up his account. Such a paper should contain a clear and definite statement of his dealing with his testator's estate, so that it can be made the subject of intelligent objections. *Solomons* v. *Kursheedt*, 307.

3. K., who at one time, qualified as executor of the will of each of two decedents, whose respective testamentary provisions were in direct antagonism, cited all persons interested in either of the estates to attend the judicial settlement of his account as representative of one thereof, and applied to the court for instructions as to the proper mode of presenting the account.—*Held*, that such instructions should not be given, but that the executor should in the first instance, solve for himself the problem which confronted him, leaving it to those interested to raise desired issues by the interposition of suitable objections. *Id.*

See ACCOUNTING ; EXECUTORS AND ADMINISTRATORS ; TESTAMENTARY TRUSTEE.

ACCOUNTING.

1. Since the amendment of Code Civ. Pro., § 2606, made in 1884, a Surrogate's court may require an accounting from the representative of a deceased executor or administrator, in like manner as it might have, from the latter during his lifetime, after revocation of his letters. *Herbert* v. *Stevenson*, 236.

2. After the letters of an executor or administrator have been revoked, a Surrogate's court cannot compel him to account, upon petition of a creditor of the decedent; its authority, in this respect, being limited by Code Civ. Pro., § 2605, to a case where proceedings are instituted by a successor, or a former co-representative. *Breslin* v. *Smyth*, 251.

3. Upon an application, by the personal representative of a deceased legatee under decedent's will, to compel the executor thereof to account, the latter filed an affidavit alleging that he, petitioner's intestate, and

another were the "only heirs at law" of their mother, the decedent, and that they had "divided and settled the estate of their mother, and passed and received releases to each other, and to deponent individually and as executor;" without setting forth the so-called releases or disclosing their character.—*Held*, that such affidavit showed no cause why petitioner's application should not be granted. *Sayre* v. *Sayre*, 264.

4. After an executor's account has once been judicially settled, the mere fact that, since the entry of the decree, assets to have come into his possession for which the decree made no provision does not, of itself, afford sufficient grounds for compelling another accounting. Considerations of economy may indicate the propriety of the postponement of another settlement, until it can embrace the results of a completed administration. *Wetmore* v. *Wetmore*, 414.

See ABATEMENT 1, 2; COMMISSIONS, 17.

ACCUMULATIONS.

See EXECUTORS AND ADMINISTRATORS, 3.

ACKNOWLEDGMENT.

1. An allegation, in an administrator's answer to a creditor's petition for payment of his claim, that one not a party to the proceeding recovered a judgment against decedent, during his lifetime, for a sum specified, and that the same is entitled to priority over petitioner's claim, is not an acknowledgment of indebtedness, of which the judgment creditor can avail himself, under Code Civ. Pro., § 376, in order to repel the presumption of payment of the judgment. *Visscher* v. *Wesley*, 301.

2. *It seems* that an affirmative answer to the question, "do you acknowledge, in the presence of these witnesses, that you signed this paper, as your last will and testament, knowing fully its contents?" is not an acknowledgment of subscription, within the meaning of the statute of wills. *Rumsey* v. *Goldsmith*, 494.

See EXECUTION OF WILL, 3, 4, 6, 8; PUBLICATION OF WILL; STATUTE OF LIMITATIONS, 3.

ADMINISTRATOR.

See EXECUTORS AND ADMINISTRATORS; LETTERS OF ADMINISTRATION; TEMPORARY ADMINISTRATOR.

ADMINISTRATOR WITH WILL ANNEXED.

Code Civ. Pro., § 2645, enacted in 1880, requires an administrator, with the

will annexed, before letters are issued to him, to qualify as prescribed
by law with respect to an administrator in intestacy, and makes the
provisions of the article containing § 2667 applicable to his official bond.
The latter section, which was enacted in the same year, and prescribes
the requisites of the bond of an administrator in intestacy, was amended
in 1882, by adding a provision that, "in cases where all the next of kin
to the intestate consent thereto," the penalty of the bond may be limited in a manner specified.—*Held*, that the former section, and the latter
as amended, are to be construed together, as if enacted simultaneously,
and that an administrator with the will annexed may avail himself of
the provisions contained in the amendment of 1882, upon obtaining
the consent of the next of kin, although they may have no interest
in the decedent's estate. The existing statutory rule on this subject—
criticised. *Curtis* v. *Williams*, 63.

AFFIDAVIT. :

See VERIFICATION.

ALIENIST.

See EXPERTS.

'ALIENS.

Alienage is not a bar to heirship. *Kilfoy* v. *Powers*, 198.

ANCILLARY LETTERS

See FOREIGN GUARDIAN.

ANNUITY.

See INTEREST, 8; LEGACY, 6.

ANSWER.

See PLEADINGS.

APPEAL.

An order of the Surrogate's court, directing an executor to file an official
bond within twenty days after service of a copy of the order, provided,
in case of his failure so to do, as follows: "It is hereby ordered that
the letters testamentary be revoked and annulled." The executor perfected an appeal from the order within the time specified; after the

expiration of which, an application was made for an absolute decree of revocation.—*Held*, that the application must be denied; on the ground that, either the order in question was itself a decree revoking letters, in which case a further decree was unnecessary,—or it was not such a decree, in which event it was not within Code Civ. Pro., § 2583, and the appeal operated as a stay. *Halsey* v. *Halsey*, 196.

See CASE ON APPEAL.

ASSETS.

A creditor of testatrix, who had recovered a judgment against the executors, having presented a petition, under Code Civ. Pro., § 2717, for a decree directing the latter to pay the same, it appeared that there was no personal property actually in their hands. The will, however, devised certain real property to the executors, in trust to collect the income, and pay the same to the children of the testatrix during the life of her husband, W., and, upon his death, to sell the property and divide the proceeds among said children. W. was dead. He had been adjudged to have an estate by the curtesy in the real property in question,—which reduced the executors' rights in the premises to a power of sale and distribution.—*Held*, no assets; and that the prayer of the petition must be denied. *Lynch* v. *Patchen*, 58.

See BENEFIT CERTIFICATE.

ASSIGNMENT.

The language of Code Civ. Pro., § 2804,—which allows a person who "is entitled, by the terms of the will," to the payment of money or delivery of property, to proceed against a testamentary trustee for satisfaction,—indicates, even more strongly than that of id., § 2717, relating to executors, etc., a purpose to postpone, until a judicial settlement of the account, proceedings to enforce claims made against a testator's estate by persons holding *assignments* of legacies. *Tilden* v. *Dows*, 240.

ATTORNEYS AND COUNSELLERS.

See EXPENSES OF ADMINISTRATION ; PRIVILEGED COMMUNICATION.

BENEFIT CERTIFICATE.

Testator, during his lifetime, insured his life in two "benefit insurance associations," the certificates being made payable to his mother, who, shortly before testator's death, assigned the same to the executor and executrix named in his will, the latter of whom was his wife, in trust for the use of the assignor during life, the principal, upon her death, to go to the wife. Simultaneously with this assignment, testator executed his will confirming this disposition of the moneys to become payable upon the certificates. Testator having died insolvent, and the executors having received the benefit moneys, decedent's creditors sought to reach the same as constituting assets of his estate.—*Held*, that it was to be presumed, from the beneficial nature of the policies, that the same were within the scope of the statutes relating to the insurance of a man's life for the benefit of his family, and that the moneys which the executors had received thereunder were not assets in the hands of the executors, and could not be disposed of as such, but should be applied in accordance with the terms of the trust, to the exclusion of the claims of decedent's creditors. *Matter of Palmer*, 129.

BEQUEST.

See CHARITABLE BEQUESTS ; LEGACY.

BOND.

See OFFICIAL BOND.

BURDEN OF PROOF.

The burden of impeaching the justness of disbursements, made by a trustee for expenses of administration, is upon the party objecting thereto. *Valentine* v. *Valentine*, 597.

See ACCOUNT, 1; PAYMENT OF LEGACY, 1; REVOCATION OF PROBATE, 3; SALE OF REAL ESTATE, 2; TESTAMENTARY CAPACITY.

BURIAL PLOT.

See SUSPENSION OF OWNERSHIP.

CASE ON APPEAL.

The provisions of Code Civ. Pro., limiting the time for taking an appeal from a Surrogate's court to thirty days from the time of service of a copy of the decree or order complained of (§ 2572), and declaring that, to render an appeal effectual for any purpose, the appellant must give an undertaking to the effect specified (§ 2577); and General Rules of Practice 32 and 33, requiring a *case* to be made and served within ten days after service of a copy of the decree or order, but permitting the Surrogate to allow further time, etc.; are to be construed independently of each other: under these regulations, the Surrogate may enlarge the time for making and serving a *case* before the appeal is perfected by filing security, if the time for perfecting the same has not expired. *Tilby* v. *Tilby*, 258.

CASES APPROVED, COMMENTED UPON, COMPARED, DISAPPROVED, DISSENTED FROM, DISTINGUISHED, DOUBTED, FOLLOWED, OVERRULED.

Babcock *v.* Stoddard. 8 T. & C., 207—followed. *Beekman v. Vanderveer* (No. 2), 619.

Barnett *v.* Kincaid, 2 Lans., 320—disapproved. *Turner v. Amsdell,* 19.

Baskin *v.* Baskin, 36 N. Y., 416—doubted. *Rumsey v. Goldsmith,* 494.

Baucus *v.* Stover, 89 N. Y., 1—followed. *Warner v. Knower,* 208.

Beebe *v.* Estabrook, 79 N. Y., 246—distinguished. *Kirk v. Cashman,* 242.

Bradner *v.* Faulkner, 12 N. Y., 472—commented upon. *Dustan v. Carter,* 149.

Brown *v.* Knapp, 79 N. Y., 136—followed. *Keating v. Bruns,* 233.

Cammann *v.* Cammann, 2 Dem., 211—distinguished. *Reynolds v. Reynolds,* 82.

Campbell *v.* Beaumont, 91 N. Y., 464—distinguished. *Kelsey v. Van Camp,* 530.

Campbell *v.* Cowdrey, 31 How. Pr, 172—followed. *Dustan v. Carter,* 149.

Christopherson *v.* Naylor, 1 Meriv., 320—dissented from. *Abbey v. Aymar,* 400.

Clarkson *v.* Clarkson, 18 Barb., 646—distinguished. *Knight v. Lidford,* 88.

Cowing *v.* Howard, 46 Barb., 579—distinguished. *Hawley v. Singer,* 589.

Decker *v.* Miller, 2 Paige 149—followed. *Warner v. Knower,* 208.

Estate of Pirnie, *Tucker,* 119—disapproved. *Hawley v. Singer,* 589.

Fraenznick *v.* Miller, 1 Dem., 136—overruled. *Tappen v. M. E. Church,* 187.

Gormerly *v.* McGlynn, 84 N. Y., 285—distinguished. *Tilby v. Tilby,* 258.

Hancox *v.* Meeker, 95 N. Y., 528—distinguished and commented upon, *Andrews v. Goodrich,* 245.

Hoffman *v.* Penn. Hospital, 1 Dem., 118—distinguished. *Simpkins v. Scudder,* 371.

Hull *v.* Hull, 24 N. Y., 647—compared. *Solomons v. Kursheedt,* 307.

Johnson *v.* Lawrence, 95 N. Y., 154—compared. *McKie v. Clark,* 380.

King *v.* Talbot, 40 N. Y., 76—distinguished. *Warner v. Knower,* 208.

Lawrence *v.* Hebbard, 1 Bradf., 252—compared. *Abbey v. Aymar,* 400.

Laytin *v.* Davidson, 95 N. Y., 263—distinguished. *McKie v. Clark,* 380.

Leavy *v.* Gardner, 63 N. Y., 624—followed. *Herbert v. Stevenson,* 236.

Lynch *v.* Mahony, 2 Redf., 434—doubted. *Carr v. Bennett,* 433.

Matter of Glann, 2 Redf., 75—disapproved. *Turner v. Amsdell,* 19.

Mitchell's Case, 12 Abb. Pr., 249—dissented from. *Hoyt v. Jackson,* 888.

Palmer *v.* Horn, 84 N. Y., 519—followed. *Taft v. Taft,* 86.

Peyser *v.* Wendt, 2 Dem., 224—compared. *Tilden v. Dows,* 240.

Pierce *v.* Chamberlain, 41 How. Pr., 501—doubted. *Carr v. Bennett,* 433.

Platt *v.* Moore, 1 Dem., 191—followed. *Larkin v. Salmon,* 270.

Prowitt *v.* Rodman, 37 N. Y., 42—distinguished. *Kirk v. Cashman,* 242.

Rex *v.* Twyning, 2 Barn. & Ald., 386—followed. *Nesbit v. Nesbit,* 329.

Riggs *v.* Cragg, 26 Hun, 89—distinguished. *Knight v. Lidford,* 88.

Riggs *v.* Cragg, 89 N. Y., 479—followed. *Beekman v. Vanderveer,* 221.

Rogers v. Squires, 26 Hun, 388—distinguished. *Fleet* v. *Simmons*, 542.

Sanford v. Sanford, 4 Hun, 753—followed. *Beekman* v. *Vanderveer*, (No. 2), 619.

Slosson v. Naylor, 2 Dem., 257—followed. *Andrews* v. *Goodrich*, 245.

Tompkins v. Moseman, 5 Redf., 402—approved. *Matter of Whitehead*, 227.

Warner v. Knower, *ante*, 208—compared. *Zapp* v. *Miller*, 266.

Waters v. Collins, *ante*, 374—compared. *Thompson* v. *Thompson*, 409.

Whitson v. Whitson, 53 N. Y., 479—distinguished. *Reynolds* v. *Reynolds*, 82.

CESTUI QUE TRUST.

Upon an application, by the beneficiary of a trust, to compel the trustee to pay to her alleged arrears of income, the respondent answered that he had expended nearly $350 for counsel fees, in defending an action brought by the petitioner for the purpose of extinguishing the trust, and wherein he had recovered a judgment for costs, which his attorney claimed was a lien on any sum to which petitioner might be entitled under the will,—such sum being less than the amount for which credit was asked by the respondent.—*Held*, that the application must be denied without prejudice. *Geissler* v. *Werner*, 200.

CHARITABLE BEQUESTS.

1. Testator, who was an illegitimate child, and died leaving no parent or issue, by his will gave his property to his executors in trust, directing that, after the death of A., who was to have the use of his farm for life, the same "be sold, and the proceeds be let out at interest, and the said interest be annually paid to" a charitable corporation named, but making no provision for the management of the property after the death or resignation of the trustees selected by him. A. having died, the executors converted the real property into money which they invested, and paid the interest annually to the corporation legatee. Upon the judicial settlement of their account, had upon their application for leave to resign their trust,—*Held*, that the bequest was not void, as contravening the statute against perpetuities, but that the principal of the fund should be transferred to the corporation, after deduction of commissions and the expenses of the accounting. *Reform Society* v. *Case*, 15.

2. The statutory restrictions upon the validity of bequests to corporations, conditioned upon the survival of certain relatives of the testator, are not obviated or modified by the fact that the testamentary provisions are of a contingent nature, and only to be enjoyed in the event of the death of such relatives. *Price* v. *Foucher*, 341.

3. Testator's will contained the following clause : "And I also reserve five hundred dollars for an *arbor vitæ* hedge around the plot in burying ground, and for other things necessary about the plot, and what is re-

maining of the above (500) five hundred to be given to some Sunday school Rye Presbyterian or charitable institution."—*Held*, that the testator intended to make a bequest for a religious or charitable use ; but that he, having failed to point out any corporate or natural person who could maintain an action to recover the legacy, the court could not supply the defect ; and that the residue of the $500 fell into the residue of the estate. *Mitchell* v. *Presb. Church*, 608.

CHILDREN.

The word "children," in a testamentary paper, must be taken in its accustomed sense, and limited to offspring in the first degree, in the absence of indications that the testator intended to give it some other meaning. *Kirk* v. *Cashman*, 242.

CITATION.

1. Under the provision of Code Civ. Pro., § 2615, requiring the heirs of a decedent to be cited upon an application for the probate of a paper propounded as his will, where the same relates to real property, a non-resident alien brother and sister of a deceased citizen of the United States, if among his next of kin, are entitled to citation ; the latter inheriting, in case of intestacy, as if a citizen, and the former in like manner, subject to a conditional defeasance, enforceable at the instance of the State. *Kilfoy* v. *Powers*, 198.

2. The practice of inserting, in citations to infants, a clause advising them that, in the event of their not appearing by general guardian, and failing to ask for the appointment of a special guardian, a special guardian will, upon the return of the citation, be appointed by the Surrogate—commended. *Price* v. *Fenn*, 341.

See SERVICE OF CITATION.

CODE OF CIVIL PROCEDURE.

[*Sections construed or cited.*]

§ 90. *Benedict* v. *Cooper*, 362.
§ 376. *Visscher* v. *Wesley*, 301.
§ 403. *Visscher* v. *Wesley*, 301.
§ 755. *Herbert* v. *Stevenson*, 236.
§ 765. *Herbert* v. *Stevenson*, 236.
§ 829. *Jones* v. *Le Baron*, 37.
§ 829. *Shepard* v. *Patterson*, 183.
§ 829. *Cadmus* v. *Oakley*, 324.
§ 835. *Hoyt* v. *Jackson*, 388.
§ 837. *Hoyt* v. *Jackson*, 388.

COMMISSIONS.

1. Where an executor or administrator has only received, and not paid out, funds of the estate, he should be allowed therefor commissions at one half the legal rate. *Lyendecker* v. *Eisemann*, 72.

2. Decedent's executor, who was appointed in 1855, voluntarily accounted in 1865, distributed all the funds of the estate then in his hands, and retained about $200 as his commissions, without objection from any of the beneficiaries. Upon a judicial settlement of his account, had in 1885,—*Held*, that, in the absence of an allowance by the Surrogate, this sum had been improperly retained, and that the executor should be charged with the same, but, under the circumstances of the case, without interest. *Wyckoff* v. *Van Siclen*, 75.

be so construed as to treat the reception of every variety of assets as a receiving of money, and the application of such assets to the discharge of debts and legacies, and to the establishment of trusts, etc., as a pecuniary disbursement. *Rowland* v. *Morgan*, 289.

8. A result of the adjudicated cases is a recognition of the divisibility of the commissions of executors and administrators, for receiving and for paying out moneys, and of the propriety of an allowance, in many instances, of half-commissions, for receiving, in advance of any paying out whatever. *Id.*

9. Upon the judicial settlement of the account of executors, a question having arisen as to the mode of computing commissions upon certain securities which, forming part of the assets of testator's estate, had been retained by the former under authority conferred by the will, and were about to be delivered to testamentary trustees,—*Held*, 1. That the market value of such securities, at the time when they came into the executors' hands, should be taken as the basis for half-commissions, for receiving; and 2. That the half-commissions, for paying out, must be computed upon their value at the time of entering the decree directing their transfer to the trustees. *Id.*

10. Testator's will, besides bequeathing various specific and pecuniary legacies, directed the executors to pay cash, or assign securities, to a trust company to the amount of $200,000, for the benefit of his widow for life, after whose death the fund was to be *repaid to the executors;* it further gave the net income of the remainder of his estate, during the widow's life, to his children equally, providing that such remainder should be held by and in charge of the executors, the rents and income be collected by them, the personal estate kept invested, and the said net income paid over semi-annually, or as often as practicable ; and directed the executors, upon the widow's death, to divide the entire estate, including the $200,000, into equal parts, and pay over or assign the same to the children. Upon an accounting in 1878, the executors were each allowed half commissions on all assets received by them, and the same upon all sums paid out, as well as upon the balance directed by the decree to be retained in their hands until a final distribution. That decree provided "that they" (the executors) "retain to themselves, in their capacity of trustees, all the remainder of said moneys," etc., "to be held and accounted for by them as such trustees, upon the trusts and in accordance with the provisions and directions" in the will. The widow having died, the executors, upon a judicial settlement of their account, had with a view to a final distribution, claimed full commissions upon the entire amount undistributed at the time of the former accounting.—*Held*, that the will required from the persons to whom the estate was committed, the employment of no other than purely executorial functions ; that the decree of 1878, in conferring upon them the new name of trustees, did not change their real character, or confer upon them any new rights or privileges ; and,

that as to such funds as had been in the executors' hands since their former accounting, their claim to commissions should be disallowed. *McKie* v. *Clark*, 380.

11. Although executors' and administrators' commissions are allowed only by order of a Surrogate's court, the latter cannot withhold them; except in certain cases, as where a will denies compensation, or provides specifically therefor. *Welling* v. *Welling*, 511.

12. Under Code Civ. Pro., § 2736, relating to the commissions of executors, etc., in cases where the decedent's personal estate amounts to $100,000, or more, over all his debts, the only conditions necessary to entitle executors to three full commissions are that the estate should be of the requisite value, and that three or more representatives should qualify and act. *Id.*

13. Accordingly where testator, who left an estate of the value of $400,000, appointed three executors, each of whom qualified, but one of whom died at the expiration of six months after the grant of letters, having acted up to that time,—*Held*, upon an accounting by the survivors, that three full commissions should be allowed, to be apportioned among the accounting parties and the representative of the deceased executor, although, by this means, each of the surviving executors would receive compensation in excess of full commissions, by reason merely of the death of their associate. *Id.*

14. A trustee, *durante minore ætate*, is entitled to commissions on amounts received by him after the *cestui que trust* has arrived at full age and become entitled to the possession of the fund, until his duties are terminated by a final judicial settlement of his accounts. *Hawley* v. *Singer*, 589.

15. A statute establishing a rate of commissions allowable to trustees is not in the nature of a contract, so as to remain in force, notwithstanding the repeal thereof, as to one who assumed the duties of a trust before such repeal. *Id.*

16. While a Surrogate's court has not power to open and reconsider, on the ground of legal error, an adjudication already made, still where full commissions have been inadvertently awarded on a fund as received and paid out, when in truth it had been received and not paid out, such a tribunal may, in a subsequent accounting, take cognizance of the fact, and decline to award half commissions again for paying out. *Id.*

17. Where the accounts of executors or administrators are subjected to successive judicial settlements, they are entitled, on the first accounting, to full commissions on all moneys received and paid out, and half commissions only on moneys received and not paid out; on the second, they are allowed the other half on moneys since paid out, and full

commissions on the increase received and paid out, or directed by the decree to be paid; taking care, however, that the total award shall not exceed what would have been full commissions, had the whole estate been finally settled, on one accounting. *Id.*

18. The executor of decedent's will, who was also trustee of a trust thereby created for the benefit of an infant during his minority, had an accounting in 1877, in the former capacity, on which he was allowed full commissions upon the entire amount of the estate, which was then more than $9,000,000. · In 1881, he accounted as trustee, and was allowed full commissions upon the amount of the trust fund, which was one sixth of the residue. The *cestui que trust* having reached his majority, and proceedings having been instituted for the judicial settlement of, the trustee's account, with a view to the· transfer of the fund, now about $1,500,000, to the beneficiary,—*Held,*. that the only compensation allowable to the accounting party was. commissions at the rate of one per cent. on the amount of increase· since the last accounting. *Id.*

See SPECIFIC LEGACY.

CONDITION.

See LEGACY, 1; WILL, 2.

CONSTRUCTION OF WILL.

1. The force and effect of a testamentary provision cannot be finally determined upon an application for an advance upon a legacy, made under Code Civ. Pro., § 2717. *Rank* v. *Camp*, 278.

2. A Surrogate's court has no jurisdiction to determine the validity, construction or effect of a testamentary disposition of *real* property, upon an application for probate. *Privé* v. *Foucher*, 341.

3. In the construction of testamentary papers, language which, tested by strict grammatical rules, refers to the happening of events in the future may be held to include past occurrences of a similar character, including those transpiring before the execution. *Abbey* v. *Aymar*, 400.

4. Upon the judicial settlement of an executor's account, a Surrogate's court has jurisdiction to try and determine a question as to the meaning of the provisions of the decedent's will, so far as necessary to enable it to direct the distribution of the entire estate. *Board of Missions* v. *Scovell*, 516.

5. A Surrogate's court may construe a decedent's will· in *any proceeding*

where it becomes necessary in order to enable it to exercise powers expressly conferred upon it. *Kelsey* v. *Van Camp*, 530.

See COMMISSIONS, 4.

CORPORATIONS.

See CHARITABLE BEQUESTS, 2.

COSTS.

1. The administrator of decedent's estate, which was insolvent, was ordered to pay to various creditors a *pro rata* dividend of forty per cent., and to retain other assets, amounting to more than $900, "to abide the result of the claims of" a creditor, S., who thereafter recovered a judgment against the administrator, for a sum, of which about $100 constituted the costs of the action wherein the judgment was rendered. The administrator contended that S. was only entitled to forty per cent. of the total amount of the judgment.—*Held*, that the costs of S. must be paid in full, and the dividend of forty per cent. be calculated upon the residue of the amount for which the judgment was recovered. *Shields* v. *Sullivan*, 296.

2. The denial of an application to open a decree is properly incorporated in an order, and not in a decree; and the maximum allowance of costs thereupon is $10 and the necessary disbursements, as prescribed in Code Civ. Pro., § 2556. *Pease* v. *Egan*, 320.

3. In a special proceeding for the disposition of a decedent's real property for the payment of his debts, no costs or allowances can be granted to a petitioning creditor, the right to award thereof, being confined, by § 2563, to the executor or administrator, and a freeholder appointed to execute the decree. *Long* v. *Olmsted*, 581.

4. In such a special proceeding, the costs of none of the parties can be fixed or adjusted so as to be embraced in the decree directing a sale, mortgage or lease. This can be done only at the time of the entry of the supplementary decree described in § 2793. *Id.*

See PAYMENT OF DEBTS, 7; SALE OF REAL ESTATE, 3.

COUNSEL FEES.

A Surrogate's court cannot make any allowance to an executor or administrator, as counsel fees in litigation in other courts, concerning the estate, until he has paid his counsel and applies for reimbursement. *Shields* v. *Sullivan*, 296.

CREDITOR.

In order to entitle one to proceed, under Code Civ. Pro., § 2715. as a creditor of a decedent, against the executor or administrator of the latter, to compel the filing of an inventory, he must either distinctly declare himself to be such a creditor, or set forth facts showing that he is entitled in that capacity (id., § 2514, subd. 11). *Pendle* v. *Waite*, 261.

See SALE OF REAL ESTATE, 1.

CY PRES.

The *cy pres* power is not exercised by any court of this State. *Mitchell* v. *Presb. Church,* 630.

DEATH.

See ABATEMENT, 1, 2; JUDGMENT, 2; WILL, 8.

DECLARATIONS.

See LATENT AMBIGUITY.

DECREE.

Before the enactment of the Code of Civil Procedure, a Surrogate's court possessed no power to open a decree and grant a rehearing, on the ground of an error in law; and no such power has been conferred by that act, the words " or other sufficient cause," newly introduced by § 2481, subd. 6, being properly referable to causes *ejusdem generis,* only. *Singer* v. *Hawley*, 571.

See JUDGMENT; ORDER.

DEFINITIONS.

See CHILDREN; HEIRS; ISSUE; PERSON INTERESTED; RESIDUE; REVOCATION OF LETTERS, 1; TESTAMENTARY TRUSTEE, 2.

DEVASTAVIT.

It appeared that the accounting executor, who was a farmer, having in his hands $500 cash assets of the estate, handed this sum over to his co-executor, who was his uncle and a man of business, in good standing, in order that the latter might pay therewith the debts of decedent at his place of business, pursuant to advertisement. The latter having misappropriated the amount and died insolvent,—*Held*, that the former was liable for the devastavit, and should be charged with the amount, but not with interest thereon. *Wyckoff* v. *Van Siclen*, 75.

DEVISE.

See LEGACY; WILL.

DISCOVERY OF ASSETS.

1. Under Code Civ. Pro., § 2706, relating to a special proceeding to discover property of a decedent withheld from his representative, and providing that "*an* executor or administrator" may present to the Surrogate's court a petition praying an inquiry, one of two co-representatives may proceed alone, without alleging a demand upon and refusal of the other to unite with him, or otherwise explaining the non-joinder. *Tracey* v. *Slingerland*, 1.

2. The substitution, in the section cited, of the words quoted, in place of "*any* executor or administrator," used in the original act (L. 1870, ch. 394, § 1), is a mere change in phraseology, which has effected no alteration in the law. *Id.*

3. In a special proceeding, brought by an executor or administrator under Code Civ. Pro., § 2706, to discover property of the decedent withheld from the petitioner, the allegations on the part of the latter may be exclusively on information and belief, without disclosing the sources or grounds thereof. The only pre-requisite to the issuing of a citation, is the satisfaction of the Surrogate that there are reasonable grounds for the inquiry. *Walsh* v. *Downs*, 202.

DISINHERISON.

See PAYMENT OF LEGACIES, 3.

DISPOSITION OF REAL PROPERTY.

See SALE OF REAL ESTATE.

DISPUTED CLAIM.

Notwithstanding the limitations apparently implied in Code Civ. Pro., § 2743,—which provides that, "Where an account is judicially settled . . . . . and . . . . . the validity of a debt, claim or distributive share *is not disputed or has been established*, the decree must determine to whom it is payable, the sum to be paid by reason thereof, and all other questions concerning the same,"—a Surrogate's court has jurisdiction, upon the judicial settlement of an executor's account, to *decide all questions* necessary to determine a dispute on the part of the executor, as to the validity of the claim of one asserting a right as legatee under the will, and to construe the will for the purpose of making such determination. So—*Held*, where the will bequeathed $500 to the trustees of the S. A. church, "towards paying off the debt of the church," and $500 to the managers or trustees of the M. C. Mission ; and the executor, seeking to procure the entry of a decree judicially settling his account, contended that the former bequest was ineffective by reason of the fact that the church designated was, neither then nor when the testator died, in a state of indebtedness ; and the latter, void on the ground that there was no existing person or institution bearing the name of the "M. C. Mission," and none competent to take the bequest whereof the will made the M. C. Mission the beneficiary. *Tappen* v. *M. E. Church*, 187.

See JURISDICTION, 5, 6.

DISTRIBUTIVE SHARE.

See NEXT OF KIN.

DOWER.

The widow of a decedent, who has accepted under her husband's will a legacy bequeathed to her in lieu of dower, is not entitled, as against creditors, even to the extent of the value of her dower interest, to priority of payment. Her claims are superior to those of voluntary legatees, but her husband's debts must be satisfied before any property of his estate can be lawfully applied to the discharge of her legacy. *Beekman* v. *Vanderveer* (No. 2.), 619.

See INTEREST, 4 ; LEGACY, 6.

DUPLICATE WILL.

Upon a petition for probate of a will executed in duplicate, one of the two originals being shown to have been destroyed by the maker, *animo revocandi*, and there being no proof that the other was in her possession at any time after its execution, though it did not appear but that it was still intact,—*Held*, that a decree might be entered denying the application. *Asinari* v. *Bangs*, 385.

EQUITABLE CONVERSION.

See WILL, 9.

EVIDENCE.

1. The provision of Code Civ. Pro., § 829, forbidding a party to a special proceeding to be examined, upon the hearing, in his own behalf, *against the executor or administrator* of a deceased person, concerning a personal transaction or communication between witness and the decedent, does not apply to a special proceeding instituted, by a creditor, to dis-

pose of decedent's real property for the payment of his debts, where the testimony of another alleged creditor, offered in his own behalf, concerning such a transaction or communication, is objected to by petitioner. The rule is for the protection of the personal representative of decedent, and he alone can take advantage thereof. *Jones v. LeBaron*, 37.

2. Where, upon the settlement of the account of a deceased executor, the accounting party was permitted to testify respecting an agreement between the former and the beneficiaries, by which a retention of commissions at the rate of five per cent. was claimed to have been authorized,—*Held*, that, under Code Civ. Pro., § 829, it was error thereafter to refuse to allow the examination of one of the objectors, as a witness in his own behalf, in reference to the same subject. *Shepard v. Patterson*, 183.

3. In Code Civ. Pro., § 829 forbidding a person, in certain specified cases, to be examined as a witness in his own behalf or interest, against *any person deriving his title or interest* from, through or under a deceased person, concerning a personal transaction or communication between the witness and the deceased person, the italicized words should be construed as being equivalent to "any person *claiming to* derive," etc., and so to include the contestant of a will, upon the hearing of a special proceeding for its probate. *Cadmus v. Oakley*, 324.

4. Upon the hearing of a contested application for the probate of a will, a person named as legatee in the paper propounded is incompetent, under Code Civ. Pro., § 829, to testify in his own behalf or interest (*i. e.*, in general, in support of the application), concerning a personal transaction or communication between himself and the decedent. Section 2544 of that Code, declaring that "a person is not disqualified or excused from testifying respecting the execution of a will by a provision therein, whether it is beneficial to him or otherwise," conveys no intimation that a person within its description is not, in like manner as others, subject to the limitations contained in the former section. *Id.*

5. Under ordinary circumstances, where a witness, in obedience to the command of a subpœna *duces tecum*, attends in court, and produces papers which contain matter relevant and material to the pending controversy, the same are admissible in evidence, not only upon the offer of the party at whose instance the subpœna was issued, but also upon that of his adversary. *Hoyt v. Jackson*, 388.

6. Where a party to a pending controversy subpœnaes his own attorney to produce papers at the trial, which, upon their production, he omits to offer in evidence, he is to be treated as thereby giving the right to his adversary to introduce them, if discovered to be pertinent to the issue. *Id.*

See EXPERTS; PRIVILEGED COMMUNICATION; SUBPŒNA DUCES TECUM; WITNESS.

EXECUTION OF WILL.

1. **The document** propounded as decedent's will was in the handwriting of W., one of the subscribing witnesses, who was not a lawyer, and was written upon two pages of note paper, in three divisions, as follows : (1) Near the end of the first page was decedent's name with the words "her mark" under it, in the draughtsman's handwriting, and, immediately under this, decedent's signature. To the left were the signatures of W. and R., and the date. (2) On the next page, what purported to be a codicil to the will, dated the same day, was executed in a similar manner. (3) And, immediately following, was the clause, "I appoint W. my executor," similarly subscribed, and witnessed by R. and M. The testimony, though somewhat conflicting, showed a substantial compliance with the statutory requirements as to publication. It appeared that the draughtsman expected the decedent to make her mark, which, however, she declined to do, writing her name, instead; and that the codicillary matter and the executorial appointment were originally omitted by inadvertence, and the omissions successively supplied.—*Held*, that the paper, though inartificially drawn, constituted one harmonious will—even the last execution being sufficient;—and that the same was entitled to probate. *Taylor v. Wardlaw*, 48.

2. The intent of the legislature, in requiring, by 2 R. S., 63, § 40, subd. 2, a testator's subscription to his will to be "made in the presence of each of the attesting witnesses," or, etc., was not simply that the testator and witnesses should be within the same enclosure, but that the latter should either actually see the former write his name, or have their attention directed to the act of signing while the same is taking place. *Gardiner v. Raines*, 98.

3. The rule that a will may be subscribed by the testator in the presence of one witness, and the signature be thereafter acknowledged to the other—applied. *Id.*

4. Evidence for and against the proposition that testator acknowledged his subscription to one of the subscribing witnesses—weighed, and the authorities relating to the subject of such an acknowledgment—collated and discussed. *Id.*

5. It appeared that decedent, at the time of the alleged execution of his will, was, from long continued sickness, in a state of chronic stupor, from which he could be awakened, but into which he would speedily relapse, the interval of lucidity being too brief for any considerable mental exertion; that, of the subscription to the instrument,—which was in the following form: "Patrick [his + mark] J. O'Neill,"—decedent wrote only the first three letters, and then dropped the pen, saying he could go no further; whereupon R. proceeded to make the mark and complete the signature. There was no evidence of a request by decedent to R., so to do, nor of a subsequent indication of knowledge or approbation, on the part of the former, of what had been done.—

Held, that the act of R. did not constitute a subscription of decedent's name, and that the fragmentary signature written by the latter was not sufficient as an authentication of his will. *Knapp* v. *Reilly*, 427.

6. A substantial compliance with the statute, 2 R. S., 63, § 40, in the execution of a will, is all that is required. An acknowledgment of the execution by the testator, made to a witness after the latter has signed, is sufficient, where the two acts are performed on the same occasion. The several independent requirements of the statute may be joint in their execution. *Lyman* v. *Phillips*, 459.

7. Decedent, having written and subscribed the paper purporting to be his will apart from witnesses, took it to the place of business of S., made formal publication in his presence and procured his signature in attestation. He then went, with the document, to the office of B., an attorney, told him that it was his will, or his last will and testament, and requested him to sign as a witness, which B. did, the signature of decedent being, at the time, plainly visible. The evidence showed that decedent's acknowledgment of the character of the instrument was made after B. had signed, and that the latter thereafter told decedent that it was very informally drawn, specifying various objections as to its form and the manner of execution, and advised him to go to some attorney and have a will regularly drawn up; from which views, however, decedent dissented. B., who omitted to add to his signature a statement of his place of residence, testified that such omission was owing to an impression on his part that, when decedent left the office, he did so with the purpose of having the paper redrawn, and did not regard it as an executed will. Upon an application to revoke probate, it was contended that the execution was invalid by reason of the failure of decedent to acknowledge it until after B. had completed his signature; and, also, that the latter could not be regarded as an attesting witness.—*Held*, that the will was duly published in the presence of B., whose signature, as the second witness, gave to it legality and validity; and that the petition for revocation should be denied. *Id.*

8. Upon an application, made in January, 1885, for the probate of a paper propounded as decedent's will, dated November 14th, 1884, it appeared that, at the time of the alleged execution, decedent was confined to his bed by his last illness; that the paper, which had been prepared by one D., who was not a lawyer, at decedent's request, was read to the latter by the draftsman, and, its contents being approved, signed in the presence of D. alone; that D. then summoned from an adjoining room the two persons whose names appeared as those of subscribing witnesses, who, when they entered decedent's apartment, found him bolstered up in bed, and the paper lying, at his side, upon a stand whereon they wrote; that decedent was then asked by D. whether he acknowledged that to be his last will and testament, whereto he assented by nodding or bowing his head; whereupon D. said to the witnesses, successively, "you will please sign your name here," indi-

cating the place, with which request they each complied. There was no conversation between decedent and the subscribing witnesses. The paper was not sealed, and was written entirely upon one page, which lay open before the witnesses, so that they could have seen the decedent's subscription. The witnesses' signatures were preceded by an attestation clause in the ordinary form, reciting that the document was "signed, sealed, published and declared," etc., in the witnesses' presence.—*Held*, that, in view of the false recitals in the attestation clause, and the brevity of the period which elapsed between the signing and the examination of the witnesses, this clause could not be resorted to, for the purpose of raising any presumption of due execution; that the question addressed to the decedent, by the draftsman, in the witnesses' presence, called for nothing more than an acknowledgment of the nature of the instrument; and that probate must be refused on the ground of non-compliance with the requirement of the statute (2 R. S., 63, § 40), that the testator's *subscription*, if not made in their presence, "shall be acknowledged by him to have been [so] made to each of the attesting witnesses." *Rumsey* v. *Goldsmith*, 494.

See FOREIGN WILL, 2; PUBLICATION OF WILL; REVOCATION OF WILL.

EXECUTORS AND ADMINISTRATORS.

1. Payments made by an administrator to redeem decedent's real property from sales for arrears of taxes, allowed to him, in a peculiar case, as a preferred claim against the estate, with interest. *Jones* v. *LeBaron*, 37.

2. An executor has no right to buy off contestants of his decedent's will, and charge the expenditure against the estate. *Bolles* v. *Bacon*, 43.

3. An executor cannot be allowed for advances made by him, without authority from the court, to infant *cestuis que trustent*, out of the earnings of a fund directed by the will to be accumulated for their benefit until the termination of their minority. *Shepard* v. *Patterson*, 183.

4. Upon the judicial settlement of an executor's account, it appearing that he had failed to comply with directions contained in the will, requiring the income of certain trust funds to be deposited "in some good savings bank," or devoted to some other safe investment, during the respective minorities of the beneficiaries; in the absence of evidence that he had been guilty of intentional wrong, or reaped any personal advantage from the management of the trusts,—*Held*, that he must be treated as if he had pursued the course prescribed by the will, and be charged with interest, compounded semiannually, at the rate of five per cent., upon all sums received, from the expiration of three months after the receipt to the date of the 'filing of the account, and at the rate of three per cent. thereafter, until the entry of the decree of settlement. *Id.*

value occurred, between 1870 and 1885, of more than $6,000. It was contended that the trustee was liable for the loss, by reason of mismanagement, and that, under the will, he could lawfully invest in the stocks named, only on failing to find suitable investments in bonds secured by mortgage on real property.— *Held*, that the terms of the will did not indicate the preference contended for; and that the trustee was not liable for the decrease in the value of the fund, especially as it appeared that the shrinkage in the principal was more than offset by advantages secured in point of income. *Valentine* v. *Valentine,* 597.

See ACCOUNTING, 4; ADMINISTRATOR WITH WILL ANNEXED; COUNSEL FEES; DEVASTAVIT; MORTGAGE, 2; OFFICIAL BOND; PAYMENT OF DEBTS, 4.

EXEMPTION.

"Where a man having a family" dies, leaving a widow, the appraisers are authorized to set apart for her (1) the articles of personal property specifically enumerated in 2 R. S., 83, § 9, as amended in 1874; (2) "and also other household furniture which shall not exceed one hundred and fifty dollars in value " (id., subd. 4); and (3) " necessary household furniture, provisions or other personal property, in the discretion of said appraisers, to the value of not exceeding one hundred and fifty dollars " (L. 1842, ch. 157, § 2). *Lyendecker* v. *Eisemann,* 72.

EXPENSES OF ADMINISTRATION.

A claim by an attorney employed by an executor, for services rendered in conducting proceedings for the probate of decedent's will, and otherwise in the settlement of the estate, and for moneys advanced for disbursements therein, is against the executor personally, and not against the estate of the decedent. *Budlong* v. *Clemens,* 145.

See BURDEN OF PROOF.

EXPERTS.

The prevailing system of presenting, in the courts, the testimony of medical experts upon the question of sanity,—criticised, as being poorly calculated to assist in arriving at the exact truth. *Potter* v. *McAlpine,* 108.

FALSA DEMONSTRATIO.

The designation of "St. Frances Hospital," as a legatee, *held* a curable misnomer for the "Sisters of the Poor of St. Frances." *St. Frances Hospital* v. *Schreck,* 225.

FEES.

See COSTS; COUNSEL FEES.

FINDINGS.

Although Code Civ. Pro., § 1023 has no application to a Surrogate's court, which, therefore, cannot be required to determine particular questions before rendering its decision,—its authority to pass upon proposed findings, after such rendition, is expressly recognized by id., § 2545. *Tilby* v. *Tilby*, 258.

FOREIGN GUARDIAN.

A foreign general guardian is not entitled to recognition by the courts of this State. He should apply for ancillary letters, under Code Civ. Pro., § 2838. *West* v. *Gunther*, 386.

FOREIGN EXECUTOR.

See JURISDICTION, 4.

FOREIGN WILL.

1. Under Code Civ. Pro., § 2476, subd. 3, prescribing the jurisdiction of Surrogates' courts to take the proof of a will in certain cases, and id., § 2611, providing that a will of personal property executed, without the State and within the United States, as prescribed by the laws of the place of execution may be proved here, a Surrogate's court may grant probate to a will executed, in and according to the laws of another state, by a resident thereof who dies therein, leaving personal property in its county, without waiting until the instrument has been submitted to the proper judicial tribunal of the decedent's domicil. *Booth* v. *Timoney*, 416.

2. The paper propounded as the will of the personal property of the decedent, who was a resident of the state of New Jersey, where she died in 1884, and where the same was executed, was in decedent's handwriting, and embraced upon one page of a half sheet of note paper, upon which her name appeared only in the opening clause: "If I, Cecilia L. Booth, should die within the year 1884, I leave," etc. The paper was subscribed, at decedent's request, by two witnesses, who attended for the purpose of attesting it, and in whose joint presence decedent declared it to be her will, intentionally placing it before them so that her name stood revealed, though it did not clearly appear but that one of them was in an adjoining room, when that name was written. Decedent left personal property in the county of New York, where the instrument was presented for probate.—*Held*, 1. That the Surrogate's court of New York county had jurisdiction to take proof of the will, in the first instance. 2. That the validity of the execution depended on the law of decedent's domicil. 3. That the instrument was duly executed, according to the provisions of the New Jersey statute of 1851, which required a will to be "signed by the testator," and the

signature to be made, or by him acknowledged, in the presence of two witnesses present at the same time. *Id.*

See JURISDICTION, 4.

FUNERAL EXPENSES.

Upon the judicial settlement of the account of the administratrix of decedent's estate, objection was made by certain of the next of kin to an item of $56, expended for mourning goods for the widow, who was the accounting party, as excessive, and not properly chargeable against the estate. It appeared that the decedent left no children, and that the condition of the estate was such as that a surplus of several thousand dollars would remain after the payment of all debts.—*Held,* that the charge should be allowed, as a part of the necessary, or, at least, proper funeral expenses. *Held,* also, upon the same accounting, against a similar objection, that the widow should be allowed a reasonable expenditure ($19) for the disinterment and re-burial of decedent's remains,—the place where they were first deposited having been discovered to be undesirable ; also $175 for a mortuary monument; and $40, the purchase price of a lot in a well kept cemetery, the title to which she was allowed to take and hold in her individual name. *Allen v. Allen,* 524.

See MOURNING APPAREL.

GENERAL GUARDIAN.

1. Where the guardian of an infant's property takes the responsibility of encroaching upon the capital of a trust fund, of which his ward is entitled to the income, he must make out as clear a case, for the subsequent sanction of his course, as he would have been required to do, had he applied, in advance, for authority to adopt it. *Oakley v. Oakley,* 140.

2. The temporary guardian of an infant, whose estate consisted exclusively of his interest as *cestui que trust* under a will, pursuant to which a fixed annual income was regularly paid over by the trustee to the guardian, for the infant's benefit. having expended in that behalf about $400 in excess of the amount of trust moneys which had come to his hands, asked, upon the judicial settlement of his account, to be allowed the amount specified, to be paid out of future income to be received by his successor. The referee, to whom the account was referred, found that, in view of the necessities, prospects and social standing of the infant, the expenditures in question were properly made.—*Held,* that the propriety of those expenditures must be judged by a different standard from that which had been applied, and that they should be disallowed, upon the ground that they were beyond the infant's means. *Id.*

3. Upon the failure of the general guardian of an infant to give the security required as a condition of the payment to him of a legacy bequeathed to his ward, the executors should be directed to pay the same into the Surrogate's court, as if there were no guardian. *Toler v. Landon*, 339.

See GUARDIAN AD LITEM, 1, 2 ; INTEREST, 7.

GENERAL RULES OF PRACTICE.

See CASE ON APPEAL.

GUARDIAN.

See GENERAL GUARDIAN ; GUARDIAN AD LITEM ; TESTAMENTARY GUARDIAN.

GUARDIAN AD LITEM.

1. Although Code Civ. Pro., § 2531 recognizes the authority of the Surrogate to appoint a special guardian for an infant at the latter's instance, that section must be construed, in connection with id., § 2530, as authorizing such appointment only where the general guardian does not appear, or the Surrogate is satisfied that the latter is disqualified to adequately protect the interests of his ward. *Farmers Loan & Trust Co.* v. *McKenna*, 219.

2. Where, therefore, an infant having a general guardian applies to a Surrogate's court for the appointment of a special guardian, to represent him in a proceeding therein, he must give to the former notice of the application. *Id.*

3. In a special proceeding instituted for the disposition of decedent's real property for the payment of his debts, the citation having been duly served upon certain infants, interested in the estate, who were under the age of fourteen years and resided within the State of New York, and a special guardian having been, before the hearing, appointed for each, upon his parent's application, without the notice to the infant required by Code Civ. Pro., § 2531, the purchasers at the sale under the Surrogate's decree objected to the title upon the ground of the omission of such notice.—*Held*, under Code Civ. Pro., § 2784, subd. 1, that the omission in question was not of such a character as that it "would affect the title of a purchaser at a sale made pursuant to the directions contained in a judgment rendered by the Supreme Court in an action," and that the objection taken must be overruled. *Price* v. *Fenn*, 341.

4. It is the proper practice, in proceedings in a Surrogate's court to which an infant is a party, where no application is made, upon the return of

, the citation, for the appointment of a special guardian, for the Surro-gate to appoint such a guardian upon his own motion. *Id.*

5. Where an intelligent and competent person is appointed special guar-dian for an infant in a special proceeding in a Surrogate's court, the decree binds him as much as it would an adult. *Singer* v. *Hawley*, 571.

See CITATION, 2 ; GENERAL GUARDIAN.

HEIRS.

As to what is the proper judicial interpretation of the expression " legal heirs of the estate," occurring in a will—*quære. Buchan* v. *Rin-toul*, 353.

See ALIENS.

IMPROVIDENCE.

See LETTERS OF ADMINISTRATION, 2; REVOCATION OF LETTERS, 1.

INFAMOUS CRIME.

See LETTERS OF ADMINISTRATION, 2.

INFANTS.

See CITATION, 2 ; GENERAL GUARDIAN; GUARDIAN AD LITEM; TESTA-MENTARY GUARDIAN.

INJUNCTION.

See EXECUTORS AND ADMINISTRATORS, 6.

INTEREST.

1. Notwithstanding that, by 2 R. S., 90, § 43, legacies are, unless the will otherwise directs, not to be paid until after the expiration of one year from the time of granting letters, interest upon a general legacy, in an ordinary case, begins to run at the expiration of one year *from the death of the testator. Dustan* v. *Carter*, 149.

2. At the time of testator's death, K., who was appointed executor, held moneys belonging to the former, amounting to nearly $170,000. Sev-eral months previously, the parties had·made an agreement, indefinite as to time, that K. should be chargeable with interest on such moneys in his hands at the rate of four per cent., per annum. The will gave the executors full and absolute discretion as to the form, manner and extent of any and all investments of the estate. Upon the judicial

settlement of his account as executor, K. contended that he was not bound to discharge his debt immediately upon receiving letters, but was at liberty to exercise his discretion as to the time of payment. A referee reported that the executor must be treated as if principal and interest, due when he qualified, had been moneys of the estate then in his hands, which he failed to invest ; and that he was chargeable with interest at one per cent. less than the statute rate, commencing to run six months after the issue of his letters.—*Held*, that the executor's contention must be overruled, unless the will could be construed as giving him power to make new loans of the estate funds, at four per cent., without security—which it could not; that, however, the statutory provision declaring an executor liable for his own debt "as for so much money in his hands at the time such debt or demand becomes due," etc., had not the literal application implied by the report ; and that K. should be charged with interest on the principal of his indebtedness, at the rate of four per cent. until his qualification, and six per cent. thereafter, until he actually collected or set apart the amount of the same for the benefit of the estate. *Warner* v. *Knower*, 208.

3. Testator, by his will, gave all his property to his executors, in trust, to reduce the personalty to cash and sell the realty, and of the proceeds to invest $15,000, the income whereof they were directed to collect and pay to his minor adopted daughter, M., then living with him, for life ; with remainder over. The personal property was of insignificant value. The will made no other provision for M. Upon the executors' accounting, it appearing that they had in their hands only about $16,000, proceeds of a sale of the real property, which, after payment of commissions and expenses, would not suffice for the investment directed in the will; the court was asked to determine from what date interest, payable to the life beneficiary before the permanent establishment of the fund, was to be calculated—whether (1) from the testator's death, or (2) the end of a year thereafter, or (3) the time when the proceeds of sale of the real property were realized.—*Held*, that the real property became personal at the death of testator ; and that M. was entitled, as one to whom the testator stood *in loco parentis*, to interest from the date of that event. *Keating* v. *Bruns*, 233.

4. A legacy to a testator's widow in lieu of dower carries interest from the testator's death, although its value exceeds that of the dower interest. *Matter of Combs*, 348.

5. Testator, by his will, gave a legacy to his daughter, V., a married woman, directing his executors to pay it "as soon as practicable" after his death; and, by a later clause, provided that, "after the payment" of V.'s legacy, and "as soon as possible" after his death, the executors should invest a specified sum, and pay to his widow the interest and increase "commencing from my (his) decease."—*Held*, that no feature of the case took the bequest to V. out of the operation of the general rule, that interest does not begin to run on a legacy, until the

expiration of a year after the death of the testator, in the absence of an express or implied direction of the will to the contrary. *Vernet* v. *Williams*, 349.

6. *It seems*, that inability on the part of a legatee to take a legacy, at the time when it has become due, and when the executor is ready to pay it, will ordinarily prevent the running of interest thereon during the continuance of the inability. *Simpkins* v. *Scudder*, 371.

7. But where the father of an infant legatee, during the year succeeding the testator's death, advised the executor of his intention to procure the appointment of a general guardian who would be entitled, as such, to receive the legacy, and, in consequence of delay in applying for letters of guardianship, an appointment was not made until after the expiration of that year, the executor continuing to hold the fund in his hands,—*Held*, that the legacy should have been invested for the infant's benefit, pursuant to 2 R. S., 91, § 48; and that, though the executor was exonerated from personal liability, the infant was entitled to interest at the rate of six per cent., commencing at the end of a year from the death of the testator. *Id.*

8. The object of the statute (2 R. S., 90, § 43), directing that legacies are, unless the will otherwise directs, not payable until the end of one year after the grant of letters, is, first to give the executor ample time to reduce the estate into money; second, to allow him time to publish, for six months, notices to the creditors of the testator to present their claims, which notice cannot be published until six months after the issuing of letters; and, third, one year is allowed, after the recording of a decree admitting a will to probate, for persons interested in the estate of the decedent to present a petition praying that the probate thereof be revoked. It was evidently not the intention of the legislature, in postponing the payment of legacies, to change the old and well settled rule as to the interest thereon. *Carr* v. *Bennett*, 433, 455.

9. Testator, by his will, after providing for the payment of his debts, funeral expenses, etc., gave to his adopted daughter, J., an adult married woman living with her husband, the farm on which testator resided, and the household furniture, absolutely, and further directed his executor to invest $4,000 in a specified manner, and to pay the interest, after deducting commissions, annually to said daughter; the principal, at her death, to go to her children. The estate was adequate for the payment of all debts and legacies; more than $4,000 thereof being, at the time of testator's death, and continuously thereafter remaining invested as specified, and drawing interest. The life legatee asked for interest on said sum from testator's death; the residuary legatee, on the other hand, contending that interest did not begin to run upon the legacy until all decedent's debts were paid.—*Held*, that the life provision for J. was a general legacy, not falling within any of the exceptions to the general rule, whereby interest on such legacies begins to run only at the expiration of a year from the testator's death. *Id.*

10. Authorities upon the subject of payment of interest on legacies—collated; and the rules governing the same—stated. *Id.*

See EXECUTORS AND ADMINISTRATORS, 4; MORTGAGE, 2; PERSON
     INTERESTED; WAIVER.

INTERPRETATION OF STATUTE.

1. An act was passed by the legislature, in 1866 (L. 1886, ch. 201, §7), declaring that the corporation thereby created should be "subject to the provisions of title seven, part first, of chapter eighteen of the Revised Statutes, in relation to devises or bequests by will." The R. S. contain no such title; but, in a compilation, published as the fifth edition of the R. S., in 1859, a so-called seventh title was appended to the chapter in question, consisting of Laws of 1848, chap. 319, the sixth section whereof contains a restriction upon devises and bequests contained in a will not made and executed at least two months before the death of the testator.—*Held*, that the reference in the act of 1866 was to the act of 1848, appearing as the added title in the compilation referred to. *St. Frances Hospital* v. *Schreck*, 225.

2. Under the rule of construction established by § 3355 of the Code of Civil Procedure, sections 90 and 2511 are to be read together, the prohibition of the last named section being subject to the exception contained in § 90. *Benedict* v. *Cooper*, 362.

INTERPRETATION OF WILL.

See CONSTRUCTION OF WILL.

INVENTORY.

1. Testator, by a codicil to his will, provided: "Nor shall my executors and trustees be obliged or compelled to file with the Surrogate any inventory of my estate." Upon the application for probate,—*Held*, that it is against public policy to permit such interference with the forms of procedure established by law, removing the barriers designed to protect estates from misappropriation; and that the clause in question was invalid and of no effect. *Potter* v. *McAlpine*, 108.

2. Code Civ. Pro., § 2715 establishes the only method of procedure for compelling an executor or administrator to return an inventory. The order, made pursuant to that section, requiring the respondent to make a return, or show cause why he should not be attached, is one of those mandates which must be issued as the result of a judicial determination, and not one which can be properly issued, as of course, by the clerk of the court; it must be personally served upon the delinquent. A summons requiring the representative to appear is improper. *White* v. *Lewis*, 170.

3. An inventory, made and filed by an executor, of the assets of his decedent's estate, has not the effect of binding, even presumptively, his successor in office. *Solomons* v. *Kursheedt,* 307.

4. An unverified list of a decedent's assets cannot be treated as an inventory thereof, within the meaning of the statute relating to such instrument. *Loesche* v. *Griffin,* 358.

See CREDITOR.

INVESTMENTS.

In order to justify the removal of a testamentary trustee, upon the ground that, by an improper application of trust moneys, or an investment in securities unauthorized by law, he has demonstrated his unfitness for the due execution of his trust, within the meaning of Code Civ. Pro., § 2817, it must appear that his acts have been such as to endanger the trust property, or to show a want of honesty, or of proper capacity, or of reasonable fidelity. *Morgan* v. *Morgan,* 612.

See EXECUTORS AND ADMINISTRATORS, 9.

ISSUE.

The word "issue," in a will, where no light is thrown upon its meaning by the context or extrinsic circumstances, must be construed to denote the lineal descendants, in the first degree, of the ancestor indicated, to the exclusion of remoter kindred. *Taft* v. *Taft,* 86.

JUDGMENT.

1. Whether a judgment entered against an executor or administrator after the revocation of his letters can be enforced against the decedent's estate, *quære.* If it can, the method is by application, under Code Civ. Pro., § 2609, for leave to sue upon the judgment debtor's official bond. *Breslin* v. *Smyth,* 251.

2. The death of a judgment debtor within the State does not defeat the operation of the statute regulating the presumption of payment of the judgment ; nor does it affect the rights or remedies of the judgment creditor, except that the personal representative of decedent is substituted as the person whose recognition of the validity of the judgment may serve to take the case out of the statute, and except, also, that one year and six months are added to the twenty years, within which the creditor is bound to enforce his rights or be treated as having abandoned them. *Visscher* v. *Wesley,* 301.

See COSTS, 1 ; PAYMENT OF DEBTS, 6 ; STATUTE OF LIMITATIONS, 3.

INDEX.

JUDICIAL NOTICE.

The courts cannot take judicial notice of the aptitude of bonds and mortgages to escape the vigilance of the taxing officer. *Valentine* v. *Valentine*, 597.

JUDICIAL SETTLEMENT.

See ACCOUNTING; EXECUTORS AND ADMINISTRATORS; GENERAL GUARDIAN; TESTAMENTARY TRUSTER.

JURISDICTION.

1. A decedent's discharge in bankruptcy may be attacked collaterally, in a special proceeding in a Surrogate's court relating to his estate, and declared void, as against a creditor as to whom the same was fraudulently procured. *Jones* v. *Le Baron*, 37.

2. Testator, by his will, gave certain property to his executor, in trust to receive the income and apply the same to the use of E., his widow, for life, who he also provided should be paid an annuity of $250, in lieu of dower. The annuity and income not being duly paid, and E. having presented a petition praying that the executor be compelled to file an account, and for the payment of the same, respondent set up an agreement between himself and E., whereby, in consideration of an increased allowance, she withdrew her opposition to the probate of the will, and released her dower; which agreement, it was contended, ousted the Surrogate's court of jurisdiction, and rendered resort to another tribunal necessary for its enforcement. The agreement contained a clause expressly negativing a waiver by E. of her rights under the will.—*Held*, that, notwithstanding the agreement mentioned, the Surrogate's court had jurisdiction to compel the execution, in E.'s favor, of the provisions contained in the will, and that the prayer for the filing of an account should be granted. *Howard* v. *Howard*, 53.

3. Jurisdiction over a non-resident respondent can be obtained only by voluntary appearance, or by service of a citation in the manner specified in Code Civ. Pro., § 2524. *Saw Mill Co.* v. *Dock*, 55.

4. Where a non-resident of the State died without its limits, leaving personal property in New York county, which was taken into actual custody by a domiciliary executrix before the filing of a petition in the Surrogate's court of that county, in pursuance whereof the will was admitted to probate here,—*Held*, that the court had no judisdiction in the premises, and that the decree must be set aside, and the letters issued to the petitioner revoked. *Townsend* v. *Pell*, 367.

5. A Surrogate's court has no jurisdiction to try and determine the question of the validity of an assignment, procured by the administrator of an intestate's estate, from one interested therein, of the interest of the latter, where the same is attacked on the ground of alleged fraud in its procurement. *Woodruff* v. *Woodruff*, 505.

LACHES.

LAPSE.

tion contained merely words of identification; that the habendum operated as a limitation; and that the legacy lapsed under the general rule. *Bolles* v. *Bacon*, 43.

See LEGACY ; WILL, 9.

LATENT AMBIGUITY.

Testatrix, by her will, directed two fourths of the residue of her estate "*to be divided equally between the home and foreign missions.*" The context furnishing no evidence tending to identify the intended recipients of this charity, the next of kin objected, upon the executor's accounting, that the provision in question was void for uncertainty.— *Held*, that the case presented was one of latent ambiguity explicable by extrinsic evidence, including declarations of testatrix made after the execution of the will; and that, upon such evidence, the legacies belonged to the Boards of Home and Foreign Missions, respectively, of the Presbyterian church in the U. S. of America. *Board of Missions* v. *Scovell*, 516.

LEGACY.

1. Testator by his will, directed his executors to complete the building of his house, if unfinished at the time of his death, at an expense not exceeding $50,000 in the aggregate ; and if the same should not be furnished at that time, to pay to his wife as desired "not exceeding $15,000, as an additional specific legacy, to enable her to furnish the same." He then devised the house to his wife, and her heirs and assigns forever. The devisee sold the house unfurnished, and received from the executors $15,000, as an absolute legacy. Upon objection to such payment,—*Held*, that the purpose mentioned in the legatory clause was not of the substance of the gift, which was an unconditional one ; and that the payment by the executors was proper. *Lounsbery* v. *Parson*, 33.

2. A gift, by will, of "all the money left in the W. S. Bank, after carrying out" (certain prior directions contained in the will), is a specific legacy of a chose in action, which the legatee is entitled to receive *in specie*, together only with such increment as may have attached thereto. No claim will lie, under any circumstances, against the executors, for interest, *eo nomine*, thereon; nor are they bound to make the same productive. *Larkin* v. *Salmon*, 270.

3. The statute does not contemplate the assumption, by a Surrogate, of responsibility as custodian of *chattels* bequeathed to an infant. He can be called on to receive a legacy so bequeathed, only where its subject-matter renders it capable of investment for the infant's benefit. *Toler* v. *Landon*, 339.

4. Unless a testator distinctly indicates that one or more of his beneficiaries

is to be preferred to others, or one or more of his bequests is founded upon a consideration, and is not, therefore, a mere bestowal of bounty, the courts will presume an intent that all should be paid alike, and, in case of a deficiency of assets, will direct a ratable abatement. *Waters* v. *Collins*, 374.

5. Testator, by his will, directed the establishment of a trust fund of $50,000, for the use of his daughter G., for life ; and, by codicil bequeathed to C., one of the persons named as executors, $700, which sum, he declared, "is to be over and above any and all commissions that he may be entitled to receive as one of the executors," and was given upon condition that C. qualified and acted as executor, which he did. There being a deficiency of assets, it was contended, on the one hand, that the trust provision in G.'s favor took precedence, as being made for the support and maintenance of a daughter ; and, on the other, that the legacy to C. was not mere bounty, but was in the nature of a compensation for services expected from and actually rendered by the legatee.—*Held*, that the two legacies must abate proportionally. *Id.*

6. Testator, by his will, gave all his property to his executors, in trust (1) to discharge his debts; (2) to pay to his widow, for life and in lieu of dower, the interest or income from one third of all his property; (3) to pay to his mother $100,000; and (4) to dispose of the residue as directed. The condition of the estate was such as to leave a large residue, in excess of the mother's legacy, and after setting apart one third of the entire estate for the widow.—*Held*, that the widow was entitled to the interest or income of one third of all the property, after payment of debts, without a deduction of the amount of the mother's legacy. *Thompson* v. *Thompson*, 409.

7. As to whether, in case an assignment, to the life beneficiary, of one third of the estate, after payment of debts, left less than the specified amount of the mother's legacy, the provisions contained in clauses (2) and (3) would abate equally—*quære. Id.*

See ASSIGNMENT; INTEREST, 1, 5, 6, 8; LAPSE; WAIVER; WILL, 3.

LETTERS OF ADMINISTRATION.

1. The withholding of letters of administration from one who, if not by some cause incapacitated, would be entitled in priority, under the statute, is never justifiable, except in cases where his disqualification is declared by the statute itself. *O'Brien* v. *Neubert*, 156.

2. Under 2 R. S., 75, § 32, providing that "No letters of administration shall be granted to a person convicted of an infamous crime . . . . . nor to any person who shall be adjudged incompetent, by the Surrogate, to execute the duties of such trust, by reason of drunkenness, improvidence or want of understanding,"—*Held*, 1. That, in order to bring a

case within the statutory prohibition, the *crime* in question must be infamous, within the definition of the statutes of this State, viz. : one punishable with death, or by imprisonment in a State prison ; and that the *conviction* must have been had in a court of this State, for an offense against the laws thereof ; 2. That a conviction, in a court of another state, of the crime of larceny, was not evidence of *improvidence* on the part of the convict, which would justify an adjudication, by the Surrogate, of incompetence to execute the duties of an administrator. *Id.*

LETTERS TESTAMENTARY.

See REVOCATION OF LETTERS, 2.

LIFE ESTATE.

1. The testator of testatrix, by his will, gave to the latter "all my (his) real estate of every name and nature, whatsoever, and all my (his) personal estate, goods and chattels of every kind, together with all book accounts and debts due, etc., and also a lawful right to buy and sell and dispose of a part or all of the above mentioned real estate, personal property, goods and chattels, as long as she retains her sound mind, and is capable of doing business and is not insane, during her natural life;" and, after her death, all the rest, residue and remainder of the estate "which is above willed and bequeathed to my (his) wife" to another and his heirs and assigns.—*Held*, that this provision expressly created a life estate in testatrix, with a power of disposition during her life; that so much of the personalty as remained undisposed of at the time of her death constituted no part of her estate; and that the executor of her will was not bound to account therefor. *Tompkins* v. *Fanton*, 4.

2. Cases where a will bestows property without specifying the nature of the estate, and gives to the donee a power of disposition—distinguished. *Id.*

3. Testator, by his will, after making certain specific dispositions, gave the remainder of his farm, and all his other real estate, and all his personal estate not otherwise disposed of, to his wife, S., to have and to hold during her natural life ; providing that she might use and employ the property so devised and given to her as she might see fit, for her own benefit, and might dispose of such part of said personal estate, from time to time, as she might see fit, or as might be proper for the best management thereof, for the benefit of those concerned, as she should direct ; and ordering his executors, at his wife's death, to sell all his real estate, and all his personal estate, or the produce thereof that should then remain, not disposed of by him in said will, or by or under the direction of his wife, and distribute the proceeds of sale, after paying his debts and those of his wife, in a manner specified. S. claimed the right to expend the personal property for her own

benefit, and that the executor should be directed, from time to time, to pay over to her, without notice or application to the court, such part of the principal fund as she might desire to use.—*Held*, that S. had the right to the life use, only, of the personal property, and that the executor was bound to turn over to her all such property in his hands, to be held and managed by her as a testamentary trustee for the remaindermen. *Kelsey* v. *Van Camp*, 580.

LIFE TENANT.

1. While it is the general rule, that as between life tenant and remainderman, taking under a will, the expenses of administering the trust must be borne by the former, and paid out of the income, the same is subject to exceptions, as *ex. gr.*, in the case of a disposition of the residue, to ascertain the amount of which such expenses are necessarily incurred. *Reynolds* v. *Reynolds*, 82.

2. Testator, by his will, after directing his executors to pay all his just debts and funeral and testamentary expenses, and making certain specific bequests, gave the net residue and remainder of his estate to his executors, in trust to manage the same, collect the income, and, after deducting all proper costs, charges and expenses pertaining to the trust, to pay over the net residue of rents, etc., to his wife for life with remainder over; and appointed his wife and another, executrix and executor thereof. The widow alone qualified. Upon the judicial settlement of her account *as executrix*, had with a view to handing over the funds to a trustee,—*Held*, that the expenses of administration and commissions were chargeable to the *corpus* of the estate. *Id.*

3. Where a will gave to testator's widow the income of all his estate, "after deducting taxes, assessments, interest on mortgages, if any, *and other charges and expenses*, for and during her natural life,"—*Held*, under the doctrine of *ejusdem generis*, that disbursements for funeral expenses, transportation of decedent's remains, and services of his attending physician, were chargeable to the *corpus* of the estate, and not to income. *Zapp* v. *Miller*, 266.

See STOCK DIVIDEND.

LIMITATION.

See STATUTE OF LIMITATIONS.

MENTAL CAPACITY.

See TESTAMENTARY CAPACITY ; WILL.

MARRIAGE.

Upon an application, made in 1885, for a decree granting to petitioner, as

decedent's widow, letters of administration on his estate, it appeared
that petitioner had been married in 1874 to one D., with whom she
afterwards lived as his wife, and whom she last saw in 1875. There
was no evidence that D. had been seen by any one since 1878. In
1883, petitioner was married to decedent, who was cognizant of her
prior marriage to and relations with D.—*Held*, that there was better
warrant in the law and in the evidence, for holding that D. was dead
than for holding that decedent and petitioner were guilty of a bigamous marriage; and that the prayer of the petition should be granted.
Nesbit v. *Nesbit*, 329.

See ABSENCE.

MISCONDUCT.

See REVOCATION OF LETTERS, 3.

MORTGAGE.

1. Testator, by the fifth article of his will, directed his executors to pay, out
of the residue of his personal estate, "the mortgages now being existing liens upon . . . . . two dwelling houses (describing them), to the
end that said dwelling houses may be free and discharged from mortgage liens, as soon as practicable after my decease;" and further gave
his real property, and the residue of his personal property, to the
executors, in trust "to pay over the entire net annual rents of said
real estate, after payment of all taxes, assessments, insurance, and
repairs of and upon said real estate, and the interest" of the personal
property, to his wife, for the maintenance and education of his minor
children, with remainder over. The mortgages fell due after the death
of the testator. A referee reported that the interest on the mortgages,
accruing after testator's death, had been improperly charged to the
corpus of the personalty.—*Held*, that the will contained an "express
direction," within the meaning of 1 R. S., 749, § 4, requiring the mortgages to be satisfied, both as to principal and interest, out of the personal property. *Alexander* v. *Powell*, 152.

2. Decedent, during his lifetime, assigned a certain leasehold to Z., who, to
secure a part of the consideration, gave back a bond, and mortgage
thereof, conditioned for the payment of $3,700, in semiannual instal-
ments "until the whole principal sum is fully paid, and interest on the
amount from time to time remaining unpaid . . . . . at the rate of
seven per cent., per annum." Z. assigned the lease, subject to the
mortgage, which the assignee assumed and agreed to pay, to M., who
assigned to another without mentioning the mortgage. Thereafter M.,
having been appointed executor of decedent's will, which disposed of the
estate for life, with remainder over, caused the mortgage to be satisfied
of record, and filed an account charging himself with no indebtedness
in the premises. Upon a judicial settlement of M.'s account, had

after the death of the life tenant, and to which the latter's representative was not a party, no evidence was given of the payment of any part of the principal of the mortgage, or interest thereon.—*Held*, that M., by his assumption, became decedent's debtor in the amount of the mortgage, and was chargeable therewith, in favor of the remaindermen, with interest at the rate of seven per cent., from the date of the instrument, save for the period between the death of the decedent and that of the life tenant. *Zapp* v. *Miller*, 260.

See JUDICIAL NOTICE.

MORTUARY MONUMENT.

See FUNERAL EXPENSES.

MOTION.

See PRACTICE, 2.

MOURNING APPAREL.

It being the almost universal practice for the family of a deceased person to wear mourning ; and a change of wearing apparel being thus rendered necessary as a part of the preparation for the funeral, and as a mark of proper respect for the dead ; this expense, when reasonably incurred by those for whom he was bound, in his lifetime, to provide, should be borne by his estate. *Allen* v. *Allen*, 524.

See FUNERAL EXPENSES.

NEXT OF KIN.

Upon a judicial settlement of the account of the administrator of intestate's estate, a decree was rendered in July, 1884, whereby the distributive share therein of J., a son of the intestate, against whom proceedings supplementary to execution were then pending, was fixed at $212, which the administrator was ordered to retain until the disposition thereof should be directed by a court of competent jurisdiction. Thereafter the wife of J. applied to the Surrogate's court to open the decree so rendered, and amend the same by directing said share to be paid to herself, alleging, substantially, that J., during the lifetime of his mother, had conveyed to the latter all personal property to come to him from the grantee's estate, or from any other source whatever; and that said grantee had forthwith conveyed the same to petitioner.—*Held*, that it was not in the power of any person, by any such process as that described, to introduce himself into the category of the next of kin of another; that petitioner, being neither a creditor nor one of the next of kin of intestate, nor the assignee of a distributive share in her

NOTICE.

OFFICIAL BOND.

ORDER.

See Costs, 2.

PARTIES.

Testator, by his will, directed the executors to invest $100,000, and pay the income to his wife B., during her life or widowhood. This provision, which was declared to be in lieu of dower, was accepted by the widow, who for a time received interest upon the amount mentioned; but ·no sum was ever invested as required. B. having filed a petition with the Surrogate, alleging that the value of the estate had depreciated far below its appraised and estimated value, and praying that the executors be directed to pay to her an amount equal to her dower interest, as a purchaser for value, it appeared that there were several alleged creditors of the estate, whose aggregate claims exceeded the estimated value of the latter, and none of whom had been cited.—*Held*, that, whether the testamentary provision in petitioner's favor called into exercise the functions of the executors as such, or as trustees, those claiming as creditors must be brought in as parties, unless petitioner chose to discontinue and institute a proceeding for the judicial settlement of the executors' account. *Beekman v. Vanderveer*, 221.

See Citation, 1; Discovery of Assets, 1; Notice; Temporary Administrator, 2.

PAYMENT OF DEBTS.

1. The executors of decedent's will filed an intermediate account in 1882, whereupon a decree was made, pursuant to which the assets then realized were distributed among the creditors whose claims had been presented and proved. A creditor company which held a claim secured by mortgage, did not present the same, but, after the distribution, foreclosed the mortgage, obtained a judgment for over $2,000, deficiency, and, upon a judicial settlement of the executors' account, asked to be allowed, out of the assets then on hand, the same dividend to which it would have been entitled, if its claim had been presented upon the intermediate accounting, before the declaration of a second dividend. Decedent's estate was insolvent.—*Held*, that the demand in question was proper and should be allowed, being justified by the provisions of 2 R. S., 87, § 28, which prohibits a preference in the payment of any debt over another of the same class. *Home Ins. Co. v. Lyon*, 69.

2. In a special proceeding, instituted under Code Civ. Pro., § 2717, to compel payment of a claim, the petition alleged, substantially, that decedent's estate was indebted to petitioner in the sum of $267, without setting forth the nature or basis of the demand; whereto respondent interposed an answer, averring, upon information and belief, that the pre-

tended foundation of the claim was the rendering of services and incurring of expenses, in and about decedent's estate, and denying that the same was done at decedent's request.—*Held*, that the answer did not set "forth facts which show that it is doubtful whether the petitioner's claim is valid and legal," etc., so as to necessitate a dismissal of the petition under Code Civ. Pro., § 2718 ; but that respondent was entitled to a direction, to the petitioner, to state the nature of his claim with greater particularity. *Budlong* v. *Clemens*, 145.

3. In a special proceeding, instituted under Code Civ. Pro., § 2717, to compel payment of an alleged claim against a decedent's estate, an objection, properly interposed, whereby it is insisted that the demand is excessive in amount, necessitates a dismissal of the petition,—the issue so raised being one which the Surrogate's court has no authority to determine. *Koch* v. *Alker*, 148.

4. The statute, 2 R. S., 84, § 13,—providing that "the naming of any person executor in a will shall not operate as a discharge or bequest of any claim which the testator had against such executor, but such claim shall be included . . . . . in an inventory, and such executor shall be liable for the same as for so much money in his hands at the time such debt or demand becomes due," etc.,—must receive a restricted interpretation, made in view of the mischief designed to be thereby remedied : it was not its purpose to place a debtor-executor in a position more favorable than that of other debtors of the estate. *Warner* v. *Knower*, 208.

5. Where a creditor receives, from the estate of his debtor, dividends upon a debt partly secured by the guaranty of a third person, such dividends should not be appropriated exclusively to the *excess* of the debt, above the sum guaranteed, but should be applied ratably to the whole indebtedness, thus relieving the surety from liability, to the extent of the dividend on the part secured. *Richardson* v. *Kidder*, 255.

6. Decedent who, in his lifetime, was appointed guardian of K., then an infant, and filed an official bond, in a penalty of $60,000, upon which R. was a surety, died insolvent, and indebted to K. in a large amount. The latter, having recovered a judgment for more than $70,000 against decedent's executors, commenced an action against R. which was compromised, R. paying $33,000 and obtaining a release from further liability. The appropriate dividend upon the whole amount of the judgment having been paid into court, by the executors, out of the insolvent estate, K. claimed the entire dividend, while R. contended that he was entitled to a share thereof proportioned to his payment.— *Held*, that the dividend must be divided between the claimants, in the proportion of the paid to the unpaid portion of the judgment. *Id.*

7. 2 R. S., § 28, forbidding preference to be given in the payment of any debt of a decedent over other debts of the same class, and declaring that the obtaining a judgment against the executor or administrator shall not "entitle such debt to any preference over others of the same

class," does not undertake to provide respecting *the costs* of an action for the collection of such debt, the same not being one of the "debts of the deceased" (§ 27). *Shields* v. *Sullivan*, 296.

8. A creditor of a decedent cannot, at his own option, divide up his claim, placing a portion as a demand against the personal, and the remainder as against the real property. An administrator of a decedent's estate, having no power over the realty, an arrangement to such an effect, entered into by a creditor with him, would be void as against the heir. *Mead* v. *Jenkins*, 551.

9. One N., who was indebted to decedent, at the time of his death, in the amount of a promissory note for $222.50, and interest, was appointed administrator of his estate, and omitted this item of indebtedness from the inventory and from the account filed by him as such administrator. Upon a judicial settlement, certain creditors objecting to the omission, it appeared that the debt had not been discharged, and that N. was totally insolvent.—*Held*, that the administrator stood in the same position as any other debtor; that the amount of the claim should be added to the sum of the inventory; and that, in case he subsequently became possessed of means, he might be compelled to account for, and pay over the amount, in the same manner as if he had, after an accounting, recovered, from a third person, a doubtful claim, for which he had received credit thereupon. *Burkhalter* v. *Norton*, 610.

See PAYMENT OF LEGACY; TAXES AND ASSESSMENTS; TEMPORARY ADMINISTRATOR, 4.

PAYMENT OF LEGACY.

1. Where a creditor of a decedent petitions the Surrogate's court, under Code Civ. Pro., § 2717, for a decree directing payment of his claim, subd. 2 of § 2718 casts upon him the burden of proving, "to the satisfaction of the Surrogate, that there is money or other personal property applicable to the payment or satisfaction" thereof. *Lynch* v. *Patchen*, 58.

2. Code Civ. Pro., § 2718, relating to an application to compel *an executor* to pay a legacy, and id., § 2806, containing a similar provision in reference to *a testamentary trustee*, have essentially the same purpose. They establish modes of procedure whereby a beneficiary under a will may obtain prompt relief, where it is plain that the rights of other persons cannot be thereby prejudiced; while, on the other hand, where the grant of such relief may prove prejudicial to others, the latter are required to be allowed an opportunity to be heard. *Beekman* v. *Vanderveer*, 221.

3. During the pendency of a special proceeding, instituted to procure a decree admitting to probate a paper propounded as the will of decedent, one of the latter's next of kin, who was named as legatee in the disputed instrument, having applied for a decree directing the payment to her of

a sum of money, to be reckoned as part of her distributive share, or of her legacy, according to the event, the executor filed an answer setting forth that the applicant was opposing the admission to probate of the alleged will, which contained a clause declaring that, in case any legatee should contest the validity of the instrument, the provision in his favor should cease, and fall into the residue.—*Held*, that the facts set forth showed that the applicant had rendered "doubtful" her claims as legatee, and that, under Code Civ. Pro., § 2718, subd. 1, the petition must be dismissed. *Rank* v. *Camp*, 278.

4. The direction—which, it is provided by Code Civ. Pro., § 2748, must be inserted in a decree for the distribution of a decedent's assets—to the executor or administrator to pay to the county treasurer a legacy or share which is not paid *to the person entitled* thereto, within a time specified, is generally of no practical importance, and may in most cases with propriety be omitted. *Koch* v. *Woehr*, 282.

5. Testator, by his will, gave the residue to "my (his) brothers and sisters now living, and the descendants of any deceased brothers and sisters." Upon the judicial settlement of the executor's account, it appeared that decedent once had a sister, A., of whom nothing further was known.—*Held*, that the share of A., if living, or of her descendants, if any, could not properly be left in the executor's hands, subject to a direction, in the decree, to pay the same to the county treasurer, at the expiration of two years, in the contingency specified in Code Civ. Pro., § 2748, but that a reference must be had to determine who was *the person entitled* thereto. *Id.*

PERSON INTERESTED.

A special proceeding instituted, under Code Civ. Pro., § 2685, to procure a decree revoking letters of administration, is entirely distinct, in its nature from those referred to in id., § 2514, subd. 11 (second sentence), which declares that, "where a provision of this chapter prescribes that a person interested may object to an appointment, or may apply for an inventory, an account, or increased security, an allegation of his interest duly verified, suffices, although his interest is disputed; unless," etc. Hence, where such a decree of revocation is sought by a widow of the intestate, who has assigned her interest in the estate as widow, by the procurement of the administrator, though she alleges fraud in such procurement, her proceedings will be dismissed,—the Surrogate's court being unable to set aside the instrument for fraud ; until which is done, the petitioner is excluded from the class of persons interested in the estate, as defined in the first sentence of Code Civ. Pro., § 2514. *Woodruff* v. *Woodruff*, 505.

PLEADINGS.

PRACTICE.

1. Where there is manifestly a *casus omissus* in the statute, respecting practice, owing to inadvertence in amendment, it is the duty of a Surrogate's court to adopt the practice formerly pursued in similar cases by the Court of Chancery, and more recently by the Supreme Court, in its exercise of equity power. *Matter of Whitehead*, 227.

2. Under Code Civ. Pro., § 2481, subd. 6, which authorizes the Surrogate, in a proper case, to vacate a decree of his court, and provides that the powers thus granted "must be exercised . . . . . *in the same manner as a court of record and of general jurisdiction exercises the same*," the manner indicated is that sanctioned by a court of the character mentioned, in proceedings to set aside or open a judgment; the same being properly initiated by a notice of motion or order to show cause. *Cluff* v. *Tower*, 253.

See GUARDIAN AD LITEM, 4; NOTICE.

PRESUMPTION.

The presumption of the continuance of life shown to have once existed must yield, in case of conflict, to that of innocence of crime. *Nesbit* v. *Nesbit*, 329.

See ACKNOWLEDGMENT, 1 ; MARRIAGE.

PRIVILEGED COMMUNICATION.

The privilege established by Code Civ. Pro., § 835, which declares that "an attorney or counsellor at law shall not be allowed to disclose a communication made by his client to him . . . . . in the course of his professional employment," is that of the client and not of the attorney ; and, where the former is a party to a litigation, this privilege exists, notwithstanding the abrogation of the rule which rendered *parties* incompetent as witnesses. *Hoyt* v. *Jackson*, 388.

PROBATE OF WILL.

1. The court, when asked to reject an alleged will, can pay no heed to such considerations as that the same is mean, unjust and inequitable; or that it withholds the absolute ownership of decedent's property from his own children, or makes unequal provisions for them; or that public sentiment and the moral sense of the community condemn the instrument and its author. *Potter* v. *McAlpine*, 108.

2. The enactment of Code Civ. Pro., § 2622 has lent a new sanction to the doctrine enunciated in Delafield v. Parish, 25 N. Y., 34,—that the proponent of a will 's bound to prove to the satisfaction of the court that

the paper in question declares the will of the deceased, and that the supposed testator was, at the time of execution, of sound and disposing mind and memory. *Cooper* v. *Benedict*, 196.

See CITATION, 1 ; EXECUTION OF WILL ; REVOCATION OF PROBATE.

PUBLICATION OF WILL.

Upon an application, made more than thirty years after the date of its alleged execution, for the probate of decedent's will, F., one of the subscribing witnesses, testified that he signed it as such, and saw it signed by the decedent and by the other witness, since deceased; that, according to his best recollection, which, however, he admitted was indistinct, decedent signed while seated at a stand in a room of her residence, thereafter yielding her seat to F., who, after signing, gave place in like manner to the second witness. The only other evidence was that afforded by an attestation clause, which lacked the usual completeness of form, being to the following effect: "Signed and acknowledged by said (decedent) as her last will and testament in our presence; and signed by us in her presence."—*Held*, though with some hesitation, that there was sufficient evidence of a virtual acknowledgment, by decedent, of the testamentary character of the instrument, and request to the witnesses to sign as such; and that the petition for probate must be granted. *Nicholson* v. *Myers*, 193.

See ACKNOWLEDGMENT, 2 ; EXECUTION OF WILL ; SUBSCRIBING WITNESS.

REAL PROPERTY.

See SALE OF REAL ESTATE.

REFERENCE.

1. In a special proceeding instituted for the revocation of probate of a will, the citation was duly served upon all the necessary parties, including decedent's infant son, a special guardian for whom was, however, neither applied for nor appointed. By the consent of all the parties who appeared and took part in the subsequent hearing, a referee was appointed to take testimony and report the same to the Surrogate; who decided, upon the testimony reported, to revoke the decree of probate. The executors, respondents, opposed the entry of a decree, contending that, because of a failure to appoint a special guardian for the infant party, the order of reference and all subsequent proceedings were unauthorized.—*Held*, 1. That, by the service of the citation upon all the necessary parties, including the infant, the court had acquired jurisdiction of the proceeding and of all the parties thereto; 2. That the testimony taken in pursuance of the consent of parties should not be tossed aside as worthless at the instance of those so consenting;

3. That a special guardian should be appointed for the infant, to ascertain and report whether it would be for the best interests of the latter to set aside the order of reference and the proceedings subsequent thereto, or that the same should stand, and a decree be entered in conformity with the decision already made. *Benedict* v. *Cooper*, 362.

2. A referee appointed by a Surrogate, pursuant to the authority conferred by Code Civ. Pro., § 2546, having, by the terms of that section, the same power "as a referee appointed by the Supreme Court for the trial of an issue of fact in an action," the procedure before him is governed by the provisions of General Rule of Practice 30, which excepts testimony, taken upon the trial of the issues in an action, from its requirement that testimony taken before a referee shall be signed by the witness giving the same. *Matter of Russell*, 377.

See STENOGRAPHER.

REHEARING.

See COMMISSIONS, 16.

RENUNCIATION OF LETTERS.

1. One who has become invested with the office of executor may resign, but cannot renounce the appointment; still less can he retract a renunciation. *Matter of Suarez*, 164.

2. Where a person, who has actually received letters testamentary, performed, for a time, the duties of the executorial office, and procured, upon his own application, the revocation of his letters, he becomes a stranger to the estate, as regards any right or privilege previously belonging to him, by reason of his nomination in the testator's will. *Id.*

3. It is the manifest purpose of the provision of Code Civ. Pro., § 2639,— allowing the renunciation of an executorial appointment to be retracted in the cases and manner therein specified,—to sanction the doctrine of the courts, which permitted one, who had not only declined to undertake the duties of an executor, but even solemnly declared his refusal to act as such, to withdraw his declinature at any time before the estate should be put into the charge of a representative, or thereafter, when it should cease to be in such charge. *Id.*

RES ADJUDICATA.

Where the claim of a creditor of a decedent has been fixed in amount by the decree of a Surrogate's court, rendered upon an accounting to which he was a party, he is concluded thereby, in a proceeding subsequently instituted by him for the sale of decedent's real property, in order to procure the payment of an unpaid balance of the claim. *Mead* v. *Jenkins*, 551.

676   INDEX.

RESIDUE.

A *residuum* of a testator's estate is nothing more nor less than what is *left*, after satisfaction of all express or prior dispositions. *Thompson* v. *Thompson*, 409.

REVISED STATUTES.

[*Sections construed or cited.*]

REVIVOR.

See ABATEMENT, 2.

REVOCATION OF LETTERS.

1. Testator, by his will, appointed his son T. and one C. its executors; bequeathed sundry legacies, which he charged upon his real property; and gave to the executors a power of sale of the latter, in order to carry out his testamentary provisions. C., who performed most of the executorial duties, having found an opportunity to sell, at a fair valuation, a parcel of the real property which, both before and since testator's death, had been occupied as a residence by T., the latter refused to join in the deed upon the ground that he ought to have the property himself at less than the stipulated price, at the same time stating that

It was worth more than such price to an outsider. On account of this refusal, the contract of sale was abandoned. Upon petition, by the residuary legatees, for the revocation of T.'s letters,—*Held*, that T. was not a testamentary trustee within the meaning of Code Civ. Pro., § 2819; that the power to sell and distribute the proceeds of the realty was so inseparably connected with the office of executor that no distinct proceeding to remove him as trustee, or donee of a power in trust, could be had; and that, while the delinquency of which he had been guilty could not be construed as improvidence, within the meaning of Code Civ. Pro., § 2685, subd. 2, it was such misconduct in the execution of his office as rendered him unfit for the due execution thereof, within the meaning of that subdivision, and that the prayer of the petition should be granted. *Oliver v. Frisbie*, 22.

2. Testator having, by his will, nominated M. and J. as its executors, and letters testamentary having been issued to M. in June, and to J. in September, 1878, the former, in October of the same year, filed a petition setting forth his wish " to renounce the said appointment as executor and all right and claim to letters testamentary," and embodied, in the account filed by him, a declaration that he had renounced the same; whereupon a decree was entered, declaring the acceptance of M.'s renunciation and revoking his letters. J., who thereafter entered upon the execution of the duties of the trust, having died in 1884, leaving assets unadministered, M. applied for letters testamentary, filing what purported to be a retraction of renunciation.—*Held*, that the case was one for the grant of letters of administration with the will annexed, pursuant to the provision of Code Civ. Pro., § 2643, which requires such letters to be issued where the office of legal representative is vacant by reason of the revocation of letters; and that the petition of M. should be denied. *Matter of Suarez*, 164.

3. The will of decedent contained a clause, whereby his executors were fully empowered, authorized and directed, at any time after his decease to sell any or all of his real or personal estate, not specifically devised or bequeathed, with a certain exception ; also giving unto them full power and authority to execute and acknowledge all necessary conveyances to carry the will into effect. The surviving executor having been required to give security for the faithful performance of his duties, filed an official bond in a penalty of $11,000, with two sureties, to whom, for the purpose of indemnifying them against loss by reason of their recognizance, he at once conveyed a farm, and assigned a contract for the purchase of another farm, both belonging to his decedent's estate. Upon an application, by persons interested, for the revocation of the executor's letters, on the ground of misconduct in the execution of his office, within the meaning of Code Civ. Pro., § 2685,—*Held*, that, the indemnification of the sureties in the executor's bond not being one of the purposes contemplated by the power of sale contained in the will, the act of the executor was illegal and improper ; to uphold which would be to subvert the very principles upon which

such a bond is required; that the act complained of was clearly within the spirit of the section cited, and that the prayer of the petition should be granted. *Fleet v. Simmons*, 542.

See ACCOUNTING, 2.

REVOCATION OF PROBATE.

1. Under Code Civ. Pro., § 2652, requiring the Surrogate, if he "decides that the will is not sufficiently proved to be the last will of the testator," etc., to make a decree accordingly, the rule laid down in Delafield v. Parish, 25 N. Y., 34, is applicable where the proceeding is, in form, one to revoke a decree of probate already granted. *Cooper v. Benedict*, 136.

2. A petition for the revocation of probate of a will should not differ essentially, in its statement of the grounds of objection, from an answer to a petition for probate. Upon the principle embodied in Rule No. 4, in force in New York county, which regulates the contents of such an answer, averments of matters of evidence are generally out of place in a petition for such revocation, and may be stricken out, on motion. *Henry v. Henry*, 322.

3. Where, upon an application to revoke a decree admitting a will to probate, the court finds *grave reason to doubt* whether, at the date of the alleged execution, decedent was physically and mentally capable of participating in the essential formalities, and whether he subscribed the instrument according to law, the prayer of the petition should be granted. *Knapp v. Reilly*, 427.

REVOCATION OF WILL.

See DUPLICATE WILL; TRIPLICATE WILL.

SALE OF REAL ESTATE.

1. In a special proceeding instituted to procure a decree directing the disposition of the real property of a decedent for the payment of his debts, the Surrogate is bound, under Code Civ. Pro., § 2755, upon the return of the citation, to take proof of the claims of all who appear as creditors of the decedent, including those which have been presented to the executor or administrator, and rejected, or not allowed, by him. Actual creditors and those claiming to be such, have the same right to appear and establish their demands. *Turner v. Amsdell*, 19.

2. In a special proceeding instituted under Code Civ. Pro., § 2750, *et seq.*, to procure a decree directing the disposition of a decedent's real property for the payment of his debts, the fact that an alleged creditor's claim has already been presented to and admitted by the personal represen-

tative throws the burden of proof upon a party objecting thereto. *Jones* v. *Le Baron*, 37.

8. In a special proceeding for the disposition of a decedent's real property for the payment of his debts, a creditor other than the petitioner, whose claim has been contested and allowed cannot be awarded costs under Code Civ. Pro., § 2561, notwithstanding the *general* character of that section, inasmuch as no provision for the payment of such an award is made by § 2793; after compliance with the directions of which section, the entire proceeds of the disposition will have been exhausted. *Long* v. *Olmsted*, 581.

See COSTS, 3, 4; GUARDIAN AD LITEM, 3; JURISDICTION, 7.

SECURITY FOR COSTS.

A Surrogate's court has no authority to require a party to a special proceeding therein to furnish security for the payment of his adversary's costs. *Loesche* v. *Griffin*, 358.

SERVICE OF CITATION.

1. Code Civ. Pro., § 2527, providing, among other things, that a Surrogate, where he has reasonable grounds to believe that a person to be cited is mentally incapable to protect his rights, although not judicially declared to be incompetent, may "make an order requiring that a copy of the citation be delivered, in behalf of that person, to a person designated in the order," authorizes an *additional* service; the regular and ordinary service is not dispensed with. Hence, where application was made for an order for such delivery, in behalf of a resident of another state, alleged to be of unsound mind,—*Held*, upon granting the application, that, in order to acquire jurisdiction, the citation must *also* be served upon the non-resident, by publication, or by delivering to him personally a copy, without the State, pursuant to § 2524. *Matter of Cortwright*, 13.

2. Upon an accounting by the executors of the will of decedent, the citation was served upon one of the next of kin of the latter, who was a resident of the county, but was at the time absent in England, by leaving a copy at her residence, with a person entrusted by her with its charge, of the age of about sixty years, on the 5th day of August. The citation was returnable on the 22d day of September, following, and a decree was not entered until the expiration of two months from the return day.—*Held*, that the service was made "under such circumstances that the Surrogate had good reason to believe that the copy came to her knowledge in time for her to attend at the return day," as required by Code Civ. Pro., § 2520, and that the decree rendered in the proceedings, wherein the party so served failed to appear, was binding upon her. *Mead* v. *Miller*, 577.

See JURISDICTION, 3.

SPECIAL GUARDIAN.

See GUARDIAN AD LITEM.

SPECIFIC LEGACY.

It seems that no commissions are allowable to an executor upon the value of articles specifically bequeathed. *Hawley* v. *Singer*, 589.

See LEGACY, 2.

STATUTE OF LIMITATIONS.

1. Letters testamentary under decedent's will were issued in April, 1861, and the executors, in July of that year, filed an inventory of the estate; but their account was never judicially settled. M., a legatee, attained majority in February, 1879, and applied in April, 1884, under Code Civ. Pro., § 2723, for an order compelling the executors to file an account. The latter pleaded the statute of limitations (Code Civ. Pro., § 2723, subd. 4; id., § 396, subd. 1, and clause *ad. fin.*).—*Held*, 1. That, the object of the proceeding being manifestly to ascertain the petitioner's share in testator's estate, the same was subject to the limitation of an action for a legacy. 2. That, by Code Civ. Pro., § 1819, the statute commencing to run against such a cause of action only when the executor's account was judicially settled, petitioner's remedy was not barred. 3. That petitioner's delay in instituting the special proceeding was not such laches as would justify a dismissal. *Collins* v. *Waydell*, 30.

2. Decedent's sole surviving executor, having instituted a special proceeding for the judicial settlement of his account, and omitted to charge himself, in the latter, with several items of assets set forth in the inventory, which was thereupon offered in evidence by objectors, for the purpose of charging him with the omitted items, he pleaded the statute of limitations as a bar, nearly twenty years having elapsed since the issue of letters testamentary, and the account never having been settled.—*Held*, that the executor had waived this plea by his voluntary institution of the accounting proceeding. *Wyckoff* v. *Van Siclen*, 75.

3. Decedent, a judgment debtor, died within this State, and an administrator of his estate was appointed, within twenty years after the date when the creditor was first entitled to a mandate to enforce the judgment. Upon a judicial settlement of the administrator's account, the creditor, who sought payment of his judgment, failed to prove a partial payment or written acknowledgment of indebtedness, made by decedent in his lifetime, or by the administrator before the expiration of twenty-one years and six months after the date mentioned.—*Held*, under Code Civ. Pro., §§ 376, 403, 1. That the question as to the statutory bar could be raised by any other creditor, or any of the next of

kin, even without the administrator's co-operation, and against his wishes ; 2. That the judgment in question had lost its priority, and its validity as against other persons interested in decedent's estate, and could not be revived by the administrator. *Visscher* v. *Wesley*, 301.

See JUDGMENT, 2.

STAY OF PROCEEDINGS.

See APPEAL.

STENOGRAPHER.

The stenographer of a Surrogate's court is not within the scope of Code Civ. Pro., § 90, which prohibits the appointment of a clerk, deputy-clerk, etc., of a court of record to act as referee, or in other specified capacities, except upon the consent of parties not in default; nor of id., § 2511, which contains a similar prohibition as to a clerk or other employe in a Surrogate's office. *Benedict* v. *Cooper*, 362.

STOCK DIVIDEND.

The residue of testator's estate was given by the will, to his executors as trustees, in trust to collect the income and pay the same to designated beneficiaries for life, with remainders over. At the time of testator's death, a portion of the estate consisted of certain shares of the stock of a railroad corporation, whose entire capital was divided into 14,000 shares, of which only 13,052 had ever been issued, the balance, 948 shares, remaining in the treasury. Thereafter, pursuant to a resolution of the board of directors, whereby it was determined to distribute the unissued shares ratably among the existing stockholders, the executors received, as their quota, 22 shares, which they sold, realizing by the transaction the net amount of $1,741.25. Upon a judicial settlement of their account, the question arising, whether this sum was to be regarded as an augmentation of the capital fund, or the whole thereof was payable to the life tenants, as income.—*Held*, that the case was to be distinguished from the ordinary one of the declaration of an extra corporate dividend, payable in stock, in that, here, the stockholders merely received a *pro rata* distribution of what already belonged to them, viz.: a portion of the original capital,—the company acquiring no additional property as an equivalent; and that the increase was to be credited to the *corpus* of the estate. *Knight* v. *Lidford*, 88.

SUBPŒNA DUCES TECUM.

Where a witness, in obedience to a subpœna *duces tecum*, attends in court and, after being sworn, produces papers which he thereupon places in the custody of the court, either party has thereafter the same right, which he had when the witness was present, to insist that the papers shall be placed at his disposal, for use as evidence in the cause. *Hoyt* v. *Jackson*, 388.

See EVIDENCE, 5, 6.

SUBSCRIBING WITNESS.

The signatures of attesting witnesses are effectual, in this State, only where preceded, in point of time, by the signature of the testator. *Knapp* v. *Reilly*, 427.

See EXECUTION OF WILL; PUBLICATION OF WILL; WILL.

SURETIES.

It seems, that a surety, who has engaged himself for the whole of a debt, cannot, by paying part of it, become entitled to stand in the creditor's shoes, and cannot successfully prosecute his claim against his principal until such creditor has been fully paid. *Richardson* v. *Kidder*, 255.

See PAYMENT OF DEBTS, 5; REVOCATION OF LETTERS, 3.

SURROGATE'S COURT.

See JURISDICTION.

SUSPENSION OF OWNERSHIP.

Testator's will contained the following clause: "All the rest, residue and remainder of my estate I bequeath to my executrix, *to remain with her forever*, upon the following trust, however: to be devoted and applied in such sums and amounts as she may see fit, to preserve and keep in order my burial place or plot in B. cemetery."—*Held*, that the trust attempted to be created was for a purpose for which the law recognizes the right of a testator to make provision; and that since, by its terms, the entire residue might be at once consumed, the bequest was not open to objection as involving an unlawful suspension of absolute ownership, or of the power of alienation. *Pfaler* v. *Raberg*, 360.

See CHARITABLE BEQUESTS, 1.

TAXES AND ASSESSMENTS.

A tax or assessment upon a decedent's real property, which has been levied and confirmed before his death, being one of the "debts of the deceased" which his personal representative is, by statute (2 R. S., 87, § 27), required to proceed with diligence to pay, a devisee of the property is entitled to have the incumbrance discharged out of the decedent's personal estate, unless the will contain directions to the contrary. *Matter of Noyes*, 369.

See EXECUTORS AND ADMINISTRATORS, 1.

TEMPORARY ADMINISTRATOR.

1. Letters of temporary administration upon the estate of a decedent can be granted only where an application for letters in chief is pending, and under the circumstances specified in Code Civ. Pro., § 2668, subd. 1. An original independent proceeding by a creditor to procure temporary letters, to enable him to collect his debt, is unauthorized. *Saw Mill Co. v. Dock*, 55.

2. Upon an application for an order directing a temporary administrator to pay to the applicant a sum of money on account of a legacy or distributive share to which he is entitled, a citation is properly addressed to and served upon the administrator alone. *Rank v. Camp*, 278.

3. The Code of Civil Procedure makes no provision for the trial of issues raised by means of objections filed, by parties opposing the probate of a will, upon an application by the temporary administrator of decedent's estate for leave to discharge certain items of alleged indebtedness. *Mason v. Williams*, 285.

4. Under Code Civ. Pro., § 2674, providing that "the Surrogate may, upon the application of the temporary administrator, and upon proof to his satisfaction that the assets exceed the debts, make an order permitting the applicant to pay the whole or any part of a debt due to a creditor of the decedent," the only limitation upon the authority of such a representative to pay debts, in his own discretion, as if he were an administrator in chief, is the necessity for satisfying the Surrogate that the total value of the assets exceeds the amount of all the debts; this requirement being satisfied, the Surrogate should grant permission to discharge a debt whose validity is attested by the administrator's oath, and which bears no indication of mistake, exorbitance or fraud, subject to such objections as any person interested may interpose upon a subsequent accounting. *Id.*

TEMPORARY GUARDIAN.

See COMMISSIONS, 3; GENERAL GUARDIAN, 2.

TESTAMENTARY CAPACITY.

The sanity of every man, and his capacity to make a will, are to be presumed until the contrary appears, and the burden of proving mental disability is on him who asserts it. *Potter v. McAlpine*, 108.

See EXECUTION OF WILL, 5; EXPERTS; PROBATE OF WILL, 2.

TESTAMENTARY GUARDIAN.

A beneficiary under decedent's will, who had recently arrived of age, applied to the Surrogate's court for the opening of a decree rendered in 1877, judicially settling the account of the executor of said will; and for the like relief in respect to two decrees rendered on subsequent accountings by the same party, as trustee and testamentary guardian of the applicant; so far as to permit him to contest the allowance of commissions made to said executor, as such, and as trustee and guardian, by said several decrees, alleging that the same exceeded the amounts allowable under the statute, and that some portion thereof were illegal by reason of being based upon the estimated value of certain shares of stock claimed to have been specifically bequeathed; and also to permit him to contest certain items of expenditure, allowed for law expenses, and legal and other services, and also to contest the direction in said decree contained, as to said stock, and the distribution of the proceeds of certain realty.   On each accounting a special guardian was appointed for the applicant, then a minor.—*Held*, that the errors alleged were errors of law; and that the application must be denied, for want of power.   *Singer* v. *Hawley*, 571.

TESTAMENTARY TRUSTEE.

1. It is the duty of a testamentary trustee to defend any actions whereby the trust estate is attacked; for which purpose he may lawfully employ counsel ; and, on the settlement of his account, he will be allowed credit for such reasonable and necessary sums as he has, in good faith, expended for the protection of the estate.   *Geissler* v. *Werner*, 200.

2. Notwithstanding the definition contained in Code Civ. Pro., § 2514, whereby the term " testamentary trustee " is declared to include a person designated by a will, *or by any competent authority*, to execute a trust created by will, the provision of id., § 2815, allowing a Surrogate to require security from a testamentary trustee, in the cases therein specified, applies only to one named in a will; this exceptional meaning being " plainly apparent from the context." *Matter of Whitehead*, 227.

3. From the provision of Code Civ. Pro., § 2818, requiring a testamentary trustee, appointed as successor to one who has resigned or been removed, to qualify in the same manner as an administrator with the will annexed, no inference is to be drawn, of an intent to relieve the successor of a deceased or insane trustee from the like necessity.   *Id.*

4. The only matter determined in Hancox v. Meeker (95 *N. Y.*, 528) declared to be—that the right of a testamentary trustee to make periodical rests in his accounts, and at such times, even without presenting such accounts for settlement, to withhold his lawful commissions, is not limited to cases where by statute, or by general rule, or special order of court, such periodical rests are required or permitted, but extends,

also, to cases where, by the direction of his testator's will, or for the proper administration of his testator's estate, he is required to, and does, make periodical payments. *Andrews* v. *Goodrich*, 245.

5. A Surrogate's court, in the exercise of its power to require from a testamentary trustee security for the performance of his duties, is not confined to proceedings instituted by a petition filed under Code Civ. Pro., § 2815, but may make an order to such effect, where objection is duly taken, on a motion to open a decree rendered upon an accounting and modify it by delivering property to the applicant, who occupies the position of trustee under a will. *Kelsey* v. *Van Camp*, 530.

6. Under L. 1882, ch. 185, entitled "an act in relation to trustees of personal estates,"and L. 1884, ch. 408, re-enacting Code Civ. Pro., § 2818, the Supreme Court and Surrogates' courts have concurrent jurisdiction over the appointment of a successor to a deceased sole testamentary trustee. *Matter of Valentine*, 563.

7. Neither "poverty" nor "insolvency" being specified, in Code Civ. Pro., § 2817, as grounds for the removal of a testamentary trustee, the entry of an order, requiring the giving of the security prescribed by id., §§ 2638, 2815, and neglect or refusal to comply with such order, are essential preliminaries to the Surrogate's removal of such a trustee upon the ground of insolvency. *Morgan* v. *Morgan*, 612.

8. M., one of two trustees under decedent's will, being the owner of an undivided interest in certain real property in the city of New York, conveyed the same to one P., who thereupon executed a first mortgage thereof to the trustees to secure a loan of $35,000, the proceeds of which came to the hands of M., and were subsequently used in the business of a firm of which the trustees were members. The mortgage afforded adequate protection for the repayment of the loan, and, for aught that the evidence disclosed, yielded a rate of interest as large as was obtainable at the time when the loan was effected. Upon an application to remove the trustees for a breach of trust, by reason of the premises,—*Held*, that though they might have become amenable to some of the consequences which follow from a trustee's acting in any manner for his own benefit, in regard to the subject of his trust, the trustees had not been guilty of any such palpable breach of trust as to demonstrate their unfitness, under Code Civ. Pro., § 2817, to be continued in office, and that the application must, accordingly, be denied. *Id.*

See ACCOUNTING; COMMISSIONS, 6, 14; OFFICIAL BOND, 2; REVOCATION OF LETTERS, 1.

TIME.

See SERVICE OF CITATION, 2.

TRIPLICATE WILL.

Decedent, who died in April, 1885, executed a will in 1875; and, in 1880, executed, as and for her will, three identical instruments, making a different disposition of her property, and containing a clause expressly revoking, in general terms, "all other or former wills" made by her. The three instruments of 1880 were severally entrusted by her to three different persons, one of whom was an attorney, P. Shortly before her death, she insisted on sending for the three last mentioned papers, declaring her intention to revoke them. Accordingly, P. attended upon decedent, and wrote at the end of one, and upon the back of another of these papers, a formal revocation, each of which was read to the testatrix, who declared that it was "all right," and subscribed it in the presence of P. and another witness, who thereafter subscribed their names to an attestation clause in the usual form. The third paper, which was in P.'s possession, he omitted to cancel. Upon an application for probate of the will of 1875, and a cross application for the probate of that of 1880, it was—*Held*, that both wills were effectually revoked, and that decedent died intestate. *Biggs* v. *Angus*, 93.

TRUSTEE.

See TESTAMENTARY TRUSTEE.

VERIFICATION.

In order that a petition, sworn to in another state, as permitted by Code Civ. Pro., § 844, be deemed *duly verified*, the certificate authenticating the act of the administering officer must show that the latter was authorized by the laws of that state to take and certify the acknowledgment and proof of deeds to be recorded therein. *Matter of Wisner*, 11.

WAIVER.

Testator, who died in 1869, leaving a small estate consisting exclusively of real property, by his will, bequeathed $1,000 to his son M. ; devised the residue to his widow for life, with remainder to his children ; and devised his real property to his executors in trust to pay debts and legacies, with power of sale. The widow and all the children except M. resided on the real property until 1884, when, the former having died, the executor made a sale of the property which yielded $2,000, whereof M. claimed about $1,900 for the principal of his legacy, and interest thereon.—*Held*, that the will would have been properly performed, if the executors had made a sale within a year from the grant of letters, paid M.'s legacy, and invested the balance for the widow ; that M.'s omission to enforce his rights having been tantamount to an agreement to waive the use of the legacy in favor of his mother, he could not now recover from his brothers and sisters what he had given to her ; and that his legacy was payable without interest. *Cobb* v. *McCormick*, 606.

See STATUTE OF LIMITATIONS, 2.

WARD.

See GENERAL GUARDIAN; GUARDIAN AD LITEM.

WIDOW.

See DOWER; EXEMPTION.

WILL.

1. Testator, by his will, provided : " On the arrival of my youngest child at lawful age, I direct that my said estate, or so much thereof as shall be remaining, be divided equally between my said wife and children." Testator left, him surviving, besides his widow, two children each of whom attained majority. Upon a judicial settlement of the executors' account, a question having arisen as to the relative rights of the three beneficiaries in the residue,—*Held*, that the widow and children took, each, one third thereof. *Morgan* v. *Pettit*, 61.

2. The sixth subdivision of decedent's will made the enjoyment, by one of his sons, of the income of a share of the estate conditional upon the beneficiary's not living with, or in any manner contributing to the support or maintenance of his wife.—*Held*, that the condition was precedent, and illegal and void, being both against public policy and good morals, and one which would require a violation of the statutes (Code Crim. Pro., §§ 899–904); and that the gift was discharged therefrom and valid. *Potter* v. *McAlpine*, 108.

3. By the terms of a trust created by the will of testatrix, the trustees were directed, upon the respective deaths of two life beneficiaries, A. and B., to divide one half of the principal fund equally among the children of the one so dying, each of such children to receive his or her share on becoming 21 years of age; it being further provided as follows: "Should the said A. decease before arriving at the age of 21 years, leaving no issue, then on her death I direct her share to be divided among the issue of B. . . . . . Should B. decease leaving no issue, then I direct that her share be divided among the surviving issue of A." B. having died leaving C., her only child, her surviving, and A. having died *at the age of* 37 *years*, leaving no issue, C. received one half of the fund, as the child of B., and claimed the other half under the clause of substitution.—*Held*, that the half primarily given to the children of A. was diverted to B.'s children only upon the happening of three contingencies, one of which—the death of A. *during minority*—having

become forever impossible, the gift over was ineffective, and the amount thereof fell into the residue. *Morgan* v. *Darden*, 203.

4. Testator, by his will, gave a share, in remainder, of his residuary estate, after the death or marriage of his widow, "to his sister M., if living, and if not living then to her children." At the widow's death, M. had died leaving, her surviving, sons and daughters and certain grandchildren—children of a son who had died before his mother. Upon the judicial settlement of the executor's account, the context furnishing no evidence favoring an exceptional construction,—*Held*, that the surviving sons and daughters of M. took their parent's legacy in equal shares, to the exclusion of the children of their deceased brother. *Kirk* v. *Cashman*, 242.

5. Testatrix, by her will, after bequeathing, absolutely and in trust, divers preferred pecuniary legacies, amounting to $51,300, directed the executor, in order to satisfy them, to use any bonds or securities she might leave, having a market value not less than par, reckoning the same at par (including accrued interest), without regard to the ruling premium, as if they had been specific legacies, so that all the legatees should receive the same proportional amounts out of her estate; and authorized the executor to retain any securities as trust funds or to sell any thereof for the purposes of distribution. She left municipal bonds of different cities, commanding a premium in the market, of the par value of $38,500, which the executors sold, and also other securities.—*Held*, that the preferred legatees were entitled, *pro rata*, to the proceeds of the sales of the $38,500 bonds, with the accrued interest, and the premium realized, and also whatever increase had attached thereto, but not to interest, *eo nomine*, on the proceeds; and that the deficiency, ascertainable by deducting the par value of such bonds from the aggregate amount of such legacies, was payable as general legacies, with interest, in the respective cases, from the death of testatrix, or from the expiration of one year thereafter, under the ordinary rules. *Bliss* v. *Olmstead*, 273.

6. Testator, by his will, executed in 1881, appointed his mother, S., executrix, and two others, F. and M., executors of his will, giving them the residue of his estate, in trust to retain the same, or convert it and invest the proceeds, and pay the income of all or any part thereof to S. for life, with remainder over ; further directing his executors, at any time, upon his mother's written request, "unless declared by her family physician and two other trustworthy doctors to be mentally unsound," to pay and deliver to her any part, not exceeding one half, of the principal, in absolute ownership. This latter provision was, by a codicil, extended to include the entire estate. S., who alone qualified as executrix, shortly after receiving letters, executed, with the knowledge of F. and M., a written instrument, declaring her election, in pursuance of the power vested in her, to take and hold in absolute ownership, all testator's estate, with certain exceptions delivered the

same to M., and thereafter died, leaving a will of which she appointed M. executor. M. having qualified as executor of the will of S. and also of that of testator, and rendered his account in the latter capacity, in which he recognized the instrument executed by S. as a transfer to her of the estate of testator, the residuary legatees under the will of the latter, objected that the acts of S. were ineffectual as an appropriation of such estate.—*Held*, that the testator could not have intended that the failure of F. and M. to qualify should deprive the chief object of his bounty of the privilege accorded to her by his will ; that S., by executing the instrument in question, became invested with title to the property, though M. at the time of its delivery was not executor,— provided she was then of sound mind ; that it was not yet too late to determine the question of her competency ; and that the entry of a decree upon the accounting should be deferred, to permit such determination to be had.   *Solomons* v. *Kursheedt*, 307.

7. Testator, by his will, bequeathed to O. the sum of $5,000, gave to his wife a life interest in the residue of his estate, and established a scheme for the distribution of the remainder after her death. A codicil to the will contained the following clause : "In the second article of my will of the bequest to Rachel Oliver, my wife's sister the sum of $5,000 I revoke and instead bequeath unto her the sum of $300 to be paid to her annually in equal quarterly payments during her natural life at which time will cease and go to the legal heirs of the estate in equal sums to be paid by my acting executrix and executors." The widow died after O., who had received her annuity of $300, though no fund to produce it had been specially set apart. The estate being about to be distributed, decedent's next of kin claimed to be entitled to $5,000 by virtue of the clause quoted.—*Held*, that so much of this clause as followed the word "cease" was void for uncertainty, and that the estate should be distributed as if the codicil ended with that word. *Buchan* v. *Rintoul*, 353.

8. Testator, by his will, directed that, upon the death of his sister, J., his estate should be divided into fourteen parts, one of which parts, it was provided, "is hereby given to and shall be vested in the children of my deceased niece, H., in equal shares. And in case either of the children of said H. *shall die* before my said sister, J., leaving lawful issue surviving, such issue shall take the share which would have been taken by such deceased child of H., if living." H. had left her surviving eight children; of whom seven survived the testator, and one had died before the execution of the will leaving a son, F., who survived the testator. Upon the application for probate of the will, a question having arisen as to the construction of the clause quoted, it was contended, on the part of the seven children of H., that the bequest in dispute was primarily given to a class in which no person other than themselves was included, and that F. could not take under the substitutionary clause, not having been a member of that class, at its creation; while it was argued, in behalf of F., that the primary benefits of

the bequest were extended to a class consisting of (1) such children
of H. as survived J. and (2) the issue of others *at any time* dying,
leaving issue surviving.—*Held*, that F. took the share to which his
parent would be entitled, if living. *Abbey v. Aymar*, 400.

9. Testator, who died in 1844, by his will, directed his executors to sell his
real property, place the proceeds at interest, and dispose of the same
as follows: his widow, S., to have them during her natural life; if she
should have heirs of his body, they to be supported and educated out
of the fund, and, at majority, to have one half thereof, and, at the
death of S., the remainder; if, at the death of S., there should be no
heirs of his body living, the proceeds to go in equal shares to two
nephews, N. and C. There was a posthumous son of testator, H.,
who died after attaining majority and before S. N. died after testator,
and before H. The net proceeds of the sale of the real property, viz.:
$3,000, were retained by the widow, who died in April, 1884. Upon an
application to compel the distribution of a portion of the proceeds,—
Held, 1. That the will effected an equitable conversion of the real into
personal property. 2. That the taking by H. was not absolute but
dependent on his surviving the death of S.; and was, therefore,
defeated by the happening of a condition subsequent. 3. That N.'s
legacy lapsed by his dying before S., and that, therefore, as to one half
of the fund in question, decedent died intestate. 4. That the other
half was payable to C. *Hulse v. Reeves*, 486.

See Duplicate Will ; Latent Ambiguity ; Life Tenant, 3 ; Mortgage, 1 ; Payment of Legacy, 3 : Suspension of Ownership ;
Triplicate Will.

WITNESS.

The provision of Code Civ. Pro., § 837, to the effect that the rule compelling *parties* to answer relevant questions "does not require a witness
to give an answer which will tend to . . . . . expose himself to a
penalty or forfeiture," cannot be invoked to justify the contestant of a
will in refusing to furnish testimony which would establish the fact of
the validity of the disputed document. *Hoyt v. Jackson*, 388.

See Evidence ; Reference, 2 ; Subscribing Witness.

Ev. Y. a. a.